HARP SONG
FOR A RADICAL

HARP SONG
FOR A RADICAL

The Life and Times of
Eugene Victor Debs

MARGUERITE YOUNG

Edited and with an introduction by Charles Ruas

ALFRED A. KNOPF   NEW YORK   1999

THIS IS A BORZOI BOOK
PUBLISHED BY ALFRED A. KNOPF, INC.

Copyright © 1999 by the Estate of Marguerite Young

Library of Congress Cataloging-in-Publication Data
Young, Marguerite, 1908–1995
Harp song for a radical : the life and times of Eugene Victor Debs /
by Marguerite Young ; edited and with an introduction by
Charles Ruas.
p.   cm.
Includes index.
ISBN 0-679-42757-0
1. Debs, Eugene V. (Eugene Victor), 1855–1926.   2. Socialists—
United States—Biography.   3. Working class—United
States—Biography.   1. Ruas, Charles.   11. Title.
HX84.D3Y68   1999
335'.3'092—dc21
[b]   98-50290
CIP

Manufactured in the United States of America

First Edition

Contents

Introduction

Harp Song for a Radical: The Life and Times of Eugene Victor Debs is the work to which Marguerite Young dedicated the last two and a half decades of her life. This biography of Debs is a monumental achievement, the culmination of everything Marguerite Young believed in and worked for as a writer. In the tradition of Walt Whitman, she writes with the lyric vision of poetry and the sweep of history to give us a life that is also the ballad of an age, and the story of a nation.

In a career of nearly six decades Marguerite Young produced a small but formidable body of fiction, nonfiction, and poetry that attracted a fervent readership, while she also attained legendary status as a teacher of creative writing in New York. A resident of Greenwich Village for over forty years, she became the living representative of its heyday as a literary center. People pointed her out and greeted her on the street. She was a colorful presence, strolling nonchalantly down Bleecker Street in her long crimson dresses, with a gold embroidered vest, her black Polish nursemaid boots worn with pink stockings, toes peeking through, and a floor-length red woolen cape thrown over her shoulder.

Over time her face acquired a craggy monumental quality, which she shared with her friend W. H. Auden; like his, her expression was forceful but meditative in its intelligence. She had naturally red hair, which she always wore shoulder-length, with bangs cut straight across her forehead. When her hairdresser passed away and the beauty parlor on Bleecker Street closed, Marguerite Young bought a wig the same color as her real hair and had it cut the same way, and thus her appearance acquired the timeless quality she strove for in her work.

Marguerite Young was born in Indiana in 1908, when, as she liked to say, "Indianapolis was the Athens of the West." Her parents separated when she was three, and she and her sister made their home with her grandmother, who encouraged her talent. It was after graduating from Butler College, while teaching and pursuing her graduate studies at the University of Chicago, that she brought out her first volume of poetry, *Prismatic Ground,* in 1937. The publication of her second volume, *Moderate Fable,* in 1944 coincided with her move to New York. The following year she published her first work of nonfiction, *Angel in the Forest.* It is the history of two failed utopias—one a religious, celibate millennial community led by Father George Rapp, the other a rational sect, founded on the perfectibility of man by Robert Owen—one following the other in the same village of New Harmony, Indiana. In *Angel in the Forest* Marguerite Young came into her own. According to the poet Amy Clampitt, she turned from writing poetry to prose because of her spirit of inclusion, wanting to stretch each line to encompass every historical fact of her subject.

It was a technique she took even further, to encyclopedic dimensions, when she published her only work of fiction, *Miss MacIntosh, My Darling,* in 1965. This massive, demanding novel is an inquest into the disappearance of Miss MacIntosh, an old nursemaid, which takes the narrator, Vera Cartwheel, from the coast of New England to the Midwest. It portrays four archetypal characters with the double consciousness of one life lived and one unlived. Through them the author explores the subjects that enthralled her: the misfit, the wrecked, the impossible, and the forgotten. *Miss MacIntosh, My Darling* caused quite a stir on publication; it was the controversial epic novel that actually took three months longer to write than *Ulysses,* as Marguerite announced to Joyce's sister at the Gotham Book Mart.

I met Marguerite Young in the fall of 1973. Every morning at the same time we both had breakfast at Rykert's Coffee Shop on Sheridan Square in the Village, she in preparation for her literary work, I to get ready for the classes I was teaching at Columbia University. I would see Marguerite sitting at the counter reading the newspaper over her innumerable cups of coffee. One day when I was late for class, I passed her my *New York Times* as I dashed off into the subway to catch the uptown train. I learned that she read all three New York papers every morning before work, and that's how our friendship began. Subsequently, in 1974, using the text of *Miss MacIntosh, My Darling,* I produced a yearlong series of weekly readings from her book by poets, novelists, playwrights, and theater and screen actors, which were broadcast by radio station WBAI in New York and distributed nationally. My conversations with Marguerite started in those days and lasted throughout the rest of her life.

In 1967, she started writing a biography of James Whitcomb Riley, the "Hoosier poet" who created "Little Orphant Annie" and was a drinking companion of Eugene Victor Debs. The humor and fantasy, and the elegiac treatment of childhood of Riley's nostalgic, homespun lyrics, she felt, recreated a whole world and revealed the unconscious psyche of the poet and his society.

During this period, Marguerite was drawn into the larger social issues of the late sixties: the civil rights marches in the South, the mounting protest against the war in Vietnam, and the plight of conscientious objectors. Every issue made her think of Debs. When she was asked to join a panel of women writers against the war in Vietnam, she realized that she was hearing a modern-day recapitulation of all the issues that had motivated Eugene Debs. Half a century earlier, during World War I, under Woodrow Wilson's draconian Alien and Sedition Act, Debs had been imprisoned as a conscientious objector for protesting U.S. participation in the war.

An equally powerful influence on her decision to write about Debs was those aspects of the protest manifested in the music and poetry of the "counterculture." The Flower Children made a cult of nature and the American Indian, and returned to nineteenth-century dress, with women wearing long hair and long dresses and men, earrings, beads, and beards. It was a nostalgic yearning for a lost America. All of these cultural phenomena made Marguerite Young understand that the youth of America had unconsciously returned in a fragmented way to a deeper ideological bedrock than Marxism, one predating Debs; they had gone back to the utopian ideals of the early settlers and of those mad dreamers, Fourierists and Saint-Simonians, who were so profoundly a part of the American spirit.

One hot day, as we marched together in a rally on Hudson Street in Greenwich Village with a contingent of writers to protest the war in Vietnam, the air around us ringing with the songs and slogans of student radicals, black militants, hippies, and conscientious objectors, Marguerite told me she was writing a biography of Eugene Debs. She saw in all the young people around her a great need for information about Debs and his era to guide them through the present political conflict, and chaos—for there had been a struggle and a social upheaval even greater than this in the American past. They needed to know about Debs.

In looking back over her life, Marguerite felt that she had pursued the same theme in every work. As she told Professors Miriam Fuchs and Ellen Friedman in an interview, "I believe that all my work explores the human desire or obsession for utopia, and the structure of all my works is the search for utopias lost and rediscovered. This is true of *Prismatic Ground, Moderate Fable, Angel in the Forest,* and *Miss MacIntosh, My Darling,* and my biography of Debs. All my writing is about the recognition that there is no single reality. But the beauty of it is that you nevertheless go on, walking towards utopia, which may not exist, on a bridge which might end before you reach the other side."

This underlying vision is also her definition of maturity in the artist— the essential coming to terms with human experience. As she phrased it, she also had looked into the abyss. "When you have examined all the illusions of life, and know that there isn't any reality, but you nevertheless go on, then you are a mature human being. You accept the idea that it is all mask and illusion and that people are in disguise. You see the crumbling of reality and you accept it."

To her the world was imprinted with the ideas of those who passed through it. "So I show all the different colors entering into the making of the utopian quest, and one of my themes is what Oscar Wilde said: 'If you show me a country which has no map of utopia even though there is no utopia anywhere, it's not a country I would ever care to live in.'"

Marguerite used to say that in life she was like the seashore: she accepted whatever the tides brought in. People came and went, but she remained constant. She was like Prospero in his cell, sitting in a coffee shop in the Village, smoking her packs of Lucky Strikes, and always holding her key ring in her left hand, for some reason. Her conversation was mesmerizing; she ignored all interruptions unrelated to the subject at hand. Listening to her one grew oblivious of the surrounding world. She waved her cigarette and looked at you squinting, and punctuated her sentences with jabs in the air, and when you spoke she would pause and take a sip from her cup of black coffee before answering.

DEBS'S FATHER named him Eugene Victor, after the French novelist Eugène Sue, and the great nineteenth-century French romantic poet and novelist Victor Hugo. Early in our friendship, I found a set of Sue's works translated into English, which I gave to Marguerite. We discussed Debs's interest in Sue, now primarily remembered for his anti-Jesuit novel, *The Wandering Jew*. In works such as *The Mystery of Paris* and *Jean Chevalier,* he dealt with stark social issues such as prostitution and religious revolt, which she thought had influenced the young Debs. But Debs's favorite novel would remain Hugo's *Les Misérables,* which he read and reread all his life. Marguerite, who had studied French, preferred Hugo's *The Man Who Laughs.*

In those days I had just completed a dissertation on the historian Louis, duke of Saint-Simon, an ancestor of the utopian Claude de Saint-Simon. I used to bring Marguerite the latest critical works on Charles Fourier and other utopian writers after the French Revolution, who were the precursors of socialism. Over cups of coffee, we debated the French invasion of Mexico as opposed to American aggression, the conversion of American Indians, the parallel between the widowhood of the Empress Carlotta and

Mrs. Lincoln, labor issues in the novels of Charlotte Brontë, George Eliot, and Emile Zola, the trains in *Anna Karenina,* Dred Scott, the Molly Maguires, and the accomplishments of Woodrow Wilson as an educator and as the founder of the League of Nations. Remarkably, even then we were discussing every aspect of the Debs biography. In college I had actually met Norman Thomas, Debs's successor as head of the Socialist party, with whom Marguerite discussed the last years of Debs's leadership.

I often felt that I had entered a long running conversation about writing that Marguerite had begun with other people long ago and others would pick up where I left off. Marguerite found no contradiction in writing a biography, devoting herself to historical research, after having spent eighteen years on a novel. She had worked in many genres, and she believed that the same creative process applied in all of them. As she described it to me, her approach was to immerse herself in the period she was studying, reading about every detail, no matter how minute, until she made it her own. "The beautiful thing is that as the research piles up, it begins to assert a life of its own. You can have the same thematic relationships to that research, the flood, the ebb, the flow of history. But the river is a dream—imagination. You have the same relation to it as you do to the unconscious. It takes over, and you can do the same artistic writing."

Her strategy in writing the Debs biography was to use the historical figures of the times as the focus for discussing the crucial political events and thereby create a palpable sense of the cultural climate in which Debs developed. "The people are the vehicle of dreams through their actions and all their activities," she explained. "There are great personalities who are phenomenal in themselves, like Debs for example, or William Randolph Hearst in another way, James Whitcomb Riley or John Altgeld of Illinois, one of the most beautiful people I know, Susan B. Anthony, or Clarence Darrow, or Joe Hill. There are so many beautiful people who have conveyed ideas and dreams. I find that I'm fascinated by them all."

For Marguerite, recovering the unknown or forgotten past was doubly illuminating: it restored a piece of our collective history and simultaneously identified the vital origins of the present. Part I of *Harp Song,* "Prelude in a Golden Key," encapsulates Marguerite Young's dual objective of exploring Debs's quest for utopia while also unlocking a vista on nineteenth-century America. "I focus on the human fallacies," she said, "the great prototypes and their fallacies and their positive aspects, because out of every dreamer something good comes. It might not be heaven on earth, it might only be an eight-hour day. But these people are bigger than life, that's why they are leaders, reformers, activists. They are caught in some greater time."

In her biography of Debs, Marguerite Young reveals the evolution of the American psyche, which began to take shape in the uncharted wilderness, onto which all the fears as well as the dreams of unlimited human potential were projected. The story ends with Debs in prison coming to terms with the reality of American society. For Marguerite, the values of the early settlers in their struggle for survival are the same principles that motivated the labor movement in forming unions against the unchecked powers of industrialism. Like Henry Thoreau, Debs would bring to his vision of society the values based on individual self-reliance and the survival of the collective that differentiate American socialism from its European counterpart.

Yet Marguerite affirmed her belief that history is directed by the individual. "I'm interested in these tremendously big archetypal figures, of whom Debs is one of the greatest. Also in the pitiful human side of all the great ones, including Abraham Lincoln."

Our understanding of Debs deepens as our perspective broadens and as we grasp the people and the forces in the nation that shaped him. Through the journey of Wilhelm Weitling, a German visionary utopian, the author presents a bird's-eye view of the utopian settlements in the West, communities that perished, were in the process of disappearing, or even triumphed. At this time, the 1840s, Debs's parents traveled westward, eventually to settle in Terre Haute. Their son Eugene grew up imbued with the stories and memories of those seemingly pastoral days before the Civil War.

Marguerite Young's focus remains on Debs's gradual emergence as a man of heroic, visionary stature, as he comes into contact with different segments of the American people. In her view the process began in earliest childhood. "When I'm telling you about Debs's childhood, for example, when he was a little boy *not* going to Sunday School, or going to Sunday School. That was the year when things were happening in the nation, the White House, the gold rush, when the president visited Indiana and nearly drowned in a sea of mud. His father Daniel Debs's memories of the French radicals, and of people like Victor Hugo and Eugène Sue. His father's background, his coming to America, the towns he passed through. His being in Cincinnati, and what Cincinnati was like then, it's all important in Debs's history. I simply build the landscape, the time-scape, and there's the little boy. He happened to be the son of an extremely intellectual father, who would talk to him about these things. He taught him French poetry when he was three years old. They had evenings like Henry James's family in which the children were taught by intellectuals."

Adapting the techniques she used in *Miss MacIntosh,* Marguerite starts subjectively, deploying a series of multiple consciousnesses but ultimately arriving at an objective record of events; in contrast to a strictly linear structure, her narrative resembles spokes radiating from a center. Her profound grasp of psychology is revealed by the characters' actions, which then reverberate through the lives around them. Thus, the building momentum of the narrative is psychological as well as historical.

What I'm doing is giving the most dramatic and, I think, revelatory things, and linkages, and passages, to know exactly where it is at all times. Who it is and what was said when and by whom. I don't leave anything to speculation. I will give a portrait and then I can switch and come to another. For instance, the portrait of Eugene Field, which I have already done, and I am now bringing into relationship with Debs and the Socialists. But you know who Field is. When Roy Baker first met Debs, he said, "He reminds me of a combination of Abraham Lincoln and Bill Nye." Well, if you don't know what Lincoln looked like according to the cartoonists of the earlier age, or what Bill Nye looked like, you don't really get the comedy of the peculiar thing. Bill Nye was . . . one of the craziest, wildest, most beautiful men who ever lived, and was Pulitzer's favorite comedian, who was often with Debs. He was a rival of Commodore Vanderbilt—he had a perpendicular farm built on a mountainside, straight up and down, and the house stood this way over Vanderbilt's great estate.

So vivid were the ironies and absurdities of history that Marguerite Young would burst into hearty laughter and tell them as if they were current jokes.

The not-so-still center of all this is, of course, Debs himself, whose maturation process begins as he absorbs the social and professional reality around him from the vantage point of his first job, when he was a teenager, as locomotive fireman. Then he makes the transition to chronicler and statistician, gathering facts about the working conditions on the rails, and reports them in the union paper. From his deepening understanding of the workers' plight, a vision begins to evolve that propels him in his course from a railroad union organizer to the idealist and social reformer he becomes.

In prison he understood that labor issues were the issues of society as a whole, and he began to embrace socialism. Becoming the voice of the voiceless, he defined the rights of the workingman and the dignity of labor.

When Marguerite Young spoke about the writing of history, there was a blurring of distinction between creator and creation. She writes in a rich, imagistic style that captures the beliefs, the lore, and the language of her subject. Through it she conveys the underlying dreams of the people in all their variations and the multiplicity of myths alive in the culture. "It is marvelous that they use the same metaphors in their search for heaven on earth. The fact that all these people, no matter who they were, and of which political party or whether they were opposed to utopia or not, they all had a lingua franca, which all understood and which was based upon poetry, like Whitman, Melville, or Longfellow, or Lowell. They all spoke in metaphors. And Debs was one of the great lovers and users of metaphors."

The Debs biography grew in scope as Marguerite pursued her research, but she saw that the same moral and social imperatives that motivated him to organize the American Railway Union would cause him to found the Socialist party of America and stand up to Woodrow Wilson in protest against American involvement in World War I, and consequently to run as the Socialist candidate for president from inside the Atlanta State Penitentiary. Marguerite Young believed that Debs and the issues he fought for were eclipsed by the Depression and the New Deal. But she felt this half-remembered chapter of American history was essential to an understanding of the current social issues, especially in a global economy. During the last decade, when Marguerite Young's health began to fail, she witnessed the downfall of that great Marxist dream in Russia, but this only increased her belief in the relevance of this biography, she told me.

Like her favorite novels, Sterne's *Tristram Shandy* and Gogol's *Dead Souls,* Marguerite Young's biography of Debs stands by itself, a complete creation, without having been entirely finished at the time of her death in 1995. She was writing the chapter on the great Pullman strike, or the Debs strike (it led to his first prison sentence and would form the conclusion of this book), when she first became ill and was hospitalized. It is not clear how much more she had written because when she was in the throes of composition no one was allowed in her apartment for years on end. But during her stay in the hospital, her apartment building was renovated, and in the turmoil the different drafts of her enormous work became mixed together. A couple of friends helped her collate one complete draft of the manuscript, which I then photocopied and distributed to each of the friends, to be returned when she resumed working on the manuscript.

In this version of the Debs biography, which Marguerite Young was preparing for publication at the time of her death, she foreshadows his founding of the Socialist party of America and his eventual nomination as a candidate for the presidency by the recurrent depiction of presidential campaigns of that time—a mad, comical sequence of elections from Grant to Tiller to Blue Jeans Williams. Debs's imprisonment is anticipated by the unforgettably harrowing scene of Dostoyevsky being led to his near execution as a Fourierist sympathizer. The scope of the present biography is the period of American history that formed the historical Debs as we know him.

Although Marguerite Young never regained her health, she continued to write and edit the manuscript through her illnesses until the end of her life, and she bequeathed this work as her testament. Indeed, her portraits of Debs and his family, Heinrich Heine, Wilhelm Weitling, Brigham Young and the Mormons, Mrs. Lincoln, Susan B. Anthony, Allan Pinkerton, the Molly Maguires, Pullman, James MacNeill Whistler and his mother, and Dostoyevsky—to name only a few—are unique in contemporary American writing. She entrusted to Victoria Wilson at Alfred A. Knopf the publication of her work, and I was enlisted to prepare the manuscript for publication. Marguerite Young's papers and manuscripts are deposited with the Beinecke Library at Yale.

Not surprisingly, *Harp Song for a Radical* is a summation of her writing life, and with it she returned to her origins. As the narrator of *Angel in the Forest* went back to New Harmony, Marguerite Young did in fact return home to Indiana. After several bouts of hospitalization during which her condition worsened, her niece Daphne Nowling, with her children, moved as much as they could of Marguerite Young's New York apartment to the Nowling house in Indianapolis, where they re-created her rooms down to every detail. There they nursed her until well nigh the end.

Charles Ruas

Chronology

1855   Eugene Victor Debs born on November 5, 1855, in Terre Haute, Indiana. His parents, Jean Daniel Debs and Marguerite (Marie, or "Daisy") Bettrich, came from Colmar in Alsace, France. His father names him after two favorite authors, the novelist Eugène Sue and the poet Victor Hugo, both social reformers. Eugene is the third of six children, born after Marie Marguerite and Louise, and followed by Eugènie, Emma, and Theodore.

1861   The Civil War begins. Debs's father educates him in the ideals of the French Revolution, and passes on a love of the Enlightenment and the French and German romantic writers.

1869   At the age of fourteen Debs starts working in a railroad shop in Terre Haute and eventually becomes a locomotive fireman. Continues readings with his father.

1875   Debs elected secretary of Vigo Lodge, a newly formed local branch of the Brotherhood of Locomotive Firemen, and devotes himself to building up the union.

1880   Elected national secretary of the Brotherhood of Locomotive Firemen.
Becomes editor of *The Locomotive Firemen's Magazine.* He is laid off during a depression, and looks for work in Saint Louis.

1879–83   City clerk of Terre Haute.

1885–87   Member of the Indiana legislature.

1885   Marries Kate Metzel in Terre Haute on June 9.

1893   President of the American Railway Union, which he founds when the various railroad craft unions refuse to unite to realize his goal of "federation for mutual benefit."

1894   Successful strike against the Great Northern Railroad.

1895   May–September, sentenced to six months in jail for contempt of a federal injunction to halt the Chicago Pullman Palace Car Company strike. His imprisonment destroys the American Railway Union. During his prison term his broad reading includes Karl Marx and Victor Hugo. A close-up view of prison conditions reveals to him that labor issues are not separable from social issues, which makes him critical of capitalism and introduces him to socialism.

1896   Campaigns for William Jennings Bryan for the presidency.

1898   Debs establishes the Socialist party of America to further the cause of labor; the name is legally adopted in 1901.

1900   Debs is Socialist party's presidential candidate, winning 96,000 votes.

1904   As Socialist party's presidential candidate, Debs wins 400,000 votes.

1905   Debs founds the IWW (Industrial Workers of the World), but eventually withdraws because it becomes too radical; members are popularly known as Wobblies.

1908   As Socialist party's presidential candidate Debs receives 400,000 votes.

1912   As Socialist party candidate for the presidency, Debs doubles his votes to over 800,000.

1916   Debs refuses his party's nomination.

1918   Debs is sentenced to ten years in prison for his opposition to Woodrow Wilson's policy of U.S. entry into World War I and for his criticism of the government's persecution of conscientious objectors, who have been charged with sedition in violation of the 1917 Espionage Act. During the trial he makes the famous speech, "Your Honor, years ago I recognized my kinship with all living things and I made up my mind that I was not one bit better than the meanest of the earth. . . . I said then, I say now, that while there is a lower class, I am in it; while there is a criminal element, I am of it; while there is a soul in prison, I am not free." Major political and intellectual figures around the world, from George Bernard Shaw to Lenin, plead for his release.

1920   Runs for presidency while an inmate in the Atlanta Penitentiary, receiving unanimous vote of prisoners as well as his highest number of popular votes, 915,000, 6 percent of the total votes.

1921   Massive demonstration for amnesty for prisoners of conscience. President Warren Harding releases Debs from prison; he is in broken health. He does not regain his citizenship, which was abrogated when he was convicted of sedition.

1922   Debs becomes editor of the Socialist weekly, *American Appeal*. Debs separates the Socialist party from the Communist party.

1926   Dies on October 20, in Elmhurst, Illinois. His best-known writ-
        ings are a pamphlet, *Unionism and Socialism,* and his book, *Walls
        and Bars,* published in 1927.

1976   Debs's citizenship is restored.

PART I

Prelude in a Golden Key

[I]

Twice in his life Eugene Victor Debs took the long leap to the Ultima Thule of prison, passing beyond the realm of the acceptable into the nonacceptable, from respectability into the criminal community of the monster who was an enemy to the people. Twice on his way to the socialist state that should have its genesis in the utopias which this world should be when it was transformed from the present irrational to the rational state by man's brotherhood to man in a universal sense and without limit of creative possibilities here upon this earth and not upon some other star beyond time, beyond space, Debs was cast into a prison cell by those who had on their side the pomp and power and glory of immediate circumstance. Twice a prisoner repudiated by the great plutocrats who were like the toad dreaming of being the largest toad in the world, larger than all the other toads combined, he who had had no inherent instinct for martyrdom had welcomed this fate of incarceration by the masters of rails and iron and steel and lead and coal and coke and oil, whose desire was to stamp down the least evidence of the independence of the human spirit.

He would come to the apparent end of his career as a visionary labor agitator and eclectic Socialist, as much subjected to reproach as if he were a fiend—this Abel who would be branded Cain by the murderers of workingmen, by the ravagers of their widows, children, and old mothers and fathers, if there were any who had survived the depredations of industrialism in the age of the ever-accelerating machine. Capitalism was an institution as sacred as if it had been handed down by God to man, probably along about the time of the eviction of Adam and Eve and the fencing of the Garden of Eden. Debs would end his career in the twentieth century as a voice of Socialist war protest, possibly even of an essential pacifism crying aloud in the wilderness of war, this World War which was to end all wars forever throughout the world, according to the then president, Woodrow Wilson, who believed that in order to have universal peace the way must be prepared by universal war and so threw Debs into the burning ash heap with the dead souls of America.

Debs was just one of the jackass Socialists who would not keep their mouths shut. He was a man of complex character but of simple honesty whose right hand knew what his left hand did. He has been called Debs the Unpurchasable by those who knew him best, as by those who did not know him. Few in this nation have elicited so wide, so deep, a love. A Socialist of the native grain, he was an American folk hero who, both stalwart and fragile, would outlive in moral legend and human consciousness and conscience all the members of the megalomaniacal power structure who defamed him and would have blasted him to eternity and a step beyond if they could have. But he was a stubborn fellow who took the incalculable risks that many others, including former Socialists, avoided for the sake of immediate survival and possibly also for the pecuniary rewards which were given to some of them for upholding the war, which was supposed to spread democracy to the rest of the world.

According to the Reverend Norman Thomas, who would preach Debs's funeral sermon from the front porch of his home at Terre Haute, Indiana, Debs was one of the world's darlings in the Emersonian sense— that is to say, the Transcendental sense.

Surely there were many men and women as well as children to whom he had been and would remain the saint of an enlightened labor movement as of that all-inclusive socialism, which he piloted through the raging storms of modern industrial wars and which he did not abandon during the World War, as did many others, because they lacked the abiding sense of the true cooperative brotherhood of workers in all countries and all spheres of life and death.

They would agree with Norman Thomas's evaluation that nothing constituted so black a page in American history as President Wilson's failure to intervene in behalf of the many conscientious objectors who were thrown into prison under the Espionage Act. The absolute vindictiveness of President Wilson's treatment of conscientious objectors, including those who, often dwelling apart from the world, usually under the leadership of some bearded patriarchs, had refused to answer the call of the greater power who was not God, had baffled not only Norman Thomas but many apologists for wood-headed Woody Wilson.

The conscience was not corporate but was individual, and no state had the right to ask a man to cede his conscience to it as to a higher power. Also, pacifists and war objectors who were not members of religious bodies had the right to express themselves, even as did any lone individual.

It had seemed to Norman Thomas and to others in many walks of life that those who had disputed the rigid Wilson's paradoxical and often self-contradictory justification of the war had sinned against the Holy Ghost. Or possibly it was as if by his harshness toward them Wilson could silence his secret and lingering doubts, which neither his eloquence nor the applause of the multitudes could wholly stifle. Thomas observed: "He who dared to proclaim abroad America's faith in freedom of speech and opinion used none of his great power and greater influence to modify the cruelty of our Espionage Law or the preposterous rigors of its enforcement. . . ."

Indeed, it may be that Wilson wanted Debs, with his smashed utopian dreams, to suffer as he suffered in what seemed an increasingly doomed search for his version of utopia. As his face twitched, as he staggered onward, he perhaps wanted Debs's face to twitch and wanted him to reel, stagger, faint, fall upon the road to universal peace and justice.

The man whom the self-righteous Wilson had consigned to a prison sentence had been four times a candidate for president of the United States under the Socialist banner. And, indeed, through all his political life— which was a life of failure to reach that high office where he could never have been called chief executive, for with his election the United States would have ceased to be a capitalistic country, would have gone out of business, as some of his enemies thought—there had been thousands upon thousands of his disciples who believed that there would come some time, some blessed March 4, when they would follow the inaugural parade and Debs's carriage into the White House, as would be recalled by Norman Thomas.

Debs would run for president from the Atlanta Penitentiary in 1920, winning in his district hands down, as he—old and puny gentleman who might never live to be released—would laughingly remark, the tears running down his cheeks. The fact that the votes of his fellow convicts could not be counted did not rob them of their value to him but were rather to be remembered by him as the most precious straws that had been cast.

The departed Debs had had that comic sense which must sustain a larger tragic sense than most people know, especially if they confine themselves to personal or egocentric horizons shutting out history as a thing of no concern to them. He had come up the hard way, from locomotive fireman on the train that was this world speeding through darkness with no headlight but that which was given by man's humanitarian consciousness, and he had clung to no desire for an easy way. He had had, moreover, no capacity to acknowledge failure and defeat. That was what he had said when he was in the prime of his manhood and in the heart of the industrial conflict. But when he was old, he had experienced in the darkness of the prison cell, where he wore a convict's garb, the sense of despair that had always been the twin of hope. Hope and despair were two of the most famous twins of the nineteenth century.

According to Horace Traubel, Walt Whitman's secretary and literary executor and thus a living conduit to Debs's great love for the author of *Leaves of Grass,* Debs had ten hopes to your one hope and ten loves to your one love. When Debs spoke a harsh word, it was with tears.

He was a great lover, indeed, with a miraculously magnetic personality—a magnetic hand which seemed charged with energy pulsing, drawing toward it all weaker creatures—but he was also the great hater of that injustice which was created by man and not by God, was not given in the nature of things.

He was an Aesopian fabulist in the realm of socialism, one who had employed in his most ordinary and extraordinary discourse the time-worn, often antique coins of speech that were current in his day and by which he had hoped to speak directly to the hearts of all the orphans in this orphaned world and make himself understood in an intuitive sense, as might not have been the case if he had relied upon arid abstractions.

An early commentator believed that Marx's philosophy might have done better sledding in America if it had not been called dialectical materialism and thus not alienated from the beginning those who were in love with the spiritual values in this most materialistic nation.

Some were of the opinion that Marx's surely not soporific philosophy would have done better if the most unread red book in America had not been called red, thus evoking the memory of the red man who had been slaughtered as the colonialists, wave after wave, expanded their domain from the East to the West—only utopians usually regretting this slaughter, which amounted to the all-but-total extermination of the red people.

A socialist by instinct who had yearned for the Brotherhood of Locomotive Firemen, the union for which, under the aegis of the Knights of Labor, Debs had worked with passionate devotion as an organizer, so that it might become, with his assistance in the founding of new chapters and the drawing up of new charters, the continental brotherhood reaching from sea to shining sea and even into the Canadian wilds—and who then, having been dissatisfied by a union of the skilled, by whom he had felt restricted as if in chains, had begun to enlarge the ideal of union into the American Railway Union, that of the unskilled, which he hoped would grow into a union of all workers in universal brotherhood, irrespective of race, color, or creed, excluding not even the least paint scraper or wheel wiper who was scraped of his paint and wiped by wheels of locomotives passing over him until he was a handful of dust. He was never the abstract theoretician, although certainly he had thumbed through the pages of Marx at the time of his transmutation from labor unionism to socialism in the evening of the nineteenth century and the dawn of the twentieth century, when it would seem that he had no future in the real world if such there ever was, that he was the lost leader of only the lost battalions, that he was the Roland who would raise up only the dead with his winding horn.

He would be looked back upon by some modern Marxist dialectical materialists as if he had been a wandering spirit, the old grandfather of Dickens's *The Old Curiosity Shop* or even the golden-haired Little Nell of socialism or even the Tiny Tim, something of another era like an old rag doll thrown upon an ash heap and left to burn, although crying with a human cry, which should be heard upon the farthest stars.

Once when Debs was running for president on the Socialist ticket and was asked by a flock of baying, barking newspaper hounds on the steps outside his hotel in Chicago what he thought of the restriction against Chinese immigration to the American shores, he had answered briefly, consulting his watch as if he had not a moment to spare, "The souls of Chinese children are yellow butterflies. Good afternoon, gentlemen"—then had turned and walked rapidly away without having given any but this surely not world-shaking news from which to provide a sensational headline.

Among the many statements that Debs made regarding childhood and one that was the brief summary of many such remarks throughout the years was that in which he compared children with flowers. It was an archetypal image of death and resurrection. He was a big rough flower himself with something of Buddha in his nature, something of Oriental serenity about him, Carl Sandburg would observe of him when he was an old, thin-boned gentleman sunning in his garden without a hair upon his head and none could have dreamed that he was so near his death.

Debs had said, "The sweetest, tenderest, most pregnant words uttered by the proletaire of Galilee were: 'Suffer little children and forbid them not to come unto me, for of such is the kingdom of heaven. . . .' Childhood! What a holy theme! Flowers they are, with souls in them, and if on this earth man has a sacred charge, a holy obligation, it is to these tender buds and blossoms of humanity."

Debs was of the belief that socialism had been sleeping in the womb of time long before it was born. The shape of future things had been implicit long before they had appeared, as no reform that was simply spontaneous and without preparation could be more than transient.

No doubt the peace-seeking President Wilson whose somewhat ambivalent policy of Preparedness was leading step by step to war—and indeed, America was already in the war except for the technical fact that the pro-war fever was not yet at the boiling point at which the president could safely ask for a declaration of war and believe that all the people would follow him over the brink into the bottomless abyss—was disturbed but not surprised when the terrifyingly incandescent bomb was thrown upon the San Francisco Preparedness Day parade, wounding many people and killing some, including those who dissolved into bloody foam. To the somewhat isolated Californians who had not been greatly impressed by the sinking of the Cunard liner *Lusitania* in the North Sea off the coast of Ireland by the German U-boat with the loss of a thousand lives, the reality of the war had been brought home in such a memorable way that some wild people of unalterably radical views would always entertain the thought that the poisoned fruit had been dropped at the instigation of the warmongers themselves. This carnage had occurred on a vast scale on July 22, 1916, and it would be marked upon the calendar of the nation's grief.

The throwing of the bomb would be traced by deliberate and intricate logic, founded upon the shakiest premises, to five well-known labor agitators, among them two of the most famous scapegoats of that guilt-ridden time: Thomas Jeremiah Mooney and Warren Knox Billings.

Tom Mooney had been with Debs on the Red Special in his 1908 presidential campaign against the two Bills, Bryan and Taft, and like Carl Sandburg, who would go over to Woodrow Wilson when he was promising peace by way of war but who would later regret this defection, had been for a time a Socialist fellow traveler and reporter spreading red like paint upon red barns.

Mooney's father had been a Hoosier coal miner and one of the first organizers of the Knights of Labor and had participated in the strike against the coal-mining barons in the little town of Washington, David County, Indiana, where he had been shot in the leg by a hireling thug and, tearing the smoking pistol from his hand, had shot him in the chest, acting in self-defense against a strike-breaker; then, with his wife, who was a migrant from the auld sod and three little children of whom the oldest was Tom, had crawled away on his ever-bleeding leg and had hidden out several nights and days in the fields and woods until told by a fellow striker that it was safe to return—that he had killed no one—that the wound in the chest had been superficial.

When Tom was ten years old, his father had died of coal-dust-shrouded lungs, although his widow had attributed the mortality of this crippled Knight of Labor to the corrosive wound that had been given to him by the labor scab during the strike. Actually, miner's pneumonia was caused by the negligence of the coal barons, who preferred to attribute this to one of the many which were acts of God.

Upon the shoulders of this apple-headed, red-cheeked little boy had fallen the responsibility of helping to support his widowed mother and the little children for whom she could not have earned enough wages for bread when she became a sorter of rags in a paper mill at Holyoke, Massachusetts. He once remarked, "I suppose the urge to serve the labor movement was born in me."

He had become her helper as a ragpicker in the paper mill by day, a laundry worker at night at his mother's side before becoming an iron molder apprentice, a ladler of iron in its liquid state giving off showers of sparks from the long-handled spoon which he would carry before him, his body naked from the waistline up lest any shirt he wore might catch a flying spark and turn him into a ball of fire.

He had become a member of the International Molders' Union, a brotherhood in which he would keep his membership through all the years of his life.

Formerly an iron molder for the Gould Coupler Works in Depew, New York, he had managed to save fare for third-class passage from the New World to the Old World, where with a *Baedeker* in his grimy hands from which all the waters of the Tiber could not wash off the dust of the mills, even as his face glistened with the marks of iron and steel and glass particles, he had made a tour of European countries, mainly the art galleries.

He had been standing before a Rembrandt in the museum at Rotterdam when a well-dressed, well-heeled American who had recently attended the International Socialist Convention at Stuttgart had offered to him the glad hand of fellowship and had suggested that he consider how the workers of Europe lived or did not live. Those who lived under the ground in Europe had more in common with those who lived under the ground in America than with those who lived above the ground in any country.

The America to which Mooney had returned was going through a dollar crisis so chronic that for the poor folks it was as permanent a state as if it had been the collapse of a dying father's lungs.

The impatient young man, it was said of him, had a tendency that he would never lose—and that was to see all things as black and white, good and evil, right and wrong—and his were swift judgments, choices between two alternatives in which he was always right by being left.

When this son of the fallen Knight of Labor with the barrel chest and the shock of wild black Irish hair and the preternaturally red apple cheeks had made his presence known to Debs on the Red Special and had asked him what he should do for the advance of socialism, the presidential candidate running against the two slow-moving Bills—William Jennings Bryan and William Howard Taft—Debs had advised, perhaps sensing something hawklike in the man's bright eyes, "Go and read more books." He should study to improve himself for service to the poor of earth.

So had he done in his own essentially materialistic way and not only had become increasingly involved in industrial unionism but had lent all his strength to opposition to the war preparedness movement, which would permit the American plutocrats to snatch babies from their cradles in order to send them to distant wars and would bring in scabs to run their mines and mills when the doughboys were shipped to foreign battlefronts.

The reason they were called doughboys, according to one comic explanation which had a grain of tragic truth in it, was that they were the flour, the very flower, of American manhood. Colonel George Harvey, who spent his time pinpricking Wilson, believed that Newton D. Baker should not be secretary of war. What was required for that bloody office was not a man named Baker—it was a man named Butcher.

No one knew or would ever know who had brought sudden midnight to so many lives of innocents at the early afternoon parade. Some enthusiasts, even should Mooney and the others who were picked up be found innocent, had wanted them to hang, much as if they because of being associates with radicals should suffer the same fate as in the long ago had been the fate of the Haymarket victims whose crime had been engagement in freedom of speech.

Mooney was to spend more than two decades on death row waiting for the executioner whose coming was continually deferred because of the uncertainty as to his guilt and the obvious perjury of some of the witnesses and the almost familiar pattern of the frame-up, which had official sanction by some of the ruling powers, and the continual loudmouthed intervention by men and women of ethical conscience in his behalf.

The first execution had been passed by because President Wilson had quietly asked that the date which Mooney had upon the calendar to meet the hangman should be deferred while research was done to find some other cause for bringing him to justice. For as a president engaged in bringing peace to the world by way of war, the pale-faced man, even if not to the point of blushing to the gills, was embarrassed by the protests against Mooney's hanging, which were coming from the Allies and other nations and even his own nation, which had cried out its opposition to the execution.

[2]

THERE HAD OCCURRED on the day of the San Francisco grand Preparedness Day bombing—which would help to lead this blind, stumbling nation to war—the death of James Whitcomb Riley, bosom friend of Debs, in the poet's house on Lockerbie Street, Indianapolis, which had been known as the Street of Dreams because the bard of childhood lived there as life's most charming guest and that was where he could be seen in his old age sunning in his garden, his large umbrella shadowing him and the children of his dreams. "Oh, my God! Little Bud has been taken from us," President Wilson was remembered to have exclaimed as the tears splashed down his granite cheeks. "Now what will become of us?"

He had sent a wire of condolence to the poet's relatives in that state capital where the mirrors in the state house were being draped with black. For some time the poet would have no burial, as he had expressed the desire to be buried at home in the old graveyard on the Brandywine where his mother and his father and his little brother Hum were—Hum was a drunk—and he had expressed also the desire to be buried at Crown Hill, the capital city necropolis which was so vast a place that if ever he had awakened in the night there, he would not have known how to get out. The pressure brought by the advocates of the vast necropolis had won out over the little country graveyard.

And how could America live without that Little Bud who was the poet's imaginary child and thus, having never been born, could never die?

The truth was that Little Bud was the little long-ago boy who was Riley, just as almost everybody knew, and in his age he said that Little Bud was the only child he had ever loved—that he had studied real children in order to understand better this child of his dreams, of his imaginings—Bud, who was invisible to others but visible to him, walking in a crooked way along the sun-splashed, tree-shaded streets of that Indianapolis, which he claimed to be heaven's counterpart right here on earth, and followed by so many pigeons because he would offer so much popcorn to real children in his wake. In one pocket was the popcorn for Little Bud, but in the other pocket was something for Pa, as he would say—a bottle of corn.

When the poet died, the newspaper elegiasts had consigned him to that heaven to which Little Orphant Annie would lift him up the golden stairs to where the little red apple trees were, a land of childhood where the heart grows younger and all men are children in eternity, the old man becoming once more the babe pillowed on his mother's breast.

A great admirer of the Hoosier poet's "Little Orphant Annie," just as Debs was, President Wilson used to dance a jig in which he acted out the clowning role of the bewitched little orphant girl for his first wife and their three daughters. Lloyd George would later recall that he would never have gotten through the night bombardments of London if he had not had Riley's Little Orphant Annie by his bedside within reach of his arm—the book, of course, and not the little girl.

When the news of Riley's death reached Debs, he had taken time out from his vocal opposition to the coming war to write his most personal elegy for the old-timer who had been a fellow traveler on life's grassy highway and with whom he would catch up when he rounded the last bend on the ever-bending, mist-shrouded road.

People who knew Debs well were surprised by what seemed his withdrawal and silence. He was ailing, indeed, and looking back upon his past in a personal sense as he prepared for publication in book form his "Pastels of Men," a collection of five miniature elegiac biographies of the key or master spirits of his life which he had begun with his impressionistic recollections of James Whitcomb Riley, the Hoosier bard of the old home place and the days of childhood that had been so happy before the Civil War, or should have been, Riley having ever preferred, if anybody asked him, the antebellum to the postbellum world.

The other key spirits of whom Debs wrote were Wendell Phillips, the Civil War abolitionist who—a Brahmin of Brahmins in Boston—had outraged his fellow Bostonians by preaching Karl Marx's red revolution from Beacon Hill's golden dome; Robert Green Ingersoll, the passionate pagan of Peoria, who was a believer in no miracle but who in his life achieved one—that of being both an avowed atheist and critic of the mistakes of Moses and Republican Speaker of the House; Eugene Field, the iconoclastic Puck whose column "Sharps and Flats" in the *Chicago Morning News* had almost no musical criticism but was very much devoted to sardonic portraits of the follies of men and who—the author of the elegy "Little Boy Blue"—had become Debs's friend a short time before he died; and last but not least of the beads upon this Arabic rosary, John Swinton, martyred, self-immolating newspaper reporter whose "Striking for Life, or Labor's Side of the Labor Question" had been one of the finest accounts of the non-soporific Debs Rebellion, back in 1894, against the despotism of the purple-robed, many-crowned George Mortimer Pullman—emperor of Pullman Palace sleeping cars, or land barges, his name as wide as sleep, according to an essay on him in the magazine Debs edited, the *Locomotive Firemen's Magazine,* long years before the strike that had threatened to stop all the trains running in this country and almost did.

AT THE TIME OF WRITING his elegy for his Old Pard Riley, Debs had felt increasingly his isolation and loneliness, as even many who had professed socialism and pacifism had jumped from the dashboard to answer their country's call.

Debs had not for a moment claimed that the author of "Little Bud" and "Little Orphant Annie" and "Little Wesley" and "The Happy Little Cripple" had shared his views as to a political and economic cure-all by which to heal society's woes, woes, woes.

When toward the end of the poet's life, newspaper reporters had come to his door to ask what he thought of the probable entrance of the American nation into the far distant European war, he would say that he wanted to talk about something really important, and that was Little Bud.

At the same time, however, Riley had been writing to his "beloved Camelot," Miss Edith Thomas, editor of *Harper's,* to warn her that the Preparedness Day people were bound to have their way—that this nation would be catapulted into war in spite of all the protests of pacifists, among them in the peace parades this transplanted Ohio poetess who in her gray rain bonnet and long gray ulster with violets at her throat signified all that to him was good and true and beautiful in the old Ohio from which she had come to the great harbor city and to which she increasingly returned in her thought-haunted songs as the war hysteria mounted and American farm boys were being shipped over there. Some would sing that tune to the words "underwear."

DEBS WAS OF THE OPINION in his "Pastels of Men" that the day when James Whitcomb Riley was born, "Nature, in love, certainly crooned above the cradle and dowered him with her most precious gift as he opened his baby eyes upon the world." His childhood had been spent along the winding bank of the little creek Brandywine rioting with other boys from the little red schoolhouse. He had gone down to the old swimming hole, had wandered among papaw and hazel thickets and persimmon trees. He had fortunately never been a victim of that artificial education that, in the words of the seer Ingersoll, polishes pebbles and dims diamonds. He had listened with rapture to the songs of feathered choristers. "Like the vagrant butterfly, he loved to flit, in perfect abandon, from field to field, from flower to flower extracting the native sweets his riper genius was to distill into the dripping honey of his melting melodies."

DEBS GAVE PRAISE to Riley's "When the Frost Is on the Punkin" as the Hoosier psalm of life. Because of the political importance of this bucolic poem by a poet who had never tilled the soil in his life except in his pastoral poems, which he had written under the mask of an old-time imaginary farmer, Benjamin F. Johnson of Boone, the Hoosier campaigners crying up and down the state at election time, "I'll see you all at the polls / When the frost is on the punkin and the fodder's in the shock," *Rolling Stock* editor Elijah J. Halford, who ran a tight shop at the Republican president-making *Indianapolis Journal* and had known what guilty party chewed the eraser and what guilty cockroach swelled himself up by eating the paste from the pot, had dismissed, under the influence of Debs, his economical assumption that no up-and-coming city newspaper needed a poet in the office braying at the moon—and so had kept Riley on even when he was trying to cut expenses to the bone. For this, Lije Halford, who had become President Big Ben Harrison's secretary and keeper of finances in the White House, where he watched over the national finances and the fate of rolling stock with a gimlet eye as he watched over every paste pot and postage stamp and saw that no rats chewed away the carpet in Lincoln's bedroom, deserved his country's praise.

In this funerary piece in which even the hawk-eyed President Wilson could have found no treason, for Debs was expressing what Riley would have called his embalmed or embalming thoughts, the old man who was hunched up in bed suffering from broken lute strings in his long throat, which had been enflamed by anarchic antiwar speeches inviting strangulation by the noose, did not mention the difficulties in giving birth to labor speeches and articles which he wrote with infinite pain and great awkwardness, as the pen was not made for his paw, his horny hand, which could handle a fireman's shovel better than a pen.

Although not given to self-congratulations for any possible achievement of his own, Debs believed that he could claim credit for having been the first to give to Riley the name Little Bench-Legged Poet. The name had been suggested by Riley's recollection of his father at his old workbench in Greenfield, shaving dolls and hobby horses for his children as the golden shavings drifted around him in the dim air of the old barn and as Bud, the little shaver or shaveling, played among the shavings strewn like baby curls or chicken feathers at his father's feet. Perhaps one evening when Debs and Riley were coming home by buggy down a velvet road and the crescent moon was drifting in the clouds overhead, Debs, upon hearing these and other recollections of the old father at the workbench, had exclaimed in a jocular way, "Oh, I see it all now—you are the little bench-legged poet."

There was nothing so fine, in Debs's estimation, as Riley's impersonations when he recited such country poems as "When the Frost Is on the Punkin" or "Nothin' to Say, My Daughter," or "Out to Old Aunt Mary's." Nothing could be more wonderful to the music-loving, clowning Debs than the wooing, cooing old-time frontier fiddler of Riley's word portrait whose fiddle was his pigeon sweetheart with the ribbons around her neck at the square dance in the old red barn in the long ago when the music unraveled like webs at the dancers' feet.

The greatest line that Riley ever wrote, according to old Debs, was that with which he perhaps wished to reproach, at a subliminal level, the Croesus capitalists who thought that as Croesus rhymes with Jesus, they must be the same, for Riley was now their public idol and their mascot and the proof of their essential goodness—"There's nothing 'at's patheticker than jes' a' bein' rich." Debs was profoundly convinced that the money that came to Riley in his later years had added nothing to his inspiration, nothing to his fame, and nothing to his happiness. "His clothes, like his words," Debs noted, "had to fit to perfection. . . . He was always clean-shaven and neat as a fashion plate."

Debs had been filled with praise for Riley's talents as fiddler, banjoist, cartoonist, and decorator or sign painter. He did not stop here to recall the youth of the poet when he had been a traveling performer with the Wizard Oil medicine wagon and had recited from the wagon step to country audiences his little red hen and baby chick poems and then had moved among the crowds selling bottles of cure-alls for your guitar, all having usually an opiate base and good for everything that ailed you—and bee stings, too—and guaranteed to grow a crop of hair on the bald pate, enough grass to require a garden rake, and keep you safe through a long winter of sleep until you should awaken with the flowers in the spring.

. . .

THE POET'S PASSAGE from this world to the next world which would be the repetition of this world from beginning to end would seem to many to have come at the same time as the death of that American innocence which, of course, had never been unless in dreams. But who could say, Debs had asked as he considered the problem of what was real and what was unreal, that the child world of the Little Bench-Legged Poet was not after all the real world, the sweet and sane world where love and peace and innocence and kindness reigned and war and strife and hatred were unknown? Certainly Debs, an old man who would soon be cast naked into the storm, could not. The spirit of Riley had gone home where a man ought to be. "He sleeps in the sanctuary of the elect, in the blessings of the children he loved—and they will wear garlands of old-fashioned roses, fresh with the breath of morning, in memory of their poet and friend through all the coming years."

Although meeting many times in pubs along life's highway or at the bar of the old Dennison House in the capital city or on a flowering bank, both Don Quixotes in quest of the golden world of happiness and harmony and peace, simply and absolutely, Debs had never been able to convince Riley that the earthly paradise of man's earliest imaginings and dreams and the transformation of the masses of mankind could be achieved through the overthrow of the corrupt capitalistic governments of the world, all the old money kings who had gold and silver dollars outnumbering the stars in the sky.

Debs and Riley had not expected to agree with each other. The poet had recalled in his old age that he had never voted but once, and that was when he had intended to vote for Big Ben Harrison, but as his wrist had trembled he had cast his vote, quite inadvertently, it seemed, not to the right to the Republican slot, but to the left to the Democrats' slot, when, as everybody knew, the Democrats were the upholders of pubs and a man's need for a little apple jack with which to wet his whistle. The Republicans were supposedly dry.

[3]

SOCIALIST CHILDREN for their attendance at Sunday School or camp meetings, like the old camp meetings of Baptists and Methodists when the Middle West was all a wilderness where the birds outwarbled the preachers on muleback going from settlement to settlement, learned from Uncle Henry Schnitkind's biography of Debs in an idyllic and symbolic way what must have been his childhood and the first impressions made upon his awakening mind, for which there was no documentation. Schnitkind had borrowed details from the mythologies of mother and child. Debs's mother, Marguerite, a mystic in many ways, had been called Daisy by all the children even before, as Riley would have said, she had gone to push the daisies up, as dead sweethearts and mothers did then.

The grass was God's handkerchief, Daisy had told Eugene. God had just finished making the world when He saw a little boy playing on a precipice. "Careful, sonny!" God had called out to the little boy. "You're liable to fall over the precipice and get killed." The little boy was so busy chasing a butterfly that he did not hear God's warning, and when the butterfly flew out over the edge of the cliff, he went right on chasing after it and fell to the bottom of the abyss and got crushed but was not dead. "Go on," Gene urged Daisy every time she told of this catastrophic event. "Then what happened?" Daisy said that God took pity upon the little boy and began to cry, and His tears made oceans and lakes and rivers all over the world, but He had nothing to wipe His eyes with, so He made a handkerchief of the green grass, with which He wiped away His tears, and thus the dewdrops were the tears of God. "But why," Gene asked, "did God make all those precipices and butterflies and little boys to chase them?" "God made," Gene's mother said, "the whole earth, with everything in it, because He wanted to have a pretty toy to play with. Earth is the marble God spins." Gene thought that just as his pockets were bulging with aggies and glassies, God's pockets were bulging with stars and planets.

When he first heard of the death of a baby, he became very angry and stamped his foot and cried out, "Shame on you, dear God! Why did you do it?" He began to think that maybe God would take him away and hide him, too. After several days of brooding over the mystery, he said, "Tell me, Daisy, why God takes children away from their parents." His mother explained, "He wants them to be out of harm's way. For God is a beautiful king, and we are all His children, and He loves us all."

When the little boy heard the whistle of the night express, the train became a living thing to him. Daisy told the little boy that the sparks of fire flying upward out of the engineer's caboose were the golden bees flying out of a beehive.

[4]

DEBS WAS THE SON of Jean Daniel Debs, whom everybody called Daniel and he and the other children called Dandy, and no doubt he seemed to them like the bearded lion who lay down with the lamb or like the "dandy lions" that were strewn as bright as little yellow suns in the grass.

Dandy had been born in Alsace-Lorraine, at Colmar, in an ancient high-shouldered five-story house in the shadow of the Cathedral of St. Martin. Throughout his life Debs had wanted to visit the house where his father was born, as he also would have sought to locate the place where Marguerite was born, although it might have been by comparison only a poor stone house, as she was a poor little mill girl, a wage slave before she came to this country in search of happiness—or so he would sometimes describe her when he was working to help the poor little mill girls and boys who were wage slaves in America, many of whom died of old age and its attendant woes at just about the time when more fortunate children were starting school.

Debs's father's father had been an owner of numerous farming interests and textile and grain mills, where Marguerite Bettrich had worked as a beater of flax, a spinner of thread, perhaps also as a sifter of grain.

Daniel had fallen in love with Marguerite at first glance—perhaps when he saw her with bundles of golden flax under her arm, perhaps when she was in midpassage of the millstream, perhaps when she was separating grain from pebbles and sand. His father had opposed the boy's interest in the poor mill girl, as they were not in the same social stream even if they were in the same millstream, down by the old red mill.

Fortunately or unfortunately, although the brooding young moon calf had been sent away to school in Paris and Wildersbach, where he was a student of French poets and romanticists of every stripe as well as skeptics and deists and agnostics and atheists and revolutionaries by the ton, he had found his love for the little mill girl growing by leaps and bounds and had been unable to give her up for even a moment in his mind.

Although the Debs ancestors at Colmar had been active in the French Revolution, the father was altogether too bourgeois to believe in the equality of all or that a bridge of love should be built over the abyss dividing the classes. The young man had burned with revolutionary fires as with the fires of his love for the little girl who was forbidden fruit forever beyond his

reach and without whom there could be no paradise on earth. Perhaps revolution was always love, love of common humanity, love of the poor.

The unyielding mill king was about to yield, or perhaps would have
yielded if only there had been a deathbed scene in which he could state that
he had had a change of mind, a change of heart, when quite suddenly and
without warning that he was suffering from any ailment of the heart he
had passed away, leaving the son free to marry the poor little fairy-tale
goosegirl if only she could be persuaded to accept the hand of this persistent
lover whose love would lead her to a distant and largely unknown land,
from which she and he would never return. They would be able to start life
all over again with that part of the estate which was his, and which was
greatly reduced by theft even before he sailed.

Not Africa but America was then the mysterious continent for most
Europeans, even as it was for most Americans as to its vast interiors, mountains, rivers, lakes, deserts. Marguerite had feared that in America there
might be the injustices that there were in France—and thus perhaps it
would be better if the land of which her suitor dreamed remained a land
for which he would set sail only in his dreams, as it would be better if he
should give up his desire for union with her. Not once had she claimed that
his was an unrequited love. She had known that there would be no other
love for her as he had known that there would be no other love for him.

She had consented, however, that he should go ahead of her to what he
considered to be a more promising world than the old, when in Bloody
June 1848, that month which should be the month of weddings and roses,
the revolution had been stamped out by commercial interests, and many
revolutionists were driven underground or were in flight to foreign
lands—especially America, with its vast, unpopulated regions, places
where a lone horseman might travel all day without seeing any other
horseman, unless it was his own shadow on the fog.

This was also the year of the discovery of gold in a creekbed in California, although only the first trickles of gold seekers were coming through
from the blasted European lands in which the poor were turning into
skeletons, the impetus to a greater migration occurred the following year,
when the gold dust was confused with the City of Gold which was in the
sun and was the place to which had always migrated the souls of the dead,
who were fireflies and gave to the setting sun its glow.

Daniel had sailed for America in 1848—but while the four-masted
schooner with its disorienting figurehead, perhaps of the admiral with the
golden cup or the captain's twins or the captain's widow, was still pitching
through high storms in heavy winter seas, plowing the waves upon

which—unlike those of history—would be left no mark of the plowman, he had been gulled out of a sizable part of his inheritance, the French equivalent of six thousand dollars, by an American confidence man who had represented himself as a successful tobacco speculator with knowledge of a surefire way of getting rich quick. Arriving in New York harbor on January 20, 1849, Daniel had turned over almost all the rest of his money to the persuasive confidence man, a master of a magician's disappearing act so complete that he had left no trace and not even a tobacco leaf or a cigar butt for the poor young man to chew on as he thought of the little sweetheart who he was determined must be his bride. For without her, he could not live.

Not being a tramp used to sleeping on a park bench or in a gutter or in a darkened doorway, Daniel had stayed for a time at the Shakespeare Hotel which—located at the corner of Duane and William streets—was frequented by many French and German and other radicals who were in flight from European capitalistic corruption and were seekers of a New Moral World such as America should be when they had transplanted socialism or communism to this amorphous continent where—as it was imagined—the habits and modes of being and institutions of the past were not so deeply rooted as in the Old World, with its furrows cut by habit through so many ages that it resisted change.

The neighborhood down around City Hall was full of radicals of every breed who seemed permanently amazed by the utopian prospects that seemed to be opening in this millennial land where there were as many folding as opening. There were utopian philosophers of every kind mixing with clowns, politicians, confidence men, rich men such as the Astors and Vanderbilts, who in the lexicons of socialistic anarchists, with their dreams of a moneyless, propertyless world, were confidence men who had made good in this age of expansion, which had expressed itself in the Mexican War and was expressing itself further in the movements of gold rushers rushing pell-mell not merely to golden rushes growing by silver streams in a paradise which would be beyond this world. There were scriptural communists with secular dreams prompted by mystical origins as there were followers of Robert Owen, Charles Fourier, Étienne Cabet of the Icarians, Brisbaneites, Perfectionists who were believers in society's reform, whether immediate, as if by sudden transfiguration, or remote.

When the youthful Walt Whitman of the *Brooklyn Eagle,* the entire cosmos not yet enclosed within him although it must have been there in an only semiconscious form, had casually strolled in to cover the world's convention of radical theorists of reform in Clinton Hall, New York, he reported under the heading "Quixotic Labors" on June 6, 1846, having noticed that Robert Owen, the philanthropist and human reformer, had arrived again in this republic. Walt Whitman had predicted that in all probability Robert Owen would do no harm but would also do no good. Whitman had not known whether to laugh at the convention of world reformers as a humbug or commend it as containing the germ of a bold though fruitless inquiry into the wrongs and evils of the world. The attendants at the convention had seemed to him, with the exception of the patient and dignified Robert Owen, the last ones who should come forth as reformers of the world. Walt Whitman had found some truth in Robert Owen's speeches and addresses, had listened to two or three of them with much pleasure, and yet was of the opinion that it was utterly chimerical to attempt to remodel the world on an unalloyed basis of purity and perfection. God had not seen fit to do so, and he could hardly expect the thing to be accomplished by Mr. Robert Owen.

When Walt Whitman had allowed the ideal of utopia to mull in his mind for a few weeks, as surely it would always mull in his mind whether it was of the future or the past, he was willing to announce under the headline "Philanthropy" that this word, signifying the "love of man," was one of the most beautiful words that our language had inherited from the Greek. "It has a musical sound, and the very utterance of it begets pleasant thoughts and inspiring prophecies of good."

Perhaps under the spell of Robert Owen as well as Albert Brisbane and others with their inflated dreams of allying age-old or newly minted utopias with society's reform, Walt Whitman had seen "a vision, however far off, of the relation existing between all men as members of one great family; the duty and pleasure of loving and helping one the other; the dwelling together of the nations in peace, as being of the same flesh and blood and bone and bound together by the ties of a common brotherhood. . . ."

These were the thoughts and feelings that for the good gray poet—not yet the crazy old Walt he would become as the elegiac author of "When Lilacs Last in the Dooryard Bloom'd"—must have lived somewhere in some hearts in the olden time and, struggling for existence, had given birth to this beautiful and musical speech. "Let us rejoice in its existence and seek to give it divine second birth in action."

[5]

Staying for a time at the Shakespeare Hotel, where Daniel had taken shelter while waiting, praying that his little Marguerite would set sail before the late summer, when her ship might run into winter storms, had been one of the most colorful of the picaresque socialistic characters streaming then onto the always millennial continent. Wilhelm Weitling had sought refuge here as an exile in 1848 but had returned to Europe sub rosa when the revolutionary forces were about to boil over in France and Germany and Austria and inundate the Old World, and then had returned to the harbor city in the New World in 1849 in flight from the failure of the revolution, in which the red caps storming the barricades had been mowed down by the military representatives of international capitalistic interests whose kingdoms knew no boundary lines but those between rich and poor, and the cobblestone streets were turned into seas of blood, red as the red roses in that June, which was the month of brides, dead brides, dead bridegrooms.

Wilhelm Weitling was ten years older than Marx and not about to take his cues from the younger man. He had not been able to plow through Marx's dialectical materialism or all those vast abstractions looming in his way—all as cold and impersonal as icebergs. The philosophy of monolithic Hegelianism was enough to put Wilhelm Weitling into something worse than a polar fog, whether arctic or antarctic, that absolute which was incompatible with divine transcendence, in Marx's view relegating the religion of Christ to the status of a hot water bottle for some individuals. The utterance of the word "bird" was evidently not the same as the bird itself.

Among the many pre-Marxist philosophers who had influenced Wilhelm Weitling was Pierre-Joseph Proudhon, the swift-thinking philosophic anarchist of change who could still state—when it seemed that the fires of revolution had been extinguished except for buried sparks—that he could envision a future in which it would be easier to conceive of society without government than of society with government. "Society, just now, is like the butterfly just out of the cocoon, which shakes its gilded wings in the sunlight before taking flight. Tell it to crawl back into the silken covering, to shun the flowers and to hide itself from the light!"

Wilhelm Weitling was the bastard son of a very theatrical, musically inclined young French officer of the Napoleonic artillery who before his departure into the realm of snow and ice that was the dominion of the Sphinx, or Talma, of the North, Czar Alexander I—a journey from which he would never return—had deposited the seed of his loins into the not stony ground of a poor little housemaid who was the daughter of a stonemason in the beautiful cathedral town of Magdeburg on the Elbe, where the marketplace was dominated by the statue of Otto the Great, a medieval emperor before whose feet the fishing folk had laid on a May day each year bundles of field flowers and glasses of pale liqueurs that caught the light of the sun.

The child had lived in such abject poverty that there would not have been even an old cock's head or feet for the soup during the invasion of Magdeburg by the wild-maned Cossacks on their wild-maned horses if he had not helped his old grandmother peddle matches, lamp wicks made of loosely twisted threads, tobacco for clay pipes, coffee mixed with chicory, playing cards—whatever might appeal to the Cossacks, whose emperor was a believer in numerous aspects of ameliorative social reform although well knowing that human gratitude was as rare a thing as a white raven.

One of the troubles springing up like brambles in the way of the czar, who was the representative of Christ, was that the devil Napoleon by his betrayals had slowed up the utopian movements of reform that he had hoped to introduce into darkest Russia in such a way that it would be his kingdom which would provide beacon lights to the world when it was in storm. Appalled by the savage spirit of Napoleon when he had caused the execution of a member of royalty, he had expressed his disapproval to him and had received the reply that a sense of moral outrage seemed strange, ill-fitting when it came from an emperor who had also slain a member of royalty.

The man whom Alexander I had killed, according to the Emperor Napoleon, had been his own father, the tyrannical Paul I, who was rumored to have worn the crown of the Romanovs even at family dinner parties and who was convinced that his children were spying on him. When he had spoken of chopping off a row of heads as lightly as if they were the plumes of dandelions, he had seemed to have his children in mind and particularly the one who would be the next czar.

Grand Duke Alexander had never wanted to be a czar at all and had planned to descend from the throne before he had ascended it—to go into exile. He had been persuaded, however, by revolutionaries to abandon this self-centered existence, to remain at the center of temporal power at least for a time before his spirit should take flight—time enough to bring calm where there had been chaos and to provide for his suffering people a freedom that would be upheld by law and would be something more than a constitution in name only, for it would have teeth capable of biting despotism in its many manifestations.

Alexander I was to remember—when half his mind was shadowed by an elegiac sense for the father whose death he had witnessed and had unintentionally made possible by admitting the revolutionaries into the dark red Mikhailovsky Castle with the idea that they were only going to ask for his abdication—the awesome fact that his father's reign had begun with many reforms running in all ways all at once.

Alexander I had been lifted prematurely to the throne by the murder of the old czar, which he had described as an act of God—at the same time that he who had seen his father's multi-fractured, multi-broken body had been infused, it had seemed, with the divine mission of alleviating the sufferings of his people in orderly ways, among them the giving of relief to farmers. For surely it could not be that, as in some old myth of the soul's passage, the diabolical spirit of his dead father had passed into him, the vessel of God, and would allow to him no peace for the bringing into darkest Russia of that light of reform which might ultimately provide, perhaps when he himself had suffered death and transfiguration, a beacon light to the world.

[6]

PRESIDENT THOMAS JEFFERSON, who had gone into office at the same time as the young Czar Alexander I's reluctant ascension to the throne, had been very grateful to this new ruler for having come to the rescue of one of our frigates when, during the period in which Napoleon was doing violence to the laws of nature, it had been stranded on the coast of Tripoli. President Jefferson had expressed his sense of exalted pleasure in the various acts that the czar's administration had achieved during the short time he had been on the throne in his country, all seeming to flow from virtue and wisdom. To be sure, President Jefferson had been writing at a time when history seemed not the stumblings of blind gods or blind fate but an exercise in the principles of morality and immorality. Man had a choice between forward and backward movements. "Sound principles, pursued with a steady step, dealing out good progressively as your people are prepared to receive and to hold it fast, cannot fail to carry them and yourself far in the improvement of their condition during the course of your life."

Alexander I had been attracted by such spirits of reform as the wildly eccentric utilitarian philosopher Jeremy Bentham, to whom, when the old hermit was living in splendor as a tenant in the manor house Ford Abbey near Chard in Somerset, its surroundings so resplendent that they might have been a miniature palace fit for a czar, he had sent a footman bearing a diamond ring in a box, which was returned to him with its seal unbroken—for what the old hermit had wanted was to codify the Russian law for the czar.

Among those potentates who had come to Bentham for help with the constitutions of the republics that they hoped to build were Aaron Burr, with his dream of establishing an empire in Mexico, and General Miranda, with his dream of liberating Venezuela.

Alexander I had also been attracted by Robert Owen's *New View of Society;* at a convention of kings in Frankfurt he had been approached by this great propagandist of a classless utopian society who had not yet found a place for the demonstration of his ideals and who had offered the czar a copy of his scroll, for which he had no pocket. The czar had invited Robert Owen to come to his rooms at some later date for a discussion of spiritual redemption, a subject of the greatest personal concern to one whose political advisers included the spirits of the dead.

At this time, the discrowned Emperor Napoleon, who was exiled upon the lonely island of St. Helena, where he was dying of cancer of the stomach, his eyes almost blind, was said to be reading a copy of Robert Owen's *New View of Society* while still considering the old.

The czar of all the Russias, with his mind seeming permanently befogged, his broken beams, his lack of any true sense of direction, and his desire to retire, had been attracted not only to Benthamites and Owenites but to the teachings of Charles Fourier, who was considered by many to be a forerunner of Robert Owen, a rival whom he himself had always considered a usurper of that utopia upon which he alone should have the patent rights.

What had held Czar Alexander I up in the enactment of reforms that should be carried out not only in spirit but in substance had been not only his betrayals by Napoleon, who had robbed Alexander of his peace of mind and had engaged him in war, but also the objections of the conservative vested interests in his own society, who were not interested in the release of the serfs who were his children or, as they called themselves, his little pigeon souls, and dependent on him for the least grain of corn they might find on a harvest ground that had been swept bare by the rich landlords.

The czar had begun to feel, quite early, that he could not trust any of his living advisers, that all were scoundrels. They would soon make of him, if he did not take care, a dead pigeon soul in the snow.

Alexander I's own historian had warned that Russia had been founded by the autocracy and that it would be disastrous to try to modify its structure. "Our political principles are not inspired by the Enlightenment Encyclopaedia edited in Paris but by another Encyclopaedia infinitely more ancient, the Bible. Our Czars are not representatives of the People. . . . They are the representatives of Him who rules over all empires. . . . The Emperor is our living law." He had clung less to the ideals of the often split radicals, who were attempting to achieve the harmonies of universal reform, and more to the Bible as time went on.

In thinking over his Book of Kings in March 1810, the former president Thomas Jefferson had remembered, in his retirement at his Monticello farm, the inadequacies of the various kings who had come before either his magnifying glass or telescope.

The king of England was a cipher, he had written to his old fellow revolutionary John Langdon. The crowned heads of Europe had been weakened by their interbreeding just as cattle would have been if kept in the same barn and begetting their calves only by each other. They would have produced animals who were all body and no brain, like the present royal heads over whom Napoleon, it seemed, had triumphed.

Among those whom the retired president considered to have been fools were Louis XVI, the king of Spain, and the king of Naples, the queen of Portugal, the king of Denmark, and the king of Prussia, the latter a mere hog in body as well as mind. "These animals had become without mind and powerless, and so will every hereditary monarch be after a few generations. Alexander, the grandson of Catherine, is as yet an exception. But he is only of the third generation. His race is not yet worn out."

ALEXANDER'S DEATH, which had purportedly occurred in December 1825, was a study in ambivalences just as his life had been. He had apparently preceded Thomas Jefferson to his grave by only a few months, the sage of Monticello having spent his life in opposition to the rule not only of foreign kings but of American moneybags who flirted with the idea of putting on crowns and coronets and who, as their power increased, would often be likened by anarchic socialists to such sleek, fat hogs as often did turn down the canyon of Wall Street.

Thomas Jefferson, as shown by his last letter on earth, which was written to Roger Weightman, librarian of the Patent Office in Washington, had been convinced of the justness of the American Revolutionary cause, which had brought to this country a half century of peace and prosperity achieved by refusal to submit to the sword of a king.

The mournful Alexander I, who had been on a tour of the Crimea, had contracted a cold, a chill and fever shaking his bones, and had apparently died, so far as all that was mortal was concerned—had given up the ghost at Tagalog. Eight days had been required for the news to reach St. Petersburg, and an even longer time for the arrival of the corpse in the long coffin, not upright, of which the lid was closed all along the way before entombment in the burial vaults of his dead ancestors in the Peter and Paul Cathedral, there to wait for resurrection, when it would be seen whether the rumor that the czar had never died, had only simulated his death by pretending to be dead when he was sleeping with one eye opened for his escape, was right.

[7]

WITH THOUGHTS of his mysterious father always weighing on his mind, Wilhelm Weitling had been fascinated at an early age by the faces of angels in the cathedral and the face of Mary, mother of the Christ with whom he had identified himself as with the crucified Christ who was hung between two thieves and had promised them that the next day he would see them in paradise. The question of future revolutionary anarchic socialistic communitarians, such as he was to become in his quest for harmony through worlds of sectarian discord, would always be why these thieves who were strung up with Christ were not thieves of mines and mills, why they were petty thieves of bread crumbs for their starving children or thieves of ribbons, spools of thread, needles, pins, strings of old lace, buttons. Those who stole a country's treasures from the poor were not punished by corrupt governments—for if they were fined, the penalties were less than the rewards.

The land in which Wilhelm Weitling spent his boyhood was filled with ancient romances. There were invisible elves. There were dead horses whose legs might turn into legs of gold. There were talking birds. There were sacrifices of little red shoes made to the god of the snow which would never stop falling unless the little red shoes were put out in the snow. It would be remembered that Wilhelm Weitling had been kind to dogs and could not have believed that even the mangiest old dog who was a community nuisance, howling all night long, should be beaten with sticks and stones and chased out of town with all the community sins placed upon his battered, bleeding head so that the sleepers might sleep in peace.

He had been educated only in the lower grades and had learned to read and write a beautiful Gothic script and was never slow to speak, was not the kind of boy who had to be fed a dog's tongue in order to learn to bark or a bird's tongue in order to learn to sing. It was a socialist's problem: Which came first, the bird or the word? Word was bird.

Wilhelm Weitling, who was apprenticed at the green age of twelve to a tailor in whose home he had lived for six years—his workplace a bench where, with his legs crossed like the legs of a frog, he had sat stitching acres of linen and wool and velvet and silk for clothing for men and women from before dawn to after dusk, his jaundiced skin mottled with shadows or shriveled as if he were a frog under a log which no sunlight could reach—for he had suffered at times from probably hallucinatory illnesses, possibly caused by long hours and sedentary habits and a poor diet and no apples either green or red or gold at his master's table—had become at the age of eighteen a wandering tailor.

He had decided to be a helper of mankind. He was a tailor by trade who became a utopist and believer in the dictates of the heart, which even if smashed and pulverized should be reassembled and made to beat again through man's intuitive desire that the dead should live, and who knew or imagined that he knew how to cut the cloth of an unreal reality in such a way that even the poorest of God's children should be clothed in a material and a spiritual sense. There was no such thing in nature as a bastard left upon a rock, for all children were the same in the eyes of God.

He was an agnostic who had remained under the spell of the icons of Catholicism as well as biblical myths of creation and salvation such as those of Noah and the ark, which were symbols of numerous utopias, and Joseph and his many-colored coat, which was brought by the envious brothers to his father to prove that he was dead although yet he had lived at the bottom of a well and would return, Christ, who multiplied one loaf into a thousand loaves and one fish into a thousand fishes by miracle, and also old pagan mysteries, which were of measureless influence upon the dreams of renascent socialists in the age of the great power looms, the despotic machine that was threatening to stamp out hand workers, all to become tramps upon the roads if they were fortunate to live.

Of course, throughout the nineteenth century, with its elegiac literature of deathlike sleep and dream, that of a perambulatory somnambulism of the walking dead and of the awakening, there was always the specter-haunted thought that the many who had been transmuted and translated to the Island of the Blessed were the fortunate ones.

[8]

THE WANDERING COMMUNIST tailor Weitling had prayed constantly to Jesus to bring His kingdom down out of the clouds and had cried out—as he would continue to announce when he fled to America—that communism would be the kingdom of the saints that had been promised eighteen hundred years ago to those who lived in communal harmony with the worker Christ Who might at any moment appear. "The boundaries of nations will crumble when the Son of Man comes to judge the quick and the dead."

He had written in 1842 while in exile at Lausanne his own Christian communal system in *Guarantees of Harmony and Freedom,* in which he had trumpeted loud enough to shake the clouds, "We want to be free! Free as the birds of the heavens—free to travel through life as only they do, in happy flight and precious harmony." A member of the swan brotherhood who had tailored only when he needed money for his bread and the print-ing of his perfectionist socialistic pamphlets, he had thrown his scissors into the lake with the hope that he would never see them again. But alas, he was to be pursued by scissors the rest of his life, even unto his grave.

The message conveyed by Weitling's song was very similar to those of Chartist agitators in the British Isles, of whom one had been Allan Pinker-ton, the wanderer upon the Scottish moors, who when he came to America in the year of the gold rush had his mind upon the heavenly city of gold but would change his mind when God—if it was God and not the devil—had opened a way to him to become a sleuth of the first magnitude, a detective hounding labor union organizers and labor strikers and anarchic rebels as in the case of the Molly Maguires.

Wilhelm Weitling's wanderings in Europe as a sower of seed of propa-ganda for a "new moral world" and not as a sewer of sleeves, pants, coats, skirts, had been made with a horsehair trunk of utopias of every cut and plan and every color there was, particularly that of Robert Owen, who in the long ago when his "phalanstery" at New Harmony on the Wabash River in Indiana had already been wrecked had announced that he had crossed the Rubicon between the old immoral world and the new moral world—a river that, ever widening, seemed to be bereft of a shore on either side, for he was still crossing it—as the romantic ex-tailor had come under the influence of Charles Fourier, the former textile mill owner and salesman who suffered from the fixed idea that the former cotton lord Robert Owen's utopia had been stolen from him, the only begetter and bearer of patent rights for his phalansteries by which he would exile winter from the earth and would provide a cure-all for society's ills more effective than any magical blue flower could be.

The seeker Wilhelm Weitling had known personally and had listened with fraternal sympathy to the promises of the earthly paradise which, to be a somewhat monarchical commune or joint stock company in which the workers pooled their gold, had been made by the French lawyer Étienne Cabet, an undiscouraged Owen disciple who had attracted associations of idealistic utopia-minded migrants to America for ill-starred foundings of transient communes in imitation of his novel *Voyage to Icarus,* the symbolism of the name to be shown in time to be an unconsciously accurate prophecy in the new millennial world of America. As the wings of the possibly original Icarus had melted when he had flown too near the sun, so also the communities of the Icarians were to be as insubstantial as if they with their canvas stretched on wire struts and swan feathers glued on with wax by an inexpert tailor had also been consumed by fire, their survival not to be long in the Texas of the monolithic land grabbers or upon the bluffs overlooking the Mississippi River, the Father of Waters, at Nauvoo, Illinois, when they made their precarious settlement upon part of the old Mormon burned-out City of God and parcel of farmland after the legalized mob murder of the divinely inflated but secular many-colored utopian prophet Joseph Smith and his brother in the prison cell at Carthage, a place also aptly named.

Wilhelm Weitling had also known the little books of the little French Catholic priest Hugues Félicité Robert de Lamennais, who, because of his revolutionary messages equating Christ with communism, had suffered the anathema of excommunication placed upon him by the ecclesiastical powers and was fortunate not to have been executed by the secular powers or lords temporal. Sometimes when revolutionary seekers after a better world could not be found, their books were brought to trial and executed in their place by burning and drowning, now as in the past.

Brigham Young, a man who could not spell the word "millennium" but with the spirit of reform on him could speak in bird tongues, angel tongues, foreign tongues, tongues of prehistoric peoples, had preached in the streets of London, where he had made fewer converts because of the competition given to him by street preachers of other millennial faiths—some with only their dreams and no kingdom on earth to offer—than he had made in Manchester, where the *Millennial Star* was edited and thousands of Mormon hymnals were published on the eve of the Chartist riots.

Brigham Young had seen boatloads of migrants off from busy English shipping wharves, many so poor that he had had to advance them the money for their fare lest they should never be able to reach the land of promise. The elder Young had been the harvester of the souls who were to join the community of Saints, where the quick and the dead were always in communication with each other. He was sure, as he had written to his brother Joseph Young in the autumn of 1840, that the Saints had so much the spirit of gathering in them that they would go to America even if they knew that they would be set upon by the mob as soon as they got there and would be driven on and on. "They have the spirit of the times here as well as the Church there."

[9]

THE FALLEN-AWAY ROMAN CATHOLIC Wilhelm Weitling, who in Switzerland had continued to employ the sacred images of Roman Catholicism while attacking orthodox theologians, had caused some rival socialists to look upon him as an incendiary tramp without much substantial thought—and others to suspect in him an ill-founded messianic illusional state—and one of his disciples to believe that he with his parody of the Lord's Prayer was guilty of entertaining the ambition to become the new pope of communism. Whatever he had intended, it was not to be the pope's nose. He had fed crumbs to the swans on the lake.

To save the money he would have had to pay for a laundry bill—for he had needed every cent for the printer's bill, the strewing of his seeds of propaganda—he had begun to go without underwear or socks. To symbolize the revolution which was about to come he had begun to wear the red cap that symbolized the martyrdom of the worker Christ.

He was the one who knew the way to the earthly paradise which was to come—the golden way gleaming through clouds of darkness—and knew it simply by instinct. Utopia was that which was outside of history. It came because it must.

The bastard had cried aloud in workers' cells that all children should be equal in the eyes of God. "We are all children of one father, and we all have a common destiny—to be happy here, and then forever in the great beyond."

Wilhelm Weitling had not believed that coins should be stamped with the heads of emperors and kings. In their stead there should appear such emblems of labor as the hammer and the anvil and the chisel and the saw and words that proclaimed, even to a blind man reading Braille with his fingertips, the promise that their value was worth one loaf of bread or one pound of meat.

For his increasingly radical writings and revolutionary speeches, which threatened to start avalanches burying old societies for the sake of others, the humble man spreading the word of the red Christ had been closed in on by the police at three o'clock in the morning on June 9, 1843, and thrown into prison, there to wait for trial for having committed no crime but the crime of spreading his anarchic socialist or communist messages, which seemed to be gaining converts by the ton.

Zurich was yielding to the pressure of German and Austrian and other emperors and kings, who had sent their detectives to watch Weitling's every move and report on every word he said or wrote.

Condemned to a prison cell in Switzerland for his mockery of the words of God and his verbal attacks on social and economic institutions, which were in general even more sacrosanct than the words of God, he was found by the Swiss to be no threat to the government nor to the established religious and banking institutions with his revolutionary red cap messages, but they had determined that he who was already a borderline case, a dweller in a fog-bound kingdom between the sane and the insane, should return to prison. When he was released, he would be sent entirely over the borderline that divided Switzerland from other lands.

He had already served four months and now had six months more tacked on to his sentence before exile for five years from every Swiss canton there was in an intricate country where, as might be seen when an avalanche occurred, there were more cantons than anyone knew there were.

Wilhelm Weitling's last speech before the court had been mainly an attempt to refute the charge of blasphemy. He had shown Christ as a man who had loved to pick flowers. Christ had been such a very human man that he had aroused, because of an insult he had paid to Judas, the vast response of his betrayal by the Judas cock, without whom there would have been no crucifixion and no resurrection and no millennial cock like that which was promised, now that Christ would soon return or perhaps had already returned or perhaps had never really left the earth or had been in and out many times as some mystical communitarians of the Swedenborgian or older supernatural assumptions believed, in view of the awesome fact that there was no exact borderline between what was possible and what was impossible.

The *Communist Chronicle* of London had announced, as Wilhelm Weitling had been returned like a ragged tramp to his tomb in a Switzerland where the poor in some cantons suffered as much as the poor in other countries, a tragedy made evident by the number who seemed believers in the artisan communal earthly paradise which was to come and who wanted to get out in order to go from the Old World to the New World which was at present phantasmal, a dream in men's minds,

> Our dear Brother Weitling is now a martyr. . . . The blood of the martyrs is the seed of the church. The bruised geranium leaf smelleth more sweetly. . . . Meanwhile, although not free in person, the thoughts of Weitling are commingling with ours and flying abroad like down-winged seeds over our common earth of green and gold. . . . Since the French Revolution of 1791, we enumerate three illustrious communist martyrs—Babeuf of France, Joshua Jacob of Ireland, and Wilhelm Weitling of Germany. . . . Blessings upon them, as far as they should be blest.

When Weitling was told that fifty francs were on the way to his assistance, he had assumed that fifty brothers from Frankfurt were coming to batter down the walls. No army had come through the night to his rescue.

He had suffered as much derangement of his senses in his cold, dark prison cell as if quicksilver had been packed into his ears. He had heard knockings in the walls, voices, cryings, shoutings. He had seen the eyes of the Austrian detective staring at him continually through two peepholes in a wall so that he in his isolation had enjoyed no sense of privacy whatever. He had developed strange burnings in his chest and could not sneeze without the sense that he was being killed. He had been afraid to accept a clean nightshirt from his jailer lest they should attempt to strangle him and hang him up by its long sleeves. He had refused to accept a cup of water or a cup of wine lest it should contain a few lethal drops that might put him into a sleep from which there would be no awakening, some people always to think that the world of sleep and dreams was his.

He had heard continually the sound of a boy blowing a wooden trumpet—a dog barking at a bone by a lonely shore—as he had remembered the holy images of mother and child he had known in his youth. He had declared that a letter from his poor mother who was living, he believed, on public alms in Magdeburg, just such crumbs as the community would allow to her, was not in her handwriting. It was a forgery, for the spelling was not hers, and the words were not those which she would have written to him. He had been driven almost completely out of his bird by his sincere but erroneous belief that the sons of Calvin had stolen from him the letters and the strand of his grandmother's hair and the strand of his mother's hair that he had carried on his person throughout the years of his wanderings and that were more precious to him than strands of silver and gold.

To try to save his very nervous mind and frayed nerves and broken strings from total collapse into the primordial chaos he had begun to pass the time in his tomb by combing with a fine-toothed comb the Bible in search of new pearls of wisdom to add to his crusader's shield if ever he should emerge. He had been sane enough to continue with his studies of the English language. For he was planning to migrate to England and possibly also to America in quest of the site for an earthly paradise or New Jerusalem that would operate in accordance with his visionary system and was not left to chance.

He had not particularly wished to go to America, possibly because that would have been for him another and lasting exile, possibly because for him as for others it was the great unknown—possibly because it was the known.

While in the prison trying to evolve his thoughts upon the subject of the universal tongue, Wilhelm Weitling had been sure that the universal tongue which he envisioned would require that complexities be replaced by clarities as in the language of children.

In the process of evolving it, he had worked on his very individualistic verse, which expressed his shattered ego. Although he might seem to himself a second Christ, he did not think of himself as a genius in the writing of poems but felt that they might fill a vacuum that had never been expressed before in the German tongue, as no one before him had suffered or recorded an experience which was unique. He had had the talents with which to do so as he also had the love of old romance from the days of his childhood in Magdeburg, that place which he most feared and loved.

The poems that recorded his "Wounds" as the bastard son of the little toy soldier who had disappeared in the Russian snow had included, along with "Conscience," "Temptation," "The Betrayer," addresses "To My Judge and to My Prosecutor," his sufferings under the gaze of "The Monster," who was the Austrian detective staring at him through the peephole in the wall, "Forty-eight Hours in the Dark," which told of the flutterings of his pulse, the rush of blood to his head, his hunger, the coughings of the sick in other cells, and "Night," which told of the jailer making his rounds and rattling his keys, and the beautiful "Morning," with its first faint beams of light, which had made him wonder if he would ever see the light of the day bringing his release and for how long.

Poems entitled "The Little Bird," "The Sun," "The Moon," "The Christmas Tree," and "Do Not Despair" were among those providing "Balsam," as were those containing memories of his mother and those asking for strength to bear his cross.

To some of Weitling's critics he was just plain cuckoo, the kind of bird who had no nest of his own and wanted to lay his egg in some other bird's nest, even as he wanted to take the meadows which were not his own and give them to the workers of the world.

While still in the prison cell wearing his red cap, clutching in his hands the sheaf of his poems as he waited for the lid of his coffin to be lifted for the release which he both welcomed and feared, jailbird Wilhelm Weitling had seemingly continued to turn a blind eye and a deaf ear to an offer of free passage to the utopian cooperative community which Andreas Dietsch, who had been a brush maker in the Swiss Alps, had recently founded in darkest Missouri and to which he had invited the seekers of light to come and share the plans devised and described by an idealistic utopian of no education but that which had been of the red heart in this little pamphlet entitled *The Thousand Year Kingdom,* in which he had pointed out that the sufferings of the poor caused by the present unjust social and economic order had not been the work of God. "Father in heaven did not want it so; only man has made it so"—the community at New Helvetia— that which would so soon fade, no sign of its passage but a few graves soon to be covered over by the long grass, its founder to die alone in St. Louis of a broken heart because of his betrayal and abandonment by those in whom he had placed his idealistic, idyllic faith.

[1 0]

S O FAR AS UTOPIAS were concerned, they might disappear because they failed in a pecuniary sense, or they might be killed by envious capitalists because they succeeded in a pecuniary sense, as has been the fate of the expanding Mormons in Ohio and in their Missouri colonies and in their beautiful temple city at Nauvoo, Illinois.

It was in the summer of 1844, following the May day of the enraged, curious, squalling Wilhelm Weitling's release from the Swiss prison or tomb by the Zurich police, that the Mormon prophet Joseph Smith, would-be candidate for the presidency of the United States who was never to run or be elected to that high office, for he in the view of his followers would be elected to a higher office, had been killed by mobs of military vigilantes who with their faces painted black and red to suggest that they were radicals had stormed into the prison at Carthage, Illinois, where the door to the stairway had been left unlocked by the watchman, acting in accordance with higher orders.

The Mormons had already been driven out of Ohio, where they had lost their beautiful temple to fires as if they were not the wheat but were chaff before the wind.

Brigham Young, who had been upon a complex missionary journey in America trying to arouse sympathy for the besieged head of the Mormon "harts," as he spelled "hearts," had been weary but happy in his calling which he spelled "cauling," by that meaning the web or veiling over the face of the newborn son who might become the sage or saint because born in his shroud.

For a long time, ever since he had worked in the city of Manchester to increase the sheaves for the church, Brigham Young had prayed that the God of the Mormons would creep out of His hiding place soon, lest his own constitution should fail.

In September, when he had finally reached Nauvoo, his mission of publicizing Joseph Smith's proposed candidacy for president of the United States having been most sorrowfully interrupted by Smith's murder—his body had been hidden away by his followers in order to keep the thieving mob from hacking him—the murdered prophet's suddenly refulgent, resurrected spirit had seemed to all but the black-garbed widow and her small party to descend upon Brigham Young, upon whose stalwart back with its excellent melon head it had been placed. And Smith's spirit also spoke through him to whom had been left the keys of the kingdom and the seer's faith in the Jerusalem of holy quest and who had been sure that the remnant Mormons in their enforced migration to nowhere would survive, as theirs was the true church combining the mysteries of Mohammed and Moses and many bird tongues and that they would have done so even if they had had no leader at the helm but the resurrected spirit of the female Jesus Christ, Mrs. Ann Lee, who had gathered money for the celibate Shaker movement by washing and shaking and hanging out and ironing the mud-stained, dust-stained shirts and drawers of clowns and other travelers down by New York's City Hall at Ye Old Shakespeare Hotel.

As the fire in the breast of Father Rapp of Württemberg had been kindled by Moses on Mount Sinai, prompting his immigration with his flocks to America, so the fire in the breast of Mrs. Ann Lee—a poor mill girl in the depressed but millennial city of Manchester—had been kindled by Moses on Mount Sinai, prompting her immigration to America, where she would be the founder of the long-lived Shaker community of celibates at New Lebanon, New York, the utopian child of her breast, which she did not live to see.

The fire in the breast of many a dreamer discontented with the Old World had been kindled also, over a period of time, in the breast of Wilhelm Weitling of the swan brotherhood. Could a swan fly if one wing and then both wings were cut off? He could if he was a man.

When Wilhelm Weitling finally went from the Old World to the New World, he would go with the knowledge of what had happened to the Mormons and the Icarians and many of the early utopias that had disappeared or were in the process of disappearance, thus he was not as ignorant as a newborn might be if asked to figure out all the odds against a millennial community which should be made of the twice-born, the dead souls awakening to life.

Yearning to see his mother again before he should disappear, fearful of murder by the German wolves who would tear him to pieces if he—like the naked lamb—should be delivered to them at the Swiss border, Wilhelm Weitling had fought tooth and toenail against the police when they attempted to take him out of the Swiss coffin where the smell of the grave was in his nostrils and only when chained by heavy iron manacles around his delicate tailor's hands and his long feet had been hoisted bodily into the carriage from which he had tried to kick his way through the glass window—with the result that his sleeves had been torn out of his coat and his arms and legs were bleeding. His eyelids were swollen like red geraniums, and his reddish hair was torn, and he was so incandescent with grief and rage that he might have burst at any instant into fire, fire which no water could quench.

It was not until noon that he had finally been handed over to the German police in the frontier town of Baden, where the watchman with his long striped pole had given him over to the German police for passage through the gates which would lead him from the darkness to the darkness and not to the light—and it was only after a journey of many days because of the delay caused by his imprisonment in various tombs from which, if he had escaped, he would have been shot down by the arrows of the great huntsman, the universal detective whose eyes were always on him—or so he with his paranoidal persecution manias believed—that he had at last been brought to the outskirts of Magdeburg and permitted to continue under his own steam—small steam, as the burning coal was in danger of being reduced to a cold clinker, so worn out was he by the rough road and the turmoil of his spirit, as one who was not looked upon by the conservative rulers of state as the Christ in man with His eternal power but was rather looked upon as Beelzebub or a poor fool or a crazy goat with a big mouth.

He had committed no crime but that of failure to keep his big mouth shut. In the eyes of the authorities this bastard prodigal son had brought nothing but disgrace to the cathedral town of Magdeburg, which had inadvertently produced him one night among the horses and the sheep and the lambs, the chickens and the cats and the dogs, and he was ridiculous beyond measure and certainly was not the Christ in the heart of man he seemed to think he was.

He was one at whom old dogs barked as if in recognition, but they would not possibly have remembered him—for he had been away since more of them were newborn pups, long enough to have found the Holy Urn several times over.

When finally he came to visit his mother, whom he had first been forbidden to see, for she was living about two and one half hours away from Magdeburg—a long way if one had no means of transportation but still bleeding feet—she at first had not known who this tall stranger was, but then, tracing the lineaments of his infant face in this present face and possibly also the face of his mysterious father who had disappeared in the Russian snow and might be dead, might be alive, had burst into tears as he had burst into tears and she had placed his head against her breast.

The widow of a simple tailor, she was not living on the crumbs provided by the Church and had been able to earn her living for herself and her daughter by working as a maid in a schoolmaster's house, so now could contribute a little support to her son, whose curiously dualistic position in Magdeburg was that he could neither go nor stay.

What had been his crime? He had known that socialism could be presented outside the biblical frame but had felt that the biblical frame was that which provided sacred images of Christ, which would be an anchor to the seekers of the earthly paradise. History, however innovative, was not forever outward bound to an unreachable point. History was member and was founded on the desire of the lost sheep to return to the sheep fold and not, of course, to the wolf fold.

Weitling's watchers had also forbidden that a first and last supper should be given in his honor by journeyman tailors and various trades in that region at a time when society had laid out—reflecting the will of the emperor or ruler who had his likeness in other countries—the table where the rich feasted on not imaginary viands served on plates of silver and plates of gold while to the poor were given only the crumbs. He had clung to his passport although his retention of it meant that he was subjected to the military service that he had avoided in the past. He had seemed in many ways a lost child or a revolutionary in embryo rather than the real thing, and so he would always seem. His teeth had chattered. He had been given over to strange cryings and to stranger silences.

The only way by which the city fathers of Magdeburg could get rid of this unwanted, perpetually bastard son was to provide for him passage on a steamboat down the Elbe to the free city of Hamburg and money for his passage to England and America—still not enough to give him a free ride for the rest of his life.

While dwelling among the Hamburgers before embarking upon the *Neptune* which would deposit him upon the British shore, he devoted himself to preparing his manuscripts of the poems for *Wounds and Balsam* for printing in pamphlet form, which he, the revolutionary pan-utopist, could sell for coins to help him upon his rugged way to wherever he was going.

[1 1]

IN THE TWILIGHT of the fog-shrouded streets of Hamburg where there were medieval craft guildhalls and banking and mercantile establishments and many gilded steeples and towards and weathercocks—city of manor houses and of a crumbling ghetto in which the poorest Jews lived—city of many phantom travelers passing to and fro, many whose true identities were masked and cloaked by mystery or did change as they journeyed from one world to another world—city where sudden cackles in the fog might be those of migratory storks and those of congeries of mournful clowns or wooden-faced puppeteers giving their shows with wooden puppets under globed streetlamps like fallen moons surrounded by the continual whirlings of moths and gnats, there were also eyes of spies watching every move that the fallen Weitling made as if he, the unpredictable anarchist, were capable of going by winged chariot over the sea road or by winged ark over the earthen road.

There were also eyes of sympathizers—shoemakers, hatters, coat and trouser makers, mantle makers, blacksmiths, whitesmiths, ships' caulkers, who seemed to believe that the cooperative socialism coming now into being upon all shores was that by which it would be possible to take away the canker from the rose and heal all wounds.

He was on his way to check on how his brainchild *Wounds and Balsam* was panning out when he had seen behind the oval window which was cobwebbed by gold of a lamp's flame in his publisher's bookstore the wavering silhouette of a man outlined against the white wall—someone who might have been only a phantom or a shadow—and a voice had whispered out of the fog into his ear that what he saw was none other then Heinrich Heine.

It was, indeed, in possibly uncertain ease and ailing flesh, the long-exiled poet Heinrich Heine, the clowning and satiric but sentimental and mournful lyric genius within whose narrow frame there seemed no space for epic themes but space for many selves including the masks of himself and his double whom he could hardly reconcile unless by wild vagaries, who had come over from France for one of his rare visits to the German toyland to visit his mother.

He had known that while Germany would endure, his mother would not. She was after all older than he was, and she was living in Hamburg in extremely straitened circumstances such as did not quite befit the sad widow of a poor, gifted, tragicomical gentleman who had not known how to make money but who was the brother of the great self-made banking millionaire Solomon Heine, the nonphilosophical and nonliterary patriarch, who although with his far-flung commercial interests was capable of numerous objective philanthropies and was even in some ways fond of his mercurial nephew kept his purse strings drawn very tight with reduction of coins as a penalty for the expression of revolutionary or profane thoughts that might bring embarrassment to his house.

Heine loved his father, who was a weak Samson, one who would neither tear down the pillars of capitalism nor build them up and whose love was all for wine and roses and beautiful velveteen coats and breeches and silvery powder on his golden hair and many lady loves but who had failed in the textile business just when his eldest son needed him most. Heinrich Heine would remember all his life and unto his dying day his father as he had last seen him—the vision coming to him as in a recurrent but possibly not deathless dream.

His father had been wearing his white powder mantle as the barber sprayed onto his golden hair the white powder, which surrounded him like a cloud. In his delight at seeing his father again, the son had wanted to rush up to him and kiss his hand. But strangely, the nearer the son came to him the more everything became blurred and changed its shape. For when he had bent to kiss his father's hand, he was seized by a deathly chill—the fingers were dry twigs and his father himself a tree without leaves and covered with frost.

[1 2]

EVERY AGE MUST SOLVE the problem of the Sphinx and when it has solved it must fall into the great abyss toward which all travelers were headed, according to Heine, who with his Christian mother and his Jewish father had become a convert to Christ yet was one who never went to church and without resolving his dualities considered himself to be a wandering Jew.

And the mounts that he would climb were both Mount Sinai and Mount Olympus, since he had been determined to cast his lot with the Greek gods who had already lost.

He would always be embarrassed by the fact that it was not until a year after his birth in Düsseldorf that his loving parents had been permitted to marry, and so he had moved their marriage up a year and his coming into this world up a year to 1799, and then up a year to 1800, in order that he might be the first poet of the new century which had been born out of the old.

He became this dapper, well-suited, well-heeled, almost ethereal gentleman whose eyes had been failing for some years—one already blind, the other curtained by the web of a cataract—and whose tall, sloped forehead ached with discordant thoughts and whose long-fingered hands trembled as if they were trying to get away from him and who—like a tree bending in the wind in which he was determined to fall backward and not forward—was beginning to experience the signs of a dissolving spinal column and the many fragilities caused by the mysterious failure of his bones to manufacture marrow—the soft tissue of vascular structure that should be in the natural cavities of man's bones and without which he would see himself turn into a ghost.

Like Frederick the Great he found that everything German had jarred upon his nerves from the beginning of his literary career, possibly even before that time, as the true beginning had been so early that it could hardly be traced. When he had reacted furiously to the insults that he believed had been dealt out to him by other students in Berlin, his patriarchal adviser Moses Moser had chided him. He should remember that he was only an idea—Hegel had said so.

He had understood when he first went over to enlightened France from the dark ages of Germany—he had been resolved then never to return to Hamburg, but for literary and economic reasons had not been able to keep the promise of permanent self-exile to himself—that the revolutionaries who had dreamed of the emancipation of downtrodden peoples would not live to realize their dreams of the dawn which was to come and which was in the psyche of the poet of the romantic quest who was Heine, with his unrequited love for his cousins—first, for the beautiful elder sister Amalie (he considered that he had known her in a former manifestation of life); second, for the younger sister Thérèse, who bore in relation to the ideal that of her possibly unreal reflection in a clouded mirror. They were the daughters of the magnificent mercantile and banking prince Uncle Solomon, whose lack of a sufficient generosity had made of Heine a rootless semi-orphaned wanderer with his sense of being a ghost while he was alive.

Where was Heine to find a resting place? "In Germany I could no longer stay," he had written just before going over to France, where he who had been the martyr of Hamburg would be the martyr of Montmartre, still in the view of many superficial people nothing but a fool with bells.

Very popular among old Hamburgers had been his "Weaver's Song," regarding the strike of the hand- and foot-loom weavers not only against the great power loom, which was their rival and which was quickly aborted but of which the spirit lived on. His often-quoted lines read:

A curse on the fatherland, false and faithless,
Where shame and infamy flourish scatheless,
Where every flower is broken in turn,
Where decay and corruption nourish the worm.
We're weaving, we're weaving.
The shuttle flies along the loom,
Whilst day and night we weave the doom.
Germany, we're weaving your shroud and worse—
The warp and the woof of a threefold curse.
We're weaving, we're weaving.

Heine had written his *Germany: A Winter Tale* when he was suffering from an attack of almost total blindness and the weaver who was Death was weaving a shroud for him who was already in some ways his own ghost. He was very grateful to his earthbound publisher for the dissemination that he gave to his works, which were the children of his brain.

Right now, as his forthcoming volume showed—and it was certainly to be no flash in the pan quickly burning out as would be the mortal fate of the poor swan tailor Wilhelm Weitling's *Wounds and Blossoms* and even in spite of the fact that he with his uncertain spelling was the resurrected Christ to whom Heine sometimes referred as his first cousin, one who fortunately had lived before the printing press had been invented and there had been no censorship to delete from a book on the problems of heaven all parts that applied to the world—Heine's cosmic but minuscular rage had been directed against those who would not permit the freedom of a poet of his revolutionary views to express himself and were willing to murder either him or his book. Indeed, according to numerous eyewitnesses regarding the hangings of French revolutionaries, when the author of an incendiary book could not be found, his book had been condemned to the fire in his place.

Heine's call upon the enigmatic publisher Campe was one in which he must have wished to assure some immortality to the children of his brain, which—in his publisher's self-serving estimation, it would be shown increasingly as time went on and Heine tottered toward his grave—were merely mortal and would not deserve to be brought out in a final edition when he who had been dying for so many years was really dead—and not because there might always be a poem from his hand when he was in his grave. His publisher's vow was that a mediocre rival deserved frequent collections but that Heine's brainchildren were so very transitory that they did not deserve to be resurrected and redeemed.

Another of the reasons for Heine's concern with the present and future publication of his work was that he was afraid to die and leave almost destitute as to worldly funds the dumb wife Mathilde whom he had married after several years of jealous love of her and at a time when conjugal relationships, always tentative, had ceased—and to whom he felt, nonetheless, that he owed his life and whatever happiness was his—and who had not the slightest idea of what his complex and many-leveled works meant and attributed more importance to a fashionable bonnet and her pet parrot's jargon than to whatever revolution might sweep over all the nations of the world.

When coming into Hamburg, Mathilde had been in a terrible accident at the dock. The pet parrot who had been like the devil's own bird intervening between the idiotic wife and her husband—and to whom she would listen in order to know what his always dying groans and grunts were—had suddenly flown off its perch and bitten the hand of the family member who was carrying its high pole through the fog, the result being that with unthinking reflex it had been dashed against a cobblestone where its feathers had turned into a mass of bloody red and its brain had suffered seemingly mortal injury. But the injury had been repaired by a skilled bird-brain doctor who probably enjoyed a large practice among the human-sized bird-brained parrots in Hamburg.

After a few days of misery to her at Uncle Solomon's dinner table where the French language was not welcome nor was the parrot on its perch, be it even bilingual, the very vocal but dumb Mathilde had been sent with her bird back to Montmartre under the protection of a bodyguard who her protective husband had hoped would keep her away from the German exiles in Paris to whom she might give her easy and indiscriminate favors, although among them would be, masked as clowns, secret representatives of the Prussian king.

The original German laws had been written in rhyme. It was during the rule of the poetry-loving king who knew that God was on his side or ought to be that the pettifogging censors at the fog-bound borderline had turned back—as if it were incendiary—the communal or socialist magazine which, printed in England, carried German translations of foreign luminaries whose works were not intended to throw a dreaming emperor off his throne—their sparks those of fireflies which had no heat and could set fire to no tree, whether dead or alive, in all the dark forest or spectral-ridden marshland. That which had given offense to the censors was a small advertisement of a new edition of Dante's *Divine Comedy*. How could anything which was divine be a comedy? How could it not be?

[1 3]

W HEN HEINE HAD FIRST GONE over from Germany to Paris after the French revolution of 1830, he had come under the spell of the departed seeker after a better world Claude-Henri de Saint-Simon, whose followers would divide into various movements as if they were birds flying through skies where the magnetic beams had been broken by storms, storms of every kind, ripping them apart.

The mystical count of Saint-Simon, whose followers were soon to be divided between the material and the spiritual, had planned his Christian socialist reform while dwelling in extreme poverty caused by the loss of much money in his schemes to cut the long swan's neck of Panama with a canal by which to unite two oceans as if they were one.

The Christian utopian society of his imagination was that which would extend the mantle of its protection to those who were sometimes dismissed as flotsam and jetsam, the no-account, the very poor to whom had not been given that reward of heaven on earth which had been given to the rich who were the few.

In 1823—two years before his death—the almost-all-seeing God who had seen a divinity in all things had led the ailing count of Saint-Simon's bony finger to the biblical passage that had given at least the skeletal outline for his dream or scheme that society should be reorganized in such a way as to divide its resources with the poor. The worker bees should be sharers of the honey which they made in their great hives and which was now not for the worker bees but for the kings of gold.

But when the count of Saint-Simon had stepped out of his mantle and left it on the ground, there had been no one to step into it, and his followers seemed to have torn it apart as some went one way and some another way to the earthly paradise.

Under the leadership of Barthélémy P. Enfantin, some who had been joined by belief in the mystical divinity of the flesh had helped to set up, near the forest of Rambouillet, a community after the pattern of Fourier, the cloth merchant who had not made the mistake of trying to attract workers by promises that they should all work. In fact, they were to do only the work which attracted them and were to live for beauty and love and were to follow whatever obsessions were theirs.

When Fourier found that the architect of this earthly paradise had built a large pigsty with a stone wall eighteen inches thick and no way in and no way out, he had been absolutely sure that his great idea had been undermined by pig-snouted Saint-Simonian followers who wanted to make him look like a fool.

Heine's *Germany: A Winter Tale,* written under the spell of the Saint-Simonians, who were not believers in the division of body from soul as in this present charnel house of life—but rather than split and divide themselves were believers in the joyous acceptance of the divinity of both—had included a vision of the kingdom of the future in which everybody would have not only bread and cake but roses and myrtles and beauty and unrestrained pleasure.

One of the utopian dreams affecting Heine's imagination then as well as that of flocks of visionary socialists before and after him had been that described by the Athenian poet Aristophanes in *The Birds,* which contains divine elements as well as those mysteries and miracles which might make utopia most attractive by placing it beyond exact imitation by man.

The most beautiful city with a wall so broad that charioteers in their chariots could pass each other even if they were drawn by steeds as big as the Trojan horse had been built by birds, birds only.

While under the spell of the windblown Saint-Simonian followers Heine had foreseen a city which should be made of human gods who would wear purple robes and enjoy all the beautiful sensual things of life while in this present state of being—nectar and ambrosia and perfumes and music and the dance of laughing nymphs—he to wane thin as a thread or crescent moon in the ensuing years as his dumb Mathilde was to wax fat as the full moon, and the only community that he might have with the beautiful word birds had been that of the parrot conveying his grunts and groans to her and her wild laughter to him.

Mathilde might have seemed, to anyone but Heine with his search for the divine earth mother who was larger than he was—he being like the pearl sleeping in the shell—a poor substitute for the two sisters whom he had loved, or even for a poor dancer, a street woman of Paris who had told him when she was dying that she was born in her mother's grave where grave robbers had found her and had released her and had brought her up to be the dancer. Had they not heard the infant's cry in the graveyard then, she might have died among the waters of her mother's grave.

Heine understood, however, when he first went over from Germany to France, where he was to be called the "*Voltaire au clair de la lune,*" that the revolutionaries who had dreamed of the emancipation of all mankind would not live to realize their dreams of the dawn which was to come. The sunrise would not redden their cheeks nor warm their hearts—as they died away like the waning moon—for the course of man on earth was all too short, and at the end was the inexorable grave.

The well-heeled, properly tailored Heine—a gentleman who valued his sense of personal privacy—was of a self-isolated nature that forbade unsolicited intimacies. He did not like to be slapped on the back by any wild-eyed stranger lest he who was so fragile should be knocked over.

The trouble with the recently resurrected worker Christ Wilhelm Weitling was that he had not asked for any favor and had not waited for recognition by the wandering Jew Heine, when suddenly out of the spectral-producing fog had rushed this wild jack-of-all-trades whom he had never seen before but whom he dimly recognized from some of the same kinds of cartoons that made fun of him.

[1 4]

THE TAILOR WILHELM WEITLING—with his red cap upon his geranium-colored locks, his short red cape held together by pins, his long workman's blouse hanging loose, his short knee breeches, his red shoes with broken heels and their soles tied on by ropes—had danced around the sweet-smelling Heine with loud squawks of a mutuality of interests that he recognized he shared with him as his long-lost revolutionary brother and fellow bard and had flopped himself onto a bench against the white wall and had not removed his red cap but his red shoes, which had no splayed toes such as he should have had if he had been a swan or some other kind of feathered bird man as—true to his habits as the wandering apprentice tailor—he had propped first one leg up under his chin and then the other leg, and he—who with his passion for cleanliness had devoted himself since his release from among the prison shades to washing his long-tailed shirts—he who with his long razor had also been for some time scraping the blue prison mold from the soles of his bare feet where it had been heavy enough to leave flowers in his tracks, had shaved and scraped away the red wounds which like flowers spotted the skin of his bare, bleeding legs—at the same time that he had spouted on and on to the bemused, startled Heine that Jesus was about to bring His kingdom down out of the clouds: "The boundaries of nations will crumble when the Son of Man comes to judge the quick and the dead."

Weitling's messages, which he had seemed to think were a unique contribution, possibly because of certain eccentric weavings or crochetings of his own upon what might be called the great universalist socialist loom, had not been too different from those of the Chartist agitators who proposed the same ameliorative vision as street-corner salvationists with their belief that in the world to come there would be corn for all the mother quails and all the little quails who had not one grain of corn and were left to starve. "We are all children of one father, and we all have a common destiny, to be happy here, and then forever after in the great beyond."

So far as the poor people were concerned, Heine had given to them his sympathies—for after all, he was poor, haunted by the threat of poverty, and well knew that until the moneyless state arrived, if it ever should arrive, money was a necessity for the support of his life as it would be for his widow's life when he was gone over the great abyss, which never accurately divided, in view of so many shifting clouds, this world from the next. He had crossed back and forth so many times.

As Heine would recall on his mattress grave in Paris, when after some years of leading a life that had been death in the midst of life and thus had transpired on a shadowy borderline between life and death, he was at last dying and gave up his wandering thoughts to his childhood home in Germany to which he, the wandering Jew, would never return—not even when he was dead and in his coffin—he had left the request in his will that he should be buried at Montmartre, where he had so long been the ghost— so that if his had been a seed carried in a clump of earth on the foot of a bird plowman, it would have fallen on no German clump of earth; he had thought much of the flight of the unemployed from Germany to other lands in search of employment—the artisans in search of work as hod carriers, bricklayers, tailors, weavers of cloth.

> Thou tookest thy flight toward sunshine and happiness—naked and poor returnest thou back. German truth, German shirts—one gets them worn to tatters in foreign parts. Deadly pale are thy looks, but take comfort—thou art at home! One lies warm in German earth, warm as by the old pleasant fireside. Many a one, alas, became crippled and can get home no more! Longingly he stretches out his arms—God have mercy upon him!

Wilhelm Weitling, too, immigrating to America, once for a brief visit before his permanent return to the land where he had hoped to found in some dim, distant Western state his workers' paradise—his Zion, which was never to be realized but took a long time dying as in a dream that never really dies as some other dreamer must take over the dream, which transcends the individual.

So far as the impressionistic old bird gentleman Heine was concerned, his relationship to the inner world of his unconsciousness was very much of the same mysterious chaos as that to the outer world of his acutely sensitive consciousness, which was endowed with historical imagination presenting itself in many symbolic forms. Illusion might be reality, and reality might be illusion. It was said that his was a world of drift.

He had distinguished between mediocrity of talents and his own genius, which had filled the heavens with the perfume of the rose, causing intoxication among the gods. He was not careless as to the children of his brain, no mere flash-in-the-pan numbers having been his. He had written to a fellow poet when he was still the fledgling poet himself his plea that he should not spare the critical scalpel, even if it was his dearest child that might have been born with a little hunchback, goiter, or other excrescence. To be strict with oneself was the artist's first commandment.

His horizons were never made of a choice between the Either on the one hand and the Or on the other, just as he knew that the real wound for which there was no balm was the creation itself in which—as had been described by the embattled eighteenth-century philosopher Denis Diderot, master of dreams, who was under the spell of Laurence Sterne—thought depended upon associations of images streaming at random through the dreamer's mind like the music caused by the vibrations of strings.

It is this vibration, the inevitable resonance, which holds the object present while the mind is busied about the quality that belongs to the object. But vibrating strings have yet another property—that of making other strings vibrate—and that is how the first idea recalls a second, the two of them a third—so that there is no limit to the ideas awakened and interconnected in the mind of the philosopher. This instrument makes surprising leaps, and an idea once aroused may sometimes set vibrating a harmonic at an inconceivable distance. If this phenomenon may be observed between resonant strings that are lifeless and separate, why should it not occur between points that are alive and connected, between fibers that are continuous and sensitive?

Being himself a citizen of cloud lands, Heine had come up before Karl Marx with the idea that religion was the opium provided by despotic emperors to the people upon whom they placed their rule in the age of iron and steel—but still and all he had been closer to the angel-infested Swedenborg and opium-drenched Coleridge than to the beloved infidel or agnostic Robert Owen, with his almost undisturbed, almost unquenchable faith that the mechanical genius of mankind would bring this world from the darkness to the light—the golden light of the new moral world—if only the parts of human nature were known and understood in a way to make possible the universal brotherhood.

Yet Heine had long ago lost faith in the idea that the machine would bring reform. The machine, if anything, had contributed to his sense of tragic woe in a way transcending the immediate scene, in a way that was not merely national but international.

Among Heine's poems that showed distrust of industrial progress was one that told of the white horse among grasses craning up his neck as he and a thistle-chomping ass watched the lightning speed of the steam locomotive and coach and the steam car as they went rattling by, black smoke issuing from the funnel like a flag. The rattling had been everywhere and had frightened the white horse in the farmyard. Trembling in every limb, he had sighed to the thistle-cropping ass that if nature had not made him white, he would have turned as white as chalk. For he had realized that there was no future for the equine species—the future that lay ahead for the white horse was cruel and stormy, black as the black smoke emitted from the iron beast, which provided a steam-engine competition with which horses could not compete.

For when men learned that they could drive without the help of a horse, there would not be a horse left alive and there would be no hay and there would be no grass. No one would feed the horses in their stalls, for men's hearts were hard as stones and would give nothing free, and the horses could not steal like people and did not fawn like men and dogs.

The ass, chomping upon two thistles more, had not feared the terrible fate which might lie ahead for the haughty horses—so that whether they were white or black or dapple or bay, they would be packed off pell-mell.

It was as if in the midst of a revolutionary battle for freedom from despotic powers Heine had charged about upon his battle horse striking at his enemies with his sword, yet had never been gripped by the fever or the joy or the fear of the Battle and had kept an inner calm such as might have occurred in his lands of fable and dream.

Not surprisingly, in view of his tendency to break himself into two or more persons whom he reluctantly recognized might be one of many pluralistic particles like sand grains, each with its individual portrait, Heine had noticed that his thoughts had sojourned elsewhere.

According to the revolutionary Ludwig Börne, whom God had captured in His butterfly net in 1838, Heine with his attacks upon demagogues, whether they were of the higher orbs or of the lower depths, had caused him with his revolutionary claims to be of no help but a hindrance to the progressive movement before which he had gotten into the way very much as if he were a boy chasing butterflies on a battlefield—which, of course, in Heine's eyes must always have been mist-shrouded.

His memory of the three days' Reign of Terror had been that he had not enjoyed mounting the scaffold and having his head cut off every day as had been his experience then.

Heine's revolutionary theory was that there would be plenty in this world for everybody if only there were fair play—wine and roses and myrtle and lilies and bread for all men, women, and children, and sweet peas in little peapods for them to feed their little mouths on.

He had seen how the rich, well-fed people raised up a barricade of laws by which to protect themselves from the starving poor, how they had at hand judges, hangmen, rope, and gallows for those who crossed the barricade.

He was a believer in the democracy of the gods, but surely the individual genius of the great poets should not be beaten down with hammer and nails by the forces of mediocrity as if all were members of the same guild of journeymen tailors even like Weitling, this poor tailor who imagined that he would become the king of tailors in a new utopian world and who, with his long legs like a grasshopper's folded under him, supposed that he knew a way by which to protect all grasshoppers from the winter blast which was to come.

Weitling's revolutionary philosophy was old hat to Heine. He knew that when an avalanche was getting ready to fall, it took its own course.

He had written to his friend Karl Marx to complain of Wilhelm Weitling's nauseating familiarity, his assumption that he was his colleague and fellow revolutionary poet and sharer with him of his enthusiastic desire to reform the old world of capitalism and bring in the new world of cooperative communitarianism which would spring up out of the grave of the Old World.

Heine, now as he approached his coffin bed where he would lie for years with his limbs as soft, as helpless to give him support as if they were cotton under him, came increasingly to view communism as that which would cut down the very flower of civilization.

There should have been a broad ground in which the anarchist Heine discovered that there were aspects in which he could be in harmony with the anarchist Weitling, but their brief meeting had been a time filled with discords grating upon the nerves of the neglected author of "A Silesian Weaver's Song"—and now they were both windblown birds of passage going in different ways, one to his grave, one to the New World, where he was never to realize his golden utopian dream.

[1 5]

WHEN KARL MARX first heard that Heine was dying, who was already as lonely in some ways as the great auk who would never hatch little auklets recognizable by him as the children of dialectical materialism—for he parted company with his disciples unless they were wholly like him, as none were—he had written from Paris to his friend, perhaps an even lonelier bird of passage, that of all the people he was leaving behind him in Paris, Heine was the one he would like to pack and take with him into his place of uncertain refuge.

The martyr of Montmartre had enjoyed his conversations not only with Marx but also with his aristocratic wife, who looked upon her husband's endless work as a poem and, although trying to understand, was not always able to understand the sacrifices which were made for its sake.

It was Marx's belief that his writings could be published only when they were an artistic whole so well rounded that he could see the entire pattern, he thus not having the opportunity to submit segments or fragments like those of the fairy-tale writer Jacob Grimm.

While visiting with the Marx family during their temporary exile in Brussels, the old man Heine, who was already thin as a reed and was to grow thinner with the years, had been able to save Marx's little daughter Jenny's life by turning her upside down and slapping her on the back when she was choking on a fish bone.

Marx was so poor that, as he forecast the future of the star that was this world of maelstrom caused by capitalistic greed, when discords were replaced by communistic harmonies and there should be—perhaps only after some time trapped in the Kingdom of Necessity—wine and roses, roses all the way, it was a wonder his children did not drink soup made entirely of the boiled bones of starfish, cuttlefish, little birds' feet, shore grasses. He had believed that man must look directly into the eye of the scarecrow which had been put up by the philistines to frighten him and that he must show that he was not frightened.

Having read Heine's *Germany: A Winter Tale* and other incendiary fables, many pertaining to no limited utopia but the enormous inequities which were fostered against the poor and the lowly upon the international scene by the great powers of an expanding imperialism on every front, Marx knew of the borderline or customs house problems which had been those of the old long-legged poet when he had first crossed over into Germany with his head a bird's nest filled with his ideas for world-shaking books.

Now languishing in Brussels, Marx was beset by these same troubles with censorship, so kept his messages brief or took advantage of a messenger to deliver a letter to Paris regarding his book on Börne, which was bringing a very loutish treatment from Christian German jackasses. Marx was intending to come to the defense of the living Heine in a controversy that had kept the dead man Börne in the realm of the living dead, just as did occur so often in Heine's ghost-ridden poems, which should have themselves suggested that he was not a man of the dialectical materialistic persuasion but rather the nondialectical spiritual persuasion in which the ordinary laws of nature did not pertain. Indeed, Heine's faith in the age of the machine, which would bring the advancement of mankind, was so altogether minimal as to be almost nonexistent.

When Heine thought that he would like to be exempt from the monolithic communist state which he could allow in no way to weigh down on his ego, crush him like the butterfly beneath the iron wheel of progress, it was impossible for him with the cataracts like snowflakes blotting out the vision in his eyes to get beyond the first chapters of the great opus of which he had cut the pages open with his knife but perhaps could peruse in only a random sense—and he had refused to believe that he must explore the mysteries of the great Hegelian iceberg, which for him was an abstraction filling the void with the theory not so much that what was rational would be but that what was rational must be—Marx had understood that Heine with his breakages was a poet and must go his own way.

Heine, who in his dreams had explored strange landscapes such as had been explored by real geographers and such imaginary geographers as Herodotus and Fourier, the latter an influence upon Edgar Allan Poe, demented but lucid visionary, who saw in America strange lagoons, waterlogged marshes where lilies cried with human voices and grasses running wild as if they were in panic cried aloud—icebergs enclosing the spirits of the dead—had seen Hegel as the mariner who had gone around the entire intellectual world and had fearlessly advanced far up to the North Pole of thought where one's brain froze when wrapped in abstract ice capes.

Lying for years upon his coffin mattress where he was held down by pins, he who was the lover of the phoenix had recalled that his first great breakdown or collapse had occurred while he was visiting the statue of the Venus de Milo, it having been his sad fate to fall like a clattering skeleton or heap of bones when he had journeyed to the shrine of the marble woman who—unfortunately for him—had an arm broken above the elbow and so could not reach out to save him.

When the news was spread by Heine's enemies that he was dead, he had come up with what well might have been a wandering Jew joke—he was not dead but sleeping—the news of his death having been greatly exaggerated.

And yet after this false propaganda had been spread about, he had felt increasingly that sense of death in the midst of life that had always been his and that was so much a part of the opium-drenched nineteenth-century psychology of madness and death and dreams, dreams of awakening again, dying again but to live.

It would be remembered of the delicately strung Heine when he was passing away and certainly could not have had the strength to stop the mill wheel of the revolutionary spirit by throwing his body against it that he had looked like a cross between Mephistopheles and Christ. When the revolutionary opium lady Elizabeth Barrett Browning heard of Heine's public repudiation of atheism for that which seemed a journey of return to the religion of his fathers about which, wailing as if there were a Wailing Wall built into him as would be said of every wandering Jew with his religious songs, the transformation of his openings had seemed pathetic to her eyes and heart. "He has joined no Church," she had written to a friend, "but simply (to use his own words), has 'returned home to God like the prodigal son after a long tending of the swine.' It is delightful to go home to God, even after a long tending of the sheep." She knew that Heine, the martyr of Montmartre whose songs had inspired her to endure her own sufferings, had lived a sort of living death for years in which he had been quite deprived of his limbs and had suffered tortures to boot.

When Heine, pinned down like Gulliver by Lilliputian pins upon the striped coffin mattress where—as he believed—the grave's cold clay would soon stop his mouth from singing his birth and death songs, had given up the god of the pantheists as one he could not use, he had thought that he had done so because of his need of a god who could reach out to help him—

and that was why he had sought the transformation that might come if he should achieve his journey of return to the god of his father.

Poetry had remained, through many deaths, many resurrections, his best friend. Even in his youth he had fallen into that yawning mouth which had opened into the great abyss which was his grave and had taken such a long time spiraling downward that he had not known when he reached his journey's end, for he had awakened from the dream that he was dead.

[1 6]

I T WAS BECAUSE OF George Eliot's pioneering work in the *Westminster Review* that upon the battered brow of the fallen knight Heine had been placed the laurel leaves as if he were only a sleeper in the dark woods who would awaken to the sound of the winding horn. He himself when he was dying had apparently not heard that sound. He had been distracted by loud piano music. The seemingly melancholy but cheerful, horse-faced George Eliot—who had praised Heine as a poet in the realm of that prose which, as we know, is many-fringed, seeming to move less of will than of desire, not all its fringes revealed to any one human consciousness at once, for they change from light to darkness—had seen that there was common clay mixed in with the ethereal elements and that his dramatic works were covered with smallpox.

Clear to the end, the dying clown Heine had carried on his quarrel with the god who had created the great joke which was this world. In his last poem, he had written of time as the worst syphilis there was.

Elizabeth Craigmyle, translator of the untranslatable Heine when his songs were on all lips, would agree with the evaluation of the dead martyr of Montmartre as a defrocked romantic belonging to the modern school of reality but not marching under its banner. She would find it not surprising that the landscape of Heine's ballads had been mystical, ghostly—in a word, uncanny—in view of the opening of the gates of his passion by the Red Sefchen's beautiful mouth and the fact that his first love when he was a boy had been the executioner's niece and that his first kiss had been snatched under the shadow of the sword which had taken the life blood of a hundred doomed wretches—these images of love and castration or execution having inspired a modern cynic to remark that every man walked through life with the bacchante of sexual sensuality on his left hand and the skeleton of Death on his right hand while leering at the one and making prayers against the other.

Heine had neither scourged himself nor murmured prayers. "Throughout his life he had eyes only for the beautiful, unveiled form of the bacchante till the grisly skeleton became the daily companion and couch mate of the nine years spent on his mattress grave."

[1 7]

WHEN IN THE EARLY MORNING of February 17, 1856, all the morphine Heine had taken out of his medicine bottles having not eased his pain or having eased it only to the extent that he did not awaken again—unless he who had gone over to the realm of the skeleton Death who was the winter king and would awaken again in some far spring of some far year which was the realm of the flower-crowned nymph and the flower children and butterflies and bees and birds, the wandering Jew who was said to have the Wailing Wall built in him—some listeners had claimed that they had heard a wailing sound coming from the shrouded body of the dead man when the coffin lid had closed down at last over him. There had been approximately one hundred mourners—could one ever say a hundred and one half?—who had gathered at the very simple, nonclerical interment of the long-dying poet of Montmartre under the gray sky streaked with snow clouds like swans.

In March the *Illustrated London News,* reflecting an opinion for which George Eliot had plowed the ground, expressed its sense that Heine's death had left a vacancy in the world of continental literature. *Blackwood's Magazine*—in the following October when the leaves in nature's crucible were turning from gold to gray—had elegiacally remarked upon the end of the jest that had been Heine's life in Paris. Indeed, as was to be remembered many times, the martyr of Montmartre had intended to ask God why He had endowed him with such a high sense of humor and then had overlaid him with such great sufferings as his. There had also been a project forming in his mind to bring God to trial before the Society for the Prevention of Cruelty to Animals.

In the following year in September, Matthew Arnold had paid a visit to the Montmartre cemetery. The controversies raging over the body of the dead poet when he was alive had continued like bitter spirits poisoning the peace of his last abode. Perhaps they were right who thought that a poet abused God's gift of song if he made of it a vehicle for satire such as had been his when he declared that the great were hollow and dull and that other artists were envious of him and that the mob was profane.

Matthew Arnold's belief at this point was most curiously that a singer should rather help us forget such barren knowledge. But something had prompted him not to turn away from Heine's grave with that last word which should be the expression of pity or half censure—rather with awe should be hailed the passage from this earth of a soul scattering lightnings:

> *The Spirit of the world*
> *Beholding the absurdity of men—*
> *Their vaunts, their feats—let a sardonic smile*
> *For one short moment wander o'er his lips. . . .*
> *For its earthly hour*
> *The strange guest sparkled; now 'tis pass'd away.*
> *That was Heine! and we,*
> *Myriads who live,*
> *What are we all but a mood,*
> *A single mood of the life of the spirit to whom we exist,*
> *Who alone is all things in one. . . .*

[1 8]

THOSE WHO KNEW of Heine's fiscal problems, which came largely from his conviction that he should have been or was a prince but was an orphan and a pauper, could only have been amused or bemused by his concern for money, his desire to leave a nest egg for his fat widow when his mouth was stuffed with clay. "Bugs, bugs, bugs!" He had cried out upon his coffin mattress that there were bugs, bugs, bugs crawling all over him and that they were not gold bugs—they were bedbugs feeding on his blood.

Marx with his own fairy tale—which was that communism would one day bring the death of the illusion of capitalism to the world if the paths shown by him were followed—had felt in the midst of his impoverished and lonely exile in London twinges of grief for the passage of the cantankerous old poet who had tended to believe that Marx and Engels had stolen the godhead for insertion into the cells of their own bodies.

So far as Heine was concerned with his many egocentric egos pulsating in him who had yearned to find the Fountain of Youth described by Ponce de León and had been opposed to America's war with Mexico and the abuses of red and yellow and black people and had been dead set against the Missouri Compromise—and who as a matter of biblical principles had identified himself when he was on his coffin bed with Harriet Beecher Stowe's poor old Uncle Tom, who—when he was dying in the deep American South where there was more water than land, and where all the people should have been heron-footed—had been lifted upward to heaven by the angelic ghost of the golden-haired Little Eva. The Hegelian world spirit had been in relation to reality the reflection of a drunkard's large red nose thrust forward like a promontory among the reflections of twinkling lights—like the lights of stars in minor galaxies.

He had understood during the revolution of 1848 that the proletarian rats running in gutters were not motivated so much by the revolutionary teachings of Mirabeau as by the soup-bowl logic—the desire for bread in which to set their large teeth, and most particularly the desire for a fried codfish which had been made golden by the butter of the sun.

Marx had written from London to Engels in Manchester to express the twinges of irritation he had felt when reading Heine's erroneous account of the way Marx was supposed to have offered consolation to Heine when he was under attack in the German press for having accepted money from Louis Philippe.

Marx with his chronic headaches and his many griefs—those caused both by his dedication to his economic research and by his poverty, which was so great that it might almost seem the magnificence of largesse for him who wished to overthrow the nonexistent universal landlord as well as the existent landlords who owned nations as their property and private preserve, and at the same time was under threat of being thrown into the gutter with his wife and his children because of his inability to pay the rent or ever to catch up with it—had been so impatient as to Heine's egregious errors that he had not paused at this point to take under the wing of his compassion that which he knew—the fact that Heine had moved his subjective kings and queens and pawns about a subjective chessboard and was not given to an objective science of society but to a science of dreams by which to prove whether or not his little ego or its reflection existed—which was real and which was dream. Marx, beset with his own apparitional things in the life of the individual—those that could not be dismissed in unsteady correlation to the objective society which was itself based upon the appearances of the ghosts of illusion as if they were real—had been grimly hopeful, when the revolution had apparently failed, that the people who were starving like crows should not be held back in their search for corn by some old, raggedy scarecrow guarding despotic empires.

The good Heine, according to the somewhat impatient, impetuous analysis dashed off by the ordinarily patient Marx, had deliberately forgotten that his intervention on the poet's behalf had occurred in 1843 and thus could not be connected with what had come to light after the revolution of February 1848. "But let it pass [in English]", Marx had continued—he was at this time practicing such simple English phrases as "So be it" or "Hang it" or "What to do" or "You see to what low state of spirit I am depressed" or "I am so poor that I am almost buried in sand," the latter indicating how very difficult it was for him to keep his wife and family alive in these chronically hard times, which were a continuation of the past and would be of that future which was left to come.

In March, the death of the Marxes' little boy Edgar—whom the father had once likened to a bright little pint bomb packed with enough energy to give off the rays of the sun if it ever went off as it was threatening to do as the little boy was always bouncing around—had permanently darkened the skies.

There had been no way by which the aristocratic, beautiful, ailing wife and the obsessed diagnostician of the ills of capitalism could be permanently reconciled to the loss of this bright little creature whose energy had fizzled out in his father's arms and who when he was interred—so far as the future which would be his in this world was concerned—might just as well have been a little bundle of pink sand laid in a place of wet leaf mold.

Two other children had been lost in infancy. They were Heinrich Guido—called by Marx the red fox—and the little daughter Franziska—who had gone quite early to Death's realm. He could not dismiss a bundle of pink sand to nonbeing, of course.

What blinding headaches were suffered then by the future father of red Marxist socialism, which would have as its other father or surrogate father, Frederick Engels, who, as a young poet in Germany, had been a translator of part of Shelley's "Queen Mab" from English into the language of grunting, groaning hogs, and had believed that from the combination of Hegel and Ludwig Börne—one with eternal snow upon his brow, one with red cherries between his lips—would come the communal world.

Few German exiles, keeping close tabs on such remarkable exiles as

Heine and Börne, could have failed to know that before they ever met they had seemed as closely woven as Siamese twins—but that from the time of his coming to Paris the poet who had once looked upon Börne's *Letters from Paris* as brightly burning paper missiles lighting the German fog had shown no desire to interweave with the absolute revolutionary in Montmartre—where there was also a good deal of fringed fog—and when their attacks and counterattacks had broken loose had accused Börne of being only a little drum major envious of the great drum major because he had taller plumes and more gold medals than he.

Börne had once stated that if ever a king should reach out to touch his hand, then he would purify it by a baptism in fire. Heine had replied that if a member of the dirty gutter proletariat should reach out to shake his hand, he would wash it with soap.

The little bona-fide traveler—as the English called the newborn—had been the youngest of Marx's daughters who would live into adulthood. She was Eleanor—the other two were Jenny and Laura. Eleanor had been welcomed into the crib although it might have been easier for the mother and the father with their abiding sense of grief if she had been a boy, to take, so far as possible, the place of the little Edgar who quite early had gotten off that train which, when Engels had first embarked on it—and no doubt there was no sound of mournful bells—had seemed to him the train to the future.

There never would be another son who was the fruit of Mrs. Marx's loins—no cherry-lipped boy to take the place of the dead Edgar. A child born after Eleanor would be in a state that Marx called nonviable—meaning not fit for life—something in defective embryo—and that was all right—it was evidently all right to fall from the womb into the grave and thus miss most of the experience of life. Over the door to Mrs. Marx's womb a funeral wreath of pale winter leaves with black and red ribbons might just as well have been laid. She was never to be consoled.

Household pressures on Marx were very great, his poverty so acute that he had considerable difficulty keeping up with his payments to the milkman or paying for yesterday's stale bread or a soup bone or a few old, half-rotted potatoes for a thin soup and no egg like a great magical eye floating in the pot to ward off evil as in a primitive fairy tale. Indeed, had it not been for the angelic Engels's help, Marx's children might have been stunted of growth with little potato eyes set close together, their skins brown and shriveled like brown potato skins as were the skins of the children of the poor who worked in mills and mines and seldom saw the light of the sun— or else because of his inability to pay the rent to the local landlord, he whose communistic philosophy was opposed not only to local landlords but to the universal landlord who existed only in capitalistic mythologies might have been tossed out with his family into the rain-swept, muddy gutter with pots and pans and his wife's precious chinaware if it was not already in hock at the pawnbroker's shop—and thus might have seemed not too different from others of the dispossessed and other often lowly wanderers who were the sediment at the bottom of the social scale and had no rational ideal and might easily be misled by false signal lights.

Sometimes Marx was so poor that he could not afford the paper and envelopes and quills for pens and stamps for the articles which he wrote for pay for the *New York Tribune,* of which the perfectionist editor, White Hat Horace Greeley in his white hat and white coat, was receiving at this time up the dirtiest stairs in the world—or so they were called—manuscripts by foreign geniuses who were surely of no common garden variety and who included the anarchist Proudhon and Marx, the rejector of philosophic anarchism. Marx was suffering from blinding headaches.

Still and all—and although his pecuniary problems dwarfed those of Heine who by comparison with him lived in luxury and wore his long-tailed evening suits so heavily perfumed that he could have been surrounded by bees buzzing in wintertime—Marx in the midst of domestic burdens was able to let off from London, in a footnote of a letter to Engels in Manchester, a few puffs of steam, a few rasping chords by which to express his angry response to the insults paid to the recently dead Heine by Ludwig Simon of Trier in the pages of the New York *Neue-Zeit,* which was the organ of the quondam lion of the parliament of the German nation—in real life Wilhelm Löwe—who was now living in retirement in Stuttgart. The name of Simon of Trier was anathema to Marx for a variety of reasons, mainly secular.

What Engels had not yet seen in his isolation in Manchester but had been seen by Marx in his isolation in London was the article in the magazine in which Simon of Trier had pissed on the recently dead poet Heine's grave. Writing hastily and at that time fascinated by the old northern Teutonic sound, Marx had meant to say that Simon of Trier had poured his urine upon the poet's grave, which was, after all, in Montmartre.

The poet or minstrel Simon of Trier, who was also a lawyer and politician—and who would eventually become one of the emigrants going from Germany to Switzerland—was in all likelihood too competitive, too biased to be a good assayer of talents, and thus he had found that the dead poet had been no poet and had had no feeling.

Very offensive to Marx was the attack upon Heine as a man who had been filled with malice and had slandered, among others, the widow of Salomon Strauss, Jeanette Wohl-Strauss, who—as was well known—had given shelter in her household to the proletariat revolutionary Börne when both he and her husband had been alive and when some had thought that the merchant had been cuckolded and others that the radical guest had been an impotent watcher through a keyhole of a conjugal kneading together of a love that he could never share.

Marx's quick objections had been to the way the self-serving Simon of Trier had tried to bring to light now in this period of chaos for many exiles Heine's characterization of Börne's girlfriend—the Strauss woman—as a gross curly-headed mouse, muse, or she-Moses—certainly not a very flattering portrait of the probable but problematical love object of a revolutionary of whom the dead poet had once stated that his hand, unlike the hand of Börne, had not been corrupted by touching upon the dirt and filth of the gutter mob or by touching the gold of the money kings who were the killers of the poor.

Heine had believed at this point that he himself was the revolutionary on a ship that had been driven far ahead of Börne's.

Simon's *From the Exile* was in Marx's opinion nothing but a work of diluted insipidity—and every word was a schoolboyish bungle, a foppish rabbit's foot, a pretension to naïveté as it seemed to appeal to beggars—and was a soup in which were mixed the dissolved Jew cherries of Karl Grun and his platitudes. What mediocrity! What slander!

All these things were not news to Engels, of course, since it had been in August a decade before, when Marx had first been told to pack his bags and get out of France, that the cotton lord from Owen's millennial Manchester had first gone to Paris to try to dissuade German workers in exile there from joining such partial pocket cooperative utopian movements as those which Proudhon had proposed in his *Contradictions in Economics* and which Karl Grun like an off-key millennial rooster had lauded to the sky and at a time when the ways to the universal improvement were unclear and the goal was wrapped in an enigma that, like the enigma of night, was greater than the enigma of day.

Marx had only browsed through the pages of *From the Exile*. His complaint had been that he would just as soon have drunk soap water or have imbibed hot cow piss with the great Zoroaster than be forced to read through the work as a whole.

[1 9]

SOMETIMES IN THIS PERIOD of narrow straits caused by his lean purse when he was up to his ears in sand, poor Marx did envy those who could reverse themselves and by continual tumbling perhaps get rid of part of their burdens. Sometimes he did wish that he could be buried many fathoms deep—for that would be easier than to try to go on with all the financial burdens which were his in spite of the money Engels managed to send and the money from the pawning of his wife's china and silverware.

In September, when with Engels's help in footing the bill for the van and horse which was no doubt as mournful as a hearse driver's horse, Mrs. Marx big then with the child who was not viable—something that might be half cinder cherub and half dead bird with a strangled neck and that would no more complete its evolution than the Marxist political economy when its author was in the muck and was trying to get out of the hole and was in a quandary because of inability to meet with total payment of rent to the new landlord—Marx had complained in his letter to his Manchester alter ego—if such Engels was—that part of what did seem no merely momentary crisis but a continual crisis—just as things were always to be for him in one way or another and as the world itself was to be—was that his wife's inheritance from her aristocratic von Westphalen family, which he had once described as worshiping God at Trier and the devil in Berlin, had been invested in Lower Silesian railroad bonds—which were immediately shriveling, dropping down because of the raging Crédit Mobilier swindles, which had aroused scandals in France and would have repercussions throughout the railroad and banking world, touching upon many lives of people who had never owned a link in a railroad belt or a banker's daisy chain.

Engels had also suffered temporary financial embarrassment—although not to the point where he could not offer bread and wine—never enough to sustain the family in view of how many hungry mouths there were, even if one should subtract the dead child like a little gargoyle who had only a rusted rain pipe, a dead butterfly upon its lips. The dead child was the last son acknowledged by Marx, but not the last son who would be his.

What had bugged Marx and Engels from the beginning of their cooperative and coordinating relationship—as it would always be through all life's jarring storms—was why the exiles who were in their various coops and disagreed with them seemed to look upon the two as one as if they were joined each to the other like Siamese twins and thus should be a two-headed subject followed not by a plural but a singular verb.

Always of interest to Marx and probably also to Engels had been the scraping, rasping, cawing, clicking, gabbling, gobbling barnyard sound of German intellectual exiles cooped in foreign lands—and the puzzle as to who supported them, who had provided the gold for the bread.

Sometimes Alfred Meissner, reading Heine's undying poems aloud at the dying poet's bedside, had felt that what he heard was a series of calls from the beyond, the cries of a shade who upon the darkest shores of Acheron yearned for a world of sunlight.

Certainly Heine could never have responded favorably to the commandment once pronounced by Engels and shared by Marx—who was more than likely the scientific originator of the logical thought: "Physicists, beware of metaphysics!"

Heine's premise had been that there was one religion for the healthy and another for the sick—as naturally Marx and Engels—with their flight from supernatural things that had in themselves no power—could not agree, for they were sick but did not take up a mad palmer's life.

One of Heine's favorite passages from the works of Homer in this age of many wanderers was that in which Achilles told Odysseus in the world of the shades that he should not try to console a man who was dying—in the words of the Achilles with his naked heel which the arrow had reached—that poor plowman who had no rood of land allotted to him and not much subsistence to live on than to be reduced to the realm of a king over the dead—that ever-increasing empire.

He himself had foreseen, as he had written in one of his Lazarus poems, no mourning for himself—no whispered masses and no Kaddish—no grandeur, no pomp—but he had thought that if the day were a sunny one, as he hoped, then his wife Mathilde would go strolling on the high bank of Montmartre with Pauline and would strew *immortelles* of dead white and yellow as she wiped a teardrop from her eye.

Now in Marx's September letter to Engels, at a time when, as in all other times of his own mortal passage which he had seemed to think was a one-way journey, his only immortality to be—no matter what the Brahmins and Pythagoras said—that which he might find in planting his seed between the loins of that beautiful but ailing wife's body of which he was the plowman—Marx had done some rooting around in the dead poet's works in order to come up with a quotation that might well have been, although made in a random way, the correct prophecy as to how the materialistic, many-mouthed Mathilde had behaved on the day of the funeral, where she made no visible appearance among the mourners.

One of Heine's witty remarks which might still be dug up was that the bust of Klopstock was mainly important as a place to hang his hat on. Another which showed his fear of despotic powers capturing the proletariat mob was that it would be wise for little mice who had no shoes not to go to the great cat shoemaker for such provisions.

Toward the end, the incorrigible clown-poet had written his poems not by moving his plumed pen but by moving a piece of paper back and forth, no doubt somewhat like the wings of a bird.

Marx had chosen from the "Romanzero," written when the poet in his coffin bed under the blue Chinese screen was trying to provide for his wife by publication so that she might not starve when he was gone the lines which showed that the female had taken no time for mourning but at eight o'clock had drunk red wine and laughed.

That which had appealed to Marx's jackass funny bone—for naturally or supernaturally, he could not have been a believer in the necessity of boarding the train to the future which seemed to be his in the midst of so many illusory spiritual sources such as had been recognized by Heine—was that the prophecy which the dying poet had made concerning the fat widow's behavior had literally (in English) come to pass. While in Paris, where Mrs. Marx had stopped to investigate the present market value of her depressed railroad stocks, she had been told many details about the frivolous behavior of the fat woman by Reinhardt, Heine's former secretary, who for a time when the dead poet was alive had served as a conduit for messages to Marx and thus to Engels or vice versa. Many of his messages had been ambivalent of meaning.

That which had apparently given offense to Marx was that the somersaulting corpse of the old clown had still been in the death house when Mathilde with the angelic smile had been called upon and fetched away from her door by her *maquereau,* or pimp. Marx had briefly wound up what he had learned—that the worthy Meissner, who had smeared soft dung on the German public, had received cash money from Mathilde to glorify this human swine who had tormented Heine to death.

One of the contemporary recollections of the dumb Mathilde would be that in spite of the extravagances showered upon her by the dying poet—even while on his coffin bed he had played on the stock exchange in order to increase his Paris-Strasbourg railroad shares and other shares—she was a slovenly creature who looked as if she were unfamiliar with water.

[2 0]

MARX'S RELATIONSHIP with Heine was a very different kettle of fish from that with Wilhelm Weitling in the long ago, he having been a member of the League of the Just, which—as its members were journeyman tailors, hatters, shoemakers, bricklayers—had distrusted such high-flown intellectuals as Marx and Engels with their vast abstractions of thought which were not those of workingmen. When a student at the University of Berlin, Marx had written to his father, Heinrich Marx—after whom he would one day name the son who was to be the apple of his eye—to tell of his having recently completed a dialogue of about twenty-four pages entitled "Cleanthes, or the Starting Point and the Necessary Progress of Philosophy." And although the Hegelian wild, rough, craggy music was that of which he knew at this time only the fragments—he was still so young, so untried that he was not yet the bridegroom or the father—he had now as an energetic wanderer set out for the main task.

The League of the Just of which the bowlegged tailor Wilhelm Weitling was a member was a secret, proletarian, largely radical order that had broken away from the original Outlaws' League in Paris in order to spread the revolutionary words in Switzerland and Germany and elsewhere. As Engels was to recall in *The History of the Communist League,* which grew out of the League of the Just, no one when looking backward upon Wilhelm Weitling's contribution to communism could deny what Marx had said in the Paris *Vorwärtz* in 1841 on the merits of "guarantees of harmony and freedom," which with its loosely stitched leaves the man with the red cap had then been scattering over the Swiss Alps and other parts of Europe and even in the America toward which so many coatless tailors and shoeless shoemakers were going if they could find a way.

Engels's recollection was of the written praise that Marx had given to Weitling's pioneering work. His memory was that in which, with his tendency to seem a man of withered veins in relation to his gold-veined brother, Marx had worked out the idea that communism was no longer something accidental that could just as well not have occurred. The proletariat could not work out its emancipation without emancipating society as a whole from division into classes and class struggle.

[2 1]

THE BREAKUP OF WEITLING with those two Brussels sprouts Marx and Engels yielded to numerous interpretations, depending on the communistic or socialistic or political or atheistic or religious bias of the interpreters.

Weitling had thought that he with his depths and heights of experience should be the helmsman—although for Marx and Engels he was soon to emerge as nothing but a windbag and no helmsman worthy of any ship but a ship of fools, all those who had departed from the rational philosophy of materialism that they were just then trying to work out.

Weitling with his idea that the poor children of poor workers were poured into molds which were iron maidens from which they would be unable to emerge as flowers was surely not, however, proposing an image of the suppression of talents with which genuine believers in the necessity of society's reform might quarrel. His trouble was that he had seemed to think of himself as the leader who in realms of science and of art was endowed with the eye of the omniscience which would show him the way through titanic storms and who had at his beck and call supernatural powers provided by the wisdom of his own instinctive knowledge which had come to his regenerative cause without abstractions of arid reasons such as those provided by the intellectual partners Marx and Engels, for whom errant utopian dreamers were guilty of throwing dust into the eyes of whatever benighted mechanics and millwrights and wheelwrights should make the egregious mistake of joining with him to go where they knew not. Neither Marx nor Engels had dug ditches or plowed lands.

In Weitling's somewhat biased or jaundiced view, these two would-be fathers of the International Workingmen's Association who were hammering out the shape and design of the revolutionary communist movement might turn out not to be good fathers of the lowly mechanics and sowers and reapers for whom he was the spokesman. For he had been one of them. His belief was that Marx with his excessive erudition might make an excellent lexicographer but never the founder of a utopian world that might be habitable by man. He had had no room in his baggage for neo-Hegelianism—he had only his own utopian scrolls and perhaps an angel's foot or an angel's spare wing.

Shortly after his rupture with a couple with whom he had never been united, he was to sail for the first time to that America which Hegel had dismissed as a continent outside history but which Marx reflecting Engels and Engels reflecting Marx knew was a continent within history and could not be left out.

There were numerous eyewitnesses to the tentative relationships at a time when everything was tentative and Marx was in love with his own crystal ball–gazing—his own spirit of prophecy in his own way—as Weitling was with his, which accepted only his own forecast.

The well-hatted, well-tailored, well-gloved, well-buttoned tailor king genuinely believed that it was he who was chosen to preside over intricate networks of primitive Christian earthly paradises. This occurred because of his swift refusal to accept any law other than his own and that of God—doubtless for the very good reason that he was the worker Christ who was the son of God and had risen. His carpenter's awl was his all.

He had now become in his own eyes the master tailor who—when others could not see an inch before their faces through the fog caused by human stupidity—could see how to draw his thread through the needle's eye gleaming through seas of clouds.

Present in Brussels at this time, along with others exiled by various crowns, had been Joseph Weydemeyer, a former officer in the Prussian artillery who was very good at spotting rebels against the iron heels of the iron king, and at a time when—as a disciple of the utopian philosophies of Owen and Fourier—he had found that he was in a situation of unendurable paradox through the fact that he was a rebel who ought to be spotting himself and had withdrawn to become a railroad construction engineer—his skill being such that he knew how many dynamite sticks would be required to blow up the locomotive and the rails when there came the coming revolution.

The eyewitness Weydemeyer was to remember random card games at night in Brussels when Marx and Engels—with himself as the third hand—had sometimes been joined by Weitling dropping in as the fourth hand. He was always the first to grow weary, the first to drop out—it would be remembered of him.

It had been Engels's belief that Weitling's refusal to participate in the strategy of the new communist doctrine had been caused by not only his illusions of grandeur but by his anxiety over money. Money, it seemed, was required in order to found a moneyless utopia, albeit—as the jackass Weitling said to all and sundry—it was or should be of less value than the dung which made the crops grow. He was greedy. From Engels's naturally not unbiased point of view, this mournful but optimistic jester with bells did seem an irresponsible mountebank, a man made all of motley—many biases and many angles and scraps and shreds. But to Weitling the gamblers Marx and Engels who were so interrelated that they seemed able to read each other's minds and also each other's cards were guilty of blackmailing anyone who did not agree with them and were determined to put him off the rails of history—throw him aside.

Weitling's objection to Marx and Engels—as he had leapt up to say one night in Marx's house where the various revolutionary exiles were gathered at a table drinking wine as they considered the way from the old world of despotic capitalism to the new world of political and economic equality which should be brought by following their chart—was that their schemes were wholly unnecessary; he had already worked everything out and would be the pilot star providing guidance because of his relationship with God and man.

Marx, arising to his feet, had brought his fist down so hard upon the table that the goblets of the red wine reflecting candle flames and the candlesticks had jumped. Marx had ringingly declared—as would be recalled by the visiting Russian P. V. Annenkov—that the arousal of fantastic hopes in the breasts of workers such as those in which Wilhelm Weitling indulged could only lead to the ultimate ruin and not to the salvation of the oppressed.

Weitling's attempt to lead workers without a scientific basis from the old world to the new was considered by both Marx and Engels to be as false and dishonest a game as playing preacher to a congregation of jackasses listening with their mouths agape. Weitling with his utopian bundle was or was soon to be revealed as a utopian bindle stiff like many a utopian bindle stiff who had gone before him and would come after him—he was guilty of promising to deliver the goods he could not deliver, not even in America, where the millennial dreams seemed to fail, only seemed to fail.

ONE OF THE PROJECTS on which Weitling had worked while living as a tailor reformer in London's Soho as he continued to try to develop the perfect lathe was the invention or evolvement of a new universal language such as had been—along with secret and occult languages and languages of silent signs—a part of many utopian ideals, although it almost always perished before it could put on wings and get off its feet. If all mankind was or was to become one body and if all things instead of being disjointed were recognized as a part of a single and unified and endless whole as Owen with his dream of a universal language had also believed—and surely that language must be the simple carrier of simple thoughts—then why should men and nations be alienated from each other by the failure of communication?

According to Weitling's new language, the German *"Du wirst das Mädchen haben,"* which in English translated into "You will have the girl," was to become—when all tongues should be the same tongue—the instantly apprehensible "Pi Papai li sas," to give but one example of the harmony which was to replace discord. What if to some ears "Pi Papai li sas" had a ridiculous sound? To its creator it was as sublime as the music of the universe. *"Ich werde das Mädchen gehabt haben"*—"I will have had the girl"— became "Pi Papai sas." *"Ich werde ein Mann werden"*—"I will become a man"—"Pi wavivi fif."

The hissing sounds of the old Westphalian seemed not to have departed from the universal tongue in which all bird workers would speak in the earthly paradise which was to come.

Weitling was never to be in agreement with Jacob Grimm of the Grimm brothers fairy tales whom Karl Marx did Grimmly read for the beaming light which—in the midst of the foggy, foggy darkness and in the midst of much dead history which somehow lived—it cast upon the study of language as that which was more than the study of words, words, words which were not merely birds, birds, birds but a means of spading up and exploring man's past—whether immediate or remote. Of all the things which man had created, language remained, according to Jacob Grimm's tracery of the origin of language, mankind's noblest possession.

In a universe filled with the roarings of waves upon all shores far and near—dogs barking, birds singing—man's language was that creation which God had given to him with his ability to think.

Weitling—to whom words like birds had provided liberation—could not forgive Grimm's questioning of the divine authenticity of the biblical tale of the Tower of Babel, which was built upon a plain in the land of Shinar by bricklayers and stonemasons and mortar bearers when the whole earth was made of one language and of one speech. And the Lord had come down to see what was built by the children of men but had feared that as the people were of one language, nothing could restrain them from doing what they wished to do—even from building a tower from earth to heaven—so He had scattered them all over the face of the earth before they could build a city—and He had split the once universal language into various tongues.

In his passion for shaving things down with his Occam's razor in the quest for what would be a rational clarity beyond dispute and which would open the door to the future, Weitling with the thickening fogs heavily increasing on him had probably not understood that he was throwing himself against God's Tower of Babel—trying to knock it down, trying to undo God's work as if it were the work of despotic powers of state who wanted poor men to be divided from each other.

The simplified spelling of words in one tongue must have seemed to him as necessary a part of his evangelical socialism as was the gospel of which the root contained the word "spel" from which "spelling" came. In overcoming diversities of tongues, he would be going back to the original word of God. He would be doing so in modern times.

It mistakenly seemed to Weitling almost beyond the power of his conception that any man would be so obtuse as to fail to see that his Simple Simon language—if such it was—provided possibilities of clear and unequivocal communication linking the earthly paradises of the world.

Weitling's new universal language, which never did get off its feet, could only seem as abrasive as sand to sensitive ears, and had seemed to Engels—and hence possibly also to Marx—unutterably ridiculous. Weitling was a tailor's dummy. He seemed nothing more—perhaps.

When he was in London devoting himself to the ironing of straw for fashionable poke bonnets and the design of his futuristic lathe while continuing his writings as he dreamed of the Rousseau green forest in which man had dwelled in happiness before his loss of that primitive innocence to which he should be returned, Weitling had sometimes attended meetings of workingmen at their institutes and had joined in their choral singing around a piano and had delivered lectures on the forms and shapes that would prevail in the world which was to come when the utopian ideal of the cooperative brotherhoods would be made real.

Charles Dickens was also an important figure in the history of British and American socialism. Dickens was the profligate author of *Martin Chuzzlewit,* in which he had given a most unflattering and not oval portrait of America as made up of an entire society in which people lived at the thin surface hiding the profound void and depended upon hyperbolic language as the substitution for the bleakness and bareness of the reality that they hid from themselves and thus—they hoped—from others. America was the place where theft was called independence.

The tarring and feathering of a political opponent in a lonely gulch was called the planting of the standard of civilization in the wilder gardens of the American continent. Reality was taken away or left behind by such dazzling claims as that the American was a child of nature and a child of freedom and by his boastful claim to the despot and the tyrant that his bright home was in the setting sun.

Dickens had not thought that such cupidity was confined to the Americans, who in public wore masks like those of puppets to conceal their inner emptiness—many having come to the new land as migrants themselves—who when they had made good by all kinds of confidence games—all kinds of crooked deals with stacked cards and loaded dice—had blotted out from their minds, for the most part, recognition or memory of the sufferings of fellow migrants who had been and remained homeless urchins in the mud. Many of life's most essential measurements were those that were measured by no measuring yardstick but that which gauged the size of a man by dollars in his pot of silver or gold.

For Dickens it did seem that the only way from earth to heaven was the way which in its many windings led from life to death.

[2 2]

FOR A WHILE, the risen Christ of the Alps or mad sheepdog barking at a star which had wandered out of the fold like a lost sheep beyond the pale of man's experience had thought of spreading the propaganda upon the earthly paradise which was to come when the workers were united—but then, as he did not have the privilege of free travel and had only a false passport and thus risked incarceration again at any border, he had turned his eyes from the east to the west. In the late autumn of 1846 through seas turning from gold to red to gray to black, Weitling had sailed from the Old World to the New World in order to get a bird's-eye view of the American continent and the prospects offered there for his own examples of millennial reform—and at a time when many of the older utopias had failed or were failing.

He had been fortunate to reach New York harbor without the wreckage of his ship against icebergs howling like winter wolves in winter winds. His passage had been paid in part by German members of various workingmen's cells who were also dreaming of migration to the future earthly paradisal networks in the New World as a way of improving their lot should other means fail in the Old World.

Wilhelm Weitling had been led by the golden light to America with the idea that he should become the editor of the *Volkstribun* (*People's Tribune*) as Kriege, the owner, had promised him—but this publication had already gone bankrupt—had closed up as if it had been a bucket in a bucket shop where no waters were—so that he had been left to fare alone with his usual ingenuity as he had always done. He had received few funds from members of the *Sozialreformverein* (Social Reform Association) who had helped to pay his passage but were themselves German migrants of very limited means.

In New York, a busy city of many utopian peddlers of many paradisal wares, some with their visions of heaven, some with their visions of earth— many barking the news of great transportation and transformation acts— Weitling had gone to work selling a third edition of *Das Evangelium des Armen Sünders,* which he had helped to set up in red print on yellowed foolscap leaves stitched together by the prospective tailor king and for which—even with expenses scaled down to a minimum and not scaled upward to a maximum—he had paid on credit. When one day translated into the English language, that which would become a "Gospel of the Poor Sinner" would seem to have, in a universal moment of cloudlike deception, that kind of familiar ring which was the work of wilderness salvationist preachers on every street corner in lower New York with its Babel of tongues including bird tongues. He had also paid on loan for the printing of the pamphlet *Ein Notbruf an die Männer der Arbeit und Sorge,* which, as the English say, would translate into *A Cry of Distress to the Men of Labor and Sorrow.*

His intention at this point had been to attract from the Old World— where the workers were yoked to the tyranny of the past and the deadbeat forces of habit—other German workers who, yearning for new horizons, wished to be unyoked and come flocking to this land of opportunity, which offered—according to his sincere belief—the golden opportunity to establish and make real his plans for the cooperative communal society of workers. It would be an enlargement of the family system of father and mother and child, which in the prevailing system of despotic capitalistic exploitation was a trinitarian arrangement more likely to be found in hypocritical sentiments than in hard-nailed fact. The fathers so often died young because of their labors that—in this New World as in the Old with its longtime corruption—the poor widows and orphans had no protection from the howling winter winds, no shelter and no bread.

Weitling had methodically organized—as he had attempted to find cohesion and coherence in the midst of incohesion and incoherence, which would increase for many poor German and other foreign migrants, to which the American continent with its instabilities seemed to contribute, for in this land they found themselves in some ways to be suddenly altered persons—some for the better and some for the worse—and there were many transformations as there were many losses of memory—just as some who had been radical became conservative if they fared well in a monetary sense—his foolproof scheme for a utopia that would not be founded on chance and would endure so long as this old world endured—perhaps longer.

When a radical left the comparative shelter of the harbor city because he was unwilling to wait for the dustman to come along and pick him up and cart him off to a potter's field—when a man set out toward the western sunset—there was no way of knowing what he might become.

The watchword of the nineteenth century, according to Horace Greeley, who with his white hat and white coat and white beard walking through a white snowstorm looked like the ice man coming in wintertime—a time when his presence was the one gift a tramp frozen in the ice glare did not need—was reform. And it should be reform under God—but not the same God as that of the antihumanitarian expansionists who scorned poor migrant speakers of foreign tongues, including, of course, bird tongues.

In 1839 the euphoric utopia-minded and yet mechanistic ex-printer Horace Greeley had written a poem about those dreams which came to him in many a waking hour and yet seemed to madness near allied—dreams that a nation which seemed determined to scale the heights would not omit concern for the poor. "Full well I know such thoughts outmock / The mind to which no more is given / But humblest blade and loftiest oak / Alike may rear their heads to heaven."

[2 3]

WEITLING, THE SPIRIT of impatience burning within him, had organized the *Befreiungsbund* (League of Deliverance), which he intended as an answer to the League of the Just and which helped to finance out of its small funds his first of many journeys into the interior of a nation certainly not in harmony with itself but torn by national discords.

He had been unable or unwilling to cling to the comparative safety of New York harbor and so, under the influence of his own inner voices and personalized mythologies and the utopias of Owen, Fourier, and Cabet, he had set forth upon a journey with his bag of foolscap resurrectionist and redeemist pamphlets, by train as far as Pittsburgh and then by ship down the Ohio to Cincinnati and then by water road down the Mississippi from St. Louis to New Orleans—and in these busy ports he had established cells of revolutionary brotherhoods who in a nation dedicated to the idea of transcience were to be noted mainly for their transcience even like the grass to which man returneth in a material if not in a spiritual sense.

He had even penetrated into the wilds of Texas, where the original Icarian commune had been torn to pieces like shepherdless sheep driven against great cactus thorns as sharp as iron spikes on which they left their bloody wool hanging like shrouds.

In Philadelphia, the City of Brotherly Love which would not always show brotherly love to skeleton workers striking against great czars of mills and mines and railroads and their combinations, Weitling had successfully established—for this was a city of that awakening workers' consciousness which could not be suppressed by seas of burning slag—a chapter of the League of Deliverance, which was to enjoy longevity in one form or another until the century's turn when he was long gone.

The constitution of the new *Arbeiterverein* (Workers Association) to which Weitling had contributed his tutelary genius was a more or less accurate repetition of the demands of older utopias that were now expanding—breaking out of capsule forms, proposing changes which should bring the booming bustling nation from woe to weal in the treatment of men by men in a genuine and not a hypocritical democracy which gave protection to the few rich but not to the many poor.

In the nation which followed the constitution drawn up by tailors, hatters, shoemakers, bricklayers, hive keepers, and workers of other crafts as well as those who were as yet craftless but might learn to do useful work, there would be none who would be left neglected by the state. People would be treated equally as Americans regardless of what foreign tongues they spoke or if they spoke not at all, if they were mute. As to how to tell the difference between the sane and the mad, the constitution had provided no way in a land where there were and would be so many mad men including the great founders of utopias.

The Philadelphia brotherhood had advocated land reform and free trade and no high tariff wall—that which in America was looked upon as the Great Wall of China—and the abolition of inheritance tax and of the interest on capital. A subsidiary order had been devised to pay for the doctor and the pills and the oils and the muddy brook-water balms for the sick and the coffin and the earth and the spade man with his spade for the digging of the dead man's grave. For these and other benefits, there were dues of three cents a week.

As at least token responsibility was assumed for the cause of the German revolution which had abysmally failed and for the support of the waves of new refugees who were coming into Philadelphia—some with the fires of revolution still burning in their eyes and some with the fires dimmed, some who had affluence in the Old World but might now be reduced to tallow-streaked rags such as only a ragpicker could appreciate—some who had always been like the ragamuffin who with his long, musty sleeves was very much the left-over actor from an old mystery play which must go on and on in this New World which was never new. The members of the *Arbeiterverein* had formed—along with an insurance society for the dead that they might land in a potter's field or be left unburied with their faces turned toward the sky—a Building and Loan Association and a singing society—a choir of voices singing like birds, buzzing like bees who would be happy in the great socialist beehive—and had instituted betting games with the lure of prizes as a way of increasing the number of pennies in their treasury for the benefit of migrants and their urchins.

[2 4]

SAILING AGAINST THE TIDE from the New World to the old, taking his utopian chance with his joker's card, Wilhelm Weitling with his foolscap pamphlets had arrived in France and had reached Paris on a Sunday, two days before the end of the July revolution of 1830.

Louis Philippe, the citizen king who under his black umbrella had walked about in the impoverished labyrinthine districts of Paris talking to sewage workers and other poor workers and trying to find out in what ways he could help them, shelter them—he had once told Robert Owen that he wished he could do more but that the circumference of his protection was limited—had been forced to abandon his throne and under his protective umbrella traveling in disguise as plain William Smith had fled from France to England for sanctuary.

Robert Owen had written, as red republicans and Bonapartists rioted in the streets, tossing building blocks and hearse wagons and steeples and steeplejacks at each other while crying out the same magical watchwords "Liberty, Fraternity, and Equality," one of his many letters to the world. His *"Dialogue entre la France, le monde, et Robert Owen"* ("Dialogue Between France, the World, and Robert Owen"), which appeared in every Paris newspaper and on every wall—sometimes pockmarked with blood—had been as pacific as doves in a city where there were many bloody doves and few who could bill and coo through the battle although there must always have been some.

According to Robert Owen, who had never admitted the defeat of his utopia on the banks of the Wabash and who had been elected not only father of the British labour movement but father of the human race—and who was still placing his faith in his scrolls and maps, which would lead mankind out of its present morass of capitalism on to the unmoving Rock of Ages—both parties were wrong. "I come to your country in this important crisis to the history of all nations to explain in the spirit of kindness and love for you and the entire family of man in what manner you may render useless all the implements of destruction, give happiness to France, and through its example insure the permanent progressive happiness of the world."

The archbishop of Paris had been shot through the back, quite by accident, during the raging storm. There were mothers and babies bleeding in gutters. There were bloody babies' hands strewn all over the streets, men who were flattened under falling paving stones, clowns killed by falling gargoyles. Forces larger than those of war had seemed at work as in every war of the rational against the irrational and of the irrational against the rational. The earth gave off a sighing, lonely sound. Was happiness after all the instinct of the universe, for was there not universal sorrow?

WHY HAD THE REVOLUTION failed? It would be Weitling's theory, as he looked back, that two thirds of the leaders in 1830 had represented the old moneybags, and that the mistake of the proletariat—or, as Marx called it, the lumpen proletariat—had been apparently not to act so much upon original impulse or passion of feeling informing every worker's cell as to emulate the French Revolution to the extent that the revolutionary birth had turned out to be that of a babe who was a bastard.

Wilhelm Weitling had been in touch with hundreds, thousands, of the suppressed and depressed at this time. His pamphlets *Garantien der Harmonie und Freiheit,* or *Guarantees of Harmony and Freedom,* which would be its name in the English translation, were going along with other foolscap publications to revolutionary workmen's cells in France and Germany and

Switzerland and to wherever rails could reach. He was also in touch with various anarchic communal heads who believed in the flowering of the ego in an altruistic sense which might be founded according to their ideals of brotherhood and sisterhood—some who would set off on their own, some who would remain in Europe and Asia Minor and Asia, others who would come into New York harbor, where there was no harmony but discord as to what should be the golden way in spite of Weitling's having spread his propaganda to such important points as Poughkeepsie and Cincinnati and St. Louis, to mention only three rival cities which were crucial in the land of water.

Brother Weitling's passage by way of London to New York harbor had been paid in part with the profit that was raised in part by the American German disciples of the cooperative brotherhood movement by marvelous games of raffles in which it was easier to raise money for the possibly already lost cause which was the utopian prospect than it would have been if there had been no visible prizes or embodiments such as a workman's lantern or a bag of grain or a pregnant sow or rooster for the pot or a spade or a beehive.

The pressures upon Wilhelm Weitling because of his need for money had provided the motive for all he did, according to an analysis made of him by Engels in his attempt to understand what had prompted him.

On October 29, 1850, a month before death snatched the little red fox from his father's loving arms, the financial distress that Marx suffered in his exile in London was so altogether intense that he had written to Weydemeyer in Frankfurt that he should please borrow from a local socialist or anybody there the money with which to redeem the family silver in the pawnshop there—then sell the silver to a goldsmith or anybody there, pay the man from whom he had borrowed, and send the remainder to him. These were the silver pieces which his wife, then pregnant with the little red fox, had carried in a bag to the pawnshop at Brussels.

The doggedly persistent Marx, the poor man who was trying to show the way to a solution of the world's economic problems could assure the faithful Weydemeyer that he and the other man would run no risk in this transaction—for if they were unable to sell the thing at a higher price, they could always take it back to the pawnshop. "The only pieces I ask you to return to the pawnshop . . . are a small silver goblet, a silver plate, the small fork and knife in a case"—these silver pieces, of little sales value, belonged to his little daughter Jenny.

No matter how poor he was, however, he had generously shared whatever bread he had with other exiles in flight from the continent to they knew not always where. A starving exile might be found upon his doorstep almost every morning.

Little Jenny and little Laura and little Eleanor—the three daughters who would survive him—were taught the English language by way of Shakespeare's plays, which were—as Marx said—a family bible. The bright little Jenny, very asthmatic, knew her *Hamlet* very well and the mad Ophelia scattering flowers on her way to her watery grave and the speech which the melancholy Dane delivered to the skull of the jester Yorick. Little Jenny was able to judge who was the real socialist exile coming to call on Marx—sometimes to share a heel of bread or thin soup made of old potato peelings—and who was the poseur, the clown, the mountebank merely pretending to be a communist.

Marx was always to be astonished by the detachment with which most Englishmen wrote of the great monetary question which was the Sphinx of that time and was to continue to be the Sphinx—but supposed it was because they generally had money, whereas he was so nearly bankrupt that he hardly knew where the next meal was coming from—and it was the cotton broker Engels who with his generous nature time and again saved him.

So far as other socialist messiahs were concerned, Marx was embittered by their deviations away from the science of dialectical materialism and was repelled by the wild leaders who never tired of wafting public incense around the heads and feet of little great men as if they were worthy of worship.

[2 5]

THE KIND OF GERMAN IMMIGRANT to these shores whom Brother Weitling could not upon the whole idealize must surely have been the familiar figure of the beaver-coated John Jacob Astor, whose name had been anglicized from the original Ashdour or Aschdoor or Ashdor to Astor and who had come to America in 1784 with no merchandise to declare at the sign of the dollar customs house but seven suits and seven flutes and who—formerly a pearl cookie salesman on Pearl Street—had gone to work for a Quaker beaver-fur king flogging moths with his bramble stick out of the stored skins of murdered beaver cooperative brotherhoods who with their instinctive architectural and mathematical sense, which was no doubt older than that of man with his contempt for natural good, had built the honeycombs of beaver dams in American rivers and streams and lakes.

For a mere dollar to the red men of upper New York State, those who had wandered as the communal beavers had waned, Astor had been able to purchase pelts which would bring six hundred percent profit for each skin shipped out from New York harbor to London. And thus he had become not only the king of the beaver trade but the great landlord of the Astor House and all that he surveyed.

It was the wanton slaughter of the feathered red men and of the beaver brotherhood and buffalo which had contributed to the elegiac sense of the American millennial continent from earliest time onward and which would bring the awakening of the social consciousness of Eugene Victor Debs, if there was such a thing as his awakening, if it had not been his from the day when he was born.

Along Seneca Turnpike, a straggling mile was named Turkey Street in memory of turkey citizens who when being driven along this main artery to Buffalo or Rochester, that which migrant workers also took when going west, had been so worn out with their feathers wilted in the wind and their red combs about to drop off that they had cried aloud in their own cackle language, doubtless the same in all countries and needing no translation, that they had gone far enough into the land where the sun set—and so they had struck, had broken loose from the drover and had flown up into the trees where they had insisted upon remaining in spite of the long bramble with which he prodded them. They were like the poor Irish themselves who escaped from one slaughter to another. The drover had sold the turkeys off to local farmers who had enough prongs to bring them down.

Weitling had been fascinated by the economy and harmony of the nearby utopian Oneida Community, which under the leadership of the perfectionist John Humphrey Noyes, founder of a quasi-millennial commune dedicated to the ideal of no personal ownership of private property but the sharing of all things by all men—including their wives, whom they owned no more than they owned their orchards and fields and beehives and brick kilns and sawmills—who had fled from Putney in the stony land of Vermont to this place of uncertain refuge from the killer capitalistic world of the philistines for the life of the primitive Christian church brothers with their faith that no man should call aught his own. They had come here to establish their peaceful island world in the midst of the sea of capitalism. And like the wild turkeys, they were under threat from the beginning.

He had made his way through the autumnal land to establish the Oneidist community which took its inspiration by link and chain from God to Christ and from Christ to Paul and from Paul to John Humphrey Noyes, whose inspiration had come to him in a radiant light when he first started out—even as it had come to the journeyman tailor when he was a naked tailor gathering mold in the Swiss prison.

On Turkey Street, to help themselves tide the community over a valley of depression such as they had found when they first came here, the Oneidists were engaged in a nakedly capitalistic venture of their own and without shame: the operation of a steel-trap business for the catching of whatever wild birds or beasts—including sometimes the two-footed animal who was man—should make the mistake of putting his foot there.

[2 6]

WEITLING WAS INTERESTED in all forms of utopias of a millennial nature, not only the pacifist Oneidists with their communal weaving looms and animal traps which made them seem to some of their observers no different from Astors and Goulds, but also all other utopian experiments which he had seen or of which he had heard along the zigzag Turkey Trail to Buffalo, as he was also to become an expert analyst of utopian alchemies which had been brought into transient being by man's primordial dreams and by comparison with which his dreams—still evolving in the great vat—would be a science without flaws, such as had been that of Owenites, Saint-Simonians, Fourierites, Millerites, Brisbaneites, Shakers, Rappites, Mormons, and the Icarian followers of Étienne Cabet—although he with his essentially imitative mind was somewhat under the spell of all. But his objections were to those false prophets who had stolen his principles and had robbed them of their meaning while presenting them as if they were their own or had been handed down by God, who, operating on high, had no need of Weitling as his low mediator and interpreter and instrument. Before leaving upper New York he had asked that his mail be forwarded to Kolonie Kommunia, Elkader Post Office, Clayton County, Iowa, and thus had shown as great a faith in the uncertain mail service and any letter ultimately reaching him as he had shown in his own ability to keep this promise to deliver utopia to his fellowmen with the help of the workingmen who would shoulder the burden with him.

Weitling's ports of call on this journey into the still unknown and perhaps unknowable many-leveled American interior with his bags of promissory pamphlets on his back as he tried to enroll exiles in his League of Deliverance included the already beautifully burgeoning paradise of capitalists and bankers on the shores of Lake Erie—the future home of John Hay, the future secretary of Abraham Lincoln.

In Cleveland, Weitling had happily come upon a cooperative tailor shop where the women had done the sewing of cloth with needles and threads and had punched buttonholes by hand when the men had failed. Among the hundreds of migrant German workers to whom he spoke in Cleveland—many not staying to hear him out, for they were drawn to a picnic with harps and flutes and songs in the flower-starred grasses of a tree-shadowed woodland about six miles away—the poor man with his promises of bread to all was unable to gather for the Workers Association more than fourteen first payments, which for a variety of reasons including both mortality and further flight might not be followed by second payments.

At this time of the gold rushers still trickling on as well as those migrants who were in search of the gold which might be made in growing corn in the western lands, then in the mournful process of being taken away from the red men whose heads—now more rarely seen than in the immediate past—were crowned with all kinds of feathers including feathers of roosters, turkeys, swans, Weitling had passed through Sandusky on his way to Toledo with his own versions of *Jesus Save Me* cooperative brotherhood pamphlets and *Arbeiterverein* enrollment propaganda long before it became a saying in that part of the world of a man who was dying or was about to die that he had taken the old Sandusky train with its lonely whistle upon a long, last journey into the burning beehive glow of the setting sun upon a far western horizon.

Among the benefits promised by Weitling to those who would join the *Arbeiterverein* where there were fifteen at Sandusky, a small sheaf in relation to potential hundreds, were pension funds for investment in cooperative stores and other fraternal enterprises and burial funds which might be called sinking funds—as they were for the purchase of burial grounds and coffins for those who had completed their cycle on earth or had not completed it—and money also for funeral wreaths and for widows and children who might be left to starve when the winter wolf howled. Brother Weitling, flushed with hope, had promised, "We shall come to power along this road if only the leaders will remain steadfast."

He was speaking in an Ohio that contained at this time the most sinister foreign-born anarchist a capitalist king of kings or emperor could have imagined, a little dwarf child worker with a harelip and an unruly swirl of corn-colored hair and violet-blue eyes fringed with unusually long lashes, who had been brought from Germany to this country when an infant in arms and now, about three years old and wizened as an old man who never had been young, had walked before his cruel, law-abiding, God-fearing religious father with his bare baby feet bleeding on the ground as he helped to sow seed by hand on a scrappy little patchwork farm and make sure that no seeds were left uncovered by clods for the marauder birds.

The name of the little boy with the thatched hair and the pointed face and the violet eyes swimming in tears as he was forced to look down, down, down upon the earth and not up, up, up to the sky was John Peter Altgeld, future governor at Springfield, Illinois, whose way was to be that of a transcendental and yet secular socialism escaping the boundaries of self-interest by allegiance to the altruism that might be identified with otherness.

A TOKEN OF SUCCESS restored Brother Weitling's almost failing, flagging spirit at Detroit, Michigan, where all the cabinetmakers—not one dissenting squeak among them, not one door or drawer which refused to open—had joined in one body as if to point the way to the future when the cooperative brotherhoods would be joined in one universal body of which the head would quarrel not with the hands and the hands would quarrel not with the feet.

To the city of Chicago upon the shores of Lake Michigan Brother Weitling also came, with his *Cry of Distress to the Men of Labor and Sorrow* and his *Wounds and Balm* and his cures for the ills and woes of the body of society which might be brought into harmony through his economy if only enough dollars could be found to give a start to a living example of the cooperative brotherhood which he could lead as peacefully toward the pleasant pasturelands of socialism, needing no reins but faith in his magical compass and touchstone and the awakening of age-old instinctive ideas.

Chicago contained within its amorphous borders slaughterhouses and the old Fort Dearborn and the factory for the manufacture of the automatic harvester for which Cyrus Hall McCormick held the patent rights and which he had brought here in 1847—the year before the gold rush into the land of the western sunset—and which would make wheat the king of American grains.

It was said of Cyrus McCormick that he was such a tough old rooster that if you threw him into a pot and boiled him to broth, the devil himself would not sup of it. He was the son of a farmer and part-time weaver of stout Presbyterian faith and inventive genius whose various inventions— a threshing machine, a hydraulic machine, a hemp-breaking machine with a peculiar horse power adapted to it—had never been thrown upon the market for transmutation into such gold as would come to the son as time went on.

In the rapidly developing Chicago of boom and bust to which Weitling came there had been thousands of permanent or transient workers in various crafts and trades, including those of teamster, carpenter, shipwright, stonemason, shoemaker, tailor, button puncher, sailor, wig maker, hatter, dress and mantua maker, wedding-gown maker, wagon maker, milkman, gunsmith, water borer, bricklayer, cradle maker, birdsmith or decoy maker, dealer in iron and nails, salesman of counterfeit panaceas which like a utopian concern promised to cure all men's wounds and ills, preacher and barber and waiter and auctioneer and pawnbroker, baker and brewer. But the Chicago of boom and bust had fallen upon hard times for the poor, and the economic ground was as barren for them as dust returning to dust where those who had no shelter slept out all night upon the sand dunes as if they were mummified and might not awaken when someone poked with his stick. Some awakened and cried. Brother Weitling was able to bring into his harvest only one member, and that was a brewer.

In the largely German city of Milwaukee, Wisconsin—which had already become a place of the rising German brewery kings—the golden liquid assets of the rich were increased by the payment of low wages to the poor German workers for whom the prices of beer and bread were kept cheap—they had their hymn-singing societies but no money for coats, hats, shoes, and other benefits, and no money for a city lot upon which to build a dwelling place where but a few years before had been a refuge for thousands of wild mallards and other birds of passage.

Brother Weitling had had bad placer's luck in Milwaukee in trying to gather money for his *Wound and Balms* and his *Arbeiterverein* and his plans for the cooperative brotherhood. Very few farmers throughout the primitive frontier state of Wisconsin, as Brother Weitling found out upon this missionary expedition, ever saw currency of any kind except for the silver dollar which was briefly held in the palm of the farmer's bleeding hand once a year—and that was at the harvesttime when it was all that was left over for him after the payment of high prices out of low wages at the country store for those necessities of life which he could not produce. This silver dollar was slippery as greased lightning and was not to be kept long in his hand. When did one silver dollar become fifty dollars? Would it become fifty dollars when passed from hand to hand of fifty toilers of the soil for the payment of fifty debts which would leave each one as bankrupt as before and up to his ears in marsh mud and sinking fast into that long winter sleep?

[2 7]

THE WAY BROTHER WEITLING took into the Iowa territory in search of a lost horizon was not even a plank road upon which the stagecoach with its families of western migrants both foreign and native, including three children and the utopian crusader, jumped up and down in imitation of the ball of the red sun, but was a road of mud with its fringed outline sometimes lost, sometimes spilling over into seas of flower-starred mud in this autumn of the year where suddenly—almost without transition— snows as cold as Arctic snows would cover somnolent marshlands, the ice so thick that it was like a coffin lid which would not lift until the spring.

The stagecoach was often up to the hub of its wheels in mud and up to the horses' heads, so that by the time Brother Weitling came to Kolonie Kommunia with his face reddened like the harvest sun, he must have seemed the poor scarecrow or scapegoat he was, mud upon his hat, mud upon his coat, mud upon his elbows, mud upon his knees, mud upon his toes, mud to which there clung brambles and twigs and flowers and wings of moths and feathers of birds.

Weitling had enrolled his faraway brothers of the *Arbeiterverein* in a community which they would have been unlikely to see even if it had not fallen to pieces. "For the first time in my life," according to his report to tentative disciples, "I stand on the sacred soil of a communal brotherhood. This land, as far as the eye can see, belongs to us." Perhaps in the low-lying clouds which were to be so soon replaced by snow flurries, ice storms covering the loam and blotting out boundary lines, Brother Weitling could see not only with his material eye but with his spiritual eye.

The Kommunia, or—as it would be spelled in English—Communia, had as one of its main advantages proximity to other centers of German workers who had come here in search of corn for bread—sometimes before the gold rush, sometimes after the gold rush, when they had turned aside because of the gold rushes casting their reflections upon rivers and streams and because of the wild turkeys and deer and other game which might be brought down by the hunter's gun.

Located upon the confluence of the Volga and Turkey rivers—the latter containing, where it emptied into the Mississippi, Indian mounds of the effigy type—Communia was not far from Gutenberg, first called Prairie la Porte but in 1834 rebaptized and renamed by German migrants now nearly approaching a thousand, who made their living working in lead mines. Also near was the German community of Elkader, which was to be known for the harvest of grain.

The utopia in which Weitling had invested the *Arbeiterverein*'s capitalistic dollars which were not moon dollars for the promotion of the harmony and economy of communism—he had laid down only eighty dollars at first from the membership dues of a brotherhood which had wished to assure burial rites—had been founded in 1847 by followers of the dead brush maker from Switzerland whose New Helvetia in the long-tongued Missouri grasses had provided the brush strokes for this still very tentative colony when it moved to the Iowa wilds.

The departure of Heinrich Koch from the presidency of the original Iowa commune, who had first come to America after the revolution of 1830, had been caused by the accusation that he had appropriated for himself and his family the gold which was the corn and had even registered the prairie and woodlands in his own name when the place which was supposed to see the death of expanding capitalism was the property of all. With a payoff of six hundred dollars, six hundred strings of golden hay hanging from his pitchfork, this flamboyant King Koch, who was under appalling accusation by some rival communitarians of the sin of embezzlement, taking for his own use that which was entrusted to him for his care—but whom Brother Weitling believed had been guilty of no crime other than that of fiscal and material mismanagement caused by the fact that he had not had the correct key that would open the door from the past to the future—had been clever enough to utilize his talents by becoming a contractor and political leader in Dubuque, the river city wedged between the cliffs overlooking the Mississippi (Father of Waters) where Julien Dubuque, French-Canadian beaver-fur trader and lead miner, had started making his living on a grand scale.

Under Brother Weitling—when he had taken only a bird's-eye view of the Iowa commune with its busy blacksmith at the forge where the horseshoes which were hammered out were made for dray horses—that which was to rule was not concord but discord caused at least in part by the claims of rival egos for whom the only altruism there was flowed from him whose *Arbeiterverein* was like a milch cow drained and leeched and shriveling as it gave off its milk for the support of families who lived better than did the average distant member who might never live to join their acres between the Turkey and the Volga.

One of the problems which the semiorphaned Brother Weitling had sensed quite early was that the women with children and especially those still suckling at their breasts did not contribute to the economy. The mothers were unwilling to be plowwomen for the community or help at the harvest while their babes ran around like small birds with their shadowy wings in the long grasses and they might themselves be in danger of the ghostly reaper with his scythe—nor would they leave their babes sleeping on a mossy knoll to be tossed up in their blankets in celebration of good corn with red gold ears or wheat or barley or oats.

The workers in the makeshift Iowa version of a potential earthly paradise were not necessarily engaged in the profession or trade which had been theirs in the outside world. Because of the shortage of hands necessary for the building of what was to be a vast commune, Brother Weitling had tried to recruit new helpers to leave where they were and come to this wilderness within a wilderness to serve the ideal as masters of such skills as those of millwright who understood the upper and the lower millstones and the maintenance of wheels—and doubtless he should never be so drunk that he would go to sleep between two millstones—maker of bricks, carpenter, two stonemasons and two shoemakers and a fiddler for evening dances in celebration of the work from sunrise to sunset.

Nothing, however, had gone according to even the most haphazard plan in a land in which everything seemed to be left to the rule of whim or chance as was said of the land of capitalistic opportunity hedging on to these uncertain, ever-clouded borderlines. And new recruits had brought new problems. There were complaints that there were no feather beds for communitarians to sleep on.

Brother Weitling was to find many acres under no cultivation although the members themselves ate well and had dough for bread for a trough big enough to have given space and to have provided comfort for the slumbers of a snoring horse. There had been not only bread for the hungry mouths of members—there had been wine. There had been little or nothing to take to market, for there were many acres uncultivated.

One of Brother Weitling's increasingly patriarchal ambitions had been to buy an automatic reaper, for which, however—in view of staggering debts and mortgages—he did not have the dollars available for borrowing from the *Arbeiterverein*'s memorial funds.

No matter how many skilled workingmen came to sink their life savings into this communal colony, no matter how many sporadic revivals of interest there were, it would seem to be sinking fast. And there were limits to the numbers who could be given living quarters in the long wooden cabin and the small cabins which looked out upon the post road to Dubuque, proud French city where the old-time beaver hunters had made their fortunes.

Brother Weitling's enthusiasm of belief in the future of a jacked-up earthly paradise was that which had caused him to extend his hand to the hands of those who had seceded. "We arrived in the colony on Good Friday," according to his report in *Die Republik der Arbeiter* (*The Republic of the Workers*), whose members were being urged to take their money out of an old sock or bank and bring it here and bring their spades and other workingmen's tools in their toolboxes like long coffins with them if they could—for now was the time of the awakening when the scarecrow with his old tramp coat and canvas painted face and battered hat and brambles made into walking sticks flapped about in the wind of his own motion as he guarded the crop which in the seed time had promised so much—certainly a double harvest. And now was the time of the awakening of dead hopes which had never really died, had only seemed to die. If suddenly the scarecrow with the patches over his eyes showed a human face, what was so unusual about that?

There came always a wandering tramp or two or three who dropped in for a feast when the robin redbreast found that the green cherries had turned red and ripe upon the trees which in the wintertime had been shrouded with embroidered lace like old windblown demented brides who, suddenly awakening, found that they could give milk in little cups to their babes.

"On Saturday we buried the old Judas of misunderstanding—and on Sunday, the Holy Easter of the *Arbeiterverein,* we had the resurrection to the eternal glory of our good cause," according to the crazy clown who never for a moment had been beyond the range of the dialectical materialist arrows since he jumped out of the Marx-Engels card game in Brussels.

On Independence Day, twelve wagonloads of approximately forty Americans were greeted by Brother Weitling when they made a bumping, grinding journey which was not that in which each wagonload carried a banner like a great sail fringed with vermilion and gold representing one of the twelve disciples and was not that of quest for some new moon or Venusian marshland or distant lightning bug star but only that which had journeyed from Elkader to Communia.

With them the travelers had brought not only plenty of juices of the apple in a fermented state along with cheese heads and hogs' heads and melon heads but a lone, shambling fiddler who was out of tune with himself and with his instrument and knew only one tune which he broke in the middle as he struck with his bow upon the strings of a violin which was battered in the winds made by his own motions and by his sawing up and sawing down and which no doubt should have been called the coffin of music and laid to rest in silence. The dancing communitarians could not keep time with its wheezing, snoring sounds.

[2 8]

ONE OF THE CAUSES of resentment against Weitling's leadership by rival leaders more interested in their own ego-centered capitalistic ventures or nonventures which still might make them money than in his altruism was that he was adamant in his refusal to cede to the Iowans the title to the mill where the grain was ground into flour and to cede also the forty acres of land surrounding it—all purchased by the *Arbeiterverein* funds along with much else already lost to the far-flung brothers. He had tried to impose order where chaos had been for some time in the process of undoing whatever work was done.

The hay had been unsheltered for so long before being taken into the barns that half of it had been eaten by stray cattle which were not of these communal fields but had followed the scent of clover and hay from neighboring capitalistic farms. The purchase of the sawmill had been—according to Brother Weitling's evaluations of profit and loss—the worst speculation that could have been made with the funds of the members of the far-flung *Arbeiterverein* whom he was still urging to come here. And how could he blame himself? He had blamed others. There were not enough picks and shovels for the hands that were. Much construction which had not yet been completed had been left to fall into ruins. Many metals had been blighted by rust, including the iron castings for the flour mill. There were not teamsters enough for the hauling of the millstones from the river front to the flour mill, and yet the journey would have been short and would have required no miracle.

The problem of the portage of millstones seemed to be—along with many other communal burdens—the problem left on Brother Weitling's back and in a society ruled by many diversities of clashing opinions where the last word could not be his as the first word had not been his.

For a little while the gleaming of silver shining up like the eyes of birds from under the soil and shining through the crevices of rocks and shining upon the bulrushes and upon the branches of the dwarfed and twisted apple trees and the apples had led to the hope that the silver when mined could be turned into gold for the payment of loans in which only such great tycoons as Astors and Vanderbilts should have indulged themselves.

The silver dream had been disappointing. The silver when taken to the silver assayer's office had turned out not to be that silver which could have been exchanged for bars of gold—the material kind and not the spiritual kind—but the lead that the Communians could not afford to mine—so that all their harvest was likely to be no tree bearing the golden apples of harmony but a tree bearing the leaden apples of discord, those turning into the apples of dust.

As the community, no matter how hard Brother Weitling tried to jack it up, was always falling from economic chaos to economic chaos mainly because of the continuing rivalries of capitalistic egos within its border-lines, he who was doomed to failure in his attempt to provide a moral dam against the flood of selfishness with its shortsightedness as to what might be the general welfare of man and bird and beast had found some refuge in trying to unsnarl the snarled threads of bookkeeping and had found per-haps his only happiness during his sojourn there when he had gone out to work upon the completion of the physical or actual dam for which the workingmen had not completed digging up the mud—perhaps because they felt that they were underpaid or did not wish to get the mud upon their lily-white hands or stand in freezing water up to their waists as they would have had to do if they had been Russian convict laborers with close-cropped heads and almost featureless faces inside the polar ice cap some-where in the wild winter wasteland and had had no choice but to dig or die and dig and die as the snow howled around them and many were entombed under the great ice banks.

[2 9]

JOHN JACOB ASTOR, who having escaped the butcher's trade lived in his own great castle or many castles as the landlord of New York while lining his pockets by foreclosures of mortgages on other men's estates when the borrowers had outreached themselves and who by unremitting collection of rents from poor tenants—mainly the Irish immigrants living in mud hovels in New York and mud holes under the sidewalks—and who was also a many-wheeled and many-cogged money machine with a Midas touch turning lead and dust into gold—in 1848, the hog-headed fat man, his chin hanging in folds and spilling like tallow over his shirt front, the wick of his spirit burning low—had given up the hog's ghost, had sunk into his grave as water to water and dust to dust—had expired as one who had contributed vastly to the doomed diminishment of the beavers in the beaver world where the cooperative beavers according to Indian legend had caused the upheavals of the waters of creation when they went to sleep in great lakes spilling over into rivers and streams and lakes watering this earth as they passed into their last sleep from which the dead bodies of these herb-eating animals would awaken in the form of islands covered with grasses and cherry and aspen and other trees of their diet, trunk and branch and seeds and flowers and fruits and pods—as they had eaten also wild beans and berries and wild rose bushes, both bushes and thorns, and reeds and stalks of corn and ears of corn which they had used to hedge their places of refuge under the water, under the ice.

A beaver who was thirty-six miles long had turned into a beaver island—even as other enormous beavers had turned into other islands—according to the red men who were being driven toward extinction by wave after wave of white settlers and whose own islands where they might find sanctuary were being continually, rapidly reduced in size and number so that the feathered man in flight might soon be lucky if he could find one island to stand on with only one leg, the other leg lifted as he must go on and on searching for a place, an earthly paradise to which the dead beaver would return as from sleep to life.

Now in this remote wilderness regaining his health which he had nearly lost while visiting other marshlands, Brother Wilhelm Weitling, wearing a beaver hat tinted with red by the delusive sun which should so soon be pale as the moon as the ice formed, must have seemed like some old beaver king of the beaver workers' crew come back to life and with intensity of purpose. What if there were those critics of his who would not give a beaver's damn for any beaver's dam built by this uncrowned beaver king who had no desire for martyrdom but was doing a beaver's work with his hands and his feet and was not ready to lie down in the mud and let the waters roll over him and the ice form?

As to the beaver skin which was the eternal remnant and could never be replaced when it was gone—that which the red men had cherished as part of their harmony and economy, provider of their food and conserver of their land—never needlessly killing one and never without ritualistic apology to him—it had been transformed by shortsighted, unthinking beaver agents into coins of silver and coins of gold for the sake of mercantile interests when the bales of the dried-out, washed, clean hides of these cooperative union brothers with their red rodents' hair had been sent by clipper ships from the New World to the Old to be stitched into such headpieces as the continental cocked hat, the navy cocked hat, the army cocked hat, the clerical, the Wellington, the Napoleonic, the Paris *beau*—styles familiar to a semiorphaned child whose mysterious father had perished or disappeared in the great Russian snow where the winter wolves howled like the winter winds in Iowa when it was blotted out by snow gales and where the light beams of the aurora borealis sweeping down from the North Pole made a crackling, musical sound.

Among the beaver brothers most sought for was the white beaver, which could be made into a sacred robe for a priest or a wedding gown for the bride of an Indian brave for whom the future would be spectral, indeed, as these red orphans of the white government were driven farther and farther over the western plains with no refuge—just as there was to be none for them where the gold and silver touched the cloud.

There had always been the spirit-haunted sense in Indian life. Sometimes the entirety of creation seemed a white snow cloud out of which a voice spoke. All things had voices—birds and fishes and waters and stones and clouds and trees and leaves and horses and dogs.

According to a tale told by nomadic Indians, the red men who were always in flight like birds who had no safe sanctuary in the sky or on the ground—and perhaps this mythology of the red creation was tinged by the no longer recognizable theology of Catholic priests clicking their rosary beads and playing their harps and conducting their Masses to convert over to their faith the primordial worshipers of the Great Spirit who was not a body but a cloud—the original beaver builders had not only been as tall as men but were able to communicate with each other with perfect lucidity, giving instructions for building their dams out of stones, pebbles, trees, bushes, twigs, corn. But like the great god who had split mankind into various tongues when they were building the tower from heaven to earth which would be known as the Tower of Babel, an envious spirit coming out of the North had taken away the beaver language and had left them with only a cry sounding like the cry of a baby lost in the dark and had also reduced their size to their present size.

The celebration of the beaver dam by Wilhelm Weitling with his rodent's hair gleaming red in the delusive light of the winter sun had been the gathering of the members at a great banquet with roast pig and cheese and bread and apples and wine for everyone and music provided by a flutist blowing on his pipe—producing flute sounds like the cries of a migratory bird passing over a sea of clouds.

The harmony in which Brother Weitling had left his people had soon broken again into chaos.

It was now that, having failed to place his matrix and build his moral dam to hold back the selfish waters of individualism which would spill over because of many inherent flaws caused by compromises with self-centered minds other than his own which was surely centered on the otherness of his maps and charts for the otherness of universal brotherhood—that of the utopian society which he should have left in a galaxy of stars—Brother Weitling, with hope and despair burning in his bosom—the hope no doubt brighter than despair—had been able to cross over to Nauvoo.

He had been drawn to Nauvoo by two magnets. One was caused by his fascination with the legendary city on the high bluffs over the Mississippi to which the prophet Joseph Smith, at its zenith, had attracted a population of twenty thousand living souls who were in communal brotherhood and sisterhood not only with themselves but with those who were dead—those who had died in this temporary Zion or earthly paradise—those who had died in distant places—likely as not when they were either on the road coming here or were dreaming of coming here. If they did not hasten here while they could—if they delayed one day longer than necessary to come upon the immigrant boat or Mormon version of a new Noah's Ark—then they might be delayed in reaching this place while they were still alive—for it was apparently God's opaque intention to dry the Atlantic up so that it would be impossible to cross that sea of mud where would be revealed ancient ships which had gone down—Phoenician and Egyptian and Grecian and all kinds of boats which had sunken in the long ago to the ocean's floor because not under the protection of the hand of the Lord.

Even after the murder of Joseph Smith, when he had known that Illinois was not his Zion, Brother Brigham Young had tried briefly to carry out the specific will of the Lord by finishing the temple that the martyred hero had envisioned as that which would be the most beautiful theological building in the world. But the location of the communal worship of ancient gods who were not the gods recognized by the surrounding land-hungry Gentiles—the limestone blocks with the large sun stones raised into place upon the shoulders of workers, the trumpet stones and capstones, the pavements of mosaics and the roof overlooking the Mississippi for miles and miles so that any boatman might see the figure of the golden angel Moroni topping its spire—the massive pillars and carved doorways to a vast interior where were carved a stone basin and oxen for a permanent baptismal font for babes—many beauties in stone and their reflections in clouds had been smashed or destroyed by Gentile or godless farmers when the Mormon worshipers of Moses and Mohammed had been driven away. Farmers had carted away the wreckages of blasted stones, so that on back-alley cowsheds or sheep sheds or in walls made of blasted stones and rubble or in the foundations of old outhouses which had a lonely, lurching look as if the wind had blown them where they were—could be seen the eye of a fragmented god, perhaps an ear, perhaps a curl, perhaps a bird's bill. What was left as a sign of the Mormon passage when the temple was burned to the ground by vandals was little but the fallen capital representing the large, many-rayed face of the sun shedding its divine favor under the horns of plenty which were held out in the hands of that provider who was a god dwelling among men. It was said by George Miller—one of the Latter-Day Saints whose loyalty was not given to Brigham Young as new head after the murder of Joseph Smith—that in relation to the original founder whose church had been originally founded, according to some of its critics, on sand—nothing but continually shifting sand at the edge of the waters in upper New York State—that the new leader bore the same relationship to the old as that of a toad to an ox.

Perhaps, however, in the unknowable years lying ahead it would seem that Brigham Young was the solid, plodding ox by comparison with whom the clubfooted Joseph Smith would seem the toad with the toadstone gleaming like a jewel in his forehead as in the long ago it was an ever metamorphic cave where were hidden the sacred scrolls of the papyrus made from the flax which was the color of his hair and which had been gathered and beaten and spun in ancient Egyptian mills and had the power to transform itself into a golden bird or an ox or a lamb. For his had been the pluralistic art of infinite camouflage.

When forced to leave Nauvoo because of threats of new murders and mayhem such as had been dealt out to the prophet who had been killed as if he were Cain but who was Abel, the slain god of orchards and fields, it became apparent that Brigham Young was preparing to leave, for he and his Mormon followers had gathered the last crop of the pale winter wheat and had not sown another crop, and all that they had built up together had been lost by forced sale or had been abandoned when there was no buyer at any price for the beehive that could not be transported by wagon so that the beehive people would have to produce another hive in which to spin the honey of the sun—they knew not where—he who was preparing with the majority of his followers to cross the Mississippi in this darkest time of the year had heard from one of his disciples that it did seem a pity they should have to leave the beautiful and not quite completed edifice which was the temple to the moon and the sun, had answered that yes, it was beautiful. "But we have the satisfaction of taking the substance with us, leaving behind us only the shadow."

There were those who had genuinely but mistakenly believed that Brigham Young and the Mormons would someday return to the place of burned-out barns, ruined choirs.

Among the healing arts that Joseph Smith and Brigham Young had been privileged to enjoy were the curing of a dying man or woman by the laying on of hands or the laying on of a mantle which would take away the illness of a body without inhabiting the lining or the folds of the mantle which also had its shadow.

The shadow or astral mantle which had been that of Joseph Smith when he was still alive but could not make the journey by sky or water or land had winged its way to the bodies of dying disciples and had spread itself out over them so that those who had been pale and withering with the fires of life's spirit about to go out of them had been suddenly flushed with red and gold and had lived.

Nauvoo, Hebrew for pleasant land, once was an Indian village which a white captain named James White had put under his belt in exchange for two hundred sacks of green and red and gold corn and which had first been called Venus and then had been absorbed by Commerce and had been called Commerce City, its name when Joseph Smith in flight with his disciples from real and potential murder in Missouri had purchased the hills and the flatlands for the establishment of his community of saints who had been tillers of the soil and had worshiped the pagan gods of sun and moon—the crippled prophet with the flax-gold hair had been likened to Apollo—had been occupied by the remnant Icarian community in 1849, the year after the burning of the temple by incendiaries who had carted away the movable stones in wagons without respect to the eyes of fallen gods flashing among the ruins—the year after the hesitant beginning of the gold rush, which had quickly accelerated into floods of gold seekers in search of gold in metallic form. Brigham Young and his followers had turned in the long, long migrations in which many had died and had been buried along the way without their coats—for no doubt God Who was the great weaver had covered the dead with new coats in which they would be seen on the day of resurrections which was always at hand, and the old coats and other pieces of garments must be used to protect the living. Signs had been used to mark the places where the Mormon dead were buried—signs which themselves were stolen or knocked down or would be eroded with time.

The second magnet which had drawn the would-be utopia finder to Nauvoo was that it was where the sun god had fallen and the Mormons had been blamed for every natural disaster there, including God's pitching with lightning forks the hay into the haystacks and causing them to burn in the midst of the flood—their lights seen for miles like the lights of a fallen sun—was also the community of the remnant Icarians who in melancholy flight from their own ruin in Texas had moved into some of the ruined buildings in the deserted village which could not fail to be haunted by the fact that it was the lost utopia of beehive supernaturalists given over to a higher rationality than that of merely mortal men and seemingly unlike the followers of Étienne Cabet, the French author of *Voyage to Icaria,* whose wings had already been burned in the Texas experiment—so that they could not get off the ground here where they were fallen and were to find in the conduct of their economy no harmony but discord and dissension caused by rivalries of clamorous egos.

Brother Weitling had considered for a time putting his Iowa forces into an intricately interlocking combination with the followers of Cabet's fictional *Voyage to Icaria* of which this cooperative brotherhood which maintained the family system and was plowed by the males—and not by the mares and not by their three-year-olds running ahead of them, plucking up clods as in some of the German colonies as well as the farms owned by individual taskmasters in the capitalistic world—never did get around to the establishment of a relationship of his utopia with that utopia, both dying like seeds in the pod. The ghost town was three years old when Brother Weitling came.

France had not permitted Cabet with his enormous Icarian following to try out his possibly screwball ideas there. As Robert Owen had purchased sight unseen the Rappite acres at the old Harmony which was to become the short-lived New Harmony on the Wabash, so it was on his recommendation that Cabet had purchased sight unseen in 1847 the acres along the Red River in Texas where the father of world socialism had once dreamed of founding a cooperative community by which to show mankind a better way to a better world where all men should love their neighbors as they loved themselves and there should be no fences dividing the property of one man from another man.

An unfortunate choice as the agent of Cabet's dreams, the Texas Badlands was where Cabet had placed his money, where the sellers had laid out the Icarian acres in a pattern of checkerboard lots—one square communal and one square capitalistic and neither conveniently marked by red and black—so that it was impossible for an Icarian to drive the cattle home to their shelters at night without stepping from communism into capitalism—the brush where the brigands waited with their brands—and there were also poisonous fevers killing many men.

The surviving Icarians, those who had neither died nor elected to return to France—had come up the Mississippi from New Orleans on the steamboat *American Eagle* and within a month after that March voyage against rough winds and high tides had organized their version of the fictional Icaria where those who had agreed to stay on had agreed to make a second attempt in the conduct of the phalanstery under a written constitution which should have prepared them for the leaves and flowers and fruits upon the branches of apple and cherry and peach and pear trees in April and May and not the trees dripping with bloody leaves and flowers and fruits and burdened by the bodies of the dead as if in reminder of the Mormon flight from new flights of murder should they remain in this blasted Zion where neighbors resented their strange allegiances to the fallen gods of sun and moon.

Mrs. Joseph Smith—the prophet's wife with her babe who had escaped slaughter by Herod among the trampled reeds—had refused to accept Brigham Young as her dead husband's substitute and had objected to polygamy as a practice which could not be divine and had held on to the sacred scrolls and the false mummies of ancient Egyptian saints who— brown as tobacco leaf spotted with gold—had been housed in Joseph's church—and had accused this would-be protector of stealing away her beloved former spouse's wool cape—that which had used to have a flying propensity of its own.

[3 0]

Leading his long wagon treks from winter quarters through unbelievable hazards with many losses of lives and many plantings of dead bodies along the way from the known to the unknown, to the Great Salt Basin where nothing grew—and there had been not only deaths of human saints but sometimes of horses and cattle bitten by serpents for whose venom the anodyne provided by Brigham Young had not always worked—Moses and Jacob had nearly perished because of overwork—the leader had shown his desire to be at all times the untrammeled, untrampled leader who, when once a decision had been given to him in the name of God, was unable and unwilling to put up with the bickerings of the twelve loyal apostles accompanying him to the distant prospect. It was his insistence that he desired to keep his twelve apostles in his pockets where he kept his little pet ones, his wives and children—as he also kept orphans, including children whose fathers and mothers had been slain and who had been left to starve and thirst in a desert where no bread was and no water was. According to Karl Marx—who understood with his partner Frederick Engels the power which supernatural agencies, exploded and exploding myths held over communitarian irrational imagination when it still refused to yield to scientific rational materialism—the Mormon bible was a document that made no common sense at all.

At a time when the ex–prison bird Weitling was attempting to be the main voice of German communitarianism in America but still could establish and maintain no real following, and when, upon the other hand, Étienne Cabet was the chief head of France's communitarianism, it did seem that both were doomed to fail in either an immediate or prolonged attempt to pave the way by force of their shining but individualistic example to the way for the enactment of the new social gospel according to their lights, certainly not only as viewed by Marx and Engels, neither of whom would wish to wind up in a crazy patchwork utopian tent show stalled in a sea of mud and sand somewhere off history's road, which was the road to be taken by Marx and Engels when the times were right.

Little or nothing could be done in Icaria by declaration overnight. When after the Texas debacle half of the survivors of yellow fever and other ills had returned to France, they had impatiently wished to retrieve the investments that they had lost by falling for the schematic promises of a vast promised land, and they had brought suit against Cabet for fraud. The Little Icaria of the French rationalists—already shattered into fragments by debacle in Texas—had settled in Illinois among the broken ruins of the once beautiful city strewn around in fragments after the murder of President Joseph Smith with his bird tongues and angel tongues and after the flight of President Brigham Young with his bird tongues and angel tongues and had had no way of being unified in harmony and economy in the beginning, which in a psychological as well as a physical sense was never the pure beginning.

Weitling had hoped in spite of melancholy forebodings to join with Étienne Cabet in the already blasted, ruined Icarian community at the Mormon-haunted Nauvoo—but was never able to hitch up with him before he and about two hundred followers were forced to take flight to St. Louis, the great river port, where he who had placed faith in the goodness of man's heart was to die of a broken heart without realization of his dreams of the perfect millennial egg out of which his version of the secular socialism should be born.

President Weitling had found what was to be only a delusional peace reigning among the Icarian socialist perfectionists in the blood-drenched Nauvoo, where—after all the sufferings that had been endured by the Mormons—the orchard boughs and the meadows should have cried out with spectral voices in memory of murder, murder most foul and of neither wild birds nor domestic fowl but of men and women and children who had worshiped the gods of sun and moon. There was only a delusional harmony and economy among the Icarian followers who during the time in which President Cabet was involved in the trial against him for fraud which he was ultimately to win were living under a French constitution, which provided for him as the elected head for one year and four ministers and many committees and many voices and many meetings to supervise the administration of the fictional *Voyage et aventures de Lord William Carisdall en Icarie, traduit de l'anglais de Francis Adams.*

Before coming to America when he was sixty years old, the founder of the Icarians—the utopia-minded lawyer who had practiced at the bar until 1820 when he had become a leader in the carabinieri and attorney general of Corsica but had been dismissed from that high office for attacking the government in his *History of the Revolution* in 1830—and later when elected to the French legislature had been prosecuted for his criticism of the state and had been driven into exile in England in 1834—had come under the magnetic influence of Robert Owen of the busted New Harmony, who had inspired in him his desire to search for the golden fleece that would be a moneyless society.

According to the fictional *Voyage to Icaria,* which had supposedly taken place in 1836 and which had attempted to make utopia palatable by draping over its political and moral and economic abstractions the thin fleece of a tale of romantic love or perhaps just some old embroidered bridal shroud or an old lace curtain or an old lace tablecloth such as was used by farmers to protect gooseberry bushes from the winter frost in the dying or dead time of the year, so Francis Adams and the youthful Lord William Carisdall had found that rarest of all things in the age of quest for a better world—a millennial communitarian society that like a flying island had not only arrived but had lived through many threats, many storms, and had not departed this life.

The Icar who had founded the utopian family communalism was revered by his Icarian followers as if he were the spirit of a god and not merely a great socialist engineer who had laid out his family communitarian and communal society according to the correct principles, maps, charts, knowledge of living or dead statistics which he had devised and which he would have successfully carried out if instead of coming to a fruitful land he had set his city down upon a wide sea of grass where nothing grew but grass or upon a sea of sand strewn with the skulls of dead animals.

Dinaros had explained to the inquiring travelers that the Icarian communitarians were living in a system founded upon the assumption that man was distinguished from all other living beings by his reason, his perfectibility, and his sociability, without which—as past experience had already shown—happiness could not exist.

The Icarian family communitarians were members of a larger single family governed by laws intended to establish absolute equality in all cases where equality was not materially impossible. All partners in this cooperative communal community shared all personal goods, all products of land and industry in a single social capital which belonged indivisibly to the people in that kind of communal communitarianism which had always been dismissed as an impossibility but was here shown to be a possibility, a thing that had been put into practice. The Icarian associationists all had trades and worked the same number of hours and used their intelligence—should one call it gray matter or golden matter?—to make their labor as brief as possible and varied and agreeable and safe.

As the republic of the community was the sole owner of everything and determined what workshops and stores and dwelling places should be built—and as the land which was chosen for plowing by the plowmen was also chosen by the government which represented all—every family and every citizen was provided with food, clothing, lodging, and pleasure.

The Icarian republic being also the sole owner of all horses and carriages and hotels, it had exacted no monetary charge from travelers from the outside world for food within these borders and transport from place to place and beds—beds which could not have been in the mud or under the mud, one may guess, as some were in the world ruled by iron kings, coal kings, steel kings who had no care for the progeny of the poor. Buying and selling were completely useless—in fictitious fact—to the Icarians.

Everything which transpired in Icaria transpired in public and was discussed by all inhabitants, who lived according to those facts of life which they did not permit to be shrouded by mystery or mystification or ambivalence of any kind and which were always verified or verifiable by statistics, statistics, statistics distributed free.

Children were protected not only from their birth but during their mothers' pregnancy, for which young couples had been prepared by reading of books on anatomy and other subjects of concern for the welfare of the little ones while they were in the womb and—in all probability—were reading little books as they dreamed of being born alive and not dead, torn into bloody hunks and strewn over orchards and fields and isles of reeds. Members of the family and several midwives were eyewitnesses to every birth which took place in this communal Icaria. The mothers always gave milk from their breasts to their own children if possible.

The Icarian children were the most perfect in the world—and thus it could be easily seen that they were very different from the dwarfed children who worked in capitalistic mills and mines and died without ever seeing the light of the sun.

At an early age the children of the Icarians—in that French tradition—were taught to read and write and read aloud and declaim. Their handwriting which they spelled out with their little quill pens was legible and clear and neat, although their language was not the general language recognized by others in the outside world. Their language was so regular and easy and devoid of the burden of unnecessarily intricate grammatical structure that after about a year of learning at their mothers' breasts and from a little book called *The Children's Friend* they were able to make replies to those who questioned them and to ask questions of those who replied and to send their letters to absent members of the Icarian family. Every game they played was an act of learning, and every act of learning was a game.

Words in the imaginary Icaria were spelled as they sounded and thus contained no useless letters by which to bar the children's way as did the Old Man River Mississippi by which the real Icarians had come to the ghost-haunted Nauvoo where had been the worshipers of the gods of the moon and sun above the many waters of the flood which as they staggered along and went whichever way they would bore a name crossed by double s's like sandbars and suddenly apparitional isles of reeds as mud buried some settlements along its low-lying shores and unburied others.

President Weitling—who was fresh from helping to build the beaver dam at Communia and had felt a sense of inner triumph accompanied by dark forebodings of despair—had found that the families had been assigned space furnished by sticks of that which surely must have been non-Stygian furniture, and he had also found that to each family head had been allowed a garden for the growing of apple and peach and plum and pear trees and berry bushes and melons and corn and beans and peas or whatever they desired for their own use or desired to sell for coins to non-communitarians so that they might have money for their sugar and their coffee and tobacco for their pipes. The whiskey that was provided free from the distillery was good and probably—even if not mixed with bee balm or nepenthean remedies—was much needed in the freezing winter of ice gales and snowstorms making all things appear twice their size.

Behind the ruins of the temple to the gods of sun and moon and stars the Icarians had erected a long two-story house with a kitchen in an ell where the community cooking was done—and there was also a long hall where most of the members preferred to take their meals and gather on Sundays for musical concerts, harps and horns and violins and theatricals and puppet shows and discussions of socialism—what it was or would be when it came as their absent Icar had promised—while upstairs there were private quarters for families, their number altogether twenty, ten on each side of a long gallery—and evidently not one door of illusion opening onto the great abyss which had been Joseph Smith's concern—not one for the mysteriously cloaked traveler which should be the angel Moroni in disguise.

While the children of the Icarians were taken from their parents at the age of two to be educated at the left-over Mormon or Owenite or Fourierite equivalent of the little red schoolhouse where the little red book could not have been Étienne Cabet's equivalent of McGuffey's nor a prophetic rendering of the materialistic determinism of Marx and Engels as it filtered through a sieve, the children who had passed beyond the suckling state and were growing up with some detachment from their immediate families in rehearsal for their becoming members of one great happy family which should be that of the human race were never very happy in their isolated state except for the Sunday afternoons when they visited their parents in their homes. But the mothers and fathers were apparently happy with this arrangement.

What the lonely bachelor Brother Weitling had observed was that the women of Nauvoo were not expected to join with the plowmen as plow-women in the fields as in the German colonies of Ebenezer and Zoar—and thus, when there were never enough hands with which to assure that there would be bread for all in the harvesttime which came for grain as it would someday come for most men, the numbers of hands were reduced.

A German pietist commune had been established under the leadership of Joseph Bimeler, who in escaping from the rationalism of the established Lutheran church of Württemberg in August 1817 had taken flight with his followers to America, where they would establish their own millennial city upon a land spread of fifty-five hundred acres along the Tuscarawas River in Ohio where there might be no other settlement for miles—or it might be blotted out by snow and ice.

They had agreed to pay out the purchase price by long-distance payments over a period stretching out to fifteen years, when the last gold or silver would be paid out unless hoary Gabriel or a Gabriel sweet smelling as flowers should already have blown his horn—great or small—and what if he should foreclose the last mortgage upon this property of earth just when the last payment should be made?

They had called the place Zoar—meaning a place of refuge—after the Zoar in which according to the biblical account Lot and his wife and daughters had taken refuge. The ox that was used for work in the fields was something like that beast of burden who was equipped with two horns, one of which was the male and the other of which was the female and both of which were in harmony doing God's work and not the devil's work.

Celibacy had been considered to be upon a higher pinnacle of being than married love. It had been only after the original Zoar had gotten onto its feet in an economic sense that there had been restored, after the prevalence of cold-limbed celibacy up until about 1830 or shortly afterward, the lost paradise of conjugal bliss permitting the joinings of the previously unjoined inhabitants for the begetting of children—only when there were enough cradles filled with corn to fill not only big mouths but little mouths and enough left over to sell to strangers passing through, and there was enough flour produced in the flour mills for the baking of bread for the inhabitants of Zoar, this place of refuge, enough bags of flour to sell to mysterious travelers, gentlemen or bums who when they passed beyond Zoar might bake their own bread somewhere along the side of the road from here to there.

It would be long remembered of the age when water travel had seemed the golden promise, although the barges which walked on water were already being threatened by the barges which walked on land, that it was the Zoarites, the people dwelling apart, who under the direction of President Bimeler had contracted to build that part of the Ohio-Erie Canal that crossed over their flowering land spread in the Tuscarawas valley and as a matter of fact not far from the future as-yet unfounded Massillon, with its nearby limestone quarry, from which in the midst of a surrounding country made historical by numerous Moravian missionary settlements would someday see the rising up of the somewhat revolutionary crank general Jacob S. Coxey, a prosperous gentleman who with the unrespectable Carl Browne and his Army of Christ would lead the raggedy unemployed to Washington to demand employment by the laying down of free roads and to demand bimetallism and other balms and whose place of habitation where he quarried and raised beautiful mares and stallions to seed them from seeds of their posterity had been named by Mrs. James Duncan, the wife of one of its founders, after the French bishop whose distinction was that he had opened the funeral oration for Louis XIV with the infamously famous sentence, *"Dieu seul est grand,"* or, as the English would later say, "God alone is great."

In Zoar the dream of the New Jerusalem was symbolized by the beautiful community garden which, to become a cynosure for eyes of commercial or utopian travelers, imitated or tried to actualize New Jerusalem as described in the twenty-first chapter of the Book of Revelation. Occupying an entire square in Zoar, the garden had been laid out by Zoar's spiritual and material head in consultation with other trustees and God's plan, which was a geometric plan, a square in which there was a center surrounded by three concentric circles and from the third, twelve pathways radiating outward, whether as long rays of sunlight or long rays of shadow to show the paths which might lead not merely to a curbstone to all those who by following this order avoided the roaring chaos of the old mistaken world.

In the center was a huge Norway spruce with, circling its roots, a low hedge which, made of arborvitae, meaning the tree of life, was for the Zoarites the tree of heaven. Twelve evergreen juniper trees with cones gleaming like blueberries or eyes circled in a third concentric circle which stood for the twelve apostles of Christ.

[3 1]

W HAT PRESIDENT WILHELM WEITLING had found among the
French Icarians in their second promised land was a new earthly
paradise where they were squatting in the midst of the once golden but
now tenebrous and bloodstained Nauvoo, which fascinated him more than
the community of the French-speaking rationalists.

Arrangements in Icaria were necessarily so haphazard, so makeshift,
that the main community farm was located five miles away by foot or sled
or boat—depending upon what the terrestrial weather was—just as this
and other farmlands were not owned by the Icarian communitarians, who
had hoped to spread beyond their present boundaries, but were leased and
as the old farmhouses strewn here and there were rented, although still
remaining common property.

There were hostile neighbors watching everything the French did, and
where there was no visible violation of the prevailing mores by the revolutionary French Icarians, they were saved from being torn to pieces and
strewn over the fields as the Mormon martyrs had been, their numbers
including children—because of the desire of the governing powers to
prove that the state of Illinois was a pleasant host or father to those of
strange faiths who were not themselves presumed to be murderers.

Only half the shelters needed to protect the Icarians from the coming
winter's blast had been completed and only half the shelters needed for
horses and sheep, as the Icarians had included among their number not
enough skilled carpenters and bricklayers but surely enough and more
musicians than necessary to play at their harvest feast or their Sunday
meetings, thus unlike the clown Weitling's Communia, which had only
one lone fiddler or one lone flute player, although throughout the uneasy
and crumbling years before his giving up his idea of supporting cooperative
workers' communes which would be the earthly paradise in Iowa there
was a Polish barber in an Eastern Seaboard city who had continued to pay
his dues because for him this was the Promised Land to which he had
promised to come when he was old and tired of playing scissor and comb
music through the hairs and mustaches and beards of men and would
become the settlement's lone fiddler playing the fiddle in the harvesttime
and in the snowstorms and in the springtime of the year.

Coming down the many-barred and many-wandering old Father of

Waters Mississippi by packet from Nauvoo with his tin trunk containing whatever spare clothes he had and his red neckties and more important his packets of evangelical socialist utopian messages promising a better world to the workingmen of the world should they be joined in that cooperative brotherhood who up until now had had and were still having a thorny way but who would be drawn by him as the many into the one although now scattered at many distant star points, Weitling with his packets of needles and pins and threads which were also for sale should he be in want had sailed into the port at St. Louis, Missouri, at a time when it was filled with packets of the busy river trade linking the South with the North and the East and the world was not the desolation it would become after the Civil War as the bleeding land continued to bleed. Now there were whistles of hundreds of steamboats tied up along the wharves as there were whistles from the chimneys of land-locked flour mills, iron foundries, and distilleries—and there was no sign of the great fire which had swept the waterfront in 1849, the year of the accelerated gold rush, when this had become the gateway for the equipment of canvas-shrouded schooners heading in long trains over seas of grass toward the western fields of gold.

President Wilhelm Weitling, although now exuding from his porous, many-celled body which had plowed through many waters some perhaps dim, wavering rays of hope, had been unable, in spite of arduous efforts as a crusader by pen and mouth in the former French fur-trading center of St. Louis where was gathering a population swollen into a turgid, roaring flood by the continual influx of thousands and thousands of migrant workers who had been attracted there by the immediate opportunity of employment, to gather up more than sixty subscribers for his cooperative brotherhoods, which—as shown by the incipient example in Iowa—would not suddenly and as if by miracle rise up overnight and if given time eventually spread as an all-golden utopia throughout the world from which death itself might be ultimately exiled when all the poor, naked, burning, freezing children of the poor were given shelter and habiliments and beds and bread and no one should be burned in a furnace under the earth or thrown out to starve in the snow until the millennial spring of cooperative communal socialism should come.

Coming up the Ohio River in a steamboat which upon this watercourse used to be likened to a river horse as it pranced up and down with its eyeballs turning red and its nostrils emitting steam and its long tail of foam, the socialist utopian peddler would not have been himself with his obsessions upon him if he had not spoken with other travelers of the impending moneyless world which was to come when all things, even men's coats and hats and shoes, should be the property of all and there should be no theft because there would be neither silver nor gold to attract the eye of a thief.

In Cincinnati, where he had debarked, he had found that his coat and the trunk with which he had embarked were missing—either had not set sail with him or had been thrown overboard to flatboat riders following the horse's feathery foam tail.

Cincinnati, like the St. Louis which was named after the martyred Louis XI, the medieval French king, even as the Louisville on the Kentucky side which had been named Louisville in thanks for the first and second aid given to the American Revolution by the French nation and by the indolent sportsman and horse racer King Louis XVI, who was to lose his beautiful and many-curled head under the executioner's bloody blade as was the beautiful many-curled Marie Antoinette—"If the poor people have no bread, let them eat cake"—was already a city of old-time native Ohioans and New Englanders and Virginians and Kentuckians, to which had been added thousands and thousands of German workers, who had started their flight over the Rhine and what used to be called the boundless main in the 1830s, and many poor potato-faced Irish in flight from potato famines in Ireland, the latter having engaged Weitling's sympathies before he ever came to America. Fortunately having some utopian declarations stuffed under the brim of his red mouse–colored beaver hat and in the pockets of his vest and in the many pockets of his big wilderness breeches and the tops of his red leather boots as well as some money of the folding kind which made no jingling sound by which to attract thieves in the muddy bottoms of the harbor city where the poor lived as the rich lived on top, he was able to spruce himself up and provide his body with a new coat of fleece lest he should appear before the German migrant workers as the naked king of tailors.

He was able to sell subscription and membership blanks and life- and death-insurance blanks and other blanks and obtain promises of property and cash for the maintenance of his work. And yet he had attracted to his all-consuming cause only a small minority of workers from that large body of workers who for one reason or another including lethargy could not accept his solution for the cure of the ills of mankind; they were split at the seams into various factions because they were unable or unwilling to accept the somewhat wavering vision in his eyes, and where he saw the light, they saw the darkness.

No doubt if he had howled around in the Ohio woods all night shaking the blackbirds from the trees with his millennial messages he might have attracted more converts by the pretense of madness than by that of sanity, both of which were given definition by no absolute standard but the prevailing mood. The freethinkers' society, which included agnostics and atheists for whom it seemed that the god of the past was a dead concept incapable of any further flowering and that the law of progress toward that happiness which was the instinct of the universe and toward which modern man with his knowledge of machinery, big wheels and little wheels, should bring man as Robert Owen had promised to the depressed, starving, mud-bound workers of the world when they should rise up to take over the operations of the steam engines of the world and all the wheels and all the cogs—for freedom without social and economic power would crush them all under the iron heels of iron emperors—had refused to go along with some of the cooperative tailors and other workers and a mutual insurance society.

It could be said of the wilderness scout Wilhelm Weitling that he had not oared his way up the Ohio as a lone oarsman in a birch-bark canoe to tell of the wonders he had seen in his quest for the earthly paradise which should not be corrupted by the inroads made by the encircling capitalism, nor had he gone to stay a night with those poor workers and their families who lived in clay holes and in the mud.

According to the anti-Weitling attacks shot out now from the buzzing, booming Ohio harbor city, where—as in other harbor cities at this time of busy riverboat traffic—there were bodies of murdered men found in the muddy bottoms when the waves of night had withdrawn and the first faint rays of the sun had appeared, he was taking his journeys to this Ohio state of the old western midlands and to other western states and southern states for the sake of his own pleasure and possibly his health and at the expense of the workingmen to whom he was promising, of course, if only they would pave the way which had once seemed certain but was now increasingly wild and uncertain and wavering, an earthly paradise which they would not live to see or would see only when they were dead.

In the triangle where the Monongahela and Allegheny rivers flowing together in confluence form the Ohio River, up which Brother Weitling had come making his ports of call before the river should be covered with ice as hard as iron, was the city of Pittsburgh, that great future Leviathan of iron and steel and coal and limestone and potter's clay and baking, filled with many burning pits—smokestacks of chaotic factories and mills belching with chemical clouds which mixed in with the river fogs turning from red to yellow to gray to black like the phantom workers who seemed to disappear into the clouds as one watched. The utopian shepherd, intent upon looking for more lost sheep to add to his fold, had been able to gather up a few converts in relation to the large number of German migrants there, not only hand- and foot workers but workers with their heads who were employed by the rich exploiters of the poor.

The chemical clouds hanging over the harbor city and streaking the atmosphere almost from the top to the bottom had not been woven of delicate lace like veils—they had been long, drifting shrouds.

In the incipient empire of iron and steel backed by hills striated by smoke and clouds could be found the graves of early French explorers and fur traders as well as the graves of the red men of Pontiac's Confederation, who had been defeated by the mad Anthony Wayne, and the grave of the long chief Red Pole, who now might sometimes be seen against the black clouds like a long red pole crowned with burning feathers of red fire drifting over the former Fort Pitt, which was pit-marked with big and little craters of fire.

While in Pittsburgh on this trip, Weitling had added to the number of strange characters he seemed to be fated to touch upon wherever he went with his *Guarantees of Harmony and Freedom*—a possibly, impossibly, probably, improbably mad street preacher with eyes burning like coals who was assured by the Word of God in his or by his own intuition that all the religions of the world were about to come to an end with all their pontiffs and all their powers and what should take their place would be a universal Jesusville made of socialists only.

[3 2]

VERY ATTRACTIVE to Weitling's eye as he who was surely as strange a traveler as any he met while going about with his measuring tape by which to take the measurements of paradisal seekers, who might better be measured by a gradient than by a tailor's tape or a carpenter's ruler, the old communal settlement of the Rappites near Pittsburgh, now when its great days were over, provided for him a cynosure, a center of light not yet extinguished by the dawn of the new world of the machine, which ought to make all such places of refuge obsolete.

The Harmony Society at Economy, which stood on the banks of the Ohio River, was that to which after the sale of the Harmony on the banks of the Wabash married celibate communitarians had come, leaving behind them all their property which was deemed by them to be nontransportable, including the bodies of the dead in their nameless graves, which were marked by no tombstones for the sleepers to have to roll away when the angel Gabriel blew his horn, and the footprints which the big-footed angel had left outlined in limestone when he descended to earth and talked to the patriarchal Rapp—who in his tall peaked hat had seemed to have the ability to be everywhere at once—had been confident that God would provide again such patterns of being and signs and tools as they had left behind them—such houses and barns and mills and beehives as they could not have carried with them unless they had had the help of winged magicians. He had spoken with the elders who were running a community long geared by habit to the peaceful ways of shepherds and fleecers and weavers and fruit pickers and plowmen and who were always very much involved with the community's conduct of business affairs with the external world—those of which the workers in the internal world seemed to know little or nothing as to how many dollars of silver there were or how many dollars of gold.

Why had Father Rapp left the old Harmony on the Wabash, where he and his people had been doing so well? It was said that in accordance with the text of Martin Luther's original German Bible, of which he was the one mouthpiece, conduit, interpreter, he and his followers were not mere children of clay as some might believe in view of their self-effacing humility but were the living incarnation of the Sun Woman who in the Book of Revelation—as described by St. John the Divine—was a woman clothed with the sun and had the moon at her feet and wore upon her head a crown of twelve stars and was with child and cried as she in the midst of her travailing in birth was pained to be delivered of the child.

And there had appeared in the heavens a great red dragon with seven heads and ten horns and seven crowns upon his seven heads whose tail had drawn down a third part of the stars of heaven and who had cast them down to earth and who had stood before the woman before she was delivered so that he might devour the child as soon as it was born. She had brought forth a man-child who was to rule all nations with a rod of iron and who was caught up unto God and to His throne. And the woman had fled into the wilderness, where she had a place prepared by God, and they should be fed for a thousand two hundred and three-score days.

There was to be war in heaven until the great dragon with his evil angels was cast out from the heaven where they could be found no more in any place inasmuch as he had become the devil or Satan who had deceived the whole world and had persecuted the woman who had given birth to the man-child.

The Rappites were generally united by faith in this Sun Woman of whom they were the manifestation or embodiment or children—she was winged but bigger than an ox and with the bright rays streaming from her head had led them to the millennial continent which for some unholy reason was given over to the idea of transience—and had been with them when they had established their first Harmony in Pennsylvania and then their second Harmony upon the banks of the Wabash before voyaging to Economy—and then without bringing upon a flat boat the slab of limestone where the angel Gabriel had left his long-toed footprints—believed by some expert geologists to be those of a prehistoric Indian runner who had paused for a moment while running over the bluffs overlooking the Mississippi and had been purchased by Father Rapp from a poor Indian for two dollars on the wharf at St. Louis—without bringing from the old Harmony to the divine Economy the sign of the Golden Rose of Micah which had signified the coming of the golden age and without bringing the sundial which had measured time by the shadow—all such heavy freight— had established a community which was to prosper through its pecuniary interests in coal mines, sawmills, oil wells, control of manufacturies at Beaver Falls, laying of a subterranean pipeline to convey their rich deposits of oil in a golden flood for dispensation—surely not holy, sweet-smelling oil—to strings of western Pennsylvania industrial settlements, where if among mills and mines a wanderer worker named Jesus Christ should appear in a period of starvation causing the uprisings of labor strikers, the pharaohs of the ambulatory capitalism would drive Him out of town and tar Him and feather Him.

The Harmonists at Economy were to live and prosper until their gradual shriveling and extinction caused by the celibacy of these married men who had placed not their seed in the loins of their women, all waiting for regeneration when the golden messiah should come to bear them away to the earthy paradise, as had been promised in the long ago and very recently.

[3 3]

FREDERICK RAPP, Father Rapp's adopted son, had said to Frances Wright when she visited the Rappite Harmony in the toe of the Indiana boot not far from the Wabash flowing into the Ohio that if he could not eventually effect the emancipation of the Rappites from what amounted to a wageless white slavery, he would make his own escape from this community of married celibates—he was himself a very thoughtful, very philosophic bachelor—and join with the wealthy Scottish orphan in the utopian project which she had started in 1827 on the plantation Nashoba on the banks of the Fox River in Tennessee for the purpose of raising up and educating black slaves to the level of the whites and thus preparing them for what might be called the hardships of freedom.

Jeremy Bentham's ward, the friend of Shelley, the friend of Lafayette, Frances Wright—who was a link between Rappites and Owenites as she was a friend not only of Frederick Rapp but of Robert Owen's son Robert Dale Owen, as she was a visitor at both communities with their differing views of human happiness as expressed in social terms—had wished, with her two-chambered heart, to unite their characteristic features in her version of a Greek city-state.

Frances Wright would be recalled by Robert Dale Owen as looking herself like an Antinous or Minerva with her raggedy chestnut curls flying in the wind and her icicle-cold blue eyes which were not blue as violets and her sharp features stained almost black by the burning light of the sun, the sweep of wind and rain and snow as she rode on horseback through the wilderness trying to get other intellectuals to join with her at Nashoba, the refuge from which she would be forced to take flight in less than three years for the West Indies for the establishment of another commune for the freeing of the black slaves from the white, over whom she had ruled as if she were an empress before whom they wafted their purple plumes like fans with which to shoo away the sand flies from her ever-twitching face where the waves of the sea swept in and the waves of the sea swept out.

COMING BACK to the temporarily depleted divine Economy through the western Appalachian Mountains upon an April day of soughing wind and rain and lightning flashes, turning his horse's head through a dark forest, Father Rapp's adopted son Frederick had been killed by the falling of a rotted oak tree which had unloosed itself from its mooring just at the moment when he was passing with his broad-brimmed hat drawn down low over his brow and shadowing his sunken eyes and his broad-shouldered cape drawn tight around him, or else he had been murdered and the tree placed as a deception over his body as if to suggest that he had been pinioned down and could not move.

It was some weeks before he was found, and then his face was but a broken skull, and only part of his body was found. The hat was his and the gold watch and the riderless horse, which would have been left behind by no ordinary thief in this dark forest of life, but the foxes had eaten his limbs away.

Who had murdered the great pantheist? Was the nefarious deed committed by the hand of God or God's emissary here in this lonely way where apparently no eye witness had seen this murder but the eyewitness who was himself the murderer? And if so, he would not be so twisted and tormented by his conscience that he would tell who the murderer was—and thus would disprove the truth of the old saying that there is always someone watching or that there is no such thing as a perfect crime or that murder will out. Perhaps all had been an accident such as may happen in the nature of things. The hypothesis of murder had prevailed, however, once suspicion had gotten on the wind, and would be elaborated into a tale told in taverns in America and Germany.

PERHAPS THERE COULD BE few or no utopias which could be utopias unless they contained within them strange murders whether real or imaginary, the mysteries of which could not be solved by powers of reason alone, as they contained within them certain elements of the supernatural. It was to be recalled in the pages of the very ethical *Atlantic Monthly* at the beginning of the Gilded or Gelded Age and then only by hints and glints which left the reader to draw, in an uncertain and clouded and oblique way, the negative conclusion that Father Rapp had been guilty of having gelded his only real son, John, for the crime of having placed his seed in woman's body and that because of his remorse for his inexpert surgery—the son had died when he had lost, as one may say, his little man, his Little Tom Thumb—and perhaps it was buried with him in a nameless grave or had been thrown out among the hogs—the remorseful but self-righteous sire of the children of the Sun Woman had arranged for gradual transference of his community from the prospering first Harmony in Pennsylvania to the second Harmony on the banks of the Wabash.

Sheep, cows, horses, roosters, bags of beans, wheat, corn had been transported by long lines of flat boats, including that with the reed cradle in which was rocked by winds and waves the baby girl who had been the issue of the dead son's widow and who grew up to be the pride and joy of her hale, hearty grandfather, who took in a widower and his entire flock of semiorphaned children to bring up as Rappite believers and workers on his farms and whom he also loved as much as if he were his own his surrogate son Frederick Rapp, ambassador to the world.

Father Rapp had moved from the prospering second Harmony to the divine Economy for a variety of reasons—among them, a desire to move to a place providing wider horizons for his investments in capitalistic adventures, although he was already raking in ample return upon many far and near, among them the six percent interest which was paid to him for the mortgage which he held upon farmland upriver on the bluffs overlooking the Wabash at Terre Haute.

Individual farmers who had a hard time on their pea-patch farms, even like the poor squatters who had no shelter or lived in caves or in holes in the mud and sometimes had more little mouths to feed than they could feed, did resent the almost awesome fact that the Rappites who did escape responsibility for man's future life upon this planet—some of the wanderers no doubt did not know that it was a planet or that they were in the United States of America—were unlike themselves always so prosperous that they had wheat for their mills and wheat for their bread and were not known to starve. And yet squatters who lived outside the Pearly Gates and needed bread for the mouths of more children than they could feed were given bread.

Sometimes obscene messages were found tacked on fences and walls surrounding this peaceful community of married celibates who were waiting for the world to end on the banks of the Wabash—or waiting for the world to begin when the skies should open and the angels should appear and the graves give up their dead. And then the wheat would be divided from the tares. The Rappites, because of the sacrifices they had made on earth, would be the first to be transported to heaven.

As Father Rapp had had no direct confrontation with Robert Owen, so he had had none with Joseph Smith, although after the loss of a third of the stars of heaven which were drawn down by the serpent's tail in the divine Economy he had occasionally received letters from the Mormons at Nauvoo who had wished to establish solidarity with the Rappites, although they might seem worlds apart—for they were polygamists, it was rumored.

When Father Rapp had departed from the first Harmony in Pennsylvania for the second Harmony in Indiana, a new utopia had been laid over the first like a palimpsest through which one saw the gleamings of an older writing. The new owner, a German named Ziegler, had purchased the original Harmony at a bargain price, which meant a great loss to Father Rapp, who when he had fled into the farther western wilderness in his Noah's Ark was apparently of the opinion that the world was not so decrepit that it was about to fall into dust and ashes.

Ziegler had put "For Rent" signs upon the former Rappite houses and barns and farms and pasturelands and apple orchards, all but the nameless graves which were already occupied by the unrisen dead, and had opened a show of wildly dancing puppets.

[34]

IT WAS SAID OF JOSEPH SMITH that the tendency for dreaming had been born in his blood as an inheritance from his ancestral family tree whose members in earlier times had been English and Scottish Crusaders and Puritans for whom the Bible was never a complete book, for chapters had been lost or had strayed or had been stolen—and so it might be asked whether they would ever be found, perhaps rooted up from under the roots of a tree by an old hound dog on a celestial mission, baying at the moon when he found what he found?

Perhaps also Smith's dreaming propensity had been heightened when as a little boy with typhus which threatened the loss of a leg, he had refused to have that leg cut off—but without one drop of blood-red wine to lull his senses and without ropes to tie him down had sat in his father's arms while the doctor had drilled into the bone on each side of the afflicted bone and had lifted out three pieces with a pair of forceps.

The future prophet of the Mormon church had grown tall and athletic but had walked with a limping gait somewhat like that of a wounded horse, and was given to strange fits, starts, and frothings of the mouth, as were many founders of religions who, while under the spell of dreams which may be the only anodyne for an unbearably wounded reality, see the foundations of a new heaven and a new earth or that which—having been stamped out of man's memory long ago by the passage of time and the conventions of habitual thinking which keep man in one groove—will return. The prophet whose faith was in various aspects of pluralism and not monotheism once said to the followers of whom he had an ever-increasing flock, "I am a rough stone. The sound of the hammer and stone was never heard on me until the Lord took me in hand. I desire the learning and wisdom of heaven alone."

But as a matter of fact—and there was fact in a psychological landscape which was that of the inner soul turned into the outer soul—Joseph Smith had desired not only to spiral upward to heaven's gold but downward to earth's gold, he having been a gold seeker by profession, a seer who, wearing his magical peep stone under his wide-brimmed hat when it was pulled downward over his eyes, had so much magnetic power that with his willow wand pointing in his hand he could locate buried gold.

Once when digging for a bag of Spanish gold that his insight had told him should be found buried under a tree deep under its roots, he had said that it would be found only by leading a black sheep around it three times with the correct magical incantations and then slaying that obviously unwinged creature and smearing its blood upon the ground.

No treasure had been discovered, but the black sheep had disappeared, no doubt as one unfit for heaven's fold, and had appeared for the next several days in the form of a sheep's head, lamb chops, lamb stew with the lamb's eyes floating in it at the table of Smith's visionary gold-hunter father and visionary mother, who had many children with many mouths to feed at their scrawny little farm near Manchester to which they had moved because of the breadwinner's inability to make the last payment on a larger farm at Palmyra, where they could have raised enough corn to keep a ram and a ewe and many little ewelings, doubtless the playful kind—for there was always something very playful about these Smiths.

Hop-toad Joseph with his three bones missing and the spell of his dreams upon him might remind some that his paternal grandfather had been dubbed Twisted Neck Smith because of the way his head was set on a twisted neck, one shoulder higher than the other, so that with this kind of crooked pipe it was no wonder that the religion which he spouted should seem something beyond recognition as that of the Presbyterian church—itself a dissenters' faith in things which were not seen but should be seen, voices which were not heard but should be heard by those who believed in enchanted fairy realms and golden cities under the earth.

Joseph Smith had been as much fascinated by the legends of the gold buried by Captain Kidd as by the mines of Solomon. It was on a bright spring morning in the forest near his father's farm that the young man, kneeling in prayer that the light might fall on him, had been surrounded by such darkness that his tongue was bound so that he could not speak except in a deep pool of silence to God. He had felt that he was doomed when all of a sudden a pillar of light brighter than the sun had appeared over his head and had descended on him and rested on him, and it was then that he had seen those two angels who were God the Father and His beloved Son.

The angel Moroni some two years later had visited the young hunter of gold candlesticks and gold watches and gold watch chains when he was lying in his bed, perhaps under the spell of imbibing more of the blood-red wine than he should have imbibed. He was visited by a beautiful floating angel who stood in the air and was wearing a long white robe and had naked hands and naked feet and naked legs and a naked head and a naked neck and a naked bosom which could be seen as his robe floated apart and had also a countenance which looked like lightning.

The angel was a messenger from God, and his name was Moroni, and he had told the eighteen-year-old boy who was then coming into his somewhat mutilated manhood—where were his three missing bones hidden, and who should restore them to his limb?—that he knew where was deposited a hidden book which, written on golden plates, told of the former inhabitants of this continent and the place from which they sprang up. Also, that there were two stones in silver bows—and that these stones, fastened to a breastplate, constituted what was called the Urim and Thummim—and that their possession was what constituted seers in ancient or former times and that God had prepared them for the purpose of translating the book. He had also been visited with a vision showing where the golden plates and seers' stones in silver bows would be found. Once when asked what an angel who was a messenger from the Lord looked like, he had said that the true angel of light was the most handsome man there ever was.

With his magnetic sense drawing it to him as a smaller lodestone might be attracted toward a larger lodestone, Joseph Smith—although he had not found this secret treasure upon the former Rappite stamping ground which was now cut into farmlands operated by individuals, one of whom was Josiah Stoal—Joseph Smith, that obsessed seeker after the long-lost Indian bible which was capable of many transmutations into many forms and could be a sheep or a dog or a swan, had stolen away with the most precious jewel that there might be and who was certainly not a book but a bride.

She was Miss Emma Hale, daughter of the hidebound, well-heeled, tightly buttoned, upstanding, prosperous, skeptical gentleman farmer Isaac Hale, in whose house in Economy in a spare room—very spare—the ne'er-do-well gold hunter Joseph Smith had stayed while his gold-hunter farmer did the digging for such illusional treasures as a silver mine or a slice of the gold melon moon which had fallen to the crust of earth and was marked by tooth marks of little mice stars.

Isaac Hale was a firm believer in the dignity of labor by the sweat of one's brow, by dropping turnip seeds into holes in preparation for the future. He had refused to encourage or countenance the impecunious Joseph Smith's suit for his daughter's long-fingered lily-white hand, which was not stained by dust of coal mine or mill—and hers were also lace veils in plenitude and billowing satins and satin slippers long-toed as boats—she was worlds above this suitor in a personal and social and economic sense.

Joseph Smith had first become the robber bridegroom when he had fled with the love-smitten Emma Hale over the border to New York, where he had not abandoned her in a murky marshland nor drowned her in a lily-margined pool nor left her to find her own way back to her father as a villain might have done but had married her in the sight of God and the manifestation of law who appeared in the form of the man who tied the knot and where he had lustily, crowingly placed his little man in her virginal body, that which for a young man who in spite of his missing bones suffered from an overplus of vitality with its divine sparks and not the witherings of sterility in a desert land where no water was and must have seemed to him a cave hung with the most refulgent and yet taciturn, mysterious jewels where he had reigned supreme before he was born from immortality into morality and to which he like many utopian dreamers and some who might be simple dreamers wished to return as to immortality.

Brigham Young once described the Book of Mormon as that which told of a religion upon which it was difficult to put one's hand on either end, for it was the religion which moved from eternity into time and out of time into eternity without beginning or end. When he came to believe that all must be baptized in the new and yet very old Mormon faith or be lost, he was also convinced that to seek any other way to God was as foolish as to take lessons in painting in a dark forest at midnight.

Although Joseph Smith had roped himself to his forbidden love according to Christian ritual as demanded by law and she in her voluminous gown had soon swollen big as if she carried the melon moon inside of her, the little boy who came sailing out of his mother's body in approximately nine months had been born dead.

Although in order to take possession of the Indian bible which was hidden in the cave, the angel Moroni had told the pleasure-loving Joseph Smith with his battered old tramp's hat and his hair sticking out like corn-silk through the holes in his hat—someone who might have made a good scarecrow as he leaned upon a fencepost or as a fencepost leaned upon him—the terms of his discovery, that he must go through a probationary period of four years in order to be worthy of a treasure that was of unknown value in any material sense whatever at that time and that he must have a wife and a male son of whom he would be the father as the son would be in his image—the fact that the little son had been among the thousands of stillborn births occurring in America at that prodigal time had not been held against him. He had been told to avoid wine and beer and cigars in order to purify himself for the coming gift of the golden plates which were hidden away in the cave in the Hill of Cumorah where he had first seen the holy, true, long-concealed word of God which should be written in foreign tongues beyond the poor lad's comprehension at that time, and two stones in silver bows which were fastened to a breastplate and went by the name Urim and Thummim and constituted the most magical, most mysterious, most omniscient seers' stones, which would enable him to translate ancient hieroglyphics into the English language or, more strictly speaking, the American tongue, its mutilated mutation.

During the four probationary years in which Joseph Smith had waited for the golden plates that should be found in the cave of which the door was concealed by a large stone, he had been forbidden entrance by characters who might not seem representatives of God's Word—the guardsmen including a lowly toad and a dwarf and a thug, all subjected to the metamorphosis taking place in the memory of a young man who was given over to the dream of connecting the broken arches of ancient rainbows so that there would be bridges with pots of gold at either end. The last of these characters had been a living dead man, a mysterious Spaniard with a long beard like moss hanging from his chin to his waistline, his throat slashed from ear to ear and the blood running from his wounds and the sockets of his eyes, although he might have perished or disappeared some time ago.

There were those who believed that Joseph Smith's encounter with the mysterious Spaniard had been inspired by his fascination with the adventures of Captain Kidd, who had been employed to protect Colonial ships plying the coast or driven by gales into Spanish waters through which, had he been gifted with double vision, he might have seen the sunken temple of the lost Atlantis, but who—a law upholder in pursuit of pirates in their galleons waylaying ships carrying gold and other treasure for burial—had not turned his eyes downward to see what lost sun and moon gods might be under water.

No one knew precisely where Captain Kidd's treasure was buried—some people thinking that it might be at Gardner's Island, others that it might be found under the mud and sand of a southern coastal island, others that it might go by tidal water almost anywhere.

Captain Kidd had lost his pleas for his life just like a simple watch or snuff thief but was strung up on the hangman's tree at the Executioners' Wharf of the Port of London as a warning to all sailors going out to sea that they who heard the clankings of the captain's chains as the crows pecked out his eyes and heard the cryings of the sea winds should be honest men lest they themselves should be hanged like this former upholder of the law who showed what a poor puppet thing life was for those who became pirates of other men's gold. Captain Kidd, although protesting his innocence until the end, had also been condemned for murders of drugged men in the hold.

[3 5]

WHEN JOSEPH SMITH, looking through his peep stones Urim and Thummim, was translating the golden plates, which—according to one version probably intended as a joke on everyone except himself, the country jackass—had started out as about forty pounds of gleaming wet sand wrapped in his shirt, as if, so lovingly did he carry it home to his father's fireplace, it was or might have been a baby in his arms, but which must have grown heavier and heavier along the road—indeed, had grown to the nest of golden plates for which he had waited four long or short years before admission to the cave guarded by the mysterious Spaniard, an archetypal figure in search of El Dorado, a city of gold with turnip towers, spires, domes—the tonnage of the golden plates had seemed to increase miraculously at times by leaps and bounds—at one time was twelve hundred tons like a resurrected city or chip a man could scarcely be expected to carry in his gloveless work-scarred hands unless he was an angel or a messenger of God—although quite suddenly, of course, the ever-problematical golden plates might shrink to the size of a watch or a moth or an eyelid or the eye of a bird which had no eyelid and specialized in omniscience, in seeing all while not being seen.

Joseph Smith had refused to allow his wife so much as a peep at the golden plates. They were wrapped around and around with shrouds of water-stained linen and a lace shroud or bridal veil or tablecloth and laid out upon the gleaming surface of a massive table under a glass lamp of many prisms reflecting the colors of the known spectrum of the rainbow.

With his magic spectacles through which he could see even with his straw hat brim drawn down over his eyes—and could see also through the bundle of linen and lace wrappings tied around by strings—the seer could see to read between gold book covers spiraled together with gold wire such as was used in watchmakers' shops or eyeglass makers' shops the raised hieroglyphics appearing in unfamiliar tongues suddenly familiar to him as the pages turned of themselves with a whirring sound like bird wings as they emitted all kinds of little squeaks, trills, tickings, whirrings very much like bird songs.

The prophet—even like Brigham Young when he became a Mormon and the caul of prophecy was placed over his face—was an expert in strange tongues which sounded like bird tongues—those in which Shakers and the feathered red men of America also communicated, although some of the bird tongues were those of birds that had long since disappeared from other parts of the world and might be heard only on Lost Atlantean islands occasionally coming up from the waters of the great deluge upon so many pinnacles between the coasts of Ireland and Wales and the New World—many mythologies which were old and flourishing before Adam came into the world and God made out of his spare rib a wife to be his companion and she ate the apple. There were versions of visions in which she ate a rose from a rose tree and ate its thorn.

BRIGHAM YOUNG had not met or known Joseph Smith at the time of the discovery of the phenomenal, superphenomenal plates of gold in the cave—had been living some fifteen miles away as a painter and paint scraper who was dissatisfied with the Methodist faith and was more or less outside of any faith—yet would recall that on the night when the invisible plates of gold were brought out of the cave, a night when there had been no moon, he had seen the most brilliant light sweeping the heavens for several hours before it formed into men who seemed to be marching in great armies out of the northwest to the southwest. The armies had taken about two hours to pass beyond the farthest horizon.

He must have been smitten by the spirit of prophecy even at this early time and by the time of his conversion had been able to talk with bird voices to feathered angel bird men and saints long dead who came to his call.

When at last Brigham Young read the Book of Mormon, which was Joseph Smith's translation and which some people thought was real and some people thought was a fraud, he could see nothing but truth in it and was assured that this truth was the pure gold of the spirit of God and not the gold of a fool. The only truth there was in heaven was the Mormon truth, and the only truth there was on earth was the Mormon truth, and the only truth there was in hell was the Mormon truth—if, indeed, any truth of any kind could be found in hell.

The curiosity seekers who had wished to see the golden plates when they had been delivered to the golden chanticleer who was Joseph Smith in a land prepared to believe that America was the millennial continent where dead cities which had been hidden under roots of trees and where rivers should be paved with interlinking sheets of long-winged, long-headed, long-necked, long-limbed seraphim so far as eyes could see, had not been permitted to see—while the many-fluttering pages with their seemingly random and yet logical sentences and half sentences and almost disembodied phrases were in the process of discovery. For God had forbidden that these golden plates which were the source of vision and should transform the face of the world should be seen directly, even as God Himself should not be seen except in the form of the bush burning up in the midst of the flood.

Farmer Hale—reluctant host to the enthusiastic bridegroom and the bereaved bride who had lost the child of her womb but had placed her faith in what well might have been called Joseph Smith's desert sand—had wanted nothing in his house that could not be seen, even if it could be heard—and perhaps after all it must have sounded like nothing so much as metallic curtain hoops being drawn along a metallic curtain rod.

Joseph Smith's life, that of a perpetual bridegroom surrounded by mysteries out of which he would try to make some kind of order and which he would always love as much or more than life itself, was certainly and could continue to be increasingly a mare's nest. Had he not been drifting consciously or unconsciously toward the restoration of a religion that had been long lost to earth, and if he had been content to let the talk about the golden casket that contained the book die out as a nine days' wonder soon displaced by other headline news, he might have subsided eventually into obscurity.

The accident, if such it was, had become his fate in an America where, overshadowing the lives of many poor earthbound farmers dropping turnip seeds into holes on little hardscrabble farms, was and would be for many decades the dream of Mohammed's winged casket flying over the earth and casting its many lights upon the faces of the plowmen.

The true developers were not those who placed their faith in Aladdin's lamp but those great tycoons of coal and oil and steel who, already coming up, were like ancient pharaohs who needed no such dwarf as this poor gypsy to interpret their dreams according to the golden plates—they were well on the way to building their great pyramids of power which no poor gypsy could possibly overturn. For with all the sand in the world, Joseph Smith had nothing to see but an idea in his mind.

Once when asked how the golden plates and the breastplate and the

Urim and Thummim had been transported unseen from the cave in the man-made Hill of Cumorah to the door of his father-in-law's farmhouse, the crippled youth had answered that they had been delivered by a postman who had hidden them in a bag of wheat. The deliverer had been the angel Moroni in disguise.

Emma's father insisted that he had known nothing of this coming of the golden plates—the bag had contained no grain but a change of clothes, shirt and pants and underwear, the latter in short supply or not owned by him. For surely the bridegroom who was now claiming to be the successful gold seeker who had raised himself up a few notches socially from the mud and the sand had not wished to continue to look like a scarecrow, just as the bereaved bride had not wished to look like the bride of a scarecrow—her wind-torn, rain-stained, dirty old lace curtain which was her bridal veil blowing like a shroud around her when the great snows fell and the winter winds howled like hungry wolves around her as might happen if there was no corn.

[3 6]

MANY AND INNUMERABLE difficulties had attended the discovery and acquisition of the hidden plates of gold to which Joseph Smith had been led by the angel Moroni, who—albeit unknown to any lexicographers of angels up to that time—was his choice among such possibilities floating around in those days as the angel with the harvest hook, the angel with the divining rod, the angel who was made entirely of an iceberg or hailstones reaching from heaven to earth and never melting or moonstones or seas of ever-burning coals.

In his work of translating the cuneiforms of the long-lost golden bible with its cuneiforms beyond translation by any living man, Joseph Smith had sought the help of a prosperous neighboring farmer who believed in his being, no mere counterfeit of the real thing.

Martin Harris, owner of a farm spread which had included hog sties and poultry yards and orchards and pasturelands, had been at that time worth a fortune that came to approximately ten thousand dollars—no mean sum in those days—although it was his intention to increase it to what would come to him as a magnificent Medici publisher, American style, of the plates of gold once they could be seen, probably with no mysterious cuneiforms lying around in mud and sand.

He had been a religious turncoat who had gone through various probably superficial metamorphoses upon the millennial continent—had been a Quaker, a Universalist, a Restorator, a total-immersion Baptist, a Presbyterian before becoming a Mormon for a time which was not to be everlasting. Indeed, he was a weathercock whose enthusiasms seemed to shift with whatever winds there were and who was interested not merely in the gold of the dawn breaking over the waters and the land but in whatever gold the long-lost bible might bring to him when it was translated and made visible. No one who demanded verification of the dream by the reality seemed to remember that if there were hieroglyphs beyond translation, that fact alone should have been proof that they were from God.

Martin Harris had been convinced that Joseph Smith, even with a black hat drawn down over his eyes and shadowing his face—this disguise or mask giving him a furtive air—could see through his peep stones Thummim and Urim any landscape he wished to see, whether one of the remote past or far distant future.

The Urim and the Thummim to which the scaly, warty-skinned toad had led the seer to the plates of gold were those for which Martin Harris had squirreled away enough gold chestnuts with which to back the publication of these lost words of a god who could never really be lost but would always reappear because always escaping the ultimate understanding of a man who had no poetry in his soul and was as hard as the nails which had been driven into the bark of trees in order to stop their growth and which had been derived from the Babylonian-Chaldean tablets of destiny and had been engraved upon the breastplate of Aaron as a sign of his office of high priest.

Urim was the sign of the luminous speculum that consisted of the engravure of the divine name with its forty-two letters, of which the original world was created out of nothingness into something. Thummim was the nonluminous speculum in which the divine name was spelled out in twenty-two letters, the combination of these two divine names having provided the visionary magic of Joseph Smith's Urim and the oracular magic of his Thummim which inspired Martin Harris to place his faith in the invisible before it became visible.

Martin Harris had provided the money by which to become an interloper between Joseph Smith and his sacred text—that is to say, an assistant in the work of translation from ancient, long-lost, possibly fragmented hieroglyphs into the modern tongue or English as she was spoken on the continent where angels and unearthly creatures were not unknown and even wagon tongues and wheels and spokes spoke the word of God.

Angels were so polymorphous that they were not necessarily separate identities fenced off from each other but could be two angels in one body or could go into an angel's body by one door as one body and could go out of an angel's body by another door as another angel. Angels had been sparks of life sleeping in many embryonic forms before they were born, sometimes in flocks upon the clouds or upon the waters or upon the sands.

Martin Harris had been privileged to see, under the spell of his mesmeric, mesmerizing, mesmerized mentor or his own inscape or outscape, Jesus Christ and various angels of various color bars and had talked with God's son, he had told his neighbors in Palmyra, who would surely spread the word like wildfire that the Promised Land was about to come—as they must surely have heard many times before and would hear many times again.

Jesus Christ was altogether the handsomest man he had ever seen and thus had shown no sign of His martyrdom and could not have been dragging His hand-hewn cross and His bag of nails along with Him. He must have been sweet-smelling as amaranth, a legendary flower inclining never to fade. He must have washed His feet in lily ponds and scraped them with sand.

THE ANGEL GABRIEL with his one hundred forty pairs of wings—as many pairs as might be found sleeping on a white wall in a white twilight, and all these wings were also white—was said by Mohammed to have dictated to him the Koran and was believed by him to be not only the spirit of truth but the Holy Ghost, which was made of man and angel and God. One of the legends regarding Gabriel was that he had precepted the place of the carpenter Joseph when he was out of town—had planted in Mary's previously unentered and uninhabited womb—if there could be such a thing as a womb not already filled with the spirits of angels—the seed from which the Son of God was to be born.

Gabriel had appeared to Father Rapp in Württemberg and the first Harmony, where he was generally associated with the angel of the moon, and had appeared at the second Harmony on the banks of the Wabash, where he had left as his calling card the impression of his long-toed naked feet on a slab of porous, rain-collecting, dew-collecting limestone where the angel had stood and which should give proof throughout the coming years that he had either been here or should have been here. For when the footprints seemed ready to fall, they were always restored by a community chiseler, no matter what the surrounding world was or would become.

According to a Mohammedan legend growing out of the Koran, when the hoofs of the horseman Gabriel's horse had struck the earth, they had thrown up so much dust into the mouth of the Golden Calf that it was suddenly activated, its eyes lighting up like jewels, its nostrils breathing smoke and fire, its tail flashing, flailing.

As for the Urim and Thummim which derived from the Babylonian-Chaldean tablets of destiny—the Urim who was the source of such illumination as that streaming from Joseph Smith's high, shadowed forehead and was usually accompanied by the Thummim guiding the seer who was the seeker after perfection—they had been endowed with such versatility of functions that the spark of vision had evolved into a cherub in Klopstock's "The Messiah."

Martin Harris had been so easily mesmerized by the seer or himself that he would be able to increase and multiply the gold coins he had hidden away on his farm by using some of his wealth for the translation and publication of the unseen plates of gold into a bible that would found a new religion by restoring an old which had lost some of its ribs in modern times but now would have its ribs intact, scarcely a sign of breakage in them—so that when his skeptical wife had objected to his pouring his liquid assets from a bank down a rusted drain that seemed to have no bottom, he had become enraged by the evil eye she cast upon his prospect and had treated her as if she were an ugly old crone who wished to destroy him who would raise himself up from a vegetative state to a city of gold if only he would remain steady in his faith in the angel Moroni's bible.

Because of his wife's doubt in the validity of the Mormon bible's account of the upper convex and the lower convex of the mundane shell of this egg-shaped world at a time when many mystical geographers who were by their nature theologians believed that the ice floes at either end of the pole were kept from floating away from each other by golden spirals much like the pages of the gold hunter's book, he had given himself over to such hysterical rage that his mouth had frothed. He had whipped and kicked his wife time and again. He had thrown her into the garden and had chased her around and around because she had dared to question the divine angelic origin of the testaments that Joseph Smith had found in the ark in the cave and had not believed in his Urim and Thummim—or so she had claimed.

While some angels may be the angels of forgetfulness, particularly if they are in communication with an errant husband, others may be the angels of memory, particularly if they are in communication with an abused wife who cannot forget one iota of his assaults upon her.

Her memories were of the time when, no longer able to endure with any semblance of harmony or equanimity the subject of the Golden Calf which he had believed would provide endless treasures for him and probably all the jewels of Golconda or Ethiopia or the mountains of the moon and the valleys of the sun and the abysses if he did not sever his partnership with Joseph Smith and sink into the muck as one who had passed over the opportunity to become God's publisher, Martin Harris had struck her with the butt end of a whip that had been used for driving an ox to the fields and of which the butt end had been about the size of her thumb and the whip had been about three or four feet long and when lashing through the air had made a serpentine sound.

According to a legend that had its counterparts in other lands of the Near East, the Golden Calf had been slain by the wicked Mot who was death and who then was pursued over hill and dale by the beautiful virgin Anat, who had cut him down and winnowed him and ground him with a millstone and ground him into finest particles of bones and dust, which she then scattered all over the fields in order to encourage the growth of the bearded wheat of which the strands were golden like those hanging out from the mouth of the Golden Calf.

Also according to legend, although the Golden Calf was sleeping in his tomb, he had not passed into that eternal sleep which seems never to have been eternal, but had awakened and risen again—had risen many times to the clouded sky—for he was magical and was endowed with angelic wings and made a bellowing sound. Sometimes the Golden Calf was transformed into a pomegranate.

VERY FASCINATING to the Swedenborgians of this millennial time which would see the death of the agrarian world and the birth of the world of the machine had been the variety of inventive talents shown by angels in their means of transportation and particularly the feathered pharaohs who rose up out of their desert tombs each night to travel over America with wild shoutings, honkings over the sky like migratory birds—and some were bird-headed. Some were angels of a thousand eyes, and some were angels of wheels, and there were angel gods equipped with castors by which they could roll themselves, and there were angels of the lower rays of the moon and of the many mansions of the moon and also of the sun either when it was burning gold or pale as the sun.

DURING THE TRANSLATION of the plates with the spiritual spectacles that had enabled Joseph Smith to put the mysterious cuneiforms into the English language without tracing the raised figures with his thumb, Martin Harris had assisted as the polisher of the great carbuncle that, like a figure in a Hawthorne fairy tale, would provide the light of the sun and the moon to unbelievers in the invisible or the angel of invisibility for whom the discoverer did not call out for help.

Joseph Smith had been twice refused permission by God to allow the earthbound Martin Harris to take the proof of the manuscript from Harmony to Palmyra to show to his henpecking wife whose eye was on the main chance for corn and not this bypath away from future wealth, but when he had asked God or His representative for the third time, the answer of the divine intelligence had switched from the negative to the affirmative—but the permission had been accompanied by the injunction that Harris should show this new bible to no one except his wife and his brother, Preserved Harris.

When after three weeks in which Joseph Smith had suffered from anxiety because the manuscript had not been returned in any form, he had hastened from Harmony to Palmyra and there in his father's house had been told by Martin Harris that he had lost the precious sheaves—that they had disappeared, he did not know how or where.

This news had been enough to stagger a man, both body and soul—for the original words which had become the birds had perhaps already faded or were fading from his mind. "Oh, my God! All is lost! All is lost! What shall I do?" he had cried out, as would be remembered by his mother with her red berry face. "I have sinned—it is I who tempted the wrath of God. . . ."

He had recognized that he should have been content with the first answer he had received from God and should not have pressed so hard on Him. But to make a request three times was obviously, as he must now have forgotten, a part of ritual in fairy tales and mysteries. And now how could this uncompleted manuscript have disappeared after so brief a time in which he had seen and heard it through his peep stones, and where were they?

Although Martin Harris—who now was not to be a major or even a minor stockholder of a bible he had helped to translate from the mysterious

golden plates which had disappeared for thousands of years in which it had
suffered only God knew how many adventures in sea storms and then had
come briefly to the surface of life only to sink again or be lifted up beyond
reach of the hand of man or any horizon visible to his eye—had searched
everywhere for the manuscript in his own house, he had not been able to
find that which should have been categorized now as belonging to the
department of what was lost, strayed, stolen.

Have a care about the next dead dog you may see on the road. Do not
give it a kick. It may be the lost bible and may suddenly whine. Have a care
about the dead bird. It may suddenly sing. Have a care about the next pile
of dung. It may speak with an angel's voice to a poor man, for it is also
made with gold.

Joseph Smith had paced around and around and had wept copious tears
until sunset and only then had sat down to partake of bread and cheese and
wine so that after a night's sleep interrupted by much tossing, turning,
dreaming he might have the strength to rise up the next morning and
weep, weep again. He had filled the already murky atmosphere around
him with his lamentations and had shed many tears unstintingly for days
and days.

The fingers of suspicion had been pointed to Mrs. Harris by her husband and Joseph Smith. Both were sure that although the missing testament might, of course, have taken off on its own with its one hundred and
seventeen pages bound by a spine flapping like the wings of a bird, she had
been guilty of throwing this holy proof of God's conceivably unaltered and
unalterable words into a roaring bonfire where it had burned to such dust
and ashes that not one iota of its remains could be found by any sifter of
dust and ashes and cinders.

All during the nerve-wracking search, Mrs. Harris had been too cautious either to affirm or to deny that it was she who had set the fire; she
could only say to her flat-headed husband that Joseph Smith should put on
his magical spectacles and go peek for it—peek and peek and peek and
perhaps peek and peek and peek as he had already done and without
success.

There had been a miracle, however, on the day when the translation
from the golden plates had been burned, or—as it had been seen by eyes
other than those of Mr. Harris and his domestic flock—had been stolen
away by the most dreadful creature that there might be, although not the
first to engage in such a theft—a rival who like a raven would steal away
this sacred sheaf with which to line his own nest so that to him would be
brought the benefits of exposing what the true words of God were.

It seemed that the good angel of the weather had been on Joseph Smith's side and not on Martin Harris's side. For God had punished the careless or gullible Martin Harris for his transgressions by bringing upon him both temporal and spiritual sufferings in a way so plain, so unambivalent that even the dumbest ox could not have missed the point unless he chose to be obtuse as to the ways of God.

Joseph Smith's mother—an eyewitness to the darkness of that day—was to recall in her memories of the unfading amaranthine son which she provided for an amanuensis for publication some five years after his death in the courtyard of the Carthage pen when his martyrdom was not that which would cause the purple of the lily to fade—a dense fog had spread over the fields that Martin Harris owned at Palmyra and had blighted the wheat of this careless caretaker of God's word—it could only have been called the translated word by anyone devoted to the not divine art of total accuracy, that which could hardly have been the subject of her devotion since theology was always based on mythology and myth-making propensities—and although the spikes that grew from the plant were in full grain, the fog had caused such blight that about two thirds of the crop had been lost while the fields that lay on the opposite side of the road had been spared injury of any kind. The wheat on one side had lain down. The wheat on the other side had stood up. "I well remember that day of darkness, both within and without. To us, at least, the heavens seemed clothed with blackness and the earth shrouded with gloom."

[3 7]

AFTER A TIME at trying to support himself and his wife by doing a little work with his hands on the farm as if he had been the son of a clod instead of the son of God, Joseph Smith had received a visit from the Lord, Who had come to tell him that his forgetfulness as to what was in the lost text word for word need provide no difficulty that could not be solved by what might have been called a kind of hiatus, a breakage or cleft or caesura or fissure in memory. The angel Moroni was that rara avis which would not repeat himself and thus was different from those many angels of the heavenly sphere at every level who lived by repeating themselves, by saying over and over what they had just said. Joseph Smith should discontinue his weeping and continue with another version of the Word of the Lord, which could be subjected to so many interpretations, including one's own.

As Joseph Smith and Oliver Cowdery were low on coins of gold, silver, copper, tin—other than coins of speech stamped with faces of kings of Phoenician, Babylonian, Sumerian, Egyptian empires of which they had possibly also a limited supply—and as they had not ever the coins of beaver and otter empires with which to pay for bread and bed as they continued the translation of the Indian bible that would bring to the darkness of this world the honeycomb of light, they had gratefully accepted the invitation of Peter Whitmer and his sons to eat and sleep in their home in Fayette, Seneca County, New York, while the work of translation went on—not speedily as a winged horse but slow as a workman's horse.

Once more behind a curtain that divided God's prophet from his translator, although there was no partition of any kind between their two brains, the prophet with his peep stone piped out the holy words of this strange and yet familiar text which was to be but a shortened version, an epitome of the original which had weighed forty pounds and had been reduced in passage from one world to another world. Even like so many things which are lost between the conception and the act, the dream and the reality.

Helping with the translation over a period of seven months, which should have been nine in which to allow it to develop before lifting it up from the womb of time, had been Peter Whitmer's sons and sometimes Emma, mother of the child whose little imago had apparently not been protected by the talismanic angel of childbirth and who had been born dead.

Around the dining table in Seneca County, Peter Whitmer's sons Christian and David had joined in a cottage industry in which they not only served as scribes taking down Joseph Smith's dictation, which came from behind the green curtain like some great weaver's loom from which the harp music spilled, they also, although they had not yet seen the golden plates of which the discovery must be taken on faith as they heard sounds like hands moving among strings—perhaps the hand of that great creator who while in flight had let loose and dropped from his hand the egg out of which, when it was cracked, all the forms of creation had spilled—had attempted to arrange in a semblance of the logic of a creator who had antedated logic the fractured, disjointed grammar of the translation of the orthography.

Remnants of mythologies older than those of the generally accepted Bible were very real in Joseph Smith's mythology which antedated the traditional religions and had brushed upon him with their plumes as no doubt also during the period of their exile they had been somewhat under the mesmerizing spell of Phoenicians, Greeks, Cretans, Arabs, Persians, Egyptians, Etruscans, and various other pagan deities in a timeless time of many migrations, meltings, mergings, meetings, partings, and many changes in forms of gods.

The prophet's ignorance of the Bible had been so great that he had not known that Jerusalem was a walled city until one of his helper scribes told him, it would be recalled by David Whitmer in an interview in the *Chicago Tribune* of December 15, 1885, at a time when continuing strikes by usually foreign-born workers for the eight-hour day so that they might sometimes see the faces of their children when they were wide awake and smiling in the light of the sun had ripened the ground for the strike against the McCormick Reaper Works in Chicago, where the angel who presided over the works was not the harvester angel Gabriel, as what was harvested here by the reaper was not corn with the grain still on the listening ear but those poor naked cobs who were men.

The long-ago founder of the Mormon church whose people had never starved through any carelessness of his had drawn into orbit a variety of feathered bird men, including the Egyptian falcon with the eye of Horus, who when he was brought down from the skies by the arrows of a pagan archer was comforted in the lap of the earth mother Isis, who perhaps had prepared the way for the mother of Christ when He with His bloody wounds and marks of spears and flames upon Him was taken down from the cross and comforted in her lap as if He were still her little child as He was still the carpenter's son. And no doubt He was.

The trouble with Joseph Smith was that he wished to be taken seriously in spite of the joking spirit in him which was generally recognized. A toad had shown him the way into the man-made cave to show him the golden plates which were still invisible to others and which had been placed there by Moroni, a man who was not an angel in the beginning but had become an angel after he had been buried here and had ascended to heaven as a spirit who now had returned through the Pearly Gates as an angel.

Joseph Smith's pride in having the invisible golden plates in his possession had seemed to make him swell larger and larger like the mythic frog who had swallowed all the waters of the world and was afraid to open his mouth lest they should all come spewing out and he should be a dead frog as inept as a brown leaf swept along by wind.

The title page had explained in a way to appeal to the spirit of adventure inherent in the breasts of many Americans but not all that this new bible on which Joseph Smith held the copyright was an abridgement of the record of the people of Nephi and also of the Lamanites and was written to the Lamanites, a remnant of the House of Israel, and also to Jew and Gentile. "Written and sealed up, and hid up unto the Lord, to come forth by the gift and power of God unto the interpretation thereof, sealed by the hand of Moroni, and hid up unto the Lord, to come forth in due time by the way of Gentile, the interpretation thereof by the gift of God."

The book was further described as an abridgement of the Book of Ether, which was a record of the people of Jared—and if anyone wondered who they were or what language they had spoken, there was now given enlightenment as to further mysteries caused by the failure of communication in a universal tongue such as many socialists had dreamed of and would continue to dream of—the premise being that if men understood each other and if all excesses of languages buried in languages were stripped away, they would live in greater harmony and less chaos than now.

This book, reduced in form although certainly not to the smallest capsule possible—for if it were small enough, a man might have eaten it as if it were a lightning bug—had been written when the Lord scattered the people of Jared and confounded the language of the people when they were building a tower to get to heaven.

No doubt the Lord had split and divided the language of the builders into a Babel of tongues because He had had it in mind not only to discourage the search for social perfection by the mud-bound, sand-bound, water-bound children of earth but to give comfort and employment to the Grimm fairy-tale man in whom probably more Americans—whether high up or low down upon the scale of success—believed than believed in Martin Luther's god or Jean Calvin's god.

The name that Cornelius Vanderbilt had placed upon his first freight boat steaming up the Hudson had been, for example, the *Cinderella*—after that little girl who had sat among the ashes and had turned into just such gold as would the coal brought by the water barges before there were land barges or ships on rails.

JOSEPH SMITH'S SEARCH had not been for perfection but for improvement of man's lot on earth. In order to find financial backing for the publication of the abridgement of God's word into a form that was not merely a capsule assuring peace to the believers who were the children of light and not of darkness, the prophet had been told by Moroni, the son of Moron—whose muse must certainly have been not the muse of memory which was the mother of the arts but the muse of forgetfulness—that the Lord had changed His mind and that it behooved him to allow the translators to see the golden plates that had previously been hidden from them.

The bound paperbacked visions that were looking for financial backing and a publisher and were not blank pages and were bound together so that the pages would not fly apart in the wind and the messages would not be lost, irretrievably lost—although after centuries in a cave they had come to man and so ought always to be able to return—had been seen and handled by the translators who had previously been as blind as three blind mice, at least just so long as it was not a haystack burning in the midst of the flood.

The three witnesses to whom an angel had come down from heaven bearing the golden plates which they were allowed to see with their eyes and touch with their fingers were Oliver Cowdery, former schoolmaster and former blacksmith, who was to do his hammering henceforth upon the forges of the Lord; the translator David Whitmer, whose fathers and brothers were also to testify, as would Hyrum Page and Joseph Smith, Sr., and his sons Hyrum and Samuel H. Smith, beloved sons of the former gold hunter father who was not to waver in his faith that the son who bore his name was the vehicle or vessel for that which he called the genius of his wandering family; and finally Martin Harris, the black sheep who had wandered away from the fold but now had wandered back.

To Martin Harris with his purse strings drawn as tight as the mouth of a dead man trying not to cough up the gold coin for his passage through the ever-widening Stygian flood to the shores of light, God had sent—by way of Joseph Smith as His messenger and servant—a message that, had he been in a colloquial mood as he sometimes was, he should cough up, cough up.

God had commanded Martin Harris to make haste to repent, he being in the presence of the eternity of God and the potency of His punishments, of which, of course, he had already experienced some.

It seemed that if he had sinned in his haste because of his selfishness, he was to be given no time in which to repent at his leisure. If he did not immediately repent in order to piece out the payment of the bill that he had contracted with the printer at a time when Joseph Smith, the ne'er-do-well, could get no credit from the devil's printer for setting up the Lord's words, God would smite him by the rod upon his mouth and by his wrath and by his anger, so that his sufferings would be sore—how sore he knew not, whatever he may have thought, how exquisite, he knew not.

"And again, I command thee that thou shalt not covet thy neighbor's wife nor seek thy neighbor's life"—polygamy at this point having been not so much a sudden flock of startled thoughts rising up in the prophet's mind as a way of making sure his earthly paradise would have inhabitants and be not empty as a dry well. "And again, I command thee that thou shalt not covet thine own property but impart it freely to the printing of the Book of Mormon." And the Lord would not release him from bondage until he had done so, and the Lord did not want to have to speak of the matter again.

So that Martin Harris, repenting of the sins that had made him covet his own property as that which he did not wish to share with other men—the concept having not yet arrived that as one should not sequester one's own gold coins away from the all-encompassing community of saints under the protection of God, one also should not own the body of one's wife but should share her as if she were common stock in which other saints and possibly even angels had their joints as of the fruits of their loins, as more than one frog prince dreaming that he was a man might have dropped his seeds into the same many-furrowed earth tossing up and down like a sea— had been urged to borrow on his farm land or sell it outright in order to pay the printer who had gone on strike and had refused to continue with his work or word which he who might well have been the devil fallen from a high estate in the clouds to his present low estate in the mud had no reason to take on trust either the Lord or the Lord's emissary here on earth, whether true or false.

Among the many tales told regarding the circumstances of the revelation of the golden plates to the three original witnesses was that they had at first seen nothing they were supposed to see. When Joseph Smith had opened what seemed the golden box in which the golden plates had been enclosed, there had been not so much as a flash of golden lightning forks lighting the heavens and casting their reflection upon earth. Their hearts had been smitten with disappointment. "O, ye of little faith!" the prophet had cried out. "How long will God bear with this wicked and perverse generation? Down on your knees, brethren, every one of you," he had commanded, and they had knelt.

According to the possibly somewhat foggy recollections of David Whitmer in a Democratic organ, the Kingston, Missouri, *Times* of December 27, 1887—and that was in the month following the execution of the Haymarket anarchists, whose guilt was never to be established beyond the shadow of a doubt and who were tried and condemned only for having spread the drizzly atmosphere which had inspired someone else to throw the bomb in the Haymarket Square—there had appeared in the heavens the miracle that was the affirmation of the miracle for which the gentlemen had waited: a slowly floating table upon which were many golden plates piled high as a tower, a table where the members of the Church of Latter-Day Saints should share the fruits of life and the long-necked golden goose stretched out upon its golden platter in a communitarian brotherhood of saints and angels, where to all members would be given bread and not merely the crumbs or possibly not even the crumbs which in this present society of rich men were not allotted to the poor tramps and bums, who were left to starve like scrawny blackbirds in the snow—for there would be the realization of Joseph Smith's dream of a New Jerusalem rising up out of this Dead Sea of life or coming down through heaven's gates, as had been promised long ago and quite recently.

The golden plates were those which had provided material for the Mormon bible and which these three witnesses had seen for the first time as the scales dropped from their eyes and the sky that had previously been darkness without light had been filled with a light more glorious than that of the sun and they had also heard the voice of the Lord speaking to them.

According to Martin Harris, he had not seen them with his natural or bodily eyes as he might see a pencil case in the lawyer's hand—he had seen them with the eye of faith just as distinctly as he might see anything around him—although at the time of the revelation they had been covered by a cloth.

When the Mormon temple was built at Kirtland, Ohio, by the Mormon Saints, who were even then always being threatened with extinction by their persecutors, one of the ways by which man's vision had been magnetized by the convert Brigham Young, stonemason and carpenter and painter and glazier by trade—and also adept in speaking mysterious angel tongues, bird tongues, frog tongues, just as Joseph Smith was—had been for him to work with an early Canadian convert on the mixing of the plaster for the outer walls with no jewels from Solomon's undiscovered mines such as might have been preferred by the average man but with gleaming fragments of china dishes, which caught the light of the sun and the moon and which had been contributed to the dauber's bier of sand, water, lime, and sometimes human hair by the Mormon women who gathered at the dinner table. It was the way of the twelve saints who had been chosen by the three original eyewitnesses to set up stakes for the catching of an angel of the Lord if they waited long enough—Brigham Young's view having been that if one or many angels would come, they would come whether they were expected or unexpected.

Joseph Smith and Oliver Cowdery had seen at the temple various sacred characters from the past, which they believed—in spite of all the storm and stress of life—was the present and future for them and those who were sharers of their faith—among these visitors who kept the heavens busy with their traffic, the long-bearded Moses with the keys of the gathering and the return of the Ten Tribes, Elias with the keys of the dispensation of Abraham, Elijah with the keys of redemption and sealing. One of the buildings erected by Brigham Young was the post office.

Although all three of the early witnesses were to sever the cords that bound them to Joseph Smith, all three were to continue to believe in the authenticity of the mysterious golden plates when they might have joined with howling mobs to say that they were false. That pronouncement would have meant that they themselves were guilty either of plain, open-faced falsehood or biased judgment, which might have robbed them of their desire to be considered honorable men in relation to the fraud that they could see was Joseph Smith—who had seemed too much a clown to be a god and who was like a ventriloquist able to speak from a cloud, a stone, a pebble, a hole in the sand, a tree blowing in the wind at the edge of the ever-crumbling abyss and against whom the three dummies had rebelled because of disappointed opportunism in a real or an imaginary sense.

The three original witnesses, who never did recant and tell the truth that anti-Mormon watchers yearned to hear—that the Book of Mormon was of no known divine origin and that the golden plates that they had promoted in the darkness were a fraud promoted by a fraud who was interested in the money that would be brought by sales—sales of books and not sails of boats manned by angels, especially Moroni who was the head of the crew—were to enjoy greater longevity than that given to the great illuminator, his life to be cut short by the violent mob in the flower of his manhood, whereas their lives were to go on and on, possibly as a reward from God for their reticence, their keeping their mouths as silent as if stuffed with old bird's nests, pebbles, and clay when time after time they were approached after their falling away from the Mormon faith as headed by the dead or transfigured or transported prophet, they still had refused to speak the truth that would have revealed them as false witnesses. The three original witnesses had remained true to the angelic experience which they had shared.

Although Martin Harris had departed from the company of Joseph Smith, he had not fallen so far, far away from the tree of life that he could not find his way back to take another baptismal dip in the river, so that he who had been an apostate had been restored as a member of the Mormon church when God cast upon the waters His golden net to bring him in, bring him in, bring him in. He had been a flounder, so bring him in and let him flounder like a loose garment upon this shore of sand and snow and mud.

His last words when he was dying at the age of ninety-two and must have known that he was passing from the light into the darkness or the darkness into the light were remembered to have been, according to ear- and eyewitnesses who had gathered at his bedside, the words "Book! Book! Book!" After all, he had not only seen the golden plates like the flashing of sunlight inside the box—he had tried to retrieve his original monetary losses by taking greater loans upon his farm and so had become the bookmaker or publisher, as he had also become the bookmaker, the shill urging people to put their money on the four horsemen who would carry the believers in Moroni's golden plates to the Promised Land.

Martin Harris, although not an authentic carrier of the vision—for he was a money-grubber grubbing only for himself—had foreseen such a great landslide of converts to the Mormon faith that had been served on the plates of gold by the angel messenger that it was not difficult for him to bet that the United States government was on the verge of falling, and not in the remote future but very soon—for the Mormons were spreading, increasing their number, and were about to take over this land root and branch, and not leave it to its present driftage and seeming chaos as the powers in Washington seemed to do in relation to the poor, who were trammeled on by the trammelers, as they were generally called.

When Oliver Cowdery was approaching his end, he had not turned turtle by denying that he had seen the golden plates. They after all had been the initial illusion ushering in other illusions, such as those of the sacred prophets of old, who in answer to his bird whistles and those of others of the Mormon saints with whom he had parted some time ago had come out of the sky into the marshes near Kirtland in order to appear in the great golden temple before the eyes of the mesmerized members of the church. What if he now denied that he had seen Moses or Elijah or John the Baptist—and no sooner was dead than one of them would meet him with reproach?

His last words, according to Brother David Whitmer—a not unprejudiced witness—had been a reminder to him that he should not forget what he had seen and should be true to his testimony of the Book of Mormon and the golden plates from which they had translated it leaf by leaf.

What had perhaps swept over David Whitmer's mind before his physical senses faded and his spiritual senses like eyes were returned to some great cloud bank was perhaps the idea of an oversoul or an idea existing in an angel's mind. He had felt no great crackup of his brain—no splitting, no division as into two melon halves—but had been very clear and lucid and probably more than usually sane—so when beyond the help of any prescription other than that nepenthean patent medicine which should put the old man to sleep until he should awaken in paradise at the sound of the ram's horn, he had called the doctor to his bedside for the express purpose of ascertaining whether or not he was in his right mind.

The doctor had examined him with his stethoscope, telescope, microscope, tuning forks, or whatever instruments were in his bag and had assured him that his mind was shipshape—he probably was not leaking out part of his mind and was not already a mere paper skull. Whitmer had answered all questions—he had known whether it was day or night. He had known which country he was in as could not be said of all dying men. And he was going to clear the deck. He was not going to his grave without taking his revenge upon those who had believed he was a liar and had waited hopefully for his deathbed recantations.

The Richmond, Missouri, *Democrat* had reported that the old man, just before giving up the ghost, had called out to the eyewitnesses of what must have been his final passage, "I want to say to you all, the bible and the record of the Nephites is true." Thus the words carved on the tombstone that marked the grave of the rasping old man who had claimed that he was not unhinged but who long ago had fallen from the Mormon Tree of Life could have come as no surprise to those who watched over what should be called the Department of Last Words: "The record of the Jews and the record of the Nephites are one. Truth is eternal."

[3 8]

MARK TWAIN gave some small moment of remembrance that once during his travels through the still untrammeled western wilderness, through which he had gone with his brother Orion by overland stagecoach in 1862, thus ten years before the elaboration and extension of his original notes in *Roughing It,* published in 1872, he had come into contact with the Mormons, who had taken flight from Missouri and Illinois to the deserts of Utah under the leadership of Brigham Young, who was called the Golden Lion of the Tribe of Zion.

Since many had been drawn by the silver lodes to the Far West but had not reported what they had seen with their own eyes while on the ground, it had been Mark Twain's intention to help the resting reader while away an hour with his impressions of an interesting episode that he had seen during the time of the rise, growth, and culmination of the silver-mining fever in Nevada. As he had explained in his Prefatory, his fear was that, taking it all around, a good deal of information had gotten into his book—to his great regret, but it really could not be helped. Sometimes Mark Twain had been of that mind in which he would give up worlds if he could retain his facts, but it could not be.

As for the nineteenth century, it may be said that it was probably the leakiest century there ever was and so would remain.

ONE OF BRIGHAM YOUNG's memories of the long passage of himself and his ragged, dying people from Nauvoo to the utopia which was then nowhere was that flocks of angels of the Lord had leaked enough buckets of tears from their eyes to make a lake. And now the rain had swept against the broken windows of the Overland Express in which Samuel Clemens— he was not yet Mark Twain—and his elder brother Orion had traveled, so that, in order to protect the passengers from the rain, the stagecoach driver had caulked the sides of the torn curtains to the warped frames with rags made of strips of old clothes, as over appearing and disappearing roads, places of sand and stone where the roads were lost or had never been or forked between nowhere and nowhere, the coach still had made progress toward Brigham Young's utopia, which the Golden Lion had founded when it was nowhere.

To Mark Twain coming over the long shoulders of the Rocky Mountains, the long range had seemed like a great China wall protecting the Great Salt Lake City, which was the capital city in the empire ruled over by Brigham Young. Perhaps the image of the China wall had occurred to him because of the fact that indeed early discoverers of the Great Salt Lake and many coming afterward had thought that it was a sea from which they could sail directly to the mysterious Orient. Viewed from the top, the city of the Latter-Day Saints had seemed a toy village upon the distant plain.

Mark Twain had known much of the anti-Mormon conspiratorial apparatus that acted in behalf of the somewhat shaky United States government in Washington and of invasive Gentile business interests for whom the golden apples of the Mormon polygamists provided irresistible temptation to put their long, sharp teeth into the fruit of the man who had made the Dead Sea to flower—but his stay in the Mormon paradise had been only about two days and three nights, scarcely time for the unwrapping and solving of all the mysteries of what was called the Mormon question. Just as, busily sightseeing in Greater Salt Lake City, where he and his brother Orion had found sanctuary as guests of the Gentile acting territorial governor in the Salt Lake House, he had never gotten around to taking the horse and buggy ride to the Great Salt Lake which he had traveled so far to behold.

As Mark Twain and his brother Orion had walked in the long twilight through the streets of Greater Salt Lake City, they had been impressed by their first glimpse of shops and stores—and by every passing creature they took to be a Mormon. "This was fairy land to us, to all intents and purposes—a land of enchantment and goblins and awful mystery." They had yearned to ask every child along the way how many mothers it had and if it could tell them apart and had experienced a thrill every time the door of a dwelling house opened and shut as they passed and they caught a glimpse of human heads and backs and shoulders, for they yearned to see a Mormon family in what Twain described as all its comprehensive ampleness when disposed in the customary concentric rings of its home circle—the image he employed was perhaps consciously astronomical, as the Mormon home circle included both the living and the dead—and surely he knew that there were no orphans sleeping in gutters or starving for a few crumbs of bread as there were in capitalistic towns and that all orphans were taken in and sheltered by many mothers and fathers in the kingdom of Brigham Young.

The legend has come down that once when the Golden Lion found two starving, wizened little Indians, brother and sister who like desert mice had nothing to drink but the few drops of water they sucked from the roots of cactus plants, he had picked them up in his arms and when asked what he planned to do with them had answered that he would take them home, of course, and bring them up with his other children as Mister and Miss Young—and so he did.

Mark Twain and his brother Orion, strolling about through the broad, straight, level streets of the sunlit city the day after their arrival, had enjoyed the pleasant strangeness of the most unusual fact that there were no loafers or drunkards perceptible anywhere; that there were limpid streams flowing through every street from the canal in place of filthy gutters; block after block of houses built of frame and sunburned brick, each with thriving orchard and garden at its back; branches of water from the great stream winding among the vegetable beds and trees bearing fruits; and there must have been the apportioned apple tree from which hung the hangman's fruit, although there should have been—yet all was very peaceful. People everywhere were busily at work in shops and factories and all manner of industries; Mark Twain recording that there were intent faces and busy hands—he did not liken them to doves—while what struck his ears were those sounds that he remembered as the ceaseless clink of hammers, the buzz of trade, the contented hum of drums and flywheels.

The Mormon crest was easy for Twain to understand. It was simple and unostentatious—it had seemed to him to fit like a glove. "It was a representative of a Golden Bee Hive, with the bees all at work."

It was the younger brother who was providing the dollars for this journey in search of money—who had visited the foundations of the Mormon temple which was then in the process of being built upward from the ground—and had seen the Tithing House and the Lion House and many more church and government buildings of various kinds and curious names which by the time of the writing of *Roughing It* had slipped from his mind.

The two travelers from Missouri had dined with their Gentile hosts, who had regaled them with all kinds of strange tales regarding the Mormons. They had emerged from the Salt Lake House in their best clothes for their call on Brigham Young, the very thought of whom had filled Mark Twain's somewhat porous brain with awe. Merely mortal travelers, especially if from Missouri, might not have been received into Brigham Young's presence. But Orion was on an official mission, having received from Abraham Lincoln as a reward for supporting him in the presidential election campaign of 1860 the office of secretary of the Nevada Territory.

Wearing white shirts, the two gentlemen had gone to pay their respects to the Golden Lion of the Tribe of Judah, whom they had approached with as much respect as if they were paying a state visit to a king—a man who must not have seemed a caged lion to them, although a lion behind bars and hedged in on every side by contending armies was what he was—and yet from Mark Twain's point of view, he was the king.

The Lion House, in which the king lived with his numerous wives and numerous children—he who was good at keeping count of all things, including the ears of corn and the number of the dead, who continued in the Mormon greater family, he must surely have known how many there were, although, with his sense of enlarged fatherhood, he was not the kind of man who would have kicked out any poor, starving woman or stray child who had come out of the desert or out of the mountains into what others might consider a lion's fold but what to him with his shepherding instinct and his millennial ram's horn must have seemed a sheep's fold for the ewes and the lambs who were gathered in under the protective hand of God—was and would continue to be a wonder to other travelers, because this harbor for a pluralistic household was marked out by the sign of a crouching lion upon the portico of the front entrance of the gabled, many-celled, thick-walled abode where Brigham Young laughed with his wives and children after a long day's work, which might be followed by a long night's work.

The Lion House had been built to contain a schoolroom, recreation room, washroom or laundry, dish room, buttery, weaving room (for busy looms which made a sound more wonderful than the songs of harps), ash shed for the making of soap (although cleanliness was not necessarily next to godliness, these previous mud crawlers knew), and a shelter for the coachman's coach. In his compound there were also shops for the sawing of logs, sheds for poultry where no doubt the rooster reigned supreme over the hens as in a Morocco courtyard where the hens were in purdah; and there were numerous farm properties owned by him, including shelters for horses and buggies and wagons and mules and cows and a threshing machine and several plows and harrows and a sleigh and a gold watch and chain and three silver watches and six clocks of beautiful design and work-manship like everything else from Brigham Young's hands or the hands of his workers.

The place where he received his visitors—some of an eminence who might find their names unknown to him in this desert wild, for his only concerns were those of his Israel that it might not be pulverized, beaten back into the dust and sand like that through which it had come, that it might survive by begetting and multiplying and extending as God had promised—was his office between the Bee Hive House and Lion House, actually an extension of the honey hive where he kept his actuarial accounts on the progress of the living and the dead, the material and the spiritual orbs.

Mysteries were not mysteries but came through man's inadequate understanding of the chemistry of God. Mystery was nothing to Brigham Young. The Mormons were under the protection of the hand of God and had been through all the way by which, after the burnings at Nauvoo, the Latter-Day Saints had come into Utah for the erection of the Great Salt Lake City upon the desert floor by all working in harmony together for the good of all and not of one interested only in self-advancement, in buying low and selling high. Brigham Young had cried out through his ram's horn, "We have been kicked out of the frying pan into the fire, out of the fire into the middle of the desert floor, and here we are and here we will stay."

To later handcart immigrants, mainly English and Welsh and German and Scandinavian, he had advised that they should not search the sky for the angelic beings who actually, of course, thickened the air about them but should dig ditches for irrigation and dig holes for the planting of the turnip.

Brigham Young was never so wrapped up in the spiritual that he forgot to give practical advice. He understood that if any one of his twelve apostles whom he had expected to rule with him as kings over the deserts and the mountains for the good of the Mormon people should disagree with him there still would be stamped upon each of them the sign that he was and always would be a Mormon at heart. Brigham Young was as full of wise sayings as if he were an edition not of the Mormon bible but of *Poor Richard's Almanack*.

He did know that sometimes his advice went like a shuttle into a Mormon's ear and came out at the other ear without leaving so much as a thread of understanding to show that it had passed in and out. He measured every keg of water or keg of salt and struck its top with his gold-headed cane to make sure that neither salt nor water leaked out.

While underpaid stocking knitters who knit stockings by machines in the attics owned by the stocking kings in blasted industrial cities of the East were either blinded by their long hours of work or were expressing social protest by knitting stockings that would fit no feet, he had advised the women who were hand-knitters in his knitting shop to give greater care to their knitting, ribbing, and purling.

It was his belief that little children in the Mormon settlements should not be sent out into the deserts and the mountains to round up the cattle and the sheep and the lambs—they should spend their time in school in the midst of such pleasant gardens of fruits and flowers and vegetables filled with the splashings of waters and the singings of birds and the buzzings of bees that they should never wish to leave home.

The legend has come down that once when Father Young had paid a call at a home in a remote pioneering settlement—that of Anson Call who had answered the Lord's call to help protect the Mormon kingdom—he had been sitting before the fireplace with his host's little golden-haired daughter on his knees as he explained his love of the children whom he desired should be educated and play in green fields, when the cherubic child had said to him, "Mr. Young, your eyes look exactly like the eyes of my father's sow."

Walking tiptoe with the little girl leading him by the hand, he had gone out with her to the pig shed so that he might see what the sow's face looked like and had stood studying her features for some time, as if she were his living reproduction or portrait.

If the Mormon kingdom stretching out like a hog's back in the desert in the shadow of the mountains had really been a hog, then its back would have bristled with the swords of territorial troops who had been sent to watch over the Mormons and impose their peace upon the wandering remnant tribes of starving red men by making war, war that seemed to have no intent but extermination.

THE WHITE-SHIRTED Mark Twain and his brother Orion felt a certain sense of awe that they should have the privilege of making a state visit to the king whom the clowning comedian would describe as ruling over a Mormon state which was no state at all but a state of mind.

Mark Twain would have been pleasantly surprised if he had ever found out that the man who kept record of visitors calling to see Brigham Young had entered the names of the two callers that hot August day as the brothers Orion and Samuel Clemens.

The stateless king to whom they had paid their state visit was a kindly, easy-mannered, dignified, self-possessed old gentleman who had in his eye a gentle craft that probably belonged there. "He was very simply dressed and was just taking off a straw hat as we entered."

It was Brigham Young's belief that this earth had once been closer to the moon than it now was and that because of a great sin it had been dropped to this distance but would bounce back when came the millennium in which the Mormons would be reunited with their dead and would prevail, although now subjected to persecution in many forms. The Mormons who were a small stone would triumph over the Gentile intruders by breaking the large stone into fragments.

The great patriarch of the Mormons usually took advantage of the presence of visitors passing into and out of the Great Salt Lake City by scattering the seeds of propaganda which might give a better portrait of the in-gatherings of the Latter-Day Saints than they generally enjoyed in a Zion that was the envy of Babylonians.

The head of the Golden Bee Hive in this Greater Salt Lake—while discoursing upon Utah and the Indians and Nevada and general American matters and questions—had paid no attention to Orion Clemens's brother Samuel, although Samuel had made several attempts from the sidelines to draw Young out on such subjects as federal politics and that which he considered to be Young's high-handed attitude toward Congress. "I thought some of the things I said were rather fine."

Brigham Young had merely looked around at him at distant intervals—thus reminding Samuel Clemens of the image of a benign old cat which he had sometimes seen looking around to see which kitten was meddling with her tail. So that Orion Clemens's younger brother had subsided into an indignant silence throughout which, hot and flushed, he had sat until the end while execrating Young in his heart as an ignorant savage. But as for Brigham Young, he had remained calm, his conversation with the official gentlemen flowing on as sweetly and peacefully and musically as any summer brook. Only when they were retiring from his presence, Brigham Young had put his hand upon the head of Samuel Clemens, beaming down on him in an admiring way as he said to his brother, "Ah— your child, I presume? Boy or girl?"

In comparing Brigham Young with the old cat, the author of *Roughing It* had perhaps not had in mind the image of the cat who was sacred in Egypt and in other Eastern lands as a watcher over the dead and in Scandinavia as in some other Northern countries was sacred as a watcher over the corn ears lest they should be nibbled away by mice and was revered in particular for its eyes, which were as refulgent with light as the moon. The moon brilliance of the cat's eyes had given rise to the belief that the cat had healing powers.

For a while, he said, with what laconic Samuel Clemens described as the gushing self-sufficiency of youth, he had thought of staying on in the desert kingdom of salt and stone in order to plunge headlong into the work of antipolygamous reform, but that was before he had seen—according to his acidulously comic portrait, which showed largely his own biases—the poor, ungainly, and pathetically homely wives who were the wives of Brigham Young. Soon thinking better of his original sentiment, however, and not succumbing to the temptation to allow his head to be ruled by his heart, he had observed, regarding Brigham Young and the number of wives who were rumored to be his: "No—the man that marries one of them had done an act of Christian charity which entitles him to the kindly applause of mankind, not their harsh censure—and the man that marries sixty of them had done a deed of open-handed generosity so sublime that the nation should stand uncovered in his presence and worship in silence."

The gentlemen Orion and Samuel Clemens—the latter no child, although he had wished to seem more naïve than he was, possibly an "innocent abroad" in his own country—had at least in retrospect seemed to believe, when the news could have come as no news to them, the tales of Mormon violence that they had heard during their last night in Great Salt Lake City when they had sat smoking their pipes in a den of Gentiles and had been told how heedless people who came into Utah and made remarks against Brigham Young or his polygamous society were likely to disappear during the night and be found the next morning lying in a back alley, contentedly waiting for the hearse.

Their Gentile hosts had told Orion and his brother Samuel—the former Mississippi River boat pilot who had known the ever-shifting river from the ruins of Nauvoo downward to St. Louis, port city to the land of the Missouri mule skinners from which the Mormon polygamists who had already been driven from Ohio had been driven as from Iowa and Illinois—that Brigham Young's Lion House or hennery in Utah contained twenty or thirty wives, each with her children, amounting to about fifty altogether.

This number must have been by a rough count in a kingdom of so many mysteries as this which was headed by the great Golden Lion of Judah or Archer of God. And this was a kingdom in which not even the poorest Mormons and their wives and children starved while only the rich ate well. The Clemens brothers had not been given the opportunity of eating at the table of the very fatherly and motherly Brigham Young, so they had had to depend upon the eyewitness account given to them by a Gentile by the name of Johnson as to what the domestic life was like in the inner sanctum of the Lion House.

This fictional Mr. Johnson, who was evidently Samuel Clemens's alter ego, had told a preposterous tale regarding a sociable breakfast that he had enjoyed with Mr. Young in the general dining room in the Lion House. The only carnage that had occurred was when after the calling of the roll the buckwheat cakes were brought in for serving to the children—and one could imagine that they were stacked up as tall as towers upon the platters and were dripping with butter and honey as if they were manna that had come down from the clouds. But the fields from which the buckwheat cakes were made had been planted by the Mormons themselves when they were a starving tent people in this desert wild where there was no water.

How much different the plenitude of children running around like chicks all over the place in the hennery of which Mr. Young was chanticleer must have seemed to the Clemens brothers Orion and Samuel from the lives of poor children who slept in gutters in many industrial cities and who on lonely farms were often stamped down into clay and mud by their parents in the struggle for survival and many of whom were now being orphaned by the Civil War, in which the territories took no part, although in these far regions the red men with their remnant tribal family systems were being cut down and their children made into orphans by the same regiments that would like to turn their bird shot upon the Mormon flocks as of old.

But Mr. Johnson was not the kind of equable newshound who was capable of pointing this out to the travelers listening in the Gentile den, the younger with his dream of finding a mine of silver—he would have settled for gold or lead or any other metal—in order that he might enjoy a butterfly existence in San Francisco, but such was not to be his—the only veins from which he might drain the wealth being those of his comic sense.

[39]

As a matter of record, Brigham Young once stated that his formal education in a schoolhouse had not exceeded a period of eleven days—and yet he was the deviser of a system of education by which the children of the Mormon faith could be taught in such a way that they could take full advantage of their native gifts, whatever they were. When he was a little boy he had been so poor that he had carried his shoes in his hands, wearing them like gloves until he reached the church door, where he would put his shoes on his feet rather than enter a place of worship with his bare feet exposed before the altar of God.

His mother had died of tuberculosis when he was still quite young, and he was left to the care of a sister who had carried him on her hip when he was a baby and to whom he had remained very close—almost as if the two were interrelated as one, he and the sister who was the repetition of the dead mother's image.

Once when the wiry old man had gone away in search of work by which to bring grain for the feeding of these two children who were the last of the large Young flock still living with him, he who had expected to return with the setting sun had been delayed for almost three days, during which the two children would have starved if it had not been for the brave little Brigham Young's taking his father's rifle down from a wall and going out into the snow where he had spotted a robin redbreast upon whom he had placed his bead—shooting it undoubtedly without knowledge that the breast of this little bird had turned red with grief on the day that Christ was killed. He had brought the slain robin into the cabin and laid it on a table and defeathered it and wrapped it in a little shroud made of old flour leavings and water and put it into a little pan or coffin for baking into a little pie, which the children had eaten. And no doubt when the old father with his beard frozen onto his face came home at last with grain, he had found them both chirruping.

Toward his children even before he became a Mormon of that pluralistic religion in which monogamy was replaced by polygamy, Brigham Young had shown infinite care for their material and spiritual welfare. There was scarcely a town or village in any part of northwestern New York that did not have marks of his craftsmanship—a window glazed by him or a door carved by him or a fireplace carved by him or a stairway—all of most excellent skill—nothing dishonest in his joinings of beams—all as he had promised—no roof falling down before it was pitched up.

He had painted Easter eggs to hide in the hay for his little daughters to find, and never did they run around in rags and tatters like the poor little Mormon children hiding themselves away in haystacks when the Gentile raiders came to set fire to haystacks or pitch little Mormon children upon their pitchforks into the fires, which kept on burning like stars in the midst of waters.

One of the resolutions that Brigham Young had made after his conversion over to the Mormon flock was that never again would he do any work that would increase the wealth of Gentiles by even one dollar—all the dollars which he might earn must be for the increase and benefit of the Mormon Church of Jesus Christ of Latter-Day Saints, whose property, time and again, would be stolen from them.

Regarding polygamy, Brigham Young once confessed that when he first heard that it was to replace monogamy, he had been filled with such a dread sense of apprehension that he had felt he would rather be wrapped in his caul and placed in his coffin and carried on his bier to his grave than have to assume responsibility for the feeding of many wives, many children.

Brigham Young's geography was that in which polygamy was the Great Divide marking the difference between his former life and his life as a believer in the New Dispensation.

. . .

ALL THAT MR. JOHNSON, Samuel Clemens's alter ego and comic mask concealing the tragic mask of the future Mark Twain, for whom all forms of human idealism, whether of institutions or men—all sacred cows were flawed, insubstantial, subjected to shattering as into dust and ashes, and they included eleemosynary utopias such as that of the Mormons—had based on his own superficial recollections of what the affable Mr. Young had sighingly confided to him. The great question seemed to be: Was Mr. Young happy among so many wives?

It appeared that he was not, if one may believe what Mr. Johnson said to Samuel Clemens, Orion's little brother or sister who had heard earlier in the evening from the other Gentiles in their den of happiness of the Mormon elders who—greedy as big fat toads—could take all the women of all ages from a family, ranging from the old grandmother down to the little granddaughter, and then take all the men because of their belief that the brightest stars in heaven would be theirs—no one knowing in advance of the experience, of course, whether these stars gleaming in the meteor's tail would be extremely cold or extremely hot.

Mr. Young had bent Mr. Johnson's listening tin ear by pouring into it the confession that life was a sad, sad thing—for the joy of every marriage which he contracted with a new bride was so often blighted by the inopportune funeral of a less recent bride.

One of Father Brigham Young's letters to a Mormon farmer who—it would someday be divulged—had written to him of the hard times that were his daily lot as he was always bent over digging, digging, digging so that he had felt as if he were being killed, was that as his two or three wives who might have good reason for wanting to kill him had not been able to do so, then nothing could kill him and he should stop pitying himself and should keep on digging, dropping his turnip seeds for the glory of the Lord. Or words to that effect.

Father Young also had to keep close track of the tenth of their products that the Mormons brought to the Tithing House, without which their names were struck off the rolls of the saved by the recording angels who watched over such contributions and their nature as to whether they were real or false.

The depressing situation that Mr. Johnson had seen enacted before his eyes was that in which the ever-hopeful and not easily despairing Mr. Young had been set upon by one of the Mrs. Youngs rushing in and demanding a breast pin such as she had just found out he had given to another of his wives, Number 6. It evidently had amused Mr. Johnson or Samuel Clemens to label Mr. Young's wives as if they were spools of silk or some other merchandise—perhaps piled up in some great, shadowy, dimly outlined warehouse where would be galaxies of stars brighter than most seen on earth, a crown of stars for the Mormon head as for other elders of the Church of Zion when they passed through the Pearly Gates.

What Mr. Johnson had beheld with his own eyes and not with somebody else's eyes and what he had reported in an irrational language beyond summary in a rational language might well strike man's funny bone as a scene of comic chaos very much like that of a wandering puppet show such as Punch and Judy or Noah's Ark or Jack and Jill.

Mr. Young had promised to that other Mrs. Young a breast pin which would be the same as that first one, which he had bought for Number 6, but then when the news got out had been set upon by Mrs. Youngs of various numbers wave after wave with tempests of tears spilling upon him—weepings and wailings and gnashings of teeth—until altogether he had had to promise breast pins to all twenty-nine of his spouses as the price for the restoration of peace.

He had pointed out to the masked Mr. Johnson—the future Mark Twain—that what he had just witnessed was a specimen of his life. It had truly seemed that a man could not be wise all the time. He had poured into what could be called Mr. Johnson's tin ear his confession that in a heedless moment he had given to his darling Number 6 a breast pin of which the apparent value was only twenty-five dollars, but of which the ultimate cost was inevitably bound to be a good deal more. "You yourself have seen it climb up to six hundred and fifty dollars—and alas, even that is not the end."

He stated to any man who was not of the polygamous faith the doubtless awesome fact that he had wives all over the territory of Utah, dozens of wives whose numbers he did not know without looking in the family bible. "They are scattered far and wide among the mountains and valleys of my realm. And mark you," he had continued to the future Mark Twain, "every one of them will hear of this wretched breast pin, and every last one of them will have one or die." So that altogether the breast pin which he had bought for Number 6 would cost him twenty-five hundred dollars. And if these creatures got together to compare their glass gems and if one was found to be a shade finer than the rest, then they would all be thrown back upon his hands so that he would have to order a new lot of glass gems in order to keep the peace in his family. So that with his troubles seeming never to end, it was no wonder if eternal vigilance must be his.

The lion who was the paw of all the babes who were laid between his paws had also told the woeful, doleful, and curiously symbolic tale of a gentleman who once when passing through Salt Lake City had given to one of the children of Brigham Young a tin whistle, which had seemed to him a veritable invention of Satan, an unspeakable horror as his listener would understand when he related the troubles caused in his house by a child's having in his mouth a tin whistle of which the number must be multiplied because of the number of little mouths in a polygamous commune.

Foreseeing what was now to occur, the lion had thirsted for vengeance. "I ordered out a flock of destroying angels, and they hunted the man far into the fastnesses of the Nevada mountains. But they never caught him. I am not cruel, sir—I am not vindictive except when sorely outraged—but if I had caught him—so help me Joseph Smith—I would have locked him into the nursery till the brats whistled him to death."

He had been able to make the jealous mothers of the other children believe that it was not he who had given out the one tin whistle to the one child. There were a hundred and ten children in the house then—some were now away at college—and he had had to order a hundred and ten tin whistles, which had made such a shrieking noise that he and the other adults in his flock had had to talk on their fingers entirely from that time until the children got tired of their whistles. "And if ever another man gives a whistle to a child of mine and I get my hands on him, I will hang him higher than Haman! That is the word with the bark on it! Shade of Nephi!"

As for married life, Brigham Young's complaint was that it was a perfect dog's life. "You can't economize. It isn't possible." There were also such overwhelming expenses as those for wash bills, which literally caused Brigham Young to weep—expenses for cradles, vermifuge, soothing syrup, teething rings, papa's watches for the babies to play with, things to scratch the furniture with, lucifer matches for the little ones to eat, pieces of glass to cut themselves with. The item of glass alone, he had ventured to say, would have supported Mr. Johnson's family.

Rather than keep thousands of dollars tied up in the purchase of seventy-two bedsteads when the money should have been put out to earn interest, Brigham Young had sold the entire lot at a loss and had built one bedstead seventy feet long and ninety-six feet wide. But the bedstead had been a failure, for he could not sleep, all the seventy-two women who were draped on either side of him snoring so loudly that the roar had been deafening. "And then the danger of it! . . . They would all draw in their breath at once, and you could actually see the walls swell out and strain and hear the rafters crack and the shingles grind together."

Samuel Clemens had had a difficult time skimming over the Mormon bible, of which he had brought away a copy from the kingdom. So far as he was concerned, the Mormon bible was a curiosity, a pretentious affair, so slow and sleepy that it seemed only an insipid mess of inspiration. "It is chloroform in print."

To him, the imaginary history with its use of the Old Testament as a model and its plagiarism of the New Testament was a mongrel—half-modern glibness and half-ancient simplicity and gravity. Whenever things were growing too modern, and that was every sentence or two, Joseph Smith had ladled in—the image suggesting that of an iron ladler—a few such scriptural phrases as "exceeding sore" and "it came to pass." " 'And it came to pass' was his pet," wrote Johnson.

Clemens's belief was that Brigham Young (the Utah head) had been responsible for grafting the polygamous branch onto the murdered Joseph Smith's tree of life. But yet he was never one to advocate that the Mormon utopias should be driven off the face of the earth and into the sea, as was urged by some of the Gentile anti-Mormons.

Upon the publication of *Roughing It* in the *Atlantic Monthly* in its June 1872 issue, Twain had received high praise from his friend William Dean Howells, son of an old-time Ohio millennialist of brilliant mind and liberal views who genuinely believed that he would see the endless rainbow like a bridge overarching this world when the storms of life were over. "The grotesque exaggeration and broad irony with which the life is depicted are conjecturally the truest colors that could have been used"—William Dean Howells had offered a nosegay to the often clowning Mark Twain, his friend and neighbor who had come to the East out of the West—"for all existence there must have looked like an extravagant joke, the humor of which was only deepened by its nether side of tragedy."

[4 0]

IT WAS ALWAYS because of their success that the Mormons were threatened by the Gentiles. When Karl Marx with his memories of the Manchester Mormon "millennialists" whose street-corner sermons and wild trumpetings by angelic trumpeters, among them Brigham Young—he with his sensitive ears could not have ignored them when he was visiting Engels—finally got around to looking through the Mormon bible—could one look through it?—he had found it very difficult to understand and for the reason that there was not a spark of sense in it.

The murder of Joseph Smith and his brother Hyrum, who had been left unprotected in the prison at Carthage through the harmonious agreement of Governor Thomas Ford of Illinois and Governor Lillburn W. Boggs of Missouri—who had issued an extermination order against all Mormons in that state, this tool pattern for the illegal lynch murder which was permitted or instigated by the legal authorities themselves and which had been used before and would be used again, always with variation depending upon the time and the place—could have come as no surprise to such far distant analysts as Marx and Engels, joint authors of *Dialectical Materialism,* which was published in the same year as the death of Joseph Smith with all his utopian burdens upon him.

The death of Joseph the clubfooted came as no surprise to the imprisoned prophet, although he had hoped to the last moment for rescue. But the messenger who was supposed to give his message asking for the Mormons to come to his rescue had forgotten to pass it on until the death of the head of the Mormon church had occurred. The messenger's forgetfulness had been deliberate. But the memory of Joseph Smith would remain forever alive and green.

As for Wilhelm Weitling, who while in Nauvoo had acquainted himself with the history of this martyrdom, he was to have ample occasion to identify himself with it when he lost out in his own far western communes and wished that there had been an angel Moroni to protect him and had seemed under pressure to forget that yet no angel had protected Joseph Smith at the last from the howling mob.

Returning to New York by way of the Allegheny Mountains, which in the 1870s would become the scene of the execution of the Molly Maguires at the behest of the coal barons where no corn grew, Weitling had spoken wherever he could upon his own form of cooperative communism, which he held to contain the alpha and omega with all the letters in between for the redemption of suffering humanity.

The journey to the western utopian wilderness scout Wilhelm had returned from was a journey from which many who went would never return. At the old Shakespeare Hotel facing upon the original Astor House—home of the money king—Weitling had appeared as star speaker at a banquet in honor of revolutionary socialists and labor union men.

Presiding at the banquet table with its tall candles gleaming with flames which were reflected upon the wineglasses had been August Willich, a Prussian army officer who had fallen away from Marx because of some utopian dreams of his own.

As Marx had expressed himself in a letter to Joseph Weydemeyer—he who had once returned for him to the pawnshop the little silver fork and knife in a case and other little silver pieces which had belonged to his little daughter Jenny's tea set and who was now planning to sail from the Old World to the New World—what he had heard about Herr Willich and other members of the *Lumpenbundenbunde,* a band of rascally dogs, had caused him to draw a portrait far from flattering.

Willich was, in spite of his philistine-aristocratic, Spartan-broth non-commissioned officer's hypocritical airs, a thoroughly ordinary cardsharp, four-flusher, false gambler. Marx was sure that Willich—in common with other mounted knights of his kind—was determined to lead a free life at the expense of the public.

It seemed altogether fitting and proper that the actor Weitling, for whom the earthly paradise or utopia should be achieved and solidified through the act of one largely intuitive man, should have appeared at the old Shakespeare as the red-faced, sunburned, windburned speaker in the dining room at the long table decorated from head to foot with tiny red flags and little bunches of red rosebuds and red geraniums. There had been red flags stuck into the body of a roast pig.

Brother Weitling had presented to Brother Willich a secondhand sword that he had purchased from a pawnshop at Union Square, where its previous owner had not come to redeem it, which with appropriate flourishes he had handed over to Brother Willich with the rasping reminder that Jesus Christ had come to bring not peace but a sword to the revolutionary workers of the world who were awakening to their rights in all countries.

Frederick Engels would someday liken Wilhelm Weitling to a medieval Christian to whom Willich and other members of his ill-fated clique had added a fanatic Islamic element which had overlooked the laws of historical development.

The flaming speech at the old Shakespeare by the former bastard tailor of Magdeburg commanded by his enormous enthusiasm of enlarged vision the respect of those who heard his voice, and yet there had arisen in the minds of some of them who included agnostics, skeptics, unabashed materialists of almost every color imaginable in the present spectrum the question had Brother Weitling been blown out of his bird or off his branch—in his case because of old Christian theologies of which he could not or would not divest himself.

Why must he insist upon the image of the first proletaire as that of Jesus Christ who was crucified on Golgotha because of the gospel he had preached for the benefit of the poor and the oppressed? Did he not know that Prometheus upon the rock had been of the same godhead—as shown by Hegel, who had abandoned the New Testament as a texture made of messianic myths and miracles—whereas the many-eyed Prometheus had been the noblest of saints and martyrs, as it was he who had brought fire to earth in his rebellion against Zeus and had transmitted that fire into knowledge?

The trouble with Brother Weitling, in the view of many of the revolutionary German labor union heads, was that his emotional spoutings had made him sound and look like a Methodist preacher promising heaven's fire to his followers and hell's fire to those who disregarded the word of Christ, just as he had complained of Wilhelm Keil, the former tailor from Darmstadt whom he had first seen in Kentucky where taking on the local religious color Keil had picked up the inflammatory vocabulary of old-time tent meeting evangelists and whom Weitling had later encountered again keeling around in the Missouri pulpit, where he seemed to think that he himself was Mr. Christ and that his wife was Mrs. Christ, and who with his mystical sect of communitarians was to give up his land in Bethel—named after Christ's Missouri birth or manifestation—for a new location in the far Northwest which offered greater promises.

One of Keil's most attractive ways had been to welcome into his communitarian society all who had faith in the redeeming powers of Christ—he had asked not whether they were skilled or unskilled. Keil's leading of his religious-minded and yet secular communitarians in a line of twenty-four wagons upon the two-thousand-mile journey which he began at Bethel toward the end of May 1853 was one of the saddest of the utopian uprootings and journeys to the farther West there ever was and could not altogether be explained, for the communities at Bethel, Elim, Hebron, and Nineveh had not been financially bankrupt and had made a fortune in the annual output of kid gloves and had owned steam-driven plants and sawmills and barns in which had been housed the cows that gave the sweet-smelling milk—and there had been churns for the churning of butter and there had been beehives for the making of honey.

Perhaps one of the reasons for Keil's moving was that like many in search of the earthly paradise he had an itchy foot. Brother Weitling's recollection was that he, whose Catholic sentiments were never wholly to depart from him, had seen Keil shouting himself hoarse as he pounded upon his pulpit and leapt around like a mad hyena in his cage while speaking in a very ungrammatical way the message of the thirteenth Corinthians but without any encompassing sense of unity or unification.

JOSEPH WEYDEMEYER had helped to transcribe for the printer the *Dialectical Materialism* of Marx and Engels. He had had no difficulty in reading the openly bold handwriting by Engels but had had to look through a magnifying glass to try to figure out the marginal notes and corrections written by Marx—scratchings sometimes as difficult to read as might have been made by the feelers of a spidery crab who had walked through no marsh pools but pools of black ink.

Weydemeyer was up to his ears himself in the mud and muck and about to croak because of his slanderers—and they were all the German exiles who disagreed with him in any way—Willich, for example, was a communist Cromwell, just as the revolutionary soldier Weitling with his red cap and his red flags pinned all over his coat and his red rosettes on his red shoes and his secondhand pawnshop sword and his evangelical pamphlets was certainly the clown, the fool, the wild card who had jumped out of the Marxist card game and now was doing great harm to the rational development of Marxist communism in America.

Upon Weydemeyer, the future colonel in the Civil War in Missouri on the Union side, Marx had pinned his faith as a leader in the haphazardly concerted movements of German communal workers against the perverse derelict Weitling with his piecemeal proposals of one coat for all mankind. The trouble was that Weitling was beginning to believe or had always believed in his own powers to evoke miracles and seemed impervious to the discouragements he had so far suffered. He was, after all, the builder of a beaver dam for which he seemed to give no one credit but himself.

But should the principles espoused by Marx be sacrificed to a madcap joker who knew all the answers to all the questions even before they were asked?

That which Brother Weitling proposed was that America should be transformed into a vast empire made entirely by workers. And there should loom upon this continent a great pyramid, a social and moral and economic structure for the benefit of the cooperative workers at every level from the bottom to the top and the top to the bottom and thus very different from the pyramids of capitalism rearing up in this millennial world and built to resemble in many and possibly unseen ways those of ancient Egypt where the few pharaohs were at the top and the vast masses of wage slaves were at the bottom, some under the mud.

Mr. Owen had wished to reverse the pyramid, to place the many workers at the top and the industrial and agrarian and other pharaohs at the bottom.

As to the crazy clown Brother Weitling, however, the suspicion was that he was determined to be at the top, ruling over the workers at the bottom—and yet his interest in utopian settlements that should be exemplars of the efficiency of his ideals had combined with his encouragement of the then awakening but still puny labor unions of workers of various crafts who were striking for living wages.

Among the many attacks pouring like hot shots and cold shots upon poor Brother Weitling was that of an anti-Weitling German labor paper in Ohio, the editor of which was glad that most Americans did not read the German language and thus were spared the knowledge of the works of this dictator and savior whose promises to establish a blood-red republic inside the democratic nation would have driven them to the conclusion that Germany, when she exiled such madmen as this Weitling, must have been emptying all her insane asylums onto the American shores.

And thus he had not been able to organize the workers' party he had in mind as that which would include utopian cooperative colonies as well as labor unions made of tailors and shoemakers and winders of sweet-smelling cigars who believed in the messages conveyed by his socialistic *Die Republik der Arbeiter* (*The Workers' Republic*), which was the compass and the heart of his revolutionary movement for his Noah's Ark, to which he had welcomed all who paid their dues and their insurance program, a guarantee of protection against the ravagements of fire and flood and sickness and old age and death itself—his Noah's Ark which was the entire continent or the whole world as once was said of Robert Owen's vision of Noah's Ark.

Even when Weitling's communal disciples throughout the land had decreased in number, there were still those with unshaken faith in his redemptive power. A friend from Switzerland who had become a tanner in Kalamazoo, Michigan—and still cherished his faith in Brother Weitling's power to be the helmsman of a revolutionary movement that, it had been foreseen and foretold, would bring poor workingmen into the earthly paradise or halcyon state which would prevail when Weitling had established and made real the one big union, which now, however, seemed to be only a foggy, foggy dream in his mind and very far from imminent realization—had asserted his faith in him over all other rival German leaders, such as the anti-Weitling Weydemeyer, by sending him thirty golden calf skins of which he was to sell one half to the burgeoning union of the shoemakers of New York and return the profit to him and keep the other half as his contribution to *Die Republik der Arbeiter.*

To Weydemeyer, Weitling's proposals for revolutionary socialism according to his style—as expressed in *Die Republik der Arbeiter*—made that publication something so prehistorical that it would have attracted the interest of no one but an archaeologist who might preserve a copy in a museum. Yet in spite of the underminings of Weitling's utopian Castle Nowhere or Castle Somewhere—whichever it was—there were and would continue to be to the end those who, like the tanner who sent him thirty calf skins, still had believed in his redemptive powers which would bring the dead world into flower through the words spread by his *Republik der Arbeiter.*

To a German immigrant returning to New York harbor after sixteen months in Europe, *Die Republik der Arbeiter,* as he wrote to Brother Weitling before continuing to St. Louis, could only be compared with the beautiful snowdrop, the flower that delighted and refreshed the friend of nature as it raised its head above the icy plain. "Carry on, restless warrior, even though the road be rough and full of thorns—at its end you will find the most beautiful palm which a victor has ever received—you will live on in the grateful hearts of millions of workers."

While the great Jupiter who was Marx had been inspiring thunderbolts against the fool Weitling, who had only a little spark of flame in his box, yet perhaps this disciple of Icarus, as he was sometimes called—although he was the disciple of no one but himself with his positive instincts—could still encourage the buds of reform, even though seeming to jeerers and sneerers a mere clown, a wanderer to and fro and up and down. He was accused of being centered wholly upon his own demented self and warped ego and of living far beyond his means while accusing others of making no such sacrifices as he made.

[4 1]

WHAT HAD KILLED Brother Weitling, what had consigned him to oblivion, had been the continued accusations that the *Arbeiterverein* funds which he had invested in the harebrained schemes for utopia in Iowa had never been repaid by him as they should have been. How could he return to the brothers their money, however, as the colonists in Iowa had paid but little for the support of the *Arbeiterverein* to which many workers belonged and which they would not live to see, for the very good reason that the shaking community could not stand on its feet and the water dam that he had built had collapsed and many barns remained without roofs and his central treasury in New York had shrunk to such an extent that it had no money of any kind with which to make good on old promises—no more resources than dead butterflies folded in dead cocoons upon dead tree boughs?

Although he was able to prove to a judge in Dubuque that he had not misappropriated the *Arbeiterverein* funds by his refusal to turn over to the rival heads in Communia the forty acres of mill land, which represented the investments made by him in the name of the *Arbeiterverein,* there was a plot to have him arrested as an embezzler.

On returning to Iowa for settlement of claims, he had not gone farther than Dubuque, so never again saw Communia. As to the losses that were suffered by some who had placed their stock in Communia, he was deeply regretful but could not feel guilt.

"Forget that we once had brothers in Communia," he had advised the dwindling ranks of the faithful. They should remember how many losses of elephants and men had been suffered by Hannibal before he finally triumphed over Rome—patience was required. So far as Weitling was concerned, the members of the *Arbeiterverein* had not been the losers of an earthly paradise.

Certainly he who would have been the tailor king had Communia succeeded—had it not been overshadowed by the losses suffered by Étienne Cabet and the death of Joseph Smith in the jail at Carthage and the dispersal of the remnants of the Mormons—must now suffer the ignominy of being a rags and patches tailor.

Upon the cobwebbed window of his shop in New York was hung a sign advertising Zion—and it was apparent that although his face was streaked with tallow and his sleeves were streaked with chalk marks, he was still in quest of a better world, although perhaps only in lands of dreams. He still wore a red cap when at his work and red shoes.

Friedrich Engels was to recall in 1885 when the name of Wilhelm Weitling had been forgotten—he was that forgotten man who should be called the unforgettable forgotten man, of whom, of course, the number could be beyond number, for the grassy ways of socialism were studded with these red caps coming up in the spring after a long winter's sleep under the grassless ways—that when the author of *Gospel of the Poor Sinner* had first dealt himself out of the Marxist card game he was already in his own mind the great man who carried a recipe for the realization of heaven on earth ready-made in his pocket and was convinced that everybody intended to steal it from him.

It was plain to those who were his Marxist watchers in America that he had been unable to get along with anyone in a cooperative joint stock company like that which had fallen to pieces in Iowa, where, as was often said, the winters were as cold as those in the Siberian wasteland and from where he had withdrawn because he could not be the total despot.

So far as Marx was concerned, if the hysterical fool Weitling and other fools of his brand had succeeded in spreading their earthly paradises—if they had not been divided as in Iowa by their own anarchic sectarianism causing splits from within—the so-called communitarians would have lived under a repressive system worse than any ever imposed by the most cruel czar over his serfs.

Jumping out of Communia, Weitling upon his return to the lower Broadway of a thousand babbling tongues had returned to a linguistic project—the devising of a universal language. He had grown a red geranium in a pot on the sill inside his window that was to remind him that he had been the crushed geranium. He had also been treated as if he were the mad dog. Sleeping in a crescent position on his mattress on the floor at night, the deposed would-be tailor-king who had turned tailor once again had given himself over to the memories of mother and child that had accompanied him in his quest for the ideal utopian state that had seemed both motherhood and fatherhood to him, as it would seem or be to all the lost children of God.

Perhaps—as Marx once observed—when the projects for reform carried on by an essential philistine failed in the outer world, they crept back into his mind for solutions only in his dreams. Weitling had remained seethingly enraged by the failure of Marx and Engels to publicize his universal language, the discovery or invention of which had required his ranging through vast geological layers—in a subjective sense only and not an objective sense—of earth forms, mineral forms, plant forms, which his universal language would provide the key for the opening of the door of pure reason.

The bride whom Weitling chose to be his bride was a very loving, quiet girl who was half his age and the eldest daughter of a former locksmith from Wittenberg in Mecklenburg-Schwerin over whose door hung a huge iron lock and who had come to this country by sailing vessel in 1852 and had settled on a farm near Utica—burial place of the sacred stone of the

Oneida Indians and other Mohawk relics, in Herkheimer County, where there were many old Mecklenburgers—and had bought with his hard-earned savings a small farm where he had grown apples and corn and had practiced his various labor crafts, including the making of iron keys for whose who wanted to lock the doors of their barns after the horse was stolen, probably never before.

Caroline Todt was a very helpful girl who knew how to pick apples, shoo the ducks down the lane to their pond, was an excellent seamstress and knew how to make cloth shoes, red shoes—and added to the family treasury her self-help as the elder daughter who earned her room and board and fifty pennies a week as an apprentice to a milliner in Utica for the purpose of learning to make straw bonnets. That she was a straw-bonnet maker and that the former utopian head Brother Weitling had devised a method for ironing the straw for the poke bonnet could not have accounted for the feeling of instant recognition which he felt for her when they first met—nor could the domestic talents for which she was well known, such as leading ducks to ponds or feeding chickens in a yard—there would not be much chance for her to exhibit such talents in New York unless she should be a duck stealer or a chicken stealer in the muddy lanes around City Hall where the duck and chicken thieves did flourish like the Utopian thieves who might steal a man's utopian scroll.

The girl certainly had a wonderful way with the sick and the old, a feeling of compassion for those who might be wounded or might be approaching their end upon life's road, people who like Brother Weitling himself might have lost their mizzenmast and sail when their ship was blown down in a storm—might have lost all their sails and shrouds, might have been loaded with anchors so that they could not go skyward but must go earthward and must drown before reaching the end of a journey which should have had no ending.

It was while Caroline had been visiting the home of her Uncle John on lower Manhattan island in order to take care of his sick wife, Mathilde, that the former tailor king had caught his first glimpses of her as she moved back and forth with her bandages and her bottles in the workshop in the home on the Bowery near river and ocean where he frequently dropped in for passage of a lonely hour or two in the company of the uncle who loved the music of horn and harp and fiddle as much as he did and whose exquisite trade was that of making and gilding and binding gilt-edged pages into calfskin bindings for the books for the private libraries of rich tycoons such as Astors and Vanderbilts for whom the coverings were sometimes more important than the contents had been. The salt atmosphere had been filled with the smell of golden calf skins and little specks of gold like mica forming around dust motes as they dripped from the gilder's brushes and brooms, some showering onto Brother Weitling's coat as his attention became utterly magnetized by the ministrations of the angelic girl who had come from the Old World to the New World as he had and who represented evidently some kind of unity that would bind together his broken parts and provide an unbroken linkage or chain—a chain of being that would unite his past and present and future.

In fact, he was still working on and would continue to work on his lost sweetheart poems as on his universal language, which would provide the key to the mysteries of the queen of the sciences and which had led him to a study not only of the earth but of the heavens and to the challenge of Copernicus in favor of Ptolemy and to a sharp-bladed attack upon the law of gravity as it had been worked out by the very unworldly Sir Isaac Newton, who had been such a small baby when he was born that he could have been enclosed in a half-pint bottle.

Once when Newton was away from his astronomical laboratory, he had returned to find that his little poodle dog Diamond had torn into shreds and eaten up part of his map showing distant star points. Perhaps God was punishing him for his neglect of God. He had picked up his poodle from its basket and had brushed its curls with his loving hand as he—not shouting in anger—had whispered serenely, consolingly, "Ah, little Diamond! Diamond! Thou dost not know the harm which thou hast done." Some corner of the universe had been made into pulp. He had left it so.

Brother Wilhelm Weitling had shown himself to be no robber bridegroom but a very proper tailor when he had asked for and had received from the farmer and iron locksmith in the apple-growing Herkheimer County the hand of his elder daughter in marriage—and thus had saved her from what might have been the life of an old maid whose father had scared a demon lover away and who would become as sour and puckered and bitter as the one green apple which was never picked from the Eden tree.

[4 2]

IN COMING BACK from Utica to New York, Brother Weitling might have seemed to be taking the road away from his quest for the earthly paradise, which had led him into the wilderness where he had hoped to find or found a land that—like that described in a third-century Greek philosopher's utopian dream—would be a land of such plenty that the oat cakes and wheat cakes would do battle with each other to see which could get first into voracious mouths.

The happy couple who were bound in that wedlock which some people called bedrock had returned to the tailoring shop where he with his key had opened the door to the treasure box of his wife's womb at the same time that he continued with his work upon the philanthropic universal language that sounded much like babbling baby tongues—as well it should, for there would be added to their household the mouths of his children whom the mother and the father had to feed, their number to increase until there were five sons and one daughter.

Besides babblings and cryings of baby tongues, there were purrings of cats' tongues, cats' tails, and cats' eyes casting their reflections upon the white plastered wall, which was streaked with firelight and shadows and would be increasingly hung with star maps as time went forward in an objective sense if not in a subjective sense. There were litters of flower-faced kittens who had to be fed crumbs and milk. If the old mother cat in her basket had ever happened to give birth to a litter of kittens at the same time one of Weitling's sons was being born, it could have been remembered by him that he had been conceived in a church which had been used by animals and that, according to Catholic mythologies which would always cling to his mind, there had been a cat giving birth to a litter of kittens at the same time that the Virgin Mary was in the hay giving birth to the Son of Man. There were also the singings of birds. For Weitling's pets were canaries hanging in their cages from the ceiling, all singing in harmony with the purring cats and the baby tongues and the tough-necked old rooster and the clucking hens who would soon find their way to the iron pot for broth for baby soup.

Once this good German father who seemed to be living in a Hans Christian Andersen fairy-tale world with his cats and his birds and his little babies had come upon a group of ragamuffins who—in imitation of the city fathers with their cruelty dispensing itself alike to tramps and mad dogs—were beating to death with sticks and stones an old dog cornered in a blind alley—the blood spouting from his eyes, an ear hanging by a thread, a broken paw, some of his joints broken, legs broken. His had been a lonely bark, probably the only bark left in him.

Weitling had reached down into his pocket which had few spare dimes and had given to the savage street boys the one thin dime that would have been theirs if they had turned the dead dog over to the dustman who with his old gray horse and old gray dust wagon came diurnally to carry away the bodies of dead cats, dead dogs, dead tramps to what should have been their final resting place.

Weitling had carried the bleeding tramp dog home for Mrs. Weitling, who combined her nursing arts with those of a seamstress and tailor's aid to nurse back to health, clean the dust and sand and grit out of the inflamed eyeballs and many wounds and place upon them a healing balm, stitch back into place a torn ear which had been hanging like an old cocoon upon a few silken cobwebs—no butterflies in it—mend the wounded paw and tailbone, put the broken limbs into splints just as she also mended the wounded, often splintered ego of her husband when possible and when not possible waited for it to mend itself.

He had named the mongrel, who was made of a variety of mixtures such as man himself might be in the view of antisocialists if such mad-dog anarchists and the clown Wilhelm Weitling took over, by no ordinary name befitting a broken mug but by the French name Filou—and the patched dog was to become the family pet of whom it was never to be recorded that while chasing a shadow or a spot of light upon a wall he inadvertently got into one of Weitling's neatly kept pigeonhole file cases and put into his maw a part of his astronomical star roll on which his master was measuring the dimensions of the universe.

The children were taught to keep their blue bowls turned upward toward the sky, for the ones who kept their blue bowls downward would not get enough manna to keep a dog or a bird alive. The children were generous sharers with each other until they were reduced to little bags of bones hardly worth enough for the great harvester to send to the mill for grinding, even although there were times when there were so few coins in the coin box that their father did not know where the next meal was coming from nor how he should pay the high rent for his tailoring quarters—and this perpetual state which was near bankruptcy was not because of his dumb, dunce-headed inability to earn a living as a tailor but because of his sacrifice of his time to tailoring a new map of the stars.

His wife had not been blindfolded when she married him. She had understood his psychological and cosmic goals and from the very beginning of their marriage had helped to pay the piper's bill by punching buttonholes by hand and also eyelets.

At the suggestion of this loving spouse whose fingers bled as he bled all over from as many darts shot all over him as if he had been in a battle with porcupines, he had worked with infinite patience to design an idea for a machine of which he had had the conception long in his mind, and that was a buttonhole machine for stitching of edges and buttonholes and eyelets and for crimping ribbons and silk and satin cloths and clouds of chiffon for fancy dress balls and regulating the tension of thread.

He had worked on his intricate design for the automatic buttonhole machine—possibly by fits and starts—at the same time that he had worked on the universal baby language, which had awakened again his idea of a new cosmography—that to which he after long wanderings had returned with a particular interest with the birth of his first son.

His wife and her younger sister Johanna—who was not quite half the elder sister's age and had come to assist her through her first moon waxing and would stay on through other moon waxings—had helped to punch and embroider eyelets by hand in such filmy material that it was something like the ectoplasm that had first been touched upon by star needles when this world was first cut out and tailored by whatever creative force there had been and still might be until the end of time.

Weitling's first son had been given by the father the first name William and the second name Wangansky after the Chinese revolutionary leader whose patterns for reforms he believed to be more like his own—stitch by stitch, line by line—than any others he had ever heard of, but Wangansky had seemed a long name for the little boy, so they had dropped the sky out of his name and had called him Wangan. Not wishing to be embarrassed by the Chinese name, which caused other schoolchildren to ask where his pigtail was and at a time when the Chinese in America to whom the father gave his sympathies were less likely to be great mandarins than poor Chinese coolies who were likely to have their pigtails set on fire by such antiyellow mobs as were also persecutors of the blacks and the reds, Wangan had cut off the pig's tail even further by reducing his name to the initial W.

The elder Weitling's interest in the devising of a new astronomical system was something he had been dallying with since he saw his first comet streaking the heavens like a burning pigtail. He had not become seriously involved with his proposal for a new star chart, however, it was hazarded by his brilliantly pinpointing biographer Carl Wittke, until he saw the approaching head of this first son coming out of the mother's womb. His son was to become deeply interested in astronomy himself, although unable to accept his father's somewhat wandering, erratic system, which was tinctured by mythologies and theologies, even as Sir Isaac Newton's had been, and was to write several papers on his own vision of the stars which had been the elder Weitling's hobbyhorse when Wangan was a little child.

The second son had been given the names Gracchus Babeuf Robert, but the burden of two spectral martyrs with whom the father had continued to identify in the spectral-producing fog caused by his revolutionary ideals was someday to divest himself of these bleeding martyrs by calling himself Bob. He was like a bobtailed horse and no Pegasus.

The third son was Tycho Brahe Edward, to be known always as Edward, although he was named for the great Dane—the astronomer, not the dog. The fourth son was Charles Frederick, and the fifth son was Terijon, after Weitling's own mysterious father, Guillaume Terijon, whose death or whose disappearance in *les grandes neiges de Russie* in the senseless Napoleonic invasion was to leave Weitling with the unquiet sense of bastardy that would lead him to search for something royal in his life.

The last of Weitling's children—all gifted—was his one and only daughter, whose name, Caroline Johanna, was the merging of the names of her mother and aunt, who had punched and embroidered the eyelets in bridal veils by their work-worn hands as they listened to his enlightenment of the ways of the stars in the dark opaque which had aroused his interest when he began to pursue the meaning of the word "astronomy," which he had found in the dictionary while pursuing what should be the structure of the universal babbling baby language like that which he would hear in the next several years in his home. She would be the head of the first nursing teachers' clinic at Hunter College.

Although Weitling was to carry on a lifelong business of bombarding the world's great astronomers with requests for their financial or philanthropic help—and obviously, these stargazers who were located in various nations were not members of an astronomers' union, which would be the equivalent of a tailors' union—he could find no help from great scientific heads for the picture of the universe that he gave in his "Mechanic of the Heavens," and none to propagandize—in his waning years as the flame of his life was starting to sputter and burn low—the building of a machine that he called a mechanical Celeste, as it dramatically illustrated to the sensual eyes of men the wheelings of the sun around the wheelings of the earth and showed the sun to be farther away than most astronomers thought it was but left the mother moon undisturbed where she had always been or had seemed to be beyond the bare tree boughs, where she seemed caught but was never caught.

Unfortunately, he could find no capitalist who at this time of boom and bust, when many fields were being opened for the making of money, was willing to invest in his marvelous sewing machine eye-punching device with its capacity for the rapid punching of holes and intricate patterns of roses and lilies and daisies of the fields—no one who seemed to see a future in saving the eyes of poor women.

Brother Weitling's claim that the autonomous buttonhole-punching and embroidery machine was the child of his brain had been based on his claim that it was an improvement over other attachments that had been placed on the market by rival sewing machine companies jousting as in a great tournament which included not only Howe and Singer but a French father charging around with accusations of infringements on their patent rights for this revolutionary machine over which there raged a battle as intense but not so long as the War of Roses before the dust settled for the last time.

As a matter of record: Wilhelm Weitling's application for patent rights was first made in October 1861, along with applications for eight other improvements, of which five received recognition by the United States Patent Office in Washington. It cost him more money than he had in his treasury box.

It certainly took more money to press a lawsuit against infringement of Weitling's patent rights by one or a combination of thieves such as Howe and Singer than to press straw into a poke bonnet or press a pair of pants. And all this at a time when the virulent rumor was being spread by some of the fleeced Icarians that he with his fortune in royalties for his mechanical buttonhole puncher and embroiderer of reeds and roses and swans paid to him by Howe and Singer and other sewing machine heads was living royally—was living as high on the hog as a Wall Street broker, a king of tailors.

But as a matter of fact, he and his heirs to whom would be left a last estate mainly made of his utopia and sewing machine and star maps had received not pecuniary reward as had the devisers of the great Gatling gun and the International Harvester or, as it was sometimes called, ghostly reaper.

[4 3]

THE SALARY that the fallen tailor Weitling had earned for a time during the Civil War as a registrar of immigrants and a translator of the languages of certain of the foreign-born at the Bureau of Immigration in the great harbor city into which Europe was pouring its muddy waters had not been enough with which to promote and protect the marvelously synchronized and peaceful eye-punching and lace embroidery machine with attachments, which was being stolen from him by sewing machine magnates whose realm was extended while his shriveled like the wild ass's skin and whose failure to acknowledge thefts from his map for earth mechanics meant that he would have no paydirt for the feeding of his wife and sister-in-law and children and the little orphan girl who worked for bed and bread and fifty cents a week in his home.

One of the causes for Weitling's short-lived employment as registrar of immigrants at Castle Garden was that the wages of the man who had proposed the wageless society had been ten times smaller than those of a higher officer who left him to do all the work—and this injustice to him could only turn his life on the immigration docks into a mare's nest of snarling rage, had caused him to bare his teeth as he cried out to one of his superiors that he could not do five errands at once and was neither a fool nor his servant and knew more of foreign tongues than he did.

For those who could not write and upon whose hands he placed his hand to guide them in the signing of their names with their long X sign which was like a sign of flight, he wrote to their old folks or wives or sweethearts to say that they had safely arrived and that they would soon be hearing from them again. And some would not live long enough to mail another letter home unless they could find a way to send an angelic messenger with the news—"Oh, Mother, I am dead in a foreign field. My body is eaten away by crows."

Weitling's sympathies with the starving potato-faced migrants had remained so altogether dominant in him that he had refused to participate in what was looked upon as his ritual duty to persuade them that they in their gratitude for having arrived in the land of the free should transfer from the deep holds of immigrant ships to the deep holds of warships for shipment to the Deep South to rescue the black man from chattel slavery by men who had never seen a black man in their lives but the angel of death, who was either black or white or something in between—a gray fog painted on a gray fog.

The revolutionary Weitling had seen the paradoxes and self-contradictions in the Northern conduct of the Civil War, which was fought quixotically against the Southern states for the preservation of a Union that had existed largely in imagination or illusion and would leave this nation still divided into two nations—the house of the few rich and the house of the many poor with the abyss widening between them.

He had never cast a vote and was convinced that both major parties were iridescent bugbears very much like each other in their desire to lead the American people into a bog. He was intellectually lucid, or so it had seemed, but his life was made into an endless misery of nervous disorders—jangling nerves which gave him a pain which only he knew—tangled and broken threads, lost spindles, broken reeds and smashed rosettes and torn cloud film and scraps that were all edges and made him howl with rage and bare his long mule's teeth because of the failure of great moneybags to come to his rescue with their financial help so that this earth mechanic might support his brood while he continued working on his celestial mechanic and developing other ideas such as plans for a flying machine, its gears and parts and some parts not yet perfected in which he would take off from this imperfect world.

Trying his best to lift himself up from the mire so that he could support his version of the celestial mechanic, which could never be wholly rational so long as it was shadowed consciously or unconsciously by the anthropomorphism of the outward-bound voyager, Weitling had suffered great increase of his feelings of frustration, neglect, isolation, and helpless oblivion when the news had been brought to him by an old friend arriving upon the wharf of this harbor city in this time of fratricidal war that the agents of Howe and Singer sewing machines were going all over Germany, with his automatic puncher for buttonholes and eyelets and embroidery needles and reeds springing up wherever they went.

The cost of living had inflated from about a quart-sized balloon to a ton to twelve tons and might go up to twelve hundred tons as time went on, while the treasury that was in his old tin box contained only his sample of each penny issued by the United States Treasury since the nation began, of which the last would be added about a year before he died.

His collection of copperheads had not been enough to buy the piano for which he had yearned with both sides of his broken heart—had not been enough to buy a keyboard with strings and pedals and coffin life which he would have assembled for himself—might have bought only an ebony or ivory key, although he, with his great love of music and his increasingly theosophical visions which had characteristically accompanied star searches and millennial searches upon this dark continent as on other continents, had yearned for a piano which might be given to him as a permanent or temporary gift so that he with his intuitive sense of the harmonies of heaven which he had kept through all discords could work out—as an astronomer and mathematician and cooperative socialist—the relationship of musical bars to colors of planetary bars and star bars that had been sug-gested by Ptolemy in Upper Egypt when he had explored the mysteries of Pythagoras and the doctrine of the transmigration of souls about which one heard so much in America.

When he asked Charles Dana—a Republican then living in the city of Chicago, which was a settlement among the sand dunes—to help with his buttonhole punching device, the answer had been like another coffin nail hammering into him: none of his friends had money for this promotion, and America was not a country that respected inventive genius.

The eye puncher which was promoted by the government in the never-ending Civil War was, of course, the great Gatling gun, which—somewhat erratic but ultimately efficient—was to be turned against black and red and yellow and poor white men in labor wars and was already being turned against the poor.

As the Civil War dragged on, the aging William Jennings Bryan of the *New York Evening Post,* who had been a founder of the Republican party, had relieved himself of his impatience regarding the progress of the war by work in his garden at his idyllic estate overlooking the sailboat-spotted harbor in Roslyn, Long Island, where he had advised the migratory birds to delay the date of their usual departure from the North to the South. "For there is heard the bugle-blast, / The booming gun, the jarring drum, / And on their chargers spurring fast / Armed warriors go and come."

To his old friend August Schilling the quasi-tailor, the quasi-astronomer had written that he was still being cheated out of his patents by Singer and other sewing machine moguls and that he was profoundly aware that whoever was without funds in this country had no chance against those who had funds. "Heaven save humanity from such republics of the money bags," had been his prayer.

The godhead, of course, was supposed to be inside every workingman who had seen streamings of beacon lights through darkness and had known that he was a part of a larger body than his own.

[4 4]

IT WAS A DISTINGUISHED poverty in which Brother Wilhelm Weitling had spent his last years on the top two floors of a thin, high-ribbed house on Essex Street. Sometimes in those waning, darkening, fog-bound years when the skies were streaked with red and black, black veils of chimney smoke trailed over the busy harbor as he dreamed that when his eyelet puncher and embroidery terrestrial machine received pecuniary reward he might devote himself not only to his Venus or moon trap celestial machine as shown on his astronomical blueprint but to the realization of his ever-abiding dream of a perpetual-motion machine—one that when it was once started would come to no halt, no swift or slow or grinding halt, one that might even reproduce and give birth to a new part as a dead part died and fell off—and might realize also his dream of chimneys that might be taught to consume their own smoke and not darken all city lights—but he was hard-pressed to know where to get the money with which to pay for a bag of potatoes or a hog's head with which to feed his family.

The bloody rule of the carpetbaggers who were carrying so many of this nation's treasures and public lands away that they ought to have had carpets hanging from their mouths could have come as no surprise to one who had remained under the spell of Robert Owen's messages to the Chartists—the starving miners and millworkers of England, Ireland, Scotland, and Wales. Weitling's sympathies remained those of a Fenian German, in fact, at a time when so many poor potato-faced Irish—and mainly they were the young—were coming into New York that some people thought it should be called New Cork—and certainly the gutters were rolling with them who had not yet attained the status of the lace-curtain Irish, as probably most never would.

In 1868 the former alpine climber and perhaps only fleeting resurrection of Christ had suffered a most severe accident in a life that had suffered many somatic and psychic accidents—many wounds which he had tried to heal as best he could—and that was a fall on his back on a jagged slab of ice when he had gone out to clear away piles of ice from the yard of his Essex Street home and had stubbed his big toe. There had been no soft feathering of snow to protect his head when he fell, but his head, which contained the refulgent flower of the many-lobed brain, which was the chief flower upon the stalk of his body, had not been injured—the only external suffering was that of a nether part, the big toe.

A first doctor who was called in had washed away the blood of the wounded big toe and had advised rest so that the smashed jointure might knit itself—just hang in there on to the foot to which it belonged. But because of a virus causing the man to swell up so that it had seemed he might burst, a second doctor had been called in and—feeling that there was danger in waiting for time to heal this wound, for the patient might die before the wound was healed—had cut away the big toe with surgical shears and sewed together the sides of the hole where it had been with needle and thread.

The loss of the big toe which was a symbol of manhood had crippled the star voyager as if he who from now on could walk only with the help of his stout cane upon a zigzag course had heard in this harbor a silent ship's bell silently heralding the approach of his death.

His illnesses had immeasurably increased because of this accident, which did reduce his spirit to its lowest burning point as his body minus his big toe which had presumably returned to limbo and had left him with a crippled limb had swollen up with the old king virus in all his mortal cells, the gallbladder trouble which, turning his skin from red to yellow to black to gray like the gray clouds forming around him as his eyes grew dim and his eardrums seemed ready to burst, had affected his drainage pipes and had contributed to his suffering from many debilitating ills, of which he was his own best diagnostician. His wife, who had always had a strong sense of a rescue mission in her character and had followed with him through many snowstorms, had assisted this dying knight by placing over his wounded, breaking, or broken heart mustard poultices and massaging his pain-racked body with its porous pores from which the night sweats poured colder than the ice and snow in the frozen winter world where the cry of the fox was frozen like the bark of a dog.

He had continued to fight on and on for his sewing machine attachment rights and had even offered to come to a compromise with the Singer Sewing Machine Company—which, however, would continue to hum on and on without payment to his widow and children when he had passed on to what was perhaps erroneously called his last reward.

Great Caesars of sewing machines had triumphed in Gaul, while he was left in gall and wormwood up to his mouth while pursuing his *iguus fatuus* as a thing more worthy of interest than worldly wealth. The true wealth was—in his view—spiritual and not material.

The magnificence of the intentions that had caused him to elect to lead a life of poverty had not been impressive to those to whom he had paid off no loans or whom he had asked for extensions of loans. Was there one cell which was immortal, as some dreamers dreamed there might be—one which might outlast death? If he had been a Jay Gould, for example, he could have peddled a mousetrap which would have made of America a Golconda for him, especially when the mousetraps grew big enough to trap poor men and grind them to pieces in the expanding age of the machine.

He was so poor, however, in his last New Jerusalem that his father-in-law—after four years of neglect of him and his wife and her sister and his little ones, none of whom was old enough to pick up the family burdens—relented from his anger sufficiently to send to him once again—on a farm wagon coming in from his upstate farm—a barrel of pork and other produce, which had arrived in time for Christmas Day in 1869, the year following the loss of his big toe.

The quarrel between the farmer and his now largely bedridden explorer son-in-law had been caused by the father-in-law's repayment of a loan which the son-in-law in flush times had made in hard currency with soft currency—paper so debased that it could not keep body and soul together, as the winds of wild inflation beat upon the poor and would continue to beat—paper that was called shoe money because it was used to stuff into the paper-soled shoes of poor men in order that their bloody footprints might not be left in the snow as some were.

The poverty of the ever-dying Brother Weitling—now, when his steam was running out—had been such that he had been unable to keep up his dues for the Journeyman Tailors' Protective and Benevolent Union, to which he and his patiently uncomplaining automatic-buttonhole-punching wife had belonged since its founding.

On January 24, 1871, Brother Weitling had made his way over slabs of ice through needling snow to a festival of the German, French, Czech, and English sections of the Workers' International of New York and the last banquet at which he would appear in his present manifestation. Brother Weitling's host at this celebration—where he had partaken of vegetables and fruits and roots and turkey and roast apples and roast hog and to him had not been given merely the hog's snout or the hog's tail—had been the eminent communist Friedrich Adolph Sorge, who was in communication with Marx and Engels as to what was going on in the American political and economic wilderness and who was practically a listening post for them and who had been a friend of the resurrected Christ of the Alps even before his coming to the millennial continent.

A German by nativity and intellectually and musically gifted, Sorge as a young man had lain down his keyboards of ivory and ebony keys and all his chords and horns and harp strings and violin strings in order that he might take up the sword in the revolution of 1848 and had been under sentence of death—by firing squad, hanging, beheading, burning, or any other effective means—when in fear of losing both his material and spiritual life he had fled first to Switzerland and then to Belgium and then to England, from where—in a heavy fog in 1851 before the sun had cleared away the name of the fog-bound ship and its destination—he had embarked at the Emigration Wharf upon a voyage that he had supposed would take him to Australia.

It was only after the ship sailed, continually plowing through northern waters, that he had found that he had arrived in New York—and that was where he had remained. Indeed, for a little while trying to pull himself together, he had played the fiddle under corner street lamps in order to attract the crowds to Brother Weitling with his pamphlets, which told the best way to get from here to the New Jerusalem.

Sorge, the unredeemed radical labor leader who for some time had been living with his wife across the Hudson River at Hoboken, New Jersey, where he was a teacher of music who—in spite of the uproar of Stygian chaos around him—was still trying to work out a harmony of parts, did not abandon Brother Weitling, although their ways were widely divergent—for what was necessary was a movement that could embrace as many people as possible and even this lone knight.

Returning to his nontherapeutic bed of star points and thistles and thorns, Brother Weitling had suffered, along toward dawn's first light-beams before moonset, a paralytic stroke from the crown of his head to the tips of his nine toes. After a long day in a deep coma from which he could not be aroused to make any voluntary response to his weeping wife and sister-in-law and children, and no response in any language—"*Wir werden gesund geworden sein,*" "We will have become well," "by sanoa"—he had given up the breath or the spirit or the ghost of life in him—an exhalation coming like snow clouds from his lips, his eyes, his ears, his nostrils as he passed over into the great beyond—and the way it was known that he was dead was that his heart had ceased to beat and had not been followed by little ripples of response so far as could be ascertained by the physician with his stethoscope, which should have been a telescope turned upon some distant star.

Perhaps the journey of death was to be but an extension of the journal of life. Perhaps his travels were not over and there were metamorphoses yet to come.

It was because of his fellow members of the swan brotherhood, needle and thread and scissors and pants and coats men and their swan sisters who had kept up his membership, that he, who had no more earthly goods to show for his life's work upon utopia and the automatic eyelet puncher and eyelash embroiderer and the Venus or moon trap, had escaped being carried away by the dustman to the potter's field of the broken clay pots which were so many that they clogged the gutters and sewers and rivers of New York.

A surely admirable example of human solidarity was that in which the journeyman tailors joined together and were able to put their differences aside and join in harmony in celebration of funeral rites to make his passage from this world to the world yet to come. They had been able to pay out of their communal funds for the hearse horses and the hearse driver and the hearse with which to carry the fallen knight in his coffin under the coffin lid to the place where he was to be interred—members of his family and union members following in a straggling line before there was much traffic to hold them up or even conceivably knock over the hearse and knock over the coffin and knock the corpse out so that he might get up and walk as did others in the city of the walking dead.

The place where the sexton had dug up the clods for the grave with his shovel when Brother Weitling's wife and his sister-in-law and his little daughter in their black pokes and black veils embroidered by machinery and his five sons and the mourner swans had departed was in the impoverished, unfashionable section of the Greenwood Cemetery in the city of Brooklyn.

Among the few American newspaper reporters giving notice of the passage of Wilhelm Weitling had been the *New York Times* obituary writer, who had had a few tears to shed for Wilhelm Weitling, an inventor of prominence who had never received any benefit from his inventions and had left among his last effects his unfinished treatise on moon and sun and stars—the fruit of fourteen years of mental toil which competent star critics had declared interesting and worthy of commendation.

The New York *Belletristisches Journal* had given star billing to the lately departed utopian tailor. But for this obituary writer, Brother Weitling was evidently an archetype, the original pattern after which a thing was formed and which would have its imitators. The editor had seemed to be determined that to the forgotten man should be given remembrance, at least for a fleeting moment. "Wilhelm Weitling," he wrote, "is the name of a forgotten man, one of the many who, after a stormy career abroad, became lost and were forgotten and found their last resting place in America where they were confused by their own theories."

Germany had forgotten Wilhelm Weitling long ago, only the long-departed Heinrich Heine—one may remember that the dying Heine, the ghost of his father whirling around him like the Holy Ghost as he had lain on his pallet stuck by needles and pins causing his increase of sufferings, as this present elegiast for Weitling did not recall, thus not mixing one elegy for one man with another elegy for another man—had once directed attention for a fleeting moment to the philosophical tailor, the gifted thinker, the founder of German communism.

Das Evangelium des armen Sünders—Gospel of the Poor Sinner, as the English would say—deserved to be brought out again in print that all might read who had eyes. Perhaps the obituary writer should have called the book a booklet, as it had been written by the man who was to be an eyelet man.

But Wilhelm Weitling had lost his following after the fiasco of the *Arbeiterverein* and the utopian colony at Communia. "Men ceased to believe in him, and the waves tossed him upon the beach. . . . Throw no stone at him, for he proved to be a man amidst the storms of life, and his driving motive was something higher than ambition and selfishness."

Further along in the Gilded Age, Marx was to describe—in a letter dated October 19, 1877, to representative Sorge, which would reach him in his garden in Hoboken when the last of the gilded leaves had fallen in the soughing winter wind—the decades it had taken to sweep utopian socialism out of German workers' heads so that they might be as theoretically and practically free as the French and the English. But now it seemed that what had been swept out by the tide had been swept back in by the tide.

The concern of Marx had been with the resurgence of old-time German utopian socialism, which was now spreading. There had come also a chimerical game with the future of society, although in a more futile form than in its previous manifestations and thus was one not deserving of comparison with the great French and English utopians but only, of course, with Weitling.

It seems that the fallen tailor and the long-departed Heine had been much on Marx's mind lately, although they had been at odds with each other, out of joint with their time. And so had Marx been out of joint with his time and always would be, no matter what time it was.

To his communist correspondent in the frozen Hoboken garden in his letter which had come to him by no miraculous means but by mail packet with funnels blowing trails of crackling, hissing steam like snow clouds, Marx had pointed out what seemed natural to him, that the utopianism that before the age of materialistic critical socialism had concealed the latter within itself *in nuce*—in a nutshell—and which was coming now *post festum*—after the event—could only be silly—silly, stale, and basically reactionary.

AMONG THE time-yellowed manuscripts that had been left by the bankrupt revolutionary Weitling in his last estate were his sheaves of tattered and torn prison poems, socialist poems, workers' poems, poems replete with the love for mother and child which had been psychologically so great in the bosom of this bastard wanderer that he had refused to publish in any financially failing sheet bearing his millennial imprint the paying advertisements of embryo killers. Also, a poem which should have qualified him for publication in journals of sentiment in an age which must have produced from its start to its finish twelve hundred tons of rose poems and which seemed particularly to lean toward those which expressed lost love, lost lovers, lost sweethearts, was that which told of a beautiful maiden who plucked a rose and placed it upon her lovely breast, where it faded as her banished lover yearned to share the same fate—it seeming that he would die for love. "Life's Dream" was farewell to a loved one forever lost.

PART II

Harp Song for a Radical

[4 5]

DANIEL DEBS—rooked of his capital and unable to find the tobacco store the confidence man had described to him—could not have afforded to make an investment in any utopian concern even if the idea had occurred to him. Although he had come under the influence of revolutionary philosophers of liberty, fraternity, and equality and had been fascinated by some of the same iconoclasts who interested such radicals as the humanistic tailor Weitling, perhaps there could have been no rivalry in his mind between revolution and the dream of transplanting Marguerite—his Daisy—into a meadow in the New World which would be for him forever a little piece of *la belle France.*

So in August Daisy had said farewell to the cathedral at Colmar and had begun the long schooner voyage which brought her into New York harbor, where her lover was waiting at the dock with a bunch of roses in his hand and the gold wedding ring in his pocket, and they had been married in haste who would never repent at leisure.

The city where Daniel and Daisy had started their married lives was that where tides of refugees from Irish famine and the failed revolution were coming in, and there were many squatters, and there were so many stray dogs running wild in city streets so thick with them that a Saint Bartholomew's Day for dogs would sometimes be held, their corpses clogging the Hudson from shore to shore—sometimes old dogs of the two-legged variety floating with them, their red eyes staring at the reflective sky. There were districts of poor tenements jogging along side by side with districts of wealth where the worshipers of Mammon were developing Midas ears of gold.

Daniel had taken Daisy to live in a small home in Williamsburg—later to be absorbed into Brooklyn—and there she had given birth to a baby daughter who could not breathe and had died almost immediately. The little baby with the white rose under her chin and white hood and white shroud in her little white coffin who had almost bypassed earth by taking the swift road from earth to paradise was buried in the Greenwood grave-yard—where one day the socialist tailor Weitling would be buried.

When Eugene Debs was running for president and was a name revered by the poor tenement dwellers of New York, he would seek for this dead little sister's grave in Greenwood Cemetery, and had he known that the tai-lor socialist was there, would surely have dropped flowers on his grave—his constant habit was to visit the graves of dead children and poets and socialists, he being that kind of permanently elegiac fellow.

The bereaved parents had decided to move away from the blight of the city to someplace where there might be country bloom. The place which Daniel had thought might be the best for their new home was Cincin-nati—widely known as the Wonder of the West, the Infant Hercules, the River Queen.

Daniel had shipped their household linens, silverware, chinaware, which had been brought over from Colmar, by watercourse down the Ohio River—that which the French originally had called *la belle rivière* and which had moved as slowly as a flight of pregnant, large-bellied mares with a tossing foam of curls as it neighed with inflated nostrils between the Ohio and Kentucky shores—so sylvan then in pastoral quietude that mocking-birds on one side could answer mockingbirds on the other side.

There were thieves along this course who sometimes swam out into the central foam caused by a mare's tail to sever the cord between the passenger queen and the flatboats. But it was believed that because the Ohio River was in flood, the flatboat that carried Daniel's goods severed and had drifted on down the Ohio into whatever landing it nuzzled into—perhaps where lilies grew. It was never reported as found among the lost.

Where now were these bereaved parents to go? Daniel had gone by stagecoach over bumpy corduroy or mud roads while Daisy had gone by smooth river course to the Wabash river town of Terre Haute—where he had heard that there was a large French population that could well provide some aspects of the old civilization and give to this uprooted couple a sense of continuity between the present and the past. Perhaps he did not foresee the rudeness and crudeness of that little town where there would be seas of mud and a porcine population bigger than the human one—hogs on their way to the slaughterhouse sometimes so thick in the unpaved clay streets that they were like a heavy tide and it was almost impossible for a woman to walk without having her skirts brushed upon by the long snout of a razor-backed hog keeling her over where a deluge roared. The Wabash River itself was sometimes clogged with slaughtered hogs and pigs on their way to slaughterhouses—some with their throats cut still moaning with the saddest moan there was.

Daniel was willing to work hard for his living—although his were white hands which had not handled an ax but rather the rare leathers of old books embossed with the lilies that were the sign of France.

Trying his hand at various hard jobs along the Wabash River and the Erie Canal—where there was a straggling line of primitive factories and mills and warehouses and slaughterhouses, a foundry, a brewery, an ice-house, a blast furnace—Daniel had found employment laying ties for the Vandalia railroad, preparing the way for the iron horse with the apron on the front—it was called daisy chopper because it chopped down the daisies which grew between the ties—but after two days of working from dawn to dusk—fourteen hours by a clock which went so uncertainly that it might mark fourteen hours when there were more—he was so worn-out, the palms of his hands so blistered and bleeding, that he could not hold the handle of the pick, and he was told by the foreman of the road gang to go home and rest in bed. He could not do so.

Daniel took whatever job he could find and worked until he was laid off because he was ready to drop in his tracks. He went from the ice to the fire as from the fire to the ice and without a season of transition between freezing and burning, burning and freezing as he grew gaunt. He waned as his wife, big with child again, waxed like the moon. A second daughter was born and died before she could be named and was given to the cold clay in the graveyard.

When a third daughter, Marie Marguerite, was born and did not give up the ghost or the infant soul which was believed in those days to be a white butterfly, the parents had trembled with anxiety for her lest she also should perish because of the miasmic vapors coming from the marsh bogs and from the standing water in the streets which were hog wallows and puddles where the ducks quacked like the quack doctors selling their magical oils.

Daniel and Daisy had waited throughout the winter months with terror in their hearts for the little one whose cheeks glowed in the red of the fire from the fireplace and who was wrapped in red flannels to keep her from the snarling teeth of the raging winter wolf, but they had known that the spring would bring the ghostly reaper of many a little flower and that the summer would bring the plague—there were hazards in all seasons for men and women and babes, it was a fact.

They turned their faces from the West to the East from which they had already fled. But life in New York had turned out to be as difficult as it had been before and was made even more precarious by another blessed event, the birth of another daughter, Louise—who would live and whose triumph over Hades meant that Daniel now had four mouths to feed.

With their papooses on their backs, they who had waited for the summer plague to depart from the land of the Wabash had turned once more from the East to the West, arriving in Terre Haute in the autumn of the year when the harvest moon was full—and they had been grateful to be in proximity with the beautiful upland farms of meadows and orchards and woodlands and the river, where the fishing was good and the woodlands where the hunting for small game was good, and the prairies of the long grasses—the antelopes and buffaloes were gone, but there were prairie chickens and there were pheasants and quail and other game birds for the pot.

It had seemed to Daisy that the best way to assure that the little family did not die of starvation in the winter cold was to run a grocery store, where Daniel, who had learned the science of slicing the hog from his father in Colmar, could preside at the butcher's block slicing the hog right there in Terre Haute. And so the forty dollars that were left of their earthly capital were laid out to open the business in the front room of a little two-story house which was not very much more than a shack in the shambles of the factory district, built of old driftwood for the housing of a populace of those homeless wanderers who had floated like the driftwood to these shores and had stopped for temporary habitation before drifting on.

The date when Eugene Debs was born in the back room of the little grocery store, which had a scale upon which to weigh him, was November 5, 1855—and who could have foreseen that this newly arrived son who had been a long time coming would become the founder of many railroad unions and other unions and ultimately a founder of the Socialist party of America, as he would also be the perpetual presidential candidate for that which was presumably the highest office in the United States and running slowly with no expectation of winning even so much as by a majority of one? Probably there was no one who could have foreseen what the future would be and would not be—the future being, of course, then as now, a permanent enigma wrapped around with mysteries that might or might not unwind themselves.

The man in the White House then—Franklin Pierce, a previously unknown figurehead of the Democratic party—had been one of the most reluctant presidential candidates imaginable, just as his wife had been one of America's numerous reluctant first ladies and as their little son Benjamin—reflecting his mother's inordinate fears of exile in such an unholy place as Washington—had prayed that God would spare his father from the election so that he might stay in New Hampshire where he belonged.

Little Benjamin's prayers were not to be answered, although God did spare him from the White House. He was killed in a train wreck while traveling about a month after the election with his father and mother between Boston and Concord.

What had caused this wreck, anyone might ask. Of course, the railroad powers would rather have blamed God than a rod or would rather have blamed a careless workman than a corporation now brought into terrible focus by this tragic death of the president's son.

But the president-elect, not one to use his power against the corporate powers, had instructed his lawyer, General Benjamin F. Butler, to defend the railroad that had caused the death of little Benjamin and other passengers whose survivors were bringing suit for damages, and the reason for this decision, which might seem one of a curious detachment, had been that his wife's only consolation for the loss of their only son—she had already lost two other children, but not in train wrecks—was that the tragic accident had been caused by the intervention of a higher intelligence, a supernatural agency that had loosened a cog's wheel or caused a rod to break—an act of Providence by which to ensure that the father would give his entire attention to the nation.

There was a permanent air of mourning in the White House in an administration which, in 1854—the year before Debs's birth—had presided over the expansion of the empire of black slavery by nullifying the Missouri Compromise and opening to black slavery the territories of the Louisiana Purchase, which had been sealed to slavery for more than three decades by a covenant now broken by a government that gave no protection to its black and red children and none to its poor white children, whether in the North or in the South.

[4 6]

IN THE POOR little Alsatian store where in hard times like those which came in 1857 there could be few paying customers—many a poor old woman having not the money to pay for a ham bone or a bag of flour, many a poor old man having no money for a loaf of bread—where if there was stock, the father would allow credit or simply hand out a loaf, as if he were casting it upon the waters and hoping it would return as two loaves, the shelves were sometimes better stocked with Daniel's books than with the provisions for which the purchase required capital.

Daniel—to while away the time between customers—would read aloud from the works of French poets to Marguerite as she rocked the wooden cradle at her feet while knitting or sewing, the beautiful words spilling like a river of music over the little boy.

He had been named Eugene Victor by the father because the name Eugene was one that the mother loved and because the two authors whom the father had loved ever since he was a student in Paris were Eugène Sue and Victor Hugo, both of whom had profoundly inspired him by their belief that the dead and inert masses of mankind, the lowliest beings of the dust, were a species of divinity, containing within them the living sparks of redemption in a material and not merely a spiritual form—as would be the passionate belief also of Eugene Victor Debs throughout his public life as the wandering Jew in the services of *les misérables*.

What would always engage the entire being of the man Eugene Debs would be the resurrection of the workers of the smallest parcel of earth, the assertion of their pride in their manhood—that they who were the poor creatures of the clay should stand up as men.

Debs, when an old, bald-headed man headed toward his grave, was asked numerous times where he had acquired his revolutionary sympathies, how it first came about that he had given his life to the unremitting struggle for that cooperative commonwealth which, after all, had informed man's earliest dreams. He did not answer as might have been expected, that he had become a revolutionary under the influence of his father from whom he had heard, since his earliest infantile memory, the spoutings of Rousseau, Voltaire, Saint-Simon, Proudhon, Étienne Cabet, and how many others—especially Eugène Sue, for *The Wandering Jew* and his novels of the proletariat, especially Victor Hugo for *Les Misérables,* and even the revolutionary poems of Heinrich Heine. He said quite simply that his mother had taught him to be a revolutionary when he was a little boy at her knee.

Eugene was the first of Daisy's four infants not to be baptized—nor would the six others, four of whom would live, two of whom would be planted in unhallowed ground. Daisy was not in the least a nonbeliever. She was no skeptic now but filled with assurance of the ultimate goodness of mankind just as her son would be. Probably she was and always had been an instinctive socialist. She had conserved and preserved the fruits of the earth for sale in the little grocery store and would not have objected in the least if her husband had wrapped the jars or the sheep's head or the hog's jowl in brown paper covered over with revolutionary poems or messages as to a coming world.

THE SITE of Terre Haute, which had been given its name because of its location on the high land—the ridge that in early days had divided Canada from Louisiana—had been known in the early eighteenth century by French Jesuit explorers who if they had had their way would have established throughout this entire western wilderness of North America when it was in its sweetly primeval state a nascent utopia of premature heaven on earth which would be made only of themselves and the children of nature who were the red men they had converted—by hook or crook—to the Catholic faith.

Americans had first settled in the region of Terre Haute in 1811, when General William Henry Harrison—who would be the ninth president of the United States and who would catch a cold while riding horseback in the inaugural parade through a driving rain, perhaps while under the influence of the whiskery whiskey he had distilled, his reign in the White House to be only one month, during which he would take to the bed from which he would seldom or never rise again—had built in his earlier years Fort Harrison on the highlands rolling over the Wabash about three miles to the north of what was to be Terre Haute and from that vantage ground had made war against the red men, had either successfully exterminated them and their leadership or had driven them out of their Happy Hunting Ground to exile always farther west.

For the cowardly attack upon the utopian philosopher Tecumseh and his sleeping red men when they had already surrendered, William Henry Harrison would come eventually to his reward in the White House.

[47]

IN THE SUMMER of 1815, the region of the future Terre Haute had been visited by Abraham Markle—originally of Ulster County, New York, now a major in the Canadian Volunteers—and Joseph Richardson—a magistrate of Ontario County—both on horseback where the grasses grew as high as waves sweeping over the horsemen's heads and only some remnant red man or wild crane hiding among the grasses and the reeds might know that the white horsemen were here.

In Canada, Markle had been under suspicion of being of an American element attracted into the northern country by liberal grants of land that he hoped would be annexed to the States. His property had been confiscated and his family endangered because of the generally accepted, widely circulating belief that he had given secret information to the enemy regarding the defenseless position of the depot at Burlington Heights—so, escaping the net, he and a companion had come by flatboat from Pittsburgh on the Ohio River watercourse and then up the Wabash to the treeless land where he had planted cornfields and built a mill for the distillation of corn into a liquid state.

When Markle and his companion had first arrived, they had found the corn standing knee-deep in water with full red ears planted by early squatters who had already gone and had left no trace.

In 1816 a group from the Indiana shore of the Ohio River and a group from the other side which was the Kentucky shore had come only about a year after Father George Rapp's founding of the old Harmony on the lower Wabash to this high ground farther up the Wabash, where they had established—apparently without benefit of any angelic guidance—the incipient city of Terre Haute, two years later to be the seat of Vigo County, of which the exact lines were known and not left to chance. This county was not that which should have been called Nowhere.

The first Wabash River steamboat had docked at the old flatboat yards in the spring of 1822, but steamboats that nosed in there for rest before charging on were forced to remain stalled when the water to the north was low and blocked their passage—there being many shoals of bare-ribbed sand, places of water so thin that the sand cranes and the herons and other shorebirds stood as if upon phantom islands of reeds in the midst of the river exposing flats like mosaics as far as the eye could see—and thus the only way a ship could have moved would have been to take off on wings or move on wheels.

Indeed, many pioneers to the West built their log cabins on wheels which moved from one settlement to another as if to indicate that the nation itself would soon be moving on wheels to carry this continent away.

The dream that Terre Haute would become, through the establishment of an intricate system of waterways, a seaport for direct passage to New York Harbor had shriveled, because the Wabash was too shallow for a laden boat.

Until Daniel Debs with his bleeding hands had laid the rails for two days on the Vandalia, upon which his son Eugene Victor—a stripling youth who had not seen the great world—would one day be an inspector of ties, bolts, and nuts, walking the rails with his eyes downward and often kneeling, crawling to repair a broken rail or lift a dead or wooden dog from between the rails, the national road from the East had been that by which land travelers had come by stagecoach and prairie schooner.

Even when the trains went west, they would continue to whistle by like meteors in this way—for some men were too poor or too independent for a locomotive's wheels and preferred locomotion by their feet. And doubtless to some of the antitrain people, the risk to life and limb was less than to take an iron horse which did not always have the power to sprout sudden wings and sail right over the cradle-broken back of some old mule who, deaf and dumb and blind, had wandered through a hole in an old rail fence and stood so still that the birds of evening could sleep on its back. The first post office in Terre Haute had been built on the site of the old county jail. The delivery of mail had been so very uncertain then that—perhaps like life itself and the delivery of society from a state of corruption into a state of incorruption—the mail was something eternally delayed.

[48]

THE OLD TERRE HAUTE State Bank which was built on Ohio Street in the old frontier Wabash River town was the only genuine specimen of pristine Greek Revival architecture there was in the county seat then. It had not yet been decorated by sudden mushroomings of Roman domes, some of the pure Greek to be torn down or overgrown or overthrown by Roman columns and visages of Roman emperors with a peculiarly home-grown look as befitted a nation dominated less by Greek philosophers than by Roman presidents, generals, governors, senators—so many who required only a bedsheet to show themselves for the conquerors they were, over not only other countries to which their power could reach but over their own.

When someone once asked Debs's friend, the comical Bill Nye—who looked so much like him that, as they were both as tall as stepladders and very bald, they were taken to be twins, although they were in no way joined in a political sense, as Nye was of the right wing and Debs was of the left—where Julius Caesar was killed, in what part of his anatomy the sword had passed through him, Nye had answered with reference not to Rome but to Washington that he had received his mortal wound—where else but—on the steps of the Capitol.

Although Terre Haute developed very rapidly from a settlement in the wilderness into a town—some people thought that it would outrival Chicago some day as a hogopolis, its railroads flourishing as were its candle factory and its woolen mills and canneries and butcheries and slaughter-houses—some projects were slow, and one of these was the raising up of a bell over the Vigo County Court House (in which Debs as a young man would function for a time as a very Tolstoyan city clerk who was likely to favor the poor and the oppressed in his dealings as the representative of law and order).

DEBS WOULD RECALL of his childhood during the Civil War, which began when he was a five-year-old and ended when he was a gangling ten-year-old—too big to spend his time as he did rocking a baby sister or help-ing his mother putting up strawberry and cherry preserves with which to stock the shelves in the grocery store, too tall to run between his tall father's legs when he held them wide in the pattern of a steeple—that he had grown up in a town as in a state where many people had not been particu-larly sensitive to the sufferings of the black slaves in the agrarian South.

Little doubt that they were not easily incensed by the project of freeing the black man from the yoke—and this conceivably had been because of the great physical as well as psychological distances then as perhaps perma-nently between the people and the abstractions of a coldly methodical, somewhat ingenious federal government to which they could scarcely give loyalty for any fatherhood of the white slavery in the industrial North from which many people like Daniel had fled, having observed while in New York the unutterable injustices to which black men were exposed, their way even harder than that of the white wage slave, and having also won-dered—as did many other idealists, including Thoreau—how the white slaves of the blighted North who could not free themselves from the domi-nation of dollar kings should be trusted to have the wisdom of freeing the black slaves of the rural South.

Daniel, alive to the economic and political issues of his day and spouting them to his wife who shared his humanitarian views if only in a simple way and without his capacity for irony and paradox, must often have spoken the names of Dred Scott, John Brown, Abraham Lincoln—and he had also foreseen the approach of the internecine conflict that would be merely in a propagandistic way concerned with the abolition of the accursed thing which was slavery.

Daniel, schooled in the philosophies of the revolution although inclined to be peaceful when he laid his shaggy head against the bosom of his sweet-smelling Marguerite, could understand as well as anyone that the fundamental division of this nation into two nations was not the division between North and South but the division into the rich and the poor which existed in a thousand ways in the North and in the South. He had correctly foreseen that the division into the rich and the poor would be heightened and increased by the Civil War and not lowered and decreased.

Children of Debs's day had visualized the Mason-Dixon Line as a chalk line that had been drawn through this nation or as a picket fence. When Debs asked his father how the Civil War could be so cruel and yet be called civil, he was given the same explanation as other Hoosier fathers gave to their little boys who were too young to understand complexities resulting in savagery—the Civil War was not civil and was not polite as fathers and mothers wished their children to be.

Debs's father and mother, far from wishing to infuse a war spirit in the lad, had preferred that he should spend his days as the frolicsome but spirited little colt running loose in meadows of wildflowers, where his father would teach him all that he knew of birds and honeybees, which in all probability were not adverse to landing on him as he filled his hat with wildflowers for his mother. He had learned to recognize all the wild birds and their songs, which he could accurately imitate throughout his life.

As it was necessary to provide food for the table as well as for the grocery store, the little boy would go with his hunter father in search of wild turkeys and rabbits and squirrels—Daniel wearing, for such adventures, a hat with a bushy tail and a fringed jacket as they stalked for their prey that never was a nonedible owl or other wild creature one might kill simply for sport. Indeed, Daniel was called the bloody mushroom hunter by some of the townspeople because of the numbers of mushrooms he pulled up from the ground—always with the knowledge of which were edible, which were poisonous.

Little pitchers have big ears, as certainly did the future labor union organizer and socialist whose ears—seeming to prick up—had heard what was said at a supermarginal level as well as what was said at a submarginal level and would always hear the cries not only of the living workingmen but of those soon to be dead. What had mainly impressed him as to the uncivil Civil War were the hog cars packed not with hogs but with boys on their way to the South.

The boys going to the South by hog cars bristling like a hog's back with guns included many of the poor white who had drifted up to the North by prolonged and uncertain migrations into what was known as Hoosierdom and were not actually white but so burned by the heat of the sun under which they labored or by the blasts of furnace fires that they who were of Southern sympathies—if of any sympathies at all or knowledge of boundary lines—were called Butternuts. They were vast hordes living throughout all the middle western border states, and they were as yellow as the butternuts from which, following an age-old habit, they made their butter and from which they made the oil they rubbed upon their faces and their hair and made the buttons for their coats and made the necklaces which were worn alike by their bridegrooms and their brides, their men and their women and made rattles for their Butternut infants.

Now they were being shipped down south in the hog cars that had carried the hogs whose provender had been mash of corn and butternuts and oats—the old sow rarely swelling so big that when she was dancing a mad jig she would step upon her little pigs, as did this government.

The most expendable of all the products of the North were men, as the not universal draft law was enacted for the enforced enlistments of the poor boys and the exemption of the sons of prosperous fathers who could pay poor boys a bounty to go in place of their sons, who elected not to hear the Union's call to defend their homes, which were not invaded, whereas in the South the call to arms usually met with instantaneous response from rich and poor alike, since it was that land which was to be burned—and yet there were naturally spies on both sides and many Southern spies in Washington, perhaps some in the White House, which to Southern patriots with their desire to split from the Union deserved to be called the Black House.

It would have been almost impossible for a bright little boy not to have understood that the war which was the loss of limb or life for many boys brought profit to some men who, if rich before, would be big tycoons when the war was over, their profits exceeding what once had been their wildest dreams—the shipbuilders having built such unseaworthy ships, for example, that some sank to the ocean's floor with all aboard before they could get out of New York Harbor past the lighthouse from which the lights of liberty had gone out.

[49]

COULD IT POSSIBLY BE that the best way to win a war was to devise an instrument so terrible in its effects that no man in his right senses or even his left senses would wish to start a war and thus unleash forces of such vast and massive devastation that this old planet Earth itself might be stripped as bald and bare as it was before Creation when there was in all probability not a bird or a beast or a flower or a man or a woman or a child or one old cocoon left over from a previous world?

That war would be given up as a way of solving political or economic problems was the humanitarian mask of Dr. Richard Jordan Gatling's idea—a soft-spoken Indianapolis physician of southern origins who claimed to be motivated by his healing instincts and who claimed that he had devised the most wonderful modern invention, which, if purchased by the secretary of war in Washington, would shorten by many months and possibly years the weary, dreary, everlastingly prolonged, and certainly most unpopular war which there had been in America to that date—and which would, moreover, make all future wars seem unfeasible, perhaps even unthinkable, so dreadful would be the showers of burning brimstone let off at one blast by his new machine gun.

In 1862—and thus in time for the coming furies of the Civil War of which the gathering storm clouds could already be seen—Dr. Gatling had produced a crank-operated gun of which he would proudly boast as if it were after all his brainchild as it was his namesake, and would come down through generations with many issues, many other guns. His claim was that his intentions were pacific, as in a sense he may have actually believed.

Unfortunately for his accuracy as a gazer into the crystal ball which was clouded over by his own biases, the great Gatling guns and other mechanical purveyors of shrapnel that were the contributions of other steel magnates using his pattern of discord for the achievement of harmony would mow down and tear into largely depersonalized fragments by sheets of brimstone like burning meteors coming to graze on earth more hundreds of men at one turn of the wheel than ever before and would require, with accelerations of speed, greater and greater armies of the living men with which to replace for all too brief a time the dead pouring their blood from every cell as the holes which were made in the clouds did not rapidly disappear. Although, of course, sometimes, as in the ever-increasing elegiac literature, flowers would grow through those empty sockets or bees would make their honey inside those gaping skulls.

The Civil War, coming at the age of mechanical experiment, was the first war conducted in the modern sense of mass slaughter with the help of industrial enterprise—at least on the Northern side.

The boys on the Southern side had been horsemen with swords uplifted as they charged against cannonballs that had the power to thresh them like the corn or the wheat.

Abraham Lincoln, the understandably mournful redneck in the White House who had been a fighter against the Indians and had been a lawyer for railroads, was certainly enthusiastic about the efficiency and potentiality of the patriotically named Union Repeating Gun, for which, in October of 1861, he had put in an order for ten—each described by its salesman, J. D. Mills, as an army in six square feet, worth about a hundred men.

In an old, abandoned Indianapolis graveyard down on Noble Street— where better place than a graveyard for this purpose?—Dr. Gatling, if he still may be called by the title of physician who should cure all wounded men without regard for the side they fought on but whose cure would cause those greater and greater wounds which would increase with time and would never heal as the wounds to the body of this nation would be slow to heal, had illustrated by demonstration more powerful than testimonial by word of mouth the altogether remarkable efficiency of this great Gatling gun, which gave, just as he had claimed, undeniable and presumably irrefutable evidence to the eyes of awed beholders that by one turn of the handle there was such a volley, such vast foundations and showers of shrapnel like hailstones puncturing the air, that all the quails fluttering up from the long sweetheart grasses were knocked down from the four corners of the sky and suddenly red clouds like bloody rags—and the weeping, weeping willows had good cause for weeping, weeping even as would the war widows, and the graveyard owls had good cause to hoot in the daylight as darkness of storm clouds suddenly descended to earth.

Among the personages present in the graveyard at this remarkable quail shooting and greatly impressed by this prelude to many a requiem had been Governor Oliver P. Morton, who during the Civil War had adhered with increasing obsession to his virtuous belief that those not favoring the war should be held for treason, although there were not only Democrats but Republicans who had believed in the rights of the South to secede and for whom the war was so unpopular that there were riots and violences of various kinds carried on in some thirty counties along with murders of enrolling officers, who were suddenly stormed upon by Butternuts and other Southern sympathizers, or those for whom the conflict had only a negative reality or the motive of robbery of the poor, and there were wreckages also of numerous newspaper presses in various towns, including Terre Haute, the smashings of boxes of leaden keys by those who did not wish to be smashed by an army in a box more lethal than a toy army of little tin soldiers—as Morton after the election of 1862 was denied funds for the conduct of what some might consider his simply treasonable war.

The Knights of the Golden Circle, founded on Independence Day, 1854, in Lexington, Kentucky, had been particularly active in the southern part of the Hoosier state, as the river had not divided North from South but had afforded endless opportunities for water passage by those who knew the river and its moods and could come by darkness under the firefly stars and could come with silent oars.

Two branches of the Knights of the Golden Circle were the Hoosier Council of the American Knights and the Order of the Sons of Liberty, the former having originated in Terre Haute in 1863 and having spread to sixty counties, where furtive citizens met under cover of darkness, united in their belief that Lincoln's national Republican government and Morton's state government were most red-handedly guilty of usurpation of power and had committed most dastardly treason against the will of the common people—they who in general were believed to be the low-down, skulking, shifty-eyed Democrats. They had found that their votes gave them no more choice of destiny than if their ballots had been chewed up by water rats.

"The right of secession conceded, the nation is dissolved," Morton had warned—and also that it would not be twelve months before a project for a Pacific empire would be set afoot and California and Oregon would have a right to withdraw and form two separate nations. "Need I stop to argue the political, intellectual, social and commercial death involved in this wreck and ruin?"

[5 0]

DR. GATLING had come to Indianapolis not in search of a medical practice beyond his own hearthstone but in search of capital for his various inventions, including that great Gatling, which had caused the quails that had rustled like the souls of the dead in the long grasses to rise up and be shot down from all corners of the sky under the volley of hailstones, which he regarded to signify the miraculous intervention of God as if it had been the work of a supernatural agency upon the battlefield scattering these little birds.

Upon this great Gatling the doctor had taken out patent rights with which he would have more success than would the poor tailor Weitling whose buttonhole machine was made to punch holes for buttons and not holes in men, the kinds of holes in which the only buttons would be the wildflowers growing over ruined battlefields.

A Northern patriot now—and such was the impression he wished to give—Gatling had been impressed mainly, as he would recall in 1877, by the fact that the large majority of the dead had lost their lives not upon the battlefield from their wounds but by sickness incident to the service. Dr. Gatling was determined that his gun, because of its great efficiency upon the battlefield, would preempt the necessity of large armies, with the consequence that the exposure to battle and disease would be greatly diminished.

In February 1864 he had written with patriotic fervor to Lincoln, "Such an invention at times like the present seems to be providential, to be used as a means in crushing the rebellion."

The commercial interests motivating Dr. Gatling had already asserted themselves in his attempt to sell the great Gatlings to the French government. Perhaps he would have succeeded if the Washington government had not placed an embargo upon the shipment of lethal hardware to a foreign power, as the guns and the munitions were needed at home during the war—and would still be needed when the Civil War became that in which the rich turned against the poor in factory yards and railroad yards when they struck for bread and got bullets.

"The gun"—according to Dr. Gatling's recommendation to the Ordnance Department of War in 1865, when the war was almost over, Mother, and Johnny would never come marching home—"can be discharged at the rate of two hundred shots per minute, and it bears the same relation to other firearms that McCormick's Reaper does to the sickle or the sewing machine to the common needle."

The accusation would be made that all the while this persuasive doctor had been a subterranean but active member of the Hoosier Council of the American Knights—although he had been so plausible in his loudly proclaimed apostleship of the Union cause that he had been able to carry on his surgical operations with success. It would be alleged that he had chosen to locate his factory in Cincinnati so that if it went into mass production, as he hoped, raiding parties from over the river would be able to transport the

Gatlings to the other shore—thus to equalize the battle that the South was losing like a poor body which was being drained of all its blood under a bloodless sky.

The great Gatling was adopted, in fact, as an official weapon by the United States government in the year following the Civil War, which would leave this nation as a nation including many and increasing self-regulating empires, their heads enjoying more power than was given to the czar of Russia who might easily be the ritualistic puppet of warlords.

In 1868, when the Gatlings were already being purchased in other countries, the Russians bought twenty great Gatlings and ordered another one hundred, which would be used by the imperial armies to shoot down the czar's little pigeon children who were the serfs starving for corn.

In 1877 had begun in America—at a time when there were so many tramps, many of them respectable men who were unemployed drifters from city to city, shore to shore in search of jobs, that the *Chicago Tribune* advocated a little strychnine or arsenic as the cure for them, as other journals proposed stout ropes that should be thrown over limbs of trees where they should be hanged and left dancing in midair—there had begun the strikes of railroad and other workers for bread in that uncivil civil war in which federal troops would be employed to suppress what was called an insurrection inspired by Karl Marx, a man of whom few had heard and of whom most would continue to be abysmally ignorant.

As for Debs, as a veteran of the strike against the Pullman Palace Car Company in Chicago in 1894, which he had led in the face of overwhelming odds of the rich capitalists against the poor scarecrows, he would remark that the rapid-fire injunction would seem to him a great improvement over the great Gatling gun.

Great Gatlings would be used in time of peace in America for the protection of the works of McCormick's reaper—called the ghostly reaper by some poor men who would be reaped and shucked and ground to pieces with the corn—would be used by the invading federal troops at Homestead—would be used by the armies of the mine owners against starving coal miners in Appalachian coal-mining towns and against starving gold and silver and lead miners at Coeur d'Alène and Cripple Creek and Goldfield and elsewhere—always elsewhere as time went on at an increasingly rapid pace.

[5 1]

DEBS COULD NOT have spent his childhood on the controversial ground of Terre Haute without overhearing, from his revolutionary father with his abolitionist passions tempered only by his very rational fear that the irrational Civil War would not achieve unification of the amorphous nation but would leave it as the two nations it had been, the names of many legendary figures who were spokesmen for the obscure—including the name Dred Scott, which had been given to himself by a black slave who perhaps had misspelled Dread as the shortened Dreadful.

Debs would become, long before he had ended his adolescent years—there scarcely having been in a harsh world the time for transition between boyhood and manhood—an expert on the legend of Dred Scott, even as of many lovers of freedom and many abolitionists of whose number he would be one, a lover of poor men whether black or white. So far as he was concerned, they all could have been checkerboards. Or perhaps he was just as blind to color bars as would be the blind, deaf Helen Keller, the friend of his later years.

THE VERY DAY after the inauguration of James Buchanan as president of the disunited United States—and thus when Eugene Victor was still in his red wrappings—there had been issued by the Supreme Court injunctions whereby the South would be embalmed in the patterns of its planter past, and a black man, even though he had been a free man while living in a free state, would become a slave again at the instant he should put his foot into a slave state or, for that matter, should be carried against his will over the borderline by slave hunters.

The Supreme Court—which was already following elections as the hearse follows the horse upon a bumpy road—was not likely to overthrow the practices of the past—the very sacred past—and dump out of its judicial cart the hacked corpse of a black man bleeding in all his pores as the corpse bleeds to give sign that his was no natural death but murder, murder not only of his body but of his manhood and his perhaps understandable desire to belong to the human race.

The Supreme Court had handed down in 1857 its majority decision by which Dred Scott—born Sam Blow, a black slave of Peter Blow—was not only a man of color but was also a plaintiff in error, that he was absolutely and indubitably not entitled to wage suit within the all-reaching precincts of the Supreme Court or any other court in the United States, for he and his wife and children were slaves by law and thus could enjoy no recourse by appeal to the law which naturally was acting in behalf of the protection of the law.

Even if he were not a slave, he could not sue in the courts of the United States as a free man because free Negroes also could not sue in them for any cause—just as, of course, as should have been added, the reds could not sue for all that had been done to them, for they were not citizens.

Dred Scott and his family, who had been free in a free state, were not entitled to their freedom by reason of the Missouri Compromise Act, the black-robed jurymen who had not one black face among them holding that all compromises were unlawful. No doubt Dred Scott's claim might just as well have been the words of a fictional romance upon which to build the foundations of a humanistic and humanitarian utopia where there would be no more difference between white men and black men than between white cows and horses and black cows and horses.

For what the old-timers on the court had feared was evidently that there would be spotted cows and horses if a black man were free to enjoy his civil rights, and handed down a decision which included degrading, humiliating injunctions against crossing a road without his master's permission or drinking water from a white man's stream even if he brought his own gourd; nor could he turn the short way through a little wood, nor could he carry a gold watch as some free black men did, nor could he learn to read English, let alone Hebrew or Greek as some of them did—for he was a jackass, a beast of burden who should not nose among flowers but only among thorns.

The efforts of political agitators for the restriction of the slavery of the black man by the arousal of public opinion had been as vainly spent as if they were threshing a wheatfield where the wheat had already been threshed and the air was cold and bare as the barren face of earth where not a blade of wheat was left.

The owner of a black slave was as free to take him over the borderline from one state to another as he was free to take a jackass over the borderline from one state to another without losing ownership. Upon the owner of a black slave no inhibition should be placed.

THE FATHER of Eugene Field, Roswell Martin Field (Eugene Field would be one of the master spirits of Eugene Victor Debs's life, although Debs had met the poet only about a year before his death, which had found him sleeping like his Little Boy Blue), with his fellow ex-Vermonter Abra Crane had hoped for a victory in the pioneering Dred Scott case, which would open the way for the citizenship of black men in the land of the free and the home of the brave, which had not yet been given the appellation the land of the slave and the home of the grave, as it would be from the time of the great chains of industrial strikes.

Now in the North and along border states where lived many enlightened men and even in darkest Missouri itself—as some comedians used to call it in parody of darkest Africa—there were cries of protest against a judgment so altogether unjust.

Eugene Victor, who would grow up to give his life to the emancipation of the lowliest American serfs, both black and white, had been about two years old, too young to hear the news when Dred Scott and his little family were at last purchased out of chattel slavery by the impoverished bookkeeper Taylor Blow and his brother Peter, sons of the original Peter Blow who had been his owner and upon whose Virginia plantation he had been born like one of the many little brown sparrows a storm will scatter from a nest upon a windy bough.

The future friend of poor white wage slaves as to all poor black men whose way was made even harder by being black than if they had been white—all poor black railway porters and hotel porters who, even when old and bent permanently, must carry the white man's burden, his suitcases, but would never be allowed to carry the suitcase of Debs, who would lean over and help the black man carry the white man's towering burden— the future friend of every black man whom he would wish to welcome to the brotherhood of the footboard even when it was still impossible for him to do so because of prejudices encouraged by owners employing black men as scabs or in other ways turning white against black, black against white, class against class—Eugene Victor would revere the memory of every black frontiersman in the struggle for freedom and especially the memory of the archetypal Dred Scott, the heroic rationalist with a brilliantly burning mind enclosed in a frail, ramshackle body where the fires of consumption burned faster than freedom's fires burned.

Old beyond his years—seeming almost as old as Methuselah when he died although he was in his middle years—suffering from the galloping consumption—at times spitting up his blood as red as the red apples on the red apple tree, as red as the red chokecherries in a Missouri bog, as red as the red heart of a black man—Dred Scott had enjoyed his freedom, which was freedom only in an individual and not a universal sense, for only a short time in which, although unable to do the heavy work with mop and broom and unable to carry heavy suitcases upon his back and forbidden also to carry trays of food or touch with his hands the food which others ate lest he should infect them with the galloping consumption—a worse virus than his passion for freedom—he had worked as a porter at the Theron Barnum Hotel, to which his presence had attracted many travelers.

They had entered their names in the guest book because Dred Scott was the porter there, although he, even more than they were in this life's passage, was transient—would not be there for long.

During the period of his labor as a free black man who still, of course, could not vote a pro or a con, yet certainly had known the difference between a pro and a con, he had worked as long as he was able—like an old work mule who should have been turned out to crop the daisies in the fields but so seldom was given this reward for past services—to put one foot in front of the other, he insisting upon the acceptance of no charity for himself and his wife, who did not want to be daisied along.

This sense of his innate dignity and simplicity of manhood—a spirit indestructible in him and perennial as it would be in the black man in spite of every discouragement—was something beyond the understanding of Bible-thumping slave traders, whose main justification for slavery was that the black man was a heathen who must be civilized by the Bible thumpers, who also thumped him into acceptance of the ways of God.

Finally, when Dred Scott's illness had progressed so far that he was rack and ruin except for his alertly bright eyes and was hemorrhaging, spouting blood, and when his white friends had found that which was almost as difficult to find as a needle in a haystack, a white physician who would treat a black man suffering from such mortal ills as all flesh is heir to, the tall black man had been carried home on long gray slats in a wagon bed to the little old shack with its pitched roofline, from where, when he gave up the ghost, he was carried in a wagon bed in his boat box to Christian burial in the Blow family plot in the Methodist graveyard, where not long afterward he would be joined by his wife, who also had suffered from the galloping consumption shaking her frail bones from head to foot, and where not long afterward the father and the mother would be joined by their elder daughter, whose frail body had also been invaded by the galloping consumption, making her rattle in the wind like a brown leaf.

After about seven years of sleep in the Wesleyan cemetery, all three had been dug up and moved, with the Blows to accompany them, to the Calvary Cemetery because of the conversion to the Catholic church of their beloved Taylor Blow, who had not wanted to leave Dred Scott and his family to wait for the Methodist day of resurrection, even although by all calculations the Methodist opening of the heavens when the earth gave up its dead should have been nearer at hand than the Catholic awakening, which would be only the awakening of idol worshipers and not of good, old-fashioned Christians whose faith was supposed to point a direct way to God.

Dred Scott, whose faith had been in man without regard to what color he was, would always be memorialized as the man who, even although he had slipped so fast from consciousness to unconsciousness, had gone a long way toward the awakening of American consciousness—the stirrings of many dead souls with such dreams of liberation as had been his who had died in that which should have been the fullness of his manhood.

[5 2]

EUGENE VICTOR DEBS had been not quite three years old when there had been the first burial—and upon the second burial, when Dred Scott and his family were dug up to wait for the Catholic resurrection, which some believed should be in the flesh complete with every freckle, Debs was about nine years old and the nation was being torn to pieces by the bloodiest war there ever was, none bloodier than a Civil War where the enemy was within and might be any man.

Dred Scott would be one of the many men idealized by Debs for his attempt to awaken the all-too-somnolent consciousness of America to the immediate as well as the remote tragic consequences of the denial of citizenship to the chattel slaves who had been brought to this country in chains and whose slavery was perpetuated by law in the land of the free and the home of the brave.

The song of the old John Brown who lies a-mouldering in his grave and of whom the Union boys sang as they were sloshing their way through the red mud could not have been very popular with the boys of the Butternut economy who were on their way to be fed to the hogs on Southern battlefields, albeit Brown was a hero to the abolitionists as he would ultimately be to the presumably anarchic revolutionary Debs.

The year of Debs's birth had been that in which John Brown, who had started out upon his God-obsessed career—formerly a shepherd and farmer and student of social justice in both a transcendental and materialistic sense—as a kind of half-baked Buddha and a kind of half-baked Marx but probably had relied upon neither for the mandate that had been given to him by God, had joined with four of his sons and two friends on the night of May 24 in the murder of five log cabin settlers whom he had assumed to be pro-slavery when the only slaves they had were themselves hoeing their own plot—he had come upon them in the night when they were sleeping and had ignored the cries of their women that their lives should be spared. He had left one with his bloody fingers cut off, and if, as in old folktales, he had ever come before them in a trial, they would undoubtedly have pointed toward him although he had only plotted and directed this murderous mayhem.

At Osawatomie, when border ruffians came to burn him out in revenge, his son Frederick was killed. Watching from the thickets on the other side of the river, John Brown had said to his son Jason, "God sees it. I have only a short time to live—only one death to die—and I will die fighting for this cause. There will be no more peace in the land until slavery is done for. I will give them something else to do than to extend slave territory. I will carry the way into Africa."

Driving a prairie schooner through freezing winter cold, he had escaped over the border into Canada and upon reentry into the United States had attempted to establish, when there was no possibility of doing so, a republic of black men in the Appalachian Mountains where all would be equal as plowers of the soil, which—as in the red communities of the past—no individual would own, and no individual would be permitted to sell what he had not bought.

This dream being beyond realization, he had struck the blow against slavery at Harpers Ferry, and for this he had died, with noble calm, the one death that had been his to die as the martyr whose death had started the Civil War and whose figure would be idealized by abolitionists.

Debs would recall of John Brown's execution on December 2, 1859, when he—little more than four years old—was spinning a top which was not the top of this world spinning, spinning until it died down, that on the day of John Brown's execution Louisa May Alcott had christened him St. John the Just and Henry Wadsworth Longfellow had prophesied, "This will be a great day in our history—the date of a new Revolution, quite as much needed as the old one"—and that for Victor Hugo (as Eugene Victor had heard his father say many times) John Brown had been a greater man than George Washington.

[5 3]

FOLLOWING THE DRED SCOTT decision, which had taken the old judge all of three hours to read with a whispering voice so faint in the St. Louis courtroom that many words were lost, where darkness discouraged lip readers and where justice was blind and deaf and dumb even more than if it had been a stone—for a stone may see and a stone may hear and a stone may speak—Abraham Lincoln of Springfield, Illinois, had responded with melancholy cadences as to the sufferings of the black man to whom the Constitution—according to these negative interpretations—could not reach out the umbrella of its protection.

Lincoln's message employed the symbolism of keys, keys of every kind by which the black man was kept in his prison house, that which those in power had searched and in which they had left no prying instrument—how one after another they had closed the heavy iron doors upon him and bolted him in with a hundred keys that could never be used to unlock the doors without the concurrence of every key—the keys in the hands of a hundred different men in distant places as they had stood musing as to what invention in all the dominions of mind and matter could be produced to make the impossibility of his escape more complete than it was.

Could not Lincoln—the former fighter against the Crows—have used the same words in regard to the red man? But the red man had no John Brown, no Harriet Beecher Stowe, no Lincoln to make the rocks and streams cry out for him.

The attack upon the law had been futile as far as it might have any effect upon the extinction of the great evil that was black slavery, for many abolitionists were blind to the white wage slavery in the North, which was, however, emphasized by the secessionist intellectuals in the South who also saw that the black man in the free states was likely to be left to starve or be your stable boy. And true it was that there were and would be for many years after the Civil War documented cases of poor old black fathers and mothers who did not know that they were free or which state it was that they were in or that they were in the United States. All they would know was that they were the eaters of mud.

No one had told them of the martyrdom of old John Brown or of old Abe Lincoln, who—while disapproving of lawlessness in freedom's cause—had certainly admired the dignity and courage and rare unselfishness of the great martyr who had swung with the hempen noose around his neck and had never once lost his dignity—as even the governor of Virginia had testified.

In the vast crowd assembled that day to witness the death of Brown had been the future murderer of Abraham Lincoln. He was to be America's first and foremost and most noted assassin of its most noted president.

John Wilkes Booth, the pale-faced actor with dark hair shining—every hair in its groove—was dressed in a military uniform, all gold braid and glitter, and was studying for some future role the last writhings of the blindfolded eagle John Brown—and perhaps he did not quite know what role. He would become, when the Civil War was unleashed with all its furies, and perhaps by that death which had been the individual prelude to man's death, a member of the Baltimore chapter of the Knights of the Golden Circle, who were devoting themselves to hatching the black egg of assassination that would blow the rude, crude old Abe Lincoln so sky high that he might never come down to earth again.

Booth sought to immortalize himself by the murder of Abraham Lincoln that night when he shot the tall, long-limbed president in the box at the Ford Theatre and jumped upon the stage crying out, in the name of the state of Virginia, the slogan of Brutus when he wounded with more slices of his sword than could be dealt to a watermelon in watermelon time the imperial Caesar on the steps of the Capitol, "Sic semper tyrannis!"—a Latin slogan that probably less than half the people in the audience, if they had heard, had understood, they having little Latin and less Greek.

The blood of the president had spilled upon the audience and upon the scarf of a pregnant Hoosier woman who—a younger sister of the mother of James Whitcomb Riley—had been escorted away by her husband as he shielded her eyes lest the baby be born with a birthmark of blood on it caused by this shower of old Abe Lincoln's blood—the bloodstained scarf to be preserved in a little glass box in a little out-of-the-way country museum, the kind where might be found a Civil War soldier's bloodstained red cap or a bundle of Butternut blood–stained rags or a papoose's tree cradle or a stuffed, moth-eaten buffalo with four feet—two of which were fore and two which were aft—and would be laughed over in some old joke by Long Debs and the Funny Little Short Man Riley when there was nothing left of the primordial wilderness but an old Lincoln joke, when there was not even that wilderness which had been in the days of yore childhood *The Old Curiosity Shop* with its clock birds and old grandfather's rocking chair and Little Nell, always Little Nell.

The unemployed but versatile actor—perhaps with a joking spirit upon him or with a sense of the irony born of a constitutional desperation, perhaps because he really did believe in the Southern cause and had planned the way of his escape, his disappearing act—had dispatched to Hades, on of all days Good Friday, April 14, 1865, the rail-splitter president or rail president, whose death many secessionists had hoped for as for the April showers that bring the May flowers. And there were radical Republicans who had feared old Abe's conciliatory spirit.

Old Abe had presided over the splitting of the nation into two rails. What could be expected but revenge? For, after all, had not mutual enmity increased with the approaching threat of peace, which might mean only the further imposition of old Abe's will—the further devastation of the ruined South?

[5 4]

IT WAS GOVERNOR MORTON who had first given the name Butternuts to the Copperheads, who for a variety of reasons opposed the war, including the deepest of all, which was instinct—came from the muzzle ends of Sharpe's rifles that the Union boys had carried into the battlefields of the South and that had received the appellation Beecher's Bibles because their sermons were those that the Reverend Henry Ward Beecher, a Johnny-come-lately abolitionist whose sister Harriet Beecher Stowe had started the war with her *Uncle Tom's Cabin*—and could he ever forgive her?—had cheerfully recommended should be the Lord's word. His Brooklyn Plymouth Church had subscribed the money for twenty-five rifles and what had been the Church of the Holy Bibles had been renamed the Church of the Holy Rifles.

Governor Morton had been outraged by the way intellectual Southerners in Indiana had not shared the grief of the nation when the North suffered reverses. The city of Indianapolis itself was split between North and South. The Episcopal Church was split between two congregations.

Deep in the Indiana hill country where the South surely was, there had been ever since 1840 a great, shambling, many-roomed hotel at French Lick. At this wilderness hotel were three artesian springs—Pluto, Prospero, and Bowles—of which the one with the strongest waters was Pluto.

From a counter in a storeroom at the front of the hotel, the peaceful Dr. Bowles—who had been selling the all-cure spring water to pioneers who in the summer or the autumn of the year came in their red wagons with their clay jugs to stock up on Pluto water—had been operating under the counter, so to speak, as spy for the Confederacy.

In fact, he was one of the foremost Knights of the Golden Circle who now were rounded up by one long rope which would be their noose from which they all would swing for treason to the Union cause—and a terrible aspect of their two-faced treason was that some were not Southerners by origin and had no reason for their preference, even like Stephen Horsey of Shoals, whose grandfather had been a pioneer in a little town that was built upon both sides of White River.

Now why should Stephen Horsey favor the old South and answer to the winding horns of the Knights of the Golden Circle?

The most important, the most colorful of these secret plotters and thus the most outrageous, had been the Irish-born Lambkin P. Milligan—a lawyer who had once ridden horseback on the circuits with Benjamin Harrison, grandson of a president and himself a future president, who had long since come to a parting in the road with this charming gentleman whom he considered to be a traitor to his country. Milligan had read law in Ohio with Secretary of War Edwin Stanton and was a great lover of Thomas Jefferson and Andrew Jackson and was by religion a devout Catholic—and in politics, which was an aspect of the same religious faith for him, he was a devout Democrat.

Milligan's home had been situated upon a vast estate almost overlooking the Little Wabash—and not far from where William Henry Harrison, in the War of 1812, had taught Chief Turtle's nomadic Indians a lesson by burning down the model farm where under the tutelage of a Quaker missionary they had put on linsey-woolsey clothes and were trying to learn the white man's way of farming, which was made necessary because they had lost their Happy Hunting Ground, and a new mode of existence seemed preferable to ever-threatening extinction.

On his model farm, Milligan had devoted himself to the breeding of racehorses which he had paced on the oval track in his grasslands.

He had objected to the war before it began as he had objected to the war dragging on and on—the draft of the poor boys, the military arrests, the executions of spies behind both lines, the enflaming of passions by the manipulators who were in power, the promises of partial emancipations that were like promissory notes which would never be made good—the failure to end the war by negotiation rather than by endlessly extending it with all its sufferings, which brought losses of life and limb to some men, profit to others on an almost unimaginable scale.

The accusation would be made that Milligan and other Knights of the Golden Circle had been planning an insurrection that was to take place on August 16, 1864, in which Governor Morton would be kidnapped and held a hostage. But the day of the insurrection had passed without the insurrection.

To Milligan's ideal farm up at Huntington a military expedition had set out to capture—even to kidnap and bring in shackles to the military court—this outspoken redheaded Irishman who had been at one time the president of the Chicago & Atlantic Railroad—predecessor of the Erie Railroad—and who had run at too slow a pace for governor.

On the night of October 5, 1864, when the frost was forming on the pumpkin moon, a train with engine muffled and all lights out had crawled backward all the way up from the capital city depot on the railroad track to Milligan's door and had chugged back with this prize to the capital city, to throw him into a military prison to await his trial, which came with lightning speed for fear the Knights of the Golden Circle might spirit him away.

Acting as judge advocate in the trial of the Knights of the Golden Circle and serving as legal adviser to the military court had been James Whitcomb Riley's father, who had volunteered for the war to which he had gone riding away as a young man and from which he had returned as a cripple with a paralyzed arm, who had found that in his absence his law practice had withered and who now—to support his wife and little children, including that Little Bud with his yellow-chick hair whom he had hoped would be a lawyer or a judge—had taken on this task which had not made him very popular.

Milligan's lawyer had argued—and with considerable right on his side—that the military court had no jurisdiction to bring to trial and sentence an American citizen who was not a resident of one of the rebel states and was not a prisoner of war and was not a soldier but a citizen of Indiana arrested at his farm—largely given over, he should have added, to the raising of thoroughbreds. For this was a rich man and hence should not have suffered the swift retribution that was usually handed out to poor men, some of whom were shot without trial.

Predictably, however, as this was a star case and the best road show the Union cause had at this point, the judge advocate had maintained the military's right to have this trial, President Lincoln having suspended civil law in trials for conspiracy and treason.

Milligan was sentenced to be hanged on May 19, 1865, between the hours of twelve and three on the parade ground reaching from the camp which was named after Morton to the barracks which was named after the Hoosier general Ambrose Burnside.

While waiting for the execution upon the gallows which, with an excessive cruelty—as much as if a labor union head who had led a strike of starving workers were forced to build with scab labor the gallows upon which he would be swung—the military tribunal had detailed that the Confederate prisoners must nail the planks together and put up the tree for the rope upon which the hanged man, like every other hanged man, would dance as in his dying or posthumous agonies he slipped upon the air the ghostly stream that would impregnate the ground with the seeds from which would spring the hanged man's children, who, like unto the deadly nightshade, were mandrakes rooted in the ground, were half flower and half bird beating with restless wings which could not leave the earth.

Abe Lincoln had seemed inclined to give Milligan his freedom, but before he could find time to sign the correct paper among the papers he carried in the crown of his old stovepipe hat or among the folds inside his folded long umbrella, the former circuit rider who had the look of the harvest in his sad eyes had been himself mowed down.

Milligan had refused to entertain new hope and had asked that his wife should prepare for his funeral and had named the pallbearers he would have to carry him to his grave at New Hope.

On the plea of his wife in Washington, Secretary of War Edwin Stanton had asked that the sentence be commuted to a life sentence of hard labor at the Columbus prison. Governor Morton, with a spirit of charity not always characteristic of him, had asked for a delay in the date for Milligan's appointment with the hangman.

The Supreme Court of the United States had handed down a decision very unlike that which had been handed down regarding Dred Scott.

Re Milligan, the Constitution of the United States was a law for rulers and people—equally in war and in peace—and covered with its shield of protection all classes of men, at all times and under all circumstances.

When, on April 12, 1866, Milligan's discharge from his death cell was ordered, the man who had been for eighteen months in the shadow of the noose had been greeted at Huntington by the roaring of cannonballs and the ringing of church bells.

In May, the federal grand jury in the capital city had indicted him on the military tribunal's charge for a second performance of a melodramatic road show. Bail was put up by Milligan's bailsman so that he could go home, and he was not to be called back again to court although the threat of the hempen noose was still hanging over him, as if to warn him that he was entrapped by fate.

Other Knights of the Golden Circle, including the bottled Pluto water man Bowles, had been spirited out of the prison in the dead of night by their friends and would not emerge from their hiding places until the coast was clear and the episode of problematic treason was forgotten as something that had happened in the long ago.

[5 5]

ALL THROUGH THE YEARS of his childhood and boyhood, as Debs would recall when he was an old man himself and had been known for years to some as the second John Brown, the second Abe Lincoln, and the first Debs there ever was, Debs would wonder with his awakening political consciousness what on earth the tall Old Sycamore of the Wabash, Dan Voorhees, United States senator from Terre Haute, meant by his complaints that everywhere he went someone was waving a bloody shirt at him. Whose bloody shirt? And why was it waved at peaceful Dan who had not a spot of blood on his shirt? And who was waving it?

The bloody shirt was that which would be waved by Harrison against all Democrats—members of a party that in his view had a stronger instinct for taking the wrong side of a question than any other political party the world ever knew—and against in particular Old Sycamore, whom he personally viewed as the chief of sinners.

On August 10, 1878—when Harrison was running for a governorship which he was doomed to lose—he would bring up before the Hoosier voter the memory of old Jeff Davis, who, wearing hoopskirts and bonnet, had attempted to escape from this country, where if he were caught he would have been swung from that famously ambient sour apple tree. And old Abe had prayed that he would not be caught. "If a Democratic Congress should pass an act to indemnify Jeff Davis for the loss of his wardrobe, including his hoopskirt and bonnet, or to pay General Beauregard for his personal effects destroyed by our bombardment of Charleston, would Mr. Voorhees maintain that these laws are unconstitutional?"

In that particular gubernatorial campaign where Harrison had appeared upon the platform of Terre Haute as a waver of the bloody shirt, he was still waving the bloody shirt when he told a small group of gray-haired Union veterans down in an Ohio River town where the rebels had grown as wild as the wild rambler roses along the roads winding through woods and as many as the lilies swept by fingers of waters which had reached from the South to the North that he was proud to carry aloft the banner of the bloody shirt—the tattered, worn-out, old faded shirt that had been worn by some gallant Union boy and was stained with his blood as he gave up his life for his country.

"When they purge their party of the leprosy of secession, we will bury the bloody shirt in the grave with the honored corpse who wore it and not before."

Waving the bloody shirt in memory of the Union boys and opposing some Hoosier boys when they were rebels against the wage slavery of whites and struck against the Vandalia Railroad, he had threatened to have them all mowed down by troops equipped with Gatling guns such as had been used to mow down the bearded and the beardless boys in the South, and he had announced that he had come to believe that the perverse disposition to oppose everything the Republicans proposed was the strawberry mark by which one could always identify the Democrat.

Old Abe had said at Columbus, Ohio—at the time of his election when he was on his way from Springfield to Washington by way of Indianapolis and other old western towns that he had not seen again as he would never come this way again unless carried feet-first as he would be carried feet-first when he was dead, long poker toes stretched out—and some people had always wondered if he was web-footed or if he had more than five toes per foot—for he had seemed to them such an ugly and ridiculous fellow to be at the helm of the ship of state with his old black umbrella and his old black stovepipe hat and feathery rain shawl and shrunken coattails and shrunken trouser legs—"I cannot but know what you all know, that without a name—perhaps without a reason why I should have a name—there was fallen upon me a task such as did not rest even upon the Father of his Country. I turn, then, and look to the American people and to that God Who has never forsaken them."

[5 6]

THERE WAS ALWAYS in American politics a thinner chalk line between the ridiculous and the sublime than the chalk line drawn by Mister Mason and Mister Dixon between the North and the South—as old Abe had certainly known. He with his big nose and sunken forehead and receding chin and Adam's apple had given much employment to cartoonists when he was alive, as he would not by his death dispense much employment to eulogizing preachers who were busy embalming, enshrining, canonizing him.

Pulpiteers springing up everywhere were in general more concerned by the spilling of old Abe's blood upon the ground by the mad dog assassin Booth than by the spilling of his brains—for to many he had not seemed to have many brains to spill—and what was important was the sacramental spilling of his blood upon the American ground.

According to one of his many theological elegiasts upon this blackest Easter Sunday morning, God had the right to the blood of His servants as there were times when great men could do more good by their deaths than by their lives—and this was one of them. The martyred president was like unto the Son of God Who had asked that this cup pass from Him but had received no affirmative response from God.

According to another clerical patriot, Lincoln had been the incarnation of both Moses and Jesus Christ in one. The combination of Moses and Jesus in one person was certainly not unusual, of course, in an America where there were many prophets given over to the quest for Canaan as for the New Jerusalem.

Symbolically, according to one of his many funeral sermons, Lincoln, it seemed, had died for his country and had died for the world, although perhaps no one knew precisely what country it had been or in what ways he had died for the world unless he had been planning to emancipate it—he who, after all, as would be seen, had not achieved his mission here.

Old Abe's old western log-cabin jokes, old Irish-shanty, and old black-slave jokes had been offensive to some elegant Easterners to whom it had almost seemed that just as his zigzagging conduct of the war seemed to be dictated in a large measure by the rail-splitter's own simpleminded nature, so his jokes controlled his policies far more than did the wisdom of some of his advisers.

Jokes had provided a safety valve through which the steam could escape and without which old Abe would have blown up like a riverboat or a train. The joke was not only in its way full of intellectual things—strange mirrorings of strange fallacies or stranger truths—but was also the language of the skeptic brain transmuted by the faithful heart. Jokes had also their quality of Apocalypse, of resurrection and redemption, and their undying precepts.

While he was president in the White House, Lincoln had seemed to guide himself not only by jokes but by the tongues of birds and beasts in animal parables—some told by old black men whose folklore was older than Aesop or Homer—and by prophetic dreams, and he had also consulted weather prophets and rainmakers and had been known to believe in magic.

Macbeth was his favorite play, of which he had read aloud—not long before the surrender of Lee to Grant—the lines that would so soon apply to him: "Duncan is in his grave; / After life's fitful fever he sleeps well; / Treason has done his worst; not steel, nor poison, / Malice domestic, foreign levy, nothing / Can touch him further."

One of the clerical elegiasts for old Abe had been the Reverend Henry Ward Beecher, who seemed to love him better dead than when he had been alive. Old Abe had seemed too altogether cautious for him, who was a well-meaning gentleman who knew old Abe's Hoosier neck of the woods and lonely, backward, out-of-the-way places such as Pigeon Creek quite well and had not liked the rednecks of the Lincoln breed—had not understood them or their mudslinging ways.

Beecher had been a preacher for a time in the Ohio River town of Lawrenceberg, where river steamboats had charged by in the summertime on their way from Pittsburgh to New Orleans and where from his front window he could see the river traffic and the Kentucky shore—but he had not emerged as an antislavery man at that time.

At Terre Haute in this wild Hoosier land that Beecher had felt to be scarcely civilized, the youthful reverend had ventured to give a sermon one night at a camp meeting without arousing a pro-slavery or an antislavery mob in the burgeoning hogopolis.

And in Indianapolis, where the rhapsodic gentleman had occupied a fashionable Presbyterian pulpit as a preacher to all who were the elect, slavery was likely to be a taboo subject even to many who did not believe in it and had never owned a black slave in their lives.

Beecher had become at last, however—in the affluent Brooklyn church to which many Wall Streeters belonged—such an ardent abolitionist that old Abe Lincoln—a man who could be quite calm—had seemed to him just about the most inadequate, the most slow-moving, the most lack-adaisical president there ever was. He was lachrymose—no doubt not only to Beecher but to other men—and was endowed in his giant frame with a bone that tended to produce tears.

But now from the Church of Holy Rifles—not Bibles—Beecher's voice had tolled out with that loud clapper which would be muffled when white wage slaves struck for freedom during the railroad strikes for bread, beginning in the late 1870s, against the railroad owners, who had prospered beyond their wildest dreams from the Civil War and would give to the strikers, including many who had been poor foot soldiers, bullets instead of biscuits or even crumbs of bread—that the martyr was moving in triumphant march, mightier than when he was alive.

"Four years ago, O Illinois, we took from thy midst an untried man and from among the people. We return him to you a mighty conqueror."

[5 7]

To Debs as to other young social idealists, the old Wendell Phillips with his old flowered carpetbag packed with radical messages was still as he had been when a young radical—an immortal crusader on behalf of civil rights, the survivor of the martyr age when the abolitionist had been considered the anarchist and when anyone who stood up for the Bill of Rights for black men risked being torn to pieces by a mob as John Brown in an illegally legal sense had been when he stood upon the scaffold and had his head hooded for the rope. His face in his death agonies had been concealed, but it had been impossible for the hangman to conceal that old white beard burning like a meteor in the winds.

For a time, as Debs would find out when the patriarchal white-bearded train traveler Phillips stopped off at Terre Haute, Phillips had favored the complete economic and political dissociation of the moral North from the immoral South, for it had been his belief that for a white man to give countenance to the slavery of the black man in any part of this Union was to invite the same dispensation of fate to the white.

In a speech titled "The Argument for Disunion," on January 20, 1861, at the Boston Music Hall, Wendell Phillips had stated, "The Democratic principle, crumbling classes into men, has been working down from pulpits and judges' seats—through shop boards and shoe benches—to Irish hodmen—and has reached the Negro at last. . . . For this, Leggett labored and Lovejoy died. For this, the bravest soul of a century went up to God from a Virginia scaffold."

Phillips had been and always would be a nonrelativistic worshiper of the absolute, thus differing from the many-sided Lincoln, who was burdened with the wisdom of his melancholy, which came from a sense of the many and not the one truth which like the Rock of Ages would not move. Lincoln's view was that the Union represented the investment of too many human hopes which would yet come into flowering and that the breakage of the North entirely away from the South would not necessarily bring the Zion or paradise or peace on earth that the disunionist had envisioned.

The abolitionist Phillips had seriously wondered whether the despotism of the president in Washington—although admittedly preferable to the despotism of the president in Richmond—was really representative of the head ship of the government. According to his loudly ringing speech "The War for the Union," which he gave in New York and Boston, he saw violations of that very freedom the Union was fighting for. These violations were no mere child's play.

He had protested against the suspension of the writ of habeas corpus, which Thomas Jefferson had created to give constitutional power to suspend in any emergency whatever. Yet today the writ of habeas corpus, the right of free meeting, and a free press has been annihilated in every square mile of the Republic.

"I only ask you that out of this peril you be sure to get something worthy of this crisis through which you are passing. . . . I only paint you the picture in order, like Hotspur, to say—'Out of this nettle, danger, be you right eminently sure, you pluck the flower, safety.' "

Phillips was for not slow, not fast, but instant millennium for the black men—those whom he had many times described as knowing best all the secret places of America, the darkest forests, the loneliest bogs in which a black man had tried to hide himself away from his pursuers.

At a meeting near Boston on August 1, 1862, Phillips had complained that the president had no mind whatever: "He has not uttered a word that gives even a twilight glimpse of any antislavery purpose," Phillips had said, probably in recognition of the fact that there was something always of twilight mystery about old Abe. And as for the fact that he might be honest, nobody cared, Phillips had added, whether the tortoise was honest or not, as he had neither insight nor precision nor decision.

In the elegy that Phillips had delivered for old Abe at the Tremont

Temple, he had taken occasion to point out that except for the fiendish spirit that in North and South supported the rebellion, the assassin could never have dared to do such a deed as he had done.

> Suppose that when a boy—as he [Lincoln] floated on the slow current of the Mississippi, idly gazing at the slave upon its banks—some angel had lifted the curtain and shown him that in the prime of his manhood he should see this proud empire rocked to its foundations in the effort to break these chains—should himself marshall the hosts of the Almighty in the grandest and holiest War that Christendom ever knew and deal with half-reluctant hand that thunderbolt of justice which would smite the foul system to the dust—then die, leaving a name immortal in the sturdy pride of our race and the undying gratitude of another—would any credulity, however sanguine—any enthusiasm, however fervid—have enabled him to believe it? Fortunate man! He has lived to do it.

But God, according to the agnostic or atheistic Phillips, had graciously withheld Abraham Lincoln from any fatal misstep in the great advance, had taken him when his star touched its zenith and the nation needed a sterner hand for the work God gave it to do.

[5 8]

COMING BACK HOME to the old western land feet-first upon the locomotive *Union,* which had carried him from Springfield, Illinois, to Washington—and stopping in important places that he might be seen so cold and lonely and dead, not seeming about to rise up from his coffin to crack some old Butternut joke or say Howdy Do to those who were gathering to say farewell—greater and greater crowds appearing along the rails from Ohio onward—passing through town after town with all their storefronts draped in so much black crepe that there were literally rivers of black crepe streaming across this continent—black crepe like waterfalls falling from rooftops and overhead bridges and branches of orchard trees, black crepe flying from church steeples with the crosses that were Catholic and church steeples with the weathervanes that were Protestant, black crepe flying from the tops of old town pumps in little nowhere towns in which no train, not even this one, ever stopped, black crepe flying from barber poles and flying from the scarecrows in the cornfields where surely all tassels must have been black as the sable train passed as slowly as a horse-drawn hearse along the sometimes bumpy rails—church bells tolling and court-house bells tolling in places where there were churches and bells and maybe in places where there were not—but only the sound of this bell earth tolling, tolling like the bell on the funeral train—women dressed in black with black veils and black rosettes like those of the president's widow—two portraits of the dead president hanging in front of the cow-catcher—the president's car had entered the old Hoosier land at Richmond, which since the early days or, more accurately, early nights had operated through a seemingly endless night a station on the underground railroad for fugitive slaves and which now showered petals upon the roof of the president's car and laid wreaths upon the president's long coffin with one wreath for his dead son Little Willie who in his short coffin had been disinterred for this trip home and to whom was directed a note reading "Like the early morning flower he was taken from our midst."

At the Hoosier capital city, the mourning rites for the president were especially theatrical, in view of the president's having gone this way to Washington on what now appeared after all to be the circular way by which he was returning home as if in proof that in his end was his beginning and in his beginning was his end.

The president's body was put on display at the capital city's first state house, which—designed by Ithiel Town, a renowned architect of the East—was a Greek temple with a Roman dome. Over the coffin was spread a black velvet canopy sprinkled with golden stars and laced with white cords.

He belonged to his country now, however, and so was taken north through the naturally sorrowing countryside and thus he had passed by way of Michigan City to Chicago, stopping at Twelfth and Michigan, where all of a sudden—according to the *Chicago Tribune*—the waters of Lake Michigan which had been long ruffled by a storm had calmed from anger into solemn silence.

The president was placed upon a regal Pullman sleeper for his journey from Chicago to Springfield, the permanently bereaved widow with her acres of black veils having suggested the attachment of the palatial Pioneer with its luxurious appointments to the funeral train for her passage and that of her surviving sons, the delicate Tad and the stalwart Robert, future Prince of Nails who would drive the nails into his possibly mad and possibly sane mother's already broken heart and would be the lawyer for Pullman during the rebellion against the despot Pullman and would drive the nails into Debs's heart and crucify his labor union as surely as if he were nailing it up on a mound of burning cinders in a railroad yard.

Oh, how strangely unreal it would seem that this son of old Abe Lincoln would be a lawyer for Pullman, who had backed the hangings of the Haymarket martyrs and would like to remove Debs from the scene. And how inappropriate it would in all probability seem that the jackass Debs should be likened to the Pullman lawyer's father.

Lincoln had been for more than two weeks on the road, attracting more crowds than had ever been attracted by a horse-and-buggy gubernatorial or presidential candidate, when finally, with his riderless old Bob—his bay mare which he had ridden when he was a circuit-riding lawyer—he was carried to his grave with Little Willie. Now they were joined by Little Eddie, who had died in Springfield when the old gray mare had been what she used to be and was not yet what she would become.

Because of quarrels between the officials and the widow over where the president and their sons should be laid to rest, they would be moved from this to another resting place, where they would be joined by Tad—the boy who had been a stammerer—and then all four would be moved in 1871 to another resting place when Lincoln's body was placed in an iron coffin and under an iron lid as safely sealed as if it had been sealed by kings of iron and steel.

Later, the long coffin with little coffins and Tad's coffin had been dug up, and Lincoln was still there, as could be testified by the plumber who had seen him looking as if he might almost say Howdy Do before he was put into another overcoat—probably two more than he had ever had when he was alive—and he was given a new red cedar coffin lined with gray lead and was placed in a marble sarcophagus in the center of a semicircular catacomb where surely his journeys would all be done in a literal if not a spiritual sense.

In 1876, a gang of counterfeiters who let their plot be too widely known in a Chicago saloon were plotting to kidnap and hold President Lincoln's body hostage and hide it upon a lonely stretch of the Indiana sand dunes, where presumably would be no witnesses but the waters of Lake Michigan licking upon a lonely shore and the eyes of water birds among the reeds at the shore's edge.

Pinkerton's detectives, who had gotten wind of this proposed attempt and whose head had guarded Lincoln from assassination in Baltimore when he was on his way to the White House but who had lost him to Booth that night in the box stall at the Ford when the door had been strangely left unguarded and unlocked, now watched ceaselessly over him.

The ex-president's wanderings were not yet over. Once more, in 1901, the Lincoln family was moved—and Robert Todd Lincoln, who had arranged for the resurrection and reburial, had told the burial committee that he wanted his father to be buried so deep that he would never be brought up to the surface of earth and buried again.

Once more, before this last interment, the plumber had peeked in and had seen Old Father Abraham's spare face, which he knew because the skin was dark, as it had been in life, and his hair was thick and coarse, standing up like a horse's hair, just as Lincoln himself used to say, and his features were not decayed as he said Howdy Do, Good-bye in the way that had been his custom.

Now the coffin was sunk deep and stiffly corseted and surrounded by a heavy tonnage of cement which Robert Todd Lincoln had designed in imitation of the underground citadel of George Mortimer Pullman—who had feared revenge from anarchists going clear back to the days of the Haymarket martyrs and the Debs Rebellion.

How unquiet had been Father Abraham's grave.

[59]

THE CHILDREN of the Debs family with their mother a non-church-going Catholic and their father a Protestant who had given up religious faith for the study of philosophers had been allowed to attend the church of their choice or no church until they should be old enough to judge for themselves which brand they preferred. Debs's church would always be, it has been said of him, a church without walls.

The little boy, his hair smoothed down by Daisy's comb as sleek as a pussy willow after the rain, would set off for Sunday School, regardless of whatever war clouds were threatening, with a nickel in his hand for the collection plate, but the truth was that there was no church worth a nickel in his opinion then.

He had gone to St. Joseph's Catholic Church one Sunday morning for Mass on a day when the sermon was on hell, burning hell, a thousand demons and devils with pitchforks dipped in brimstone, lakes of fire in which the sinners should forever burn so fierce that he with his imagination already alert to human suffering, as he had heard the human hogs groaning in the hog cars, could feel just as if the sparks were flying right on to his highly flammable self—and had fled at one mad dash outside the church to get the flying sparks off his hair and his shirt. To judge by his later history, he probably never did.

The narrow-ribbed little grocery store with the bars over the upper window to keep the children from falling out had been inadequate, hardly a place where they might have room in which to grow up to healthy adulthood, as the sun baked the roof in summertime and in winter the ice formed like a coat above their heads.

The increase of business during the period of boom and bust which came during the Civil War had made it possible for Daniel and Daisy to move to a more substantial house on Eleventh Street and Wabash Avenue, a vast improvement over the former tenement but still not as luxurious as were some of the sprawling manor houses where the rich people lived.

Daniel, fairly indifferent to the world's goods, for he had abandoned affluence when he came to America, was less interested in financial booms and busts than in the busts of Voltaire and Rousseau that were set upon the mantelpiece of the fireplace with the French clock and his collection of pipes and were the presiding deities of this household with its beautiful steel engravings recalling France—that country which was always in his heart—and the European library for which there were never enough shelves as it was continually growing, and a place for his French cornet, which never would be used.

Daniel's precious pipe was that on which he would allow Eugene Victor Debs to puff once a year in commemoration of the year in which he became a man.

According to all accounts this was a home in which the children were happy and welcome to run about, to develop their own individualities with respect and deference and love from their somewhat formal parents to whom they gave their respect and deference and love in return. There was always a place set for the unexpected guest—whether Robert Ingersoll, the orator and Republican attorney general of Illinois, or some old coal heaver who was interested in establishing the brotherhood of man with man before coal turned into diamonds.

[6 0]

McGUFFEY'S LITTLE red-backed readers were those which, ever since the miraculous rendering of the leaden print into poems and proverbs and moral tales in Cincinnati in 1836, had been the bible to children in the little red schoolhouse, which stayed open from the last of the harvest to the spring planting if there was a schoolhouse in the ice-shrouded land and if the children had coats and had shoes with which to walk the long way to school, sometimes where there were no roads and the wolves howled at Little Red Riding Hood.

McGuffey's was as much a part of the world of the childhood of generations of men, including future presidents, vice presidents, presidential candidates, preachers of every faith, old black sleeping-car porters, locomotive firemen, lightning slingers—such a fireman was Debs to become, for he knew how to sling the words that made the lightning flash—as were Noah Webster's *Dictionary,* of which every word was truth, and *Poor Richard's Almanack* and Perrault's *Tales of Mother Goose,* Hans Christian Andersen and the Grimm brothers and Aesop's talking beasts and birds.

Children reading McGuffey's might carry away for life and clear to death itself the memory that Socrates died like a philosopher but that Jesus Christ died like a god. Or they might learn from McGuffey's what property rights were—that if you found a man's mantle lying on the ground and stepped into it because it was empty, you were a violator of his property rights as surely as God made fenceposts and milestones, big owls and little owls.

McGuffey's seemed always of the long ago before there was a Civil War, which passed without any new edition or mention of a Fugitive Slave Act or a St. Louis porter named Dred Scott and made no mention of old John Brown whose army of seventeen men had been exaggerated to seven hundred—no mention of Elijah Lovejoy, Abe Lincoln, Robert E. Lee, Ulysses S. Grant, John Wilkes Booth, the Molly Maguires.

The struggles for freedom in the McGuffey's Acropolis were always of the remote past—very early American or Greek or Roman but nothing to interpret the rapidly changing world, which changed only to become what it was as if there were no *Pilgrim's Progress.*

Actually, William Holmes McGuffey was born in Washington, Pennsylvania, had attended the old Stone Academy there, and was a graduate of

Washington College and a teacher in Paris, Kentucky. He had become a Presbyterian cleric who preached literally thousands of sermons on the elect and the damned before giving up and from 1845 onward serving as a professor of natural and moral history at the University of Virginia at Richmond. It was said by his brother that he was a pacifist so long as he was not disturbed in his Confucian meditations.

"Birds in their little nests agree, / So why can't we?" would be one of the first poems Eugene Victor Debs would learn to read aloud with other children when he went to singing school.

He would learn that George Washington cut down the cherry tree and that when his father asked who did it said that he could not tell a lie, that he did it with his little hatchet.

According to the morality of McGuffey's in its teachings of voice control, the articulation which was the utterance of the elementary sounds of speech every schoolboy and schoolgirl should learn. There were examples of ordinarily accented lines as contained in statements such as these which the children rehearsed and which were not necessarily coherent, although perhaps there was a thread running through all. "What a terrible calamity. . . . His eye through vast immunity can pierce. . . . A tempest desolated the land. . . . He preferred death to servitude. . . . God is the author of all things visible and invisible."

There were examples of a dramatic nature to encourage correct pronunciation and no slurring of words. "The magistrate ought to arrest the rogues speedily. . . . The whirlwinds sweep the plain. . . . Linked to thy side, through every chance I go. . . . But had he seen an actor in our days enacting Shakespeare. . . . What awful sounds assail my ears. . . . We caught a glimpse of her. . . . Old age has on their temples shed her silver frost."

There were exercises in inflection, whether sliding up the scale or down. "He did it voluntarily" (sliding down), "not involuntarily" (sliding up). "Heard ye those loud contending waves that shook Cecropia's pillar'd state? Saw ye the mighty from their graves look up, and tremble at your fate?"

As tempo was of overwhelming importance, there were exercises in the qualities of voice which should be long, medium, or short. There were the long, as in the following passage which required air-inflated lungs: "O righteous Heavens! e're Freedom found a grave / Where slept the sword, omnipotent to save? / Where was thine arm, O Vengeance! where thy rod / That smote the foes of Zion and of God?" Medium: "At midnight in his guarded tent / The Turk lay dreaming of the hour / When Greece, her knee in suppliance bent, / Should tremble at her power." Short: "Back to thy punishment, false fugitive!"

Children learned from McGuffey's how pitiful was the death of a child, as exemplified by the Death of Little Nell. "Sorrow was dead, indeed, in her; but peace and perfect happiness were hers, imaged in her tranquil beauty and perfect repose. And still her former self lay there, unaltered in this change. . . ."

McGuffey's by its many examples gave countenance to the belief that the wars which were the important wars were those of the Greeks and the Romans. God was an all-seeing eye, a constant presence, if sometimes clouded over, as McGuffey's would not admit. Everything which had ever happened had been the working out of the laws, the often inscrutable laws, of God.

This was what so many people believed in a world in which the wilderness had been so rapidly fenced that it all seemed to be passing away or had passed in a single lifetime. The apple trees belonged to the farmer with his barking gun. The bridges were guarded by toll-keepers with their long rifles pointed at whoever wished to cross a bridge and had no coin.

Children were taught by McGuffey's—and let there be a curse on future advocates of property which should be owned by the propertyless— that a man's property belonged to him and must be respected, even as had been shown in biblical times, probably ever since the eviction of those non-rent tenants Adam and Eve by that first great realtor who was God.

Time and time again, Supreme Court justices, when they were not taking a leaf from the Bible, had seemed to be taking a leaf from McGuffey's and to be under the mesmerizing spell of the little red-backed reader in the formulation of their oracular decisions and pronouncements. But McGuffey's should not be blamed for the ways in which it was used by small-time judges.

When it would be said of the labor leader Debs that he was the Terre Haute Rienzi, few who had ever heard or had recited great speeches from McGuffey's delivered by schoolboys and -girls on Friday afternoons would fail to remember just who the original Rienzi was, their association with him having been limited to the little red-backed reader's noble choice of his "Address to the Romans": "I come not to talk. You know too well the story of our thralldom! We are slaves! . . . And once again—Hear me, ye walls that echoed to the tread of other Brutes! Once again, I swear, the eternal city shall be free."

[6 1]

ALTHOUGH INDIANA—which from its early days had attracted not only Bible scholars but intellectuals whose bible was Rousseau—had been a pioneering state in the avowal to establish a system of free education, the Hoosiers were too poor to pay taxes for any kind of network of public schools.

The realization of the promise of education for all was for a long time deferred, outside a few ambitious centers. Father Joseph Rapp had believed in free public education for the children of others, and his learned foster son, Frederick, a secret lover of Voltaire and Rousseau, had been one of the first state senators and the real and not merely foster father of the propagation of free education.

Robert Owen's school in the New Harmony, which was short-lived in the place where the Rappites had enjoyed long life before moving on, had pioneered communal education for infants and children and workingmen.

Robert Owen's son Robert Dale Owen—future United States senator—had contributed much to the promotion of public education in the state of Indiana.

The Civil War had slowed down the pilgrim's progress toward public education. Terre Haute for many years could not afford to pay for a teacher for a public school, so Eugene Victor Debs had been sent with his chalk and slate to the Old Seminary School during those years of battle over the Mason-Dixon chalk line. Also, learning by rote without relation to the realities of things had not appealed to Daniel as the ideal way to teach the young.

He would always enlarge at home upon the education which his children received at school—would try to turn their eyes away from the limited to the distant horizon, which was not merely the next furrow in a field.

Arithmetic also had not been neglected in the Old Seminary School, for how could there be bankers coming up in Terre Haute if none knew how to add, subtract, multiply, divide?

Eugene Victor knew French—had been taught in a town where there were many citizens from France and not a few of intellectual background who knew Greek and Latin, although one did not usually wear one's knowledge on the sleeve of one's old work shirt or the toes of one's old work boots as one slopped around through seas of mud. One did not put on airs.

The father would have been happy if he could have arrived in this settlement when it was a remote part of France and would have been even happier could it have remained France. He had among his possessions a little packet of the sweet French dust that he had scraped away from the roots of spice bushes which had been brought over from France and which he intended—when he heard Roland's winding horn—to have put into his grave with him who had been and would continue to be a citizen of France all his life.

As a cracker-barrel philosopher in a grocery store talking to old French customers who sometimes came in on winter nights to warm themselves before his stove, which always had its belly full of coals and a pot of hot soup on the lid in order to melt away icicles from hats and beards, Daniel had exchanged all the legends which could be found relating to the French in America from the earliest time and the French Revolution, among them one pertaining to an old, white-bearded French hermit who had fought for Greek freedom and when it was lost had come to America in search of freedom and who—not far from the Rappite and Owenite utopias, neither of which had attracted him—had lived with a white horse in a cave on an Indian mound high over the Wabash and had never come down until he came for solace when the white horse died, and he had said to the people surrounding him that he was two thousand years old, then had returned to the cave to sleep for possibly another two thousand years.

The father had been altogether happy when, having supplemented the son's education by the reading aloud of books which never got into the Hoosier schools in that day as they were altogether too revolutionary, the public had become aware of the need for training preachers, teachers, bankers, farmers, and engineers, and this had prompted the city fathers to open a high school for white students who wished to improve themselves or whose parents did not wish to leave them in a natural state of corruption, although education was not compulsory. There were no blacks or reds or yellows—not enough to fill a lean-to.

The cheerful Eugene Victor, whose good cheer even then had not made him blind to social injustices—he observed more and more of them, always would—had been such an excellent speller that he had received from his teacher, Miss Abbie Flagg—to whom he would always feel that he owed in many ways his everlasting indebtedness for the beautiful knowledge she had disseminated if not for a gift which she gave—a Bible for not having missed a word in spelling for a term of twenty-two weeks.

That was in 1867, according to the inscription on the flyleaf, which was attended by the admonitory words "Read and obey." Debs would remark when he was a very old man who had certainly been in hell's furnaces through his very insistence upon walking in heaven's way and a jocose spirit had overcome him in a moment that should have been one of high seriousness, "I never did." He had certainly read the Scriptures for his creative purposes—at least had glanced at them.

It was—to say the least—very doubtful whether, if Lincoln had not been killed, he would have been able to enact the benevolent Reconstruction of the South that he had envisioned—for when there had occurred the death of the man who had been after all nothing but an old clotheshorse in Washington and beyond the help of any tailor, the cry could be heard as if emerging from McGuffey's little red-backed reader: "O righteous Heavens! e're Freedom found a grave / Where slept the sword, omnipotent to save? / Where was thine arm, O Vengeance! where thy rod / That smote the foes of Zion and of God?"

Whatever he knew of McGuffey's he had learned as he was riding about on his old bay mare whose head had been his desk—a very uncertain desk, as she had stopped to crop the grass along the roadsides. "Oh, why should the spirit of mortal be proud? / Like a fast-flying meteor, a fast-flying cloud, / A flash of the lightning, a break of the wave, / He passes from life to the rest in his grave. . . ."

But now that Lincoln was dead and thus proved to be mortal, his ideas had to be killed, not only by Democrats but by the most radical Republicans—not all of whom were abolitionists.

[6 2]

APPARENTLY THE HIGH SCHOOL boy Eugene Victor Debs had had no reason for wasting his precious time reading terrible Diamond Dick or other penny dreadfuls. He was emotional but without isolation or division of his ego from the highest ideals, which at any period of his developing life he could command. He was not absentminded and abstract and of a generalizing nature, which, while making him sympathetic with the large body of mankind, could still permit him to be indifferent to the sorrows etched in the individual human face.

His sympathies would always be with the pursued and not with the pursuer—as would be expected from the wandering Jew in the service of *les misérables*. Who were the pursued? They were the many.

They were and would be the many members of minorities—the red men, the black men, the yellow men, the tramps whose numbers increased after the Civil War in which the rich industrialists of the North had prospered and waxed large as the poor man waxed as thin as the sickle moon. The poor white workingmen who had no work were driven from place to place endlessly as birds of passage who could sleep nowhere.

Who were the pursuers? They were the military men who had been trained in war against civilians, and the company detectives—mainly Pinkerton's—who had gained their reputation by protecting the president from assassination every night except the night when he was killed.

Debs's youth was spent in brooding over the abyss. He was not one of those indifferent or neutral or sleeping people who, half asleep and half awake—which half was asleep and which was awake?—were never alert to any of the great historical events with which their lives were contemporaneous and which, although so momentous in passion that they tore the sky apart, passed over them like water over a duck's back and left them undisturbed, perhaps because of ignorance, perhaps because of knowledge.

The times were those of trouble, trouble, double trouble and turmoil with cries of murder, murder, murder everywhere, even now in the peace which was a tragically classic case and which continued to break out in a pattern which, seeming sporadic, was unremittingly logical. "What a terrible calamity," as had been written in McGuffey's. "A tempest desolated the land." But had not the schoolboys seen an actor enacting greater Shakespeare in the killing of Abraham Lincoln than had been given to many actors in life? And who had directed the actor in this most melancholy role?

Was it someone in Lincoln's cabinet, some lifelong dissembler like Edwin M. Stanton, secretary of war? Was it he who threw the stone that killed two birds at once, many birds, heavens of birds? "Now he belongs to the ages," Stanton had said of the murder of the president by the unemployed Booth.

Had Mrs. Lincoln—who was well known to be both hysterical and extravagant—ordered, as it was rumored, acres and acres of black mourning veils before the assassination? She would return two dozen of the president's monogrammed shirts to a Washington store for refund.

Was it she or someone else who had arranged that the door of the president's box be left unlocked for the assassin's entry at the end of the second act? And why had every road but one out of Washington to the South been closed, the one that the mad assassin had taken?

And was it really Booth who was killed and buried, and why had no one been allowed to exhume him to see whether someone else had been killed in his place?

And was it true that the reason he had killed the president was that he had been brought up by a tragedian father who had been a bigamist, a drunkard, a vegetarian, and such a great pacifist that he had taught his children to try to evade stepping on beetles and ants and not even to kill a rattlesnake and had succeeded with all his progeny except for this son, who had enjoyed shooting cats and dogs and birds and had not been punished by his father?

Booth the elder, after all, had been such a red-eyed, raving, ranting, incandescent old man. Once along the Ohio River shore, the elder Booth had found some passenger pigeons dead from the hunters' bullets in the wilderness and had summoned a preacher to bury them.

He had written to his sons, only one of whom had been heedless of his advice: "The ideas of Pythagoras, I have adopted—and as respects our accountability to animals hereafter, nothing that man can preach can make me turn to the contrary. Every death its own avenger breeds."

The pacifism of this old actor—who had committed many murders while in the guise of many kings on stage and had himself been killed—had been so profound that he did not believe in capital punishment. His son John Wilkes, his favorite son, did not seem to him to enjoy those stellar talents that would make of him a star of major magnitude—indeed, he had thought that the mercurial lad would be lucky if he turned out to be a clown with tinsel streaming from his hat.

And who had conspired with frenzied, frothing, but coldly calculating Booth? Why had General Ulysses S. Grant and his lady not appeared in the doomed box that night—for although the general had explained that they could not, due to the fact that his wife was sick, tired, worn out—yet how could she have been more sick than Mrs. Lincoln was and more tired than the president of the United States was? And had they had foreknowledge of the bloody aftermath to many bloody battlefields—the bleeding horses shot up among the boughs of bleeding cherry trees? For whom had Booth been the agent? Acting in whose behalf?

[6 3]

O N MAY 2, 1865, the new president, Andrew Johnson—the southern
tailor who had also been invited to be seated with President Lincoln
in the doomed theater box but had refused—had made an announcement
that had increased the country's uproar: from evidence in the Bureau of Military Justice it appeared that the murder of Abraham Lincoln and the
attempted assassination of William H. Seward had been incited by Jefferson Davis and certain other rebels.

When Jefferson Davis heard that he had conspired with Booth to kill
Lincoln, all he could say as an honorable southern gentleman was that God
knew that he preferred Lincoln to Johnson.

On January 24, 1867, according to another voice in the congressional
bedlam, it was obvious that the evil deed must have been done by this new
president, who had profited most by the old president's death. Abe had
been a fool when he placed his faith in Andy. Anyone who had placed faith
in him to carry out Abe's crazy policies of not penalizing half a nation for
the attempt to secede from the other half in accordance with his philosophy
of regeneration had been in all probability a worse fool.

The extremist Republicans, according to the president-by-assassination
Andrew Johnson, showed no more respect for the Constitution than if it
were an old almanac. When Ulysses S. "Unconditional Surrender" Grant
had unwilling accompanied Andy Johnson upon the tour of the East and
Middle West by which Johnson had hoped to win the people over to what
he believed was his continuation of the fallen Lincoln's policies in regard to
handling the fallen South, there had been such a wild mob of hooters and
tooters and howlers barring the way that the tailor president might have
been torn limb from limb and left with wounds beyond all powers of
patching up by any physician with his needle and glue and thread if Grant
had not brought temporary calm to the storm by remarking—as he waved
his burning cigar toward the target—"The President of the United States."

The poetry of Lincoln's soul was what some people thought had been
lost to a new race of hard-boiled businessmen—but then why had there
been shots in the Hoosier capital to stifle the voice of a man who had wished
to speak on behalf of Lincoln's conciliatory policy toward the murdered
South which would have been his had he lived, had he not been killed?

The grand old Republican party had discovered that it had made a vast mistake in having had aboard a president and a vice president of such different natures—as if when the Great Emancipator who was the Christ of the American passion play had been slain they were left with the unregenerate southern tailor who would steadily deny civil rights to black men and was just as guilty of murder as if he had stabbed Abe in the back.

Andy was not against the blacks, but he was against the continuation of the war by the shedding of more and more seas of red blood, that of both black and white men.

Andy had been left to reap the double whirlwinds that old Abe had started up without himself quite knowing how he was going to attain the peace that would not be the war all over again such as now it seemed, as shouts of treason rent the air and the president was not to be allowed to be his own man and act upon his own conscience as he saw fit for the preservation of the South against the operators of Manifest Destiny, who wished to annex it to their financial empire before going on and on to take the North and the West.

Lincoln had been so strong a president in time of war that he had had the power to do anything he pleased and a great deal more in order to subdue the enemy wherever he appeared in the North or in the South, for he had interpreted his presidency as giving him the authority to govern by the crisis law which permitted him to respond with his enigmas to the enigmas of the war, as when—acting outside the law as only a skillful lawyer could—he had closed the mail to treasonable correspondence—had ordered the arrest of potential traitors for traitorous activities which had not yet occurred—had authorized the suspension of the writ of habeas corpus with a high-handedness that even passionate abolitionists could not forgive him for as some had questioned his commitment to the cause of freedom in view of the starvation of the white wage slaves in the North and the extermination of the red men in the West and the way the labor unions had been set back in their struggle from the darkness to the light.

What Andy had seemed to see was that freedom for the little people—whether white or black—was never the true goal for the radical Republicans, who wished to warp and bend the Lincoln policy to a way very different from his, that their concordance was discordance and that if ever freedom came by their deliverance, it would come to an absolutely barren world without a human being in it from pole to pole.

BEFORE THE PILLARS of Terre Haute society who were members of the prestigious Philomethan Literary Club, which had taken its name from a daughter of a king of Athens who was changed into a nightingale, Eugene Victor Debs—who was one of the high school members and was trying to learn to be vocal—had given an oration entitled "Honor" and had appeared also in various debates on various American historical characters and their merits and demerits—sometimes difficult to assess.

A subject of debate in which Eugene Victor Debs had had to be prepared to take either side was whether Benedict Arnold or Aaron Burr was the traitor of greater magnitude of purpose—what might be called not the relative merits but relative demerits of treason.

Debs would one day remark in the pages of *The Locomotive Firemen's Magazine* that George Washington had been considered a demagogue in his day but a generation later had been idealized as a demigod—for the differences between a demagogue and a demigod were largely dependent upon the passage of time.

Thomas Paine and Thomas Jefferson had become in Debs's school days his true heroes, as they would be all his life. As to a choice between Republicans and Democrats, he would prefer—until at last, like a child who is burned by touching the fire, he came to see that they were governed by the same powers—Democrats, who, it had seemed to him, generally favored the poor, whereas the Republicans generally favored the rich and made no bones about their preference.

[6 4]

THE BESIEGED PRESIDENT in the White House was a self-made rugged individualist just as Lincoln had been but was believed lacking in the spirit of poetry that had helped old Abe to synthesize discords into concords all along his way of thorns—or so it had been hazarded.

Andy was the son of a poor North Carolina redneck who could not keep his head above the waters in this life in an economic sense—could not swim—but not questioning whether or not he could had jumped from a bridge into a river in the flood to try to save a redneck millworker who had been swept from the bridge and had been drawn down with him in a locked lovers' embrace of fellowman with fellowman and had not risen again.

Apprenticed to a cruel tailor at the age of ten because he had to work for his crumbs of bread, Andy had been a bound boy until, at the ripe old age of seventeen, rebelling against the white slavery of bondage, he had made his way over the mountains to Greenville, a little town in Eastern Tennessee, and in a two-room house that would be retained as his memorial opened his own tailoring business without any capital but his native wit.

Andy Johnson had listened to his little country-school-teacher wife read in loudly rolling tones to him until gradually he had learned to read aloud to her. He had learned oratory by exercising his vocal cords in the tailoring shop after hours.

The tailor president had had good reason to know that the millennium for white or black men was not the intention of Northern diehards, for whom abolition had been a sentimental slogan. The mourners for Lincoln might well be those who had hoped to profit most from his death and who might soon be mourners for Andy Johnson if they had their way.

Johnson had made an absolute mare's nest of his administration in Washington by suddenly changing from what had seemed the spirit of vengeance to that of conciliation such as had been that of Lincoln when he had promised a new nation born under God.

And now that this dyed-in-the-wool southerner Andy Johnson with his sudden showing of his true allegiances and his true colors had been elected not by election but by an assassination—and he would have been nothing if the awkwardly tailored president had lived, for he had been backed up by no constituency—perhaps his enemies in the North could find a way to get rid of him.

On George Washington's Birthday, 1866, Andy had said in loudly ringing tones to serenaders who had come to the porch of the White House to sing and play old mountain tunes to him, "They may talk about beheading—but when I am beheaded, I want the American people to be the witness. Are those who want to destroy our institutions . . . not satisfied with the blood that has been shed? Does not the blood of Lincoln appease the vengeance and wrath of the opponents of this government?"

These words were bold. They were seditious. They were undermining a government that ought to be conducted with law and order by men who were essentially lawless, anarchic men and had no respect for any law that was not to their immediate benefit.

Could a president in the White House who was availing himself of freedom of speech as given by the Constitution under the rule of God in a god-fearing nation be robbed of his freedom of speech and arrested for sedition and high treason and other misdemeanors?

As the tempest roared throughout the South, there had occurred—provoked by the military rule of carpetbaggers from the North—uprisings of the white-shrouded Ku Klux Klanners riding at night on black horses to make sure that the black men who attempted to vote in the white world would be given no fruit of victory but would be themselves the fruits of the hangman's tree under the bloody moon.

Andy had believed in not only a nation of small pockets for suits of businessmen but small farms, small stores, small banks—the kind where the banker could account for every dollar in the till—as he was and would continue to be opposed to the endless occupation of the South by no patriots but the Lords of Grab and Graft in retribution for the crime of secession, which he most profoundly swore had never occurred and which the late war had shown to be an impossible thing.

He had opposed the great, far-reaching tentacles of that great octopus which was the United States Bank as he had opposed the control of the nation's destiny by men who throughout the long war had placed themselves by their erosions of the old Constitution in a position to assume such vastly monolithic power as that previously enjoyed by the great pharaohs who were the plantation owners with their slave empire for whom he—a former bound boy—had no sympathy and which he had no aspirations to join.

[6 5]

THE DELUSIONS of industrial progress by Generals Graft and Grab were those which Crafty Andy—according to his upholders, who among the high-minded were few and far between—had opposed as if all their movements forward were movements backward. Crafty Andy was simply not cooperative with the power block.

What Andy Johnson had seemed to be in the age of the machine was an old-fashioned horse-and-buggy rider looking for the hitching post that used to be and was not there.

All through this war, which was, as some have called it, the war for the American soul—and yet was a war made of many ambivalences, many mysteries that time would not solve—the purveyors of shoddy army supplies in New York had buttoned up their coats with diamond-decorated buttons and had paved their voracious mouths with false teeth which were the gold of El Dorado flashing with diamond sparks, while the poor men had been toothless or else had had as many teeth missing as the pickets in the Mason-Dixon Line when it ran through a battlefield which would be a graveyard for the boys from the North and the boys from the South.

Gold-bearing lands were being appropriated by corporation land grabbers without objection from the federal government, which owed to them some reward for financing the war and so ignored as many malfeasances as it could while poor war widows and their children living in hog huts in that same North starved.

On February 22, 1868, the House of Representatives—led by Secretary of War Stanton, whom Andy had booted out of the War Department but whom the Senate had returned to the War Department with the intention of booting Andy out of the White House, if it took the cavalry to pursue him—had voted to start impeachment proceedings, a trial from which he was absent from the show of which he should have been the star—a fact which must have been as frustrating to the sensation-seeking audience as if *Julius Caesar* had been played without Brutus, or *Othello* without Iago.

As for Andy, he had been quite certain that his case was already lost in view of who the judges were—the very Congress that had condemned this nation to the rule of carpetbaggers. The tailor president was non compos mentis in the view of much of Republican Washington—as mad as a March hare.

The declaration—with a two-thirds majority, as required by the Constitution—had been made in the name of the House of Representatives and of the people of the United States that—but how did the people get into this act or any other act?—we do impeach Andrew Johnson, president of the United States, of high treason and misdemeanors. There had been twelve commandments which he had broken in the name of a god who was other than the god of their worship, but mainly they consisted almost wholly of the charge that Andy had attempted to remove Stanton from the War Department without having had the commandment of the Senate to do so.

The proceedings began on March 5 before Salmon P. Chase, who was now Chief Justice of the Supreme Court. Three times during the progress of the trial, the president had been saved from removal from his office by one vote. A vote of two thirds was necessary for conviction according to the Constitution, and on three counts the vote to convict was thirty-five to nineteen.

Senator Ben Wade of Ohio—who had disapproved of Lincoln's Amnesty Act but had stumped for Lincoln when victorious battles had seemed to assure the victory of the North against the South—had been so sure that he was going to be the president moving onto the disgraced, impeached, exiled Andy's throne that he had written his inaugural speech and Mrs. Wade had provided herself with her inaugural gown.

Both the inaugural speech and the inaugural gown and the fans and gowns of ladies-in-waiting should have been placed under glass as a reminder to future generations that he who conducts his political career in accordance with his great expectations may suffer an everlasting disappointment when the great prize that seemed so near is snatched away from him.

Although the impeachment proceedings should have brought the day of reckoning, this fate was not to be old Andy's fate. When the roll of the Senate was called, the answers of "yeah" had seemed to pile up the certainty of the stubborn, recalcitrant, mulish old Andy's infernal guilt, until from Senator William Pitt Fessenden of the state of Maine—an old friend of Lincoln's—had come the braying mule's "nay" and "nay" from Senator James W. Grimes of Iowa and "nay" from Senator Lyman Trumbull of Illinois, so that there were altogether seven "nays" from Republicans stampeding to join the Democrats.

After the trial for treason, of which he was acquitted by a majority of one and by men who perhaps revered the presidency more than the profane president who was trying to keep his sacred trust, Andy's presidential power had not increased, of course—his fingernails and his toenails had been clipped by the great power clippers. "Damn the presidency," he had remarked. "It is not worthy of the aspirations of a man who desires to do right."

Not elected a second time as he had never been elected a first, this accidental president had stopped on his way home to attend a banquet at Baltimore in his honor, and in response to the glowing toast to him that had been proposed by his southern admirers, he had said that his deliverance out of the White House had been the greatest case of emancipation there had been since the rebellion began.

After a little less than seven years, Andrew Johnson had returned to Washington as a senator and had come back with two purposes. One was to do what he could to punish the brigadiers who had led the South to desert the Union. The other was to make a speech against Grant for his use of federal troops to force upon the people of Louisiana a corrupt governor whom they had already booted out.

Andy Johnson had promptly, proudly made his speech under the dome of the Senate as he asked whether Louisiana was a commonwealth free to elect its own governor or was a government maintained by military powers by the president of the United States. "Is it his government? . . . How far off is Empire? How far off is military despotism?" He had prayed, first looking heavenward and then earthward: "May God bless the people and save the Constitution!"

Having made his speech, he had died, yet not because of the speech he made and not because he had called for restoration of peace and the reunion of North and South and for the preservation of the Constitution. It had seemed to him a document that was greatly in need of salvation and probably always would be.

Andrew Johnson was buried back home in Tennessee, wrapped, as he had desired, in the American flag—with under his head as a pillow his old, yellowed, thumb-marked, tallow-stained copy of the Constitution.

[6 6]

LYMAN TRUMBULL—one of the men who had saved President Andrew Johnson from impeachment for treason—would be a member of a legal team of three arguing, but unsuccessfully, before the United States Supreme Court in Washington in defense of the application of the writ of habeas corpus in the case of Eugene Victor Debs and his labor companions for the so-called Debs Rebellion by the fledgling American Railway Union, which had not struck illegally against the rule of the Emperor Pullman—had struck legally—and yet had been denied their constitutional rights by having been imprisoned without benefit of a trial by a jury made of men who were true to freedom's always threatened cause.

The lawyer for Pullman would be Robert Todd Lincoln, Prince of Nails, who had been as hard on his widowed mother as on wage slaves, black or white, and who had forgotten his father's sympathies with the burgeoning labor union movement, which had been retarded in its progress by the all-consuming Civil War but after the Civil War had reasserted itself in the face of federal troops equipped with great Gatling guns manned by former Civil War officers.

When in the year of the Emancipation Proclamation the locomotive engineers had refused to man the trains on all the railroads coming into Chicago, scabs imported from the East had broken the strike in only two days as these strikers who obviously were not superpatriots like the railroad pharaohs were forced back to work.

Eugene Victor Debs, who was to organize the show that published the *Locomotive Firemen's Magazine,* would write the constitution for a branch of the International Typographical Union—and he would also dip into his own lean pockets from which he gave out more than once along life's road a miraculous penny which was one more than he had.

When during the Civil War the printers in St. Louis had gone on strike, they had been faced by General William Starke Rosencranz—the hero of the battles of Rich Mountain, Corinth, and Stone River—the loser of the battle of Chickamauga. Rosencranz had employed federal soldiers as scabs to take the place of the printers who, when they wrote of their grievances to the man in the White House, old Abe, who according to Walt Whitman was the Hoosier Michelangelo, had been conciliatory—very fatherly or brotherly—and had sent back word that the military strikebreakers had no right to interfere with the legitimate demands of labor and should be withdrawn as some who had known him as a print-starved boy at Pigeon Creek should have foreseen—salvation having come to him through the printed word, which was denied to many a poor white man as to a black man.

Upon his second election, President Abraham Lincoln—as few people knew at the time—had received from the International Workingmen's Association in London—signed by the hand of its almost unknown secretary for Germany, Karl Marx—a letter of congratulation which had drawn protest from the members of the Communist Club of New York, who were united in their inability to foresee any immediate or remote prospect of a republican revolution taking place in the shadows of the colossal Wall Street where the profiteering war vultures perched. Marx had urged that the American people should give full civil rights to the newly emancipated brothers lest there should be a new war.

IN 1864—the year of the burning of Atlanta—there had occurred a bloody massacre of the red men of the West by the white men who had already robbed them of the freedom to roam over their own lands and had driven them to starve where nothing grew.

The Indians had not been that minority for whose suffrage the Civil War had been fought—and they generally had no friends unless among utopists who were trying to withdraw from the ever-encroaching capitalistic American nation themselves—among them, the Mormons, who had been victimized by the same land grabbers as the red men were—even as they had recognized—and whose Zion was under double jeopardy, and was threatened at the same time by the great scissor blade of the North and the great scissor blade of the South—the former because of the Mormons giving refuge to red men who were in flight from extinction—the latter because of their having wished to welcome the black men when they were fugitives from chattel slavery whom the Latter-Day Saints would have taken into their ranks if they who combined the religion of Moses with that of Mohammed had not been threatened by those greedy expansionists who wished to cut them to a shadow and a flame, a flame and a shadow.

Before the gold rush the territory of the Southern Cheyenne and Arapaho Indians had extended from central Kansas to the Rocky Mountains, but now the red men had been pushed into a small circle straddling a ridge with all their hunting trails closed and in 1861 had been persuaded by an agent of the United States government to sell that land, which to all intents and purposes was no longer theirs, for a piece of paper—a promissory note of $350,000 which was to be paid upon the installment plan each year over a period of five years—as also they were given for their dwelling place this new land which was depicted as a land of promise—which it was—a land of promise of which the promises were all illusion even as were the promissory notes.

There were neither fruits nor flowers nor grasses nor earth for seeds—and there was no game—neither the white antelope nor the black antelope nor the spotted antelope—and thus the red people starved.

Uncle Sam and his profiteering financiers had forgotten their broadly latitudinarian promissory note—it might as well have been something written on papyrus and hidden away under a mountain of stone when they had shaved the Indian territory down to a withered rind with the flies buzzing on it.

All the dollars Uncle Sam with his large moneybags could locate were required for the advancement of the Civil War, which had as one of its numerous illusory goals the problematical release of the black man from the halter of chattel slavery, whereas the less fortunate red men who had already been exterminated by thousands and thousands, as when they had lost their old Ohio and Indiana and Illinois homes, were scheduled to be driven off the face of the earth or into holes in the ground—it was widely known in the West, for they were of no more value than the coyote population—and the numbers of moccasin prints in the grasses were also to be reduced like the grasses of the onetime savannah and like the numbers of buffalo prints left by buffalo herds and the numbers of fishes which had been as thick in the rivers and streams as the autumn leaves falling in the autumn and the numbers of wild geese and other migratory birds—this land to be denuded and polluted by the inexorable wheels of progress.

The red men had been blown before the white men like sand grains in a storm.

[6 7]

AMONG THE CROWDS that had gathered to admire the statue of the Indian hunter in New York's Central Park which had been lifted up against the city's skyline in 1863, John Quincy Adams Ward had sensed—as a seasoned traveler who had made a long peregrination among the Indians of the West and Northwest—that this was a symbol of no living and pulsating reality but rather was a memorial to a species that was doomed to extinction.

Chief Black Kettle of the Cheyennes—having been promised safe conduct if he would give up his arms—had hoisted the American flag and the small white flag of peace high on a pole over the tents of his sleeping flock in their village at Sand Creek when on a morning in late November 1864 as the gray clouds steamed—sometime between daylight and sunrise—Colonel John Chivington and his militia had ridden upon the encampment and had slaughtered and mutilated approximately four hundred and fifty men, women, and children with a deliberation that might seem to provide some historical precedent for the slaughter of the strikers in the tent city of Ludlow and in other strikes, when corporations identified all strikers as reds.

The archetypal villain Colonel Chivington—the center of hurricanes of protest—had been cited for court martial but was never to be brought to trial. No Indian who had escaped the slaughter at Sand Creek had been allowed to testify before the military commission.

As for Chief Black Kettle, who had survived the carnage of that dawn's slaughter when the sun had turned blood red and who had decided that never again could he believe in white man's promises, he had steamed with black grief over the death of his people—that which he said was as wide as the world.

Chief Black Kettle—still spouting with rage caused by that grief without which he would not have been a human being—was killed in the autumn of 1868 in the Cheyenne camp on the banks of the Washita in the Nebraska sand hills where only the day before he had been assured by the white military officers that it would be safe for his men and their families to pass a night.

The man who had led the cavalry stamping down Black Kettle into the water had been General George Armstrong Custer, who in 1866 had been one of the many surplus Civil War officers for whom Uncle Sam had provided an extension of employment.

One of the motives for Custer's descending upon Black Kettle—the last of the peace chieftains—had been his desire to have his naked shame as a military deserter from his post covered with the fig leaf of military glory.

Custer's illegitimate half-breed son—called Yellow Swallow by the Cheyennes because his pale face and yellow, feathery hair differentiated him from the red men, whose hair was as black as the feathers of the black swallows—had been with his dead mother's people through long, long flights in desert lands as they were driven like black swallows before the wind by the white murderer.

Custer's discovery of gold in the Black Hills would attract thousands of gold seekers to the land that by treaty had been given to the red men. One of the motives that prompted the search for gold had been the need to publicize the railroad, which had been stalled in its progress up the Yosemite, as few in the East had understood why any railroad should be in a place where no one was going anyway.

In charge of the military conquest over the already dying reds had been the much bemedaled, gold-braided General Nelson A. Miles, whom Mr. Dooley of Chicago would someday describe as having faced—during his thirty-five years of army service—death and promotion in every form.

General Miles would later be the general called in from Ft. Leavenworth to be in charge of the federal troops massed against Eugene Victor Debs during the Pullman strikes and would go on to become the senior officer in command of the United States Army during the Spanish-American War, whose purpose was the extension of empire over the Caribbean Sea as if it were a lake or as if its islands could be drawn by cables to the Florida shore.

[6 8]

The time from the assassination of Abraham Lincoln and the sudden catapulting of a rebel into the presidential saddle to the time of the assassination of James B. Garfield and his succession by Chester A. Arthur would be a time through which would run—sometimes in the limelight, sometimes in the shadows—the distraught figure of Mrs. Abraham Lincoln, the black widow, as she was called by those who—often hating her husband when he was alive—did not deceive her by the respect they paid to him when he was dead and she was left to starve to death inch by inch.

The trouble was that Mrs. Lincoln had purchased by secret charge accounts of which her husband had not been apprised voluminous satins, to which she had added oceans and oceans, acres and acres by her shopping tours in New York and Washington, and her trunks and trunks—bales of chiffons and silks and velvets and lace, which had come by ship throughout the war—because of which she thanked God that he had died before confrontation with her bills for yardage, reaching endlessly, it must have seemed.

Even when her husband had been alive to know that letters of threat had been made against his life—so many that he had told her that life was hell—people who were scorpions—the radicals, the vindictives, the Jacobeans in the Republican party—what need had Abe of enemies outside that recalcitrant mob?—his enemies had tried to drive their swords through him by driving their swords through her with accusations of traitordom—for the best way to reach his vulnerable heart was by way of her even more vulnerable heart.

The *Chicago Daily Tribune* had remarked that if Mrs. Lincoln had been a prizefighter, a foreign danseuse, or a condemned convict on the way to execution, she should not have been so maltreated as she was by a portion of the New York press. Her secretary—in response—had tried to laugh out of court the implication that Mrs. Abraham Lincoln had been engaged in treason to the Union cause by remarking that if there were so many spies coming over the White House grounds like so many ghosts every night as had been implied, probably the best way to get in through the window to the sleeping former first lady of the land would be to put up Jacob's ladder and climb.

But the accusation of his wife's treason to the cause of the Union which old Abe Lincoln had believed that he himself personified in every department of the war could not be dismissed as a joke.

Before the Committee on the Conduct of the War he had ambled in one day to declare, "I, Abraham Lincoln, president of the United States, appear of my own volition before the Committee of the Senate to say that I, of my knowledge, know that it is untrue that any of my family hold treasonable communication with the enemy."

When Andy Johnson—as the new president surrounded by the bloody reconstructionists who had defamed the conciliatory Lincoln—was having his veiling problems, which Carl Schurz—a spokesman for the Deep South—had told him he could have for a long time in the wilds of the Deep South, strange land where civil liberties would be withheld from black men whether alive or dead and where a great many black women, who under the old order of things had not dared to wear black veils as an expression of their grief—for black veils had been considered the expression of white aristocracy fit for a white lady but not fit for a white lady's black maid or black washerwoman, black washer of her white feet or black comber of her hair or nurse for her young—had put on veils under the new order of things in recognition of the fact that slavery was supposed to be no more in idea or fact, and thus had been set upon by white women tearing the black veils away from their faces—such having been the spirit of revenge of former first ladies of great plantation kingdoms. What concern should the welfare of the former first lady, the president's black widow with her eternal veiling problems, be to the former tailor Andy Johnson, for whom silks and satins and long veils for the first year of mourning with diminishment in length of veil as the period of mourning diminished itself had never been his line?

It was said of Mrs. Lincoln when she was still in the White House that she—never known to deny herself the most extravagant luxuries—had been such a penny-pincher and so tight-fisted that she had had drawers for careless old Abe sewn out of the White House sheets and pillowcases, which bore the wreathed initial *M*, signifying the name of Madison. She had dismissed all laundresses but one, who was not herself—for she was no Dolley Madison stringing her washing in the damp, moldy Blue Room on rainy days in order to provide shelter from storms—had dismissed all gardeners but one—had sent back for refund a load of manure which had been intended for the White House garden and with the money had given a dinner party that, ever afterward, had been described by some of the ungrateful attendees as the manure dinner.

Poor, starving widow! Was she now supposed to eat nothing but manure herself? Was she supposed to live on a diet of worms or not enough bread crumbs to keep a bird alive as those who were in charge of the nation's breadbasket certainly did not starve themselves but prospered and grew fat with their ill-gotten gains?

In a nation of starving poor whites, where poor blacks in the mass could find no employment but to be used as scabs upon trains and rails during railroad strikes and thus suffer increase of the hatred by the poor white for the poor black, war veterans of both North and South, Mrs. Lincoln—the squat black widow with her black hat and black cherries and black veils and black ribbons making her seem an ambulatory pavilion flitting forever among her self-protective shadows—had been obsessed not only by the idea that she was the starving, homeless wanderer but that all the tragedies that came after the death of her beloved husband were and would continue to be the responsibility of those who had conspired for his removal from the White House.

She was overwhelmed by the belief that Andy Johnson had been in communication with Jefferson Davis and that both ought to be hung from the same sour-apple tree—for both had conspired with Booth.

She well knew, moreover, that she was under suspicion herself of complicity with the murderers—for who were more likely to try to throw the burden upon a bereaved widow for whom the light of the moon and the sun and the stars had gone out?—that they had spread the rumor that she had been precipitate in her preparations for what she called—surely not erroneously—her everlasting grief—that she had ordered her black widow's veils and black silk and black satin skirts and underskirts and black hats with black cherries or black roses on the brims and more black ribbons and black veils than were ever worn by a hearse driver's horse and black gloves and black snub-nosed velvet or satin pumps and black stockings and probably even black corsets before the president's murder had occurred—for she had known—no doubt with great intimacy—that the president's murder was in the works.

People were shocked indeed by the way the Lincoln widow woman had thrown her dead husband's clothes around as if to return them to the primordial chaos—the old worn clothing for which she could get no dollars—and even his bloody shirt among the bundles.

Mrs. Lincoln—clinging tenaciously to all the trunks of silks and satins and laces which had been hers and which the merchants to whom she owed money for enough mourning veils to have covered the ocean with mourning veils and enough sequins to have paved a black shoreline, enough black hats to have hatted dozens of hearse men—was believed by the thieves who were carrying a continent away in their carpetbags to be a thief herself, even if a petty kind.

What had she stolen? She was accused of vandalism by the Johnson administration, although all she took when she left the White House through the back door—as it were—so terribly alone and ignored by the people who were coming in through the front door, was just her husband's shaving mug, for which—something like a pack rat in her honest psychology of taking nothing for which she did not leave something in its place—she had left a shaving mug as near its identical twin as she could find.

She had held it against Andy Johnson that he had not written to her for nine long months after the president was killed, and then came only the most impersonal expression of profound regrets from the methodical houses of Congress, to which had been added not so much as a postscript from the man in the White House.

When Victor Hugo—at a ceremony in Paris where there were forty thousand mourners for the martyred president who had been opposed to slavery in any form—gave a medal in honor of the Great Emancipator to the American ambassador with the request that it should be passed on to the president's widow, and this was delayed in the delivery, she had become convinced that if they could only have omitted handing over to her the tangible honor of this memorial medal they would certainly have done so and pocketed it away for themselves.

Her tonnages of silks were for a long time Mrs. Lincoln's only insurance—her husband's estate when divided three ways, of which a third was hers and a third was for each of her two living sons, having not been enough to keep her moored—poor soul—as she drifted helmless in the storm.

The stalwart successors to President Abraham Lincoln had ignored his difficult widow, either because they had remembered or had forgotten that it was she who had jogged old Abe's elbow to make him write the Emancipation Proclamation sooner than he would have.

To Frederick Douglass—the distinguished leader who would be the first black man ever to be entertained at the White House—Mrs. Abraham Lincoln had sent one of the murdered president's fine walking sticks—which, in the hands of a man who had loved him, must have seemed to have had for him throughout all his future years a life of its own in the journey toward the land in which civil rights would be something more than a promised land.

As the cost of living had been higher than the cost of dying after the Civil War, when the Congress had allowed to Mrs. Mary Todd Lincoln only the salary for that one year which the president had not lived to collect—and as she had only her widow's share of Lincoln's dollars and only a little more than the ten thousand dollars raised by popular subscription for the purchase of a house into which she could retire with her black-veiled grief—the latter sum having been raised before the public knew that Lincoln had died with little more than a few pennies in the toe of an old gray sock—the sympathies of her well-wishers had seemed justifiable.

Black church folks and some who had no church or Rock of Ages to which to cling had been among those who—starving and homeless as many perpetually were—had contributed their hard-earned copper pennies—penny by penny—to the original first aid sum. But who else would be a Saint Bernard to the president's frail widow as she struggled to keep footing in a world of icy pinnacles, abysses, avalanches of snow falling over her?

Heavily disguised—pretending to be somebody else's black widow—Mary Todd Lincoln had consented while in New York to have her clothes put on display for sale—and she had also permitted the publication of letters in the Democratic newspaper *New York World* in which the Republican party members were accused of having deprived her of all means of support and having thus left her in a pitiable condition.

The black widow had been accused of blackmail on every side, her detractors seeming always to increase and never to diminish. And thus she who was of a bold rather than a timid nature had become afraid to venture out of doors for fear she would be mobbed and knocked down and subjected to highway robbery by those whose hands were claws—iron claws such as pursued and assaulted her in her night dreams as in her day dreams, which also transpired in darkness—darkness and whirlwinds never ceasing—and indeed, she had passed already beyond recognition, she was convinced—as she surely would have been wiped out from public and most private memory if it had not been for the heavy black widow's veils behind which she draped herself and which called attention to her in a nation of many widows, who—both black and white—were surely poorer than she was and had no such lavish weeds as she who was passing beyond recognition of self by self—the reflection of her face in the mirror pale and haggard—drained of all color—a mere moth—perhaps the death's head or Sphinx moth the moon sometimes seemed when it was in a cloud—her dresses like bags hanging onto her lean frame so that it was a wonder she did know herself, although, of course, she did—and in dimensions not usually apprehended by the average eye, which saw not beyond the superficial appearances of things.

[6 9]

THE WIDOW of Abraham Lincoln did not feel like shooting or stabbing the Republicans in the North or the Democrats in the South—only like taking her own life.

Added to all other nervous discords, griefs beyond measure, had been William H. Herndon's revelations, by publication and lectures, of the awful lie that her idolized husband had never really loved her who had been his helpmate and his wife and that he had gone mad—mad as a March hare, no doubt—because of the death of his sweetheart, Ann Rutledge, whom he had loved with an everlasting love and of whom the besieged black widow had never heard.

Mrs. Lincoln's husband had been truth itself in his relationship with her not only when he was alive but when he was dead—so that she had been sure in every cell of her being from the crown of her head to the soles of her feet that Abraham Lincoln's much publicized love for Mrs. Ann Rutledge had been founded upon a myth, such a romantic name never having been breathed by him who would never have cherished his love for a ghost with whom she could not compete and who was beyond the range of what was real and who existed not even in a dream—an undying dream that would go on when the dreamer was dead.

Abraham Lincoln's life, all through his marriage to Mary Todd Lincoln, had been a life of joyous laughter in which one would not have supposed that his heart was in an unfortunate woman's grave.

As for the widow of Abraham Lincoln, however, her heart was and always would be in her dead husband's uneasy grave, no matter how far she wandered. She had lost some of her buttons when she lost her husband, it was true. Agonies had smitten her between her eyes, sometimes blinding her right eye and sometimes her left—so that at least half the world was cast into darkness at either hand—sometimes to the left and sometimes to the right—she did not always know which—inasmuch as her sufferings were all-pervasive.

Because of accusations and persecutions making her almost maniacal, especially those of the dirty dog Herndon, the widow of Abraham Lincoln had fled—heavily veiled by her black veiling—to Europe with her idolized Tad—the frail and asthmatic and stuttering son who had reminded her most of Abraham Lincoln and of Little Willie, as Robert Lincoln—cold and hard and precise—never did.

She had been determined that Tad should have the finest European education there was—this flight from the New World to the Old gave great offense, however, to those who believed that he should be planted in the American millennial soil, which should give nurture to the murdered president's son and which should shape and influence the forming of his character and sense of leadership in a way that would not disappoint his dead father, who had continued to live through him and would live as long as his offspring lived—perhaps longer.

For those who had loved the former president, his memory could not be killed, could not be extinguished—but would always shine on like an undying spark in a sea of darkness for them—even as for her delicate, high-strung, nervous, stammering invalid boy—the always dying, nearly dying Tad over whom the president would always watch—no matter where he was or where they were. For to be dead was not to be dead. The advantage of being dead was that one had simply escaped the logic of time—that time which would net all fishes of the sea and all birds of the air in the end, or almost all.

The date of passage of mother and son on the *City of Baltimore* for Bremen had been October 1, 1868. In Europe—where, as not in her own country, she had expected to be treated with deference as the president's widow—she had drifted from spa to spa, castle to castle—always keeping herself amply shrouded by black mourning crepes and silks for which she was delighted to find that the price had been only fifty cents a yard—whereas in New York harbor where the evil profiteers flourished, the same material was fifty dollars a yard.

The widow of Abraham Lincoln—her mind always replete with memories of her beloved husband's body when it had lain in state in the Windy City of Chicago at the courthouse, where over one door had been written "Illinois clasps to her bosom her slain and glorified son" and over the other "The beauty of Israel is slain upon her high places"—had seen that Paris, the French city that was in France and was not a town in Illinois where the president had often set his foot as never in this metropolis filled with people who spoke French, had been crowded with the presence of rich Americans who—weighted down by their wealth which was of great magnitude and whose munificence provided a sharp contrast with her penury—for she was poor and must count each cent—had made their fortunes during the Civil War.

She had seen while in Europe—as she journeyed from spa to spa—the loud-mouthed, vulgar type of American visitors who would be the concern of Henry James.

Mary Todd Lincoln—the black widow with the permanent lines of grief etched upon her club-shaped face as with an endless rage no passage of time or change of habitat from the New World to the Old World or from the Old World to the New World could blot out—for she had recognized all too clearly that for her there would never be a resting place—had wept and moaned through ceaseless peregrinations in the Alps.

Among her numerous peregrinations had been that in which she had gone over the cloud-topped alpine pinnacles to Florence—slumberous city where she had been fascinated by the birthplace of Dante and the Pitti Palace and the king's residence, which she had visited with the keenest appreciation of historical residences and monuments and flagstones and Ghiberti's bronze doors while waiting for the passage of the pension bill which had been drawn up for the protection of the dead president's widow by Charles Sumner and which—asking for only three thousand dollars a year—had been passed by the House in May 1870 but which had been killed by the Senate when Lyman Trumbull spoke out for it—Sumner having continued to carry on the battle for the black widow's pecuniary rites even when the mud throwers threw mud on him as they were also so busily throwing mud upon her skirts that he would think they should have wearied themselves of this cruel sport in which they engaged at the expense of a most helpless, most fragile soul.

According to Senator Simon Cameron, the men and women who could not destroy Abraham Lincoln had done all they could to destroy his wife.

Finally, in July, Mrs. Lincoln had received her pension by a vote of twenty-eight to twenty, this pension to be increased in 1882 to five thousand dollars a year—so that, if she had been sensible, she might have enjoyed a certain munificence—had she not been swept away by fits of extravagance such as had always been hers.

Very probably—besides the personal aversions to Mary Todd Lincoln caused by their own sense of guilt—the congressmen were reluctant to extend compensation to women, who—no matter under what circumstances the breadwinner had perished—enjoyed no property rights at all in those halcyon days, not one iota more than had the red men.

[7 0]

Mrs. Lincoln's social consciousness, which had transcended that of many who were now become her persecutors and the maligners of her character, had shriveled to so thin a thread that she could see little or no connection between her struggles and those of the sufferings of the blacks and the reds—a relationship that she might have seen if she had not been of necessity centered upon her homeless, wandering, wind-driven, bedraggled self.

Left with only her poor widow's mite and acres of black memorial garments, she had been unable by even the farthest stretch of imagination to identify herself with the women's freedom cause and struggle from the darkness to the light as embodied in the person of the long-suffering Susan B. Anthony—that gaunt-ribbed but motherly bloomer girl who had been smitten by a sense of moral and physical outrage because the power to cast the vote at election time had been given to freed black men but not to women who had fought for abolition long before the war—as there were also those who had fought in the war.

Mrs. Lincoln had been utterly appalled when Victoria Woodhull—who had been a tramp clairvoyant in the Hoosier capital during the Civil War—had emerged most flamboyantly as a candidate for the surely sacred and not profane office of president of the United States in 1872, when her slogan had been that what she stood for—so help her God and man—and especially man—was the naked truth, which—whatever that might be— should be revealed to men, and may the devil take the hindmost—there having been only the thinnest veiling between her naked body and her followers, who, mostly men, had tossed red roses in her way so that her gossamer shroud had been torn into shreds and she stood blushing as if in a sea of roses, none with thorns.

Although it had seemed to Mrs. Lincoln that she had made many sacrifices for her country and even that ultimate sacrifice which had come with her husband's death by hands that were mysterious to others as never to her—few who had prospered having escaped her suspicion, her brightly roving eyes which could see through her black widow's veils, which were as thick as steam emitted from smokestacks of ships and factories and trains—the legend of her self-centeredness had increased—and yet that from which she had suffered acute diminishment was a loss of self—as probably could not be guessed by most of those who considered that the clotheshorse was insane and was more in love with the clothing of reality than with the reality itself—a thing which was so very plain and bare and cold and had passed beyond all memory except her own.

Only a few weeks after her return from Europe to Chicago—the ailing eighteen-year-old Tad having died from the consumption that he had caught while living with his ailing mother in too many unheated castles in Europe—Mrs. Lincoln had passed into a state of almost perfect lunacy, from which it had seemed she would not recover.

The lonely Mary Todd Lincoln had been surrounded by the Stalwarts, who were a sea of scamps—in her withering estimate. She had been isolated by their cruel behavior and driven into exile as if it were she and not they who had conspired in numerous plots for the murder of her husband—a noble man not utterly naïve—a man who could never have been taken by surprise, no matter if there was one murderer or if there were many murderers out to saw him down—if an assassin was always waiting in his path through the dark forest of this life.

Physical harm to Abraham Lincoln had not been enough to satisfy his would-be killers. Slander had also been a death-dealing instrument. Mary Todd Lincoln had had her love robbed by the malicious gossip that old Abe had loved a corpse in Illinois, the beautiful Ann Rutledge, who had died young and who was not his wife who had lived and had grown old at his side although she had remained—as he well knew and as she well knew— a child in her heart. He had been so faithful to his child wife that no memory of the dead, always mysterious sweetheart—the dead Ann Rutledge—could have displaced her—there had surely never been the ghost of a third person in her marriage bed.

Mrs. Lincoln had been accused of infidelity to her dead love, however, the false news having been spread that while in Europe wandering from spa to spa she had attracted and had not discouraged the amorous sentiments of a German dwarf who was a grand chamberlain to the duke of Baden.

Utterly mad but still not half as mad as the government of this nation was—for they should have provided her with comforts that might exceed those of a poor widow who had never been the first lady of her land and had never seen her beloved husband killed by a madman's bullet—sometimes Mrs. Abraham Lincoln thought that her husband's astral body had returned to sleep with her.

Even when at last there was no monetary problem, her habit of tight-fistedness had been so persistent in its rule over her that she had continued to pity herself for her deprivations and ask for the pity of others, and she had remained convinced of her increasing poverty, which was largely a product of her own mental and moral vision and was not real.

Worn out by his mother's maniacal belief that she was surrounded by her enemies on every side and by her inordinate fear of starvation and shelterlessness and most particularly by her vast shopping expeditions, the only living son of Abraham Lincoln had foreseen that if his mother were not checked she would soon run pell-mell through her sizable capital by large purchases of water-damaged or fire-damaged silks.

The widow of Abraham Lincoln was obsessed by her almost constant, almost unremitting fears that Chicago was going to be burned down again by a great fire, which would leave only skeletons of tenements and scorched dune from which all bushes would be burned away and by her desire that her trunks and boxes of material goods should be moved to a small town which should be beyond the tongues of fire. She did not feel that she was safe in Chicago, where she—safely ensconced with her memorial torch flaming all during the night—was determined that the fires would never find her—be they even the fires of spring—and where she could surely trust no water man of the ladder and hook society—if such there was—to come to pour waters onto the fire—pour all the waters of all the lakes and rivers and streams on her.

She slept on a mattress stuffed with corn shucks, which made a papery, rustling sound as she moved from side to side, trying to find some rest for her aching, swollen head upon its feather-stuffed pillow and rest for her inflamed spinal column from which she suffered such sharp pains that she felt that there were some discs missing as in an old many-toothed harvester machine which had broken down and had been left to rust away into nothingness or almost nothingness.

She knew so well that there were people who, whether or not they were conscious or were unconscious of the fact—her judgment refused to differentiate between them—wanted her out of this world—those who had for so long refused to provide an umbrella such as her ever-thoughtful and considerate husband had always carried over the frail creature who was of the creation but not its creator.

The ever-prudent Robert Todd Lincoln, carrying the heavy burden of familial responsibility on his broad shoulders, had been worried by his frenetic, loudly vocal mother's shopping manias—her purchases, for example, of seven thousand dollars' worth of lace curtains when she had nowhere to hang them—acres of lace tablecloths and bales of silks and jewels and gold watches—altogether three timepieces when she already had enough—including the timepiece that told the time only of some other day, some other year that was fled and would never return—would never bring her husband and her dead sons back to her whose only prospect was to make haste to join with them as hastily as she could—and she had also loaded herself down with boxes and boxes of scented soaps and bottles of eau de cologne and more perfumes of Araby than she could ever use, although she continually washed and sprayed herself from head to foot and powdered her face and applied eye shadow and painted her lips cherry red so that she would be recognized by old Abe when he saw her, for she had desired to be no poor bag of skin and bones such as he might not know. She carried her capital on her person and was made squat by so many hidden appendages that her only living son had had in her tow for about three weeks Pinkerton's detectives to shadow her and report to him how and where she spent her money.

How could such frugality and such extravagance as hers be combined in one not simple nature, and was she duplicitous or straightforward?

[7 1]

AT THE COOK COUNTY COURTHOUSE, at the behest of Robert Todd Lincoln, who, hat in hand—his attitude was both sincere and reverential, he being a lawyer for his mother's last estate and being also her only living son, he who was thoroughly worn out and who had suffered enough through his mother's temperamental outbursts and her quarrels with the Republicans and who had political ambitions of his own that made him want to keep the black widow quiescent and out of the nation's limelight—had brought Mrs. Lincoln, against her will and better judgment, to trial before a lunacy judge who had been her husband's friend and before a prosecuting attorney who had been her husband's friend and before an attorney for the defense who had been her husband's friend and before a jury, which—all things were to seem equable, fair and square as a carpenter's last—was made up of important businessmen, merchants, real estate men. All had been her well-wishers and had intended her no harm—but had wished to protect her from taking her bucket to the well so often that she should draw up all the water in it.

Mrs. Lincoln's own chambermaid who had seemed devoted to her had testified—as proof of her mistress's madness—that she could never let up on the subject of Grant, who for her—as was well known to practically everybody except himself with his winsome ways—had a defective character—was a caitiff, a mad dog, a murderer—was a coward.

Mary Todd Lincoln had hated Grant with such almost unceasing virulence that the only way to quiet her had been to give to her the laudanum drops with which she could put herself into a state in which she was half asleep and half awake.

Merchant princes had testified that Mrs. Abraham Lincoln's madness had been shown by the purchases she had made at their stores, actions that they ordinarily would have welcomed as a sign of her sanity having now become a sign of her insanity, as undoubtedly it was if this black widow thought that she was getting bargains from them who had carried to even further extremes than usual their custom of marking things up so that they might mark them down.

The jurymen had included Lyman J. Gage, who would be secretary of the treasury under President William J. McKinley—the third president of the United States to be assassinated.

Not mainly because of her hallucinations, which might have been harmless, the poor lady was adjudged abnormal, abysmally insane, her mind having been shattered possibly beyond repair, it being recalled that, in response to former and present harassments piling up like old sheets stained with blood, she had made an attempt to do away with herself by drinking from two bottles which—about the size of those in which ladies carried their tears and their smelling salts—she had asked to be filled with something to end or abort her misery, but which the pharmacist, knowing his customer well, had labeled laudanum and camphor, although both were as false as false signs along a road—for both had been nothing but water. She had been escorted to Batavia in a private railroad car as she sat upright and still, moving without rustling and without jingling and jangling—her stocks and bonds and paper bills and coins having been sequestered by her son.

While there she was so far gone in madness that she was under the delusion at least part of the time that she was in the White House still. The large part of Mrs. Lincoln's waking time, where she was surrounded by boxes and bales of the purchases that she had made at the crossroads store at Batavia, which had carried—ordinarily a decade late—the last word in fashion, she had spent her flickering, cluttering energies writing to old friends or acquaintances who were in a position of power or had contact with those in power, from whom she asked for assistance in helping her to escape from the madhouse—in which she was confined behind bars to the surrounding land of freedom, where she should be permitted to live in accordance with the style befitting a president's widow who had served her country to the best of her ability as her faithful husband had—they had been side by side through periods of darkness and whirlwind unimaginable to most people from whom had been required such sacrifices as theirs had been.

Her confinement because of her shopping manias had caused as great an embarrassment as when the black widow had been denied her pension rights by a government seemingly indifferent or oblivious to her sufferings, and thus how could Robert Todd Lincoln have expected to enjoy appointments to high office in the Grand Old Party or run for election for president of the United States if it could be said by every loudmouthed Democratic speaker on his trail that he had thrown his mother into a loony bin and left her there?

After four months that must have seemed like four eternities to her whose life was that fifth eternity which was four with one to spare until she should come to the place of the meeting of all parallels, Mrs. Lincoln had been released from the care of her keeper who had posed as her buggy driver and who had certainly treated her with a greater show of outward courtesy than was generally given to most maniacs.

Nine months had passed before Mrs. Abraham Lincoln had been at last pronounced sane, the attorney for the prosecution having turned turtle as had the attorney for the defense. Since his mother was no longer in the tightfisted custody of her son, Robert Todd Lincoln could no longer keep his hands on the purse strings of his father's widow.

Oh, what a thief this thieving son was and how undependable—how duplicitous—untrustworthy and ambivalent and two-faced!

It was perhaps understandable that poor Mrs. Lincoln, who had lost so much and all those things which had recalled to her the meaning of her life, dead life, had been like a hunter with a retriever's instinct when it came to the recovery of all her stolen property—all her losses—all the goods which she thought had been stolen away from her by her son.

To Robert—the future most important cog of the Pullman empire and lawyer for George Mortimer Pullman, who would be barely glimpsed by Eugene Victor Debs when he was leading the strike against that sleeping-car emperor and who could not have been amused by the comparison of Debs with the left-wing father whom he had never known very well—the mother in a white heat of anger had written from Springfield that she wanted the return of all her paintings, both oils and watercolors, whether framed or unframed.

One was the oil painting of the infant Moses hidden among the bul-rushes away from the cruel Herod. Another was the oil painting of fruit that had been hung above the buffet in the dining room. She wanted her silver set and her large silver waiter and her silver tête-à-tête returned to her—all her vermeil spoons and silver spoons and gold and silver forks and pewter ware returned to her—also her laces, diamonds, other jewels—silks and white lace dress, double lace shawl and flounces, lace scarf—how many acres long?—two black lace shawls and one black lace with deep flounces.

Mary Todd Lincoln had informed Robert Todd Lincoln that he had injured himself, not her. Two prominent clergymen had written to her that they were offering up prayers for him in their pulpits on account of the wickedness of this son against his mother who was of this earth like all things mortal, no doubt—he had sinned not only against his mother but against high heaven, too. He had tried, moreover, his game of robbery long enough.

Her letter to Robert Todd Lincoln containing the list of her stolen prop-erties and the threat that the extensive theft would be published in the newspaper if not returned immediately to her—who hesitated not to reveal to the public eye all that it did not see—had been written on June 17, 1876.

Thousands of families in great cities like Chicago and New York were living on as little as seventy cents a week, even like the poor Indians, now as the breed of reds against whom the great guns were turned were not the feathered bird men who had been so greatly depleted and were still being mown down but were union labor strikers who dared to question the authority of the American czars of mills and mines and rails and their punitive expeditions against all who did not conform and who belonged to some lesser orb than theirs.

[7 2]

WHILE MRS. LINCOLN might be mad as her original persecutors had judged her to be, she was beyond a shadow of a doubt sane enough to have enjoyed the collapse of the Northern Pacific and the Jay Cooke Company scandals and the Crédit Mobilier scandals and all the embarrassments which had been brought to the administration of Grant and Grab.

Returning to Europe in 1879 because she felt that she was a stranger in her own land where she could have no peace in a personal sense, Mrs. Lincoln, well knowing that there were some people in her native land who would believe the judgment which had declared that she was insane but not the reversal which had declared that she was sane, had drifted once more over Europe—from one cathedral town to another cathedral town, where history, which was always of utmost fascination to her, was visible in every stone; from alpine spa to alpine spa, where she took the waters or walked alone upon a windswept esplanade under her black widows' veils by which she hid herself from the recognition that she above all things wanted not for her own sake but for that of the great president who deserved to be honored throughout the world for having died for the cause of freedom to his fellow men and women in his own country.

She had followed world news with intense interest but had lived mainly with her memory of her beloved husband and her three younger sons whom she missed so much, seeming almost to have forgotten Robert Todd Lincoln, until one day she read in the newspaper that Robert Todd Lincoln and Stephen A. Douglas, Jr., against whose father Abraham Lincoln had won the election to the White House, were likely to run against each other in the coming election. Suddenly her presidential ambitions for her only living son had been stirred, but not for long—her mind passing to something else—she could not concentrate on one subject for long, especially if concerned with a future prospect and not with the past.

Her only living son, at any given moment, could not have told an interrogator what the address of this spectral lady was—although conceivably anybody who really wished to reach her could have located her through an old friend of Lincoln's who was living then in Paris and was handling Mrs. Lincoln's pecuniary affairs. She had exalted that she who had been neglected by her own country had received the condolences of many crowned heads, including the still beautiful widowed Empress Eugénie and the Empress Victoria, both of whom had known, had shared so well the communion of grief.

It would have been strangely appropriate if she had joined in the company of the black-veiled Empress Carlotta, widow of the Emperor Maximilian, who she had not known was dead.

The Emperor Maximilian had been toppled from his gilded throne in Mexico and executed upon the Hill of Bells by the marksmen of General Benito Juarez, who had insisted on shooting him and had not been treating him as a prisoner of war, as William Seward and Andy Jackson had asked—the revolutionary general having been determined not to seem a pawn in the hands of the American practitioners of Manifest Destiny.

The general could remember very well that the Americans had stolen Texas and Arizona and California and had already tried to take Mexico as their empire—and thus, to exhibit his seeming independence from Washington, he had refused to put the emperor on a boat at Vera Cruz—the town of the True Cross, where, bearing his golden cross, Maximilian had first arrived—had refused to lift him up like a long-legged doll or puppet with a golden cross and send him back to the Old World from the New before he had scarcely stepped foot out of the waves which were coming in onto the shore.

Juarez and his guerrillas had threatened the Emperor Maximilian and his crew from the beginning. The displaced Austrian prince was tall and pale and gentle of manner and had a golden beard—to the thousands of red men who had poured out to greet him, he had seemed perhaps the resurrection of the god Quetzalcoatl who had promised that he would someday return in the form of a white man with a golden beard.

Seward and company had done all they could by all diplomatic means to topple Maximilian from his throne and bring him to the execution, for which they could disclaim direct responsibility—they had not pulled the triggers of the rifles riddling the man who all throughout the Civil War, which he had not dared believe would not be won by the South, had been allowing traitors to come over the borders into this land. Republican clubs strategically located all over the United States of America were raising dollars at every hand for the support of the guerrilla Juarez with rifles and munitions.

The trouble with Maximilian—the scholarly, ailing, dreaming archduke who had been Napoleon III's archdupe and, as some people in Washington said, a paper emperor—was that he was not really as ambitious for power as the power brokers were—and all through the ever unpredictable and intense jungle and desert and mountain warfare waged against him with the help of Washington given at every turn had been so concerned with archaeological expeditions to the dead kingdom of the Aztecs, the preservation of the Emperor Montezuma's golden masks and golden cups and golden plates and burial boats and the preservation of the great pyramids of the sun and moon which related to the pyramids of Egypt—so interested in botanical specimens, beautiful flowers, rare jungle beasts and birds—that he had allowed himself to digress from the main chance and had not been as militant as he should have been.

The Empress Carlotta, who had yearned to wear a crown and who—a black-veiled professional widow like the black-veiled Mrs. Abraham Lincoln—had continued to wear it after her husband's premature death—had stated that she would wait for the return of the Emperor Maximilian for sixty years if that was the time required for the return of her dead husband who had been so cruelly snatched away from her. For sixty years—as if acting in fulfillment of her prophecy as she looked in all ways turning her head from side to side toward the four corners of the many-tasseled sky— she would address her remarks to her husband and God, just as Mrs. Lincoln, although knowing that her husband was not in this world but was in the next world, if there was such a world, which was always, of course, made of aspects of this world with its inherent mysteries never to be solved, would imagine that he spoke to her in the name of God.

Every morning in the spring of the year for sixty years, the demented Empress Carlotta in her black mourning clothes would step into her little boat which was moored among the lily pads upon the glassy moat of her castle in Brussels and say—only she seeing the dead emperor's living face as she surely saw it the day she died—"Today we are sailing for Mexico."

[73]

FOR A WHILE, Mrs. Abraham Lincoln did have an American competitor, albeit one who was far removed from her in attitude and kept her grief pent up. She was Mrs. Arthur Garfield, whose husband, when he was an Ohio congressman, on a random visit to New York had delivered impromptu and unrehearsed but with oracular triumph from the steps of the subtreasury where George Washington, the father of his country, had most appropriately been sworn in as first president of that democracy which would be called a dollars and cents democracy—dollars for some and cents for others—an instantaneous elegy for the prairie president Abraham Lincoln:

"Clouds and darkness are around him, his pavilion is dark waters and thick clouds, justice and judgment are the habitation of his throne; mercy and truth shall go before His face! Fellow citizens, God reigns and the government in Washington still lives!"

The wandering black widow had journeyed across the ocean four times before her last voyage of return, which could only be followed by that last of all last voyages. In December 1879, while trying to hang a picture, she had had a fall that had severely injured her spinal column.

Mary Lincoln, given more and more to stumbling, falling, had sailed from Le Havre on the French steamer *Amérique,* which was expected to make the passage in nine days although the ways of winds and waves had been—as always—unpredictable. Heavily veiled, her head whirling, her body twisted by torment, while standing at the top of a stair, she would have been pitched downward by a sudden swell had she not been saved by a lady who had kept her from falling and who had turned out to be none other than the divine Sarah Bernhardt.

The acrobatic Sarah Bernhardt had heard the gentle, dreaming voice of the little woman in black thanking her, but as her face was swathed by so many veils had not recognized her. "You might have been killed, madame, if you had fallen down that horrible staircase." The little woman had answered with a sigh that yes, she knew, but that it was not God's will.

When Sarah Bernhardt, saying good-bye, had revealed her name, the woman in black had recoiled and had said with a hiss to the one who had stood between her and the enactment of God's will, "I am the widow of Abraham Lincoln."

Sarah had divined that since it had been an actor who had killed her husband, she had no love for actors—even the most eminent. The great tragedienne before whose feet Oscar Wilde had paved a path of long-stemmed lilies during what was called the lily craze and had not been placed at the black widow's wandering feet had said afterward that she had done the unhappy woman the only service she ought not to have done her—she had saved her from death.

She could not know, of course, how many deaths John Hay's black cat caterwauling widow had died—she had died more than nine.

[74]

THE BLACK WIDOW had passed unnoticed by the crowd welcoming the great tragedienne at the dock. The veiled Mrs. Abraham Lincoln descending to the dock must have seemed a figure from the past—a cutout from a page of an antebellum *Godey's Lady's Book*—for she had not changed her style for years. She had set out for Springfield via the Hudson River Railroad, where night began as dusk, traveling on through the fog-shrouded, randomly star-punctuated darkness of the sleeping, undulating prairie states—Ohio and Indiana and Illinois—until she came at last to Decatur.

Mary Lincoln in her final phase as she lay with all her trunks and boxes piled around her bed on the top floor of her sister Ninian's high-shouldered house of limestone on the hill had seemed to arouse little understanding of her illnesses in physicians and relatives or in her only living son, Robert Todd Lincoln.

Her passionate love of money had remained the same when she had at last received the retroactive pension, which she had recognized she would not live long enough to use. She had worn her money belt around her waistline as she waxed, waned, waxed, waned, waxed and waxed and waxed large as the moon—as long as she was wide—turning, rolling in her bed—and once had insisted upon rising because she was convinced that a thief in the night had stolen from her where the sounds of the rustlings of her stocks and bonds and gold certificates had assured her that there was money for her support—that she was never to be like some old, twisted hen for whom there was not a grain of corn or a blade of grass to feed on.

Mary Lincoln had departed this life on the night of July 15, 1882. She had been in a deep coma but had been ready to sail. The funeral had been held in her sister Ninian's parlor where her open coffin had been illuminated by the flickering rays of the whale-oil lamps, which sometimes left her face among the shadows and sometimes lighted it up with sudden incandescence.

The Reverend James A. Reed, who had delivered the eulogy, had spoken with a symbolism that almost any McGuffey's man or woman would have understood, regardless of what his or her social status or class was, whether high or low. Mary Lincoln and her martyred husband had been two tall and stately pines that had grown so close together that their roots and branches had intertwined as they faced mountain storms. When the taller of the two was struck by a flash of lightning, the shock was too much for the other, and thus they had virtually both been killed at the same time—although for the one that lingered, it was only slow death from the same cause. When Abraham Lincoln died, she died.

Now, with a book made of flowers—lilies, rosebuds, tuberoses, carnations, and the name Mary Lincoln spelled out upon its cover with forget-me-nots—she was carried by the hearse men to her grave, her son Robert Todd Lincoln and members of his family and members of her family following her to the place of her interment at Oak Ridge Cemetery, which had been built to discourage those who might wish to disturb the president's body or Little Willie or the other two dead sons to take them on tour—and there she was placed in a row of coffins at the feet of old Abe, Civil War president and Great Emancipator who had died for mankind— the only living son, Robert Todd Lincoln, secretary of war, having been the only one who would not someday join with his parents at Springfield.

The year of Mrs. Lincoln's possibly final death was the year of the publication of the agnostic Mark Twain's *The Prince and the Pauper,* a tale which, based upon the cruelties of the social injustices flagrantly prevailing during the reign of Edward VI, he had intended as a mask made of the masks of rags and riches that differentiated the classes in America, this supposedly God-given democracy—the rags of the many, the riches of the few in a nation where the Mephistopheles in the government conspired with the regnant financial powers of Wall Street to acquire empires like giants dwarfing many European countries and with as great or greater power than was enjoyed by any czar—this retrogressive development in America having increasingly occurred since the time of the Civil War.

Eugene Victor Debs would come to feel that the public imagination was not erroneous when it labeled the real rulers of America the steel kings, oil kings, railroad kings—theirs the power of veritable monarchs.

[7 5]

IT WOULD BE ASKED many times how Debs—through endless trials and turmoils of his life as the great crusader for social justice—had remained Debs with the courage to be Debs and always himself.

How had it happened that he who had been born from the loins of his people and who had become a simple workman should have evolved into their chief spokesman for social justice when he could so easily have been crushed under the wheels of a train suddenly moving, as he, down on his knees, was wiping a wheel—and if it had been his fate to be left mangled beyond recognition in the mud of a train bed as a string of trains passed over him—perhaps thinkingly, perhaps unthinkingly—would God have produced another man to take his place in the long struggle which the divine intelligence—surely that of the Great Engineer—had marked for the amelioration of the conditions of poor workingmen on the tracks and in the mills and in the mines?

When Debs—who took little care of his own life and thought that he was of no importance as an individual but only the expression of the desires of many men for freedom and equality and justice—was to become the Garrison and Wendell Phillips of the day's abolitionists, the Charles Martel of wage slavery, the St. John crying in the wilderness, the preacher of the gospel of labor—a man who was all of these and a Wilberforce and a Kossuth and a Mazzini and a Chrysostom compounded—it would be wondered whether this golden-tongued agitator of the modern social problem had come into the world as a matter of blind chance or accident or whether, just as there were laws in nature assuring man's progress from darkness to light, his life had been an expression of the will of the all-seeing God.

But why—if he had ever been a laborer as he said he had been from the days of his youth—had he not worked to lift himself up from rags to riches, and why had he insisted on devoting himself to impoverished folk when he could have become a railroad president?

He must always have been thinking not merely of the railroad line and whether the track was clear ahead as far as his eyes could see—must always have been thinking also along the line of industrial revolution, labor and industry, the great struggle, and modern profiteers.

Although it was true that Debs's intellectual interests had continued during his period of heavy labor on the trains and the tracks and had even been inspired by them as he sought connections between the age of the machine and an idea of social progress, when he was a youthful locomotive fireman—sometimes called firebird—he had not attempted to read Plato's *Republic* while riding like the devil on the left side of the engineer who was the king on the throne, the god of the engine. A fireman on the road reading Plato would have given the capitalistic owners an ideal justification for an ever greater aversion to what they considered to be educated fools than they generally entertained.

With the depression which had come with the vast upheavals of the fratricidal war and the period of Reconstruction, the grocery store run by Dandy Lion Debs and his wife Daisy had seemed about to go under, as the poor folks whose wages during the war had lagged behind the cost of bread and meat could scarcely afford to keep body and soul together. It had seemed to critics of a despotic capitalism that no matter how high the wages paid to labor should soar, the cost of living must always soar higher in order to keep the poor worker's nose to the grindstone.

Ever since Eugene Victor Debs had been tall enough for his nose to reach above a counter, he had helped in the family store and had continued there, as a measuring rod was marked with notches showing his growth—he having been the pride and joy of both of his parents.

The only trouble was—and they did not discourage his dreaming atti-tude—the older he grew, the less aptitude he had seemed to have for busi-ness, was so absentminded, in fact, that he did not seem to know how to weigh out a pound of meat—although it was curiously true that a pound was never less than a pound; it was always more than a pound for which the price remained the price for a pound. Never—it would be told of Debs in the popular legends concerning his youth—did he count out potatoes for some potato-faced old woman's burlap bag—that kind the poor used for Lazarus' burial—without the miracle of managing to put in a few more potatoes than she had asked for.

Because of the depression going on and on when many small businesses were suffering the bankruptcy that had always been near, Debs had been overwhelmed by the idea that he should give up his pursuit of higher edu-cation, which only the most affluent but not necessarily the most brilliant could afford.

At age fourteen, in the spring of 1870, Eugene Victor had severed his connections with school and had done so with considerable grief, which he did not openly express. He had kept up his good cheer, had whistled like a bird in answer to every bird whistling to him, had pretended indifference to the fact that he would not be returning to class after the spring break—but when the time had come for the graduation of his class without him, he had shed in the darkness of night his secret tears.

Certain opportunities of life—as he had recognized when he had seen the harsh world of wind and rain and snow and storm, the turbulence of nature which had seemed to have no regard for the spirit of man nor care for his mortal life—had been cut off from him, in all probability. And yet as would be seen, he loved the life of the train and would never leave it—not even when he left it.

A friend of his parents'—Dandy Lion, his father, and Daisy, his mother—had been the French revolutionary master overhauler Pierre Solomon, painter of boxcars. He painted on engines and cars such mar-velous designs as those of strutting roosters, flapping eagles, owls that could not close their eyes and so were very good symbolizations for night trains on which engineers and firemen could not close their eyes.

The greatest of all of Solomon's masterpieces was the goddess Victory on the side of a boxcar. She was riding an eagle that spread the entire length of the car and carried a banner which was very revolutionary in its message to the plowman or whoever might look up.

The art of sign painting had been very highly valued in that day. The wizard Solomon, sharing Daniel's love of France as of literature, music, art, and good cooking, was a faithful visitor with Daniel at the grocery store, where they would play chess on a rare chessboard with chessmen who had been brought from the Old World, and their discussions dealt with a different range of subjects from those of the average storekeeper and customer as they moved their men over the board.

Solomon in all his glory as the Michelangelo of strings of boxcars could not have foreseen that he was stepping into the history of the labor movement as Daniel had pointed out his ambitious son's need for employment and had asked whether Solomon would recommend him to anyone in need of help. Solomon had answered that he would be very happy to introduce Eugene to the man who—known simply as Old Man Pebbles—was his boss at the old Vandalia paint shop and who—as time would tell, and whether he would enjoy the honor or would not—was to get a free ride in history by hiring at Solomon's recommendation the inexperienced but avidly ambitious paint scraper Eugene Debs.

Debs's diurnal pay had been fifty cents. He had also had to palm out one dollar for the purchase of his paint scraper—the equivalent of two days' pay—but the instrument was to be forever his. Hence he had not complained about the price. His paint scraper, which he had kept hanging on a wall in his office when he was a labor leader, was also the tangible proof to which he with his long fingers could point if anyone of a cynical nature questioned whether he had actually done manual labor, whether his hands had been blackened with coal dust or streaked with paint.

Having learned to paint stripes and lettering on boilers—having proved his mettle—Debs had been given the opportunity to see something of the larger world by travel—learning the distance from Terre Haute to the state capital by bumping along the seventy miles of track as a painter of the luminous places which would shine in the night when they were caught by the headlights of the trains if the unguarded headlights were not busted out and by the eyes of the engineer if he was not the blind engineer like the god of capitalism running this blind world.

The boy had been lifted up from the paint shop to the position of locomotive fireman, a stoker of coal, a lightning slinger—he having been suddenly entrusted with that position of responsibility because the fireman on the night shift had been too drunk to come to work—had been three sheets to the wind—had blown himself out.

Thus Debs had been precariously promoted from low to high—riding with the engineer in the fireman's wooden cab or, as it was sometimes called, the hog—his job including the services of an extra pair of eyes for the engineer, who could not see on both sides of the track at once to spot whatever obstacle might lie ahead—a cow who might have wandered through a broken pasture fence, a fallen tree, a tramp, a woman, a child, a surrey top, no driver under it.

[7 6]

IN WINTER BLASTS the snow flurries drove into the young Debs's eyes, making him seem to see two moons at once—one on either side of the rail—and when the dawn came, the morning sun would seem like a cinder in his eye, and in the winter there was the way he was frozen by glacial cold on one side and his eye fried like an egg by the burning heat on the other side when he was driving up the tracks—the process to be reversed when he was coming back.

The pay was measured not by time but by mileage. If anything happened to a railroad man along the trail, that was when his pay was stopped—and stopped whether he was injured or dead.

Debs after a long night's journey to the red dawn slept in an attic room with his red fire cap drawn over his eyes and the train whistle blowing in his ears.

It was a fearful extension of his working hours that after a night's work he would dream that he was in the firebox with the train still speeding on, running, tossing upon a mattress stuffed with corn shucks of which the rustling penetrated his thin sleep—he who made a dollar a night and was naturally not paid for his extension of labor as he dreamed he was still the fireman with the cinders burning his shirt as if they were a thousand quail shots which would riddle him into rags before the firebox of the sun appeared through black smoke clouds was now a wage slave as he believed his mother had been when she was a child in the mill.

Debs's only formal education beyond his two years of high school had been that which he had received for a few spare hours in the afternoons at a business college as a student of telegraphy—how to make the keyboard flash along the lines—bookkeeping, by which to learn the differences between profits and losses, assets and liabilities, the red and the black—but he had been listening to the music of the future, had been synthesizing various departments of knowledge.

What was the distance between utopian speculations of any kind and the possibility of their attainment? And if there could be no actualization in reality within the framework of any individual's mortal life, should not the first steps still be taken upon a road that was long—very long—longer than the longest life was?

Surely, it would be only the naysayers and never a man with Debs's faith in socialistic perfectibility who would agree with Herbert Spencer's theory, in "Man Versus the State," published in 1884, that the socialists who had diligently prepared the way were deluded in their belief that by exercise of patient skill an ill-working humanity might be framed into a well-working institution.

On Sundays when the long-limbed Debs was at home, he would spend his time riding his little brother around on his shoulders or teaching him how to recognize wildflowers and calls of birds and spotted or unspotted butterflies or how to skate on ice, which was so much easier than to skate on grass, how to unwind the cable of a kite which with its long tail would go sailing through the clouds high above the sun or the moon, and sometimes in the early twilight when fireflies were coming out would go with him to draw on a string of cardboard boxcars cut out with little windows covered with red paper through which there shone the lights of candles burning inside like the lights of trains. Children's games had reflected the adult games of the age.

Sunday evenings, as Debs would recall when he was an old man and as he had mentioned many times along the road of life, had always been those which he had held sacred and which he would spend at home with his father and mother and the other children of the family unless it was absolutely impossible for him to return in the flesh although he must always have been a presence in the spirit.

There was always a plate set out on the long table for him or any other absent child—there was a bowl—there was a wine cup—there were knives and forks and spoons, big spoons, little spoons—fine napkins and a long lace tablecloth and a bowl of flowers as a centerpiece, when flowers growing wild could be plucked from the upland meadows.

Debs would remember that his education as a humanitarian socialist had come from his birdlike little mother, who seemed to live in some ways in a fairy-tale world, and his tall, patriarchal father—beloved old Nimrod who had hunted the bloody mushrooms and rabbits for the soup and who would read aloud—until with the hoarfrost of the snows of age upon his beard and his eyes filmed with snow clouds he could no longer see—beautiful passages from French and German poets and Shakespeare's plays, chapter after chapter of *Les Misérables,* the epic condemnation of the perfidious organization of society into the caste system and its injustices to the poor Jean Valjeans of this world. When his father's eyes grew blind as stones informed by no vision, Debs had taken his place as reader to the old folks and whatever children might be at home.

[7 7]

IN THE AUTUMN of the year in which the boys of Debs's high school class graduated, minus the one who would not be the valedictorian looking forward to a bright future in a country where any poor boy who was born in a log cabin—that rapidly disappearing log cabin—could grow up to become the president of the United States or the president of a railroad, there had come with seeming suddenness another of the cyclic depressions sweeping the land with the force of a tornado—stripping the leaves from trees and blowing the roofs from railroad shacks and leaving the brakemen to hurtle on without brakes.

The Vandalia along with other railroads here and there had seemed on the verge of closing, and Debs, having been the youngest and the most recently employed on the railroad, had been thrown out of harness by the old Vandalia.

He had not spent much time waiting but had hitched a ride in a boxcar over the Chicago and Eastern Illinois line to Evansville down on the Ohio River, to which he had been attracted because he had heard—in a rather indirect way, by word of mouth—that there might be employment, but the rumor passed along had been false or greatly exaggerated, for the business of the land barge had dwindled to a thread as had that of the water barge—and so he had bummed his way in a boxcar to the Mississippi River harbor city of St. Louis, the biggest city to that date he had ever beheld with his eyes.

Though there was poverty in Indianapolis and Terre Haute, nothing had prepared Debs for the poverty of the dispossessed black folks in the city where the legendary Dred Scott had died. He had written to his father and mother to assure them that he was well but that it had made his heart sick to see men and women and children begging for something to eat. His hope was that his sisters and brother would appreciate their home and parents as he feared he had not done until he came to St. Louis.

Through the influence of Tom McCabe, fireman on the St. Louis, Belleville & Southern Illinois Railroad who had been a machinist back home at Terre Haute, Debs had been promised the first seat there was in the fire cab as a locomotive fireman.

In answer to his mother's and father's pleas that he should come home, he had written that he was determined to stay on. "I can see it better than I could in Terre Haute, for if you had any idea of the hundreds of starving people that I see daily, you would not urge me to return"—at least so long as there was a prospect of an employment by which to support himself. He had cheerfully assured his parents that they should have no anxiety for him—all would be well.

Dandy Lion and Daisy could not have foreseen then the many thousands and thousands of nights when—beginning with his career as a labor union organizer—he would be on the road and they would wonder how he fared and whether he would come home alive or dead.

Eugene reported to the folks back home that he had met a French family with whom he could speak their native tongue and thus polish his French as his father desired. He had met their seventeen-year-old daughter Lena, whose portrait he would send by a friendly fireman going up to Terre Haute. He had wanted his sisters' approval of the portrait of the beautiful girl who had attracted his attention and was someone whom he could be proud to introduce to them.

This was not to be the case of Eugene's losing the girl to some other suitor and spending his entire life in love with an oval portrait as was the fashion of the forlorn in that day, although he would spend his later years loving a married love who would never be his bride, as his history would show.

A note to his idolized and idolatrous little brother showed that a marriage bed of any kind was far from being on the shy boy's mind, be it even a bed of stone or a railroad bed. He had killed thirty-seven bedbugs in just a few minutes in one night—a news no doubt very fascinating to the future sharer of all his sufferings.

Yes—in answer to his mother's question as to whether he had known a young man named Stewart who had been killed in a railroad accident near Terre Haute—Debs had not told her as evidently he had not wanted her to fear that the fallen Stewart's fate would be his fate—and so now he had hastened to inform her that he did not sympathize with the fallen fellow a particle, for the dead gentleman had been a genuine deadbeat of the first order. And moreover, the road that Debs intended to work on was as safe as a bed and had never had any ill luck.

Thus inadvertently and for the first and last time, Debs with his blaming or seeming to blame the unhappy Stewart for his fate—that of falling—and by his failure to withhold judgment until there should be a true postmortem of an accidental death, which was not merely a commonplace event but one of increasingly horrifying magnitude in the age of the machine, had seemed to favor the management that was blind, deaf, dumb as to its own responsibilities for accidents.

In a world of more railway accidents than were allowed to reach the knowledge of the public—so many that a traveler who found that he had missed his doomed train might well thank God for having spread a special tutelary guardianship over him—there were and would be very few railroad accidents which were not attributable to God's will or human error—the error of the trainman who was dead being the perfect error, as the dead, presumably, could not speak in self-defense or ask for a continuation of pay.

[7 8]

DEBS WAS NEVER to be a lover of big cities—but the brief time in St. Louis was of overwhelming importance in his dynamic development from dreamy lad with a chivalric instinct to fighting labor leader who excluded not the unemployed and the unemployable from his great philanthropic enterprise as he saw the depredations of carpetbaggers, gold rings, whiskey rings, wars upon reds and uprootings of blacks, gifts of vast acreages for little lightning fork trains going nowhere and lasting about as long as a flash of lightning, gifts which the Crédit Mobilier had given under the table to Republicans and Democrats in high office who were as alike as Gog and Magog and of which the bombardments had caused the beginnings of the era of tarnished reputations, all or more of the corruptions which had prevailed in one way or another even before the beginning of the Gilded Age.

Every kind of gambling game and confidence game had flourished in the roisterous, the boisterous river town that had been before the Civil War the port for steamboats and now was the place for the locomotives which were the steamboats of land passage. These old kings of the river had given up to the new kings of the rails who had won the race for speed in transportation from the time of the war.

Now in the old Mississippi riverboat port, Debs had come into contact with many and never-ending legends of the river which he had known previously through the writings of Mark Twain, whose brother had been blown to smithereens when he was a riverboat pilot in the long ago.

Debs had learned also the history of land grabbers on a mammoth scale, it seeming that America had been and would continue to be based upon the grabbing of real estate.

St. Louis was a Mississippi River city which had once been dismantled and which was now flourishing and where—in spite of the surrounding darkness—torches of social consciousness had flamed through the chemically poisoned, saffron-colored mists and fogs which hung not only over the city called River Queen but over other great and small industrial cities.

St. Louis was the place where the youthful Joseph Pulitzer—a tall Hungarian with red hair and a Civil War veteran who had fought to keep this nation from falling apart, who was the main radiator of the Carl Schurz reform movement, and who had made many stump speeches throughout this part of darkest Missouri against Ulysses S. Grant and the bloody Reconstructionist carpetbag man in the campaign of 1874 when he was neither traitor nor anarchist—had loudly cried out in favor of states' rights against the increasingly iron-bound encroaching powers of the federal government.

Later the founder, in 1887, of the prestigious *New York Evening World* had believed, being himself a man of print, that the state of Missouri desired for her citizens at least the capacity to write their names and read before they voted under a government that should be based upon intelligence and not ignorance.

Joseph Pulitzer arrived in East St. Louis on the evening of October 10, 1865. He had probably been forced to be a deadbeater, had bummed his way west in a Pullman sidecar through the autumnal cold without so much as an army overcoat to cover him.

DEBS DID NOT AGREE that those who could not sign their names nor read should be the disenfranchised—the large number of the black, the red, the yellow, the poor white—as the power to control their destinies might never be theirs if dependent upon literacy—nor was literacy a measure of a man's heart or intellect. The folk wisdom that all men shared did not depend on the knowledge of the alphabet.

In mid-October 1865, when the golden leaves were falling and the chills and fogs of the dying time of the year would soon be replaced by howling winter winds and freezing snow and the body of nature would be stretched out like a corpse under the black clouds and the steam from the locomotive chimney, Debs had mounted into the fire cab once again for continuation of a work which had fascinated him although it had placed him in danger of losing his life at any moment.

He had dismissed all fears of danger, for he had held to his belief that the age of man's progress toward a better world would be opened by the progress of the machine.

As Joseph Pulitzer would one day recall of the decade of turbulence and turmoil in the post–Civil War world, the prospect of the utopian cooperative brotherhood had seemed very distant when the great tycoons were swarming everywhere with their war profits, which were their rewards for military services, and then the returning veterans who had fought for the union had found disunion and gold-braided generals everywhere in power and themselves treated for many years like outcasts—unpopular reminders of an unpopular war—neglected and unemployed cripples in the communities which, during their absence, had prospered and did not have a place for them in the new economics of war profits.

Debs would make the not original remark in the coming age of the great trusts that if the rich ever managed to travel to the moon or some other paradisal planet and found that the streets were paved with gold, they would tear the place up and bring back the gold for sale in shares on Wall Street. Nothing was safe with them, neither the moon nor the Great Wall of China.

When he was an old man who in the heart of danger had spent many years of his life warning of danger ahead—even as he would do until the end, as his messages continued to be heard by that not inconsiderable part of the public for which he had provided a voice—Debs would recall that he had been physically afraid but once in his life—and that had been when he was riding in the firebox and the engineer of his train and the engineer of an approaching train, both where they should have had right-of-way, both with their eyes blinded by fire and their ears deafened by wind, suddenly were able to see each other and had pulled the brakes only a few minutes before there would have been collision and derailment—doubtless that kind which would have left no particle of consciousness or only the smallest particle to tell what had occurred.

[7 9]

THERE IN THE OLD St. Louis where Debs had bunked with an engineer in what was called with literal correctness a railroad flophouse, he would throw himself in weariness each night upon a mattress stuffed with cornstalks, which made a rustling sound and probably a few squeaks if it was, as it might easily be, a nest for field mice and would soon be propped up reading by an oil lamp which he was careful to shield with his red fireman's cap as a guard so that the light would not stream into the eyes of the engineer who considered his red-faced roommate as strange a bedfellow as was ever turned up in God's lottery in the city of the devil's lottery and would tell him that he was a damned fool to be wasting his eyes like this when he needed sleep.

There in that old river town which had become a railroad town where the rich danced under twelve hundred tons of crystal chandeliers in halls of gold-framed mirrors and the poor lived in hog hovels and drank the muddy waters with their faces next to the ground, the innocent youth who had been startled by disparities between social classes such as he had never dreamed could be possible had been groping for a way of social order which would be a different way, for that illumination and articulation which would make of him the most radiant spokesman for the dead souls of America who could not speak and who had no words but were surely men and women with red hearts.

Unfortunately, the knowledge of train wrecks which occurred with an amazing and almost predictable regularity could not be kept from Daisy. Her anxious letters had urged her son to come back to Terre Haute, where she was sure that he would find pecuniary employment—but how could Debs give up his love of the trains which he believed were on the way to a better future for mankind, and how could he give up seeing the world from the vantage point of a fireman's box?

What had caused Debs to leave the fireman's box and return to the banks of the Wabash had not been his mother's anxiety for him but the absolute and never-to-be-forgotten horror which had been his when he had witnessed the death of a fellow worker who while working on a wheel had been knocked down, mangled, and mutilated, the train bucking back upon the buckling rail and the wheels passing over him as the rims and the spokes turned red as the sun in the red sea of his blood.

Accidents happened almost every day to someone on the road when the equipment was obsolete, and to stay on the road in such neglected times as these would certainly have been almost suicide.

Self-murder was what the company had wanted it to seem. Should Debs be pulverized, dropped off at Terre Haute like ashes in an old coal sack or a box which contained only one jawbone—that of an ass which would sing, sing, sing to tell of his murder by those great powers who risked men's lives every day for the sake of an increase in their bloody dollars? Many a poor workman who had no kith or kin to mourn for him had been shipped back to a possible point of origin with no address but "To whom it may concern" or concern not. Postage due. Nameless dead. Answered not to any name. Whistle blew for him as it must blow for every man. Was killed by error of his own and not the management. Should have seen that there was danger ahead—danger of washout, road under repair, always under repair. Footboard man made fatal mistake. Was under the influence of the lubricating oil and tried to step upon the footboard of the moving train and missed, went under the wheels.

[8 0]

AN EMINENT CITIZEN of Terre Haute who was intimately involved with the growth of the town and was one of the largest individual landowners in Vigo County had been Herman Hulman, Sr., a native of Hanover, Germany, who in the year of Debs's birth had joined with his brother Francis in the forming of a wholesale grocery business on the banks of the Wabash when the town was organized as a city.

Terre Haute was no longer a water town, had given up its dependence on water passage for its industrial and agricultural products.

In 1869 Hulman had admitted into his partnership Robert S. Cox, who would remain with him until his purchase of a distillery, when Hulman's sons would join with their father in the business which had grown to a vast wholesale empire when Debs was taken into the main office and storeroom by Hulman, his father's wealthy friend.

Out of his first pay at Hulman's Debs had taken a five-year subscription to the *New York Herald*. He had purchased, on a twenty-month installment plan, a complete set of *Appleton's Encyclopedia* by means of which—as he kept up with the dynamic and crucial events covered by a newspaper in the nation's largest city and disseminated elsewhere—he attempted to furnish his mind with the history of man and the world throughout the ages of time.

As a child he had memorized much of Goethe and Hugo, Racine and La Fontaine and some few mosaics from the works of Dante and many passages by Shakespeare and, indeed, whole plays, including *Julius Caesar,* and many poems by Shelley and Burns; and he was an early reader of *Don Quixote.*

In Dandy Lion's house with its library of rare and precious volumes, where upon the mantelpiece the marble busts of Voltaire and Rousseau were the reigning deities, taking the place of the Blue Madonna and the Christ on the Cross, sacred images of the kind one would not expect to find in the household of a fallen-away Catholic and revolutionary agnostic like the bloody mushroom hunter in the squirrel cap who had not placed his faith in heads of saints and many-eyed angels such as were painted on cathedral ceilings along with chariots of fire and trees bearing golden apples like the apples of paradise, in a household where Victor Hugo had always been idealized for his portrait of the little waif Cosette as she had been depicted in *Les Misérables,* as were Eugène Sue's *The Wandering Jew* and Little Nell of *The Old Curiosity Shop* and Harriet Beecher Stowe's Little Eva of *Uncle Tom's Cabin,* who when she was an angel attempted to lift Uncle Tom up from his deathbed and carry him heavenward, Debs would sequester a few gold coins out of his pay and not for the purpose of buying a high silk stovepipe hat and cape and suit and fine linens and braids and buttons or for the purpose of making himself into a dude who might lord it over poor railroad men down by the rails, but for the purchase of other books by which, along with the *Appleton's* coming each month, he might increase his knowledge of the lives of the poor folks who lived in America, not above the ground but under the ground—forming the crust of ashes and dust created by the great moguls of modern industrialism, who had so many ways of ridding themselves of what they did not want.

Debs had been and would always be particularly fond of Gogol's *The Overcoat* and *Dead Souls* and of the specter-ridden, ghost-haunted poems and tales of the drugged wanderer Poe who had been, like Dostoyevsky, a student of Fourier's magical beasts and birds, as he had been and would be magnetized also by the works of Balzac and Dumas and the dreadful Dick's Son—as the name of Dickens had been pronounced in the pioneering Hoosier days by those rigid, God-fearing parents for whom the author was the son of Dick—the devil himself—because of his encouraging their children to be thieves by showing them the way Fagin—the master of thieves—had tried to twist the poor little orphan Oliver Twist into becoming a thief of gold watches and whatever else he could find. Yet the works of this devil with the horns on his head and the cloven foot had outsold every book in the American wilderness except for the Bible, which was usually kept under lock and key and seldom opened except for the recordings of births and deaths with sometimes false entries by which a person might have died before he died or might have been born before he was born or might never have made it into this world, might have been blotted out completely. Debs was to see more than one of such Bibles with statistics altered or wholly missing.

He was particularly fond of Shelley and Robert Burns and also had given himself over completely to the works of Oliver Wendell Holmes, whose poem "To the Chambered Nautilus" he could recite from heart as he placed the great conch to his lips and blew, blew, blew in a way to shake the clouds. But although he was in many ways an aristocrat as to his literary tastes, he had cared not only for the great who dazzled him with their genius but for folk and railroad poets by the ton, those who in most instances never got to the top of Mt. Olympus or even to the foothills but sometimes got to the top of Pike's Peak in the Colorado mountains and crossed the Great Divide in their journey to the sunset glow—if they had not already fallen along the way where there was no net to catch them and stay their fall. They were always falling, sometimes upward, sometimes downward.

After dinner at evening with his father and mother and sisters and lively little brother Theodore who—although it was not recognized then as that which would be the pattern of his life—had increasingly reflected his elder brother's sometimes dark and sometimes chromatic moods as if by some vast and perhaps rimless mirror held up to him to catch not only the visible but the invisible features and bars and tones and cloud levels above or beneath the sun or the moon which they explored with their long-tailed kite which had been launched by them with such skillful wrist and arm movements that it would not become entangled like a golden bird among tree boughs—Debs in his old blue fireman's clothes would slip away to the railroad cinder yards to talk a spell or two or three or four with cinder-bitten railroad men about the hard times they were having.

Visiting the pig's-feet bars in the shambling shambles of the railroad yard, Debs would talk with smoke-blackened coal-barge men whose faces were so very black that there had begun to cross his mind—as he would someday recall—questions as to why poor white men as black as these should in any way consider that they were as white as the pure white lilies of the field and not as black as the coal in the coal mines under the earth nor as black as the black man for whom the opportunities in the economic realm were less than for the poor white man who did not recognize their common brotherhood and who were encouraged by the great tycoons to remain divided in order that there might be no advancement of their mutual interests.

Debs would talk to the coupler who had lost his hand between the coupling pins, the footman who had lost his foot.

Debs's interest in the coal mines of Vigo County and that entire Wabash region would gradually extend like an enfolding horizon to all the coal miners of the earth and the conditions of the men employed in them, just as his interest in the small railroads that he had known as a worker on them was already extending to greater railroads than the imaginations of most workaday men could encompass.

Being the son of his French revolutionary father, Debs had been prepared to believe that the guano of dead immigrant workers was that which turned the grasses green and caused the red flowers to bloom in places where they had been killed—even as the red prairie flowers were supposed to be red because of the blood of murdered Indians.

A way had opened for Debs, who was above all things a man of his time and for his time whose rise would be with the rise in the seventies of a new class consciousness not only in the Hoosier state but in the nation.

[8 1]

NOT CONTENT to be a bystander watching the trains go by, Debs, the wholesale grocery clerk with the large bird bill and the incense of spices hanging in his clothes, had yearned for the firebox so much that he could almost not endure his sedentary existence in the warehouse.

Slipping away from the family dinner table one cold winter night, saying that he was just going down to the railroad yards for a while, Debs had gone to a rally of railroad men by which, as could not then have been foreseen, his entire life would be transformed, so wholly changed that the man who returned home that night would never again be the man who had set forth.

For him who had so brief an experience as a locomotive fireman, it might seem that he had no more license to join the Brotherhood of Loco-motive Firemen than he had to join this gathering together from four points of the horizon to hear the clarion message of the itinerant grand master of the Brotherhood of Locomotive Firemen—Joshua Leach—then at the meridian of his life, as he urged union upon the unprotected men of the scoop.

When Debs, acting as if by that automatic reflex for which his narrow experiences and broad observations had prepared him, had expressed his desire to join with the firemen's nascent brotherhood, Joshua Leach had been very much surprised, for the young man stepping out of the crowd had both his eyes and was wearing a white shirt and a white collar and a proper necktie and a gray business suit. But upon hearing from the others that Debs was a veteran of the cars and was all right—O.K., meaning "oil's korrect," an Irish road hand's way of spelling "all's correct" in his report on the condition of the rails, the ties, the switches, nuts, bolts—Leach accepted this new crusader for human rights with the prophecy which he would repeat in St. Louis and everywhere else along the rails—he had signed up a young towhead who would do his duty and make his mark in the Brother-hood of Locomotive Firemen.

Debs would pay many tributes to the revered grand master when Leach—no longer hale and hearty as he had been upon his first coming to Terre Haute with the offer of a charter for the Brotherhood of Locomotive Firemen, which would transfer the wholesale grocery billing clerk from his position on the banks of the Wabash to billing clerk for the locomotive firemen upon the banks of the Styx as broken bodies came in mutilated beyond repair and were thrown upon the capitalistic dung heap because they were something less valuable than rusted rails and rotted ties—he had become—for the years had taken their toll—the fragile gentleman seem-ing ready to blow away like the puff of smoke human life really might be in the immensity of time. The frost and snow crowning his old head had been the sign of wisdom in that time of so many patriarchs giving guidance that if America had not been a democracy it might have been a series of cooper-ative communities under the guardianship of patriarchs who would pro-tect all orphans from the storm whenever possible and leave not one to burn or drown. It was after all a child continent, was even an orphan conti-nent in an orphan world.

Joshua Leach, who had been born near Nenagh, in the county of Tip-perary, Ireland, had become a fireman on the Erie Railroad, which he had left when he had witnessed the falling of a fellow fireman in whose memory he had founded the Brotherhood, which had given help to the dead fireman's widow at Port Jervis, New York—the first of many to whom he would bring first aid.

The Brotherhood of Locomotive Firemen, at the time of its organization, in 1863, had been known as the Brotherhood of the Footboard—its eclecticism such that it had been a harp of many strings, which should have been carried on its back as it had welcomed engineers and firemen and machinists to participate in the equal brotherhood. Right now, the chief argument for joining the Brotherhood of Locomotive Firemen which related only to the knights of the fiery scoop had been that it was a society for mutual benefit which was trying to build up a financial pool for the insurance and burial of the former lightning slingers and for benefits to their survivors.

The group that Debs had joined was—according to the statement of intention—

> an order for the protection and elevation—mentally and socially— of all classes and denominations of mankind who step on the footboard for the purpose of working their way to a higher position. The Brotherhood of Locomotive Firemen is not a society organized for evil purposes. . . . We seek not to only regulate and maintain our salaries alone, but we do more than this—let it be said to our credit—we educate our members for the position which they daily toil for—caution them against the wine cup and the disastrous results arising from the same.

The three words on the Brotherhood's banner were "Benevolence, Society, Industry."

[8 2]

FROM 1873 TO 1878 there had been times of peril and trouble for the Brotherhood of Locomotive Firemen, when the winds and tides had challenged its progress, its tenacity of purpose, its mental resources, its right to exist.

The Locomotive Firemen's Magazine had given assurance to its readers that in their editorial vision the future was bright. "Will there be storms in the future as in the past? Manifestly so. What then? Out-ride them. Ours is not 'Like some ill-destined bark that steers In silence through the Gate of Tears.' "

The correspondence that Debs filed away in chicken crates had included not only the letters he unfailingly answered but those he published in *The Locomotive Firemen's Magazine* because of his desire to encourage the use of words by those poor workers in the mud who were supposed to be too dumb to express themselves. They had signed themselves with such noms de plume, such fiery plumes as Total Wreck, Eccentric Scoop, Link-Block, Vacuum, Maple Leaf, Plug and Foam, Gravity, Smoke Box, Short Rail, Third Rail, Signal, Smoke Stack, Headlight—and not necessarily because they were shy or were afraid that their efforts to express themselves might evoke ridicule.

A greater reason for hiding under various noms de plume was the fear that they might be considered incendiaries by their employers because of their knowledge of mechanical problems or because of their accusation that many accidents were avoidable and were caused by the company's failure to replace old rolling stock with new railroad stock—old wheels with new wheels—old hand-and-pin mechanics with new foolproof air brakes.

In March 1888 *The Locomotive Firemen's Magazine,* from a seemingly inexhaustible supply of railroad and country poems which were coming in by every train, had given space to the poem "Death of a Brakeman," which was mistitled—it should have been called "Death of Two Brakemen," as it concerned not one but two.

Oh, the transience of life! In the month of July *The Locomotive Firemen's Magazine* provided space for a letter from a man who had signed himself Troy Light at Baltimore, Maryland, regarding an early trip over the road when he had seen a number of beautiful pine trees near the track. When he had returned only three hours later, they were gone. "Some one had cut them down. Let us, therefore, brethren, united here, prepare ourselves for the great union in heaven. Let us be sober men. . . ."

Not all news should be sad, of course. Brother Herman Weiss—one of the old standbys of Hickory Lodge No. 266—had been promoted from the left to the right with his left hand on the throttle and was driving piles instead of breaking coal.

But little doubt that in relation to the few who had arisen, there were the many who had fallen and were falling. On August 8, Brother Grant Hall had been taken from the Seymour, Indiana, lodge. While trying to board a train at Shoals, he had fallen between the platform and the train. The locomotive wheel had passed over him, but something which had struck him on the back of his head had knocked out his vital spark. "Watch, therefore, for ye know not what hour your Lord doth come."

A pillow of lilies had been contributed for the resting of the head of the young fireman who had met his death at the Shoals depot.

And in the September issue there had come this croaking note: "God pity us all. 'Time too soon will tumble All of us together like leaves in a gust—Tumbled, indeed, down into the dust.' "

As to railroad accidents—the nature and cause of which Debs and his firemen correspondents as well as those he knew from personal encounters were keeping track—they were broken rail, loose or spread rail, broken bridge or trestle, broken or defective switch, broken or defective frog, bad track, broken wheel, broken axle, broken truck, failure of coupling or draw bar, broken parallel or connecting road, loose wheel, fall of brake or brake beam, failure of power brake, derailments arising from operating negligence, misplaced switch, rail or bridge removed for repairs, making flying switch, runaway engine or train, careless stopping or switching, bad switching, cattle on track, snow or ice, washout, landslide, accidental obstruction, malicious obstruction, wind, men on track, rail misplaced, various causes which were unexplained, disasters occurring without collision or derailment, boiler explosions, mistakes concerning telegraphic orders.

In October 1888, tribute had been paid by *The Locomotive Firemen's Magazine* to a heroic fireman who, when a wee girl on a track outside Toronto had not moved when she heard the engineer's whistle but had stood still staring with her hands clasped over her head, had swung himself down onto the cowcatcher where he had crouched like a cat ready to spring as the baby laughed at him. He had thrown his arms around her and jumped away from the track as the driving wheel grazed him. But the baby had been saved and restored to her mother.

The Locomotive Firemen's Magazine was "the organ of a great Brotherhood in whose vocabulary there is no such word as fail"—as also there were no words giving signs of such ideas as decline, decay, wane, disappear. They and their like were not in *The Locomotive Firemen's Magazine*'s lexicon. "The New Year comes with no newfangled panaceas for the ills of mortals," according to that parson who was Brother Debs as he surveyed the scene in a nation which, of course, had depended on nostrums from the beginning and seemed to be inclined to continue to do so.

Debs was writing at a period when there were magical medicine men still plying the backcountry and winding roads with their canvas-topped prairie schooners, from which—to the tune of music—they sold as cure for bee sting and all other ills there were the contents of one nepenthean bottle.

Stupefying opiates, however—the lively *Locomotive Firemen's Magazine* editor had written from the firebox as if in antitestimonial regarding the possibilities of instantaneous transformation by *The Locomotive Firemen's Magazine* from deathly struggle to the balm of peace and cure of all man's woes, woes, woes, and wounds—were not known now in its Materia Medica.

> The lethargic, the drowsy, dull and sleepy will not keep up with the procession. . . . Victims of those who wait for good luck to turn up are victims of hallucination—among the world's unfortunates. They have faith in soothsayers and fortune-tellers. . . . The *ignis fatuous* school of philosophy ought to have long since disappeared. The screech owl omen and the hobgoblin terror ought to be things of the past. . . . The pick and the scoop are not the wands of the conjurer. There is no juggling with the fire-box, no magic monkeying with the machine. . . .

Doubtless the screech owl, hobgoblin poet James Whitcomb Riley— James Whittlecomb, Honeycomb, Haircomb, whittling and combing himself from his adulthood into short-limbed childhood with his bawling cow and lost childhood poems—was one who had laughed the most over his long-limbed labor union organizer friend's exile of the screech owl omen and the hobgoblin terror to the past—along with many other hallucinations.

"Poets," Brother Debs had continued, and anyone who knew him certainly knew that he was not going to bury them so long as they had even a shred of social consciousness, "write of the years as 'remorseless,' as 'ironhearted,' as 'tomb-builders,' as conquerors who 'muse' with satisfaction upon the 'wreck and ruin' which mark their march. Much of this sort of arrangement should be understood in a Pickwickian sense. If it be true, there is no appeal. . . . There is precious little lyrical logic in the world."

Riley published an occasional verse rhyming with hearse for *The Locomotive Firemen's Magazine,* whose editor had first discovered him and brought him to the capital city when he had been all alone and very solitary and in deep disgrace for having labored under the delicious illusion which had been and could continue to be his that he was the resurrection of the spirit of Edgar Allan Poe.

The New Year was to put to the crucial test—Debs had foreseen—the devotion of the Brotherhood of Locomotive Firemen to obligations and with a faith which was based on the evidence of things not seen.

"Speaking of rest for working men, it is now said that certain tools, like men, grow tired and require rest." *The Locomotive Firemen's Magazine* was referring to the condition of edged tools which had been vouched for by a grizzled old veteran in a letter to the *Iron Industry Gazette*. What was one to do when a tool had lost its cutting edge and temper? "The tool is all right, only a little tired—lay it away and let it rest." After a period of rest, the temper of the tool would be restored and could be used again.

A spectral white dog running beside a train in New Jersey had warned of a rock on the tracks ahead, *The Locomotive Firemen's Magazine* had reported in March. If the driver had not stopped the train to try to find the spectral dog, he would have continued speeding on with telegraph poles passing as fast as picks in a hair comb.

Not all trains, however, could be accompanied by white dogs—certainly not if a driver was not a somnambulistic driver because of having to drive on long, long journeys without sleep. "The declaration that 'it is appointed unto man once to die' no longer means that it is appointed unto man to be killed. . . . The Divine Providence theory won't wash much longer."

A young man who had been a member of the Terre Haute hook-and-ladder department—his mission was obviously then to put out fires—had become a brakeman and a fireman on the old Vandalia, his mission to keep the fires burning. Dying at Vincennes, he had had valid reason to suppose that he soon would be promoted to the position of engineer. As the cold hand of death was laid upon his vitals, his dying words to his wife had been, "I told you that I would get on the right side"—and then he had tried to lay his hand upon the throttle as he imagined that he was the engineer.

In an essay entitled "Our Brotherhoods" which had appeared in March, Debs had summed up, with many lauds, the history of the Brotherhood of Locomotive Firemen, its glory and growth during the years in which he had been at the helm.

The ten humble firemen who in 1873 had laid the foundations of the Brotherhood had done much for the world.

"It has crossed the continent. No one can know how many griefs it has assuaged nor hopes it has inspired—these are recorded only in the books of God's remembrance. . . . And yet our Brotherhood is in its infancy."

The members of the Brotherhood would not—according to Brother Debs with his burning desire for recognition of firemen by engineers—

become members of another Brotherhood affixing upon them by their laws an insufferable stigma. "Our Brotherhood will not be the tail to some other Brotherhood's kite or a modern incubator to hatch roosters to crow for others."

What was necessary was equality of brotherhood. The laws which the Brotherhood of Locomotive Engineers had designed to degrade members of the Brotherhood of Locomotive Firemen must be repealed.

In that time when many workingmen were walking around on one leg, one stump or two stumps—perhaps also without those hands which, being lost, would never require wedding rings, gloves, winter gloves, funeral gloves, and this happened sometimes in the days of man's youth—the April issue of *The Locomotive Firemen's Magazine* had mournfully reported that at Jersey City, New Jersey, when the foot of a workman had become fixed between the rails—the cruel iron frog bending his foot as the train bore down on him—he had flung himself headlong into the iron wheels rather than be crippled.

In July, *The Locomotive Firemen's Magazine*'s undimming headlight had revealed a disaster that had occurred on the Cairo Short Line—in Belleville, Illinois, which had been a terminus for Debs when he was on the fire hog in the long ago—this notice showing that the company had made no improvement in giving supports to the thin crusts of earth that divided the upper from the underworld. While passing over the Walnut Valley Company's coal mines a train had sunk six or eight feet when suddenly the ground had given away.

Debs was not and would never be a worshiper of the capitalistic gods of terminus who were the nineteenth century's gods in a world dedicated to speed—terminus to come early for some of the children of men, late for others, according to their fates.

[83]

BEFORE THE PRESTIGIOUS Terre Haute Occidental Literary Club, at about the time Debs joined the workingmen's union, he had given his maiden liberty speech, which would be remembered as having heralded the career of the greatest of all the golden orators America ever knew. He had chosen liberty as a surefire winner that would permit him to speak in behalf of those who for one reason or another were the unemployed—

those who for a long season had been laid off the rails, perhaps because they had broken their necks or had lost their hands or their feet—those who had been deprived of certain inalienable rights such as life, liberty, and the pursuit of happiness.

Gradually with the increase of ethical passions which came with his view of unethical practices against the poor worker, Debs learned to seem as natural as he inherently was and to be that which he also inherently was—himself without fear of what favorable or unfavorable impressions he might give. "No man," he once stated, "ever made a great speech on a mean subject. Slavery never inspired one immortal thought or utterance."

[8 4]

ROBERT GREEN INGERSOLL was an influence on Debs's choice of Liberty as his subject matter for his first speech and on his oratory ever afterward. Debs, not seeming to realize that he had attained his ideal of being himself one of America's greatest golden orators—indeed when he was an old man looking back upon his life—said in answer to a newspaper interviewer's question as to what he would have been if he had had his choice—that which it had seemed had not been his—that he would have been an orator, or that if he had been a woman, he would have liked to have been one of the world's great singers—for he was always an admirer of the soprano.

Ingersoll was the God-inflated agnostic or atheist who included in his attacks upon the Bible the essay "The Mistakes of Moses," which some of *The Locomotive Firemen's Magazine*'s readers mistakenly thought were "The Mistakes of Mosaics," those which were intended to pave the way to paradise. Moses or mosaics—what difference?

One of *The Locomotive Firemen's Magazine*'s little jokes of which there were as many as dandelions springing up along long-forgotten rails told of an acrostic which became an agnostic.

As Debs had been a founder of the Occidental Literary Club—which should have been named the Occidentals and the Orientals in view of his concern with the blacks, the reds, and the yellows—even as the poor whites were and always had been the subjects of his fraternal solicitude—he was able while he was still the weigher and unpacker of boxes and bales at the warehouse on the Wabash to bring to Terre Haute, the city on the mound, some of the men who would be the key spirits of his life as a citizen of this planet.

The first of the young warehouse clerk's guests was the Pugilistic Pagan of Peoria, Robert Green Ingersoll, the atheist who for some time had been passionately proclaiming himself not a believer in the dead theological past which with all its outworn miracles and promises of a world beyond this world and all its icons should be swept like junk into a graveyard or carried away in a flood and who had been for some time also a believer in the All Golden World of Now, of which he had become the lighthouse casting its beams over the dark world—some people thought—while to others who were a majority he with his false signal lights would cause the wreck of this sinful world which had been wrecked once before because of man's failure to listen to the Word of God. All hands would be lost.

Robert Ingersoll could place no credence in spirit voices, heaven's answer to man's prayers, Joshua's power to stop the sun, Daniel's power to burn in the furnace fire and be not seared into ashes and dust, angels riding at the prows of ships or riding with their hands upon the throttles of loco- motives when the engineer and the engine were dead, or in any kind of heavenly or diabolic intervention or any other miracle such as the turning of stone into bread.

Robert Ingersoll was the rising star of Republican national politics whose life, whatever his skepticism might be, was made of many mira- cles—the chief of which was that he was to gain recognition as the greatest Republican orator although he was also the most flamboyant God- forsaking infidel or agnostic—that is to say, he was both a propagandist for the Grand Old Party, which was the party of God—whereas the Demo- cratic party, of which he had been a member before he passed from the darkness into the light, was on the side of the devil and was the party in which he should have remained if he had been an honest man.

Besides being an atheist who had no fear of trumpeting his challenges to God throughout this land, Ingersoll was known far and wide for having unsteadily resisted the blandishments and threats of the unsteady brothers and sisters of the temperance movement who hung around doors of saloons promising God's thunderbolts to those who seemed to care more for the unplugged beer barrel than for the Word of God Who would lift us from the flood and carry us home.

He knew the Bible as well as any Bible thumper. For of course, in order to be a critic of the Bible, which was called the Good Book but which was full of murders as often as not countenanced by God, one had to read it and know its passages from Genesis to Exodus and beyond in the same scrutinizing but melodious way as had the old-time preacher and the preacher's mule in the old-time wilderness days, where the itinerant self-elected cleric—Methodist or Baptist or member of no church because member of all—sitting mounted on his saddle before an improvised desk which was the mule's head, had warned all listeners wherever they were to remember thy creator in the days of thy youth e'er the evil days come on thee and the golden bowl is broken like the old oaken bucket that spills more water through its warped pales than it draws up from the well just as does the old oaken bucket bird when it goes clanking up from the well of the stars and brings the rain. And the old mule would sometimes come up to the wilderness altar and join in the praises of the Word of God—sometimes with laughter, sometimes with tears.

Coming twice to Terre Haute, city of churches—once in the spring for the opening of the lecture series and once in the autumn for the closing which came before the harvest—Robert Green Ingersoll, a man whose coming could only have seemed that of a fiery devil to the old-fashioned Americans who kept on the tops of their parlor tables the old-fashioned Bible and adorned the walls of their living quarters with such flower-embroidered mottoes as "What will you be doing when Jesus comes?" or "What must we do to be saved?" or "A mighty fortress is our God" along with the picture of the winter wolf howling in the snowstorm or the Newfoundland retriever guarding the dead mother with the dead baby at her breast at the edge of the tide as had happened not only in an artist's dreams but in reality.

Ingersoll's attacks upon the old-time irrational religion offered in substitution his rational religion, which should be that of cheerfulness, good nature, good health, liberty, and intelligence.

"I had rather think of those I have loved and lost as having returned to earth, as having become a part of the elemental wealth of the world—I would rather think of them as unconscious dust—I would rather think of them as gurgling in the streams, floating in the clouds, bursting in the foam of light upon the shores of worlds ... than to have even the faintest fear that their naked souls have been clutched by an orthodox god."

In a sermon entitled "At a Child's Grave," he had cried out in his sonorous voice which seemed to open a golden path through darkest clouds, "Every cradle asks us 'Whence?' and every coffin 'Whither?' "

James Redpath—the Scottish immigrant who as a fledgling newspaperman had interviewed John Brown in Kansas and had been the first to go on a perilous journey into the South to take down into his notebook from the lips of black people at their cabin doors their testimonials on what the experience of black chattel slavery was from the point of view of those who had lived through it and died through it—had come upon a gold mine through the founding of the Redpath Lecture Bureau, which sent out speakers of every kind to bring the light of culture to the darkness of the American continent.

Ingersoll was the greatest speaker drawing crowds in America then, according to the glowing descriptions put out by Redpath. According to one of the many testimonials written by those who had heard him, "He pleaded for every right and protested against every wrong—he touched every emotion and expressed every mood of his enchanted listeners."

[8 5]

TERRE HAUTE had been warned by Debs of the approach of Ingersoll, so that some God-fearing citizens had been afraid to go out of doors. Terre Haute had been pockmarked with bills warning against the advent of this apparently godless man whose profession it was to make a great joke of God.

No man without a sense of humor had ever founded a religion, according to the pompous Ingersoll. Fortunately for him, humor had not been left out of his melancholy constitution, his body so large that it could contain the muses of both tragedy and comedy, dancing, dangling upon the same puppet stage.

The legend has come down regarding the legend-begetting man that once when the great Republican Speaker of the House was crossing a rainy gutter and was kicked at by a coach horse whose driver, in the coachman's box, had not seen him, he turned directly to the horse's head and, politely lifting his high silk stovepipe hat as he bowed with his great cape whirling around him—and it had its own musical momentum—had asked with that devastating wit that made him anathema to the Democratic party wherever he went, "Pray tell me, sir, whose Democratic candidate are you?"

At the time of the great orator Ingersoll's first visit to Terre Haute, he had recently returned to America from a Cook's tour of the Tower of London and other museums of torture instruments.

He had seen the rack—"And then priests, clergymen, divines, saints began turning these windlasses and kept turning until the ankles, the knees, the hips, the shoulders, the elbows, the wrists of the victims were all dislocated and the sufferer was wet with the sweat of agony. And they had standing by a physician to feel his pulse. What for? To save his life? Yes. In mercy? No—simply that they might rack him once again." This had been done in the name of civilization, law and order, and the name of the most merciful Christ.

Ingersoll had been speaking at a time when the difference between that medieval torture and this age of the feudal railway as ruled over by the industrial barons who generally considered themselves representatives of God and always on God's side was that with labor so cheap and in constant oversupply there would be little point in employing a physician to blow up the bellows of dead life fires. It was easier to substitute the living workman for the dead.

The day of Ingersoll's speech in Terre Haute had been a day of flood. The autumnal heavens had poured with the cold rain like that in which the waters had covered the face of the earth, it seeming as if the God of the Bible were taking His revenge for the swollen, water-loaded, porous Ingersoll's disparagement of Noah and his ark, which had had room only for couples and none for some old goony bird.

It had seemed as if the Wabash, swelling under the tumult of rain, might carry away some of the poor people whose beds here in Terre Haute were old boxes and boats half in the water and half in the alluvial mud.

The "Tall Sycamore of the Wabash"—United States Senator Daniel W. Voorhees—had assured Debs as they bumped along from the railroad station in a yellow tram to the Opera House that the downpour would make no difference. "Colonel Ingersoll is the only man in America who can attract the biggest house on the rainiest night."

The Tall Sycamore of the Wabash's prophecy had been correct. The Opera House was packed to the gills with as many people as umbrellas.

Debs had been so enchanted by the incandescent Robert Ingersoll that when, after the evening's celebrations, he had accompanied him through the ever-falling rain to the railroad station, he had impulsively hopped onto the train and had ridden all the way to Cincinnati with the beaming-faced man of that time's all-golden world of now shining as bright as the sun while the ever-falling rain—oh, the ever-falling rain of nineteenth-century literature—had continued to fall as the flood waters came up to the wheels and almost over the engine and almost over the fireman's box. And no doubt if it had, the train would have crawled on with its headlight blurred like a gold bug under a wave.

The musical, mathematical Ingersoll, a great dispenser of personal charities, had charity also for himself and would never knowingly make a mistake that would put him behind the eight ball in the capitalistic billiard game—and so had aimed to push his cue against his ball in a not erratic way that would cause him to win over his opponent, whoever he was, and not to lose.

The pagan Ingersoll was an opponent of free silver and an upholder of the gold standard—thus was a good Republican Gold Bug—whereas Debs tended to favor Silver Bugs.

The always calculating but nonmercenary Ingersoll was also the innovator of complex schemes whereby he might realize the instant gold which would not be fool's gold—all his fortune-making magician's acts having been somewhat like the world of Prospero dissolving before it could appear with even one gold vein or coin of gold or its reflection upon a living face or upon a rock.

What had impressed Debs about Ingersoll had been and would be his magnificence of character and personality and his philosophy of time's All Golden World of Now, which had made him—if no seeker after utopia in a socialistic sense and no believer in the instantaneous transformation of human society from worthless mud to purest gold by the edict of man—he had already given up placing his trust in God, it seemed—the defender of the poor and the weak, who were so many, and the dispenser of meat and bread to them out of his own not limitless means, although he always wore a suit with a large pocket in which he kept his hand for the dispersal of coins to beggar men—usually one coin per man.

Debs had been impressed by Ingersoll's having served as legal councilor for the breaking up of the forged Davis will in Butte, Montana—where because of the two hundred and fifty tons of sulfur that were burned every day by the blast furnaces he had felt as homesick as a polar bear at the Equator and had been sickened almost unto death during the course of a tortuous trial by the acquisition of greater knowledge than he needed of human chicanery, greed, deviousness, deceit, and the unreliable testimonials of witnesses whose words were as unreliable as those of Holy Writ. He had been successful as to the outcome of the trial but had not been paid a cent more than the sum necessary for the coverage of his not inconsiderable expenses which had included his medical bills for the illness that came from breathing the sulfurous air, although the widow Davis, whom he represented, had been granted a compromise settlement, which had enabled her to live very well and beyond the reach of fog and smog.

[8 6]

I<small>N LATE</small> N<small>OVEMBER</small> of 1878, Debs had been able to bring to Terre Haute another crusader on the road, Wendell Phillips. That which had kept Phillips on the road had been his crusade against the great capitalistic moguls for the eight-hour day and other economic and political reforms which should be brought into this world by the poor workingman's enlightened use of the ballot. The rich were the few, but the poor were the many and of all colors under the sun and of some not under the sun.

Doubtless Wendell Phillips would have suffered multiple violences from the red-handed brigands of corporate capitalism had there not been safety in numbers—the numbers of proposals for reforms that he carried in his portmanteau on his long tours.

A fragile old gentleman, sixty-seven years old when he came to Terre Haute, the son of the first mayor of Boston, he who was in the evening of his life had long ago been labeled by the Richmond, Virginia, *Enquirer* that "mad man and traitor to his class"—which he had continued to be.

James Redpath had prepared the members of the Occidentals Literary Club in the City on the Mound for the coming of Debs's guest, a Boston Brahmin. This was the first time Debs had met with Wendell Phillips and it would also be the last time he would come into actual proximity with the legendary collector of all the wrongs that should be righted by the reformers.

Almost bald Debs would later recall—when he had been long on the road and was likened to Wendell Phillips himself with his lecture bag stuffed with reforms including reforms of reformers—this which had been their first and only meeting, but which was not to be the last—for although the derelict Boston Brahmin had preceded him, yet surely he would catch up with him and other good companions at that Mermaid Tavern which was in heaven.

Everyone Debs loved had been a friend of everyone he loved, it would always seem, links joining with links. Wendell Phillips, for example, had been a friend of the Reverend Myron Reed who had also been a friend of Ingersoll's, and was the liberal Presbyterian divine whose sermons were delivered in a forthright and yet almost casual and random way of his own—quietly, brilliantly, as if he were talking with a friend.

The Reverend Reed had been a cod fisherman on Newfoundland's

Grand Banks before giving up his boat to become a fisherman of men's souls. He had been and continued to be an admirer of Horace Greeley, whose advice in the *New York Tribune* in 1853—"Go West, young man"—had caused a landslide of migration from the East to the West, mainly by the children of the immigrant poor, who had attributed the slogan to Greeley. But he was not the father of the westward movement. He was perhaps only the mother of all those poor workers who would perish in the prairies and in the mountains and in the deserts and along the prairie schooner wagon roads and the rails and in the places where no roads were. The true father of the slogan "Go West, young man" had been John Babson Soule, in the *Terre Haute Express* in 1851.

The Reverend Reed had also been for many years a great lover of the neglected tramp poet Walt Whitman, who used to frequent Madison Square and who was a rival pigeon feeder and was a believer—in a raggedy, disorganized way—in the brotherhood of man with man, and was also a fisherman.

What Debs would remember when he went to meet Wendell Phillips's train was that the spry, courtly old man had seemed to him a tower of strength notwithstanding his years. "Here before me stood the hero who had challenged the whole wicked, malevolent power of human slavery and had preserved unsullied the high purpose of his manhood and the precious integrity of his soul."

At the Old South Meeting House in Boston where the history of the American Revolution had been made and where the British during the Revolution had placed an academy for riding-horses—according to Debs, they were often better educated in America than the trampled working children—Wendell Phillips had stated on June 4, 1876: "Marble, gold, and granite are not real—the only actual reality is an idea."

Wendell Phillips, the darling of liberals, had been the guest at a quiet little banquet at noon in Terre Haute. He had not wanted to accept a large fee for a small audience. His host Debs had been determined, however, that the old knight, the Galahad in quest of the egalitarian society—as if it were the Holy Grail of which he had caught a few glimpses on the road, or so he must have seemed with all his great traditions of reform hanging about him and his also continuously innovative spirit, active even now—should not be paid so little that he would have no money farther on. Debs had insisted upon pressing into the palmer's palm the full fee in gold or silver or paper dollars.

And, indeed, Wendell Phillips needed dollars—he spent more than he made or gave away to other poor travelers whom he met on trains. An Ishmaelite forever on the road, Wendell Phillips seemed to have no home but a Pullman sleeping car—and no friends but engineers, firemen, brakemen, switchmen, and the sleeping-car porters who, white or black, always had a way of knowing that the old man who favored the eight-hour day was on board. He was such a perpetual passenger that it would not be surprising if he died someday while in passage. His great heroes with whom he yearned to be joined were the martyrs Elijah Lovejoy, John Brown, and Toussaint L'Ouverture.

When Wendell Phillips had preached at Faneuil Hall in 1837 his memorial sermon for the Reverend Elijah P. Lovejoy—who was also to be a hero to Debs because of Lovejoy's flaming freedom messages, which had been poured by his French revolutionary father into the pitcher ears of the little boy in that City on the Mound—Phillips's praise had been given to the freedom-of-the-press martyr who had escaped from the lynch mobs in Missouri to the free state of Illinois, where he had been murdered by an armed mob while coming out of his newspaper office in August 1835—his epitaph upon his gravestone to read, but in Latin which few people could translate, "Here lies Lovejoy, Spare him now that he is buried"—a plea to his murderers not to dig up the victim of a first murder for a second murder or not to shoot into his grave. Phillips's conservative family had tried, although with no success, to have Phillips locked up in an asylum like a mad dog.

It would be recalled that Wendell Phillips had damned the Constitution from the stage before a large audience and had tried to tear up the American flag with his teeth in hopeless protest against the tearing up of Elijah Lovejoy. The old man had told Debs that whenever he was in this part of the world on his seemingly ceaseless lecture tours, he always managed to come around by Alton, where he would pay a call on Lovejoy's grave, and he would continue to do so as long as he lived.

Not only had the many-headed reformer stood for women's rights, which had been so long denied, he was also against the imperialistic rule of the Irish by the British crown, against the stormings by Cossacks of the Jews in the ghettoes of Russia, against the exile of Russian dissidents to the Siberian wilds, and against the czars of America.

His abolitionist wife—with her concern for his happiness when he was old and frail and almost worn out, and probably with an unusual wisdom, as it was not until Don Quixote was cured of his need for quests in search of wrongs to right by wielding his paper swords that he had died in bed—would say to him until the end, "Don't shilly-shally, Wendell. Get up and go, go, go."

[8 7]

THE ELEGIAC ASPECTS of life were fortunately not the old rails the editor of *The Locomotive Firemen's Magazine* rode upon in an ever-increasing journey. The editor of the Women's Department, Debs's lively old school friend Ida Husted Harper—whose husband was the Democratic city attorney when Debs, his sidekick, was the Democratic city clerk—had volunteered to give her advice to railroad wives, daughters, sisters, mothers, and widows on all subjects that were of feminine interest and that might help them in the understanding of the world of the firemen and the problems they faced, both the spiritual and the material.

Ida, when celebrating eight years editing the Women's Department, would recall that it had all begun one cold, dark, stormy afternoon when she had been visiting with Debs's sister Eugénie—then an assistant with Émilie in the work on *The Locomotive Firemen's Magazine*—and they had knotted their heads together as they wondered why a voice should not be given to firemen's wives, mothers, daughters, sisters—all those on the distaff side.

The Women's Department, which began in the parlor where Mary was but would never forget the kitchen of life where Martha was, had been welcomed joyously by Brother Debs, who was working far beyond all union hours to make the fragile little magazine what it would soon become—the most widely circulated labor periodical in the world.

Who could possibly know, indeed, how many men and women *The Locomotive Firemen's Magazine* reached, as it was carried in the pockets of railroad men on so many reverberating rails and was passed on to fellow railroad men as in a dream of perpetual motion it went all the way from Point Barrow to Cape Hope?

When the office of the magazine had finally spilled over from the first floor and was spilling over from the second floor with nowhere to go, *The Locomotive Firemen's Magazine* had been fortunately able to move to a small office on the second floor of a business building on Main Street furnished with a long table and an old bench that had been used by passengers waiting for trains in way stations—sometimes in those stations where the trains they were waiting for had already passed or would never come, trains like the Millennial Train—and an old Ben Franklin stove such as had been used to warm the station on freezing nights but had often not been provided with coal so that the passengers and the ticket agent—if there was one, and the telegrapher—if there was one—had frozen to death at the frozen keyboard, which might make, in the spring of the year when the ice was melting, a rattling sound—perhaps of a message coming from some other star.

It would be remembered that upon the wall of the new office Debs had hung up his beloved railroad scoop, much as a knight of old might have hung up his sword.

[8 8]

WHEN IN 1880 Debs had brought to Terre Haute the formidable Susan B. Anthony, the heroine in the cause of women's freedom, he had had to do so under the sponsorship of Mrs. Ida Harper, for the Occidentals, although they had endured the advent of the atheist Ingersoll and the anarchic Phillips, both of whom were believers in suffrage for that which most men called the weaker half but which was according to one of Debs's chivalric compliments the stronger sex and certainly the nobler half of man, would not entertain this somewhat scrawny hen who seemed to want to be a cock.

No public official would allow Susan B. Anthony to appear in a large hall, perhaps through fear that it would be burned down by her incendiary message or by a mob with flaming torches, so Debs had had to rent a small, obscure meeting place for souls who had already been converted to her cause or believed that even so unworthy a cause as hers—which would break up the American marriage or leave the men to nurse the babes while the lily-white hands of women would be laid upon the throttles—deserved a forum for the exercise of her loudly honking voice in a land that granted the rights of freedom of speech.

At the railway station where Debs and Mrs. Ida Harper had waited to greet Susan B. Anthony, there had gathered a shrieking, screaming, howling mob, the women fiercer than the men—but Debs the host had been able to pilot the suffrage captain through the crowd.

They had both seemed calm in the midst of that wild tempest—and yet he had sensed her trembling at his side and had heard vibrations like those that might be caused by fear. He had intuitively known from the moment he touched her how shy and essentially lonely a fellow creature she was, and in many ways unfit to carry the cross for women that she had taken up. And indeed, hers was a maiden heart, even though some of her enemies might call her a bachelor.

At the time of her visit to Terre Haute, the courtly Susan, tall and leaning forward in her walk with the long-limbed Debs, whom some of the Locomotive Firemen brothers already compared with a strange seabird blown to the City on the Mound, was in her middle years. She should have been as unattractive as she had been depicted for some time in the lampooning publicity she received from men who would rather that paradise on earth be forever deferred and life go on in this same crippled way than admit that it was guilty Adam who had given the apple to guiltless Eve—thus establishing that ground on which she had been deprived of her civil rights ever since the historical nonevent.

The devil Ambrose Bierce—whose initials, A.G.B., his crickety crickets thought, stood for almighty god Bierce—this town crier, in the *San Francisco News Letter* some years back, had written in most rabid terms regarding the impossible Susan B. Anthony—called Susan Bee in her Bonnet by some of her deriders, of whom there were both male and female—a view very near that of the common people of the common clay whom Bierce professed to despise quite as much as some of the fragmented utopian assumptions that, although blasted, contained seeds of divinity which might someday come into flower.

"The scraggy and angular darlings of the suffrage persuasion will hold an animated yow-yow in this city on the 25th instances. Susan B. Anthony is expected to be around. We do trust Susie will not blight our hopes by staying away. We have long entertained an intense desire to walk around her and examine her points. For the furtherance of this desire, we beg her to pad as little as a decent disregard for the opinions of mankind will permit."

The daughters of Eve would always ask, however, by what right had merely mortal man usurped the authority and power of the great god Jehovah in seeking to define the proper duty of that one half of the human race which was surely woman? And had there not already arrived the barren industrial age in which there were as many female tramps as male tramps upon the nation's roads? In what home could homeless creatures stay at home?

Furthermore, the idealization of women and children by the American nation was the most gross hypocrisy imaginable in view of the exploitation of women and children at even lower than the starvation wages paid to men—as Debs would have pointed out if there had never been what fortunately there was—a Susan B. Anthony under the blue empyrean. She was always there.

[8 9]

AT THE TIME of the great troubadour Susan B. Anthony's visit to Terre Haute, the social climate, except for a few courageous friends, could not have surprised her by being hostile—for the times were never ripe for suffrage, there being a vast under-tow and upper-tow and middle-tow resistance to the cause of the intellectual freedom not only of women but of men from any type of dogma. And yet the walleyed Susan, who was almost blind in one eye, who was both taut and lean and carried upon her tall body not one inch or pound of excessive flesh in this age which favored the plump hen, had made a strong and everlasting impression of her beauty and sorrow and strength and depth of tenderness upon the mind of her wakeful escort, Debs.

She had worn her sleekly dark, shining hair simply parted in the middle and knotted in the back in the old-fashioned way—every hair in its groove—and hers had been fine-drawn classic features and a large Roman nose and a strong chin that had made her look like the impression stamped upon an ancient gold medallion exhumed from a tomb and that she had inherited from a long line of Italian forebears, of whom the last known had been a goldsmith living in Cologne—the city, not the bottle that was famous for its toilet water scented with a thousand and one flowers, with which she loved to perfume herself as she tried to keep away the gnats and dust which, when she was riding through seas of dust, had caked her gray bonnet and her gray cloak when the winds blew hard against her as she came with her suffrage messages to the wilds where few women in their right minds would venture alone—and even she had had to have at times a male escort lest she should be strung up alone on some very tall tree or cross by ruffians waylaying her.

The electric, electrifying, vibrant, walleyed, slightly bent suffrage troubadour had made her public appearances with her absolute and imperishable beauty intact, it had seemed, in spite of the many wounds that life had dealt out to her from the day of her birth onward—those of which she did not speak—for a certain secrecy of nature was hers and must be respected by all who knew her. The bloomer girls who were her followers worshiped her as if she were a goddess of old. Or perhaps one should say god—for she did not believe in the feminization of names. And if a woman was a poet-ess, she should be called a poet, as she was equal to her male counterpart.

About two years after her meeting with Debs her suffrage daughters had gathered together in Washington to present to Susan B. a long red fringed shawl. It would be this long red shawl that would be reproduced in the Susan B. Anthony portrait dolls and gold-framed miniatures that her ever-blossoming daughters wore and that for them was not a symbol of Karl Marx's red revolution—which many had not heard of—but of the women's revolution or rebellion against male domination.

Susan, the future women's suffrage captain, had been born on February 15, 1815, in the wide valley at the foot of Mount Greylock's forbiddingly masculine visage near Adams, Massachusetts—the daughter of an idealis-tic Quaker father and a pleasure-loving non-Quaker mother, who, because of her having fallen in love with him who had also fallen in love with her and never would fall out of what he had fallen into, had put off her bright gown and put on a gray gown and had given up the worldly things she loved and yet, although duty reigned supreme, was to find little or no plea-sure in the life of a childbearing mare, she who did not want her belly swollen with either the wind or a child and who wanted to do nothing but to dance at a ball, dance all night long until the rafters shook, dance until the roosters crowed and the hens cackled, dance from the dusk until the dawn. The father would not dance. He had done all his dancing in bed with her, poor creature, who had submitted to him because of her love for him or her sense of duty but had wished many times to die as she saw him approach with the love light burning in his eyes. She had tried to keep her silence but had shrieked and groaned.

Susan would always feel sorry for a mother who swelled up once a year and scarcely flattened out before she swelled up again.

The family had migrated by mule-drawn wagon first to Battenville, New York—then to a nearby settlement named Hardscrabble, most aptly named in a Dickensian sense, as they had had to scrabble hard for a living on straggly acres bearing more pebbles than corn—and from there to a farm overlooking the Genessee and the needle-thin steeples of the churches of Rochester, where they had prospered.

According to the tribute paid to the suffrage troubadour by her beloved companion suffragist—the large-bosomed and happily married Mrs. Eliz-abeth Cady Stanton, who had brought into the world many children—Susan B. Anthony had been taught at an early age to enter into the holy of holies of herself, meet herself, and be true to her revelations.

And indeed, Susan had come into her awakening in an age of the awakening of utopian schemes and schemers and dreamers of every kind and in a place particularly productive of them and their various utopias, which seemed ready to spread their flowering branches like one great tree over the American continent.

What Susan had felt when she had reached the age of twenty-five and, having lost the only masculine love that would ever be hers in life, was just such loneliness as that of any old maid who was that barren branch upon the tree of life which, it had seemed, would never break into even the most ghostly flower and would never bear fruit.

It was this loneliness that Debs had sensed without quite knowing why—although he was to pick up many secret details over the years from Ida Husted Harper, her ever-redundant biographer—Susan's lips remaining silent if not absolutely locked and sealed upon those matters pertaining to her secret heart, which was a woman's heart. And thus the chivalric heart of the bachelor Debs, at the time of their brief and all-too-fleeting encounter, had gone out to her.

What Susan would chiefly remember of her girlhood was that her overburdened mother—who had given herself over to many romantic yearnings for fruits beyond her reach—had always been embarrassed by the pregnancies, which she, under her billowing gray gown, had tried to conceal from her daughter's eyes.

Once when Susan had helped her father for a week operating a loom at his cotton mill—the strings looming like harp strings above her—she had spent her week's pay of a dollar and a half in reward for her part-time labor on six most beautiful and most fragile blue teacups for her mother, who loved beautiful things just as much as she did.

The loom in Susan's father's house had been a small loom worked by her hands upon the spindle, her feet upon the footboard. She had trembled, fluttering up and down somewhat like a bird with a crippled wing or no wing. Her father, a devout abolitionist who had not wavered in his opposition to black slavery and to white, had been—in a probably unconscious sense beyond her power to recognize at the time—her god.

What had happened to Susan's once-bright eyes was that when she was a toddler only three years old, her mother had sent her to live with her grandmother so that she would not at that tender age be present to hear the mother's cries during the throes of her labor when she was giving birth to another child.

During the period of her exile and at a time when she needed her mother most—for she had been weakened by the usual childhood ills—

Susan had been attacked by the old fiddler Death striking her with the whooping cough, which had caused her to spit up blood as her eyes watered and the tears flowed down her cheeks. Her period of recovery had been spent reading the New England infant primer in a darkened room, its blinds drawn to shut out the light of the sun, which might have added to her whoop—it had been erroneously believed.

She had emerged with her eyes crossed, both eyes turned to her nose so that her face had seemed to be cut upon a peculiar bias and was asymmetrical. Rest had returned the right eye to its correct position but not the left. The right eye had been true as the left eye had turned inward, so that for years she had bumped along like a moth in the daylight.

When she was twenty years old, a bumbling surgeon with a butcher knife—while correcting the inward turn of the left eye—had cut the cord too much, with the result that as the left eye had turned outward, the right eye had turned inward. Time had passed and the mutilation had remained. Her shame had been as great as if it were she who had been at fault.

Gradually, however, her eyes had straightened of their own accord, which had contained within it some elements of discord—in times of great stress and storm her dark eyes turned absolutely black.

It would be recalled that she had managed—when walking with a gentleman—to walk with the profile of her left eye turned toward him, as she did that day with Debs—calmly keeping the right side toward the storming mob.

[9 0]

DEBS HAD HAD A SENSE that all the firemen everywhere had been waiting for him. His suitcase had been always packed. He had traveled in all directions—north, south, east, west.

His journeys were over mountains and valleys, and his beds were in cabooses and bunks, and he was fed from the dinner pails of the swarthy stokers who had nestled close to his heart and always would until it was cold and dark.

After his first political speech in 1878, Debs had been tendered the nomination for a seat then vacant in the Congress. Although his acceptance would have been followed by his election as surely as the night followed the day, he had respectfully declined.

The conscious reason for this decision at this time was that he did not wish to leave home, but possibly also he could not see all virtue on one side of the political rail fence and all vice on the other side—apple orchards and fields of corn where the Democrats were and acres of weeds and cinder yards where the Republicans were. He dreamed already of a better way and a more comprehensive world than that of the two-party system which he would come to look upon as Gog and Magog.

Was there really much choice between the Democrats and Republicans as to their party makeup? Debs would think not when he came to the understanding that they were much the same—they were Janus-faced.

Ingersoll, during the triumphant Garfield campaign which would send the new president like a stalk of corn to his grave, had declared that he believed in good crops and was glad when a fellow found a gold mine and rejoiced when there were forty bushels of wheat to an acre—whereas in his view as surely as in that of any sensible man the Democratic party was a party of famine and a good friend of the early frost and the Colorado beetle and the weevil.

So far as Ingersoll was concerned, and thus he had differed with Debs, there was only one true Republic, the republic of one with one as a majority: "There, all are monarchs, and all are equals. The tyranny of a majority even is unknown. Reformers forget that common people—cogs and wheels—have opinions of their own, that they fall out with other cogs and refuse to turn the wheels. . . . The complex, tangled web of thought and dreams, of perception and memory, of imagination and judgment—of wish and will and want—the woven wonder of life—has never yet been raveled back to simple threads."

Had Debs gone as a congressman to Washington, he would have been there when Garfield was assassinated by the fallen-away Oneidist Charles Guiteau, who represented himself as a recipient of a message from the angel of the Lord and who believed that he had done nothing but hasten Garfield's transplant from the earthly fields to the heavenly paradise.

Debs had begun where he was. In 1879, the year in which the railroad baron Commodore Cornelius Vanderbilt had uttered the shocking statement "The public be damned!" as if to indicate that they could all go to hell in a hack as they were less important to him than Mrs. Vanderbilt's tiara or Mrs. Vanderbilt's dog's tiara or Mrs. Vanderbilt's dog's dog's tiara—the year which was also that of the publication of Henry George's even more shocking *Progress and Poverty,* which some critics called *Progress Toward Poverty,* as they did not like the single tax remedy which the ne'er-do-well author proposed for the increase of the wealth of the poor and the decrease of the wealth of the rich (with his first pay from his royalties, he purchased a flowered Brussels carpet for the parlor floor of his poor little house)— Debs was able to give up the life at the warehouse for a far more interesting life, in both the humanistic and humanitarian sense, of city clerk in the courthouse under Vigo's bell, where he would see passing before his eyes all or many of the broken shards which were beyond repair, although sometimes stuck together in one delusive body.

As if by a Wabash flood, the entire Democratic ticket of drunks and idol smashers and breakers of law—from the point of view of the sacrosanct Republican opposition, for whom all or almost all Democrats were traitors and non-Christians, who were believers in pagan Rome, kissers of the pope's big toe, and dancers of beer-barrel polkas and fiddlers on the green—had been swept into the courthouse with Debs, a good but peculiar man who had won by a majority of one thousand and one hundred bums.

In his office as city clerk of Vigo County in Terre Haute, the onetime hogopolis which burgeoned with churches of every known denomination and some which were unknown to man or woman, perhaps were known to dog and bird, Debs had shown, it was considered by some of the good, law-abiding people, a shocking kindness to drunkards and prostitutes.

True to Eugène Sue and Victor Hugo, Debs held that the poor Magdalenes of the streets—had not Christ associated with them?—were not so much sinning as sinned against, that many were debased to the oldest of professions by the cupidity of the railroad corporations and satanic mills and mines, which did not pay their fathers, husbands, or sons a decent wage and thus drove them to drink and steal. Many times while talking with the unorganized and unemployed, red-eyed men in their pig-sty bars where he did his research in a situation that would only remind him of the greater poverty in greater towns, which by its magnitude did not make that of even one poor man or woman seem less in these mudflats, Debs had seen the prowlers in Taylorsville, known also as Terre Haute's Tenderloin or its Babylon, places where there were no gilded palaces of sin at all and no palaces of the virtuous and of the rich but only tumbling shacks as insubstantial as the tumbleweed jumping along in every wind—shacks built of rusted tin cans and old fence palings and rotted rail ties and soggy mattresses and the flotsam of humanity, the castaway things that were fit for the social castaways.

He had noted that the vice kings who fed upon the poor street girls like vultures upon the body of a dead cow were never fined but flourished. He identified himself with the dregs, the very lowest depths, and not with the high ground.

Debs had refused to fine these women. He did not believe that a prostitute should be harassed by a policeman who found one on his beat and brought her to make her pay the fine that would be put into the coffers for the support of the farms for the mad or the poor which in those days were so often one and the same, as if to be poor was the same as to be mad—mad with a wound beyond any cure.

Thomas Harper had shown no sympathy for the police with their clubs and guns—perhaps because he was thinking of their attacks on labor strikers and not only the men but women and children, or of the way they would shoot tramps for merely sticking out their tongues or rubbing their noses or saying "Damn!"—and was altogether so seething that when asked to contribute a dollar toward a fund for flowers and coffin and hearse and hearse horses and musical choirs for a policeman so popular that the mourners would require no payment as might some poor man who had lost a day's pay by taking time off for the funeral of his own mother, he had answered with utter cheerfulness that he would gladly, gladly contribute a dollar for a policeman's burial, indeed, had insisted that he would give five so that they could bury five policemen while they were at it—although he did not suggest that five should be consigned to one communal grave, as sometimes happened to the poor or to the unemployed and to the unemployable who had no union such as Debs was coming to think should be theirs. Perhaps he came earlier to that conclusion than others knew or than he knew—for his were two calendars, the objective and the subjective.

And, oh, the deductions which had been made for a long time and were made at this time and would be made for a long time to come from the pay of workers for time lost on the job! The huffing, puffing, red-jowled *Locomotive Firemen's Magazine* would never let such matters rest. One of Debs's favorite Irish workmen's songs tells of that poor driller who made the mistake of lighting his pipe with the fuse.

> *Last week a premature blast went off*
> *And a mile in the air went big Jim Goff.*
> *When pay-day next it came around*
> *Poor Jim's pay a dollar short he found.*
> *"What for," says he—then came the reply,*
> *"You were docked for the time you were up in the sky."*

IN 1881, when the Democrats were buried by the Republicans, Debs had been swept into City Hall once again, but with only two more votes than the majority by which he had won in the first campaign. The fact that the organizer of the Locomotive Firemen's union had had no grave dug and no tombstone placed over his political future and Debs had outdone himself by two mouse squeaks showed that poor men had not lost their minds on Election Day and had not been left to recover them the following week.

Debs had elected not to run for city clerk a third time on the chance that there might be one more mouse squeak that would return him to his office—his confinement at his desk having isolated him almost as much as the warehouse had done when it came to organizing locomotive union chapters.

Campaigning for the Democratic vote, Debs had talked in the railway yards and coal fields and had gone all over Vigo County talking to firemen and brakemen and wheel wipers whom he knew well, farmers in their fields and barnyards, roosters and hens, had asked the old grandfathers and the old grandmothers how they were, had asked how the old cow was and how the apple trees were doing and how the mother was and how the baby was, had gathered up the newborn baby in his arms before the ghostly reaper could come with his scythe.

[9 1]

WHEN DEBS had accepted the nomination of the Democratic party for Vigo County's representative in the Indiana State Legislature, he had found himself confronted, at the national convention of the Brotherhood of Locomotive Firemen, by the proposal that an amendment to the bylaws of their constitution should forbid the holding or acceptance of a political office by any salaried grand officer, and before he could catch his breath, this restraining order had been carried quick as a thunderbolt by a loud voice vote, which nearly knocked him off his feet.

The Brotherhood of Locomotive Firemen wanted nothing to do with party allegiances, as theirs was an interest transcending politics.

Debs, supremely logical through all the illogical things of life, as a positive and not negative leader must be if he is to show the way, could not understand why a union leader should not participate in bipartisan politics and thus if gaining the allegiance of one party, risk losing that of the other which might be the next party in power and would take revenge upon the helpless union. Debs had threatened to quit in order that he might run for his people who needed a voice—all the poor workingpeople—all who were supposed to be deaf and dumb and mute. The proposed amendment was defeated by another overwhelmingly majority voice vote as quick as the first. He had triumphed.

Debs had been able to carry his torch parade to victory under a flaming banner identifying him as grand secretary and treasurer, Brotherhood of Locomotive Firemen, candidate for the legislature, while the men who were going to put him into office with their votes wore white ribbons pinned to their coats or shawls or hoods with the inscription "DEBS—OUR CHOICE."

In the Radiating Railway City where the first railroad station in this country had been reached by the first Hoosier train in 1847, the Madison & Indianapolis, having been built on the steepest standard-gauge rail in the nation at that time in order to claw its way like a wild horse with a long mane of foam up the steep hills on the Ohio River shore to Madison, there would be so many changes from the antebellum town to the postbellum town that it would be no wonder that old-timers who remembered the earlier world would sometimes speak of themselves as having been covered over by the burning ashes of Mount Vesuvius like the old Pompeii. It was, in fact, a generally American thought where there were so many rapid changes heightened by the advent of the machine, so many rapidly disappearing meadows of wildflowers inundated by burning cinders and ashes that many who were holdovers from the past felt that they were strangers in the places they had always known and perhaps had loved.

Indianapolis was in the process of a change which seemed more slow-moving there than in other great urban centers, for it was still of half a mind to be a country town where the cry of the Gabriel rooster ushering in the dawn could still be heard. The old Bates House where Lincoln had stopped on his journey to his inauguration in Washington had not yet been replaced by the Claypool Hotel, which would retain, as memorial to the dead or living past, the iron balcony on which the martyred president had stood while sensing that he would never come alive this way again—and he had been correct—he would come feet-first as church bells tolled—some with sorrow and some with something very like joy, as had happened in other towns. Cannonballs were still piled up in pyramids in the old, unkempt military park not far from the slaughterhouse where the hogs had been sent grunting in their boxcars as would be the poor Union boys who were sent grunting to their deaths in southern battlefields which might be anywhere.

The Roman-domed state capitol which was to take the place of the old Greek Revival of which the floor of the upper chamber had fallen on the chamber of the lower house had not yet been built but was in the process of being lifted up by stonemasons and with its huge copper-colored dome like a supernumerary planet gleaming through the clouds, the façades facing east and south adorned with porticos in the colonnades, with entablatures and supporting stone figures symbolizing the early days of the state, the city priding itself that like Rome it was not built in a single day, that only over a long period of time as time was measured in the Hoosier state had it arisen out of the marsh mud which had been marked into town lots for sale to not impecunious citizens.

All had been an Indian trading post. There were only a few wooden cigar-store Indians now, as in other American cities where once the Indians had roamed. The only Chinaman was a Chinese laundryman who was very good in the washing and starching and ironing of shirts, whether long-tailed like kites or short-tailed. There were black coachmen, black barbers, black shoeshine boys, black handymen, as there were Little Black Sambos who were wooden or iron hitching posts and there were turbaned blackamoors in the hallways of great houses carrying trays on which to drop your calling card.

On the lawns of many-gabled houses of wood or stone in the dignified residential regions of old settlers who had prospered and had begotten an affluent progeny as not all had, some having never gotten out of the marsh, there were weeping willows and lily-margined ponds and flocks of the iron bucks who had not yet migrated to the fenced backyards to hold upon their tall antlers the clothesline on which would be hung Pa's drawers and Ma's nightgowns flapping in the wind like the wings of birds in the age of the horseless buggy, which would wipe out the horse and buggy, the first automobile with an internal combustible gasoline engine to be built in the capital city by Charles H. Black, who unfortunately, however, used a kerosene torch for ignition so that on a windy day the flame would blow out if it did not, indeed, set fire to the driver in his long linen coat and the lady whose hat was draped by motor veils with which to protect her face from the dust.

Still in the streets where the Vigo County congressman would take his strolls, between sessions of the lawmakers who were all too slow for him in the righting of wrongs and were very good in the passage of half-baked bills, were the little old yellow streetcars driven by teams of bony long-necked mules with eyes crazily crossed, their heels dashing into the faces of drivers cracking with their whips and racing as if they were charioteers on the Roman Corso, the crowded passengers disembarking from a rear door into the middle of the road in a wilderness of traffic caused by many private coaches with coachmen blowing horns, some with Dalmatians running along the wheels—and how could they be, as Jimsy Whimsy, the little bench-legged poet with the blue eyes would ask of any companion when he was trying to get through the traffic flow as he could not follow his nondirectional sense of direction at all and curbstones were always so difficult? How could a Dalmatian be a dog? He thought the Dalmatian was a coast, just as Shakespeare or Bacon had thought.

One day a coach dog had followed James Whitcomb Riley to the *Journal* office where he had tied it to a table leg to keep company with him during the writing of his poultry poems for the advertisement of egg-laying hens, which some people thought made him not a real poet such as he yearned to be but only a poor poetaster eating asters or an illusory old farmer combing his beard, trying to turn his beard into hay. Suddenly a Republican bigwig who had come in to place his advertisement in Lost and Found—"Lost, one Dalmatian—reward, a nugget of gold"—had seen the dog chained to the post and had begun to beat the funny little mock man over his big yellow-fringed head and no doubt would have beaten him black and blue if Lije Halford or some other big-wheel editor had not come to the rescue.

All the world was looking for the golden-haired little Charley Ross, the first child of wealth kidnapped and held for ransom in America, it was generally believed, and never found since he was spirited away by horse and buggy riders, although the claimants of the reward would run into thousands and thousands, altogether ten thousand, and one or two or three golden-haired boys and girls, some of whom were dressed like Little Lord Fauntleroy. The Republican headquarters on a day so hot that one could hear bees buzzing in the streets had announced that little Charley, by now several years older than when he had been snatched away, was at the Democratic headquarters. Soon there were angry mobs in the streets waiting for the Democrats to bring little Charley out and threatening to bust the windows in if they did not do so, threatening to drag them all out and tar and feather them for hiding little Charley away from his mother.

Along with the palaces of the rich in the capital city in the Gilded Age—including that of the buggy king George A. Parry, with whom Debs would cross swords many times because of Parry's hatred of labor unions or any form of socialism whatever and his conviction that every man had a chance to pull himself up by his own bootstraps if he had bootstraps and that all utopias belonged under water like the Lost Atlantis, of which he, president of the American Association of Manufacturers, would write in

The Scarlet Empire—were the neglected districts at the western edge of the city such as Debs with Riley would sometimes visit, places like Irish Hill, Cotton Town, Possum Hollow, Rag Alley and the Crib and Pat Ward's Bottoms, Bird's Nest and Peedee and Hoplight, the places with which Debs's little bench-legged poet sometimes identified himself as the poet of Peedee who was Hoplight just hopping along with his little lights which sometimes seemed to go out in the fog but never did. He was the galactic firefly poet. Debs was his guide.

[9 2]

AS A MEMBER of the Railway Committee, Debs had dedicated his time and energies at the State Legislature to engineering through the House his bill which would make it mandatory that railroad owners should compensate their men for the accidents that they suffered on the roads and of which he had now become one of the chief statisticians in an indifferent America which did not seem to understand that it had transformed and was still transforming ironmongers into kings with powers of death's realm over workmen who helmed their trains and over passengers who made the mistake of taking the doomed trains.

A great number of accidents were caused, according to Debs's records, by antiquated or defective appliances or rails warped by rain or sun, rails with ties missing, bridges that were built only halfway across the yawning abyss, or were caused by such acts of God as a hurricane blowing a tree onto a track or lifting up an entire string of trains from one place and putting it in another or causing a mountain of marble to fall on an engineer and a fireman.

Debs's bill was for the classification and recording of locomotive engineers by railroad corporations and the rules for the declaration of an emergency.

Debs had been able to get his bill successfully through the lower chamber but had seen it wrecked a few days later in the upper chamber, quite as effectively as if the upper chamber had fallen through the floor to the lower chamber as had happened in the old state house.

Roundly defeated by both upper and lower chambers, smashed like Susan's millennial suffrage, had been his bill for woman's suffrage. Debs had crossed valiantly over the Democratic party line to vote for the Republican bill for the abolishment of all distinctions of race and color in the laws of the state of Indiana, where black slavery had presented a far less soluble problem than that of the red men, the institution of black chattel slavery in the Indiana Territory having been forbidden by an ordinance of 1787 with the exception that the judges and Governor Harrison, himself a Virginian who had seemed always to have had his shoeshine boy with him, no matter through what mud he went, had allowed white settlers who owned black men and women to make an agreement with them for lifelong slavery.

It was not until 1843 that slavery by long-forgotten agreement between master and slave had seemed to disappear. Many an old black man worked for nothing or next to nothing even now in the land of the free, and in Missouri, where an old black woman who came to Debs did not know that she was in Missouri or even in America and had asked where it was and had been told that there had been a Civil War of which she had not heard, as she also had never heard of Washington, D.C. The poor creature, only one of many black mud eaters, had continued in bondage like all or almost all those who slept under waters of which the mud increased with every mud slide and every storm.

The measure for which Debs had crossed over the line had been defeated by three votes, no doubt in the name of Father and Mother and Son.

In the antebellum Indiana the underground railway, its train bells muffled and its rails as silent as if they were really under the ground, had been allowed to operate but upon condition that it stay under the ground and would not help a fugitive settle in this state—and upon condition also that any contract made with a black man should be null and void, probably of no more worth than the famed snowflake in hell—and upon condition that to employ a black man to do any work at all, even to be your rake man raking your garden with his hoe, was to be subjected to a fine. There had been so few black men that this law had lain in a dustbin forgotten until its removal in 1881.

LOOKING BACK on his experience at the state legislature, Debs would remember with apology as one might remember a youthful mistake or even a misreading of road signs or getting off on a short spur when what was required was a long track. "There was a time in my life, before I became a Socialist, when I permitted myself to be elected to a state legislature, and I have been trying to live it down. I am as much ashamed of that as I am of having gone to jail."

[9 3]

MARRIAGE WAS A SACRED institution, no one more profoundly convinced of that than Debs was, as he had before him always the happiness of his father and his mother between whom there was never a shadow of misunderstanding, and yet their happiness was not superficial, so far as they knew or anyone knew.

Debs was one of the foremost young men of the community, not only because of his integrated character with its orientation toward a worthy goal and his altogether charming personality—he was also achieving eminence through the growth of the Firemen's brotherhoods. When he talked to fire-blasted firemen or dusty coal miners with their blind eyes burned by fires under the earth, his speech was always concerned with the unions of brothers of which the numbers daily and nightly grew and which were to bring eventually the golden world.

On May Day, 1880, long before the circling on the calendar of May Day as not that merely dedicated to the queen of the May and the flowers of the spring but also that for the celebration of the birth of the labor movement, Debs had read aloud at Terre Haute, in an essay entitled "Hard Work Versus Genius," his praise of such witnesses for hard labor as Michelangelo, John Milton, Benjamin Franklin, and Cicero—they having proved beyond a reasonable doubt that hard work deserveth all the praise, whereas Genius is a nonentity.

In October 1882, when lo, the autumn leaves were falling, falling, falling, falling here and falling there, and falling everywhere as in Bill Nye's parody of the schoolgirl's poem, the members of the Brotherhood of Locomotive Firemen had come from all over this country to celebrate their ninth annual convention at Terre Haute, which had happily received these real or potential incendiaries. They had been met by the friendly policemen, the Ringold Band, the war veterans, the members of the Occidental Literary Club, the Vigo Country Brothers, the city councilmen in carriages, and the members of the fire department blowing whistles without a thought of a revolutionary fire.

Tom Harper had been one of the eminent public-spirited gentlemen who had paid tribute to Debs and other locomotive firemen at Dowling Hall, where the manager of the Union Depot Hotel had provided roast pig and apples and bread and other fruits for four hundred and thirty-one guests at a table decorated with a painted glass lake as its centerpiece and a locomotive made of cut flowers strung on chicken-coop wires, a present from the Brotherhood of Locomotive Firemen to their benevolent host, who was Riley McKeen, president of the Vandalia Railroad and their patron. The boiler bore the initials B.L.F. spelled out in red flowers and the tender the name of the railroad president spelled out in red flowers, the floral masterpiece having been designed by John G. Heinl, who was the designer also of many a fireman's pillow of lilies white as snow or roses red as firemen's blood where those who had died upon the rails might rest their weary heads.

[9 4]

DANIEL DEBS in his little grocery store at Terre Haute had been passionately on the side of the French during the Franco-Prussian War, in which all the German states upon whose neutrality Louis Napoleon III had depended had allied themselves in the military backing of Prussia, the only country against which the war had been declared.

Daniel, already reeling from wild headaches, suffered agonies behind the grocery-store counter trying to weigh out bags of potatoes when his entire heart was in the soil of France, where the Germans were winning victories over a land whose crowned head had not expected invasion but rather to send an invasion into Germany from France.

Daniel had wept at the fall of Paris to the Prussians and had wept at the ceding of one fifth of Lorraine, including Metz, and the whole of his beloved Alsace except Belfort and the surrounding region to Germany by the vanquished France and had declared that he had been and would remain a citizen of France, *la belle France,* in every cell of his body and in every beat of his heart and in his grave when he had turned to dust, the dust of *la belle France,* for he would recognize no conqueror—certainly never the Germans.

Not condemning the innocent individual for what his country had done, no matter how nefarious that deed might be, he had given his consent to the marriage in 1871 of his daughter Marie Marguerite to the young German florist John G. Heinl, whose greenhouse in Terre Haute had been one of the first in that part of the western world to provide shelter under glass to daffodils and buttercups and lilies and other summer flowers from freezing rains and snows and winter storms which would have destroyed all.

Mrs. Ida Husted Harper would always be Debs's direct or indirect conduit to Susan B. Anthony, the wandering troubadour of suffrage who had given herself over to the love of the great suffrage cause which would release woman from her bondage to man—Ida's standards, even when she became the aged Susan's biographer, having been so wholly conventional that there was nothing she enjoyed so much as brides, bridegrooms, and wedding cakes—particularly when she did not have to bake them herself.

Marriages and not funerals were her department, for love was evidently that which had no death, and Dan Cupid was that little god of love who sometimes perched upon a fireman's shovel or put his hand upon the throttle of the engine or blew the whistle or wiped the wheels which would be wiped by daisies all the way.

On August 21, 1883, at St. Stephen's Episcopal Church, the Reverend S. F. Dunham had presided at the marriage services joining Mr. C. Odilon Mailloux of New York to Miss Émilie Debs, second sister of Eugene V. Debs, editor of *The Locomotive Firemen's Magazine.* Mr. Mailloux, an associate editor of the *Electrical World,* had first met Miss Émilie Debs at the National Convention of the Locomotive Firemen in Boston, in 1881. Ida gave praise to Émilie, or Emma as her family and friends called her, for all that she had done in the services of labor. "She was the steady coworker of her brother in his work and lost no opportunity to strew with flowers the cindered pathway of the brave brothers of the footboard."

In September 1883, two months after the marriage of Emma to the young Frenchman, the Brotherhood of Locomotive Firemen had assembled at their convention at Denver, where Debs had sat on the same stage as the Reverend Henry Ward Beecher.

The reverend had mellowed from that time when he had been exposed by the almost naked candidate on the platform of the naked truth and by her various supporters who had been both female and male and by cartoonists who had lampooned him with such portraits as that of the seduced wife of his chief parishioner sitting at one end of the divan, leaning back as she sewed doll clothes which had been cut from old skirts and sleeves and riding habits, and the divine who was the victim of something more than the love of a doll leaning back at the other end as he remarked—"Madame, the abyss is widening between us."

The silvery-haired Beecher had appeared with Robert Green Ingersoll upon the platform at the Brooklyn Academy of Music in October 1880, where ordinarily there should have been two pianos rather than two players striking the ivory and the ebony keys in praise of God's Own Party, and striking all the chords but one, their former differences in points of view having apparently been buried under waterfall and mud and silt and many stones, many pebbles—they having been introduced to a Republican audience as they clasped hands as if to show that in the name of politics, the great divide between Darwinian evolution, which was a godless thing, and religion, which was based on the recognition of the one true god, had been crossed, as both gentlemen had politely denied. The satirical sheets which appeared under the name "Puck" had noted, "The co-partnership heretofore existing between us, under the firm name of Beecher and Ingersoll as Republican stumpers, is this day dissolved by mutual consent. Mr. Henry Ward Beecher will discharge liabilities."

Actually, Beecher had accepted in his early days the theory of evolution and the higher criticism of Holy Writ in a way to make him seem unholy to the most die-hard literalists, and he had been friendly to the social Darwinian principle of the survival of the fittest as applicable to the rising labor unions to which he had not wedded himself as had some men of advanced views.

In 1877, in the sermon "Hard Times," when the starving railroad workers were on strike, he had sided with the great railroad companies in their demand that there should be a reduction of wages. There had to be, he had argued, a continual shrinkage until things came back to the gold standard—and in this process there must be an assumption of sacrifice of wages as well as greenbacks, provisions, and property. "Was not a dollar a day enough to buy bread? Water costs nothing. Man cannot live by bread alone, it is true, but the man who cannot live on good bread and water is not fit to live."

Beecher did believe, as shown in his essay "Star Papers," that the power of the mind at the top of society would determine the length of the train that could be drawn up and the rapidity of its ascent—although this might have seemed, as so many trains could not make the grade, to indicate that the reverend had chosen an unfortunate symbol indeed as he might have known if he had ever seen the railroad wrecks at the bottoms of all steep inclines. He had wondered whether the train at the bottom could ever catch up and hitch on to the powerful engine at the top, but he had been speaking not by observation but by theory as to what the social differences were.

The silver-haired, moon-faced, semisomnolent, and very good-natured Reverend Beecher had survived the revelation of his illicit affair with Mrs. Theodore Tilden and indeed may have profited from it as so many men who might never have heard of him wished to see him, perhaps envying him his seduction of the wife whose handsome husband he would have embraced with his right arm while supporting her head with his left arm if only he could have, and was trying his best to woo the labor public which he had once ignored or attacked—and so had told the workers assembled in Denver that he had walked about the city for an hour trying to find a shadow or remnant of what it had been five years ago but had found only the sense of its unfamiliarity, its strangeness at every hand—it had so greatly changed.

"You should no more pass the fireman or engineer without raising your hat to him in token of support and honor than you would pass General Grant or General Sherman," he had sonorously intoned with what must have seemed a remarkable ignorance of the treatment of fire-blasted labor in a dynamic city ruled over by many-headed gold and silver and lead kings whose empires were made of many branches and were far-reaching and many-tentacled and interrelated in both obvious and secretive ways and would increase.

Debs's *Locomotive Firemen's Magazine,* giving note to a brief version of Beecher's cordial remarks as if they were Beecher's balm, had carried in its issue of November 1883 an elegy for a man who had lost his life in the wreck of a caboose—the wreck having been caused by an act of God Who acted for His own reasons or blind Fate, which did not have to explain that it was Fate or the dead man's defective vision or a poor headlight.

Brother Henry S. Kleckner of Terre Haute had lost his life near Colfax when a tree had blown across a track and had derailed him.

In April 1884, at a reception of the Locomotive Firemen coming together in Terre Haute's Turner Hall and followed by a dance of Firemen and their wives, Debs, who had been a dancer with many of the wives, had spoken of the many homes that would have been shadowed with gloom if it were not for the Brotherhood. Out of the twenty-one members who had belonged to the Vigo branch nine years ago, only four remained on the rolls of membership. "Some have proved false—others have died—some in the quiet of home—others have met their death on the rail, at the post of duty, in a tangled wreck." The Brotherhood had caused a great change of good for the firemen—had been the widows' friend and the orphans' home.

In June 1884 *The Locomotive Firemen's Magazine* had carried the news of a mud race between a blazing locomotive and a blazing train.

Also, there had been in this same issue a description of a locomotive journeying through winter nights when the snow was flying fast and low as a good place to keep out of. The rails ran right up into the air. Nothing could be seen ahead but the jumping-off place. The windows were frozen up, the engine cawing like a crow. The locomotive seemed to have the embodiment of death's angel as it moved swiftly but noiselessly onward, its black breath snorting fire.

[9 5]

IN JUNE 1885, Debs had determined not to continue his legislative career because of pettifogging political hucksters who delayed progressive decisions for years and acted in behalf of the vested interests, the men who were the powers in coal and limestone and gas and rails, and not in behalf of those whose vests were as perforated with holes as if they were locomotive firemen riding without shelter of any screen between them and the train chimneys emitting plumes of fire so that many men were literally turned into firebirds.

But the young man's mind was not entirely upon the subject of burning to death or to a living clinker. There was a fire so intense that forty days and nights of rain upon his head could not have put it out, even if he had drowned, and perhaps he was drowning. He was absolutely burning with the fires of love, which may be, of course, in some ways not too distant from the fires of death—the same ignition starting both.

The gentle, protective young man, who had always been interested in his sisters' romances, had become now obsessed by his love for a girl who like his sisters was no blooming bloomer girl, no tramp girl wearing a man's clothes such as he might have found somewhere by the side of the road, but a very conventional and old-fashioned beauty who sang in a church choir and was involved with elaborate preparations for her coming marriage to *The Locomotive Firemen's Magazine*'s editor and not to the Locomotive Firemen to which he himself seemed already wedded and which she must accept in her lonely marriage when he was away with the trains, and their long whistles in the night might be for many nights through many years all or almost all that she might know of him.

Mrs. Ida Husted Harper would have one of the most important weddings of the year to report to firemen's wives and sweethearts as well as to their men who would want to know what had happened to their beloved editor, who, however, had not encouraged anybody's personal concern as to his welfare even though he risked his bones and his life many times while out on the road working for them who were also exposed to danger or safely slept. He was concerned almost wholly with taking the measurements of that earthly paradise which was his future bride's body and measured the length of his from tip to toe.

Walking beside him, she had carried herself so erect that she seemed elastic, her height seemingly increasing as if she had stretched herself. His steps were long and loose as if he were about to fly. Her steps were always meticulous as if she had measured every step before she took it, for she was essentially a discreet girl who would be married to a man for whom discretion was not necessarily the soul of valor. He was a man who could take risks.

Ida Husted Harper had happily reported that on the early morning of June 9, 1885, Mr. Eugene Victor Debs had been joined in holy matrimony at St. Stephen's Episcopal Church where none had proposed an obstacle which should forbid union to the stately bride who was Miss Katherine Metzel and who had been given away by her stepfather before adjournment of the party to a wedding breakfast at the Union Depot restaurant before the couple departed upon the train to the East for their honeymoon.

Debs was a pale, serious-looking bridegroom and seemed to be aware of the importance of the step he was taking, according to Mrs. Ida Husted Harper. The bridegroom had not forgotten the beautiful wedding ring, the gold hoop with its inscription promising eternal love. All that was missing from him was that he had forgotten, in his very natural excitement—the error had been noted by the ever-loving, ever-vigilant Mrs. Ida Husted Harper—one glove.

The bride was slender and willowy, her blue eyes direct of gaze, her hair red-gold, red roses in her cheeks as the transfiguring light of morning streamed through the stained-glass windows and she and her bridegroom went through this heathen wedding ceremony, as some suffragists might have called it. Kate had gone to Louisville, Kentucky, to a French couturier for her trousseau, which, although very luxurious, was very practical—a traveling outfit which she could wear while sitting upright in the train with her cheek pressed against the bridegroom's cheek and not against the window through which she might have seen, if she had had a pigeon's eye, the passing landscape.

Ida Husted Harper had reported in *The Locomotive Firemen's Magazine*'s Women's Department that the bride had worn a fawn-colored cashmere with a brocaded front, collar and cuffs of crimson velvet with matching hat and gloves and fawn-colored slippers, the crimson velvet like the crimson roses she carried and the fawn accentuating the gold of her hair.

Thus the bride was at the very height of the new fashion in the spring of 1885 when it seemed that every lady wanted to look as if she had come out of the *moyen-âge*—the middle ages, and not her own middle age, of course. *Harper's Bazaar* had reported that scarfs, handkerchiefs, wide ribbons, and fabrics were emblazoned to imitate medieval banners. *Vieux rouge,* old red, was showing two tones while the new blue was called *vielle blouse usée,* the color of an old workman's shirt.

[9 6]

KATE'S PARENTS, August Metzel and Katherine Steuben Metzel, immigrants from Germany, had been residents of Louisville. The father had shown great promise in the realm of mechanical genius but had died young, too early to demonstrate his powers.

His widow with her two children, Kate and Daniel, had been left with very shrunken means, their situation made all the more perilous by the fact that they had been stranded in Louisville during the Brothers' War. It was perhaps because of her semiorphaned childhood in a war-torn land that Kate would be obsessed all her life with the fear of poverty which would be hers when there was reason for it and when there was no reason for it. She was the kind of frugal housekeeper who garnered every crust of yesterday's bread for today's bread pudding, boiled every bone of yesterday's beef for today's broth, saved chicken feathers with which to stuff pillows and mattresses.

When the Brothers' War had ended—at least according to the official pronouncement—after the war the widow Metzel had met a German-Swiss widower who had four children and was looking for a mother to wash their faces, comb their hair, button them up, tie their shoelaces. No doubt he loved the widow for her own sake, but the situation was ideal—he took her with her orphans to bring up under one roof in Terre Haute, where he was a pioneering pharmacist, his drugstore rapidly growing to be the largest in town.

Mr. and Mrs. John Jacob Bauer had added to their original brood of six children four more who were the products of their conjugal bliss, and theirs had been a spacious house with rooms for all.

Perhaps if the well-intentioned Mr. Bauer had been Kate's father and not her stepfather she might have insisted on going away to college like her brothers—but either she had not had the courage to insist or had not known what her rights were at a time when many gifted daughters of affluent middle western families did go to fashionable schools in the East—some to Vassar, which had been founded by a rich brewer at Poughkeepsie—some to Smith, which was supported by the wealth gleaned from tobacco—some to Mount Holyoke or Wellesley. Or she might have gone to one of Indiana's burgeoning small colleges—but she had stayed at home helping her mother with the younger children and with domestic duties such as sweeping, dusting, laundering, gardening when she was not dreaming over her embroidery hoops as she stitched upon a tea cloth her monogram "K" or languidly read, and not with her green eye shade on, a novel on the subject of a faraway romance or a book of poetry depicting the marvelous life which might be hers if only a knight in armor would come to her rescue.

She had just about given up hope and had accepted the fact that she was an old maid when she had met Debs, the former knight of the scoop, who was now highly regarded as a knight of labor with a brilliant career ahead of him.

ACCORDING TO the calendar of time in that day, Kate was already an old maid, as she was, in the midst of many advantages, her mother's not enthusiastic but compulsive maid of all work who would stay up half the night ironing shirts for her brothers and had no social life and seemingly wanted none. When she occasionally ventured forth to parties, she had been as much a wallflower as if she had been stuck against the wall like a flower in the wallpaper—although it was well known that the old maid was an heiress who could bring to her marriage something more than a floor mop.

Some of Debs's intimates believed that he had probably been drawn to Kate just because of her loneliness, her singularity, her shyness, and her artistic talents for which she had no outlet, perhaps the threat that she might become the tree of life with barren boughs, the old maid who was sacrificed to the children of others—and indeed something of the solitary spirit that had drawn him toward the understanding of Susan B. Anthony may have drawn him to her who had not one bone of reform in her body, as time would tell, and yet because of her capacity for patience and her love for her husband who worked day and night for brotherhoods of poor railroad men, she would attempt to mirror the interests of her wandering lord.

Debs certainly had seemed to understand Kate's desire to escape from the drudgery of the hired girl whose folks did pay her very well for her washing, ironing, baking, brewing, churning, beating the flowers out of the flowered carpet on the clothesline in the backyard, or at the kitchen window—that was where her moonstruck lover had first seen her when he was passing in the street at night—tall and beautiful and golden-haired, leaning above an ironing board, stamping with her beeswaxed iron upon the laundry which had been sprinkled upon by the evening dew.

When Debs was asked in his middle age in which he was not as old as he would become but seemed much younger than he was why he had taken unto himself a wife who seemed so remote from the labor struggles through which he was going in his attempt to give birth to various socialistic reforms, his answer was that there had been no mystery at all in his choosing of Kate other than the mystery of love itself—quite simply, he had fallen head over heels with the girl and was still as much in love with her as he had been when his love was green.

As for Kate, she would say in the same interview that she had been drawn to Debs by his electrifying power and his brilliance of mind and that he had awakened in her many suffrage interests although she had never wished to be in the spotlight. She had been content to stay behind the scenes. She had polished the hearthstones.

For Debs, Kate was extraordinary in her awareness of many beauties in the realm of culture, especially those of literature and works of art and music, piano and violin and horn and harp, and kept him in touch with spiritual qualities he might not always have known when he was on the road away from home. There could have been no better companion, it had seemed for many years.

[9 7]

DUCKY, AS DEBS would call his golden-haired Kate, was not the wild duck whom some, and especially his brother Theodore, would have chosen for him—she was a very domestic duck and was never to accompany him on his missions in behalf of brotherhood as she might have done if she had acquired a greater social consciousness than had been hers or if she had been a poor little violet girl crushed by iron heels of iron kings in the cinder yards under the violet stars.

Brother Theodore, although often impatient in his unflattering estimates of Kate, should have stopped to consider that she was not married to him—she was married to brother Eugene, who had determined to exercise his freedom in relation to his need and hers and who had wanted no other girl among the unmarried girls who were blooming like flowers in the garden of life, many of whom had eyes turned upon this most eligible bachelor in all Terre Haute—and yet he had taken to his bosom this politically reticent bride as if she were the altruist he was and willing to give her life for labor and its endless causes. And perhaps in some ways this fine intention had been hers.

For brother Theodore, Kate had been from the beginning and always would be a self-adorning clotheshorse. She was selfish and self-indulgent and had utterly deceived his innocent, guileless brother Eugene by making him think that she was interested in social reform to the extent that he was, whether the eight-hour day or the resurrection of the workers of the world.

The only campaign in which Ducky Debs had ever engaged was that which, from Theodore's perhaps jaundiced point of view, she had carried on to catch and ensnare in her net the young labor leader who was so widely respected that he might become, and in the not distant future, it was believed, a United States congressman, a United States senator, even the president of the United States of America if he continued on his upward climb from the mud to the top—such fire and passion had been burning in his mind from the beginning until the end and long, long after her fuel was gone and she who was left alone so much of the time seemed to have lost her patience with quixotic ideals for the rightings of wrongs, all kinds of wrongs.

In the parlor of Mrs. Marie Heinl, Debs's sister Marie, who was the wife of the prospering florist, he had first met this beautiful yellow chrysanthemum of a girl whose favorite flower was the yellow chrysanthemum because it looked like her and might not have known that it was also the favorite flower used by the Romans to light up the city of the dead as if there were many bright suns fallen to this lower world.

Marie had been so happy in her marriage that she seemed to wish for everyone else to get married to everyone else and especially had hoped that her restless, vibrant brother, whose energy seemed to blow off him in showers of visible sparks, would settle down to enjoy the pleasures of marital bliss such as were hers.

But Theodore, most watchful of his brother's welfare, which was involved at all points with the Brotherhood of Locomotive Firemen and other brotherhoods, had observed that Kate had managed to be at Marie's house evening after evening in expectation of his brother's casually dropping by—her hope having been that he would escort her through the dark streets—and why not?

Debs, as a matter of fact, had dropped by more often at the Heinls' to spend an evening discussing with Marie the charts of labor mortality statistics, what new brotherhoods had been formed, what prospects there were for changes in law according to the latest word that had come in, and discussing with her botanist husband the flowers in the clay pots under the glass roof of the conservatory and what prospects there were for growing corn and squash and tomatoes and other vegetables under glass through winter storms.

Kate had been invited by the Heinls to go with them to evening dinners at the Debses' home, where she had struck up a friendship with Debs's mother and father, to whom she would return alone for talk of recipes with Daisy and talk of poetry and music and art with Dandy, whose amateur poetry in the realms of revolution and love she claimed to admire as much as his blowing of his horn and with whom she would remain until Debs, coming in from a nearby coal town, would join in the festivities until it was time to escort her to the door of her fashionable home.

Debs and Kate, under the spell of love, had gone on long tramps through upland meadows where previously the labor leader had been accompanied only by his apostolic kid brother Theodore or had wandered lonely as a cloud that floats on high o'er hills and dales until all at once he saw a cloud, a host of golden daffodils. Kate's straw cartwheel hat and Debs's fireman's cap would soon be filled with daffodils and buttercups and yellow daisies as yellow as the sun, and she was his golden girl with the yellow daisies or black-eyed susans sticking all over her dress when she arose from the grass, which was wet with dew and kept her phantom shape as it kept that of any stray cow who might lie down for a moment.

As Debs had been taught by his father Dandy Lion to imitate the calls of birds, he would call out to the birds in a mimic way that deceived them so that after a moment in which they listened with silence, they to Kate's delight would answer from all the bushes until they sang in concert. He knew also all the kinds of butterflies and moths hidden in the straggling bushes and old tree stumps and the way they would fly out with the coming of the songs of birds answering the songs of birds, and knew the marshes where there were toadstools, both edible and poisonous, the kind which would put a man into his grave, and how to tell the difference between them. He knew where the wild cherry trees were. He was like an Indian in his knowledge of nature, it was always said.

Kate would one day recall that while strolling in the highlands overlooking the Wabash they had come upon an old tombstone of the Indian days almost covered by the long, wild grasses and bearing the almost obliterated name Betsy over which Debs had mused for a long time, wondering who she was and what her life had been and whether she had had folks to mourn for her when she had completed life's vale of tears.

During the courtship, which it might seem would never end as Debs moved at such a slow and rugged pace that it might almost come to a mournful halt some night when the hoot owls were hooting, but never did—for surely his intentions were honorable—and he was not going to ditch the girl in a lonely pass somewhere or expose her to the spotlight of social humiliation because of her having believed in him—he had given to her a morocco leather–bound set of his beloved *Locomotive Firemen's Magazine,* which he called the fireman's friend that never tears, rips, or leaves him in the lurch.

Kate had been yearning to acquaint herself in a more intimate sense with what her future bridegroom's interests were, just as Debs had apparently wanted her to know what was the best of him before she knew the worst.

The best of him was always, he believed of himself, in his work for the redemption of firemen, brakemen, brothers of the footboard, conductors, especially those who were spotted by railroad detectives traveling as passengers—there were even known to be women spotters in this crooked railroad world which went as zigzag as the state legislature.

Debs had told Kate that the political grind was not for him, was altogether too slow, and that he intended to devote his life to the nuclear firemen's cell until the lines should spread and radiate through all the cells of this society. More and more subscriptions to *The Locomotive Firemen's Magazine* were coming in.

According to one of the magazine's jokes, there was a fat girl whose lover embraced part of her—the right flank—but discovered by further exploration that there was a man courting her on the left flank—she was trying to sell him subscriptions to *The Brotherhood of Locomotive Firemen's Magazine.* And Kate had laughed as Debs had laughed.

[9 8]

HAVING PROMISED Kate that he would show her the beautiful cities of the East of which she had dreamed as of art museums and nights at the opera and rides by carriage, Debs had kept his word. The happy pair had departed on their honeymoon by the early morning train, which came up from St. Louis with a merry whistle, toots and hoots, and train bells as loud as wedding bells—for the engineer and the fireman and all the crewmen, all the brothers of the footboard, all had been apprised that Mr. and Mrs. Eugene Victor Debs, bridegroom and bride, were waiting on the platform where the locomotive came slowly to a halt as the train crewmen greeted the bride with a bunch of red roses and members of their two families pelted the train with red roses, their petals catching among the wheels of Dan Cupid's car. And as was the custom, someone had thrown an old tramp's shoe or tied it to the end of the last car to go along with the couple, some old hobnailed boot hobbling over the rails like a crippled blackbird. Some of the rice which had been thrown had fallen upon the bride, some upon the bridegroom.

No doubt there were firemen who were glad to see the merry bachelor married and thus know more of their marital problems than he already knew and more of the problems of feeding little children's mouths than he already knew.

The first night of the honeymooning couple had been spent in the bride's natal place, the city of Pittsburgh—where the fires of hell had spouted in July 1877 from cars and locomotives stalled in the railroad yards during the strikes which would strip into ribbons the flesh of workers from their bones and which, as the local militia had refused to shoot their fellowmen and had fraternized with them, had been quelled by the federal troops sent in by the hymn-singing, Bible-thumping, dry-as-dust president Rutherford B. Hayes—an industrial inferno of steel and fire and smoke from factory chimneys mixed with river fog drifting in streamers at various levels as if to bisect the city where the rich lived in palatial mansions on the hills from the valley where the workmen were burned in the furnace fire to those shadows which, it would one day be revealed by the men of social passion whose consciousness was in part inspired by Debs, were the shadows outlined on sheets of steel on walls, a city dominated by Carnegie and Frick and other czars for whom the workmen were ingots, steel sheets, and iron bars, and would be beaten on the anvils by these blacksmiths into shoes for iron horses or cinders burning like the cinder stars—and yet the honeymoon night in which the bridegroom who was coming to know a wider and wider rainbow of man's political and economic woes in which all colors should be as red as the furnace fire in the depths of hell was the nearest he had ever been to paradise in his life in which he was working to put the flesh of reality upon the bones of dead dreams and make them live. Could a dream ever really die?

It was Kate who had showed him, as her golden mane was spread out upon the pillow in a hotel room in the city of shadows and fire and he had smelled the incense with which her hair was perfumed, the beautiful white cities of the earthly paradise which would come through their union.

THE JOURNEY to the eastern cities in which Debs was the experienced cicerone to the tall, willowy girl with her wine-colored toque drawn like a helmet over her golden locks and her fawn-colored suit with its tapestried panels making her seem quite regal had included many fabulosities of which she had known previously only in her dreams, among those a view of the swan boats like those which old Terre Hauteans and others of the American middle western wilderness had imagined were still passing overhead every night with the Egyptian pharaohs aboard. The happy couple had also gone to the unprepossessing yellow brick building in New York which looked like the front of a brewery or a hotel for brewery horses, retired prima donnas of the tracks who had grown old and fat, but which was the delusive shell of the magnificent Metropolitan Opera where the Vanderbilts, Astors, and Goulds and other great money kings had their plush-lined golden stalls from where their women could see part of the stage and could see each other, where the money kings could be seen with their wives and daughters wearing acres of silks and satin and tapestries and tiaras of diamonds upon their heads and diamond halters around their necks, enough to choke horses—all or almost all feeling their differences from and their superiority to the average run-of-the-mill people or even those who came to the opera because they would rather hear music than eat.

Kate and Debs had seen many fabulosities ranging from the old Gowanus Canal to the Battery and the waterfront and the enchantment of Brooklyn Bridge, reaching through the fog like a lady's long lavender lace glove. Frank Harris, future publisher of the old, balding, bald Debs's *Master Spirits* and biographer of Oscar Wilde, had been one of the sandhogs who had helped to raise the structure up as it reached through the purple fog like a long lavender lace glove.

But the honeymooning couple had arrived too early to see the statue of the goddess of liberty upon her pedestal in New York harbor with the great torch looming up and thus too early to have been able to report on their vision of her to Daniel, friend of the sculptor Frédéric-Auguste Bartholdi, who had long been inspired with the dream that at the gateway of this large nation which was America there should be something as large as the

Sphinx of Egypt or the pyramids, something arresting by its very height which would make it visible to toilers of the sea as to toilers on the land so that they could always thank God that they were not only free but had the friendship of the French nation in her struggle to be free.

Bartholdi had created the goddess, and she had been under construction in France since 1877, time of labor distress throughout the Western world and of the great American strikes and quellings of strikers with torches, swords, and guns. Generally called Statue of Liberty, rather than goddess, which might suggest a pagan origin to God-fearing Americans, she had been constructed in a foundry yard about a mile from the Arc-de-Triomphe.

Daniel Debs's beloved Victor Hugo—author of *Les Misérables* and *The Man Who Laughed* because of his idiot's grin, the frozen smile which had been cut permanently into his face by brigands seeking to destroy his noble identity in the eyes of others for whom he, the original, was dead, and yet he lived although not recognized by those for whom the superficial aspects of life were all—had come out now and then to have a look at the enormity of the girl whose thumbnail was a foot long—big enough for a poor little Cosette or Esmeralda or a poor little match girl who had gone on strike to stand on—and her right arm bearing the torch had been for a time exhibited in Philadelphia and in New York's Madison Square.

Rich people had doubted the rather angular and athletic girl's artistic value, and poor people had thought that the rich should have had something better to do with their philanthropic loose change or chickenfeed than to raise up a stone pedestal in a country where, whether in periods of boom or bust, they starved for the very reason that "The poor ye have with ye always," as was written in the good book and would have been opened upon this page if it had been a book of stone.

Of what earthly good was the big she? Some had preferred an armless *Venus de Milo* like that which would have pleased Oscar Wilde with his corkscrew curls and his eternal cigar. Liberty's disappointed creator, Bartholdi, who had labored mightily to give birth to a mountain and felt that he was being treated as if he had given birth to a mouse, had become infused in every cell of his being with the determination that the girl who would light up the darkness for miles whichever way she faced and might even be made to pivot should have a home somewhere in this nation of the free and home of the brave and not the grave, and had proceeded to offer her to bidders elsewhere, including Chicago, Cleveland, St. Louis—she to go to whoever made the highest bid and could afford her upkeep.

Governor Grover Cleveland of New York, future president of the United States, had vetoed, on constitutional grounds, a legislative bill that would have provided fifty thousand dollars for the completion of the pedestal on which the Statue of Liberty was to place her feet in New York harbor.

It did seem that he could not see a constitutional way to provide a place for the toe or even the toehold of the big girl who might have done better if she had been only the toe of her foot or the finger of her hand.

She might have remained as disembodied and chaotic as a locomotive fireman who had been chopped up by a daisy chopper, had it not been for the benign intervention of Joseph Pulitzer, once of the St. Louis mud, who had decided that it was literally an outrage that the richest country in the world had no place for this gift from France and was inspired to pass around the hat for the poor girl by throwing in the first thousand dollars.

He had run in the *World Tribune,* for the further benefit of the orphan monument for which the well-fed, well-meaning Emma Lazarus—future friend of Debs—had written the lines that might make many poor immigrants think they had reached a promised land, but the promised land for most of the poor was not the promised land of their quest and was always the promised land beyond—beyond beyond—perhaps beyond the grave—perhaps not of this world but of the next world—"Give me your tired, your poor, your huddled masses yearning to breathe free."

Many cartoons of the beggar Uncle Sam standing hat in hand appeared in Pulitzer's never or almost never sleeping *World,* along with letters from contributors—one a cigar smoker who had given up smoking and had lost twenty-five pounds and was sending twenty-five cents to light up the girl—another a little girl who would send Mr. Pulitzer a pair of her pet game bantams if he would sell them on the poultry market and give the money to the statue—she was filled with grief over the dreadful fate which would befall her pets—but Pulitzer's *World* had made a contribution that had saved them from being eaten by cannibals. And thus she would not fill the heavens with tears over the memory of these dead bantams who were dearer to her than dolls could have been and were like her children and had yellow hair like hers.

The fundraising had been about completed when Mr. and Mrs. Debs, the happy honeymooning couple, had arrived in New York just in the nick of time for the excitement caused by the fact that the ship with its cargo of disembodied parts loaded from the top to the hold with the goddess of liberty in her various crates, her head in its various parts on top deck and her torso in its various parts in the middle and her feet and arms and hands and toes in the bottom or wherever they could rest, had most miraculously survived a great storm at sea, had gone down neither in the storm nor in the calm, and on June 17 was waiting off Sandy Hook for official greetings by General Stone and various New York aldermen.

The dedication of the gray Statue of Liberty—awesome presence who had been for a long time under assembly—was not to take place until October 28, 1886, when the walrus-mustachioed President Grover Cleveland would be among those pronouncing benedictions in the gray rain under the gray clouds for the unshrouding of her face before the celebrant masses who under their waves of black umbrellas could not always see what was being revealed and could not always hear. Besides President Cleveland, there was the president of a far more important concern in the power structure of those times—Chauncey M. Depew, the president of the New York Central Railroad and supporter of capitalistic madness in relation to the exploited workers and who would be widely publicized as Mr. Dooley's Chancy Depot.

[9 9]

MOST MEMORABLE for the bridegroom Debs and the bride Kate had been the cordiality paid to them in Washington, D.C., by the Robert Ingersolls, something that would be long remembered and not tarnished by the atavistic terrors soon to tear the fabric of the democracy of these United States when it would become apparent to some of its critics that the true anarchists were not the huddled masses but the czars of iron and steel and other merchandise who, as Debs would put it, were russianizing American life.

The Episcopal bowerbird for whom the chief necessity in life would be the building of a nest for herself and Debs had not ventured forth to hear Ingersoll when he was in Terre Haute. The Ingersolls were the kind of romantic couple with whom, however, the previously solitary Kate could feel herself at home. Mrs. Debs and Mrs. Ingersoll had seemed to have much in common although they were, in fact, worlds apart. Kate in her maroon toque and tapestry-paneled suit of the mauve, gold, and brown she favored had been charmed by the beautiful Mrs. Ingersoll, who always wore wren brown to match her wren-brown hair and who told her that she was a quiet supporter of the woman's version of the Garden of Eden to which she, a deist, lent her name and gave support from her wren-brown purse—she having accepted the fact that it was Eve who had given up her spare rib to Adam as it was he who had eaten the apple first if, indeed, there had ever been an apple tree in Eden. It had certainly been no McIntosh.

Ingersoll had moved away from the old Cockle mansion at Peoria for a house in Washington, mainly because there had not been enough manna strewn around the ground in Illinois. In Washington, where the manna was, Ingersoll's house in Lafayette Square, next door to Dolley Madison's, had been famous for its lithographs of figures of Superstition, Justice, Truth, Liberty, and Human Love. There was upon a pedestal a reproduction of the *Venus de Milo,* who was to Ingersoll the supreme idea of the supreme love. The beautiful white lady of whom Ingersoll had the reproduction of the statue with the broken arms was as white as the white buffalo who had been slain in the midst of a pool in the western mountains where ever afterward, according to the legends handed down by Indian pipers, had grown only white flowers at the edge and had roosted only white swans such as might be seen in that day by those who could find the sacred pool which was hidden away from the eyes of the expansionist huntsmen for whom nature had no place in the scheme of things. The bust of Shakespeare in Westminster Abbey of which Ingersoll's was a copy brought by him from London had always struck him as having been carved by an optimist who had omitted from Prospero's "We are such stuff as dreams are made of" the pessimistic conclusion of the bard of Avon, "And our little life is rounded with a sleep."

Ingersoll was one of Debs's two friends after whom cigars were named, the honor coming to both of them rather late and arousing the reproaches of the antitobacconists quite as much as the little brown jug had caused the antiwhiskey abolitionists to go mad with fits of imitative drunken rage and even to keel over. Lighting his Bob Ingersoll cigar, offering one always to a friend unless she was a lady, he would remark, "Let us smoke in this world—not in the next."

The other friend was Debs's little bench-legged poet, Riley, after whom the Old Sweetheart cigar would be named, as would be other products: tin cans of Hoosier cling peaches and a train and a troopship.

Wherever Ingersoll lived, there had been a plethora of busts. There had been busts of many men, some of whom were Debs's heroes—among them Thomas Paine, Newton, Voltaire, Rousseau, Eugène Sue, Victor Hugo.

In the Washington house as in the New York house to which Ingersoll later moved his wife and daughters and carloads of furniture in the autumn of Debs's honeymoon year, everybody who was anybody had been entertained in lavish splendor by the genial gentleman who was known not only for his magnificence but his munificence, his huge expanse of flesh and of spirit, as the lean-boned Debs had apprehended when he first met him down at the railroad station at Terre Haute. He had drawn around himself all kinds of utopian reformers with specific reforms which were attainable in the here and now. No kind thought which had ever been spoken by a man's lips had failed to do some good was his observation—and that every man left his impression upon the air through which he moved. He was very latitudinarian as to almost all mistakes—other than those of God and Moses.

He would speak to Debs many times of the golden world there might be through an extension to society of the benevolence which man ordinarily showed to himself or his family—the humanitarian treatment of the prison convicts—the necessity of change in the laws of the courts which in their present biased operation tilted the scales of justice in favor of the rich and gave injustice in large measure to the poor.

Ingersoll himself, vast and portly and slow-moving in his walk—obesity was always a problem for him who would be an unsteadily ballooning but earthbound man who could not get off the ground into a cloud and was a God-inflated man, some people thought, while to others he was simply gaseous, filled with hot air, and ought to burst into all the fires of hell because of his mockery of God—told the ardently admiring, spellbound labor leader who sometimes walked with him when he was in New York that he had great, unbelievable difficulty in making any kind of progress in his daily walk from his Gramercy residence to his law office in lower New York, that he could scarcely steer his way in periods of hard times, which, as every man of economic conscience knew, were always hard times for the rich who profited by depression as by inflation, by inflation as by depression in their predictable cycles which he was trying to help his young friend to understand. Was there such a thing as fate or the will of God dictating these changes in climate? There was not.

Every few steps Ingersoll would be approached by beggars asking him for money for bread, not always for themselves but sometimes for their wives and children—one may imagine that some who were already dead might ask for bread for their widows and orphans. The beggars in this city of urban blight who lived in gutters or under stairways or in bare-ribbed, unheated tenements or in the shadows under bridges were no doubt not

beggars through perversity but through adversity—and what difference?
Ingersoll could no more distinguish categories of beggars, it seemed, than
Debs could. There would always be some cause for the starvation of those
who did not eat. Starvation was real, whatever the cause.

What Ingersoll had seen as he peacefully walked along were the withered hands of beggary and the lips of the man and woman who were starving to death. For whatever good was done, evil was done. God knits what
the devil unravels, he would say many times with a blurred voice as if he
were talking to himself.

He told Debs that he found it utterly incomprehensible, quite beyond
the range of his experience, that any man could die a millionaire when
there were so many of the poor in need. As for himself who was always so
handsomely dressed, he needed only one cravat to see him through, or so he
said—and probably did not refer to that cravat which was a hangman's
rope stretching his neck to the length of the neck of a whooping crane
which would whoop no more as his dangling feet danced in midair as
would happen to the Haymarket and other martyrs who were denied freedom of speech in the land of freedom because of their anarchic messages
which were based on unpopular ideals.

Ingersoll was a great believer in freedom of speech even when it was
exercised against him, when there were many Christians who would have
liked to throttle him for his attacks on Abraham, Moses, Joshua, Noah, et
al., and his pugilistic way of trying to knock Christ out of the sawdust ring.

These attacks cost Ingersoll his political future in the state of Illinois
where he must have been almost as unpopular as the martyred Joseph
Smith.

[1 0 0]

INGERSOLL WAS APPROACHED in his Washington office for a loan in the
summer of 1881 by a low, whining dog of a fellow who told him that he
needed twenty-five dollars for appointment to the ambassadorship of
Vienna and was temporarily out of funds and had come to him as his fellow
Illinoisian. It would turn out that the madman who had presumed such
intimacy of connections with Ingersoll was a fallen-away Oneidist, a former polygamist and polyandrist who had been found insane by his fellow
communitarians in the Noyes settlement near Syracuse and had taken

upon himself or, more accurately, had had imposed upon him the divine mission which, as could not then be known to others and of which he himself was perhaps not yet conscious unless in the most incoherent sense, was to shorten President Garfield's life in this vale of sorrow and tears, to promote him more quickly from the White House to the fields of paradise than he might have gone if he had had his choice.

The name of the madman who was the disappointed office seeker was Charles Guiteau, an enigma about whom Debs would come to know more and more in a world of thunder and lightning and blood, blood upon the grasses, blood upon the leaves, blood upon the skies.

Ingersoll, had he handed out the loan, might unknowingly have been financing President Garfield's murder. When the attempt had been made to trace Guiteau's bloody deed to the influence of his having passed some time at an impressionable age among the peaceful Oneidist anarchists, Ingersoll would recall his own near involvement in a conspiracy for murder based upon this loan and the dread assumption that if a murderer had patronized the same tailor or hatter or shoemaker or glove maker as another man, that man's involvement in a conspiratorial apparatus had instantly been proved.

If one of the phrenologists of whom there had been many fanatic-eyed itinerants in Debs's day had examined the labor leader's head under its thatch of straw-colored hair, he might have found a Venus bump or a socialistic or a utopian or a paradisal bump but would have been a mad dog beyond cure if he had found a money bump which might make Debs fortunate in the acquisition of wealth.

Debs, although he wished to lift his fellowmen up from the mud, fortunately had no desire to rise in the world like a hero worthy of Horatio Alger, Jr., the best-selling novelist of rags-to-riches Cinderella boys who always managed to sell their newspapers to the right rich men, and whose works included—when he knew that President Garfield lay dying in a hotel at the rich men's resort at Elberon by the sea, that Garfield was tugging at the anchor chains which had anchored him to earth and was about to take passage upon that voyage from which no man returns—the bestseller which he would rush to the press to show in an idyllic way the rise of the simple Ohio towboat boy to president of the United States and then, as this opportunistic work had done as well in sales as if the wind were blowing through all its sails, as it went sailing on, the rise of Abraham Lincoln from woodchopper log-cabin boy at Pigeon Creek to president of the United States. And both presidents had been awarded the crown of martyrdom by bloody hands of mad assassins, although their careers, which showed their rise from a lowly state, should not discourage even the poorest poor boy in his dream that he, like any other citizen born in the United States and able to cast his vote, should be able to attain to the highest office in this land—with the help of God, of course.

Debs's desire was and would always be to rise with the rising sun and set not with the setting sun but work as far into the long night as he could to advance the cause of the Brotherhood of Locomotive Firemen and others for whom he would cast a wider and wider net, especially others.

Upon their return from their eastern honeymoon, Kate must have suffered, as she was a very trusting girl and had been impressed by all the splendors she had seen, twelve hundred tons of crystal chandeliers and how many acres of cloth of gold and stage kings and queens and emperors and divas on their divine divans singing swan songs, must have felt ready to swoon away and sing her swan song when her bridegroom told her what their fiscal situation was—they were financially impecunious, as indeed could be seen when he turned his pockets inside out.

Debs had said that he was glad she had enjoyed their trip, glad—for he was broke, dead broke—had neither gold nor silver nor folding money, the latter called lettuce, and was about as busted, it would seem, as an old railway lamp with its wick worn down and no oil in it. So now they must start again at scratch.

Kate had laughed. She had swiftly realized that it was she who must take charge of family finance—small economies to be hers from the beginning, although she was no expert on the sleek hogs who ate all the corn in the Wall Street canyon and the causes of inflation and depression, which were abstractions to her. The fear of a spectral poverty was always to be hers and probably would have been under almost any circumstance, she being by nature the saving kind, the saver of candle ends for a rainy day.

The three-room apartment on the second floor had been furnished with various surprise gifts including those that had been sent by the railroad union brotherhoods.

So much freight had arrived at the railroad station that Debs would have been unable to pay for the honeymoon if he had had to pay the freight for the return of the gifts, which he did not dare to send back lest he should break the bride's heart and the firemen's hearts, too.

The seven brothers of the Locomotive Firemen's at Chicago, a city for which Debs had never felt any attraction because, as he would later describe it, this poisonous urban sprawl with its raggedy edges was a product of American capitalism and thus unfit for human habitation, had sent a regal divan of midnight-blue, olive-green, and old-gold plush with mahogany chairs upholstered in matching colors and golden fringes.

St. Louis railroad brotherhoods had pooled their resources and had sent another set complete with Turkish ruby plush upholstered divan and plush-bottomed chairs which must be stored away with mothballs, and there had been—one might have thought—a conspiracy hatched by free-love utopists as beds had come up by way of Indianapolis, the capital city, from Pittsburgh and Pottsville and Buffalo and other points east—all of which showed by their length that the members had taken the measurements of the long bridegroom with the long toes and by their breadth that there was a place for the long bride.

The couple had desired a large family like those which they had come from and would work mightily night after night to produce children with the expectation of moving someday to a larger home than Mrs. Cooperman's cramped coop, which was luxuriously furnished but gave them little space in which to move around without bumping into each other or an urn or a pedestal.

Kansas City railroad brothers had sent a silver water carafe. Boston, although the Locomotive Firemen there were not members of the Brahmin caste, that which was called, by Riley and Debs, the cut-glass set, had pooled their resources drop by drop and had sent a silver pitcher large enough for water lilies. There were silver services that had been sent by brother firemen from the four points of the compass or wherever a railroad union was. There was a Persian jar for the preservation of rose petals without which a bride setting up housekeeping in a well-furnished home could hardly expect to live in the days of Louisa May Alcott and her *Little Women,* most of whom, if they knew anything of her sad history other than that of leaning over the washboard while her heart thumped with song like a little brown bird, pitied her for having had a mad old Transcendentalist utopist for a father.

From other unions had come Oriental throw rugs of lustrous hues suggesting a thousand and two tales of the Arabian nights of socialism—and also Brussels carpets with flowers so bright that they were like newly

minted coins springing up wherever a man might set his feet, as the frangible Bill Nye with his ever breakable bones would have said with his tendency to stumble over any obstacle in his path including the flowers in
carpets.

The hanging mother-of-pearl lamp with prisms of pale-violet glass
such as Kate loved for its reflections in mirrors by which one lamp could
seem many lamps could not be hung from the low ceiling without its
prisms and flames endangering the heads of the tall bridegroom and bride
as they dashed about in their flights. There was a French rococo clock fit
for anyone who like Kate dreamed she lived in marble halls.

There were other decorative gifts from other railroad locals and friends
as there were gifts from the bride's family and the bridegroom's family of
fine bed linen and tablecloths and silverware and salt and pepper shakers
and pewter ware and china ware, the latter painted with the old Alsatian
pattern which was Dandy Lion and Daisy's love and which was like some
plates that had been lost in the Ohio storm when the boat which had broken from its wharf was never to be seen again, as there was a cabinet for
spices from the great spice mill where Debs had clerked, and there were oil
paintings and watercolor paintings of flowers and fruits and enough burning sunrises to have fooled all but the smartest rooster, the one who did not
get put into the pot.

That which had pleased Debs in particular was the gift from the Vigo
County branch of a large leather rocking chair, long of back and fitted on
long runners, in which he could rock back and forth smoother than when
he was rocking on the rails on top of a land gondola and which he would
add to the literature of the old rocking chair, which was prodigious. "There
is something more in a chair than the material of which it is made. There
are some chairs that have a psychology. They welcome you. They invite
you to sit back."

Precious beyond price was a reproduction of the statue of winged Victory which had been sent by Ingersoll as a note of luxury such as few poor
labor leaders could afford.

Numerous dinner parties were held in honor of the young couple by
Occidentals, some of whom were members of the banking and manufacturing and railroad-owning and trot-horse race sets but were backing
Debs's labor brotherhoods, whose members were so overworked that they
inclined toward peacefulness and probably never would have won the race.

The most memorable occasion was that in which Debs and Kate had
been entertained in a large hall with piano and horn and harp by brothers

from all over Vigo County, some of whom had never before seen the stately bride who with her arm through the arm of Debs was walking tiptoe through the rain and who was somewhat on the portly side—that tending to be portly, heading toward port.

There were the usual wishes that theirs might be a long voyage, a marital ship never to founder in seas of storm or even that calm which might be a greater test for some marriages than storm, and might their crossbeams never crack from side to side, and might there be no icebergs in their path or ice packs howling like a demon chorus, and might theirs be wooden and silver and golden anniversaries and a union which would be blessed by many children, those who would be the jewels in the marital crown.

Recited in honor of the conjugal couple by a gifted elocutionist who was skillful in placing her voice on the ascending scale when ascending a hill and on the descending scale when descending a hill had been the old-time ballad "Katie Lee and Willie Grey," of which guilt of parenthood was attributable to both Josie R. Hunt and J. H. Finley and which—running neck and neck in popularity with "The Old Oaken Bucket," which reminded pioneering listeners of the clanking, clinking sound of the old oaken bucket knocking from side to side as it comes up from the well and the sound of the bucket bird coming up from the well of the stars and spilling some of its waters on earth that there might be fruits and flowers and melons and corn wherever the waters spilled—shows with the ripple of a voice like a little brook two barefoot childhood sweethearts who meet beside a little brook where Katie Lee refuses to allow Willie Grey to carry her laundry basket up the hill because of her insistence that he carry only half, as boys are as weak as girls, is that which brings them to marriage, share and share alike.

Close beside the little brook
Bending like a shepherd's crook
Washington with its silver hands
Late and early at the sands
Is a cottage where today
Katie lives with Willie Grey.
In a porch she sits and lo!
Swings a basket to and fro
Vastly different from the one
That she swung in years agone.
This is long and deep and wide
And has—rockers at the side.

[1 0 1]

ONLY TOO SOON, Debs had had to leave his bride in the three-room flat, although she had begged him to stay in her arms or take her with him—which he would not do—and so she had been left alone with her golden hair spread out upon the pillow with its correctly initialed monogram as she thought of him, a restless spirit who could never rest from labor's cause, passing somewhere in the night out there, perhaps through wind and snow and ice so thick that it might bury a train until the spring of the year when the resurrection of the dead workers of the world would come and the train would move on. The time would come when she would almost feel as if she were married to a train whistle and not to a man. It would seem that she lived in a woman's world and he in a man's world.

Kate was fearful of what the future might be if the cooperative brotherhoods should fail to take a real foothold on earth and the old wolf capitalism would move into her chicken coop with snarling teeth, with bloody fangs such as she sometimes read about in labor books. She had been conceivably even more alone after her marriage than she had been before, when waiting like Cinderella for a prince to rescue her, for now she had seemed to be crumbling into dust and ashes again because of Debs's profligate generosity to poor brothers at every hand and feared that she would ultimately be left as destitute as a poor railroad widow whose husband had neglected to take out insurance in expectation of that day when he would be blown sky high as a kite and would not come down again and would be left without chick or child to console her or grandchildren to flock around her in her old age—unless there should be a child.

There would be no need in this household for the little trundle bed. If there had been a cradle, there would have been no use for it except to fill it up with firewood for burning in a stove or with *Locomotive Firemen's Magazines* and other labor magazines which were sacred literature to them. The couple would try for years to conceive before they gave up hope of bringing a child into the world. It would finally be discovered that Kate was barren. She had a tipped womb.

Although there was a doctor in Louisville who claimed to know how to unlock the door of Debs's wife's womb, the surgery was still in that infantile or pioneering state which made Kate's mother fear for her daughter's life, even as her husband did. Kate, if she had followed the inclinations of her heart, would have submitted to the surgical knife, for she well knew with what nostalgia her husband yearned for a child, but she did not have the door of her womb opened for the deposit of her husband's seed—perhaps because she feared that death which would leave him a widower—and one without a child—and perhaps she would also come sometimes to think that if she had been left a widow who would suffer starvation because he had blown up, she would have had no second little mouth to feed with bread when she had no money for bread and no money for milk and none for rent.

And although no progeny would ever be his or hers and they who were childless would live as if they were the father and mother of each other, she apparently could live without fear that the husband would be unfaithful to the faithful wife or might someday go away and never return because he had been caught on the daisy catcher by some other beautiful blue-eyed girl.

Kate was to find, more and more as time went on, that her only rival for the love of Debs was the hull world, as James Whitcomb Riley would have said—all the poor people in the world whose interests would always take prior claim over hers and over his. Unfortunately, she was living in no doll's house from which she could try to escape. Her career was that of a dedicated labor organizer's serious-minded wife who tried to help in every way she could with the advance of labor and who knew that she must share her marital bed with all the dusty heads of all the poor workers whom he would ever take into his arms.

And yet in spite of forewarnings, she could not possibly have known what life would be like with Debs—and if she had, would she not have yielded to his magnetic charm just the same? All these grimy coal men, coal gondola riders, brakemen—one whose body had not been found but whose thumb had been sent to his widow for burial in a rose garden where it might grow to be a man—were not as real to her as they were to her husband, nor did she see the world which he saw as he went about to far places organizing chapters, giving his advice, sometimes when there might be only one man showing up because of the fear of the reprisal by the management.

The men who wrote letters pouring out their problems to Debs were those of whom Kate must have known when he gave her *The Locomotive Firemen's Magazine* bound volumes as a seal of their engagement even before he purchased the golden hoops, letters which, continuing down the years, were signed with anonymous names—Signal, Dirago, Smoke Stack. Headlight, Third Rail, Eccentric Strap. Vulcan, Link Block, Vacuum, Short Rail, Back Track.

Kate would hear from Debs of the sufferings of men who for the most part were only shadows to her, although she shared her husband's pride in the growth of brotherhoods which would be reported in *The Locomotive Firemen's Magazine*—names of lodges growing all over the land— Orphan's Hope, Arbitration, Stone Ballast, Silver Mountain, Snow Flake, White Breast, Flowery Land, Home, Tried and True, Deep Water, Covenant, Friendship, Nauvoo, Maries des Cygnes, the last at Osawatomie, Kansas, where old John Brown had dreamed of freeing the black slaves who had no wages and for their sake had set a deadline on his dreams which must not always be dreams—he must realize their goal.

[1 0 2]

TIME HAD HUNG HEAVY on the young wife's hands when Debs was gone on a labor mission and she had nothing to do but hang the Oriental carpets on the line to beat the living daylights out of them until the flowers flew like moths in the foggy dew or talk sometimes with Mrs. Cooperman, who was the landlady, or talk with her mother on the subjects supposedly dear to women's hearts. Except for her husband and her family, the Bauers, she probably wanted no one. For she would usually prefer, when Debs was at home, to go to his family's home for the Sunday evenings which were the ritual of his life and would be as long as his parents lived.

Busily knitting a gray muffler for Debs to wear around his throat in winter winds or mending an old workshirt which looked as if it might have been torn by devil's claws, Kate might well consider, in the words of the great golden Republican speaker Ingersoll who never gave the shirt off his back to anyone and knew that charity begins at home—that God knits and the devil unravels, that God mends and the devil tears. It was a wonder that she did not unravel the scarf she had just knit—thus to keep her fingers busy with the illusion that she had knit not one but many scarves.

Feeling that she had already contributed enough to charity, even her husband's shirts, she would never volunteer her services to help with the foreign missions of women's groups, would pack no woolens in boxes to send to the naked children of God on paradisal isles where they ate the fruit of the breadfruit tree, would not contribute to the mission her petticoats and light summer dresses and out-of-style straw bonnets decked with flowers for shipment to Eskimo girls in lands of ice and snow, some so far up in the polar cap that they probably had never seen a flower—not even one small blue violet, where the ice did never melt and no small bird did ever cheep in welcome of the spring.

Kate's contribution to charity had been, all too soon after the return from her honeymooning journey, her beloved husband when he tore himself away from her arms for a transcontinental labor union journey.

During his absences, she had spent her evenings improving the shining hours by the reading of books—tons of novels, the classics, the best-sellers, and those neglected masterpieces which had gone from the publishers' houses to their graves as quickly as locomotive firemen on neglected rails, some to be forever forgotten, some to be resurrected from under leaf mold by later generations whose perceptions would be as sensitive as hers. She did not have to hear the world's affirmation in order to know when a work was a masterpiece.

The wife had shared her discoveries of treasures with the husband, for whom she had soon become the source or fountainhead of literary and artistic knowledge.

When Debs was at home, when he had to do work at his office and not where he preferred, at the dining-room table within proximity with his wife as she busied herself with her embroidery needle and thread, she would wrap around her a dark cloak and put on an old gray hat and take his lunch pail to his labor headquarters and would set the stew in its pot where he would find it to heat upon the station stove when he awakened. For sometimes he would have lain down on the long table for a fitful sleep, and she would lay an old gray flannel blanket over his feet and tiptoe out without awakening him.

Under the placid surfaces of their lives in Terre Haute, the Debs couple had known great fissures in the American society which might split apart the fabric of life and did cause eruptions as of volcanic ashes which simple people thought they could ignore as not pertaining to them—and yet these conflagrations promised greater conflagrations if there were no amelioration of the prevailing injustices. There must be improvement now of the lot of the workingman about whom the editor of *The Locomotive Firemen's Magazine* was gathering statistics not only on the individual but the mass scale in the time opening like a fan upon the labor strikes at the inappropriately named Homestead—the appropriately named McCormick Reaper—some would call it McCormick ghostly reaper—hangings of the Haymarket martyrs for their engaging in that freedom of speech in which no man could ever truly indulge himself until he was in his grave, according to Mark Twain—and the philanthropic strike which would be called the Debs Rebellion against Pull-men-down.

Could Kate have foreseen the dark future, the long night there would be before the dawn, she would have been more frightened by the specter of poverty than she already was.

Kate was the saving kind. She was a salvationist. She was a savior of candle ends for rainy days and probably would have been under any circumstance. She threw out no old tallow ends but melted them into new candles. The domestic exchequer being that of which she was in charge with no questions asked as to what she did with her money, she could have given a lesson to the United States government in how to make both ends meet on a limited budget.

According to brother Theodore, unhappiness came into the Debs family not long after Kate came. No love would be lost, in fact, between Kate and Theodore, the kid brother who was her husband's alter ego, almost his other self, it had seemed to some who would believe that no one who loved brother Eugene—his lovers would run into the thousands, even the millions, and were beyond anybody's ability to count as in a countinghouse presided over by the labor Eros, the potbellied god of love—could truly love him without loving brother Theodore. Indeed, it would seem that brother Theodore's lifelong history of devotion to his brother Eugene and all his passions of reform that the majority opinion in this case represented no tyranny such as an unthinking majority may be capable of—that the majority was not wronged by this double who was as empty as a straw man in Kate's eyes—she was wrong.

[1 0 3]

DISTRUSTING BANKS and bankers and all the fluctuations of capitalism, Debs would never appear at the bank teller's window to deposit whatever coins remained in an old grocery sack after he had paid some of the union's debt. He would take his sack of coins to Bauer's drugstore for his brother-in-law to keep in his safe and did not seem to realize that from there it would be carried to the bank.

Gathering sugar in the cracked blue sugar bowl which she kept on a high shelf, Kate now and then took her grocery sack to the bank where she had a secret account which collected interest year after year. When her aunt in Louisville had passed on, leaving to her a small inheritance which she had added to her original nest egg, upon the advice of the alchemic half brother, whose drugstore was prospering and who was on the way to becoming a millionaire, she was able to make in her own name with all her women's rights about her some investments in stocks and bonds which would permit her to finance the erection of a house most desperately needed for illusions of ghostly grandeur as they grew throughout the years and for a larger arena for her scrubbing and washing and boiling shirts and sheets and stamping with a hot iron than could possibly be hers in narrow rooms where the chandelier swung so low that it might send her or her husband crashing through a wall of glass when they tried to dance. They were truly a wonderful dancing couple, it was said by all who saw him whirling with her.

The Locomotive Firemen's Magazine had been transferred to the ground floor which had provided luxurious quarters in a new building in a new block. This new building, which had been built by Riley McKeen of the old Vandalia, had contained an office with a large vault and elegant appointments and room for every ledger, record, book, pamphlet, and letter, all of which could be located at a moment's notice.

Debs, although happy with his new office—it might be almost embarrassing to an old railroad bum like him and might suggest an affluence which he and no one else enjoyed—had considered his own comfort by using the old upstairs room for his hiding place, meeting place.

Not all men with their coal-blackened faces and bloodshot eyes unaccustomed to the light of the sun and muddy boots could be brought home by this host whose heart was big enough to make him wish to be, not even his enemies could deny, the host of the whole world. But what of the hostess with her floors so highly polished that they were like the light of the sunken sun, so shining bright that they were enough to make Bill Nye, Joseph Pulitzer's favorite *World* comedian, lose his balance and fall, skid like his famed Wyoming mule and break his ever-breakable bones? Even Debs would walk in his stocking feet for fear of leaving the mark of a hob-nailed boot on Kate's floor.

People for years would know when Debs was at home because of the fact that his dusty boots would be out on the porch. When they were not there, he would be absent.

Scarcely before the paint could dry or the last nail had been driven into a wall, Kate and Debs had moved into a new house at 351 North Eighth Street in 1890, thus at the beginning of the Gay or Gruesome, Gray or

Golden Nineties, or Moulting Nineties, the latter name indicating the changes in so many habits, sentiments, attitudes which had once been considered true as Moses but were now like unto that season when the serpent sheds its skin to put on new skin and the horned animals cast away their horns that they may grow new horns and the furred animals take off their furs that they may grow new furs and the birds lose their feathers that they may grow new feathers.

There was nothing pretentious about the house, nothing to suggest what its historical importance would be in the legend of all that is truly good and beautiful upon a continent of so many rapid movements and changes that the sense of memory may be short and where only a few houses and monuments may be preserved and then perhaps more by chance than by intention. The house was simple and was no luxurious, many-pillared manor house or Taj Mahal for a ruler's dead wife with endless porches, galleries, gables, spires, towers such as a rich man's house might be, nor was it surrounded by acres of gardens with lily-margined ponds and sundials and weeping willows and iron fawns, iron cranes.

There was something delusively typical of the old-fashioned America of the middle way about the frame house which called no attention to itself by any eccentric feature, something which might suggest that the owner was of the same status as members of the middle class who on the whole believed that all poor men, instead of cursing against their fate, should put their noses to the grindstone as they had done so habitually that it was a wonder they had not ground their noses and themselves away.

The corner plot of land on which Debs's house was built had an alley behind it but no stable for the fringe-topped surrey and the old Dobbin who was such a beloved horse that a New York editor of popular literature would automatically reject for many years any country story that had not an old Dobbin in it, the kind of old Dobbin that went awingin' like the red, red robin down the road. There was a toolshed, but there was not a chicken coop for the Jerusalem cock which would crow hallelujah to welcome a socialist dawn, nor was there a grassy nest where a hen could lay an egg for which she would cackle her benison to God, nor was there a dovecote for the doves who might flutter down to sleep upon the back of old Dobbin when he was sleeping perhaps the sleep of ages and would not awaken until the dawn.

The house, five years under construction by the hands of Debs in his leisure hours and with the help of a handyman who would lend him his hand when needed, had been built in an affluent neighborhood where Kate wanted it to be and with no view of the cinder yards from where in a high wind a burning cinder might land upon her roof but within sound of the train whistles if not of the grinding wheels upon the reverberating rails.

Debs, who had designed the house and had shown the blueprints to Kate for her approval, had fulfilled his wife's desire for numerous fire-places and mirrors and spacious rooms. The frame of the house was cladded with clapboard. There were eight rooms like boxes set on each other, nothing very ambitious, and there were the usual parlor and bed-room floors and an attic under the rhythmically sloping eaves with dormer windows looking here and there, all as neat as an old woman with her many-flounced bonnet tied by a ribbon under her chin. A wooden porch like an apron ran along the front and one side, where there was a side door. There was space for wicker porch furniture, clay flowerpots, and wooden boxes for petunias and other flowers. From the top of the porch to the ground there were strings where curled morning glories opened shop every morning. The hedges were always clipped and neat. There was a beautiful shade tree.

The house which, long neglected, would be preserved as a memorial mecca for students of humanistic social vision, cooperative brotherhoods, seekers of millennium coming from all over the world, would become in its own way as famous as Hawthorne's House of the Seven Gables, the houses of Lowell and Longfellow, James Whitcomb Riley's house on Lockerbie Street—the street of moonbeams at the edge of the capital city where he had spent many years of his adult life as the guest although seeming during his later years to be the host who had with him the ever renascent Little Bud, the imaginary child who would be well understood by Debs—and also the Wren Nest of Joel Chandler Harris, author of *Uncle Remus,* whose talking animals prompted the big-game hunter imperialist to remark that he never met in the western wilds a kindly, genial, gentle Uncle Remus wolf. Debs was the kind of anti-imperialistic humanitarian who respected the rights of beasts and birds and would have added that the Uncle Remus wolves were certainly not men of wealth tearing to pieces the chickens who were poor men. The house would be known by some as the House of the Rebel or the House of the Devil and by others as the House of the Martyr or the House of the Saint—most particularly when he was gone.

He would be remembered in Terre Haute as a good neighbor and friend, Genial Gene, a man who on a rainy day never had an umbrella, had always given it to a friend or a stranger—every stranger whom he met might be a friend. What he had wanted was an umbrella wide enough to reach over this nation which somehow, as Al Smith would remark when he was the presidential candidate rising from the sidewalks of New York and

Debs was in his grave, never believed that the sun would cease to shine, never believed that there would be a rainy day, never had an umbrella spread over its head.

The richly figured Victorian glass door had been designed to open into a spacious reception hall with a stairway, upon the newel post of which was set a small bronze statue of the winged Mercury branching into bronze boughs with gaslight bulbs gleaming like flowers. Where the stairway turned, catching the filigreed light which streamed in through the glass front door, had been placed a stained-glass window with patterns of roses and daisies and abstract flowers, which cast their fugitive reflections as light answered light.

The rooms had been papered with pastoral scenes, leaves and flowers, including one of Kate's favorites, water blue with long white lilies as if in memory of the maid Elaine floating down to Camelot upon her barge which was no coal barge, of course, as Camelot was no coal town.

Crystal prisms on lamp shades had tinkled with unlegislated music when the wind blew, stirring the long white curtains to billow like the veils of brides or the sails of boats, and there was a hanging crystal lamp in the shape of a many-colored dome decorated with green leaves and white lilies and bulrushes as well as other chandeliers with patterns of purple grapes and green leaves and enameled flowers, all casting their reflections upon gleaming fireplace tiles and marble tops and polished wood.

There was a fireplace in every room but the maid's room on the second floor, the omission of a place for a maid-of-all-work to warm her toes having been caused by no unthinking lack of democracy on the part of the Debs couple who would let the poor girl freeze while they stayed warm as two bugs in a rug—for the house had been built for Kate so that she might be what she had been before her marriage—the poor little semiorphaned maid-of-all-work working for her board and keep and working not only at keeping house with no loose change for her salary but helping her dear husband in every way she could with his labor correspondence and articles and speeches for the Firemen's Brotherhood of which the chapters continually increased.

Evenings when the housework was presumably done and she was left alone to pine as she thought of the long nights on the road and where her husband might be sleeping—in what railroad bed—she would sit before her choice of six fireplaces of which the firewood was lighted in only one at a time and in winter the drawing room was closed off to save the firewood. Her peregrinations were made from fireplace to fireplace during the long winter months when Debs was calling on White Breast or Orphan Daughter or even Two Orphan Daughters—the latter very confusing to a correspondent who wanted to know whether there were two chapters who were Orphan Daughters.

The mantels of the fireplaces were of carved golden oak except for that of the library, which was of mahogany from Honduras and provided place for the French rococo clock which looked far distant from the world of railroad time and train whistles and railroad strikes and which conceivably looked as out of place as the French clock with cupids in the Kremlin would seem to Trotsky with its startled chimes when he and Lenin moved into the palace of the czars of Russia and all he could say was—"They will have to get used to us"—as they never did, of course.

The French clock, chiming away the hours in the home of a step-by-step labor reformer who to the hard-boiled men of the future would seem altogether as antiquated as the deacon with the one-hoss shay or the little yellow locomotive upon the beeline buzzing along like the bee and as bright as the sun or the sunflowers against which its sides had brushed.

Debs was going to hear and had already heard a great deal of talk about the nation's convulsions when all America would seem a universal Leadville because of the flying lead which was turned upon strikers for bread when every railroad tower in every railroad town would seem a Leaning Tower of Pisa leaning farther and farther down.

The tiles in the library and dining room and master bedroom were Kate's favorite rain-washed blue. There were amber tiles in the parlor and green tiles in the guest room, the entire house seeming both a glowing and peaceful bower. There was the stately dining room with space for buffet and butler's pantry—there was no butler—and a large mahogany dining-room table with which Kate, even as when she had been at Mrs. Cooperman's, would rehearse for the dinner parties which she had once dreamed of giving but seldom gave, although laying the long linen and lace tablecloth and setting out her hand-painted bridal china and crystal and silver and pewter ware and dreaming that the centerpiece would be a basket of yellow flowers when she would wear her yellow gown and gold chains and Debs would wear his stiff collar and swallowtails—all very different from what would be when he came home with the ashes of his travels upon him and needed, in her view, simply to sleep at her white breast but only after he had bathed the black dust and glass splinters from his skin, he having often slept for many nights without a bed to sleep in.

His journeys would be upon an ever-expanding horizon as he tried to unite the forces of social and political and economic justice in behalf of those poor workingmen who, when unemployed or blacklisted by their

former employers, were left to rot like old busted boxcars with the linch-
pins pulled out of their left wheels and their right wheels and the slats broken. Kate knew what blacklistings were. The conspiratorial apparatus of
the railroad owners and managers with their blacklists doomed to a perpetual purgatory of unemployment whatever men dared to strike for that
bread which was the staff of life.

The employer who would no longer hire the man whose union had
struck would send him on to another employer who would send him on to
another employer—always with a splendid letter of recommendation on
business stationery headed by the company's name and embossed with a
watermark which could be seen only when the paper was held up to the
window light. The watermark indicated whether or not a man should be
employed. The watermark, which appeared innocent enough, showing a
tall crane with broken legs, had signified that the man had no union or that
the union had been broken as had the man's spirit.

The man who still believed in the union would be sent on and on ad
infinitum, carrying a letter with a watermark showing a tall crane standing
upright on its legs—the symbolism signifying to the prospective employer
that the man was a member of a not quiescent but active union and should
not be employed, should be shot down or forced to fly as the long-limbed
bird for whom there would never be any safe nesting places among the
clouded marshlands or the transient islands of reeds, the mountains or the
valleys from now to kingdom come which was always coming but would
never come.

[1 0 4]

A T NIGHT, when woman's work was done—but was it ever done?—
Kate would keep her lonely vigils, knitting or, tiring of this endless
stocking which was the subject of endless sentimental nineteenth-century
literature just like the old wooden bucket that sometimes went down to the
paradisal or utopian well one more time than it could, had whiled away her
time as she read carloads of romances which made her surely one of the
most artistic and intellectual women in her region of the country. For Debs,
she was the fountainhead of poetry and music and art and the wisdom of
life which she shared with him.

He thought of his wife not only as his love who kept the lights burning for him when he was away—she was also his good companion who carried upon her shoulders the burdens of labor unions, all his griefs or almost all and all his joys.

The guest room to the left at the top of the stairway with its carved balustrade and oblong pictures hanging upon the wall in a step pattern had been called the Riley Room by the hostess and the host long before it became the custom to name hotels for James Whitcomb Riley in memory of a time when he, the Hoosier Theocritus, Robert Burns, Edgar Allan Poe of the Kokomo Bourbons, and even the Hoosier James Whitcomb Riley who for Debs was precious beyond gold, was so poor and bedraggled that he did not have one thin dime or even a hope of a dime for a country hotel.

The poet of "Old-Fashioned Roses" and "There, There, Little Girl, Don't Cry," and "Little Orphant Annie" had certainly been charged no bills for his room and board in this Terre Haute boardinghouse which had the Riley Room waiting for him, all that a poet would require.

There had been a lamp upon a table piled up with books of poetry by the bedside for him to read with his owl eyes when he lay down, a little man lost in a large bed with duck-feather mattress.

Upon the broad mantelpiece above the fireplace with its green tiles the little bench-legged poet would set out those icons with which he traveled on what he called life's grassy or grassless way. The miniature bust of Dickens who by his example had shown him how to gather the lecture gold which was not merely the Transcendentalist and ethereal gold of a dream veining this mortal fog—the bust of Keats whose name was writ in water—the little chany dog with the yeller eyes which he always said was his muse and which had been his ever since he was a rose-leaf baby in his little firewood cradle boat which his mother had rocked with her foot before the fireplace while knitting. Riley's mother had believed that every physical thing there was on earth had a spiritual form and that doors and keys and carpets had souls.

The master bedroom opposite the Riley Room had upon the mantelpiece with the blue tiles Kate's Dresden figurines of that translucent porcelain which took its name from *porcella,* little pig, so called because of the resemblance of the curved Venus shell to the back of a pig—and there, of course, was the wide and long honeymoon bed for the long couple—the wife who would increase the burden of her fleshly weight in her middle years before growing lean again in her old age and the lean husband who never would put on weight.

There was, very impressive to all who saw it, a mahogany dresser with a mirror and brushes and combs with which Kate unbraided and brushed

and combed and braided her long hair which for a long time had showed
no natural bimetallism, no silver threads among the gold, and could make
hair music as she brushed and combed her shining golden locks, the sparks
electric flying around her like firefly stars around the broad mother moon
with her long feathers trailing gold.

As for Debs with his head balding like that of Old Baldy even in his
youth so that it could never be said in his age that he had lost his hair in the
services of the Lord, although some people would always think so, his little
chestnut bush grew so thin above his big ears that every hair was like a
separate hair smoothed down and about the only comb he needed was a
typical little whalebone comb which signified, as did the whalebone corset
and the whale blubber used in oil lamps, the martyrdom of whales and
which he carried in the breast pocket of his gray suit when he was on the
road spouting messages as to the need of a resurrection and renewal of
social consciousness, the arousal of the man in the bog to declare his manhood.

In the wardrobe were the boxes where Kate kept not her husband's
manuscripts which showed a variety of religious visions and experiences
and lives of saints but her hats, whether the broad-rimmed capitalistic garden variety or the socialist turban or toque, for her nights at the opera or
the theater and also her dresses which she stitched in the changing styles
and her skirts billowing or narrow and her blouses when they became the
rage and were never known as shirts but blouses and were punctured with
eyelets, hers never to be the peekaboo kind which revealed parts of ladies'
skins not publicly revealed and caused a starving tramp flea to ask a well-
fed tramp flea where he had gotten his dinner, to which question he had
received the answer that he had gotten it while moored on an eyelet in the
back of a lady's blouse.

Debs's study opposite the mistress and master bedroom had contained
his large desk over which in his later years there would be a portrait of Karl
Marx, whom he mainly knew in his early years from skimming through
old copies of the Marx correspondence which, published by Debs's beloved
old White Hat Horace Greeley, the dispenser of crumbs to Owenite and
Fourierite communes of the Brisbaneite faith, had kept Marx's little children from living on nothing but boiled potatoes and which he knew also
from old copies of the correspondence which, along with advertisements
for that savior of modern woman's eyes which was the sewing machine,
had been published by Susan Bee in her Bonnet Anthony, Marx being for
her not so much as a bee in the hive of woman's suffrage or a butterfly in
her net or a bird in her bush.

There was space on the mantelpiece for the busts of Voltaire and Rousseau and Victor Hugo and Ingersoll and for other memorabilia which would accrete throughout the years as there were shelves for books which had spilled over from the library and other parts of the house, Debs's collection seeming to grow by kangaroo leaps and bounds until it was larger than the rental or public libraries in many small towns, some of which had no libraries or what James Whitcomb Riley called lead works because of the lead printing blocks that had gone into their manufacture.

The housemaid's room where the lady who was also a housemaid and a railroad lantern polisher sometimes rested herself and her feather duster and her mop and her broom was also where she kept her ironing board as well as baskets of letters to Debs and magazines and newspaper clippings which every now and then would be carried up to the attic by her or a neighborhood hired hand for storage with discarded busts of outlived heroes and heroines and perhaps a dressmaker's form, the kind which might have been used as a wire cage by some women in which to enclose, imprison the bird which was her husband's heart.

Kept along with labor and socialistic memorabilia would be also, perhaps tied in little ribbons of blue but certainly with no lock of her wandering husband's hair, the diurnal love notes or the nocturnal notes which he sent to her throughout the years when he was away.

Sometimes he would leave a note addressed "To that Old Sweetheart of Mine" pinned to the pillow of their marital bed before, not awakening her from her sleep, he would steal out of the still house in the wavering dawn so early to catch a train that the cock had not yet crowed and upon the bony fingers of the starlight might still be seen the marriage ring of the moonlight slipping away as the arriving sunlight blotted out the finger and the ring.

[1 0 5]

SHORT WORKING HOURS were as unknown to Debs, according to his brother Theodore, as if he had been the citizen of another planet. His mind was never for one moment off the subject of man's lot. Tenants in the building where he kept his office for thirty years referred to him as the early bird and the man who never sleeps.

Upon the walls of his office there would always be, so long as he was a tenant, large pictures of Victor Hugo, Ingersoll, and Rodin's *The Thinker,* that figure of great sculpture which was somewhat like Debs's dream of the perfect world, even as he recognized, for the dream of *The Thinker* had been outlined in the stone in the quarry before the stone was lifted out and had been in the stone before the sculptor with his chisel had lifted it out.

There was not a region of a large map of the United States which Debs had not been in, as pin heads showed. Those travels were no doubt in some ways the cause of troubles which did not always express themselves directly or at the surface, for they separated Debs from his wife. He seemed to give his love to the whole world as if it were waiting for him, and when he was in Terre Haute was at everybody's beck and call except, of course, his wife's.

IN AN ESSAY called "The Vitality of Labor Organizations" in *The Locomotive Firemen's Magazine* of January 1888, Debs would summarize, as a result of the strikes on the Chicago, Burlington & Quincy Railroad in which the Brotherhood of Locomotive Firemen had been brought into conflict with a powerful corporation, "It has been written that Life is either a problem or a joke. It may be both. It may be a drama or a dream, a storm or a calm."

The men who were engaged in carrying forward modern labor organizations were problem solvers. "They are avant-couriers, path-finders whose faith is in the substance of things hoped for, the evidence of things not seen, and it is always active and ever more so than in the face of battle."

Luminously, in the time of the great mythmakers of whom Debs by his words as by his deeds was one not lightly to be dismissed, he could spout the fact that, as he wrote in *The Locomotive Firemen's Magazine* in its October number, the subsidized press employed to dwarf the importance of labor gave proof of its validity. "Monopolies do not employ cash to overthrow myths," or so he had seemed mistakenly to assume. "Men do not go a-gunning with rifles and cannon for fireflies or sparrows."

Another little human being, according to Ida Harper in her baby column, had come to grace this fair world. "This dear little atom of humanity is the son of our gifted and graceful writer," whom she identified as the author of *The Wife of Barnabas,* a work of which probably few people and not even the Locomotive Firemen knew. The father of this newborn baby who far surpassed Titania's brightest dreams was J. S. Selby, and the mother was the former Eugènie, Miss Jeannie Debs, who had given many years of faithful service to her brother's magazine and brotherhood.

That was in March 1888. The birth, which was celebrated in April

1888, in the house of Debs, was that of a child who had escaped death in infancy because an angel of the Lord was watching over her.

Colonel J. B. Maynard, a Civil War veteran who was the friend of labor brotherhoods and liberal causes and understood the wage problems of Brothers Throttle, Reverse Lever, Sand Box, Old Tool, Old Spade, and Broken Lamp, or thought he did, had read aloud to the happy couple his tribute to the birthday anniversary of Mrs. Kate Debs and the wooden wedding anniversary of Kate and Gene, which had been some days apart but now had been joined as one, her birth having naturally preceded the wedding day which had been ringed upon her husband's labor calendar.

Kate had been born in April, the month of showers, the wedding had been in June, the month of roses:

> *The melodies which Æolus sings*
> *When evening zephyrs sweep the strings*
> *Of his viewless harp*
> *Never tells*
> *Such loving tales as marriage bells. . . .*
> *And however winds may blow,*
> *However tides may ebb and flow,*
> *May natal days still come and go,*
> *Come with friends*
> *And friendship of the soul*
> *True as magnets of the pole. . . .*

[1 0 6]

S TRICT IN HIS VIEWS of marriage at this time, Debs although so often absent from his wife who might someday learn to live without him and come to look upon him as the ideal husband simply because he was away although she kept the porch light burning in expectation of his return, had been unable to understand, in spite of his liberal views which were generally inclined to be left-wing and not right-wing, any man's infidelity to his wife or his having an affair of any kind with another man's wife—that kind of affair which if kept secret was, as was said by Oscar Wilde, a romance, but if revealed was a scandal.

In his "Essay on Parnell" in *The Locomotive Firemen's Magazine* of January 1891, Debs had felt that the name of the great Irish hero would now be everlastingly associated with that of Mrs. Kitty O'Shea.

Charles Stewart Parnell's love affair with Mrs. Kitty O'Shea had cast an ominous shadow on the Irish nationalist cause, according to some of the Fenians with whom Debs was in sympathy.

From *Shandy Magazine* had come to *The Locomotive Firemen's Magazine* an amusing reply which had no doubt tickled Debs's funny bone, which was a large funny bone indeed:

> *Dear Debs—You've no mercy at all for a fellow*
> *Whose heart is enraptured by womanly wiles!*
> *Though made of cast iron, 'twould soon become mellow*
> *And fuse in the flame of her ravishing smiles!*
> *The angels, Tom Moore says, came down for a season*
> *Bewitched by the charmer, on earth here to stay—*
> *Think you that Parnell, void of infinite reason*
> *Was proof against beautiful Kitty O'Shea? . . .*

IN JUNE 1886, one month after the Haymarket bombings, Debs with diurnal and nocturnal hopes of man's redemption by way of labor unions was trying to steer the Brotherhood of Locomotive Firemen across a bridge which would not be a Bridge of Sighs, a Bridge of Lies, and crumble into the chaos created not by men in search of justice but by those capitalistic powers who did whatever they pleased and did not seem to care how many trains and train men were destroyed because of overpasses as untrustworthy as if they were tons and tons of steel and iron and wood upheld by toothpicks and often so pressed upon by heavy traffic that rose petals thrown upon a rail and adding to that weight might cause a total collapse with loss of many lives, not only those of train men but of passengers in parlor cars and passengers in boxcars, the latter including cattle and tramps.

Debs had recognized, during President Grover Cleveland's first administration—which would be followed by the administration of the Hoosier president Benjamin Harrison and then by the second Cleveland administration, the two Cleveland administrations being likened by comedians to two slices of bread as hard as tombstones or railroad station bread between which the Harrison administration was a thin slice of withered ham and was a sandwich that would break your teeth off if you tried to bite into it—

the awesome fact that differences between the two major parties were mainly delusional, for the Democratic Moses who had once advocated silver bugs had switched over to gold bugs and had become no longer a champion of the poor man but of the creditor class, bankers and banking, capitalists, and bondholders.

Boycotting, however, was still for the crusading labor man a foreign importation and not an outgrowth of American institutions—Debs seeming as cheerful as William Dean Howells in his soon-to-be-shattered assumption that the conditions of American life were not those of Russia. "[Boycotting] could not have been born in the United States," according to *The Locomotive Firemen's Magazine*'s article of June 1886, which had necessarily gone to press before the Haymarket bombing which would close the eyes of the free-speech martyrs and open the eyes of Debs. The reason that boycotting could not exist was simply for the reason that the unreasonable conditions which had made it necessary in a foreign land had not existed in this heaven-favored land of freedom.

"Boycotting had its origin in Ireland and was the product of conditions of the most harrowing infernalism such as cannot be inaugurated in America while its rivers flow to the sea."

Eight or nine years before, just after the organization of the Irish National Land League, Debs had summarized, a Captain Boycott, an Englishman, owner of landed estates, had made himself obnoxious by arbitrary methods of dealing with his tenants and others over whom he had power. He was a resident magistrate who had exercised his sweet will over the poor Irish who had decided neither to buy of him, sell of him, work in any capacity for him until he should change his ways.

Among those who had joined the boycott and had spoken for the Irish National Land League had been the beautiful Maud Gonne, whose rejected lover, William Butler Yeats, had correctly believed that he had lost her to his rival, which was politics.

It seemed unfortunate to Debs that boycotting had been imported to the United States, and he felt that boycotting was an instrument that should be adopted only when all else had failed—as a last resort—although it was Debs's natural hope that the workingmen had discountenanced boycotting as a means of redressing wrongs surrounding them.

Now for a time Debs's hope had been to achieve recognition of the Brotherhood of Locomotive Firemen from the Brotherhood of Locomotive Engineers. And now the brotherhood was large enough to be seen, its boundaries the horizons of the continent, its lodge fires spreading beacons of progress from the Dominion of Canada to the Republic of Mexico. It had received congratulations from men in public esteem—as Debs had letters to prove.

Yet the Brotherhood of Locomotive Engineers had taken the position that no locomotive engineer who was a member of the Brotherhood of Locomotive Firemen should ever become a member of the Brotherhood of Locomotive Engineers and that no member of the Brotherhood of Locomotive Engineers who was also a member of the Brotherhood of Locomotive Firemen could ever be a representative at their annual convention.

The grand chief of the Locomotive Engineers, Peter M. Arthur, argued that the engineers could go along with the management in case of a strike by brothers of the lower class. And yet how often both, in the case of railroad accidents, fell together into the mud.

[1 0 7]

JUST WHEN the Haymarket martyrs were being rounded up and were being thrown into the Cook County jail for that execution which would be legalized but would remain illegal murder, Debs with his voice stifled by various fears for his Firemen's Brotherhood had chosen for reprint in the August 1886 issue of *The Locomotive Firemen's Magazine* in the "Car and Locomotive Builders" section, a letter from a Roundhouse Foreman, who had written in reply to a letter which had appeared in *Age of Steel,* signed G.D., thus of Debs's own authorship, and who in his letter had subjected engineers and firemen to a vulgar abuse exceeding anything which this spokesman for labor had ever seen in print, and which now he shared with his readership.

The average locomotive runner, according to the acidulously satirical Roundhouse Foreman, was a man of mediocre intelligence to start with—and the average runner was a promoted foreman—and the average foreman was a common laborer with a laudable ambition to get on the right side of the cab for no reason but the money that was in it. The average runner possessed no knowledge of steam engineering, little of the practice, and had even less concern for it—all he wanted was to get his train over the road on time.

Obviously, this antiromantic Roundhouse Foreman could not see in the engineer or fireman knightly virtues such as Debs attributed to them and they attributed to themselves.

The "man of careful thought, cool judgment and unfailing self-reliance," as the G.D. puts it, is not to be found in the average runner. "Physical and moral courage," "practical sense and intrepidity," "a certain indefinable, etc., belief in history," "his obligation to go forward, to take the chances, to dare the lurking malevolence of fate, etc.," as painted by the G-D——, is all very nice and will no doubt surprise the average runner when he reads it.

But what the Roundhouse Foreman had observed was that in an impending collision or derailment the average runner jumped if he could and if he could not, then stuck to his post and died a hero.

All these semi-supernatural qualities attributed by the G-D—— man to the Knights of the Locomotive are nothing more nor less than diligence on the part of the runner that he may give satisfaction in the performance of his duties and thereby hold his job. . . . The average runner, instead of being the "modest, humble, and patient" mortal so graphically depicted by the G-D—— is a different kind of hair-pin altogether.

The Roundhouse Foreman objected also to the newspaper writers who were wont to dish up a lot of stuff headed "The Romance of the Foot-board," "The Hero of the Throttle," et cetera—praise which to the general public might seem gospel truth but to the practical railroad man of long-standing years of experience was simply nauseating.

[1 0 8]

THE PROPERTY of the railroad financier Jay Gould, whose worldly possessions only a few years before had been nothing but a patent mousetrap, now extended from ocean to ocean—thus was nothing less than the properties of this nation, which the owner toured in his private Pullman palace car *Atlanta*—and as was well known out in the western regions but was not mentioned at this point in the pages of the *Magazine* was equipped with rifles for shooting Indians, anarchists, tramps, strikers, buffalo herds, whatever moved. This monstrous Gould whose name signified gold had made his fortune in iron as he ruled over the iron rails and the lands through which they passed.

Was Jay Gould, as Debs had asked in *The Locomotive Firemen's Magazine,* the chief of sinners in his line—a victim of total depravity and without parallel? Was he sui generis? Was he like vice? "A monster of so frightful mien / As to be hated needs but to be seen?" From Gould himself there came no answer but the golden silence. "His mission in the world is to make money. . . . He likes to be viewed as inscrutable, unfathomable, dark."

The mousetrap king's belief was that men, like railroads, stocks, and bonds, were purchasable, according to Debs, who was trying to evaluate Gould as best he could and who would be dubbed some day, and with good reason, as may be remembered, Debs the Unpurchasable.

Now as Gould bordered upon the sere and yellow leaf, the November of life—"We see him with lots of gold," Debs had described him in glowing terms.

> A mask of gold hides all deformities—Gold is heaven's physic, life's restorative. . . . Has he the power to change water into wealth? Others possess the miraculous faculty. . . . Jay Gould is only one of a thousand of the same type who pursue the same methods in different enterprises. . . . As a matador he has slain a good many bulls and bears and taken their hides. As a trapper he has been a success. . . . He may lack conscience and soul because he can't buy such things and trap them. . . . If he prefers gold to God as an object of worship, he can play pagan to his heart's content, and if he wants a monument when he dies to perpetuate his name and deeds, he can build it while he lives or direct how it shall be done when he is dead.

Debs had hopes for Gould's future. Gould, *if* he kept his railroads in good order, paid fair wages to his employees, and dealt justly with men who earned their bread in the sweat of their faces, might be allowed by St. Peter to pass through the pearly gates.

WHAT WERE RAILROAD SCABS such as were employed to take the place of men on strike? They were men who never had an aspiration above those counterfeit men who crawled on their bellies in the dust and would rather be a flea in the hair of a rich man's dog or a louse in the hair of a king than one of nature's noblemen.

Indeed, Debs had believed that perhaps some scabs could be converted to the understanding of union labor but as a general proposition had deemed it quite as probable that a tree toad could be transformed into an archangel.

The toad who became the archangel had no doubt been suggested to Debs by those images of transformation of tree toads into archangels or golden talking birds into heaven's messengers which had occurred time and time and time again with something almost like regularity in American religious communal societies such as those of the Shakers, the Rappites, and the Mormons as well as other sects which had in them elements of a secular cooperative communism even if under the control of many and sometimes provable and sometimes unprovable supernatural agencies, evading any kind of documentation by any living eyewitness. And even Robert Owen's labor communities had relied upon the surely anthropomorphic premise, as Ingersoll had pointed out, that the universe is rational and that happiness is the instinct of the universe. Could Fourier with his thought of universal discord and limits upon eternity have been more nearly correct?

DEBS HAD CONTINUED that fortunately all workingmen outside of labor organizations were not scabs:

> Thousands of them are thoughtful men who act upon convictions. . . . Labor has a press. It has a literature. It has knowledge. Labor organizations have succeeded in getting labor into politics. In saying this we have no reference to partisan squabbles over the loaves and fishes. We refer to that higher plane of politics which relates to the enactment of just laws for the protection of society, in which labor has vital interests.

How ancient seemed the Brotherhood of Locomotive Firemen to Debs even when he knew that the firemen's organ and the brotherhoods had not reached their maturation as he nursed new chapters from the earliest seeds and embryonic forms into the vitality of manhood.

In celebration of the portrait of Joshua Leach, Debs had recalled, in *The Locomotive Firemen's Magazine* of May 1889, in which Mrs. Ida H. had reported upon the magnificent inaugural ball of President Benjamin Harrison and the reception which he had given to Indiana congressmen and friends—"These frequent revolutions are the salvation of our government.

They sweep over our country like a thunder storm in summer, cleaning and purifying the atmosphere."

Debs, who was at this time no old grandfather in the gloaming in his rocking chair rocking back and forth—he was more likely to be rocking at the top of a coal gondola on his way from here to there—had celebrated the progress of the Brotherhood of Locomotive Firemen which he could prove by citation of mortal statistics generally concealed from the riding public.

Men are living still in the prime of their manhood who remember the time when there were 70,268 miles of railroads and 20,000 Locomotive Firemen with not a Locomotive Firemen's Union—each fireman alone in his perilous work with no brotherhood grasp of the hand, no sign of recognition, no place for exchange of feeling and thought.

How fondly the world cherishes names, when known, of men who have planned the cathedral or triumphant arch, sculptured a Venus, painted the scene of The Last Judgment. We do not write to under-estimate a Phidias, a Michael Angelo, or a Raphael—nor to over-estimate the labors of men in humble walks of life—but the man who has built a house for hospitality stands high, eternally higher, than the man who has sculptured a Venus de Medici or planned St. Peter's dome.

Debs had been thinking much on the subject of the lowly Irish rail builders as he had been thinking of the Molly Maguires who, never for long quiescent although those of the American branch were for the most part in their graves, no doubt had been pushed to the surface of his thoughts by the Haymarket conspiratorial murder of the literate spokesmen for the redress of wrong.

Joshua Leach, the grand master of the Brotherhood of Locomotive Firemen, had embarked upon stormy voyages of union work because of the death of a fellow fireman. Leach and his fellow firemen had provided the bloody corpse with a Christian sepulcher—for that purpose had passed around the fireman's red cap to gather up the coins with which to pay for the burial of his body in his grave—his entire body or all that was found of it—for there might have been a missing foot, a missing hand—who knew what missing, blasted parts—some which might be under water, some which might be under sand?

Joshua Leach was now verging on becoming a veteran of half a century's work on the rails. He had served as grand master for three years and since 1877, when he had severed his connections with the Erie, had served on various roads—had been a fireman in Nebraska—was presently located in Sedalia, Missouri, where he was now a sedentary employee of the Missouri Pacific. His noble wife deserved honor as having designed the first set of regalia ever made by the order which was that of romantic name— Knights of the Scoop.

A man in Ireland had recently bequeathed some of his property to the devil.

[1 0 9]

According to Genial Gene—whose nature was not merely that of the smiling, cordial man he seemed, for he had as much capacity as Matthew Arnold to see the dark side of life and not only the storm clouds gathering upon a far horizon but those which had already permanently formed in the terrible deluge which capitalism without purifying effects was pouring at that time over this American continent—the craft union was an ark even less spacious than Noah's Ark, which had taken in two of a kind of every beast and bird or almost every beast and bird.

There had been forming in Debs's mind for a long time the necessity of finding a more comprehensive way of salvation than now appeared as the waters swept up to the portholes which were men's eyes.

His future history, even in these troubled eighties, was dropping from the skies as Debs, his patience rivaled only by his impatience, became editorially unable to remain in a small box of brotherhood for mortuarial purposes regarding that which would not and could not cease to be of concern, the death of the individual and the living death of the masses of men under the iron rule of the American czars who were making America, in spite of the pleasant surfaces of small towns, a nightmare of such inequities as those from which the immigrants to these shores of the free had escaped, only to find that the New World to which they had come was not new but was old—growing older in industrial corruption every day and every night.

G. M. PULLMAN was but one of the capitalists of gilt and glut upon the American scene, his Pullman car builders having gone out on strike early in April 1894. "Pullman is several times a millionaire," according to Debs in the burning July 1887 issue of *The Locomotive Firemen's Magazine,* "and to read of the town [Pullman, near Chicago] one would think it an earthly paradise"—a utopia such as, in his view, as he considered the subject over and over again, one would not expect to find in northern Illinois, the state of Lincoln and Douglas. He was writing at a time when he had not yet visited this strange town of which he had heard a great deal—many complaints as to the treatment of workers who lived inside it or at its edge—and evidently these complaints were festering in Debs in spite of his desire to be fair and square in his judgments of all parties. "Steel mechanics have had their wages reduced to a point where they say it cannot afford them a living."

As to Pullman, there had been no moral progress from January 1887 to May 1889—no reason for Debs to have withdrawn his objections which no doubt had increased like devil's taxes.

THE TERM "Pullman" had already become stigmatized as synonymous with almost anything odious, heartless, crushing which a degrading monopoly could suggest to the minds of honorable men, Debs had observed.

Pullman means purple and fine linen, sumptuous living—silks, satins, diamonds, palaces, and a herd of cringing, fawning lickspitters who do the bidding of King Pullman, submit to kicks, cuffs and such other degradations as are known and practiced in dominions of czar, sultan, shah, or khedive.

In Pullman's realm, there is no independence for working men. The decrees of the rulers are as autocratic as are known in benighted lands where men prostrate themselves when heralds shout "The King is coming!" King Pullman owns towns—he owns houses, highways, parks, ponds, churches, school houses, rinks—he has under his sway morals, education, religion, and amusement—he is all powerful in his little principality in Northern Illinois.

Debs attacked the private ownership of all the iron highways of this country—"Highways chartered by state and built with money of the people and supported by money of the people." It was these public highways where Pullman had reached the extreme limit of all that was infamous in the industrial enterprises of the United States.

The keen-eyed Debs had objected to the way the conductors and porters were subjected to ceaseless surveillance. The charge had been made that they tried in some way to filch from the passengers in the sleepers enough to compensate for the difference between fair wages and the starvation pay which Pullman allowed to his workingmen. "The 'New York Times,' in a recent article, exposes the unspeakable infamy of the Pullman policy by which he increases his wealth, regardless of right and justice," in a way of which the legitimate fruits were, according to *The Locomotive Firemen's Magazine,* fraud and widespread demoralization. Fruits of the Dead Sea of American industrial life, Debs should have added, the emblem being often used by left-wing critics of such ill-gotten profits—as simply by those who saw the land stripped bare of its bushes and turkeys—or their faces stripped of their beards and mustaches. The article bristled all over with citations of those atrocities which, now brought to the light of day, should excite universal indignation.

Pullman, by his policy, had seemed to be saying in effect, "I am an unjust man—I am pursuing a course well calculated to make my employees thieves—and to guard my coffers I will put spotters, always scoundrels, upon their track. I will employ men innately villains to watch men who are in my employment and by virtue of their meanness are liable to become thieves."

Debs's point was that the public had a right to know all about the Pullman iniquities and inequities practiced on men who attended to the night-shrouded sleeping cars.

Debs, however, was not thinking at this point of passengers through the night but of the conductors and footboard men and sleeping-car porters whose pay from Morpheus for long passages was so minuscule that it did not sustain human life and upon whose unjust pay he was gathering facts and figures as busily as a jackdaw picking up all the sticks which the wind had blown in every way.

Among the items on Debs's list of grievances were the following: Spotters were alert to mistakes in every journey which the train might take. Fines made big holes in salaries that were already cut to the bone. Errors in diagrams as to where passengers' berths were selected when passengers desired transfers, sometimes in the dead of night, were penalized by fines which might mean, of course, that the sleeping-car porter might have no money with which to buy bread and ham and apples for his wife.

"Such is the history of the Pullman reign on the road, and if anything can be brought to light more detestable, it has yet to occur. It is such detestable practices that breed the unrest and vindictive spirit abroad in the lands and keep alive the cry that there is irrepressible conflict between capital and labor, when the conflict is between right and wrong."

And how did Mrs. Pullman travel? The question, once it was asked, must be answered again and again. Away back in October 1886, when Debs was already boycotting Pullman for two reasons, his moral outrage and his impecunious state, he had considered in a bemused way the peregrinations of Mrs. George Mortimer Pullman, wife of the emperor or king of the sleeping cars.

Mrs. Pullman had traveled with four children, twelve servants, five horses, and three carriages in her husband's Pullman cars. Her stable cars were fitted with six horse stalls and room for three carriages and a sitting room for the grooms and hostlers, who evidently, unlike what might have been their fate in the magnetic palace of a Sleeping Beauty moving on wheels, did not sleep upright on their carriage seats with whips to crack when the spell was lifted, nor were there passengers sleeping inside the carriages, including Mrs. Pullman herself, as would be seen when the boxcars opened upon a pastoral slope covered with blankets of grass and flowers.

Mrs. Pullman's drawing room was equipped with Turkish divans which might have come out of an Oriental dream, and bowls of roses and lilies standing on brackets, and there were finest crystal long-stemmed cups and finest pieces of chinaware in her private dining room, and the plate glass windows of her car were shaded with lace curtains and silk draperies which her servants might always draw closed for her when there were howling mobs waiting to see her pass on, as there would be at the time of the Pullman strike.

When this gentle lady embarked upon a journey, she stepped from a house that was built over a cellar to a house that was built on rails—thus preserving the spirit of privacy which had always been and would always be essentially hers.

As for the sleeping-car conductors who were certainly not going to fare well, no matter what the economic situation was in the country at large, whether inflated or depressed, they had a mutual-aid society which, if they worked for Pullman, ought to be several mutual-aid societies, as Debs had reported in *The Locomotive Firemen's Magazine* in January 1887, the same month in which he had come out in protest against the condemnation to death by hanging of the Chicago Haymarket martyrs but all too late to save them from the executions backed by Chicago and other maggoty magnates including Pullman and had come out also with his protest against Gould's proposed organization of the Knights of Capital whose special mission it would be to defend the rights of property against anarchists, madmen, mad dogs starving for bread.

[1 1 0]

DEBS COULD STILL WRITE, and with pride in the union's achievements,

> The New Year comes with no new-fangled panaceas for the ills of mortals. Stupefying opiates are not known in its Materia Medica. . . . The lethargic, the drowsy, dull and sleepy will not keep up with the procession. They will be ditched or side-tracked—and the same will be true of the croaker, kicker, and disgruntled. . . .
>
> Victims of those who wait for good luck to turn up are victims of hallucinations—among the world's unfortunates. They have faith in soothsayers and fortune tellers. . . . The ignis fatuous school of philosophy ought to have long since disappeared. . . .
>
> We welcome the New Year because it will put to crucial test the devotion of Brotherhood firemen to obligations.

Debs had continued, as might be expected, his objections to the idea that the engineers were of a higher caste than the firemen whose presence, according to Colonel Maynard, was no doubt that which was required to keep the firebox of the sun going—as without it this entire planet would turn into ice, and there would be no economy at all—no matter what the Wall Street tycoons said.

The Locomotive Firemen's Magazine did try to arrest in every way possible the lack of a true democracy within the ranks of labor—the Indianpagan idea of caste which Debs believed so repugnant to American institutions that it was deserving of rebuke by God.

Engineers, firemen, switchmen, brakemen were men of such great interdependence in matters pertaining to life and death that the idea that the members of one group enjoyed superiority over the members of another group was sheer nonsense.

Labor created the wealth of the nation but remained poor—tilled all the fields and harvested all the crops but remained poor—manufactured all the clothing, the hats and shoes, but had to be content with scanty raiment.

Labor built all the houses and barns for cattle and yet had been compelled to inhabit shelters unfit for human beings. They had the ballots, but
the laws were so framed that their interests and rights were ignored.

[1 1 1]

CHARLES A. DANA, proprietor of the *New York Sun* had said in an
address before the members of the eastern branch of the Brotherhood
of Locomotive Firemen on May 15, 1887, as reported in the blazing-hot
issue of *The Locomotive Firemen's Magazine,* that men should be grateful to
be American citizens because they enjoyed more liberty here than any man
anywhere on earth.

This exalted intellectual luminary had failed to distinguish between his
exalted work and the work of labor hands.

The honorable Charles A. Dana's boast had been that he worked fourteen hours a day and thus, if he was to be believed, and he probably was, got
up long before the sunrise to put out the morning edition of the *Sun* and
worked until long after the sunset to put out the evening edition of the *Sun.*

Perhaps he was in a perpetual fog, for he could not see for the life of
him—his life, of course, apparently did not depend upon his seeing beyond
his own self-protective obscurantism—how for some time to come Americans could get along with fewer hours of toil than were now the practice,
days as long as his. Nor did he stop to think of women and children in
mines who did not see the light of the sun for years.

Dana had said that farmers worked about fifteen hours a day and
Chauncey Depew, the next speaker on the program, said eighteen to
twenty hours a day. So what was all this eight-hour talk about?

Chauncey M. Depew, a Mephistopheles to the power brokers in the
view of Debs, had expressed himself as utterly outraged by his encounters
with a class of men who wanted to get along without work—were they of
the leisure class? At this time Chauncey Depew had earned a salary equal
to that of the president of the United States.

How SHORT would be President Grover Cleveland's memory of the fact
that he owed his life to a locomotive fireman.

"Blow, blow, thou winter wind! Thou art not so cruel, unkind as man's ingratitude to man"—Debs should have quoted from Shakespeare in relation to the fact that the Buffalo, New York, president, Grover Cleveland, and his wife and prominent friends owed their lives to a fireman who had given his life to save them from hell's fire.

President Cleveland, of course, would show himself possessed by loyalties to men who were wielders of industrial powers of greater magnitude than that of this government, which was in thralldom to iron and steel and gold and silver and copper and lead. Metals were kings over presidents.

According to an elegiac note in *The Locomotive Firemen's Magazine* of October 1887, the fireman John Perego, while hauling a special car with President Cleveland and his party aboard, had crawled through hot steam to shut the engine off when the engineer was dead at the wheel, having been struck by the driving rod that for two miles or more had been pounding the rails and tearing many of them into splinters. The cab had been rocking like a cradle, the train speeding at forty miles an hour with danger ahead.

John Perego could have jumped from the cab, could have considered only his own life, but had died for his fellowmen.

"But does anyone propose a monument to perpetuate the name of John Perego, to keep in everlasting remembrance his deed of noble daring?" the firemen's brotherhood's tombstone cutter had asked. He then had answered in an unconsciously Dostoyevskian way: "Not a bit of it. . . . Does the President of the United States remember that John Perego doubtless saved his life and the lives of those with him? There is no record of any such recognition—it was ever thus.

"But we say, all hail! John Perego. There is kept somewhere a book of God's remembrance, and when the roll of the good and the great is called, John Perego's name will be in advance of Jay Gould's, Vanderbilt's, and many other magnates who now esteem themselves the crème de la crème of the inhabitants of earth and heaven."

[1 1 2]

A GREAT RAILROAD calamity had occurred near Chatsworth, Illinois, on the Toledo, Peoria, & Western Railroad when an excursion party in sixteen cars bound for Niagara Falls, while crossing a dry creek known as Piper Creek or Vermilion River, had gone at a little past midnight at the speed of wind over an old wooden bridge which had collapsed as sleeping passengers were plunged into the Valley of Death, the scene of wreckage one that not Milton nor Dante could have described, as would be said by Art Young.

The coroner's jury had blamed the section boss, a man of such ill repute that he could not secure bail. There had been no watchman at the bridge, which had been too fragile for the long line of cars, each dragging the other over into the abyss.

"Flag the train" had been the last words of a dying engineer on the New York Central. Edward Canaar had spoken these warning words with the death rattle in his throat: "Flag the train, save life, prevent another calamity."

The image of paradise had overcome the tombstone cutter's mind in behalf of an engineer whose position on earth had been certainly above that of the fireman, the brakeman, the wheel wiper.

DUCKY, READING the mail from Tallow Pot or Moonlight or Innocence Abroad or Orphan Daughter or Two Orphan Daughters when she was not dusting with her feather mop—clipping newspaper and magazine articles when she was not clipping streamers of silk for her hat—could not escape the knowledge of celestial mechanics vast and bewildering as that system of cosmic order and economic disorder with which she lived.

"We read about the 'Wheels of Time,' and the metaphor is usually accepted as appropriate. The earth, it is said, turns on its axis, and at the same time goes whirling around the sun on its shining circuit," it was observed by the pilot of *The Locomotive Firemen's Magazine* as the year wound up in December 1887, grinding slower and slower but not to a halt.

"All the bodies in space move in circuits—there are wheels within wheels, and yet there is order. Every planet reaches its station on time and moves on. There is no stop, no way station, no grand depot.

"Men talk learnedly of time, of time past, time present, time to come. It is convenient. No one can grasp time any more than he can space—or eternity, or the universe, or life, or death. . . . They are fruitful themes."

The most Debsian view of this celestial machine was that all along the way as the wheels of time turned were the mounds that rose above those who were our faithful dead, whom the Judas Iscariots had betrayed.

But when the old year had gone, the pilot of *The Locomotive Firemen's Magazine* could engage in no universal elegy.

"Our memories are not catacombs. . . . True, they had laid aside the scoop, relaxed their grip upon the throttle. What then? A transfer from the cab to the chariot, now the psalm and the song, the eternal holiday."

The past was valuable for its historical treasures.

Methuselah, when he handed in his checks, had seen less of the world and had had less knowledge of it than the youngest knight of the scoop and throttle who guides and feeds the iron steed on his modern track of steel. . . . In starting out upon this voyage of 1888 let us see that our good Brotherhood ship is in good trim. Ours is not "Like some ill-destined bark that steers / In silence through the Gate of Tears."

The *Railroad Gazette* shortly thereafter had reported the case of a brakeman in South Carolina who, regularly employed on a freight train, had been transferred to a passenger train for a night's run through falling snow when the platform where he must plant his feet was coated with ice. The air brakes on the train were out of order, and the brakeman had understood when he went on duty that he was being put into the ice hole for that reason, as he must have recognized again in that blinding instant when, as the train was running down a steep grade with reverse curves, he was thrown from the top and was killed. Was the railroad company or the dead brakeman responsible?

The members of the Supreme Court, certainly no more unbiased of judgment than if they had been participants in this poor man's death upon an assignment which he could not have refused without being fired so that he would have no bread with which to feed his mouth or his wife's mouth or his child's mouth if, indeed, he had a child to whom he, like the father bird, must bring worms, had ruled that he had taken his chances and had been killed and that his widow had no just claim—the company was obviously as guiltless as the howling wind, the falling snow.

THESE DUMB BEASTS who manned the trains and intricate machineries in factories and set sticks of dynamite in sides of mountains to excavate tunnels for rails or reduce mountains to plains and who by one miscalculation could bring slabs of marble tombstones falling on every man's head within a range of a hundred miles, marbles like eyes flying into his empty eye holes, and who thus must be masters of infinitesimal mathematical skills, were not the wolves who ate the children of their she-wolves.

The wolves who ate the children of this nation who should have been this nation's treasure by employment of them at long, long hours in mills and mines were the wolves of Wall Street, those who ate also the fathers and the mothers and the grandfathers and the grandmothers and who, if only they could see any money in it, as Debs had not been the first to observe, would have blown the earth from its rail and the dead moon from the sky, with the result that there would be the stilling of all tides everywhere.

So long as the great tycoons had their pants pockets stuffed with nuggets of gold and rocks in their bank vaults in their catacombs, what difference could long hours of workingmen and short pay make to them who were or claimed to be unable to understand that all men were sharers in man's fate, as would be asked by Debs and other men of a transformist reformer's tendency at this time so rapidly swinging between hope and despair that the great star pendulum was never still, was always in transit?

IN THE STATE of Virginia, a coupler had been injured because of the defective condition of the bumper, or drawbar, although shortly before the accident he had uncoupled the same cars and thus, according to the ruling of an undemocratic court, should have known of the defect—if it existed—and should have been able to determine—if he was not blind in his right eye or blind in his left eye or almost blind in both his eyes—what kind of link to use. Because of his failure to observe the disparity in the height of the drawbar, he had used a straight link and thus had recovered no damages for his body's wounds.

Similarly, if a man on a new employment had not been instructed by a fellow employee regarding a specific danger in a factory or mill and if after only three minutes he had taken a misstep into a vat of burning steel, it was no fault of the management that there had been this failure in guardianship of the older over the young brother and even if there had been no older brother on the job—if he had already stepped into the vat.

From the Savannah, Georgia, Blue Mountain Lodge had come a letter signed Devil's Elbow, probably named after the terrain and not reflective of the correspondent's nature—although a demon engineer or fireman was just as much a part of folklore as a demon buggy driver—the Devil moving fast and not slow.

"Nellie Harland, A Romance of Rail and Wire," which had reached *The Locomotive Firemen's Magazine* in manuscript form and which had been written by a practical telegrapher, should be of rare interest to men of rail and wire. Of the romances of rail and wire, Debs knew much from the railroad and wire love poetry of his little bench-legged poet who was always humming even when not talking.

From North Springfield, Missouri, had come a complaint from a woman who had described herself as a hopeless cripple. "We have a Sisterhood Lodge from which we hear not a sound—Harmony is its name. Could you urge them to change the name to Cyclone, Hurricane, or Matrimony, which are synonymous, in hopes to draw forth some fine articles for the magazine?"

Brother Grant Hill had been taken from us at Shoals, which was a town surrounded on both sides by the White River at a place so shallow that one could walk on streets of water and that all its citizens, makers of pearl buttons from mussel shells, should have been web-footed, as perhaps some were.

At Shoals, trying to board a train when it was already in motion—its wheels turning, its whistles blowing, blowing for him—Brother Hill had fallen between the station platform and the train. The Locomotive Brothers had contributed a pillow of lilies to the coffin bed of the young fireman in the water town where the lilies had grown wild before the age of industrial blast and chemical poison.

"Watch, therefore, for ye know not what hour your Lord doth come," *The Locomotive Firemen's Magazine* had quoted—and in another month, when the autumn leaves were falling, had continued, "God pity us all. / Time, too, will tumble / All of us together like leaves in a gust / Humbled, indeed, down into the dust."

COLDLY STATISTICAL was Debs's list of railroad accidents, their nature and causes, which he bared for inspection in that autumn issue when the gongs for the eight-hour day had been so muffled that they might seem only like bells gonging under the ground.

Causes for railroad accidents were many and diverse. Broken rail, loose or spread rail, broken bridge or trestle, broken or deceptive switch, broken or defective frog, bad track. Broken wheel, broken axle, broken truck, failure of coupling or drawbar, broken parallel or connecting rod, broken car, loose wheel, fall of brake or brake beam, failure of power brake. Things which had caused the railroad fireman Debs to rise crying in his bed, flailing, reaching out his long arms to the broken brake beam or throttle as he dreamed of them night after night when he was at home.

There were derailments arising from so-called negligence in the operating—misplaced switch, rail or bridge removal for repairs, making flying

switch, runaway engine of train, open draw, careless stopping and switching, box switching—few of these in relation to rails and equipment.

Unfortunate accidents also—cattle on track, snow and ice, washout,
landslide, accidental obstruction, malicious obstruction, others and unexplained.

Accidents occurring without collision or derailment—boiler explosion,
mass falling on running track, mistakes relating to telegraphic orders.

A lover of great, snow-pinnacled mountains because of their power to
prevail and abide, Debs had believed that the firemen's brotherhood was
like the mountains and would endure. The religious crank Elliot F. Shep-
ard, a Vanderbilt brother-in-law who had found within the gilt-edged
pages of the Bible special cause for the collapse of railroads, had made less
impression upon the editor of *The Locomotive Firemen's Magazine* than a
feather drifting on a cloud.

About the collapse of the railroad, the religious crank had said, "The
Lord blew upon it, and it failed." It did seem very curious that the Lord
should have blown the railroads—trains and tracks—so directly to the
Vanderbilts. "This thing of introducing the Lord as a blower up of railroads is a new departure." It seemed safe to say that if the officers of the
railroad could get wind of such catastrophes, they would speedily take in
sail.

[1 1 3]

AT THE ATLANTA convention in October 1888, Debs could report that
the assemblage of representatives of chapters of firemen had been
from start to finish a thing of beauty and a joy forever.

The governor of Georgia had found the trains of the brothers coming
into the queen city of Georgia a succession of keynotes. An Atlanta divine
had preached a fine sermon. There had been a ball with firemen and their
wives dancing the "Debs Waltz," "Wilkenson Polka," "Switchmen's
Quadrille," "English Polka," "Firemen's Lancers," "Troy Tempo," "Joint
Quadrille," "Tallowpot Waltz," "Oilcan Schottisch," et cetera. This first
convention of the Locomotive Firemen to take place beneath the Mason-
Dixon Line in the city which General Sherman had burned down in that
great inferno of which many horrors had been concealed, although there
were people still alive with memories of men and women and children and

cats and dogs who had been turned into cinders by Sherman with his flaming torches lighting up the sky and the ground for miles.

AN ARTIFICIAL-LIMB manufacturing company in Pennsylvania at this time was advertising the efficiency of its wares by employing, for its sawyers of wooden boughs from trees and polishing of wooden limbs for men, not one man who did not wear at least one artificial limb.

THE TWO GREATEST WORDS of the English language were, immediately following the note on the brotherhood of men with mutilated limbs making wooden limbs—"federation" and "arbitration," according to a correspondent to *The Locomotive Firemen's Magazine.* "When we had advanced to that stage where we could think of one another as brothers, then we could look forward, no matter what position we were in, and we would be nearer the Millennium."

Colonel J. B. Maynard, who in the long ago had taken Horace Greeley's advice to come west, young man, and grow up with the rest of the country, was like the Reverend Myron Reed not only a most beloved friend of the Debs couple but a friend also of Riley's.

Colonel Maynard, a gentleman of widely ranging mind and profoundly socialistic and humanitarian principles, had gotten no farther toward the wild West than the Hoosier capital city's little old Lockerbie Street, where the pavement ended, the street of childhood dreams in which Riley with his china-blue eyes, an old pop poet of the rapidly vanishing pastoral world, a dream farmer, had been wrapped around with many historical or pseudo-historical visions going clear back to Egypt, many of which were among the creative influences playing upon the unfolding consciousness of Debs.

At a Knights of Labor picnic in celebration of Labor Day at the state fair grounds, Colonel Maynard had given himself over to airing his thoughts on the subject of the Egyptian slaves who had built the pyramids and he had ventured that they in that burning desert sand had prayed for a Labor Day as a Labor Day had also been prayed for by the men who built the gates of Thebes and by the men who built the palaces and hanging gardens of Babylon.

The Reverend Reed, at a meeting of locomotive engineers at Denver, where his subject was Robert Burns, had said in the quietly casual, conversational tone which was always his, "One man alone is so feeble; men in

mass are so mighty. . . . When any man anywhere calls another man comrade, there is a new force in the world."

A preacher outside any orthodox religion at Denver, the city of the gold
and silver kings, which was also the city watched over by Pinkerton's, the
very latitudinarian Myron Reed gave honor to all clergymen who in such
places and surroundings were preachers of the gospel of the Federation of
Labor and not of the solitary, lonely, nonunionized man of whom, of
course, there were thousands and thousands still beyond the reach of the
nascent ideal of solidarity which was the religion of Debs.

[1 1 4]

THE IRON TRACK and the iron steeds had wrought in a short time,
according to *The Locomotive Firemen's Magazine* as it looked back
upon the passage of this year 1889, changes that staggered the minds of
humanistic philosophers who had not ridden as Debs had with his reflective face turned downward toward the cinder track where he could see the
eyes of men staring up at him—had never looked down into the shafts of
mines which had been the tombs of the dead—had never lived through his
experiences. These changes, according to *The Locomotive Firemen's Magazine*'s lonely toots upon the track of time, defied the wealth of human
hyperbole to describe.

The Brotherhood of Locomotive Firemen had acknowledged as Debs
had become increasingly concerned as well as active in the realm of social
consciousness that it could not turn aside the shaft of death. But what of the
record when death had done its work?

Time must now be defined again by the socialistically burgeoning
philosopher of time and its passage but in an objective sense, although Debs
was aware of the inner subjective sense in which time was not compart-
mentalized, just as a poet of the immortal rose like Riley's must be aware
and in the sense in which Ingersoll spoke time and again of the All Golden
World of Now.

What Debs had had in mind was railroad time, factory time, mill time,
mine time. The time when the time could be measured by the shadow on a
sundial in a garden of wild hedge roses and broken lilies was gone, at least
for the poor whose day was extended into night and would have had no

mark of the sun's passage upon the buried dials if the employers could have their way. And perhaps they could.

"We are in favor of all the sub-divisions from seconds to years," Debs had written. "We like the hour, the day, and the month. We are glad that these boundaries are fixed because, were it left to caprice, it would be difficult to fix wages, and in many instances the pay-car and the pay-day would be like the visits of angels, few and far between."

Fortunately, the brotherhoods had never been so strong as now. "True, Austin Corbin and the like of him have Russianized the anthracite coal regions of Pennsylvania."

According to Debs's caustic comments regarding labor organizations, the mine owner Austin Corbin's demands were that there should be no agitators or agitation of labor topics and of wage questions throughout the entire anthracite coal regions. "He wants stagnation, degradation, slavery," Debs had summarized, thus hoping to arouse some men from cinder beds. "He demands that his word shall be supreme—that when he takes snuff, his serfs shall sneeze."

WAS DEBS HIMSELF an angel, or was he a jackass or a combination of both who might also inspire master painters? Not one to speak in personal terms by which to dramatize himself—indeed, a self-effacing man if there ever was one in not only a symbolic but an actual and literal sense—he was perhaps a big-footed and big-handed worker angel of the Christ who was hung on the cross, as he would be someday called; and he was certainly—as he would also be called by those who loved him and by those who did not love him alike, even when perhaps suffering twinges of guilty conscience because of that fact—a jackass of the first order if there ever was one.

He had certainly favored the cause of the overburdened jackass laborer in every crisis that came up, there never having been a time when there was not a crisis coming up somewhere like the red flowers which were incarnadined by the red blood of men who like the worker Abel had been slain by the capitalistic Cain.

Debs was trying to give help against Cain in all ways in which he was Abel. He was certainly as faithful in giving signs of danger as that famed jackass who could eat anything—rusted tin cans left by tramps along the ruined railroads, old tramp boot with broken sole, old red flannel shirt pockmarked by cinder fires—and had coughed up the old red flannel shirt and waved it like a flag to warn a coming engineer of a wrecked train lying in the fog.

In "How I Became a Socialist," in the April 1902 *Comrade,* which would be the Socialist party's vehicle, Debs would recall of those early years when he was first the bachelor and then the bridegroom and had been filled with what now seemed to him quenchless zeal and consuming vanity as he answered the call of all firemen everywhere, and they were all the world to him whose mission was to unite them in brotherhood, "My grip was always packed, and I was darting in all directions. To tramp through a railroad yard in the rain, snow or sleet half the night or till daybreak, to be ordered out of the roundhouse for being an 'agitator' or put off a train, sometimes passenger, more often freight, while attempting to dead-beat over the division, were all in the program and served to whet the appetite to conquer."

One night in Elmira, New York, a conductor on the Erie had in a kindly way dropped him off into a snowbank where, as he clambered to the top, he had run into the arms of a friendly policeman to whom he had told his story and who had become his friend on the spot.

Elmira, from the time of the advent of the Erie Railroad in 1849, had been important for woolen and lumber mills and from the 1860s onward had been a dynamic center for iron, rolling stock, and furnaces, as it was famous for a pacific national graveyard for nearly three thousand Confederate soldiers who had died in a prison camp there during the Civil War. Elmira was famous also for containing the skeletons of those who had died in the French and Indian wars and had been dug up and brought here from other graves. The town was also the summer home of Mark Twain, who had married the conservative daughter of a conservative businessman, and for whose sake as well as for that of a general respectability he had tried to hold his tongue on a great many burning social issues, and who would someday be laid to rest in a grave adjoining hers from where he could enjoy, if he was right, that freedom of speech which he believed no man could uninhibitedly enjoy while he was alive.

To Debs the dead did speak, as he spoke in reply and increasingly to those dead or dying men whose bruised and bleeding bodies were always on his mind. "How could I but feel the burden of their wrongs? How could the seed of agitation fail to take deep root in my heart?"

The incident at Elmira, that night of snow and whirlwind in the railway yard of the iron town, would be elaborated upon in a mythic version many years later by his uncle Henry in his fairy tale of Debs's life, which, published by the Working Men's Institute of Boston, had been written for the enlightenment of the children of Socialists as of men with child hearts and which was no mere artifice and was founded upon substantial realities.

Gene Debs had been huddled in a freight car, according to Uncle Henry, the frost needling his long fingers, when he was discovered by a brakeman who did not believe the dirty bum when he said who he was and, advising him to give his lecture to snowflakes, had thrown him off into a snowbank where it had turned out that the kindly policeman into whose arms he had stumbled had advised him not to wrestle with the blizzard and had offered him the jail and had wished that there was someone to organize cops, they being now all dressed up and as vain as paycocks.

Debs had nearly frozen to death that night in the storm. "Limping angels would have to wring him out before they recognized the soul of Debs, who imagined himself trying to get into God's presence and could not get in. The door of heaven was slammed in his face."

Debs had peeped through the keyhole of the golden gate and had seen an angel in overalls with a silver mop swabbing the puddle and another angel scattering sawdust.

He had dreamed that the figure of Death would rock him in the storm and that the lights of Elmira would not rest.

At Elmira, there had come to him a vision of a world where happiness would flourish like a garden and where justice would cover the earth like waters of a peaceful sea. His words, which still might be heard, had been like singing birds with golden wings. "Build for yourselves a heaven right here on earth. Get together. Again and again, let me repeat the words— Get together!"

[1 1 5]

ALL THROUGH these years of organizing such chapters as White Breast, Marie des Cygnes, Madeleine, and Two Orphan Sisters, Debs had been traveling toward what he would call the Ultima Thule of labor federation but certainly without the thought that the farthest limit when he reached it would be cold, barren, dark as a cinder yard.

He was living in that time when machines were displacing men with a rapidity that made their quest for economic justice seem atavistic to the owners, for whom dead brakemen were less valuable than dead engines piling up in the junkyards which were industrial graveyards. Blood upon a rusted wheel. Dead eye staring from a spill of oil.

In June 1891, *The Locomotive Firemen's Magazine* reported on a dispatch from "The Machine and the Man":

We are told that man is of "more value than many sparrows," that a sparrow that is sold for half a farthing cannot "fall on the ground without our Father knowing"—and the question, can the great boon of the labor-saving machine relieve a man of work and wages, let him "fall on the ground," force him into idleness and starvation without the notice of our Heavenly Father, and if such notice is had, how is it manifest? . . . The sparrow hath found a house and the swallow a house, but the machine has taken the "house" from the working man. He is less fortunate than a prairie dog or a fox.

The Locomotive Firemen's Magazine had been proud of publishing James Whitcomb Riley's poems and had also given notice of the *Nye and Riley Railway Guide,* which had not a word about railways in it. There was nothing more confusing to Bill Nye and Riley, these Siamese twins of American comedy, as Mark Twain had dubbed them, than the railway schedules which they claimed they could no more have read than if the timetables had been written in Egyptian hieroglyphics upon a desert tombstone.

Once at the Union Depot in Indianapolis the lecture partners had engaged in a wild debate as they consulted their mismated watches upon what exact time it was according to the departure dials of twelve railroads which they seemed to think should be telling the same time. Only when a stranger had intruded to explain to them that the clocks overhead were mock clocks had they been persuaded that they did not tick and would not strike.

Coming in at the Union Depot from the little hub, which was Terre Haute, to the big hub, which was Indianapolis, Debs would sometimes run into his bespectacled little bench-legged poet even when he was not looking for him and once had had the great pleasure of racing to his rescue when he had seen him wildly waving at him from the window of a train and had wondered—was he waving farewell? It was departing time. When Debs had approached, running along the rail, the truly anxious, shaking poetaster had asked him if he could tell him which train he was on—was he going east or going west? Was he going north or going south?

Debs, examining the baffled, befogged poet's ticket which he fortunately had had in his hand, had seen that he was going west—in the opposite direction from what he had intended—and had been able to get him off the wrong train and onto the right train, which was going east and was also just charging up.

Debs, the great statistician of railroad accidents, was unwavering in his compassion for Riley's fear of railroad accidents, about which, as a subscriber to *The Locomotive Firemen's Magazine,* he could certainly read as he could well believe tales of spectral dogs, trains going over thin shells of ground that collapsed under the wheels, tall brakemen who got their heads knocked off by low underpasses, and he probably knew of more infernal nightmare train accidents than any railway accident inspector ever heard of. Riley had feared being run over by wheels like a poor little rabbit.

Nye had once engaged in a conversation with Mr. Chauncey M. Depew, who had told him that Garfield had given warning to him quite early in life that if he wished to advance as a statesman, he must throttle every desire to make a joke, for a sense of humor was fatal to political preferment.

Nye had answered about as follows: "If you really want to put yourself where Mr. Garfield is—viz., in the bottom of a dark grave, two or three miles from town and far from postal facilities, in order that your vignette may be printed on the face of a five dollar bill which lies at the bottom of the ill-ventilating sock—now is your time to throttle the heaven-born smile and the light-hearted bon mot."

The nonvoting Riley, bosom friend of Debs, a man who had been praised also by every presidential candidate and president from Garfield onward, including Debs, had given no offense to the presidents of ironworks and railways who were casting their blight over this land and who could be as pastoral in their ideals as this country-bumpkin poet seemed.

Very popular with tillers of the soil as with the men of iron heels who were slicing the workers in mills and mines to death and were slicing the big farms to farms so little that they might be only poorest pea patches with not enough soil to raise a pea pod with two peas in it or an ear of corn, the kind who listened to what the poet had to say or listened to the silence or to the fiddle music, had been, written in his early years, the bucolic "Mister Hoptoad," an early poem which Debs had enjoyed so much for its tale of the poetry plowman's meeting with the hoptoad in a time when to plow was like slicing cheese and the sod was lopping over and the clod was soft and deceiving, there having been the rich loam.

Sometimes when Debs had come to Indianapolis in the spring or summer or autumn before the iron frost of winter, in Riley's words, had closed over the skies like a coffin lid nailed down by the stars, he and the poet Riley, driven in a permanently wind-addled hack by an old black handyman who had one blind eye and one seeing eye, and who was also Jumpin' Jamesie's very special friend and fellow fiddle player, had gone stumbling out at a slow gait through the bewilderingly speedy current of the traffic flow on Washington Street, once the Gold Rush Road, their destination an old still away out west a mile or so by the old canal which had been there before the trains ate up the flowering woodlands and meadows and where Riley, ignoring the blight, found, out of time's way, a magnetic palace in the Sleeping Beauty wood, in a neighborhood where there was a flour mill and proximity to slaughterhouses and railroad towers and all kinds of industrial developments springing up overnight.

He had written in praise of many an old tramp's shoes and the Hogans who wore brogans, as he had written in praise of the old shoemakers' Knights of St. Crispin, his ideal of the brotherhood of man with man having derived from his schoolboy association with Tom Snow, an old shoemaker in Greenfield who, an immigrant from England and a Chartist sympathizer, had snowed all his wisdom on Riley. Snow had taught to Riley not only the arts and meanings of shoes but had also been an authority on the arts of mimicry in many forms and once, when an unemployed actor in London's Drury Lane, had seen the dapper Dickens strolling along.

One of Riley's old-fashioned raggedy dialect poems, translated into the English language which he would always have preferred to use, but there was no money in it for this honey poet, is an allegory regarding that honey which in common parlance signified money as well as prosperity, with reference to the land of milk and honey which the poet considered to have been his in the days before the Civil War.

The message he gave in "Fessler's Bees" was not likely to cause at any time red-eyed anarchists to rise up in swarms against the keepers of great hives of honey which were steel or iron or lead where the workers were such drones, as some people thought all men would become in that socialistic state, which, of course, Riley thought probably would not come even with the millennium as the imperfections of life were always important to him and no perfection could be found except for the imperfection of the way things used to be clear down to a plant missing from a front porch or a broken garden gate or a wheel leaning by a well.

An expert on bees, old Bee Fessler had been able to step in among a swarm of bees and rake them back into their hives with his naked hand, never a bee stinging him—this immunity to bees having been very much like that of Riley's Old Uncle Noey, an idyllic figure of whom he had written in his poems on the Long Lost Childhood Land. Old Fessler, unlike that moon-faced old man with the heart of a child, had been possibly too shrewd a businessman for his own good.

He had a bee shed about half a mile long with a thousand head of hives, all buzzing worse than telegraph poles, and that was when strangers from town would come and stop at the kivvered bridge just to see them come. Old Bee struck upon the theory that honey was the same as love, something you could make both day and night. He figured that if he could get the bees to Florida where there were blossoms all the year around, he could get twice the work out of them that he now got and twice the honey, and so he had loaded the glass hives onto the railroad cars and took them to Florida, where he had acted as the overseer while they doubled the production of honey but grew bilious with the sweat upon their foreheads as they panted and groaned and limped about.

They argued that this was about the longest summer they had ever seen or wanted to see and moaned at their honey making and acted as if their heads ached and would have nothing to do with Bee and would not work at all—the old-time narrator of this delusional enterprise, Ike, winding up as to the retribution suffered by Old Bee—" 'Never know'd a man,' says Ike, 'Take advantage of a bee 'at affliction didn't strike 'round in that vicinity! Sinners allus suffers some and old Fessler's reck'nin' come! That-air man today is jes' like the grass 'at Scriptur' says Cometh up and then turns in An jes' gits cut down ag'in!' "

As for his failure to choose between the two political parties, Riley would often explain that he was neither Democrat nor Republican but guessed he was a Publican. What he had meant was that he would have liked to have been a pub keeper in the flowering wilderness before there were infernal railroads.

Riley was also a Celtic revivalist—for although he perhaps mistakenly believed that there was not an Irish bone in his body, he could be as Irish as Paddy's pup and could fool many a native Brogan with his brogue, his speaking as if there were a burr under his tongue. He was a down-to-earth believer in the sanctity of the poor Irish workingman who carried on his back the hod instead of the cross.

[1 1 6]

WHEN DEBS and Riley were in the old Irish pub—investigating the lower depths in the cinder yards of Terre Haute's Tenderloin— there was always something of an uproar of joy as suddenly the workmen coming in for drinks realized that the great poet was among them, whereas the presence of Debs was taken for granted.

There was celebration as in "Chairley Burke's in Town," one of the poet's "auld sod" numbers which tells of the devil's own time at a bar called Jamesie's Place. The poem had been written before Riley knew Debs, who, however, had known some of the works before he knew the man.

In early days when the rain fell, Jumpin' Jamesie had sometimes had no shelter but the hedgerow under which he had sat with the hen and her chickens. He had sometimes slept in an unheated country inn with no blanket on his bed but piles of newspapers to keep him from freezing to death under such headlines as "Gold Falling." He had made with his lecture agent a contract that was so unfavorable to him that he had considered himself in virtual serfdom to the money grabbers.

Unfortunately or fortunately, Riley had not become the neighbor of the editor of *The Locomotive Firemen's Magazine,* which proudly published his poems.

The reason for Riley's missing the opportunity to be next door to Debs and say "Howdy" to him every time he passed him on the street when he was at home was that his letter of acceptance had lain for about a year in the dead-letter office at the Terre Haute Post Office, which had apparently achieved inefficiency, and by the time the lost letter had been found and delivered, he with the assistance of Reverend Reed had been ensconced at the *Journal* in the capital city of Indianapolis.

In Riley's room at the Dennison House, which was his refuge before he found refuge at the home of Major and Mrs. Charles Holstein in Lockerbie Street and which had continued to be his refuge when he was drinking more than he could hold and was like a ship ready to go down, there had been a wild chaos on his dresser, a jumble of manuscripts, shirt fronts and collars and cuffs and neckties, as there had been manuscripts in neat script piled up on his bed and in the coat closet—according to several eyewitnesses—and piles of empty whiskey bottles, including Old Grandfather's

Rocking Chair and Shut Eye and Four Irish Rings—the whiskey having been used for medicinal purposes, it almost goes without saying.

February 18, 1890, when he was all laid up at the Dennison House of which the bar was a favorite watering place for politicians and bankers and other aristocrats who could trace their ancestry to the pioneering realtors of the old mile square which had been this town, Debs had sent to his drinking companion in the magical Sleeping Beauty woods out by the old flour mill not far from little houses bullet-marked by the Southern sympathizers during the Civil War in this northern border city a floral remembrance with which to speak the language of his big, always bleeding heart, a basket of roses, for which Riley had written—when Debs, who was holding between his big paw hands a small bouquet, had been prancin', dancin' around in courting or had been the bridegroom who had already won his love, that which was forever old and forever new—a thank-you note expressing gratitude for all, he who sometimes described himself as a loveless lover who had no one to love in all this living world, no wife and no child and no chick, not even some little ball of yellow fuzz like a fire cheeping: "As Tom Moore sings in effect—you may break—you may shatter the little bench-legged poet if you will, But the scent of Debs' basket of roses will cling to him still!"

The split with Bill Nye, which had caused the poet to suffer a public humiliation from which he had feared he might never recover, just as he would sometimes fall off the water wagon no matter how many vows he took, for he wanted to be something greater than a chicken and egg poet and yearned to be a poet of the Lost Lenore like Poe, had been caused not only by such headlines as "Riley Leaves Nye for Bourbon" or "Riley Leaves Nye for Rye" but by Nye's having attempted to disarm the press by explaining in an offhanded, somewhat oblique, somewhat laconic way that the reason for Riley's failure to show up at their Louisville performance was that when he was a baby in his high chair, he had reached too far out over the edge to catch a butterfly and had fallen on his head—with the result that when his mother picked him up again, lo, he was a poet.

[1 1 7]

Dᴜᴄᴋʏ'ѕ ʜᴜѕʙᴀɴᴅ and Riley, the Hoosier Robbie Burns, had been men always in the public eye—so no wonder that Kate had been afraid that they would be subjected to vast repercussions of social criticism by those unable to understand the causes for a man's taking a snort, perhaps by temperance clowns who drank more than they did but who would rip them to pieces by thunderbolt after thunderbolt if ever they drank one drop too much from the little brown jug or hiccupped like old, lonely Death with his fiddle music. According to Riley, Death was an old man dancing in a red nightgown.

Ducky would always remember when her tall, bony husband with his almost bald dome and continually flapping hands and flapping feet and way of running with long leaps, sometimes seeming to run ahead of himself, had gone out with drowsy and drooping Jamesie very early one morning while she, left at home to wonder how they fared, had waited all day long with her anxiety increasing moment by moment as she wondered what kept them away so long, as Riley used to say of those who died.

About his adventures drinking with Debs, wetting their whistles when both should have been as dry as dust, Riley had written to the ever frangible, breakable Bill Nye, "Have latterly returned from a brief visit to Debs, at Terre Haute, who wants me to remind you of him in a taking way. Mind, I say a brief visit—for first dash out of the box, he must drive out to that blessed little vineyard where they serve you, out under the trellis, with such tantalizing lunch, one needs must handcuff one's appetite, else plunge head-long into their seductive wines."

Riley's personal writing paper had carried as its watermark a lightning bug that glowed against the light and had under it the letters ᴇ ᴀ ᴛ ʜ ʟ, signifying Each According To His Light, according to the *Indianapolis Press* of December 9, 1894, when any new book which had been written by the Olympian bard's pen was hailed as if it had dropped out of heaven onto earth.

His notes to Debs had been cherished by the labor agitator whose collection contained these translucent sheets through which shone this lightning bug, which had also been reproduced in one of his many gift books to the Poet's Room in the Debs shrine, which would be sacred to labor struggles.

As Riley not only slept in the Poet's Room but often did his writing there where he might be as happy as his old John Henry dreaming of mother and home-baked bread when at last, some time after dawn, he sank his head into the pillow, the Debs couple had known how often his poems were based on imaginary or hallucinated events, as might be expected from one for whom the unreal things were real and made lasting impressions.

There had come to disturb the silence of the night the poet's moaning, groaning, chanting, rhyming, chiming, dancing about as he gave birth to the baby poem that was as difficult to bear as a rough-shod baby colt which he would rock in his arms at dawn as he cried, cooed, laughed, swayed back and forth before a window in his long white nightshirt or his red flannels, which were supposed in those days to have the propensities of a magical cure-all warding off disease and death from the freezing cold in winter in places where there were no coals or the fires had gone out.

Charles Philips, with whom Riley had spent a week in one of the happiest homes he had even seen, had called these nocturnal poems the poet's "red flannel" numbers and was greatly relieved when he was gone.

And as for Debs, when he had been up all night at his desk writing a speech on the subject of labor unions or the world of socialism, which would finally emerge as the meaning of his life, he would tell the childless wife, who for a long time was his helpmate or critic in the revisions but who perhaps envied him his children and so might turn her face away as she could not share his commitment to the search for the Ultima Thule of the one great union which would provide the motivation for his life on earth, that the labor was every bit as difficult as to give birth to a rough-shod colt. Kate's rival was, it would often be said, the world.

[1 1 8]

WHEN RILEY was in town taking traveler's rest with Debs and no notice had been carried in the local presses that the pennyroyal poet had come to town, the children in the neighborhood would get scent of him and track him to his hiding place.

Children from all over everywhere would come streaming like a migration of chipmunks along the walks, and they would perch in the trees and on the roofs and on the chimney tops of the neighboring houses waiting for Mr. Riley to come out on the front porch and act out the role of that Little

Orphant Annie who was now up in the clouds and who, long in a state of evolution, had washed the cups and saucers up and shooed the chickens off the porch and told the witch stories about that little boy who wouldn't say his prayers and was snatched away when he went to bed one night. Or he would tell of that Little Hum who was chased by a big bear up to the top of the sycamore tree or would tell of that Little Long Ago Boy to whom he would call out—"Halloo, halloo! Don't you hear me calling you?"—until all the children would respond, the children of the cloud lands joining with the children of the earth in that magical moment of childhood's eternal enchantment when all of a sudden dreams are real, that Little Long Ago Boy who wore a bright robin-red coat would step out of a cloud or out of the ground. Many resurrections were his.

[1 1 9]

RILEY'S POEM "Regardin' Terry Hut," which had appeared in the Republican house organ the *Indianapolis Journal* in February 1886 and in the following year in the volume *Afterwhiles,* could scarcely have been foreseen as the poem which from the time of the Pullman strike led by Rebel Debs—who never again would be removed from the great crucible of social conflict and in a profound sense never had been outside it, had always been a man in the burning crucible with his fellowmen, and would continue to be in the heart of fire through all his presidential candidacies, including that last one when he ran for president from the dark, dank cell in the Atlantic Federal Pen, where Mr. Wilson would put him to moulder away until the grave's moss should grow over him—would be an important part of the Debs elegiac folklore when he was dead—"Away."

"Regardin' Terry Hut" had been launched with reference to a Professor Star-tailer who had been actually one of Riley's numerous noms de plume at a time when he was not sure that he knew what poets knew and wished not to disgrace his father who had made the vast mistake of naming him for an Indiana governor.

THROUGHOUT THE DEPRESSION in the seventies when Debs had gone to work as a fire hog upon the trains, burning cinders sometimes showering over the roofs of houses too near the rails or barns, as some old-time farmers complained, train whistles scaring cows and horses and flying embers with their fires not yet spent burning the back off the plowman's shirt—time when Riley in the Wizard medicine man's wagon where he preferred to be packed with the bottles in the straw between towns on the old corduroy roads where in random villages or settlements which had sprung up for no reason at all he had recited his lost Eden poems and had sold bee balm or essences of flowers to the crowds who had heard the poems—he had signed some of his fugitive newspaper pieces with the name of Professor Star-tailer, he having taken that name as an act of revenge upon one of numerous confidence men whom he had branded in that way and who, traveling also under the names of Corduroy or Seersucker, depending on the time of the year or the forgetfulness in the spring of the man who had been Corduroy in the autumn and who now was Seersucker, had included this very plausible Professor Star-tailer who had sold him what might just as well have turned out to be a county at the bottom of the sea or on an undiscovered star. In fact, it could have turned out to be two counties.

Professor Star-tailer, holding him with his gimlet eye, had sold him monopolistic rights for the selling of a patent butter churn, no doubt very much like that which the young poet had dreamed might churn out the butter of the sun or a poem, and the territory for which he had paid had been made up of two counties upon which he was to have a royalty on every butter churn he sold where no one else would be allowed to sell even one butter churn anywhere along the road or off the road.

The trouble was that of the two counties, one was a fictitious county which he searched up and down and in and out for and never found on any map or anywhere in the Hoosier state from the top of the boot to the toe.

The other county for which Riley had bought the patent butter churn monopoly had been the surely nonfictitious Vigo County, and long before he knew who Eugene Victor Debs was.

"Regardin' Terry Hut" recalls, in tribute to his visits as a poetry reader at the Old Operay House in Terre Haute.

> *Sense I tuk holt o' Gibbses' churn*
> *And b'n a-handlin' the concern,*
> *I've traveled 'round the grand old State*
> *of Indiany, lots o' late!*
> *I've canvassed Crawfordsville and sweat*
> *Around the town o' Lafayette*
> *I've saw a many a County seat*
> *I ust to think was hard to beat;*

At constant dreenage and expense
I've worked Greencastle and Vincennes
Drapped out o' Putnam into Clay
Owen, and on down thataway
Plum into Knox, on the back-track fer home ag'in—and glad I'm back!
I've saw these towns, as I say—but
They's none 'at beats old Terry Hut!

The consummation of the poet's praise was that which he gave to his host who was the labor leader and who would someday bring to Terre Haute a greater fame than it enjoyed through its having been the birthplace of Nancy Hanks, the fastest trotter in the known world in her time and not the certainly fast, mysterious mother of the rail-splitting President Abraham Lincoln, he with whom Debs would as often be compared as with Tall Sycamore of the Wabash, the famed United States senator Daniel Voorhees.

"And there's Gene Debs—a man 'at stands / And jes' holds out in his two hands / As warm a heart as ever beat / Betwixt here and the Jedgement Seat!"—according to this praise which would live as long as Debs did and long afterward.

[1 2 0]

THE MOST IMPORTANT of the gentlemen of whom Riley had written in his bread-and-butter letter "Regardin' Terry Hut" had been, of course, the Tall Sycamore of the Wabash, Daniel Wolsey Voorhees, who had been born in Virginia and was called Cardinal Wolsey by some local humorists, probably Republicans.

The first Tall Sycamore of the Wabash had been William Henry Harrison, the successful Indian fighter—and the second Tall Sycamore was Voorhees—and the last Tall Sycamore would be Debs, who would also be a second Abe Lincoln, a second John Brown, and a Debs First, who, it had seemed, was going to stop all the trains of the nation.

In Fountain County, in the days before the Civil War, Voorhees had been a friend of Edward A. Hannegan and lived for years in his house. Hannegan, a man of fiery temperament who had enjoyed a meteoric rise in his career from early wilderness circuit rider to prosecuting attorney of

Fountain County to United States congressman to United States senator, had become a part of the Voorhees legend. Daniel Webster had said of him who had set the woods on fire, "Had Hannegan entered Congress before I did, I fear I should never have been known for my eloquence."

But an Indiana governor who knew his rivers as he knew his men had cast a dissenting vote. "Start Hannegan down stream at high tide, and he can gather more driftwood than any man I know, but he isn't worth a curse to row up stream."

Under the administration of the unimaginative but canny president James Knox Polk—a former Kentucky crossroads storekeeper who had been embittered by the perverse Hannegan's phrase "Fifty-four, forty, or fight!" with which during the Hoosier campaign, where alliteration counted, he had opposed Polk's spirit of compromise with the British over the northwest boundary, give a yard, take a yard, give the unsurveyed coastal land which would become British Columbia, take Alaska and all its ice floes and polar bears, but who had seemingly forgiven Hannegan when he had backed the war which the gold-hungry Congress had declared had existed by no act of their own but by an act of Mexico and as a reward for casting the deciding vote in a party caucus he had still been disposed of— Hannegan had been shipped out as minister to Prussia, where, forgetting that he was no longer engaged in Hoosier baby-kissing politics—oh, those babies in women's eyes!—he with his democratic assumptions and his chivalric instincts who had forgotten that he was a being of a lesser orb had reached out and bowed to kiss the blushing hand of the fair queen of Prussia, to the absolute rage and horror of her jealously watchful, frenetic husband the king of Prussia, who was ready to start a war over this offense and sent him back to Covington on the Wabash, his whole life wrecked, it would appear, by this one fatal kiss upon the hand of a lady whose face he had perhaps not even seen. If it was love, it was love of a blushing hand, and yet he had meant no harm.

Failing to be returned by Indiana to Washington, blindly groping as in a heavy fog which curdled the fields like soured milk, it was said, and his spirits wilting and no honey in his horn, he was determined to get back to Washington by running for the presidency for the purposes of wreaking a Democrat's democratic revenge upon the stiff-collared, insufferably haughty king of Prussia by a declaration of war for reasons which would be acceptable to the voting public and which would provide a mask for a war in revenge for the kiss which he, a Hoosier gentleman, had placed upon the queen's ungloved, lace-cuffed, bejeweled hand.

Wars had been fought and would continue to be fought for far less cause. It was ever thus.

Nine states had declared for Hannegan, when, returning to Covington for a rest, all worn out and heavily imbibing enough whiskey to dance an Irish jig, his nomination seeming certain and the chance to take revenge upon the king of Prussia would be his, he had gone upstairs to drink and rest for another battle when his well-intentioned brother-in-law, sure that he was ruining his life by drink, had reproached him for being a drunken sod who saw his enemies when they were not there and, as Hannegan had become increasingly enraged, had tried to bring him to his senses by slapping his face until it was as red as a red beet.

Suddenly and without warning, having drawn his golden dagger from the sheath where it had hung upon the wall, Hannegan had drawn it straight through his brother-in-law's throat before he could give one wild rooster squawk.

Bleeding to death, he with his broken throat cords had lived long enough to exonerate Hannegan from any drop of conscious guilt for the shedding of his blood. All had happened as in a drunken dream—a fact that might not have helped in the case of a poor drunk who had no powerful friends in court.

Some years later, practicing law in St. Louis, Hannegan had failed to make himself heard in a public speech as a backer for the cause of Douglas, his once golden voice reduced to a whisper because his tongue was as thick as a lotus bud, and the next morning he had been found at his desk dead from having taken, after many flirtations with the idea of death, an overdose of whiskey and the morphine which is the bringer of sleep and dreams from which there may or may not be awakening.

Lew Wallace, author of *The Fair God,* which he was working on in Covington while acting as prosecuting attorney for Fountain County, had been unwilling to conduct a trial against his friend Hannegan and so had been happy to transport himself from Covington to Crawfordsville.

Daniel Voorhees, Wallace's successor as prosecuting attorney and also a Democrat like Hannegan, had refused to take action against his old friend and former prosecuting attorney in a trial for a murder of which he had been unconscious at the time and had been subjected to so many stabs by his political enemies that it had seemed his political future was entirely in the past if he stayed on in Covington.

Moving downstream to Terre Haute, Daniel Voorhees had been elected to the United States Senate and had become the Tall Sycamore of the

Wabash who was always bending to the will of his constituents and had protected every interest they had wanted protected, as he would recall when he was the old patriarch of his people, who believed that he had not ignored the rights of the children of the soil and that no one had been too lowly to come to him for whatever counsel or help he could give.

General Benjamin Harrison, when running for the Senate, had charged that Voorhees had declared war on the federal army in the South and was trying to undermine the power of President Hayes to use troops against those large and overwhelming sectors of this land which ignored the decisions of federal courts.

The people had preferred the Tall Sycamore to Harrison, who instead of going to Washington had gone back to the pastures of his law practice to munch the daisies, which were dollars in Indianapolis, a city where cows no longer grazed in the circle in the center of the mile square as they once had done, although occasionally one might still be found straying loose with its eyes bloodshot by fear of the slaughterhouse.

When Harrison finally did get to the Senate, great had been the rejoicing of his fellow Republicans. He had received a message of congratulations from Charlestown, Indiana, for a speech in which he had put some slashes and hacks into the Tall Sycamore for his hypocritical attempt to pose as a friend of veterans in order to win their votes when God knew he had opposed the war—although Harrison had not managed to fell Voorhees as his faithful correspondent had supposed—had caused perhaps only a shaking, sighing of his branches, which would not so much as awaken a sleeping bird.

A particular assault suffered by the Tall Sycamore had been that dealt out by Senator John J. Ingalls of Kansas, a tall gentleman who, with a neck long and scrawny and a thatch of dark hair parted in the middle and myopic eyes equipped with eyeglasses which were no thick window glass such as were worn by half-blind war veterans but had triple lenses so that he might form an image in the fog, which was surely always heavy in Washington where as to this nation's good almost all men might seem myopic in those days, perhaps even all, few and perhaps none not becoming confused by the far which seemed near and the near which seemed far, and whose facial foliage included a mustache and a goatee which had a way of lifting in the winds of his oratory as he stretched his long rooster neck, which was wrapped around by a bright red cravat, his high silk hat not collapsible in any wind and his long-tailed Prince Albert protected by a checkerboard ulster which showed him ready for whatever inclemencies there were and possibly for more than there were and who was certainly a

Hogarthian or Dickensian figure of high visibility, just as were other faces who listened to his words as he had accused the Indiana senator of scorn for the Union dead and wounded. His manner was so scornful and his sensibilities so outraged that there was never enough time in which to say all that he wished to say, and all he could do when he had dropped the subject as the senators were going home in the evening was to pick it up again as if it were the setting and the rising sun, both the same sun, although in some mythologies believed not to be, especially if one did not know how long the night was and one might not last as long as the night lasted.

These metallic attacks had gone on with little relief until finally in 1888 the long-suffering Voorhees, losing his dignity but not his reason, had leapt to his feet and shouted, loud enough to blow the dome off the Capitol and cause a lurch in the Washington Monument which many had predicted could not stand up against all the hurricanes blowing in Washington, "Liar! Scoundrel! It is not I! You are the dirty dog!"

The cynic Ingalls, who along with other jokers in the Senate deck of cards would oppose the Sherman Antitrust Act by trying to weigh it with so many amendments that it would be like a racehorse running with all four legs tied, would pronounce in 1890 the religion of his flaming branch of politics: "The purification of politics is an iridescent dream. Government is force. Politics is a battle for supremacy. The Decalogue and the Golden Rule have no place in a political campaign"—it having always seemed quite clear to him that to defeat the antagonist and expel the party in power had been the purpose from the beginning and that the thin gruel of idealism, all water and mud, had been never enough to assure triumph over the other side, whatever it was.

These attacks were altogether diversionary. They were good sport. They had permitted the eyes of the public throughout these troubled, rapidly changeful years to turn away from the bloody shirts of workingmen who had been struck down by Pinkerton's men in cinder yards or in a dark forest or pursued to their graves, some which had names and some which were nameless, in this new Civil War of the rich against the poor upon whom would be turned great Gatling guns when they asked for bread and received bullets like showers of hailstones darkening a summer's day, as had happened in the quail war.

[1 2 1]

IN A GREAT Democratic rally in 1888 on the outskirts of Terre Haute, Debs had appeared on the speakers' platform with the Tall Sycamore of the Wabash and had spoken out against the Republican presidential candidate, the antilabor Benjamin Harrison—he should have said that he hated fiddle music or anything which came out of a bottle and would make the corn grow—had urged that when the frost was on the pumpkin and the fodder was in the shock, all should cast their votes for the return to the White House of Grover Cleveland, a man who at this time had so much backbone that he had instructed his managers to use the motto of his previous campaign—"Tell the truth"—which everybody was telling without knowing what, indeed, the truth was.

Could it have been his acknowledgment that he might have sired the little boy of the beautiful Maria Halpin when he had answered the cries of the Blaine outfit at every stop along the road—"Ma! Ma! where's my Pa? He's in the White House, Ha! Ha! Ha!"—by saying, to the delight of Henry Ward Beecher, who had come out for an honest Democrat, a fact that could not have pleased him if he was to get the home-keeping husband's vote. And what kind of man would he have been to let an orphan starve?

But as to what the truth was, it would have to wait for an act out of the Book of Revelation, for it was Harrison who had gathered up the votes of the many poor who were the majority and had won his way to the White House and had done so with frequent denials that he had ever been unsympathetic to labor or that during the violent labor strikes of 1877, when many strikers had been shot down throughout the land, particularly the East, he had said that sufficient pay for a day's labor to any workingman was a dollar a day—or as some would report he had said, ninety cents a day. All he had ever done in 1877 was to stand for law against resistance to law.

He had won out over Cleveland in spite of the fact that in Steuben County in the Hoosier northland he had been plagued by terrible circulars showing to whoever saw them that as the general breaking the railroad strike in 1877 in Indianapolis he had said to the strikers that he would force them to work by the bayonet or shoot them down like dogs and had said that to the pickets before the old Union Depot where the soldiers had used to come in like dead or still-squealing hogs.

It had also been circulated throughout the nation that Harrison had believed that cheap meat was the food that should suffice for a cheap people, the lowly workers.

It had been widely rumored that Harrison had organized a private army equipped with Springfield rifles with which he had drilled his citizen soldiers and had marched them down to the depot with the intention that the strikers should be riddled with showers of bullet holes like the face of the clock, which had also been striking—they did not deserve the formality of a trial which would be followed by hanging.

These pro-Democratic and anti-Republican allegations had been denied by the eloquent, painstaking General Ben Harrison everywhere but at the point of origin, the Hoosier state. He had also been accused of having spoken outrageously against poor Irishmen at a Republican rally in the presidential campaign of 1876, when he had depicted them as those derelicts who filled half the country's jails. The Irish could never accept his denials of this anti-Irish position.

Harrison's own position had been that the Irish joiners of labor unions had been motivated by radical Democrats and were at too low a level to be countenanced by any reasonable American citizen, as would be shown when the votes came in and the roll was called up yonder and as time would tell.

[1 2 2]

BENJAMIN HARRISON, during the campaign of 1878, when he was running for senator against the Tall Sycamore of the Wabash, had suffered even greater injury because of the continually resurrected accusation that during the Vandalia strike he had boasted that he would wade up to his fingertips through seas of the blood of the workers if they refused to go back to work.

At the Congress Green Cemetery near North Bend, Ohio, where General Ben and his wife and others of the family had gone to inter the body of his father, the former congressman John Scott Harrison, in the family plot near the vault of Old Tip, the former president of the United States, it was noticed by the mourners that the resting place of the recently interred nephew of the congressman looked as if it had been trampled over by a drove of long-snouted hogs, for where there had been grass there was mud.

Indeed, grave diggers of a capitalism extended beyond normal procedures had been at work. And for this reason the former congressman, an almost bankrupt and certainly benevolent farmer who had lectured recently on the world's race for wealth, had been buried in a metallic casket sunk into a deeper grave than most and buried under a number of heavy marble slabs cemented together and covered by a mound of earth so heavy that no mortal man should have been able to lift it up without help of another mortal.

As this was a time of many disappearing bodies, causing people who came to bring flowers to their loved ones to suffer great shock when some grave robbers had not bothered to throw in the sod again and had left open and yawning graves—Where had Father gone? Where had Mother gone? Had someone buried alive dug his way out and torn away the tombstone if there was a tombstone?—it was suspected that the snatchers of the body of the brilliant young man who had died with his whole future before him had been stolen by a resurrectionist who was employed by the Cincinnati Medical College for the purposes of anatomical research, the place having long been under suspicion as a buyer of the bodies of the dead.

While searching for the young man at the Cincinnati Medical College, which had a back alley where mysterious wagons were known to slide down a coal chute bags which were not bags of coal, General Ben Harrison's brother John and a constable had drawn up by a windlass from the bottom of a shaft at the Medical College not the body of the young man who was their quarry but, as had been seen by the policeman when he lifted the mask from his face, an old man. It was the body of the former congressman who had been drawn up and whose startled son had stared into his face with the cry—"My God! My father!"

The ophthalmologist behind his foggy eyeglasses had been unable to see what difference there could possible be between the ex-congressman in his grave or the ex-congressman whose life services were to be followed by his death services to science for the benefit of his fellowmen—for would it not be all the same when Gabriel blew his horn on that Resurrection Day when the graves would be opened and give up their dead and the mutilations of the past would all be healed and the golden world of the millennium would begin, as it would be almost impossible to live in Cincinnati or this part of the world without knowing?

The janitor who had received the body of the ex-congressman had been arrested, and the members of the medical family had rushed to his defense—perhaps because they knew that his condemnation was bound to be followed by theirs.

The search for the ex-congressman's kidnappers, with the help of

Pinkerton's sleuths who always got their men when they were really looking for them, when they were not planting a substitute, had been carried on
at the instigation of General Ben, who had been enraged by the medical
faculty's denial of complicity and by its oblivion to the morality of the issue
and had prayed that the members would be preserved from the knowledge
of the depths of human nature which had come to him from the discovery
of the body of a father hanging by the neck like a dog in a pit. His father's
grave clothes had been found piled up in a laundry basket or casket. They
were to have been offered for sale to churches or other institutions of
charity.

It was just at this point in the campaign for senator that General Ben
Harrison, addressing a meeting of Republicans at their state convention at
the Metropolitan Theatre in the Hoosier Radiating Railway City which
was Indianapolis, had delivered, with constant interruptions of wild
applause, the keynote speech in which he had enunciated the principles of
the Grand Old Party as those which brought peace, permanency, and prosperity to the nation.

To delay the nation's return to prosperity was to keep laborers' wages
down, for it was certain that prosperity could never return in the midst of
turmoil.

The grave robbers who had soon been turned up had been revealed as
Charles O. Morton and his wife, who had dressed as a man in trousers and
an old coat and old gray hat and old brogans when she was out digging
with her husband in this business of the resurrection of the dead for which
Cincinnati was a shipping center for railroad passage to such stations as
Fort Wayne, Indiana, and Ann Arbor, Michigan, where there was a charnel house in which the body of the young man was found.

The graveyard robbers had been indicted and condemned.

In the autumn of that year in which Little Ben had campaigned for the
repression of lawlessness, communism, and class hatred, for currency on a
sound basis and faith in God and the brotherhood of man with man, the
Tall Sycamore of the Wabash, by comparison with him a radical who
believed in paper money and to whom some scraps of the old Jeffersonian
democracy still adhered, had been swept into the Senate.

[1 2 3]

"THE KNIGHTS OF LABOR," according to Terence Powderly, who had been the head of the noble order for fourteen years when all it stood for had been anathema to most capitalists and who, a fallen warrior, his visor down, his sword broken at his side, would recall when he was old, sleeping like a knight in effigy upon a tomb, for he had long ago given up the fight against the overwhelming odds as a jouster against the kings of rails, "had aimed at rescuing man himself from a tomb, the tomb of ignorance. The aim was to roll away the stone from that tomb that he might know that moral wealth and not wealth should constitute individual and national greatness."

Terence Powderly believed in the maintenance of the neutrality of the Knights of Labor and had believed that during the Vandalia strike they should keep their mouths cemented shut.

When Knights of Labor were resurrecting and spreading far and wide the dollar-a-day scandal against Ben Harrison in 1888, Debs had known the chronology of the strike as it had occurred, keeping track as if from a watchtower of the progress of the strikers and the strike from flocks of bulletins which had been scattered on Sunday morning, July 23, to churchgoers as the bells were ringing them to church and there were more people than usual on the streets. "Arise, railroad men! There will be a meeting held at the State House yard on Monday evening at eight o'clock sharp for the purpose of sympathizing and taking action with our starving brothers in the East who are now being trampled under the feet of railroad bond holders. Let us all have a hand in the breaking of the railroad monopoly."

The men had walked off the Vandalia lines, and the locomotive firemen of the Hoosier city and St. Louis had joined them, and after the meeting in the state house yard the crowd had seized the depot for their headquarters and had disconnected all cars except those carrying the mails.

The Democratic governor James D. Williams, called Blue Jeans Williams because of his sympathy with the workman and the farmer, had refused to call out the state troops to protect the U.S. mails and the federally operated line lest he should lose the labor vote and the farm vote.

General Ben had offered mediation with the errant strikers at the same time that he had prepared to take an army of citizen volunteers in tarpaulin-covered wagons filled with bayonets into this new or protracted civil war against the mudsock workers if they did not give up the depot from which the grunts had been shipped to the old Civil War when Dr. Gatling had been designing his machine guns of which there were enough now to tear poor men into rags.

One of the helpers stationed at the rear of the Post Office Building and thus somewhat out of danger until the actual battle began had been Lew Wallace, former Civil War hero who had been among the lawyers on the staff trying the hooded conspirators with Booth in Lincoln's murder and who had desired them to speak, to name a network of conspirators in this wanton butchery of old Abe before they were hanged, but they had been kept as silent at their trial as if their mouths were stuffed already with the earth's cold clay.

When the strikers and their sympathizers, forced to arbitrate or be dispatched permanently to their graves, had not yielded quickly to compromise, there had been property-loving citizens in Indianapolis who certainly had wanted to dispatch them to their graves with full speed ahead if that was what was necessary to preserve the peace. But General Harrison had stated that he was unwilling to shoot his neighbors down.

"Businessmen," he had told the negotiators for the strikers when at last they who were being starved out had come with their hats on their heads— he had made them take off their hats before he would speak to them— "have been nearly bankrupted by the stoppage of their drafts," then had asked them what right they had to seek redress from law-abiding citizens by breaking the law.

He had promised that if the strikers would go back to work at the current rate of pay—it had provided no living wage, but what booted that?— he would do his best to influence the Citizens' Committee and public opinion in their favor—and thus he had been able to bring an end to the strike without the shedding of blood which had been threatened and which would have left many widows and orphans.

[1 2 4]

DEBS HAD DECLARED at the Brotherhood of Locomotive Firemen's Convention in the Hoosier capital city shortly after the end of the midwinter 1887–88 strikes,

This continued reduction of the price of labor was the direct cause of the recent strikes which terrified the entire nation. A strike at the present time signifies anarchy and revolution. . . .

The question has often been asked—Does the Brotherhood encourage strikers? To this question we must emphatically answer—No, brothers. To disregard the laws which govern our land? To destroy the last vestige of order? To stain our hands with the crimson blood of our fellow beings? We again say No, a thousand times No!

But the wheels of time did not have long to turn over the bodies of dead workmen before Debs came to see the fact that in the compromise which Little Ben, wearing an oversized stovepipe helmet with a raven's feather and an oversized waterproof coat, had arrived at they had been robbed of almost all the benefits for which they had gone on strike down at the Union Depot in the first place.

WHEN LITTLE BEN, by then Big Ben, left the White House in which he had been, during his presidency, as lonely as God, Cleveland having pounded down to the wire for his second term, many attributed his failure to the Homestead riots, which had caused the vast body of the labor vote to go over from the Republican to the Democratic fold, the dour-eyed and unsmiling and ever mournful Indianapolis president, who had recently lost his wife as a martyr to the tapestries which she had overworked herself by weaving for the walls of the White House, which were as cold and dank as the walls of a tomb.

What he had mainly regretted was that the Democratic administration coming in with the second term of Cleveland, who must have been a fiend for punishment such as Harrison was not, would destroy all that he had worked for—the protective tariff, reciprocity, and shipping legislation, which had been dear to his heart.

"The workingman," he had explained to a friend, "declined to walk under the protective umbrella because it sheltered his employer also."

Debs had understood that Harrison had been Carnegie's man, root and branch. But whose man was Cleveland?

[1 2 5]

O F   T H E   C O N S P I R A T O R I A L   apparatus of the kings of coal and silver and iron and steel and lead and the gold bugs of Wall Street who had flourished during the Benjamin Harrison administration which broke unions and put out thousands of strikers as if they were as fragile as the matchsticks which, with their flames extinguished, would supposedly not be lighted again with the flames of social protest, Henry Adams had observed, "A banker's Olympic became more and more despotic over Æsop's frog empire. One might no longer croak except to vote for King Log or—failing storks—for Grover Cleveland, and even then could not be sure where King Banker lurked behind."

Debs had known quite early of the Molly Maguires and that they, with a name which was supposed to strike terror in all hearts, were not the kinds of wild Irish girls for whom Jamesie O'Reilly, America's greatest pseudo-Irishman as he was called because of his perfect command of the brogue and his love of the Cork, would sing "My Wild Irish Rose" while all joined in the chorus with him who was wildly whirling around like a top and little Kate would be swung around and around in the arms of men as all the trains stood still.

The Molly Maguires were not old-fashioned Bible thumpers but were coal thumpers trying to strike hammer blows, fist blows for that which they considered their right to economic survival, freedom, and justice such as had not been theirs in the old country under the British crown and had not been theirs in America under coal and railroad kings with virtual power of life and death over their expanding empires.

The Molly Maguires, if there was any order at all by that name, if it was not simply a prejudicial label nailed to them in order to make all lawless hearts skip a few beats of that music which, once silenced, would never start up again, had been a secret labor organization whose members, greeting each other by symbolic handshakes and signs and speaking a language of signs which only they might understand, living their lives and dying their deaths by images and hieroglyphs and symbolic patterns which were messages an outsider could scarcely interpret and could not answer in kind under almost all conceivable circumstances, had devoted themselves to the assassination of repressive railroad barons and railroad owners and coal-mine barons and their sycophantic bosses in the anthracite barrens of Pennsylvania, which had as one of its coal-mine centers the coal-mining town of Pottsville where the not distant mountain ridges were populated by ever-watchful, soaring hawks to whom would be given permanent sanctuary and who in the years of the Molly Maguires and other poor workers struck down by the powers of capital had never lacked for human carrion, for eyes to pluck out.

Some of the leaders of the Molly Maguires had been perhaps chosen as sacrificial scapegoats, there having been perhaps no direct guilt for murder, according to a few enlightened sympathizers who had refused to believe that they should be railroaded to hell for crimes which no one could prove beyond the shadow of a doubt had been the colorful and articulate members of an unpopular, much disparaged minority.

The leaders of the mudsock Irish who had helped to build the rails and mine the mines of this country in reward had gone to the scaffold in the late 1870s when justice was revealed as that injustice which was no surprise to them, some with roses or Madonnas or crucifixes between their earth-stained paws as the jubilant crowds of spectators watched in the same spirit of mockery and amusement as had the crowds who had witnessed the execution of John Brown, and which had not been very different from the spirit with which, then as now, they might have watched the last act in a road show brought by a Wizard Oil van. And no doubt this was what it was, as the kings of coal were the kings of oil.

IN THAT MEMORIAL SPIRIT which made Debs pass over in his calendar no acknowledgment of martyrdom upon the day of the executions' anniversary, with further knowledge that the Pinkerton's operative who had been responsible for the trapping and deaths of the Molly Maguires was still alive and had been steadily employed for well nigh thirty years in his nefarious work of railroading men from this world to the altogether problematical next world and was still so engaged, Debs would recall in a delusively peaceful way the nontutelary execution of the Mollies who, like the numbers of the individual firemen and engineers killed by the trains and like many labor strikers and labor martyrs since that bloody day giving affirmation to this undoubtedly not first great abortion of justice to the midwives of capitalism who were the judges and the jurymen in rigged courts, had aroused and disturbed his humanitarian imagination and fraternal sympathy when he, a young man wearing his battered fireman's hat and patched blue jeans when he was out at night listening to all the tales which ran like the Indian telegraph from coal yard to coal yard, the spirit of these Mollies who, perennial in memory, had died because of their protest against the industrial tyrants who in their own esteem were certainly the rational opponents of the irrational and for whom the always overemployed, never underemployed capitalistic hangman stringing them up like wild cranes who would dance upon the clouds but for a few minutes, had drawn the knot tighter than the marital knot, that which everyone knew could always slip loose and for a thousand reasons including the poverty and starvation of men and women and children that they all had protested their innocence and that all had died game.

"Not one of them," Debs would remember in the "Appeal to Reason," "betrayed the slightest evidence of fear or weakening, not one of them was a murderer at heart. All were ignorant, rough and uncouth, born of poverty and 'buffeted by the merciless tides of fate and chance.' "

The method of protest employed by the Molly Maguires had been both drastic and secretive, it was true, but this should cause man's remembrance of the fact that their hard lot had brutalized them, that they were the neglected children of poverty, the product of a wretched environment, in the all-encompassing view of Debs.

The execution of the Molly Maguires of the warped, eroding Allegheny anthracite regions which were under the iron heel of the czars of coal and rails and were the regions of the damned had been no solitary episode; it had been the archetypal crime of capital against labor as it had contained within its schematic pattern other patterns of lesser or greater or equal magnitude, none so sporadic or solitary as it might seem to those who saw no logic or connections between events apparently not connected in space or time. The forms which avarice took would be recognized by Debs as would the transmutations taking place within the life of an individual.

Was it possible that a man who had been in the Old World a Chartist with a price on his head and thus had been associated with a movement that had worshiped the socialist Robert Owen as the father of the international labor movement with its millennial dreams of awakening in the new moral world should become, by his transatlantic migration, the enemy of labor unions in the new world? And how did this great transformation take place?

His social philosophy not bound by loyalty to principles, Allan Pinkerton had reflected the colors of the surrounding world and had changed his act when the opportunity changed. The gifts of the man were many and volatile and far-ranging.

The Pinkerton sleuth who—acting as his own manager and playwright and costume man and makeup man and hairdresser and cooper who trained infiltrators to enter the battle of capitalists against labor and who also provided private police forces for public forms of public murder would have been better employed in a creative sense had his Chicago central agency been a theatrical agency for the casting and training and rehearsal of actors whose bloody talents were often native to them and unfortunately not confined to *Macbeth* or *Julius Caesar* or *Romeo and Juliet* road shows such as would have entertained country crowds by apparitions of Lord and Lady Macbeth in their bloodstained nightshirts or Caesar with a bloodstained nightcap and nightshirt or feuds between the Capulets and Montagues instead of duels between coal kings and Molly Maguires who by comparison with him (Pinkerton) were no one. He actually had had behind the scenes in the Windy City as part of his business a costume supply depot complete with mustaches of the handlebar and beards of the waterfall variety, hair dyes of every shade including green, stand-up collars and wing collars and cuffs and all kind of stickpins and cufflinks and buttons and coats and breeches and hats and shoes, pumps for British lords on grand tours or brogans for Hogans or soft-soled shoes for hard-boiled sleuths, patches for eyes, ways to make a man look like an unemployed hearse driver who had had a little trouble with the higher powers, a lone horseback rider who had sneaked past the sleeping toll-bridge keeper before he knew, as it was the dead of night, that there was no bridge over the river, no doubt being the same kind of man that Pinkerton was, and he was the kind of man who would never be stopped by flood or fire—had been a once-flashing riverboat gambler who had fallen on hard times, had been euchred many a time when he was learning the game, had had a long run of spades like blackbirds and had been down on his dukes and had had no card to play out but a faceless card—had been a wandering ex–labor strike leader whose face was black-and-blue because of all the lumps of coal which had been thrown at him by the guards in the coal yards and who had been willing to help overthrow the men who owned all the lumps of all the coal in all the cars, had been a saloon keeper who had made the mistake of drinking the coal oil he served and had had a match put to him by a mean customer who had seen his chance for revenge, had been a barber with a sharp razor and a patent rights salesman and a jewel thief, a shepherd of sheep.

But was there no sign by which nature always revealed, as in ancient folklore which was universal in all countries or almost all in which there had been ritual murder, not only in far-flung primitive societies but in modern society, where the memory of the same flora and fauna persisted in man's retentive heart, the identities of the murderers, even when they might be the accusers, and did not the rocks and the clouds and the waters and the earth cry out, and should not the tongues of birds and the tongues of living men speak for the dead whose tongues could not speak for them- selves, as surely no one could place the severed head of a man upon his shoulders to make him walk again?

Such questions would be those which Debs would come to ask him- self—at first in silence—then with a voice to shake rocks and clouds and waters and earth with the names of man's murderers.

[1 2 6]

A MAN WHOSE LIFE was in some ways as bizarre as any of the strings of murder mysteries he had ever solved, Allan Pinkerton with his undying hatred of labor unions could honestly boast that he was the only antilabor detective who had ever been a labor union organizer himself.

He had been in his deprived youth in hard-ribbed Scotland the kind of activist Chartist who had not consented to be cooped up in his dreams of bringing a new moral world to mankind, a new sense of conscience, an awakening from the sloth of dark ages to a golden dawn, and had been indifferent to paradisal principles which were altogether as distant of real- ization, as mummified as if they were already the sleepers in deep tombs under the earth.

Pinkerton never went to kirk but once in his life, and that was when he was a wee babe carried there by his rational, agnostic parents who claimed that they had their own way of believing in God. He was apparently as sure of his virtue, however, as he was that virtue would triumph and that Pinkerton's sleuths should be men of the highest moral rectitude while in his services—and what if they sometimes captured immoral criminals by immoral means in justification of moral ends—men who understood, as well-trained and virtuous actors in the intricate drama which every mur- der mystery was or is, the characteristics of the criminals of whom they were in hot and cold pursuit, as in the famed literature of Diamond Dick.

The immoral criminal, once he was trapped, should be treated by Pinkerton's sleuth with that courtesy and sympathy which a man should show to a man in deference to their brotherhood as sharers of the common clay and which would ultimately have the effect of drawing from him the confession of his guilt, even if it might be followed in some instances by the drawing of the noose around his neck.

How did one get a man to pour out the confessions which might bring him to the hangman's tree? According to Pinkerton's agent, one had to play the music by ear in order to get the right response from the man's vocal cords—even give him, now and then, a drop of cough medicine if he was suffering from a rusted windpipe. He might want to hang in the midst of this nightmare and might pour out more crimes than Pinkerton's man had ever dreamed of and some which might be imaginary crimes made to seem real as real crimes might be left to realms of imagination by Pinkerton or his agency which naturally could not unearth all. Pinkerton believed that the murderer was always dying to confess his guilt, to divest himself of its evil burden. Only Pinkerton seemed immune.

Born August 25, 1819, in the lowest depths of Glasgow where gangs dedicated to the snatching of living bodies roamed the streets in the gloaming without the formal courtesy of waiting for a grave digger's job by which to dig their graves and bury them when they had perished of rampant diseases caused by poverty and certainly without waiting for the grave robber's job by which to dig them up again as if these were old turnips or potatoes, Allan Pinkerton, future founder of that agency which, claiming omniscience, would have as its early trademark The Eye That Never Sleeps, the same as that of the czar of Russia's all-seeing eye which had been depicted upon tents along the railroads built by starving, rheumatic serfs through lands of snow and ice, had been the son of a blacksmith who when the boy was eight years old had been an apprentice to a tool pattern maker and then, as there was no future in any such work but to be a skeleton, had become an apprentice to a cooper, still at a starvation wage which ultimately would not have kept body and soul from falling apart, and had become a member of the Glasgow coopers' union which had the active intention of pitting itself against that toll keeper who was old mortality by improving, in all ways which might seem possible, man's lot.

A tramp cooper, he had gone about the countryside making or mending boxes and barrels and coops and hoops and staves for the small pay of which he had never forgotten to send a share home to his poor millworker mother lest she starve for bread as many a poor millworker widow did, or lest she should freeze because of the lack of a lump of coal or a piece of firewood.

Giving up after about a year his existence as a tramp cooper sleeping with other tramps under hedgerows or on the open moor, Allan Pinkerton had returned to Glasgow and had become a member of the Chartist organization which had given vent to the expression of the unrest of the pauper class who were the employed and the unemployed workingmen under the reign of the tightfisted William IV, whose chief fears were that the Russians were about to invade England and that the czar of all the Russias was now to include England among his possessions and would exile to the land of the polar bear all who might oppose him.

At Glasgow, where the poor were as poor as in any city on earth, it was believed that the Chartists had had no goals but to turn the social pyramid upside down so that the masses which were now at the bottom would be at the top and the rich who were now at the apex would be at the bottom, as Robert Owen had been advocating for some time to the poor folks and to emperors and kings. The Chartists of Glasgow had had as their goals, however, the improvement which should have been realizable within this mortal frame and had included such simple things as equal electoral rights, universal suffrage, payment of members, no property qualifications, vote by ballot, and annual parliaments which should not be, of course, parliament of fowls.

Unfortunately, like the socialists in America as in other countries, who in the search for the union of man with man split themselves into factions so that social progress was like a horse which was weakened by missing two shoes and could only go at a hobbled gait so long as disagreements continued, the Chartists had soon divided into those who believed in moral force and those who believed in physical force.

Allan Pinkerton had agreed with the advocates of violence and not with those of peaceful means.

All Allan Pinkerton had needed for his happiness and comfort had been a wee house, a wee garden, a wee wife to sit by a wee fireside. His hammer in his hand, his muscles had swollen with pride as he thought of the general strike in which he was to strike a blow for freedom and equality and justice. Unfortunately, the strike which had been secretly planned in the autumn of the year at Birmingham at a Chartist convention to which he had gone as representative of the Glasgow coopers had not panned out, had been as abysmal a failure as that of Beelzebub when he fell into the bog for trying to make war on God.

In the spring and again in the autumn of 1839, as the Commons had turned a deaf ear to the moral arguments of the Chartists, and when after many secret meetings on the windswept moors making their exact charts for a military expedition, the Chartists had gathered to march for the release from the prison in Monmouth Castle of the fellow Chartist Henry

Vincent, Allan Pinkerton with his cooper's hammer on his back had been one of those following the leadership of a man most aptly named Jack Frost, all carrying lighted rush torches in their hands as they joined in singing to give them courage through their clandestine fellowship—"May the rose of England never blow, / The Clyde of Scotland never flow, / The Harps of Ireland never play / Until the Chartists gain their day."

This was not to be their day, however. A rat informer had squealed. Some branches of their Chartist army had failed to meet them.

All suddenly from behind the windows of the Westgate Hotel at Newport, and much as Pinkerton's men from their concealed positions would fire on labor strikers in America as at the Homestead of Pittsburgh steel and as the czar of Russia would fire on those striking for bread with showers of bullets, King William's redcoats had responded to the invasion with volleys of shots which covered the cobblestones with seas of blood—but Allan Pinkerton had not been wounded or killed and had fled down the back alleys to Glasgow feeling like a thief as he tried to stay close to the shadows near the wall and out of the way of the moon like an eye shining intermittently through the darkness and shining on him. Perhaps his life as a phantom had begun.

ONE OF THE MEN who had spoken to the Glasgow coopers and other Chartists at their nocturnal meetings on the moors had been George Julian Harney, a well-known jailbird. As fragile and bedraggled and windblown a creature as ever had burned with a revolutionary spirit, he had been a gifted orator in spite of his suffering from a congenital quinsy, a chronic throttling of the throat that had caused him to shake continually from head to foot as if he might already have been hanged and cut prematurely down, as also his hearing had been severely impaired by that deafness which was, of course, never truly silence to those who suffered from it and made medleys of interior sounds like church bells, ship whistles, train whistles, wild winds sweeping over the moors, barking dogs, sounds of four lakes pouring out water in a desert land, coming up from an old well of which one had lifted the lid. He had a voice so mighty that he could outshout any crowd.

Pinkerton had sponsored him as a speaker at Glasgow's Lyceum Theatre, where, as he was greeted by roars of protest by those trying to drown him out, his protector, who was to be the great detective in pursuit of such anarchic radicals as these, had roared in response like a great phantom bull until the crowd was silenced and had listened or had not listened to what

Harney had to say. He was one of the many who, some nameless, some with names, might be these trailblazers who were Debs's heroes.

A pale-faced, anemic, phlegmatic gentleman, a passionate orator in behalf of social justice, which must come in this world and not in the world to come, he had believed absolutely that communism was a cure for the world's ills and that there should be no delay until next year or some other year—he could not wait for the great change, and mankind could not wait—nor did he with the rackety-clock cough and the collapsed bellows believe, one may suspect, in any miracle such as that if one bellows of a pair of broken bellows was buried in one lake and another bellows in another lake, yet still would come that blessed day when each bellows should fly out of the lake to join with the other bellows and there would be the resurrection of the dead and the socialist millennium should begin as something which did not depend upon the will of coal kings and tin kings but rather through the will of that great God or Over-seer Who was not in their employment.

The enthusiastic, somewhat irrational rational Harney's claim during his brief tenure on this earth where he like many other houseless Chartists had no house, not even the nest of the capitalistic owl who should keep watch over and protect from himself and other predators the socialist mice, was that he would always hold high the banners of the dialectical materialism which he knew could be made to work and in a spiritual sense beyond dispute, for he was no lightweight and was in good standing with Karl Marx and Friedrich Engels who were his icons taking the place of all other leaders and all other gods—although to Marx and Engels with their intricate intertwinings and intermeshings of thought he was no heavyweight in realms of purpose which step by step must slowly evolve and might as well have been a little tin soldier marching in a rainy gutter with a toy drum—they who were not always serious and shared many jokes almost as if they were a necessity to the understanding of the occult which they wished to make explicit in the new world which was to come when the baggage of the past should be thrown overboard had dubbed this frenetic, overworked leader in his raggedy, tallow-streaked clothes the Hip, hip, hooray man because of his marching and drumming enthusiastically for every radical cause there was and apparently without sufficient understanding of the way, the great way they were mapping out on their chart of the monolithic Hegelian universe which had as one of its difficulties the question—Can stones think? The answer was—Yes, they could.

[1 2 7]

IN THE TIME of the mystical pre-Marxist utopias springing up with the help of angel apple pickers in the case of the Shakers, for whom the golden apples of paradise were shaken from the trees and the angels had even pinned notes upon the apple boughs—the tutelary visit of the Angel Gabriel to Father Rapp on the banks of the Wabash and the repetition of that visit in Economy near Pittsburgh—even the attribution to the secular Robert Owen of the characteristics of an angelic guide who would pilot all mankind from the old immoral world to a new moral world—the presumption of Swedenborgian transcendentalists as to the sacredness of mankind in a state of socialism, whether Owenite or Fourierite or a duke's mixture of both—the many-branching legend of the discovery of the lost Canadian bible which showed the transformation of an angel into a postman carrying in his bag along a New York country road Joseph Smith's *Book of Mormon* or the angel in Illinois who, twenty feet high, a prehistoric Indian mound builder, had come up like smoke from a hole in the ground to give to Joseph Smith his tutelary advice—this continent had been swept over by so many wild waves of cooperative communal spiritualism that for a time it had almost become a communal nation and, although the passion for spiritual regeneration by brotherhood had undergone some degenerative influences during the Civil War, still might have reacted favorably to Marx's most mystifying dialectical materialism if only it had been called dialectical spiritualism and thus had not alienated so many people by its suggestion that unrefined, coarse worldly goods like corn and coal and oil were its chief concern.

ALLAN PINKERTON had gotten wind, with his weathercock mind always on the alert, that he was about to be cooped up by the redcoat police in the name of the Crown and so with his bride, Joan, who had been a soprano in the choir, had taken secret passage on April 9, 1842, on a mail steamboat from the Clyde to Nova Scotia, at last reaching the New World with a fitting symbolism which might have been employed by such weird mystery writers as Edgar Allan Poe: their mailboat had been able to hound its way through packs of ice floes with the wind howling like white wolves, and they had not perished when the ship had keeled upon a jagged rock as the waters of the sea filled her hull, and she was about to go down into her grave.

The Pinkertons with other passengers had taken to the lifeboats through hissing, churning waves and veils of snow and ice.

When after a few months in Montreal hammering barrels for shipments of beef and for the containment of parts of cattle Pinkerton had been confronted by the specter of unemployment such as he had always known, he had decided that the thing to do was to take the lake boat from Montreal to the thriving hogopolis of Chicago, the city of wild garlic beds where surely there would be no dearth of cows and hogs for the cooper's hogshead casks and where the continually swelling population would soon be under the domination of cow and hog kings.

When Pinkerton told his wife that he had paid for their tickets to take this passage, she had carried her high soprano notes higher than he had ever heard them before as she broke out in a wilder and wilder soprano of protest that she could not, would not sail, for she had put a down payment on a wee bonnet and would rather lose her life than have to sail without it o'er the inland sea and thus lose both her down payment and her wee bonnet—it would be his fond recollection.

He had roared his altos which could not drown out her soprano, and so he had stayed on for another week as a handyman hammering in the staves and the hoops before the wife wearing the wee bonnet and the husband with his hammer had set sail, arriving without incident in the new country, their ship having not gone down, the lake waves as calm as the ruffles on a lady's skirts.

When his Joan had pointed out to this Darby that the ship from which they had canceled passage the week before had gone down and that they owed their lives to her wee bonnet, he had vowed that never again would he stand in the way of any wee bonnet which she had determined must be hers.

THE CHICAGO in which the Pinkerton couple arrived, having first been robbed of some of their possessions but not among them the wife's wee bonnet, was that hogopolis where an Irishman, John Whistler, a traveler with Gentleman Johnny Burgoyne's army, had been captured by the American Revolutionary forces and had turned turtle by becoming an American soldier in Chicago before Chicago was born, the founder and commander of Fort Dearborn, a stockade with barracks which had been burned down in the War of 1812 by the first reds in America who were the dispossessed red men and whose wholesale slaughter by the colonizers of the western plains had been so great under every administration that President Rutherford Hayes, under whose administration the execution of the Irish scapegoats would occur as only an extension of the cruelties to the exploited Irish who had come here to escape the potato famine and whose beds were the mines under the rails, would be so embarrassed by the violences of the conquest over this continent that he could only express something of what would remain a stain upon that most problematical of all entities, a nation's conscience, in his speech to some of the members of the governing body at a time when there were members absent—"When I speak of Lo, you all know who Lo is. He is Lo, the poor Indian."

Captain John Whistler, the father of Major George Washington Whistler, who would help to lay the first mile of the Baltimore & Ohio Railroad track as well as other spidery rails and who by 1843 would be in Dostoyevsky's St. Petersburg as a builder of rails with the employment of freezing, starving serfs, the czar of Russia's little pigeons falling in starving, bloody flocks along the rails through lands of eternal snow and ice under the supervision of The Eye That Never Sleeps. He was the father of James MacNeill Whistler, for a time an unlikely drawer of surveyors' maps for that same B & O upon which would begin on July 18, 1877, at Martinsburg, West Virginia, the great strike that the owners of railroads had chosen not to avoid but rather to invite for intimidating purposes.

The hogopolis to which Allan Pinkerton had come in search of work did not become an important shipping center until the completion of the dredging of the Chicago River and the opening in 1848 of the Illinois and Michigan Canal by which the city which was the head would be joined with the river and the river with the Mississippi as a watery spine which should make of Chicago the king of water transport as it would also be, with the advent of railroads, the king of land transport.

The former Glasgow Chartist would have had to be more brilliant than he was to have seen the jewels of the future gleaming in the Chicago mud. What was of vital importance had been to keep his wife's wee bonnet on her head with a ribbon tied in a bow under her chin lest the lake winds should attempt to blow it off and blow his shirt off his back and sand grains into their mouths.

Auld Bobbie Fergus, who was the Pinkertons' host when they had no roof-tree of their own, not even a coop for the wee wife with her wee bonnet, had taken the couple that summer to an old-time Scottish revival tent meeting when they were as poor as lice in the lands of the bald, and there they had heard the auld Scottish soul saver direct his flaming messages to a man whose ruling passion was to the acquisition of dollars and who had, in spite of his love for the poems of Robert Burns, only the most superficial understanding of those who stepped aside from the path of virtue which would be a part of the religion of American socialism as of the chief of its labor spokesmen, Eugene Victor Debs, when he was trying to reach out to every worker above the crust of earth and even some perhaps permanently or perhaps only temporarily below the crust.

The advice that Burns had given in his "Address to the Unco Guid or the Rigidly Religious" had apparently made no lasting impression upon the man whose belief was in the golden hand which should shake the golden hand in a brotherhood of rich men more meaningly than the brotherhood of raggedy men of whom he had been one before his migration to that which would be for him truly the land of opportunity of which he would avail himself at every turn.

> Who made the heart, 'tis He alone
> Decidedly can try us;
> He knows each chord, its various tone,
> Each spring, its various bias;
> Then at the balance let's be mute,
> We never can adjust it;
> What's done we probably may compute
> But know not what's resisted.

[1 2 8]

FROM CHICAGO in the autumn when the cold winds were blowing across the lake with promises of colder winter winds to come, Allan Pinkerton and his wife in her wee bonnet, and other articles of apparel, had removed themselves to Dundee, Illinois, on the Fox River about fifty miles to the north of Chicago, where while working as a cooper with his sign hung out over his cabin door and steadily minding his own business and following what would be his adages all his life such as "Early to bed and early to rise / Makes a man healthy, wealthy, and wise" or "A bird in the hand is worth two in the bush," he had been interrupted in his usual routine by a most curious incident indeed.

By a series of stratagems showing his close powers of observation and native wit and ability to turn into cash whatever dollars might come his way and through no crooked deal, for he considered himself not only a law-abiding but a virtuous man as he at this time no doubt had been, at least at a superficial level, no temptations having tempted him to depart from the ways of the just, this busy cooper who had no horseflies reading on him and was always very alert had been able to bring to the coop of the law a gang of horse thieves and counterfeiters who had been doing their nefarious business in a nest among the reeds of an island in the Fox River which in memory of these transients would be called Bogus Island.

When Allan Pinkerton, who had put on his suit and hat and coat and muffler and shoes in order to make a respectable appearance, had gone through prairie grasses up to his chin and above his head to report to a Chicago bank whose head had happened to be a fellowman of the auld sod that he had captured a covey of counterfeiters and had come for his reward, he had been nearly ripped to pieces with a ripsaw and might well have been left as nothing but a pile of golden shingles on the bank floor by the Scot for having done his work behind his back and without his foreknowledge and without any contract which would bind him to pay with good money for counterfeit money, nothing but a bag of bogus bills. Allan Pinkerton had finally been paid but with the warning that he would not shell out peas from the pod again, so that from this time onward he would never do any job of apprehending anyone—would never stick his head out again—would probably not even have apprehended Jason if he had happened to spy on him when he was stealing the golden fleece that was hanging from the withered tree—unless a contract had been put out for the capture of the thief.

Besides that, not all thieves—especially the biggest thieves like those who were stealing this continent, in the view of radicals—were wanted by the police or by the government which had its noose out to bring in poor men whose greatest crime was that in this land of opportunity they were poor, the flotsam on the river of life, the scum of the earth—and that fact was something for which they had no one to blame but themselves.

Back home again in Dundee, where his fame was not particularly appreciated by the auld Scots of the kirk, who had once been Presbyterian but had backslid into total-immersion Baptists, and they had voted him unfit to run for high office as theirs was a gathering of souls providing the only intoxication there was and he who while running for a county office on the Abolitionist party ticket had not been as dry as was required of him and had been a secret drinker of buckets and buckets and barrels of whiskey when he thought no one was looking, and he had parted company with them in other ways as when he had circulated the diabolical message that Jesus Christ was an illegitimate child and not a divine visitor and that his mother had been tossed in the hay by something other than an angel of the Lord who had planted in her the seed of the bairn that was born in the hay manger with the cow and the donkey and the sheep and the goats and the rooster and the owl looking on. *Who-oo, who-oo,* the owl had asked.

Because of his inability to disperse the lies made against him by the elders of the church, Allan Pinkerton and his wife with her wee bonnet on her head and her bairn William in her arms had gone by buggy to the great radiating railroad city of Chicago where he had become, in rapid succession, a deputy sheriff under William L. Church—who was the sheriff of Cook County at a time when the city which was to be an important theater in the life of Debs was practically buried under a mudslide of the corruptions caused by the crimes committed by crooks of every kind so that there might never be an end of them although the city should perish—and he had also become Chicago's first detective and a United States mail agent, and by 1850 the head of the Pinkerton National Detective Agency which guaranteed throughout the Middle West the detection of offenders, the procurement of arrests and convictions, the apprehension of or return of fugitives from justice, the recovery of lost or stolen property, and the obtaining of information by which, in one way or another, the offender would be put out of business.

Allan Pinkerton's agency had become, by 1855, with the help of the railroad corporations which had paid for the extension of protection by his operatives of the rolling stocks and properties of railroads over as wide a terrain as their rails covered, the head of a flourishing business including among his clients the Illinois Central; the Michigan Southern & Northern Illinois; the Chicago & Galena Union; the Chicago & Rock Island; the Chicago, Burlington & Quincy—their numbers to increase during the boom which was brought by the Civil War. In 1859 Allan Pinkerton helped John Brown and the fugitive black men whom he sheltered under his wings to escape to Canada by gathering up, at a meeting of the Chicago Judiciary Convention, contributions of dollars for their escape to Kansas by the Illinois Central—and thus although he was a keeper of the law had been, with the connivance of judges and government officials, a violator of the law who in another neck of the woods, if ever he was caught, might have been the victim of old Judge Lynch's necktie party strung up on an unbending bough.

The last words which John Brown, whose head had been wanted in

Missouri and Kansas and whose neck would soon be broken by the hangman's rope in retribution for his raid on Harpers Ferry, had spoken to the freed black man John Jones and the great railroad detective Allan Pinkerton at the Chicago railroad station, which might seem to the average unthinking man to have little direct bearing upon moral issues and might be subjected to various interpretations—"Friends, lay in your tobacco, cotton, and sugar because I intend to raise the prices"—a surely accurate prediction of the economic state when prices for commodities would climb as the war brought an increase in the wealth of the rich and an increase in the poverty of the poor, and one could make no bones about it or only the bones of the poor—skeletons of poor men hanging from many trees, some making weird music as the wind crashed through them, some sounding like the harps which hung in Tara's halls.

One of Allan Pinkerton's close friends, his very *beau idéal* of military presence coupled with aristocratic grandeur, had been George Brinton McClellan, vice president of the Illinois Central, who had thrown much business his way and had shepherded many trains of many lines like sheep into his keeping at a time when there were not only train wrecks caused by natural agencies such as fallen or falling trees but those caused by train wreckers of all kinds and for a variety of reasons—the most important of which was the war which some thought was fought for the liberation of black men from chattel slavery and some thought was fought for the expansion of northern railroads into lands where they were no more welcome than would be wolves in a sheep's fold or a fox in a poultry yard.

The former lawyer for the Illinois Central, Abraham Lincoln, who had won his way to the White House which some of his enemies had vowed he would never reach alive and on both feet, owed his life to the dour Pinkerton, who, very methodical in all his ways, had warned the former wood sawyer of a plot for his assassination of which he had heard when in the services of the Philadelphia, Wilmington & Baltimore Railroad, where his job was to guard trains and bridges from the explosions of dynamite laid by Southern sympathizers—and had been able to give warning in the nick of time, although there would be other plots, of course, as there had been from before the beginning and would be until after the end.

Pinkerton, posing as a Georgia abolitionist, had met with the barber Fernandina in a Baltimore bar, where he had justified the Free Baptist Church of Dundee's accusations that he was a sympathizer with blacks and was a drinker.

The Baltimore barber had told the Georgia secessionist that he had the chief marshal of police on his side and that his plot to put Lincoln into his coffin was so well nailed together that any attempt to spare Lincoln's life would be as futile as to try to blow away the Washington Monument with his breath.

Lincoln's impression had been that the railroad detective was victimized by an overactive imagination, but he had followed the advice of his military attendants, had taken heed at a time when he had been filled with his own fatalistic premonitions of coming doom and had indicated this persistent image of death long before he had left the Hoosier state on his journey from the Middle West to the East, where he was never to be happily at home but would feel himself in some ways a stranger who had few or no friends in whom he could place his total trust.

Wearing a felt hat with the brim drawn down over his forehead and casting a shadow over his eyes, carrying over his arm a long fringed shawl to keep him from the cold, Lincoln had slept all the way to Washington in an unlighted train over the Pennsylvania Railroad, all the telegraph wires cut so that no one could be apprised of his coming and lay the dynamite egg to blow the train up with the president-elect in it, and had arrived in Washington in the dead of night, his disguise so perfect according to the false report of a newspaper writer who probably knew of Allan Pinkerton's mastery of the art of disguise, that nobody could possibly have recognized the president-elect as the tall man wearing a Scottish plaid cap and a long shawl and a long military cape, that which was his usual traveling costume. There was probably no way to keep the much-cartooned president from looking like himself.

[1 2 9]

WHEN MRS. O'LEARY'S COW had kicked over the burning lantern that caused the Chicago fire, what had caused Allan Pinkerton's intense regret was the loss of his Civil War documents and the loss of his rogues' gallery, although there would be other rogues to take their place, no portrait among them of the Chicago merchant and rail heads who had profited at the expense of the poor during the Civil War and when given funds for the rebuilding of the city after the fire had demonstrated their spirit of philanthropy by channeling the golden sluices to themselves, and no doubt if justification were needed for what anarchic intelligences would consider the fraudulent abuse of power could claim that they were doing the work of the protection of the poor and of the incompetent and of the chronically disarranged, for some of the waters of prosperity would trickle down to the dispossessed burning like cinders in cinder yards, burning like the cinder stars.

Allan Pinkerton, wishing to bend the twigs in the way the branches should grow, had trained his sons William and Robert from the days when they were taken from their mother's breast to put their baby footprints into the footprints of the great sleuth who was tracking criminals to their lair, to keep their weather eye peeled to see every evidence of crime that they might inherit his place in the Pinkerton agency when he, if a man's death may be illuminated by his life and he may continue his work, had gone to track down some great, universal mystery or even clap his coop on God, the author of it all, and accuse Him of this crime which was the fiction of the world.

As to the way people die, Susan B. Anthony would say that when she died, she would not go to some distant heaven—her astral body, should she have one, would be hanging around the earth, waiting to see if woman got her right to vote. It would be said of Debs when he died that if there were canal workers on the planet Mars, as some people thought, he would be chartering them into brotherhoods.

Allan Pinkerton's agency—at a time when the Crédit Mobilier scandals had revealed that macrocosm of crime which in its own way would inspire all kinds of thieves and counterfeiters to the imitation of the robberies of the nation's treasure and the payoff of stock to high officials in the government, secret cooperators in the theft so vast that this continent itself might have been carried away as easily as by piano thieves stealing a grand piano with scarcely a trembling of its cords or tinkle of its ivory keys which represented the martyrdom of elephants slain for their tusks in African jungles, at a time when there were vicious caricatures in the press of nascent labor union members who, if they had saved the dues they paid, might not have been reduced to beggary for crumbs of bread from that great continental table where the rich men dined and wined—had been filled with the determination that crime did not pay the criminal. One of the most tempting of all the elusive targets whom the law-and-order men had been determined to capture and bag and bring to trial had been the gang known as the Reno brothers.

Living at Seymour, Indiana, near Rockford, which they had reduced to a ghost town by many mysterious fires and which was their robbers' roost at the junction of the Yellow Band Trail and not far from a conical mound which had been one of the many mounds used by prehistoric red men for the burial of their dead and their jars of corn, these Reno, or Renault, brothers had raised hell all through the Civil War as bounty hunters and so could not have enjoyed the admiration of Allan Pinkerton, whose spy services, in the name of abolition, had flourished without such inhibitions as should have been observed in times of peace but to which it seemed that he could not return. And what was peace but an extension of war, war against low-grade train robbers, counterfeiters, anarchists, murderers as wild as wildcats in the woods?

On October 6, 1866, the two Reno brothers John and Simeon and their fellow thief Franklin Sparks, all wearing masks, had boarded an Ohio & Mississippi train and, just as with a farewell toot it was pulling out of the Seymour station for the next feeding and watering trough, stopped the engineer only three miles out of town by pointing a gun at his head and had slugged the Adams Express Company messenger and had thrown overboard two trunks of gold where there were horses waiting for their escape into the surrounding woods.

The train robbers had not been efficient safe crackers, for this latter art having shown such a high disregard as to indicate that they thought there would always be more safes coming from where these had come from. They had found it impossible to open the heavier box containing the heavier load of gold and so had left it hidden among the reeds, where, if it had been found by a mystical tramp in search of the earthly paradise with only a little larceny in his soul, it might have been looked upon by him as a miracle dropped by an angel messenger from God on high, even though in all probability the angel messengers were getting thinner and thinner every year just like the wild geese.

In the course of searching for and roping this infernal Reno gang, the Pinkertons had employed an infiltrator who had posed as a saloon keeper in Seymour, helping to put the brothers under the spell of the demon rum by serving liquor until their eyes nearly popped out and their tongues hung loose and they accepted him at face value as a riverboat gambler who was dressed to the nines as a riverboat gambler should be, complete with embroidered waistcoat and high silk hat and polished pumps—what was a riverboat gambler worth if he was not a dude?

They were self-assured and had not foreseen the nature of the duplicitous structure which was being piled up against them by law-and-order men for whom murder was old hat, to say the least, and as they surely knew. But they had apparently been mesmerized. They had discussed the next train they were going to catch and had done so without knowledge, of course, that the nation's greatest sleuth would be on the train waiting with his men, his fellow passengers, to put the manacles and chains of the law on them the moment the train had left the depot, speeding wildly ahead with other Reno brothers in hot pursuit but still unable to catch up or bar the way at any crossing or arouse the sympathetic horsemen of the countryside to join with them.

The judge at the court to which Allan Pinkerton had roped them in had been a regular Judge Lynch who, if he could only have had his way, would have hanged them from the highest tree and wasted not a moment of his or their time. Over the jail gates had been the familiar sign, "The way of the transgressor is hard—Admission twenty-five cents."

Allan Pinkerton had been lucky to escape alive from a country infested with Reno sympathizers springing up like toadstools, the poisoned kind. Under the direction of William Pinkerton, by various ruses capturing other members of the Reno gang who had committed a robbery in Council Bluffs, Iowa, where the incriminating evidence had been half burned in a stove before the Pinkerton's agents could reach out with their hands to retrieve the partially seared bills, they took their captives by train to the Indianapolis depot and then by train to Seymour through a darkened countryside upon a journey slowed by so many long-drawn-out stops that it seemed as if it would never end or that the lives of the captors would end before it did.

Reaching the Seymour station too late to take the westbound train—was this what the locomotive engineer intended?—the Pinkerton's agents took a wagon in which their captives were forced to lie down on a journey to Brownstown, where there were a courthouse and a jail, but three miles out of Seymour the horse and driver were brought to a halt by weirdly non-apparitional swarms of red-masked men leaping out of the bushes from every side and screaming with blood-curdling cries which filled with fear the hearts of all who heard and who, even if they knew no Latin and not even pig Latin, recognized the slogan under which they operated: "*Salus populi suprema lex!*" Their intention was to commit murder. Whom did they intend to kill?

Obviously, not the Pinkerton upholders of the law, for these men in turkey-red flannel masks were upholders of the law who made no attempt to defend their murderous captors from their murderers. The agents' horse's head was turned around, and they were told to go back to Seymour. So there was no all-seeing eye who saw this bloody deed, not even perhaps the eye of the moon which went behind a dark cloud, when the Renos were hung from the trees and left hanging all through the darkness and long after the dawn that all who had heard what had happened might come to see with their own eyes a crime which, it was ruled by the coroner who had also been the judge, had been perpetrated by persons unknown. Unknown even by the Pinkertons, who after all had not been given a contract to search for some two hundred men believed to have made up the mob. And some might have been church deacons, lynch law having removed from them in all probability an individual sense of guilt for murder.

The Pinkertons had gone on searching for the surviving members of the Reno gang, who in retribution for this lynching party had left as many bloody heads strewn over the fields as watermelons in watermelon time, dead men in treetops, dead men in tree hollows, and who were also devoting themselves to far-flung train robberies and who when they were rounded up and, in spite of warnings by the vigilantes that they would not be safe in any jail, were brought by train from Indianapolis to New Albany because of the governor's unwillingness to admit that the New Albany jail or any other jail in the Hoosier state would not be a safe place for them.

The old stone and brick county jail at New Albany, a town which has at its front the beautiful Ohio River and at its back the range of the Silver Hills which were formed, according to legend, when the Great Spirit dug up the ground for silver with which to make the silver stars in the sky, was sleeping, it would be long remembered, under the light of the silver moon and silver stars by the silver river when, on the night of December 12, 1868, had occurred, when there were no soldiers to guard them, the lynching in the jail of the remnant of the Reno brothers by the mob of men with their red masks as red as turkey combs who, having traveled upon the Jefferson-Madison-Indianapolis train with its darkened cars, had descended upon the jail with cries of "*Salus populi suprema lex!*" and, having wounded the jailer in order to get their prey, had strung up what had been left of the Reno gang, dispatching them to hell with such rapidity of motion that one of the men, a man named Charlie Anderson, had asked for five minutes in which to pray for his soul and had been told by his impatient executioner that his soul was not worth praying for.

The hangman who had tied Simeon Reno's necktie had not been efficient. He had left him hanging in such a haphazard way that, his toes almost touching the floor, he had taken an hour to die as the caged prisoners who were there for other crimes and had barely escaped being lynched by the overzealous mob had watched with pity and horror the death dance of this poor man whom none could reach out to rescue and who was a victim of murder.

Allan Pinkerton and his son William, hurrying from Chicago to Indianapolis, had joined with this negligent governor in expressions of regrets over the executions which had occurred through the operations of the vigilantes, parties unknown, who they had sworn would be found and brought to justice, that kind which asked for an eye for an eye, a tooth for a tooth.

The masked men had taken off their masks and had reverted to their roles as upholders of civic law and order, those who had committed crimes in its name and undoubtedly no isolated crimes, perhaps had committed crimes against their horses and their wives as by these infernal doings they had acquired the taste for blood—as would be pointed out someday by Debs and other experts in the realm of crime and punishment.

These lynchings had saved the government the expense of a trial although not all the Reno brothers had been captured, and there had been a sudden outcropping of mysterious horsemen wearing red masks who held up and robbed lone travelers in the land of the Silver Knobs, stole their horses or their silver or spirited the travelers themselves away or left them dead or wounded by the side of the road in a dark forest, as if there were imitators of the Reno brothers, who had always had their imitators, or as if some of the vigilantes had taken over the concern and were carrying away watches and watchmen and church towers. The Pinkerton solution had not decreased the numbers of the Reno brothers, whether true or false, but had increased them, as had been the intention.

[1 3 0]

ALLAN PINKERTON had suffered, in the autumn following the lynching of the Reno criminals, a paralytic stroke which could surely not have been caused by guilt causing his limbs to wither and his face to twitch and his eyes to bleed and his tongue to thicken as he thought of Simeon's dance with the long neck stretching and the long body stretching and the long toes stretching with the attempt to put his feet on the floor and loosen the noose and walk away.

ALLAN PINKERTON had known that life was not a rose garden and should not be a rose garden for criminals as it could not be for the detectives who were out to catch them—it was a wilderness of bloody thorns, a hedgerow made of porcupines for the protection of the properties which were the sacred groves of railroad and banking interests and were the properties which were the nation's properties and had been stolen by the rich from the poor, according to just such American anarchists as the Chartists were when they were followers of Robert Owen or Karl Marx. And suppose the Reno brothers had never heard of either one?

They were French, their name originally Renault, and they had ridden with Morgan's Raiders and were the kind of laundrymen who had strung up bloody shirts of Union men from every orchard bough and thus could not have been other than reprehensible to a great detective who had been a spy hunter during the Civil War. The Reno brothers and their infernal crew had been, according to the somewhat jaundiced view of Allan Pinkerton, only a type of scavenger such as flourish before, during, and after a war and must be exterminated.

From 1869 to 1871, Allan Pinkerton was at least partially but not totally incapacitated. His tongue was as thick as a lily bulb. He could not speak or make himself heard for a long time and then for a long time could do so only by a whir. He had to learn to crawl before he could walk.

He was partially cured by bathing in and drinking the salt waters of a recently discovered magical spring on the Pine River near St. Louis, Michigan, that which would be called a bugless town because of its manufacture of D.D.T., a brand of chemical signifying, as time would tell, death to all kinds of bugs even if it should mean the dismantling of earth of all its trees and all its flowers and all its fireflies and all its birds and death to babies at their mothers' breasts and death to mothers and fathers and husbands and lovers and sons, even as Pinkerton's agency in its own way would be increasingly during the long strike which was at hand and had already started to assert itself by various eruptions and rebellions an exterminator of bugs, labor buggers with buggy eyes, labor strikers lighting themselves up like human lightning bugs signaling to each other in the darkness of this mortal bog, firebugs.

The convalescence of the private eye Allan Pinkerton had been largely spent at his private estate, the Larches, about eighty miles to the south of the central office in Chicago and thus under cover from the not all-seeing public eye from whom had been concealed the extent of his impairment and the weakening of his eyes and the roaring of his eardrums as his sons carried out his orders for the overtaking of anarchic gangs of train robbers in a nation from which the poor people were awakening from the stupefying sloth of war to the realization that the products of the land and the land itself were being stolen from them by the owners of banks and trains and that the government in all its branches was still carrying on, as often in subterranean ways which were invisible as in ways which were visible, the war of money against the moneyless.

It was while he was at the Larches trying to recover his shattered strength that Allan Pinkerton, still reeling from the first blow, was dealt out, as by an unthinking fate hounding him as he might hound a wicked man or one adjudged to be wicked by the higher powers who were the guardians of democracy, a second blow when the city of Chicago had burned like a box of tinderwood which had been waiting for the flame, unfortunately not one traceable to any incendiary other than Mrs. O'Leary's cow—naturally, it was an Irish cow.

No sooner had Allan Pinkerton recovered from this second blow than he was struck a third blow by the renewed activities of the James brothers of Missouri, a mocking gang of cutthroats who had been raising hell all through the Civil War against the Northern cause and had no respect for any civilized cause and were deserving of hanging by a long rope if ever caught and all for the obvious cause that they had never learned to say their prayers at their mother's knees when they were young, had never been brought up in some old log cabin with lavender wisteria trailing at the door and smoke like lavender wisteria trailing from the chimney pot and an old fireplace where the mother rocked the baby with her foot and there were shadows thrown by flames upon a wall and there was a wall hanging of black velvet stitched in red yarn with some old morality or old mortality such as "Murder does not pay" or "An eye for an eye and a tooth for a tooth" to remind them that the way of he who transgresses against Pinkerton's is hard, very hard.

Pinkerton's operatives, although by necessity furtive and underhanded and masters of disguise as of every means of transport, were mantled by law which protected them from any true investigation of themselves in case one should take a step away from law into lawlessness.

While seeking to bag those wild ducks who were the James brothers and refusing to use their native gifts so that they might advance from the world of the horse to the world of the train like other sharers of the spoils of capitalism or, more accurately perhaps, the rewards, two of Pinkerton's duck hunters had been killed.

Allan Pinkerton, brooding in his ivory roundhouse, would have been willing to die to exterminate these amoral beetles skittering around in darkest Missouri and in all ways under cover of the amoral darkness, feeding upon the odoriferous body of capitalism.

According to Allan Pinkerton in 1878, his agents throughout the country at large had reported to him that the great strike which had begun to assert itself in the previous year had been caused by the Workingmen's party of the United States. "On every railroad that was held by lawless men, in every city where violence reigned . . . this accursed thing came to the surface."

To the agents of The Eye That Never Sleeps, the Workingmen's party which might have reasonably claimed that theirs were the eyes which never slept through the working day which began before the dawn and lasted until after the dusk had suddenly but surely revealed itself as the motivating force behind the strike of the Baltimore & Ohio Railroad.

Pinkerton's covert murderous expeditions against the Reno and the James brothers had kept his lethal plot in fine fettle, which, with variations according to time and circumstance, could be used over and over again and never miss, whatever its errors and miscalculations might be, his objective, which was that of bringing profit to his business.

Beyond comprehension by the head of the Pinkerton agency when he was at the Larches and his sons who carried out their duties according to a map which naturally could not locate every tree or bush which might seem to move in the fog like that opacity which masked men's criminal nature, the huddled horsemen moving as if the bushes moved, the horses whinnying or not whinnying, a pebble rattling or not rattling, would be the accruing legends which romanticized and idealized the James brothers as if these robber horsemen with their mockery of life were the American variants of Robin Hood and his merry men robbing the rich in order to give to the poor, handing out of the loot which they had lifted from stagecoach passengers or train passengers gold watches and chains and rings and earrings and pearl teardrops and in a period of raucous publicity when the so-called robber barons with their trains and banks and empires of public land, railroad depots and farmlands would be under great and increasing attack as if by men with arrows and not by red men but by white men who were red with blood.

The train which had departed in subzero cold in a January night in 1875, through darkest Missouri from Kansas City to Clay County under dark clouds and the moon like an eye with its lid half closed had not encountered, although it had traveled with its headlight not lighted and no lights within its cars and with its train whistle silenced to give no warning, any obstacle of a mortal kind.

Pinkerton's detectives—perhaps like an army, perhaps like a well-rehearsed lynch party or a combination of both in this distraught time when military tactics were being employed by private armies—had carried their army and navy revolvers in their hip pockets, although they wore no uniforms but business suits, probably ill cut, and might have passed for commercial travelers, book agents or Bible salesmen or buyers of mules to skin or horse buyers or parsons who were looking for new pulpits as they had jumped out of their old pulpits if anyone had wondered at their errand upon a night ride into the land of outlaws.

In a Kansas hotel room, they had gone over plans for the expedition with William Pinkerton, and every detail had been considered except that of reality itself, those wild contingencies which they had checked and checked upon and which they had taken into consideration having still contained obviously missing factors as might every map of a wilderness beyond man's grasp.

[1 3 1]

O N BOARD the train with the Pinkerton lynch party had been a Kansas City newspaper reporter who, a tall man wearing a long gray ulster—waterproof, fireproof, blood-proof—had been aflame with ambition to scoop his rivals with the possibly world-shaking news, even to those for whom Missouri was on the back side of the moon where it ought to stay, that while this continent was sleeping The Eye That Never Sleeps had been wide awake and that the mission which had been kept secret in every detail had been successfully completed—for while their horses had been sleeping in the hay a sleep so deep that Jesse James's pinto had never whinnied once to warn them and while these bloody corsairs with their cocksure ways were sleeping in their beds at Castle James with no inkling that, if they were not to be brought back alive in their red flannel shirts with their red bandannas which would no more wave over the fires of all the burning lakes of this Missouri hell where no traveler's life was safe, they would be brought back dead as dead pigeons. The guard of the Adams Express which was footing or should be footing the bill if Pinkerton delivered the goods according to their contract—a conductor who was or would be believed to have been a stool pigeon, no doubt of that lowly race of workingmen who had scores, diabolical scores of their own to settle with the Pinkerton's employment of secret but well-known spotters of railroad and streetcar conductors and other poor creatures all over this land so that he could never fly in freedom again and would be caged, or else if he was not acting out of revenge was still a very parochial sympathizer with the men of Castle James or was in their pay as a small sharer of their stock—had given warning that the bugs were coming down the line this very night.

This voluble conductor, whether he was the guilty party or not the guilty party, was later shot down by the James brothers when Allan Pinkerton, his sense of omniscience understandably shattered by the ambiguities of life and death in Missouri and elsewhere and by their strange interchangeableness in a world of camouflage where the eyes of an owl in a treetop might be the eyes of a man or a man might be an owl, had been certain that they had not been in hiding and that they were dead. Dead, deader, deadest.

Death may surely be, in matters so problematical as these in an age when the dead lived, a state made of as many comparative degrees as the state of happiness.

Perhaps some of the seemingly substantial, important, conservative citizens of Clay County who had called on William Pinkerton in a Kansas City hotel room in order that he might clear the way with them as to what the fearless agency men proposed to undertake for the benefit of all mankind in this country and elsewhere to ascertain that the night-riding horsemen would soon have seen their last sunset and their last dawn had also been duplicitous, speaking only out of one side of their mouths when they had seemed to give their tactfully beatific approval to the grave-digger shovel birds for the return of these erroneous creatures to the common clay where they belonged.

Its bell muted, the train had come with no sound but of pebbles rolling under the wheels, the black plumes filled with those incandescent sparks that might set roofs of sties for human pigs on fire along the way. Outside Castle James while the men with their guns cocked and their eyes peeled to a shining brightness had waited for their prey, two agents had stealthily tried to pry open the sash of a side window in the rear room of the old log cabin in the clearing without knowing that the blackness concealed the blackness quite as much as if there had been a black heart on a black card.

All suddenly and not included in their map of the contingencies, possibilities, unknown factors that might always assert themselves in any expedition such as this—but could even Pinkertons with much native wit and more experience in rustling up strange birds than most men have seen them all in a world which was not made entirely of logic but rather of the unpredictable following the unpredictable—an old black woman who had been the servant and friend of this nomadic family for years, and the Civil War and all its soldiers could be damned, had been aroused by that rattling of the window which could not possibly be caused by the rattling of the wind and had given as loud a squawk as the hen when the thieves try to break into the chicken coop where she is warming her egg. All the glass-smashers could do was what they had originally intended, smash the glass and toss in through the hole a bomb which they claimed afterward was not a real bomb, was only, one might say, a baby bomb and very appropriate for the work it had done, for it had killed a child who had been asleep in Castle James that night.

The bomb had been no great cannonball such as would be used in labor wars even up to the time of Debs as a contentious labor leader and long afterward. It had been only the kind of flare that had an iron base and a copper top with two curved wicks like insect whiskers and its insides stuffed with cotton dipped in the volatile oil which was turpentine, just such a heady glow of light as was employed by canvas-shrouded Wizard Oil wagons to light up the darkness in nights at the edges of country towns for the barker who had with him such exhibitions for the promotion of his products which were patent medicines, nepenthean cure-alls for all that ailed you or even more mortal woes and ills than ever ailed you in this life where very few or none escaped the bounds of old mortality, few or none achieving to immortality, a white male comedian in blackface dressed as a wild Zulu girl who had been captured by an American headhunter and brought back from darkest Africa to show that you could grow on your bald pate a bush as big as hers if you polished your head with his product, which was also good for drinking, for then it would burn like live coals in your stomach all winter long while your hair grew until the spring of the year and your long sleep was over and the birds were singing in your bush out of which the butterflies of resurrection would emerge.

Actually, this first bomb had been but the beginning of bombings of the interior of Castle James, the little white house with the green shutters where the James brothers had not been waiting to kill or be killed but the rest of the family—their mother and their stepfather, Dr. Samuel, and Archie Payton Samuel, the half brother who came not yet up to the hip of Frank and Jesse James—might as well have been ducks in a shooting gallery as was true of an old Negro mother and her little black baby who received a not fatal slice from the fragment of one of the four shells tossed by the Pinkerton window smashers.

The old-time Kentucky-born Dr. Samuel, who was interested in the healing arts and not the arts of war, would recall that after the first ball of saturated waste to which a lighted match had been applied had lighted up the entire space which had been nearly pitch black, the entire family had rushed into the kitchen, where he and his wife had picked up tobacco sticks and begun rolling the blazing ball toward the hearth with the object of getting it into the fireplace before it could set the house on fire. Suddenly through the window had come another bomb of greater size. "The second fireball," in his words, "was not like the first, though it looked like that one—it was a bombshell. It was thrown into the room while the fireball was still blazing. It was light enough in the room for any person not over thirty yards off to have distinguished our faces. The detectives were not thirty feet distant." The tobacco sticks which they had used to push the fireball off the floor were still in their hands but were too light to move this second shell. "I then got the shovel and began to push it toward the hearth, and just as I had succeeded, the shell exploded. It seemed to me all at once that the room grew black as night. I was blown against the ceiling and heard a tremendous report."

The right arm of the James brothers' mother, Mrs. Zeralda Samuel, had been so badly mangled that it would have to be cut off, and in the side of their little half brother Archie Payton Samuel there had been torn a hole so wide that birds could have flown through it.

Little Archie had died before dawn, after suffering the most frightful agony during the long night, in which Dr. Samuel and the old black woman who had found love and shelter with this family had tried to save the little boy's life and had tried, without avail, to save the right arm of the bereft Mrs. Samuel, whose left arm would remain the arm with the hand which she extended in greeting to the mourners for Little Archie, who had done to no one any harm and who would be mourned by many who had not known him when he was alive but would know him when he was dead and was a child who could not die, who came in many dreams of many men and women and was seen walking along the ground.

Three days after this nocturnal raid about which much would remain unknown—the names of the leaders of the posse and whether they included, as would be denied time and again, William and Robert Pinkerton, the sons acting in their father's place the night the child was killed like a dirty dog—the frozen ground, hard as iron, was dug up by the man with the spade for the planting of Little Archie, who was remembered to have died in the midst of his bleeding and of whom the Kansas City newspaper hound reported that as the coffin was lowered with the body of Little Archie inside, the curses which were hurled at the Pinkertons were both loud and deep.

Enraged that he should now be considered what might be called a lynch artist and depicted as Little Archie's murderer, Allan Pinkerton had written to his son Robert in New York that the mother of the James brothers, Mrs. Zeralda Samuel, had met with a merited and fearful accident. No doubt to him she deserved her fate as the bloody mare who had foaled this bloody brood.

[1 3 2]

DENIAL OF RESPONSIBILITY for the carnage at Castle James, failure also to capture the James brothers and thus unable to produce their dead bodies as evidence, had been made by the great detective, who had not been able to collect his reward from his employers, who were the Western Express, as he had falsely but honestly believed although he would come increasingly to question in his own heart whether the James brothers were dead or alive or, if dead, might still come riding up from their graves to wreak their vengeance upon him.

It was rumored that at the Larches, which he had designed to be his fortress, he had slept with his gun at his side. And how could he not have spent many sleepless nights with at least one eye cocked open and not because of Simeon, the hanged man dancing like the tattoo of the rain upon the roof, not because of the ghost of Little Archie, not because of the sound of the wind against the window glass, but because of his fear of the revenge which might be wreaked upon him in retribution for the role played by the Pinkertons in the deaths of the Molly Maguires, two by two dancing in the air?

But perhaps, of course, conscience took no toll even in this last case through which Allan Pinkerton would live to see the final wind-up, the tying of the knots around these rebels' throats, the apparent end which was never the end.

THE LARCHES, where Allan Pinkerton spent most of his time while attempting to restore the tree of life branching through his body, was a better refuge for him than his Chicago home and office would have been. According to the reminiscences of an old uncle of the James brothers who ran a country store and spoke out only when he knew that the brothers were dead, Jesse James had spent four months incognito in Chicago shadowing the Pinkerton agency—for in revenge for Little Archie's death and his mother's mutilation, her forever bleeding arm, he had been determined to shoot Allan Pinkerton as full of holes as an old tree pecked upon by a thousand woodpeckers—indeed, had had Pinkerton's son many times in sight but had wanted the father and not the son and also to make sure that Pinkerton knew who his executioner was, that Jesse was not a dead man, that he was Little Archie's brother coming to dispatch him to hell and not to heaven where Little Archie was.

Unfortunately, although he had seen the old man passing many times, his prey had not given him the five minutes he needed in order to pronounce damnation upon his soul and maybe—who knew of what greater flagrance than that of which the sometimes chivalric outlaw was capable?

The Missouri Democrats had even offered amnesty to the James brothers for all the crimes they had committed before and during the Civil War if only they would give themselves up alive for a fair trail—for the Democrats' sympathies were obviously for the Jameses and not for the great god Pinkerton who was of the G.O.P., God's Own Party. They had not come out of their hiding place. They had had no more faith in the Democrats, it would seem, than in the Republicans.

To add to Allan Pinkerton's woes, a Pinkerton's man who had been in the Missouri raid had been fired for a theft and had threatened, unless he was paid off in the currency manufactured by the United States Treasury, to report to the whole world a great secret regarding the nocturnal train ride in the old Hoosier mossbank land when the Reno brothers were strung up on the bloody hangman's tree in the state pen at New Albany where not only murder but mayhem had occurred. Was it possible that not only the tool of lynch had been designed by the former tool designer but that he had acted with the acquiescence of the pillars of state of Clay County and with only some variations had used it again in the aborted attempt to put an end to the James brothers, who, if all went well, should have been as easily put out of this world and sent to the next world as clay ducks in a Chicago shooting gallery might be shot down?

Upon the walls of the estate that had been purchased by Allan Pinkerton from the Illinois Central Railroad, uniformed sentinels with great Gatling machine guns were always on watch with spyglasses and searchlights by which to detect and illuminate any mysterious traveler, any lone horseman or bunches of lone horsemen coming along the roads from any direction at a time when lone horsemen, if they wanted to survive, should always have bound themselves into some kind of cooperative unity or corporation or trust just like the men who had stolen and were stealing the nation blind.

There were four separate entrances guarded by Pinkerton's private soldiers in uniform. There were magnificently uniformed blackamoors waiting to take the coats and hats and canes of important visitors when they came through the villa's door, and they were such honest men that they handed them their coats and hats and canes again when they were going out. The black men wore silver buttons on their uniforms and were as deferential as if they had all worked at some time on Pullman's sleeping cars.

The estate in the midst of the prairie undulating with grasses and grains like an inland sea pulled by the same moon which pulled the tidal waves was rich with pasturelands for prize cattle, longhorns and shorthorns, poultry yards for prize Brahmans, pasturelands for beautiful horses, stallions and mares and foals, a horse-race track, flowering meadows and fields of grain and formal gardens with lily ponds and fishing streams and spreads of orchards of apple and peach and pear and cherry trees with never a hangman's tree among them, so far as was known, never a cherry tree dripping not with cherries but with blood, and with a private graveyard for the burial of the Pinkerton family's pet animals, none guilty of sedition against the higher powers, none guilty of individual and mass murder such as those which were engaged in or countenanced by coal and steel and iron barons, none unlike their human owners guilty of any greater crime than that of the cat which had caught the early bird which had caught the early worm when it was out too early in the morning for its health's sake.

Dropping away from the Illinois Central Railroad depot at Kankakee where was still the unspoiled marshland which was the feeding ground of thousands of wild ducks, and wild ducks and wild geese honking like the honkings of locomotives in the sky as they passed over the Larches were following a less erratic course than that of the Illinois Central Railroad which could be used by Allan Pinkerton for transport by boxcars of horses, cattle, farm machinery, building material, whatever his heart desired for this peaceful refuge near the Illinois Central depot at nearby Onarga in the midst of some of the richest prairie land there ever was and one cleared of Lo, the poor Indian, who had moved through reeds and grasses so tall that he was not seen and had not disturbed the nest of a bird among the reeds, the undulating waves of grass and grain which were punctuated here and there occasionally by windbreaks of trees reaching on and on to the ever-shifting horizon world without end until, having built his white villa and his barns and his granaries and his stables, he had determined to reproduce the romantic, ever-shadowed atmosphere of the great properties he had seen in Scotland through the gates on the wrong side of the grillwork when he was the tramp cooper with a price upon his head and had quickly repaired the almost treeless vista by bringing in eighty-five thousand stately larches.

The first shipment of eighty-five thousand larches in their sapling state which had survived the danger of the North Atlantic and long churning through heavy seas had been wrapped in such thin burlap shrouds that they had frozen to death while waiting for shipment on the ice-covered New York docks. The Pinkerton sleuth who had been supposed to keep his eye on them and never once let them out of his eye had left them unsheltered during the long night of rain and storm and had spent his night in a dockside saloon on Jane Street. Obviously, the man had no backbone and was the kind who, if he could not protect trees, from Jack Frost or any other murderer, should not be trusted with any errand for the Pinkerton agency again.

He had been fired and a second cargo of eighty-five thousand larches had been shipped over the waters and then by boxcars to Chicago and then to the station at Onarga and, very similar to the larches in American swamps but probably not found in such large numbers, had been planted in eighty-five thousand holes in the ground for their qualities of durable growth and for their needlelike leaves borne in whorling clusters at the ends of short spurs, the needles and cones which would carpet the ground of the place which had been called the Larches even before the larches had arrived.

Probably the bullet-headed Allan Pinkerton was essentially unchanging, it would be hazarded, and was unaware of paradoxes in his own nature although he was schooled in seeing, of course, the paradoxes in other men, and undoubtedly not merely those who were anarchists with bombs, also those who were capitalists with bombs and were plotting for the increase of that inept mass anarchy by which the great leviathan of capitalism increased its illegal powers. Otherwise, he would have been utterly naïve and would have remained, little doubt, the cooper of small coops in a small town only dreaming that he might become a lord, according to the retrospective evaluations of some of the disappointed migratory people for whom America had seemed a land of promise but which was also covered with such thickness of ice that bonfires of protests although brightly burning for a while would never seem to burn away the ice, the great ice lakes and escarpments and pinnacles of a self-justifying capitalism.

A certain duplicity had always been that of this complex detective. And no doubt he was capable of capturing a larcenist because there was a larcenist in his nature, a counterfeiter because there was a counterfeiter in him, a spy because there was a spy in him, a murderer because there was a murderer in him, according to those who were not his admirers.

[1 3 3]

In St. Louis, Missouri, in January 1861, when Debs in Terre Haute was starting out to school with his little red cap and little red book by which he was learning to spell god, the word that was dog spelled backward, the American Miners' Association had been born as a benevolent fraternal association with ideals widely different from those of the detective who was the builder of the Larches.

Although the American Miners' Association had been short-lived, the sentiments in its songs had prevailed and grown in spite of the murderous outrages of the Civil War in which poor men had worn Mr. Lincoln's dog tags or, if they had rebelled, had been the very ones who were most likely to become labor agitators in the continuing Civil War of the rich against the poor. But utterly peaceful had been the intention of the miners' union, a fraternal outfit founded on benevolence, charity of man for man, mutual help in time of need. "Step by step the longest march / Can be won, can be won; / Single stones will form an arch / One by one . . . / Drops of water turn a mill, / Singly none, singly none."

In 1888, when Allan Pinkerton had long since gone to his Maker and when his agency had committed great crimes of which he had not lived to see the outcome, Debs had written in *The Locomotive Firemen's Magazine* that he did not expect by this notice of the crimes to increase the area of their notoriety. There were many Napoleons of crime. When any of these gilded, colossal scoundrels engaged in crime, they went for all that was in sight.

They shake down fortunes as earthquakes do buildings, and being educated, they are able to cover up their tracks. As crime increased, Pinkerton's thrived. . . . Who are these bloody, murderous Pinkertons? What of their character? What of their antecedents? Only

God and the Pinkerton Agency know. They come as carrion crows come to a carcass. They go as bloodhounds go into a chase.

In earlier days Debs had likened cutthroats to Apaches waiting on the rocks to descend on stagecoach travelers or lone horsemen or foot travelers—but he had long ago come to recognize that the thieves of the nation's treasures were men whose capacity for theft included the theft of mountains which they carried away as lightly as if they had been bags upon the backs of bindle stiffs or stones in a wagon. This nation had been built on wheels, as any observer knew when he watched it being carted away by the great tycoons who were the czars of American rails, mines, mills.

To *The Locomotive Firemen's Magazine,* under its headlight from which streamed the intellectual radiance of an editor who had been schooled from his infancy upward in a variety of utopian thoughts, the words if not the deeds by which they should be made real, these Pinkerton marauders were not merely sporadic bands but in ways not simple were intricately organized and interwoven with capitalists who were the coopers and the tinners and the mousetrap salesmen and the ironmongers, the blacksmiths who had gone astray, had stepped aside from the path of virtue just as the great detective had.

According to *The Locomotive Firemen's Magazine,* right in the midst of its seemingly endless business of attempting to resurrect the dead souls of American workmen, those who were stirring, those who refused to act as if they were corpses beyond the power of action or will as they refused also to play the role of opossums treed by hunters, pretending to be a part of the surrounding canopy of leaves, a role very difficult to play when the trees were bare,

> They are beetle-browed ruffians who have no more regard for the welfare of society than would be accorded to the same number of vagabond dogs. The list of cold-blooded murders these wretches have perpetuated horrifies all right-thinking men and has earned for them an eternal night of ignominy. . . . When in slave times the bloodhounds were put in pursuit of the slave fleeing for liberty, who thought of denouncing the hounds?

Behind these monsters were monsters still more inhuman than the Pinkertons, and these were the creatures put into power by the vote of the workingmen.

The Locomotive Firemen's Magazine with Debs as pilot may be likened to a principle of light seeking its way through the smog, fog, and darkness provided by the capitalistic entrepreneurs who had been themselves so often the children of the darkness but had remained in the darkness as those who wished to light no way to any better world of now for the weak and the poor, the men whose gift from God did not include personal survival unless in terms of their tendency to procreate in the midst of most barren circumstances and thus by their numbers provide an endless labor supply, the lowliest creatures of the rails, the mills which were not only mills but were crematories where men were pressed literally into thin sheets of steel for walls on which one could see the shadows of the cremated men who had fallen into the burning pit, the coal mines where children who were the slate pickers died of the diseases of senility at the age of eight if they, poor little dwarves very much like human toads who had lived in darkness under the ground and could not see the light, were fortunate or unfortunate enough to live that long.

When *The Locomotive Firemen's Magazine* was under great threat because of the long railroad strikes preceding and running tantamount with the plot of Pinkerton's against labor agitators and the so-called Molly Maguires, when Debs was a stripling trying to organize his chapter and at a time when there might be perhaps only one member present at a meeting and that was himself who certainly was easy to organize as he was all of one piece, his head receiving the messages of his heart and his heart the messages of his head and his entire arterial system at work with the dream of man's brotherhood with man in a social and economic sense which was for the salvation of the species which was money and should not be extinguished by any form of government, however sanctified by beatitudes upon its own virtuous self detached from the millions and millions of selves constituting the human race, it was probably impossible for the fragile funerary order to take an active part in the cruel labor war which was going on with the slaughter of the innocents increasing at every hand.

The lists of the railroad accidents which *The Locomotive Firemen's Magazine* carried were not those caused by Apaches, James brothers, Younger brothers, recalcitrant engineers, or railroad strikers but those caused by the capitalistic negligence of men and machines which was the same in times of peace as in times of war. There was within its pages almost audible lament for every known individual or workman or passenger as for every unknown tramp killed along a road, just as there would be until the end.

Clara Uply, train smasher, was the way a lady registered herself at a hotel. A telegrapher in a Pennsylvania railroad office, she had caused by negligence of one of her duties the collision of two trains—but no one had accused her of being in cahoots with the labor strikers who were then running loose or of being a female Molly Maguire.

In March 1877, *The Locomotive Firemen's Magazine* reported that the followers of Confucius had torn up the railway of China, six miles long. "The heathen Chinee will make a failure trying to butt the locomotive."

In August 1877, the whole country had been thrown into wild confusion by what was considered the greatest strike then known, the railroad corporations having from time to time reduced the pay to their employees who now starved. The president of the United States was sending troops to protect the railroad property as naturally he would, and Jay Gould was predicting that a monarchy would soon rule over this country.

The Locomotive Firemen's Magazine asked, in a way that was intended to elicit response,

> What does it mean? What can it mean save this: Let the Republic perish; better the downfall of freedom than the loss of any of my ill-gotten but nonetheless precious money? . . . To the great majority of the American people that declaration of the impotent railroad monarch was more repulsive than Shylock's "I would my daughter were dead at my feet and the jewels in her ear! Would she were hearsed at my foot, and the ducats in her coffin."

[1 3 4]

FAMILIES OF THE IMPRISONED railroad strikers in Indianapolis had been left in a nearly destitute condition, *The Locomotive Firemen's Magazine* with Debs at the helm had reported in September when strikers or their loved ones who had died would have no coffins but those of paupers.

Employees of the Bee Line had scraped together sixty-four dollars and twenty-four cents and out of this had given money for bread to four families.

What were men striking for that some were willing to die in opposition to corporations with their increasing powers, the railroad owners who set the terminal station for the workman's life ruling that the hours of labor should be as long as the hours of life should be short? What, indeed, were the infantile labor unions in those early days trying to steal?

They were trying to steal sixteen hours out of twenty-four—eight for their day of work should have left eight for their ordinary pursuits such as eating, visiting with their loved ones, going to church if they were church-goers, tossing horseshoes if they had a village green on which to do so, dig-ging up potatoes from their gardens, if they had gardens; eight for sleep in which to try to renew their ever-waning strength. Overwork was cutting many lives short, although overwork was only one of many factors discour-aging longevity. They were trying to steal time. They were trying to steal life.

The Locomotive Firemen's Magazine had pointed out quite simply, as a truth which should be beyond the shadow of a doubt—"Skilled labor has built up the country. In the name of all that is sacred, let the laws be so framed that soul-less corporations cannot starve it to death nor drive it out of the land."

In view of the tragic ground of this new Civil War when the Gatling guns were being turned on strikers in numerous cities and towns and vil-lages, there was comic relief to be found by locomotive firemen in the inter-view of a local engineer from the Baltimore & Ohio Railroad with a newspaper reporter in Detroit. The locomotive engineer showed himself to be a folklorist in the grand American style.

He had run the last train over the road which had been allowed to pass the strikers. All the train officials had been heavily armed and many of the passengers also. "We expected that the strikers would displace a rail, let us through a bridge, or switch us into some distant gravel pit, and just before we left the station I kissed my wife and told her where she would find the sum of $38,000 which I had buried in the garden."

His fireman, feeling that he would not live much longer, had confessed to him that he was the abductor of little Charley Ross and that he had once murdered a man in Missouri. The name of the fireman was Tom Colliers.

The conductor, also prepared for death, had returned to the railroad the $2,558,654.13 which he had knocked down during his connection with the road, and so he had humbly asked forgiveness. He was very much disap-pointed that he had not invested his share of the plunder in the founding of an orphan asylum. He owned up to having killed an old woman or two but had forgotten their names or whether they struggled very hard when he was choking them. The pale-faced young reporter, busily taking notes on these exploits, had been planning to scoop the *Free Press* stone blind.

The description of the bandits could seem an exaggeration but was all too near the reality of this time of railroad and mining strikes except to some of those old folks who managed to live out their idyllic lives far away from trains and mills and mines, had no business but to drive the old cow and the calves through the pasture gates just when the cow moon and the calf stars were coming out through their pasture gates into the fields at night, and celebrated no May Day but on soap-making day the rose petals were mixed with the ashes in the pot.

As to these bad men, the engineer had on one side of him a Derringer, a revolver on the other, a musket loaded with one hundred seventeen buck-shots strapped on his back. The fireman had on him four revolvers and six one-pound cans of glycerine.

The train had gone full speed at forty miles an hour, whizzing through cuts, dashing past farmhouses and across highways, when far ahead, in the dim gleam of the headlight, two men were spotted on the track. The engineer had thought that he should put all steam on, but the fireman had entreated him to confess that he had been hiding the Bender family in the bedroom. There was something in the fireman's hand—and what was it but a whiskey bottle?

He had wanted to ride seven miles down the track to the next station for an old jackknife and a drink of half a bottle of whiskey, the best he had ever tasted—with apparently total disregard of the oath of temperance he had had to swear if he was a member of the Brotherhood of Locomotive Firemen and not just the kind of drunk who in a dream might have stepped off the footboard when the train was running or might have provided a dinner for crows at a time when the bodies of men were the meat for crows and in a strictly literal sense.

The Anti–Horse Thief Association, in 1877, had come around to the belief that to string a horse thief up in places where the government was powerless to act was justifiable. Thus no doubt Pinkerton and his employers had been justified by advocacy of lynch law as that which should reign supreme in regions where the population sympathized with the condemned.

The two-year-old *Locomotive Firemen's Magazine* had expressed some memory of a dream of Eden which might be restored by the frail but continuing brotherhood—the hope that this might come through the following of a natural law which had held true to its course since the Creation. The attitude expressed toward religion was not that of an orthodox theology but was rather that of a loosely woven humanistic and humanitarian socialism.

When Adam was asleep in the Garden of Eden, perhaps dreaming a long wish for companionship, God had known his dreams when He said,

"It is not good for him to be alone." He had made Adam a helpmeet who was poor Eve and by so doing had aroused the disapproval and disappointment of Susan Bee in her Bonnet Anthony:

> From that time on, everything in nature had been governed by one law of association. Even the inhabitants of the seas, from Him who maketh the great deep to boil like a pot, to the smallest living creature whose native element is water, are formed for association. . . .
>
> Union in action and effect for the accomplishment of this work is everywhere and at all times marking the conduct of men, and history teaches us that no great and lasting good comes without association.

[1 3 5]

DEBS FROM THE BEGINNING of his labor activities had been aware of the small-time cockroach capitalists who fed upon the ignorant workman in regions of such poverty and ignorance of human rights that they might as well have been upon some other planet so far as working hours were concern. The line between the nonunionized workingman and the unionized workingman was almost illusory as the specter of unemployment faced both.

From his fortress at the Larches, Allan Pinkerton had looked for business with which to support his empire with his arms like those of an octopus reaching out to snap up whatever rebels there were against the military establishment which was now upholding the united corporate powers.

Keeping charge of every expense in a time of great strikes against the coalfields which had brought sufferings to miners through reductions in pay to the extent that the employed starved as if they were the unemployed and as a result were in a worse condition by far than those who slept with mice in haystacks or in old boxcars long since derailed on nowhere tracks, Allan Pinkerton had wondered how he could create a bonanza by which to keep his agency from going under. What better than to go where murder was, to decrease murder in the long term by increasing it in the short term for the general good, by stamping out rebels, revolutionaries, labor agitators in relation to a corporation with a large purse.

On May 17, 1872, he had written to the Pinkerton detective George

Bangs with the command that he should call on Franklin Benjamin Gowen, president of the Reading Railroad, to suggest to him one thing or another which might seem so feasible to him that he would give work to the agency.

Gowen, although he represented corporations of which the purse was lean when it came to the needs of railroad and mining hands, could always provide an ample expense account for the great detective whose interest necessarily was not the feeding of poor men like the raggedy quail in a barren world but in shooting them down, in secrecy if possible—and if not possible, then with great Gatling guns, as would be seen.

Those now worthy of less consideration than the lowest beasts, whether horned or unhorned, were the so-called Molly Maguires, whom Pinkerton operatives identified as a secret order of revolutionary Irishmen setting fire to coal and wood, the most inflammable material there was, burning up coal tipplers and coal yards and wooden rails around Pottsville, Pennsylvania, until it seemed to give off a permanent glow. As it was Pinkerton's operatives who first unearthed this secret gang of terrorists who were the Molly Maguires, as there was no organization by that name until the detectives discovered that there was such a spectral group, there were speculations always upon the possibility that they were the invention of the fertile brain which had provided the agents to discover them.

Actually, the men who were labeled Molly Maguires were members of the Ancient Order of Hibernians, a mutual-aid society with branches upon both sides of the Atlantic and thus many in America with the green of the auld sod from which these people had come as transplants in search of survival, just as Allan Pinkerton had come. The Ancient Order of Hibernians, probably not a Marxist among them but many a Marist, had been organized for raising funds for the aged, the sick, the blind, the deaf, the dumb.

As to the burial of the dead, they were sometimes provided free graves in the bottoms of the inefficiently operated coal mines, and so they were spared the expense of hearse and hearse driver and horse to carry them to Catholic graveyards, there to wait for their transplantation from earth to fields of paradise on some grand day of a universal or almost universal awakening.

They had come to America because of the potato famines when, as noted by Robert Owen, priests had squirted holy water on potato fields with prayers for the increase of potato crops which had failed in a season of great, sunless cold and which were considered now a sacred plant providing the very staff of life in a country where there was no grain for bread and no land upon which to grow the grain, this land being honeycombed with many waters where were eyes of water birds like the souls of the Irish dead staring from bogs through perpetual fogs of that mystery with which and by which the Irish lived and lived even when they died. They could take many shapes. How easily a bug could turn into a bear. The coal rings, with the help of Pinkerton's, had made of the Molly Maguires a bugbear with which to frighten the countryside. They were the seven Gabriel hounds or whistlers who never broke rank and whose whistle could sometimes be heard as they cut through clouds and waters or sped along the ground in pursuit of birds which had fallen or were falling to earth.

The potato, when first introduced into Ireland, had been feared as first cousin to the deadly nightshade, as that inducing sleep and dreams, even as Bronson Alcott in America thought its dream-inducing power was because of its being a downward-pointing vegetable, a seeker after the darkness of Hades and not the sunlight. The poor potato Irish, some of these children of the earth with eyes so small and blind that they were like potato eyes which could not see the light, had been subjected to such wholesale uprootings by the diabolical agents of cruel landlords that they had died by carloads and there was not room in graveyards for them, no place to shovel them under for their storage place until their graves should open when angels or angel dogs blew their trumpets and the earth gave up its dead, and so they had been carried out to sea in old burlap bags and had been cast into the sea to the sound of the mournful harp, prayers for the souls of the dead who should be seen when the sea gave up its dead—as every day it did. In Ireland, the living mixed with the dead and dined at the same table and slept in the same bed. They had their fellowship.

[1 3 6]

To ALLAN PINKERTON with his dependency upon murder for his livelihood and the support of the Larches and fourteen mouths to feed, what worse thing could there be than a period of such absolute, such halcyon and unnerving calm that a socialist utopia might have arrived all suddenly in the coal barrens and not a spider should weave a web for the catching of a fly, as now when the detective spider was weaving his web for those poor flies.

These Molly Maguires were, as he had written to Bangs of his eastern bureau, a species of thugs such as had operated in India. Theirs had been the religion of murder by which they chose their victims, arranged to strike against the upholders of law and order, and were sworn to divulge nothing even if brought to the stake. "They are bound to stick by their oath and carry out their revenge. He who they think does a wrong is marked out, and he must die."

From his long experience in the business of detecting real or imaginary crime, Allan Pinkerton could place no faith in the jury system, his fear being always that there might be a plant in the jury, a Molly Maguire in disguise, a dissenting voice.

> It is impossible to believe that a jury in the mining districts would not give a verdict of guilty against the M.M.'s should they be brought to trial, but I believe that someone on the jury would hang on and get the guilty men to escape. The only way then to pursue them as I see it is to treat them as the Renos were treated in Indiana. After they were done away with the people improved wonderfully and Seymour is quite a town.

And thus it may be seen that he was seeking to repeat in Pennsylvania the road show he had played with such success in Indiana and elsewhere that it seemed to him like an old tool which, perhaps never resting, he could use again with just such innovations as were required by a different theater of circumstance.

Why, however, did he want to make sure that all the people would see this carnage? No doubt he wanted to teach the lesson that murder did not pay. "It is awful to see men doomed to death—it is horrible." He was not anxious, however, that the lynch mob should be identified and rounded up both as to the actual participants and their instigator, the prompter who cued them at every juncture from behind the red curtain.

Secrecy was necessary for the carrying out of the penitential punitive expedition in the land of the Molly Maguires, many of whom were sons of fathers who had been born in Ireland or who themselves had come from Ireland to America in steerage boats where they were packed more closely than steers and were less valuable than larches, and so the ex-Chartist had advised that his Philadelphia agent and Robert Pinkerton should get up an organization as soon as possible and that when they were ready for action they should pounce upon the M.M.'s when they were in full blast, take the fearful responsibility and disperse.

If Mr. Gowen understood what had occurred in view of the hazards necessarily accompanying such an undertaking and the fact that they might be imprisoned, bail hay would be provided for the release of the vigilante horsemen about whose possible ride there were already rumors running like wildfire through the mountains as there were notices in newspapers, whether to warn the Molly Maguires of their approaching doom or warn the horsemen that the rocks had eyes and the rocks had ears.

[1 3 7]

Aᴌʟᴀɴ Pɪɴᴋᴇʀᴛᴏɴ was a believer in phrenology, the taking of the measurements of a man's head by which to judge what were his native gifts or their lack. His ways of reassuring men were as punctual as those of an undertaker who could never look at a stranger without automatically, in his mind's eye, measuring him for his coffin and a suit of clothes—only the front of a suit for the poor as the dead were not expected to get up out of their graves and walk although they often did. He had to choose a master of disguise to send into the disputed anthracite regions of Pennsylvania in search of those Molly Maguires, who, the most revolutionary agitators against the establishment which was the union of industrial powers with the bureaucracies of the federal government, were responding to coffin notices by pinning up coffin notices of their own in all kinds of public or out-of-the-way places as if in warning against those encroaching upon human rights as steadily as if the polar ice cap should suddenly be unpinned with death to all who could not move fast enough to escape the icy escarpments and seas of ice devised by capitalists to be for poor men an age of ice.

As for the poor who had no shelter and no place and whose bones should rattle on naked tree boughs, they should wait for the spring which might come to others but never to themselves to whom had been given no promissory note other than that which might or might not be honored when this old world itself folded up shop, struck off, lay down, and there should be a highly problematical new world with streets of gold for the capitalists and beds of straw for the bricklayers, just as before, nothing changed.

About four years after what was erroneously called, in the Horatio Alger, Jr., sense, success, the great detective would recall his vision of the ideal operator who, as he could not foresee, for he had no crystal globe in which to spot the crack which was only his own cracked eyeball staring back at him through mists and fogs of human stupidity and shortsighted-ness, was one of the strangest men who ever crossed the stage of American labor history, not only in this long road show which would result in the spectacular hangings of the so-called Molly Maguires but almost thirty years later, when Allan Pinkerton had gone through the pearly gates, when this great detective employed a stooge or numerous stooges to do murders which would be pinned on the revolutionary miner heads in Denver, Big Bill Haywood and Charles H. Moyer and Charles A. Pettibone, when Debs would risk for their salvation his life which he had risked so many times that it could be accurately described as a life which was a risk.

For his choice of the hunter after the Mollies, Allan Pinkerton had not relied upon wigs, glue pots, or paint pots to make him presentable although he had taken into his account the size of the man's brain box, hands, feet, complexion. The man who would answer to his specifications as the hunter of the Mollies not only as to the external but as to the internal measure-ments must be no ordinary man.

"He must be," he had written to his son Robert at the eastern branch, "an Irishman and a Catholic, as only this class of person can find admission to the Molly Maguires. My detective should become, to all intents and pur-poses, one of the order, and continue so while he remains in the case before us. He should be hardy, tough and capable of laboring, in season and out of season, to accomplish unknown to those about him a single absorbing subject."

To this portrait, Robert Pinkerton had added some brush strokes of his own—"The man had to feel that he was serving his church, his God, his race and his country; otherwise it would be impossible to get anyone to undertake a work which involved death by assassination."

[1 3 8]

ALTHOUGH JAMES McPARLAN was the one agent who could come into the limelight, yet there had been numerous James McParlans who had left no signs of their footprints in sand or water, just as there were no organizations known as the Molly Maguires, their only order having been that of the Ancient Order of Hibernians who had generally opposed the British Crown and in the Pennsylvania mountains were opposed to the rule of coal miners by the owners of mines which were owned in large part not only by American kings of finance but by British capitalists who were clippers of their coupons in Mayfair and other regal environments very different from the cinder yards where the exiled Irish starved and played their harps and sang in praise of that greatest of all in the roster of kings who was "King Coal! He's the miracle maker, / King Coal! He's the wilderness breaker! / The dreamer—the universe waker—King Coal! . . ."

ALLAN PINKERTON, his big western hat sheltering his face with a permanent shadow, had been riding along on a trolley car in Chicago on his way from his Monroe Street residence when, praise be to all those diabolical forces which were released in the war of the rich men against the poor, he had spotted the man who was that spotter who would bring the Mollies into the spotlight of the nation's attention while throwing upon all labor strikers the suspicion that they were under the influence of the Mollies and deserved no more mollycoddling than the Mollies deserved for their killing the bosses of coal mines and rails and the bureaucrats who were the enactors of an imperial ownership.

James McParlan, aged twenty-nine, had come from Ulster County, Ireland, about a year before Allan Pinkerton had taken him off the streetcar. He had worked as a spotter since the Chicago fire, which had wiped out the wooden coop in which he had operated a saloon which, unlike many saloon keepers, he had not contrived to open again along the lakeshore where the dispossessed and homeless poor had spent their last dimes for foam in which to drown their grief over the property losses which had seldom been theirs in any reality other than imagination.

A man of many employments, something of a drifter himself before he was invited to call at Allan Pinkerton's home, James McParlan had led a busy life as a clerk in a grocery store, a teamster driving an old workhorse about whose care one would suppose he had little or no concern as teamsters were well known for their curses of old horses they worked to the bone even as old coal miners were old workhorses for whom, upon their retirement, no pasturelands were reserved, a driver of a meat wagon filled with just such carcasses of sheep and lambs and cows and calves as old workers should be in capitalistic slaughterhouses, a deckhand and a lumberman and a private coachman.

When told what his new job would be and was given assurance that he would continue to be the spotter in Chicago if he did not want to go to Pennsylvania, he had chosen the game in which all the cards in his pack would be deuces and there would be nothing in the Mollies' pack but those twos of clubs which signify death—death and no second game.

McParlan's hair was red, and he did not comb it for at least ten days so that it would have a bushy look. He also did not go to the barber to have his face shaved nor did he try to do his own shaving with an apple knife, so there grew around his lips and upon his chin a thin, straggling red stubble.

He had not a spare inch of flesh on his tall, lanky frame. He wore old, battered clothes stained by the dust of the road, old brogans with blind eyelets, broken strings, an old felt hat such as might have been a nest for naïve field mice who did not sense that he was a man with the mind of a mousetrap, and he carried as his only luggage just the kind of old carpetbag which had given the carpetbaggers their names as those postbellum Northern adventurers who, carrying all their possessions in carpetbags when they went into the South, had carried away, by exploitation of chaotic conditions, ownership of rails, banks, public offices, plantations, lands, and their natural treasures—all that was above the earth, all that was under the earth, all that was hidden but might someday appear.

His true identity concealed, James McParlan had become the roughneck James McKenna who, as Irish as Paddy's Pup, had appeared as a drifter in the Pennsylvania coal patches where he had let it be known in every pig's-feet bar that he was on the lam—that he had gotten into a little trouble in Buffalo—had been forced to do a disappearing act because of a little thing called murder—the charge that he had killed a man.

Thus the first thing that this mysterious traveler had done in his quest for communication with the murderous Molly Maguires upon whom he would pin, according to his correspondence with Pinkerton's agency, coffin notices—much as if one bored an iron nail into the bark of a tree in order to prevent its further growth—was fly from charges of old murders whose mysteries had never been solved and which had been committed long before his arrival and charges of others which would be committed during the two and one half years before his work was completed. His success was admired by many law-abiding citizens who feared that they might be murdered in their beds although they might inhabit regions not known to be frequented by Mollies.

If James McParlan had killed a man in order to make the murder real, to give to the murdered man an embodiment not merely of his sterile imagination—that fact could not be established in a land of so many vast agrarian and industrial upheavals, so many and violent changes that perhaps only a local sheriff with one eye closed would look for the murderer of any of the thousands of homeless tramps, roustabouts, wanderers who suffered, for one reason or another, not only loss of limb but loss of life and whose absence from society seemed to make no dent upon the numbers of the unemployed and whose disembodied heads, if gathered together and laid side by side, row by row, could have been a crop of bloody murders reaching to the horizon's end where the red of the sunset also bled.

These poor lumps of coal dust and cinders and slag Debs with all his compassion about him would someday describe as the rude, crude, untutored children of nature who had protected themselves against their exploiters as best they could and whose culture, it should be pointed out, was not that of the written word, for they in their native Ireland had rarely had their noses between the pages of a book, even as those who had been born in America had almost never gone to any school and had not been scholars in the little red schoolhouse and had never had their violent ways tempered by exposure to the heroic or tender sympathies of McGuffey's little red-backed readers although near Brownsville had been the birthplace of William McGuffey to whom someday, in an unforeseeable future, would be erected by Henry Ford a monument to mark the birthplace which would be carried away by him lock, stock, and barrel, chimney and chimney smoke for the establishment of his old American pioneering town.

The gumshoe James McParlan had walked with postage stamps concealed in the toes of his boots. He could thus report on his activities without going to a post office to buy stamps but was never under any circumstances to communicate directly with Mr. Gowen, who was supposed to have no guilty knowledge of his existence although he was footing the bill.

Mr. Gowen was at least a part-time representative of the British Crown. But Allan Pinkerton was not revengeful. He was a man of flinty outlook and hard common sense and a forgetful nature as to any possible injustice which had been done to him and fellow labor agitators, even those of a Marxist nature, in the Old World, which was the world of the past.

He doubtless could never have been a reason for not allowing bygones to be bygones and thus was not like those troublemaking M.M.'s who, cloaking themselves with the mantle of the ancient Hibernians, who upon their knees had given their sacred oath of allegiance to the emperor of France and Don Carlos of Spain, were also bound by oath to murder the representatives of mining powers and challenge their assumption that it was better for a man to work for half a loaf of bread than to go on strike and that any form of brotherhood was a conspiracy which should be penal-

445

ized by exile from the brothers' places of employment and slow or sudden death.

During the revolutionary labor strikes that Allan Pinkerton and his employers were determined should be broken, there were so many burning bushes, firestorms, and whirlwinds that a man of a religious, old-time evangelical faith might hear the Lord speaking out of the burning bush, out of the whirlwind, out of the water, and it might seem that the end of the world which had been long looked for was at hand, millennial dreams persisting in this age of industrial blast oven over which the nonsalvationist Bethlehem Steel Corporation and other such outfits reigned supreme.

Not far from Reading, where James McParlan had done his research on the Molly Maguires, were the birthplaces of Mordecai Lincoln, ancestor of old Abe, and of Daniel Boone, as there were Lincoln and Boone or Bonne family members sleeping in the same graveyard along the road between Reading and Pottsville. In an America which had no center by which to establish harmonies for all and not nearly the discords necessary to maintain the entanglements of great capitalistic enterprise, the so-called Molly Maguires had tried to establish, in their own individualistic way, their center of cohesiveness by which to keep themselves knotted in fraternal brotherhood and which would not accept with stoic cheer the wasteland where the miner passed his life, the place described by one of their songs—"The trees are black with dust and smoke, / The grass is burnt and sere, / The noxious gases from the coke / Pollute the atmosphere," or "the valley drooping as with a blight where was no vivid green and all was grim and bare. . . ."

Franklin Benjamin Gowen, named after Benjamin Franklin, was president of the Philadelphia & Reading Iron and Coal Company which depended upon the Philadelphia & Reading Railroad of which he had also served as president and thus was ideally situated to do the bidding of one in behalf of the other. His left hand seemed to know what his right hand did.

Thirty-three years old, Gowen had been educated at John Beck's Academy with scions of Pennsylvania ironmasters and coal heavers who had been able to rise to the power of Gog and Magog. He had an essentially dramatic cast of mind which he would display in the courtroom in his description of the Molly Maguires as he turned and twisted and distorted the truth into the heavy ropes by which they would be hanged and by which all other strikers with just grievances against the corporate powers of this nation, all others who made response to unendurable ills would be made to seem, as the strikes increased, lineal descendants of these red-eyed fiends, not human beings but lower than the lowest beasts as if they were mandrakes, the members of no family but that of the deadly nightshade, the children who, both winged and rooted, trying to fly upward with their wings as their roots pulled them downward, were spawned from the seeds of men hanging on the hangman's tree, their fate that which should have been a warning to all men, as in the Old World, where the gallows had been at the crossroads, that they should not invite what might be considered just retribution by some men and martyrdom by others.

This example of mass execution had resulted in no diminishment of the ranks of labor agitators but rather had been an open invitation to martyrdom in the greatly expanding civil war by which the dominions of the rich would be increased and syncopated and synthesized, often in secret ways or by shibboleths presented as divine truths when they were profane and showed no respect for the divinity of man or beast or bird or flower, none for the things of this earth.

Debs, future exhumer of the Mollies and other labor and freedom martyrs possibly beyond number, would always insist, throughout his life of struggles for the rights of poor men, that clarification of the truth was the first necessity and that mysteries feeding on mysteries were essential to the domination of the poor.

[1 3 9]

BECAUSE OF A VICTORY which Gowen had gained over the Pennsylvania Railroad when as head of the legal department of the Reading Railroad he had been promoted to its president, he had been well on his way up the rungs of the ladder of success when in 1870, acting as a mediator between the railroad and the strikers of the Workingmen's Benevolent Association, he had poured oil upon the troubled waters which had turned into a sea of fire and naturally for no reason but the usual labor strikes striking their matches where oil was.

What he had suggested, that beast of famine which was called the Gowen Compromise, was that the brutally depressed wages of miners which had already been cut to the bone should be further depressed, that their pay for their backbreaking labor which they could scarcely perform without the bread sufficient to keep them alive, even when they ate whatever wild berries they could find, should be linked to the rise and fall in the price of coal, but the trouble was that the price was always falling and bore no relationship to the cost of living or the cost of dying. If the price had not been falling, if it had been rising, the cost of bread or a bag of corn would have risen in a way to keep the workers as near to starvation as they had been before.

Although there was as yet no one great union, yet there had been shown, in the freezing winter of the Gowen Compromise, a sense of man's brotherhood with man and most especially the sense of identity most ordinarily shared by the miners under the earth and even when they might be cut off from each other by distance and ignorance and darkness, when sometimes they might not be able to write their names or leave last wills and testaments. Many a poor coal miner, entombed when the tons of coal fell on him, could only carve out, with his jackknife on slate, his X by which, should he ever be discovered and brought back to his wife and children, should the company excavate so deep, he might be identified when individual features had disappeared.

As the workers were making all the compromises while the company continued with its happy reports to stockholders, even raising the price of coal from two dollars to four dollars a carload without sharing this escalation of profit with those poor miners, the miners of the northern coal fields and the miners of the southern coalfields had united in striking with the beginning of the New Year, and that was when the so-called Molly Maguires had begun to crawl out of their holes where many before them had been burned to death by sheets of flame and many had drowned because of the breakages in walls.

Jefferson Davis, at a convention of National Railroad heads in St. Louis, November 23, 1875, where the hall was decorated with banners emblazoned with such flaming slogans as "Westward the Star of Empire Takes Its Way"—"There Is the East, There Is India"—"Twenty Millions of People Seek an Acceptance Route to the Pacific"—had been chairman of the Mississippi delegation but had declined to sit on the dais after protesting that if all the commanding generals from either side of the late war were to sit in the place of honor, there would not be enough room for him.

Pennsylvania was west, west of New York, probably west of everything but the West itself and the millennial isles and the Great Wall of China. Some of the Irish workmen who had located in the anthracite regions in the eastern mountains had advised their homeless friends in New York not to come out west in search of work—there was none.

Scranton, which after the massacre of white settlers by red men in the eighteenth century had been abandoned for many years, had been resettled and was become a civilized center with churches and stores and offices of railroads and mines; and Wilkes-Barre, which was the second-largest town in the coal-producing region and marked the spot where the Iroquois had been slaughtered, was almost civilized. Civilized also were Mauch Chunk, Pottsville, and Tamaqua, where wealth clustered. Some of the retired coal operators had accumulated enough wealth to enable them to retire from their business and grow in their gardens Chinese peonies as big as bleeding miners' heads.

At the bottom of the social and economic heap, as should have come to no one's surprise, were the many less-developed settlements which were entirely composed of miners and laborers and those whose business was connected with the administration of mines in behalf of owners who were like czars robed in purple and gold. Many of these fugitive settlements—some to have their names changed, some to cave in, some to be absorbed by larger developments—were inhabited exclusively by Irish miners who were of two classes, the good and valuable citizens and the outlaws and desperadoes.

In a land of many kingdoms, many powers joined in a monarchical monolith such as had no business in a democracy of which the principles worked best when no attempt was made to clothe the word with flesh when only the words should have sufficed without the demonstration as some of its critics averred, how easy it was for the Allan Pinkerton agency to make these so-called Molly Maguires, although few in number, seem many and of the same brand as the Reno brothers, the James and Younger brothers, and most especially as the poor Irishmen who had come to the anthracite barrens before the Civil War in search of survival and had bitterly resented being dragged from the coal pits and tied hand and foot, slung like corpses over horses or tied by ropes and dragged along the ground to the draft headquarters for shipment to the southern battlefields as those who, wild dogs although they were, had been unwilling to wear Mr. Lincoln's dog tags. Some had not wished to die for any kind of philanthropic philosophy whatever—for they had come to these blessed shores in order to live, to have a second chance for life.

They had not differed from an overwhelming number of thoughtful people for whom the war had been an illegal adventure employing illegal means such as the suspension of the writ of habeas corpus, for example, and had enriched the war profiteers by not taxing them but by passing the burden on to the poor who had fought the war in which the rich had acquired those properties they now protected by great Gatling guns turned against the poor.

This was and had been and would continue to be a period of cannibalism throughout the American nation when the rich industrialists and railroad lords ate the poor people as surely as if they had been boiled in a black pot like Lo, the poor Indian, and the red men and the black men and the yellow men according to an ancient ritual which had been practiced by the Indians, who drank from the broth in which they saw the eye of an old witch who seems to have been very much like the eye of the czar of Russia which never sleeps or like the eye of Allan Pinkerton's agency which also never slept.

The premise on which Sir William Blackstone, who was a hero to the McGuffeys, had explained the law of property—the sacred right of any man to lay his mantle on the ground and not have another man step into it and walk away with it—was ignored by the rich man who walked into every mantle he found and considered it just as much his sacred right to do so as if God had placed it for him to find on the ground. The mantle of the law also cloaked the rich thief as one who served his country and his god by exploitation of the poor, for the law did not pertain for the rich man who stole a continent and carried it away and did come down like iron nails upon the poor producers of wealth who were starving to death and stole a mere ear of corn such as starving mice might steal and carry away.

The awards for the perpetrators of great thefts and the penalties for the perpetrators of petty thefts would often be pointed out by Debs although without justification of the small crime by comparison with the great crime, even as a small murder could not be justified by greater murder—as his history would show.

[1 4 0]

THE LAW WAS MADE into a mockery of law, as would be shown in the case of the Molly Maguires whom James McParlan would unearth. His plot against the Molly Maguires is suggestive of the design of the mines which had no exit for them, as doubtless hell would have none, for the one exit there was would be blocked by fire so that the men entombed in them should not appear again upon the scarred surface of the earth as these underlings were representatives of all those who were making trouble, blowing up firestorms, not content to be slaves of nabobs with more than Oriental powers in this country which seems to have been so foreign to the

United States government in Washington that there should have been a foreign policy in relation to it. And perhaps there was.

When the confessional of James McParlan as to his having been a spy against labor to railroad the Molly Maguires to eternity with no way back had been completed, Gowen had said, in answer to the question as to whether he thought it was fair for a corporation to employ a spy against labor, that he saw nothing strange in the arrangement, for the United States employed spies in foreign countries and in foreign wars, so why should the company not use them here in labor wars? As to Gowen's evaluation of James McParlan, a liar and a squealer if there ever was one: "He was red wine, one hundred percent."

Posing as that very loose tongued imaginary murderer who would make imaginary murders real in a country where murders by the ton were real, very real, indeed, although not called murders, simply called those accidents which were inevitable in the promotion of great works—in Schuylkill County, for example, as the result of company negligence 566 miners were killed and 1,665 maimed within a period of seven years, which brought great unhappiness to their old mothers and fathers, widows and children, should there be such survivors left to moan and keen and tear out their hair and beat their bosoms and gnash their teeth before they, too, should be called home by God—James McParlan had crawled from pub to pub, had moved from town to town, had managed to make himself visible in bars in Swatara, Tremont, Rausch Creek, Donaldson, and Trenton City, and had drunk with other men a glass of whiskey or red wine while secretly trying to locate the stamping ground of the Molly Maguires of whom every Irishman he met might be one—and yet he had kept sober enough not to betray himself as in some drunken pub confessional to a bartender or by seeing all things of things which were not there, more snakes than St. Patrick had ever driven out of Ireland. His way was to set up drinks for others in Irish pig's-feet bars so that they, drunk as blind pigs, might squeal to him the great secret that they were under sacred or profane oath to murder bosses and managers of mines, who, having raised themselves up from the bottoms of mines, had come to identify themselves not with the poor pigs in the Reading slaughter yards but with that great Gowen who was the slaughterer.

The money with which James McParlan paid for the red wine was not counterfeit, nor did he have enough money to arouse suspicion. Just a few loose coins had jingled in the pockets of this poor Irish bum who had been such an excellent spotter on the Chicago streetcars that no thief could escape his eye and was now on the side of the mine bosses who stole from poor miners in every way they could—even in such petty ways as payment for a ton of coal only after the slag had been removed from it, false clocks by which an hour of sixty minutes was seventy minutes long and altogether less accurate than time as it had been measured by the Indians who before the white men came to drive them away into the fires of some far distant sunset glow had measured time according to the position of the sun upon the great rock which, still standing, was called the Dial Rock because the shadow moving over the rock was far more accurate than factory time or train time, the latter not that which a poor miner had to know as he was going nowhere but into the mine from which he might or might not emerge.

James McParlan had spoken loudly of his hatred of the owners of mills and mines. They were the equivalent of absentee landlords for whose benefit the bosses had betrayed the poor miners by committing thefts for those who had in their mines the coals which were black diamonds and had required centuries to build up and would require centuries to exhaust.

James McParlan had understood, it seemed, their sufferings and their resentment of scabs who took the places of strikers against those corporations, which, everybody knew, had no souls and no sins to confess.

And he knew not only old Irish Catholic songs against Cromwell's conquest of the auld sod where their land which had been communally and tribally owned had been largely taken from them as in America the land was being taken by the kings of mines and railroads—he could also join with them in songs about corporations which blasted labor strikers and set them wandering over the face of the earth unless they gave up their pride in manhood.

> *And thus the matter stands. We do not dare*
> *to look a loss in the face and whisper Bah!*
> *Unless we wish to join the mighty train*
> *of miners wandering o'er the earth like Cain,*
> *And should you wish to start upon a tramp*
> *O'er hillock, mountain, valley, plain and swamp*
> *Or travel as the Pilgrim of John Bunyan*
> *One talismanic word will do it, Union.*
> *Just murmur that, and all the laws of the State*
> *or Congress will not save you from your fate,*
> *They'll drive you out, forfeit your goods, degrade you*
> *Just like the British did in old Acadia.*

Bursting into Pat Dormer's saloon, the wild-eyed, raggedy, half-crazed drunk James McParlan, who traveled under cover of a false name, had thrown himself into the wildest Irish jig there ever was, whirling himself around and around with other dancing men, some who would end their lives dancing at the end of a rope because of him, had sung in a tenor loud enough to break a homeless heart the melancholy song of the Molly Maguires of Donegal, county of hidden lakes and branches of the sea and treacherous bogs, ways of stone and thorn and mountains and sand hills where Muchish, the hulking shape of a pig, had dominated the sky in ways not to be forgotten by the Molly Maguires in the wilds of the Pennsylvania mountains where Mucky, the hulking shape of a pig, was that great corporate power represented by the united coal-mining and railroad powers.

During the great famine of almost thirty years before, according to Maud Gonne in her lecture at the Catholic University of Luxembourg upon that hunger which was the great crime of enforcing suicide upon the helpless masses such as those who were the worshipers of wayside Madonnas like some now to be found in Pennsylvania's anthracite barrens, men and women had eaten the dogs, the rats, the grass of the fields, and some had eaten, when the food was gone, the bodies of their dead.

> Whole families, when they had eaten their last crust and understood that they had to die, looked once upon the sun and then closed up the doors of their cabins with stone, that no one might look upon their last agony. Weeks afterward, men would find their skeletons around the extinguished fire of the hearth.... If you come to my country, every stone will repeat to you this tragic history.... It has seemed to me at evening on those mountains of Ireland, so full of savage majesty when the wind sighed over the pits of the famine where the thousands of dead enrich the harvests of the future, it has seemed to me that I heard an avenging voice calling down on our oppressors the execration of men and the justice of God.

To summarize James McParlan's many-clawed career, which would extend far into the future and would cast its shadow over the life of Debs, the singer of old ballads of Donegal who was going to euchre the Molly Maguires and send them all to the Stygian bog to be pecked upon by crows, as euchre is also the death card or sign of death, had engaged that first night in Pottsville in a game of euchre in which he, the representative of the agency with The Eye That Never Sleeps, had discovered one of the sleepers whose secret union was that of the brothers of the hearts playing with

six cards instead of five and had knocked him out cold, then had propped
him up and poured red wine down his throat.

Pat Dormer had admired the redhead for his pugnacity and his acrobatic performance as well as for the fact that he could sing out clear and
loud—just as he would sing out clear and loud in the courtroom before a
jury heavily weighted in favor of hanging the Molly Maguires on largely
cooked-up charges. Dormer had given to McParlan a letter of introduction
to Muff Lawler, the body master twenty miles to the north at Shenandoah,
from where he was sent on to a meeting with Jack Kehoe, who operated
the Hibernian House at Gerardsville and had seemed to be lulled into a
perhaps uneasy sleep.

Although McParlan claimed to have been at some time in his past a
Hibernian himself, he had not been able to respond to the secret sign by
which to establish his credentials. Jack Kehoe had seen that he knew
nothing of the present and had understood when he had said, "It is a long
time since I have been inside," and had accepted him as an authentic son of
Erin. Staying with the Lawlers at their hostelry, he was able to get a job
hauling coal twenty hours a day for ten dollars a week from the coal
barons, always with great expectations of greater pecuniary rewards from
the Pinkerton agency when he had done his work to their satisfaction, if
not entirely to his.

Twenty hours a day for a week might have killed him, but after only
five days in the freezing February cold his hands had been smashed by a
carload of coal, temporarily incapacitating him for the strenuous work that
was after all for his keeping body and soul together or at least body
together, for he had perhaps no soul to lose.

And why should any coal miner live to be old, a burden to himself and
others, an old dwarf who might pass for a child in such an occupation as
separation of slate from coal where the children who died young were old,
shriveled toads without one tree-toad song among them? Life was but a
puff of smoke.

When McParlan's wounded hands were healed, he had reported to his
secret employers in Philadelphia that the retributive murder of a higher-up
at Centralia had been done by a secret labor union branch called the Chain
Gang. Other secret branches in the mining regions were the Sheet Iron
Gang, Iron Clads, Sheet Irons. All, of course, were related to the Molly
Maguires, the name which he preferred for the identification of workmen
in iron whose labor unions represented the attempt of the isolated individual to escape from the intolerable burdens, over which, as would be pointed
out in one way or another by numerous humane and humanitarian social-

ists in time not far distant, among them Debs, who was onto Pinkerton's trail quite early. The laborers had no more power in setting the conditions of their employment or their freedom to draw up labor contracts as to pay and working hours than if they had been blind horses trying to read.

Few Americans at the time of the Molly Maguires had been able to believe that their democracy was not the land of opportunity for men whose poverty was but a transient state—few had seen that the nation was made up of the few masters and the overwhelming masses of the hired men to whom was forbidden the privilege of asking for the amelioration of their working conditions.

James McParlan, under a false name with a largely false history but no socialist imagination to burden him, had wormed his way into the inner core of the red apple of the so-called Molly Maguires to whose head, Frank McAndrew, he had been introduced by Muff Lawler, when the members of the Ancient Order of Hibernians were gathered together at Lawler's place. McParlan, very much on the alert, as he should be who represented The Eye That Never Sleeps, had not known whether he was to be invited to join or was to be murdered because of their having smelled the rat in their midst. They apparently had suspected nothing which might cause them to turn him into meat for crows. They had welcomed him into their fellowship. McParlan had fallen upon his knees like a knight of old, a Crusader who might be going to Holy Lands, and he had made the sign of the cross, of which the euchre is also a symbol, as he had taken the vow by which his life was now dedicated to "Friendship, unity, and Christian charity. . . . Should I hear a member ill spoken of, I will espouse his cause," he had promised to these brothers, the Ulsterman who, wearing an ulster to shelter him from stars dripping blood, would speak against the Molly Maguires as the self-revealed hired man of Allan Pinkerton and Gowen and company and other conspiratorial despots with murder in their hearts.

Doubtless more impressive to the secret agent who had to represent himself as a murderer in order to get into this order was the American bylaw with which he could agree with every cell of his brain, every bone of his body when his nerves were so tightly strung and his pulse so irregular that his alertness to possible danger made him ready to pin up his eyelids rather than close his eyes—"If any member of this Order be convicted of robbery, perjury, or any other atrocious offense, he shall be excluded from this Order for life."

For the privileges of membership, the mysterious traveler had paid the sum of three dollars from the funds that had been provided by his employers, of course, and as one absolutely opposed to the rule of British ducal despots had drunk a toast of the blood-red wine to the emperor of France and Don Carlos of Spain.

This ritual had occurred on the night of April 13, 1874, and had been reported in code to his employers in Philadelphia. He had sharpened his own quill and had made his ink from the bluing with which Muff's wife, when she had washed the coal dust from the sheets, had blanched them white as ghosts before hanging them out to dry in the backyard of the hotel where the man who was writing his secret letter with the blue ink was that informer because of whom the Molly Maguires would be hanged.

THE ANTHRACITE MINERS of Schuylkill County had laid down their tools in 1842 before they had a brotherhood of any kind to forge themselves together as one great tool in a brotherhood, which had soon been broken by the authorities for whom coal mines were the equivalent of gold mines. In 1849, the year of the accelerated gold rush when lone individuals in search of gold were streaming into the West of the setting sun which was made of fireflies, the souls of the dead, the miners of Schuylkill County had had a union and had struck against payment of wages in coal miners' scrip, but this strike had failed, and one of the reasons was that John Bates—the ex-Chartist who was their leader—had simply disappeared with whatever money was in their pot.

After other starts and stops in the growth of brotherhood, John Siney, in 1864, had organized the Workingmen's Benevolent Association of Schuylkill County as part of the larger union which would give to every homeless wanderer a home, leave no one out alone under that great coffin lid which was the coal-blackened sky nailed down by iron nails which were the stars, according to the elegiac spirit of the nineteenth century.

"Our eyes are being opened, and we look back to our folly for not sooner uniting ourselves for our mutual benefit," John Siney had said, and he had declared himself also in favor of ways of peace.

Indeed, it could have been said of some poor workers in mines and mills then that their working lives were longer than their lives on earth—they were the working dead, the dead souls of America whom unions would try to bring back to life by blowing one spark of that energy which was the divine spark and could not be extinguished by any man.

Anyone who did an act of violence against the law, according to John Siney, would be expelled not only from the union but from the six anthracite counties, and yet this peace had not prevailed when under the rising and falling wage scale in relation to the price of coal the wage had fallen so low that there had been no bread for miners and their wives and children.

An answer to this problem was that miners should have had no wives and children, that they should be as lone as the lone yellow men who were not allowed to bring their women to this country, as all were as polygamous as the red men or Mormons.

Gowen's monopoly had shown, in the fight against these present reds, these white men who were nonidyllic savages, how easily the union of capitalistic monopolies could be employed as one great power to crush the unions of labor strikers wherever they might assert themselves by their refusal to be supine or disappear into an elsewhere which must be nowhere for the blacklisted wanderers over the denuded face of the earth.

With the Ancient Order of Hibernians giving shelter and giving its mask to the Molly Maguires, there could certainly be no way to attract capital to the mountains of Pennsylvania or any other mountains where such mad reds flourished, so Gowen had been quite easily able to combine the retributive resources of the Philadelphia & Reading Railroad and the Philadelphia & Reading Coal and Iron Company with those of the Lehigh and Wilkes-Barre Coal Company as instruments by which to lessen the overgrown powers of the labor union and to exterminate absolutely, if possible, those very Molly Maguires whose murderous deeds against members of the establishment were most strangely increased when James McParlan came to join with players of the mournful harps and flutes for the Irish dead.

In the summer of 1874, according to Gowen's count, which had been prepared by him for presentation to a state legislative committee, the Molly Maguires had been guilty of disturbing the peace of the anthracite barrens by ninety-four crimes. These included assault and battery upon mine bosses, all as peaceful as shepherds could be when their flocks were made entirely of black sheep or those blackened by the company, the burnings of buildings and coal in coal yards and gondolas or cradles, attempts to derail trains, and the derailing of trains, which must naturally have caused as much loss of life and limb and coal as were the trains which no engineer might ever leave somewhere along the rail no matter how long his run was or even if it was longer than his life, for to do so would be to invite wreckage.

[1 4 1]

Here in Pennsylvania where the age of the machine flourished and the Ancient Order of Hibernians must have seemed somewhat anachronistic, somewhat out of time's way as if they were children of the bog and had no lights but those provided by burning reeds as if the world electric had never come with all its great profits for the rich and starvation and early death for the poor, there had been given the widest publicity possible to their excommunication if for no other reason than to damn them in the eyes of other Irishmen throughout the nation and even in the eyes of the antipapal Christians for whom the pope wore the number of the devil on his forehead and the devil himself must have been an Irishman complete with saucer eyes and horns and tail and hunting dogs, some who made a mournful whistle.

Although the archbishop of Philadelphia had been apprised by Gowen six or seven years before this resurgence of Molly Maguires which had come with the Pinkerton's detective that he intended to bring in spies and agents provocateurs, yet there was issued, by a group of Catholic priests in the anthracite barrens in 1874, a reminder that Ribbonmen and kindred societies had been condemned by the Holy See.

Thus it seems that the spirit and acts of the Hibernians had aroused the papal ire and fire because not in keeping with the plainest teachings of the Decalogue, and should the rebels against that great god whose viceroy Gowen was here on earth not give up the labor unions, they must be driven from the Church—must take their choice between Molly Maguires and Mother Mary. The question was, however, would Mother Mary ever really give them up to the mercy of these predators directed by a Philadelphia lawyer who, because of the violences promoted by such dubious characters as James McParlan, was able to absorb small competitors as if he were one great sponge sponging up a sea of blood, and break the labor strikes when for his convenience all labor unions would seem the same as the plotting, murderous Molly Maguires who burned up telegraph stations and knocked coal cars over on their backs and set vast fires which were like the fires of heaven drawn down from the sky to make a hell of earth or were the fires of hell casting their reflections on clouds so that there might seem to be always more fires than there were?

The list of the members of Molly Maguires that James McParlan had written down had come to only three hundred and forty-seven names, some of which were those of sleepers who were already in the graveyard, some who were yet to be put there, and they did not include James McParlan.

Thus he had been very much startled when he had heard the priest read, with his name at the head of the list of names as mournful as the passages of hearses to an unblessed grave, the names of the Molly Maguires whose souls were among the souls of the lost and for whose souls the congregation should pray.

From whom had the priest received the list of the Molly Maguires who were unfit to rest in sanctified soil and if their old Irish mothers and fathers or their wives and children should have been buried there were forbidden to join them? Who had placed McKenna, né McParlan, at the head of the list? Was he supposed to fool God by being a Protestant in a Catholic graveyard? Should he be buried with his rosary or with a list of the condemned?

If this was a battle in this civil war between the rich and the poor, the iron and coal cossacks and these rebellious serfs, the authorities might deliberately shoot him down as a very well known, conspicuous Molly Maguire, a part-time counterfeiter by profession, a conspirator plotting the murder of money capitalists, a low-down believer in the fact that the democracy founded upon the myth of private ownership was a fraudulent democracy and should be destroyed by whatever weapons there were, and he might find himself buried under a false name without people's knowing who he was or was not unless they should be other Molly Maguires weeping their copious tears of blood. Under such enormous pressures as might any man be under caught behind the lines in a new civil war, that of the war between classes such as was now raging on many fronts, it was no wonder that he lost so much weight that he looked like a skeleton.

An instance of insurrection observed by James McParlan with his own concern that he should be not with the tares but with the wheat on the day of resurrection of all souls was that in which a Molly Maguire named Brennan had died in Shamokin, the site of an Indian village, and although it was known that he should be given no sanctuary in a Catholic graveyard, come hell or high water, his mournful brothers who had danced the jig with him and were the wearers of the shamrock and worshipers of that old St. Patrick who had driven the snakes from Ireland had been determined to plant the corpse where he had his right to be sheltered, where the Madonna of the flowers should watch over him, but a priest named Father Koch had refused to allow the hearseman with the hack containing Brother Brennan in his box to pass through the gates, had barred the way.

The hearse driver, when told to go through the gates, to speed the horse up with a crack of the whip, had refused to do so, no doubt lest he should then become the devil's own hearse driver who would just have to go driving on and on until he should become a phantom hearse driver driving a phantom horse in an America made of phantoms—perhaps more phantoms than men, it sometimes seemed.

This refusal had made the mourners so mad that one of them had knocked the hearseman out of the hearse as easily as if he were knocking a euchre out of a deck and, taking his place in the driver's seat, had broken down the fence in his determination to get into the graveyard, had assaulted Father Koch when he would not allow the grave digger to handle the spade, had thrown the priest out of the graveyard, had dug the grave himself, and had buried brother Brennan in his grave without, of course, entertaining any suspicion that he and his brother mourners, on the testimonial of a fellow mourner whose specialty was every kind of fraudulence there was, would soon be hanged as poor scapegoats upon whose heads would be heaped the iniquities of the corporation magnates themselves and who would be buried in graves already yawning as wide as an abyss.

The coins that the blacklisted Molly Maguires had wished to contribute to the Church for the celebration of the birth of Christ in the hay of a lowly manger on Christmas Day and the coins which they had offered in commemoration of the resurrection of the poor coal-miner Christ on Easter morning were also refused, although there was great need for candles and lilies in a church in the impoverished regions of the anthracite barrens.

By Christmas Day of the year 1875, Gowen had provided by speed-up enough mountains of coal for the heating of parlor stoves in the homes of individuals who had homes and for the great furnaces of industries devouring coal, and thus there had been preparation for the strike of miners against the wages, which had plummeted like a miner without a cable rope falling into a deep hole beneath the level which would sustain human life or pay for a newborn baby's swaddling clothes or even one shoe for one foot. The coal market could afford to pay the previous year's prices but had simply wished to cause the breakage and dispersal of members of the Workingmen's Benevolent Association whom the corporation identified with the Molly Maguires at the same time that the legitimate union claimed to know of no such illegitimate branch in the land of crows and coal.

The Molly Maguires themselves, although radical leaders within a comparatively conservative union which had denied knowledge of their essentially subterranean existence, had not known that they belonged to the Molly Maguires and that they had altogether about seventy thousand members—that there were Molly Maguires in far-distant Jersey City, for example, as in the bogs of every low-down Irish settlement even if no bigger than a pebble scratch or a fallen log.

Upon a skull-bare mountain top on a wild, windy April night when the rain was falling like harp strings, Allan Pinkerton's ever-busy spy whose plots against the labor agitators would know no end until they had come to their Gethsemane had begged two masked Molly Maguires not to follow the blueprint which they had laid out just like murderous Reno brothers or James brothers for the blowing up of a bridge on a Reading line.

For it was after all not his own sudden death that he intended but the death of the Molly Maguires who should be cut down by the great reaper like the tares they were, the noxious growths poisoning and polluting the atmosphere and certainly likely to throw him over a mountaintop or trestle bridge or bury him in a deep pit if they ever saw his face behind his mask and knew that he was not the fellow conspirator they thought he was.

He had been able to persuade them that if they tried to blow up the trestle bridge, it would be as suicidal as for mice to walk into a mousetrap. And no doubt it was true that before they could plant those unholy dynamite sticks which would break into the incandescent flowers of hell, they would have been spotted by the watchmen on the bridge who were always looking for mysterious men carrying dynamite sticks, and so they would be shot down before they could light a match.

The blowing up of the bridge had been deferred, for it was evidently in such good condition that its demolishment by blasting would have been an inconvenience at that time, and the coal cars were not yet so obsolescent or defective that they were ready for abandonment. These revolutionary murderers discussed with him everything but the eight-hour day or the loaf of bread which was a loaf of stone, their civil rights, their desire for economic justice and equality and manhood.

When a little later two carloads of iron slag had been uncoupled and the locomotive, suddenly gaining an abnormal speed when relieved of this burden hanging onto its tail, had nearly missed collision with a slow passenger train at a darkened crossing—this near brush with death or actual death occurring almost every day in America when for a variety of often mysterious reasons cars quite often uncoupled themselves and the brakeman's hands from his body—the two fellow conspirators had confessed to him that they were the uncouplers who had done the work.

In the *New York Tribune* of September 27, 1871, Mark Twain had written an indictment of the moguls whose values ruled the country in the age of such corruptions as would be seen in the anthracite barrens. Who was God, Mark Twain had asked, then had answered—"Money is God, Gold and Greenbacks and stocks—father, son, and the ghost of the same— three persons in one; these are the true and only God, mighty and supreme." He had pointed out that the training of the young which had been prized in former days—those of Washington, *Poor Richard's Alma-nack,* the *Pilgrim's Progress,* and the Declaration of Independence—was no more. This was the age when a man attained to his chief end in life by furnishing imaginary carpets to the courthouse, apocryphal chairs to the armories, and invisible printing to the city. As to what were the best-prized Sunday School books in this age of greater enlightenment than that of the past, he had answered with what might be a street Arab's litany of the names of robber barons and their political cohorts such as America had permitted to thrive and would continue to thrive when the masks were changed—"St. Hall's Garbled Reports, St. Fish's Ingenious Robberies, St. Camochan's Guide to Corruption, St. Gould on the watering of stock, St. Barnard's Injunctions, St. Tweed's Handbook of Morals, and the Court House edition of the Holy Crusade of the Forty Thieves." And was there progress? "You bet your life."

The Gilded Age, which was published late in 1873 and to which Charles Dudley Warner had contributed the romance and into which Mark Twain had thrown, as into a laundry hamper, all the dirty facts, would become a part of the mythology by which the buccaneers of industry and finance, the worshipers and milkers of the Golden Calf, would be described to such men of activist idealism as Debs, who would grope his way through the age of the Molly Maguires—whose lives would be brought to an end by hangings as in a long, foggy night—with scarcely a lightbeam showing in his path, perhaps only that pilot lightbeam shining from his own breast as from the breast of a crane in flight, as was once believed, before there would burst upon him the red dawn of his social consciousness of which there would never be a sunset so long as he lived and not even when he was dead.

As the anti–Molly Maguire plots developed, running wild as ragweed in a land where nothing else grew, what had become a source of anxiety far greater for James McParlan than the coffin notice put out for him as a

Molly Maguire who ought to say his prayers was that the Molly Maguires who were under a threat of a raid against them something like that upon the Reno gang or Castle James had begun to entertain the suspicion that there might be an informer against them, a Molly Maguire who was working with the coal and iron police and was working to turn them in, and that although for a time they had not been able to come up with the name of the spy, they had at last come up with the thought that it might be or was himself, and what was worse—they were correct.

He was caught as between the upper and nether grinding stones in his old murder mill, yet had not lost courage, as the passage of time had provided opportunity for the mysterious shooting of union heads here and there by the coal and iron police and other secret agents who naturally would not look for the murderers who were themselves. No great hue and cry would come from the authorities when someone who was known to be a union man was felled. The spotlight of publicity was saved to be turned on when an antiunion man bit the dust, was given his one-way ticket such as a Molly Maguire might have for the trip back—they were so many, it seemed, as many as the sands of the sea, the sands of the desert.

[1 4 2]

THE TRIALS of the Molly Maguires, the long immortality shows playing in 1876 and 1877, should have put a permanent quietus upon the labor movement as if a cancer cell should spread to every cell of the body of any brotherhood which asked that poor workingmen should be sharers in this democracy.

The list of the obscure men who were subjected to the ritual of hanging in 1877 came to nineteen official executions of those who were wrapped in these mortal coils and who were not beseechers for the mercy of God, with Whom they seemed at peace and Who was not the god of Gowen and company, for they according to their lights, and in a profounder sense than that of their individual and mass murderers, were the only lights they knew, the servants of God, even if depicted as monsters worthy of no response but the triumph of law and order and lawlessness, intrigue, conspiracy, and murder.

The names of the men who were killed in 1877 and over whose history, so far as it could be known, Debs would come to brood, were Thomas

Munley, James Carroll, James Roarity, Hugh McGeehan, James Boyle, Thomas Duffy, Michael J. Doyle, Edward J. Kelly, Alexander Campbell, John Donahue, Thomas O. Fisher, John Kehoe, Patrick Hesser, Patrick Tully, Peter McHugh, Peter McManus, and Andrew Lanahan. The names of those who were killed in 1879 like a pair of bloody doves or game birds were Charles Sharpe and James McDonald, to whom, just after their dance in the air, the governor had issued a reprieve intentionally delayed so as to seem in keeping with the desire of that part of the public that wanted them hanged and that part that had not wanted them hanged—and he had wished, moreover, to close the old show before there came the repetition of the old climax.

The struggles of labor had not been stilled by the hangings of these men whose obscurity had been very great until the execution by hanging and had continued even then and long afterward. The struggles of labor had been heightened, in fact, by these and many other miscarriages of justice, although the question would always be whether the public heart if there was such a thing as a public heart could be educated to remember them and recognize them and their repetitions in the past which man was doomed to relive if he did not know—could not see it coming around again like an old merry-go-round not made for an amusement park.

When the many who were to be hanged had been rounded up, there were still so many Molly Maguires in America that James McParlan had been quite fearful that if he came to Pottsville for the trial, he would never get out of the courtroom alive, which he had argued with the Allan Pinkerton agency, and it also did not need publicity as to what its role had been—yet because Gowen had needed his services and because of promises of some new utopia or Zion or earthly paradise for a detective who had become expert in the planting of false evidence and who might now have his own hired men to plant the murder tree, he had consented to risk his life.

He had feared for his life in vain. He was accompanied by two Pinkerton guards when he came into court. The barber who had shaved him had done a neat job of shaving away the anarchist's beard. The man from Ulster wore a suit of the finest cut, not the kind of gray suit that would turn indigo blue in the first rain, a fine shirt with a collar which was not a fly-away collar which would fly away in the wind, nor was it paper which would melt into pulp, and he wore a properly folded handkerchief in his coat pocket and a gold watch on a chain and fine gloves which showed no stain of blood and fine shoes which showed no stain of blood. There was not a speck of blood upon this essentially bloody man who had gone a long way toward putting down the revolution, of whatever nature it was, in Schuylkill County, and would work also to do so in the vineyards elsewhere.

It would be reported that when the accused men at the defense table saw upon the witness stand the man whose name they had not recognized when it was called out by the bailiff and recognized that James McParlan was James McKenna, one and the same, that the former bum to whom they had given refuge was now this smooth-shaven, well-dressed gentleman who was, of course, playing another role—for he had always been a killer in his heart and always would be—they had literally blanched.

James McParlan had described, in an account well rehearsed beforehand with the proddings of Gowen who had also known the details as they occurred, the evil deeds of this murderous crew even when he had been the earwitness to plans but not the eyewitness to sporadic executions of victims mainly chosen for their symbolic values, as were the union leaders themselves. The defense lawyer had tried in vain to impress the rigged jury with the idea that James McParlan bore some responsibility for a plot for which one of the murderers had rehearsed in McParlan's raggedy coat. McParlan had been only five miles away from the proposed victim, Sanger, and he had not walked over to tell the victim that he was to be mowed down. "I would not risk losing my life for all the men in this court house. . . . Walking five miles was nothing. . . . I would walk twenty, but it was the saving of my own life I was looking to."

The entire county was at the time of the trials under what amounted to martial law. Coal and iron guardsmen had surrounded the courthouses of the anthracite regions lest there should be a raid of Molly Maguires or their sympathizers upon the temples of justice, as they were called, although they should have been called temples of injustice. The prosecutor who conducted some of the trials and who was a legal adviser for the coal company of which the district attorney was the president had worn his Civil War military uniform as a way of reminding the jury that the Irish miners, their faces blackened by coal dust, had been rebellious against the cause of freedom for black men during the late, late Civil War.

If McParlan had deceived the Molly Maguires, why could he not deceive the jury, too? When the high and mighty Gowen was asked how it had happened that these men had been permitted to escape from what must suddenly have appeared as a wide-meshed net for some but a small-meshed net for others, he had answered as might have almost any reader of the literature of the Diamond Dick school with its theme that crime does not pay—"Pinkerton's Agency may sometimes permit a man to believe that he is free, who does not know that he may be travelling five thousand miles in the company of those whose vigilance never slumbers and whose eyes are never closed in sleep."

As would be the case when other labor agitators whose chief crime was that they believed in the undying cause of labor unions found themselves confronted in the courtroom by witnesses who, even if sincere, might be as unreliable as color-blind critics of paintings or deaf critics of music, witnesses who might also be insincere and fearful of their own fates if they should be uncooperative with the operators of such vast murder mills as those of coal and iron and steel magnates, many of whom were taking close note of the progress of the trials, the defense had questioned the validity of what had seemed a wholly subjective and fragmentary, highly impressionistic evidence of a fleeting nature now peculiarly fixed and hypostatized as if it were an essential part of a thing and should be treated as real and distinct and unchanging, and yet it was that which was subject to continual change, depending upon incalculably changing moods.

The witness Robert Heaton, while on his way to breakfast the morning of the murder, had seen several men sitting on a fence about three city blocks away and had noted that one of them had been sitting in a peculiarly constrained position, which, he said he believed, when prodded by the persecution, could have been that of only one man on earth. He could hardly have seen from such a distance the face of the murderer and yet had been able to identify the face of two murderers, whom he had seen only partially, one of whom had turned to look back at him in that swift moment when they were at the rear of the number running away from the murder scene; and one of them was the face of the man he had seen on the fence in the distance, and that face was now that of a man who was sitting in the courtroom in a peculiarly constrained position, that of Thomas Munley, a face which in the murky distance might have been as recognizable as that of one tree toad among a dozen tree toads, one moth in a row of moths.

Gowen had thought the face of the individual less important than his constrained way of sitting, whatever that might have been—although it could not have been as certain and unchanging as the color of his eyes which could not have been seen from the distance, even by The Eye That Never Sleeps.

Gowen, this duplex combination of the Philadelphia & Reading Railroad and its subsidiary, the Philadelphia & Reading Coal and Iron Company, was a man of his time in pointing out new devices of detection, and he was also fascinated by mechanical appliances that rendered identification instantaneous. "The art of the photographer has discovered a method whereby, in an instant of time or less than an instant, in a pulsation of the heart, in a winking of an eye you can take the picture of a man while he is moving at full speed before you."

As would someday be the case in the trials of Sacco and Vanzetti, where there was no door marked Exit but the door out of this world, a case in which Debs would passionately interest himself step by step although he was destined to go before them to the next world, there were quarrels about other most transitory, fleeting sensory impressions upon which, even under normal circumstances, few persons may come to agreement as some may see that a man wears a hat and another that he wears no hat or that the hat is a cap. Such transforming things were never fixed and unchanging in a universe of change.

[1 4 3]

ON JUNE 14, 1862, the year in which the Count Leo Tolstoy, in a letter from Yasnaya Polyana to the Countess A. A. Tolstoya—his beloved Granny, as he called her, who was in many ways a sharer of his spiritual development and a guide and who also because of her powerful position in the imperial court at St. Petersburg was able in innumerable ways to protect him from threats of persecution by both Church and State and possible incarceration or transportation to Siberia for such unorthodox ideas as equality with his plowmen in brotherhood and their education by which they should be brought from the darkness of serfdom to the light of liberation and the education of the farm children—recommended that it was essential for her to read Fyodor Mikhailovich Dostoyevsky's *The House of the Dead,* written during his imprisonment in Siberia for reading Fourier and Proudhon, F. W. S. Langdon, while out walking near his colliery in this land of the anthracite coal barrens which had its equivalent of "houses of the dead," had been stoned by a crowd of angry, poor Irish bogmen for whom he was the representative of the tyrannical powers, the Goliath who had the mountains of coal and before whom they were as puny as David with his pebbles in his sling, although to James McParlan and his kind they were the Goliath who must be slain and the David was the capitalist with his pebbles in his sling.

Mr. Langdon, although hit by rocks which had left him as bruised as peaches on a peach tree attacked by wasps, had not died, had walked a mile the very next day and was three more days above the earth before quite suddenly he had died, and no one had known then who among the crowd had thrown the fatal rocks against the breaker boss. Only after almost a decade and a half had passed with its accrual of heavy fogs like those of oblivion covering memory, itself never clear, could it be established by McParlan that not only had Jack Kehoe been in the milling crowd that had thrown the stone but that he had been the thrower of the stone that had killed Langdon, as only a man standing in the crowd could possibly have seen, and that the man who put the spotlight on him now had been himself one in danger of execution for murder by the man who had kept the log upon murders which were, were not, were yet to be.

This method of hanging Jack was surely more efficaciously direct, even through its various indirections in the Gowen maze.

There had been no point in reaching out the long rake of the law to bring in some of the weeds on Gowen's pointed prongs when they were not the important men in the capitalistic hierarchy of values in a country which seemed, as would be pointed out by Debs and others of a liberal vein, a country made of many countries including those ruled over by the American czars, the great tycoons of mills and mines with magnitude of wealth which staggered the imagination of most men so that when they were sober, they might reel as if dead drunk.

There had been also the excavation of the murder on October 17, 1868, of Alexander W. Rea, a mining superintendent for whose murder Patrick Hesser, John Donahue, Michael Prior, and Thomas Duffy had been arrested as the four horsemen shooting at him and had been imprisoned. It had been too early for the Apocalypse.

IN THE NOVEL *Democracy,* by Henry Adams, which was published in 1882, the heroine Madeleine Lee exclaims of the prospect that the experiment of democracy may destroy itself with universal suffrage, corruption, and communism, her own faith being in the survival of the fittest and the necessity, if the age was to be beaten, of dying in the ranks, and winds up her fears with the statement: "I want to go to Egypt. Democracy has shaken my nerves to pieces. Oh, what rest it would be to live in the Great Pyramid and look out forever at the polar stars."

FEDERAL TROOPS had not been rushed in for the rescue of the doomed Molly Maguires from the rigged executions which had taken place in the name of justice and which had provided a pleasant diversion for people of strong nerves. Indeed, there had been a festive crowd to celebrate the enactment of the law of the survival of the fittest and the suppression of those who were unfit to live. The audience had included a flock of young girls who in their light summer dresses and straw bonnets were about the age of Debs's sisters and had been taken by a number of Presbyterian clerics and their Sunday School teachers to view the machinery of the scaffold and have explained to them the cogs and ropes which made possible such deaths as these would be, and without a hitch or only a hitch or two or three, as these primordial monsters were hung in rows from hangman's trees and the crows gathered for the picnic which was to come.

[1 4 4]

O N THIS DAY virtue had triumphed over vice, for the man who had recently been elected to the White House at a time when the people were tired of corruptions multiplying corruptions under the somewhat absent-minded administrations of the whiskey-drinking, cigar-smoking, apple-eating president Ulysses S. Grant, a man who according to Mark Twain was as innocent as a baby who had put his foot into his mouth, the man who followed Hiram Ulysses Grant—H.U.G.—into the White House had been a God-fearing and law-abiding man who, as dry as dust, had not a flaw or blemish upon his record, so far as was known, and had never stained his bib with beer or wine and had gone into office with such miasmic mists and fogs hanging over him thicker than the polar fogs in a Siberian labor camp, and he had been placed on the throne through the wielding of such intricate mechanisms of force and fraud by the capitalistic powers that the title to the presidency was not clear, just as he had known, nor was it in his nature to sympathize with the whiskey-drinking Irish of the bog who were generally Democrats and thus of the devil's own party, not of God's party. It was Samuel Tilden who had been elected, yet Hayes became president who had not been elected either by a popular majority or an electoral majority except for that one Republican vote which had been produced by failure to count all the Republican votes.

Of the Hayes administration, Robert Green Ingersoll would remark that it went into office by one majority and came out by none.

THAT DAY in June when had occurred the transportation of the Molly Maguires by the one-way ticket which had been punched for their free passage across the River Styx at its high flood by the coal and railroad powers with the help of Gowen and his staff—greatly to the triumph of the many-clawed Allan Pinkerton, who, keeping himself remote, had sent not only McParlan but others to this Pennsylvania coal country as spies against the labor-union men whom he had accused of traitordom to old king coal and of being revolutionary communists and who had evoked no memory in him of the raggedy ex-jailbird Charney for whom the Chartist movement had seemed as provincial as one small patch of red earth in comparison with the red revolution which was to come—took place under the coldly falling rain, the dark storm clouds.

The rain, pouring in buckets like the rain which was believed to spout from bucket birds going over earth, had wilted summer dresses and straw hats of those who had not brought their umbrellas to the Gowen picnic, although fortunately some had brought baskets of bread and ham but not for the feeding of the poor. There had been so many umbrellas going up that some had had to stand on platforms or chairs in order to get a better view. Over the heads of Gowen officials protective umbrellas had also been lifted just like those with which the state and federal governments protected corporation heads from the rain, the rain which fell not upon the rich as it fell upon the poor men to whom no shelter was given even upon the day of their death which was deserving of the tempest and the storm. But what difference could the ever-falling rain have made to the Molly Maguires as they whose eyes were turned up to the sky were hastened two by two to the gallows to suffer that death by hanging which is said to be most like drowning as their necks were stretched long as the necks of wild cranes and their legs were stretched long and their arms flapped like wings and their feet danced like wings and their souls took flight as those who would never die in the left-wing legends and histories of labor martyrdom but would circle the earth forever and forever or as long as there might be an earth to circle in the wide universe of stars? The men who had gone to the gallows had been attended by priests and had carried crosses and madonnas and roses and flowers, some already fading, wilting.

It would be remembered that Doyle, carrying a red rose in his left hand, had frequently raised it to his nose on that last journey of about two hundred steps. McGeehan had carried, besides a small brass crucifix in one hand—who could have afforded gold?—in the other hand a statue of the Madonna. He had worn two roses, red and white, in his buttonhole.

The witnesses in the jailyard, some relieved and some disappointed, had been spared the visages of men in their death agonies by the white hoods which had been slipped down over their heads after they had spoken their last words, some with smiles, none with any tears but those which were indistinguishable from the tears of heaven falling as the skies turned black and the sun seemed but a red spark which might also go out like the spark of life which had been theirs.

The sky, it would be long remembered, was like an iron coffin lid over Mauch Chunk and the crust of the earth frozen and broken with tracks of ravenous corporation thugs in Gowen's realm on the January day when James McDonald and Charles Sharpe had gone to the gallows just before the message of reprieve arrived from Harrisburg—this delay of reprieve for the condemned until he was dead having been an instrument which had been used before and would be used again.

The nail-head stars had been nailed into the coffin lid over the corpse of Molly Maguirism, it was believed, in the counties ruled by the czars of coal and rails whose triumph, however, was not complete and should be looked upon as the close of a parochial victory which had not brought the everlasting peace which would have put all sleuths, old or young, out of business.

The anti-Hibernian priest who had attended James Carroll and Michael Doyle when they had been among the prison shades in the House of the Dead had tended toward the profound conviction that Thomas Duffy had not murdered the policeman–lamp lighter Yost and had tended toward the almost equally profound conviction that James Carroll also had not done so.

The trials against these men had been conducted with flagrant paradox and contradictions annihilating each other in the Gowen court in which a self-confessed murderer had been allowed to go and a man who had not been accused of murder for which he was hauled up by the halter where the sky was brightened by no shaft of the truth—trials in which the great detective had been also the man who had been present when the blueprints for murder were laid out.

James McParlan had been shocked although not to the point of speechlessness when asked by the lawyer for the defense whether during these labyrinthine conspiracies for murder by the Molly Maguires he had gone to confession or had participated in communion. The very idea of doing such a thing had seemed sacrilegious to the Ulsterman. He had neither poured his confessions into the ear of the priest who had the pipeline to God nor tasted of the bread which was the body of Christ nor of the wine which was the blood of Christ.

Could a man of conscience have only temporarily denied his conscience while bird-dogging the Molly Maguires and other union men who could not be smashed and reconstructed into the image of Gowen—and would conscience hound such a man as Gowen to his grave—after all, catch up with him?

When Gowen, having retired to private law practice, had almost succeeded by his extravagant management in bringing Reading to the edge of that famed bankruptcy, that financial abyss which in America was the Grand Canyon into which men toppled and was Wall Street, a place where in times of panic it was dangerous to walk lest one be smashed like an egg by a hurtling body, his death from a shotgun wound in a room in Wormsley's Hotel in Washington, where he had been pleading before the Interstate Commerce Commission in a rate case against Standard Oil, would at first be believed to be not his suicide but his murder by a revengeful Molly Maguire who had planted a smoking pistol in his hand. The planting of such delusional evidence had been countenanced by him when he had sent the Molly Maguires to their premature graves. Molly Maguires would insist that he had not been murdered by an avenger of the dead but would attribute his taking of his own life to that remorse which had been caused by his conscience at last catching up with him.

As to Allan Pinkerton, he was not to be cut down by a Reno boy or a Jesse James still in mourning for Little Archie or a survivor of a corpse-snatching gang. He had been at the Larches when he had received the word that Jesse James had been shot down by Bob Ford while hanging a picture on a wall in his St. Joseph home.

It would be Bill Nye's theory, as he would tell Debs, that Jesse James had not died as a result of that bullet which had been shot by the dirty little coward Bob Ford, as the ballad would have it: "The dirty little coward / Who shot Mr. Howard / Has laid poor Jesse in his grave." What had really killed Jesse James in Nye's view was the famed American parlor stove.

[1 4 5]

In 1876, when Gowen had been prosecuting Molly Maguires wholesale, when farmers were also subjected to abuse by railroads and wholesale foreclosures of mortgages by banking powers, as was happening elsewhere in America, there was also increasing domination by the machine which would employ one worker for a thousand and thus increase the army of the unemployed.

As for child labor, was it not a miracle that a little girl who might have stuck herself all over with pins to make her bleed as did the children who were slag pickers in meadows of gray slag, meadows beyond the light of sun and moon, could operate, as shown at the Philadelphia Centennial Exposition in an exhibition of the Pyramid Pin Company, a machine which stuck one hundred and eighty thousand pins into pin papers every day which was, of course, as long a day as it had ever been? There was a machine which could make forty thousand bricks in a day. There might soon be a technique of putting up a brick city hall in a single day, complete with hanging ivy and the goddess of justice and her scales, as there would be a technique of taking it away in a single night without loss of a single brick, and probably there already was. City halls were as frequently put up as stolen.

William Dean Howells, in his report in the *Atlantic Monthly,* had commented upon the magnitude of the Corliss engine, its vast and almost supernatural power: "In the midst of this ineffably strong mechanism is a chair where the engineer sits reading his newspaper, as in a peaceful bower."

This engineer had seemed to Howells a potent enchanter there, as this prodigious Afreet, as he called the machine, seemed a slave who would crush him past the semblance of all humanity with the lightest touch. "It is, alas! what the Afreet has done to humanity so often, where his strength has superseded man's industry. . . . Yes, it is still in these things of iron and steel that the natural genius most freely speaks."

The Bethlehem Steel Corporation, in line with the numerous power blocks in the age of the hydraulic ram, announced that it would fire anyone who was, had been, or would be in any way, shape, or form connected with the Molly Maguires.

When nineteen had gone to the gallows, a small number compared with the seventy thousand who were still said to be running wild over this country and who were still having their secret meetings in the Allegheny coal countries from which they had not been swept out by Gowen's automatic carpet sweeper, the *Chicago Tribune* had greeted the mournful news with greater shouts of joy than might have been theirs if the skies had opened and a new heaven and a new earth had appeared—especially if it was socialistic, some version of the earthly paradise in which the usual order of events should be changed, and the lion who now lay down with the lamb and ate the lamb would be eaten by the lamb—as would be said by Debs when he became the chief spokesman for social justice and often relied upon old proverbs, saws, jokes in order to make an abstraction real, a thing at hand, visual.

The *Chicago Tribune* had engaged in a very premature celebration with great rejoicing over the awesome fact that the organization of the miners had been smashed, killed, pulverized—for it had been a thing of abnormal growth, a monstrosity such as might be seen but once in an age.

For the *Pittsburgh Gazette* in the city of steel where the Pinkerton police would function with bolder brute powers, the corporation heads covering old corporation crimes against the coal union men by greater crimes, as a murderer may do when only another crime of a wider-circling whirlpool of blood can wash away or leave to human forgetfulness, to the tendency of memory to blot out whatever is unpleasant or should not be directly faced, and most especially prevalent upon the American continent dedicated to the idea of progress which had so much to forget or ignore as an earlier crime no one but a madman would wish to resurrect, there had been no more sympathy for the proposed deaths of these Molly Maguires than if their labor unions had been cocoons upon a dead tree from which, if they were not swept away in one almighty blast, butterflies of a new moral world might emerge, probably red monarchs, and capitalism would be as dead as a dead horse.

"The Molly Maguires"—according to the *Pittsburgh Gazette*'s premature elegy for these shady characters on May 9, 1876, when it was known that they were to be swept away into the dustbin of the past—"represented the spirit of French Communism and enforced their views by secret murder. The principle involved was simply that of permitting them to dictate the operations of labor."

Yes, it did seem at this unenlightened period that the only combinations which were criminal by their very nature and intent were those of workingmen, whereas the combinations of capitalists were as sacred as if blessed by God, and there was nothing so fat as an overfed trust.

Had there been answer to the petitions and resolutions drawn up at mass meetings of workingmen in great urban centers against these death sentences which for symbolic purposes were carried out by the Gowen courts in haste and repented not at leisure, had there not been the butchery of the Molly Maguires like hogs in slaughter yards occurring in time of peace as if it were time of war, then conceivably the railroad strikes of 1877—which were either a continuation of earlier strikes and their enlargement or were a widespread and wildly instinctive, spontaneous response to the deaths of the labor union leaders upon that festive day in June which was Pennsylvania's day with the rope and which caused revulsion in many thinking people for whom might did not make right—would not have happened.

Low passenger fares on the Pennsylvania Railroad had helped to contribute to the masses of visitors flocking into the Philadelphia Centennial Exposition in Gowen's city, which could hardly be called the City of Brotherly Love—that city where Terence Powderly, two years before the opening of the fair, had been sworn into the secret order of the Knights of Labor.

The secret society contained many sons of the auld sod and would often be identified with the Molly Maguires—but Terence Powderly was disgusted by the association of his nonrevolutionary labor union with his fellow mistaken Molly Maguires or similar outfits and got very tired of hearing of Allan Pinkerton's association of the Knights of Labor with the anthracite coal barren martyrs or other trouble-making outfits.

As for Allan Pinkerton—the only great antilabor detective who could claim to have been a radical himself and thus could speak with authority on the magnitude of the communist plot and its inclusion of Molly Maguires and Knights of Labor and drifters, tramps, bums—the internationalism which had landed on the doorstep of the Workingmen's party of the United States was made up of men who were responsible for the railroad strike of 1877 sweeping across this nation, leapfrogging from one town to another and in a way that could not have been unplanned. "This accursed thing came to the surface. If its members did not actually inaugurate the strikes, the strikes were the direct result of the Communistic spirit."

The exposition grounds had been located between the depots of the Pennsylvania Railroad and the Philadelphia & Reading Railroad on the Schuylkill side. Although the Pennsylvania Railroad had brought in fewer multitudes of passengers than the Philadelphia & Reading, it had enjoyed the monopoly on freight.

Among the distinguished passengers coming in to celebrate Ohio Day had been the dark horse Republican presidential candidate Rutherford B.

Hayes, who would abandon the black men of the South and who would be a hard moneyman in a nation overrun with the unemployed and whose inauguration would all too soon be followed by that great ball which was the dance of the hanged men, the Molly Maguires, and only one month later the virulent outbreak of the great railroad strikes spreading over the face of this land with the pustular eruptions which like those of smallpox might leave permanent marks upon its skin.

Perhaps the strikes were like craters of volcanoes spouting deluges of burning cinders as they had been ever since the beginning of the Civil War. Bitterness as acrid as a curtain of smoke and fire, all through the depressed economy prevailing since 1873, had hung not only over the crowded cities of the starving, homeless poor who could naturally grow no ears of corn for their bread but also over the impoverished farmlands where the price of corn had sunk so far beneath the threshold that there was no profit in shipping it to a marketplace and the best way to dispose of it was to use it for fuel, set fire to it, or leave it to rot in the rain.

[1 4 6]

WHEN THE GREAT STRIKE had raged for two months in New York in 1872, thus continuing the Civil War of the sixties with the civil war which was that of the rich against the poor, the poor against the rich, the demands for justice had been the same as would be those beginning with the long strike of 1877 circling around the earlier strike which had been like a pebble starting up, causing wider and wider whirlpools which would not seem to exhaust themselves.

But the capitalistic powers had been prepared by the great strike for the long strike and had tried by every means to keep alive the idea that, as they had indicated in 1872, discontentment causing upsurges against those who were responsible for American progress were inspired with the searing breath of communism and were the work of foreign agitators speaking to foreign audiences in five languages which were alien tongues, tongues of fire, and that they were at the bottom of the movement for the enforcement, in New York State, for example, of the eight-hour day which might as well have been written in the language of the dead so far as its enforcement was concerned.

Drivers of horse-drawn cars, among those whose patience had been so great that they had not stopped their horses in their tracks and had not brought all of traffic to a standstill as in some Sleeping Beauty world which would not awaken until there came the eight-hour day, which had become Debs's love, had continued with their seventeen-hour day at two dollars and a half a day in which some might drive while nodding into sleep to the clippity-clop sound of horses' hooves striking on cobblestones suddenly flashing into phosphorescent streaks where the iron hooves scraped.

But walkouts of factory workers all the way from the Battery to Harlem, no Statue of Liberty yet rearing up with her promises of liberty to all who had come here in search of a better life, had taught the great capitalists what responses to make as the wages fell like stones upon a narrow reef.

To those workers who had built the cloud-capped city, Debs would pay memorial tribute when he became outwardly that which he had been inwardly—the socialist for whom the many should never be sacrificed to the few as they had been in ages past and had continued to be in this present delusional world of an only delusional progress.

The strikers had carried—in a parade all the way from the Bowery to Harlem, including both white men and black who were ordinarily supposed to be pitted against each other—the slogan of Karl Marx's International: "Eight hours—peaceably if we can, forcibly if we must." No one among the curbstone watchers had hurled bricks at this motley crew of worse than circus freaks, probably more deserving of bouquets than bricks.

As in the years when Debs gave himself over to trying to educate the Locomotive Firemen to the knowledge of that brotherhood which should reach out, by ways of peace, toward the human solidarity which was and would be his ideal through periods of increasing storms caused by the failure of the myopic capitalists to recognize the just claims of their fellowmen for the conditions by which to achieve an improvement of circumstance for their wives and their children, should the fathers remain above the sod, there were objections to the strike movement from workers who, although underpaid, held to the ideal way of self-help in the land of the free and the brave which was surely not the land of the slave and the grave, no matter what eccentric radicals might say—and they really ought to keep their mouths shut.

Businessmen would certainly, with few dissenting voices, be as unified as would be the jurymen in the case of the hanging of the Pennsylvania union leaders and as would be the jurymen in the case of the hanging of the Haymarket martyrs when Allan Pinkerton would be no more although his evil deeds, far from being interred with him, would live after him upon a widening horizon.

The Employers' Executive Council of New York, not forced to wear black masks or black gowns or issue their orders in code, so far as the public knew, had issued the bold statement against all these eight-hour-a-day protestors for whom the wound of one was to be an injury to all if it were within their power to make it so, and surely the greater fire powers would be those of the rich against the poor, were unitedly determined that they would take flight, would pull out of this city and state with their objects of manufacture, which brought employment to the masses of the workers, rather than have in their hire anyone who would not work ten hours a day, as also they had warned that workers who had fallen victim to the disturbing activities of those labor unions whose heads were engaged in any act looking to the arbitrary establishment of relations between employer and employed should be fired.

The First Division of the National Guard, equipped with great Gatling guns considerably improved upon since the day they had torn up the quails in the Indianapolis graveyard, were ready to shoot at any possible revolutionary mob which might assemble—and if someone was trigger-happy, he might shoot from his hip at a mob just for the sport of it or because he had seen an anarchist's beard and thought he should be shaved by that old barber Death. And so the great strike had trickled or, as the *New York Times* had reported in a column that should have been called "Column of Premature Obituaries," had died of sheer inanition, as it had seemed.

The stamping out of poor men had gone on with that unflagging energy, that increase of momentum which comes with each triumph of the strong over the weak, the organized few over the disorganized many who included all kinds of human wrecks among the unemployed and a larger number of men who were not professional ne'er-do-wells but were those who could find no work in a country which kept its markets oversupplied with workers and undersupplied with work even when the times were good by comparison with these hard times but were never intended to be absolutely good.

In Chicago, communist and socialist and labor union spokesmen had called a mass meeting in protest against starvation in the freezing cold where the workers' only shelters were makeshift tents and boxes along the shores of Lake Michigan where the seagulls were frozen upon the piled-up ice billows and had presented a petition for relief to the city council, which had made the promises it had been no more prepared to keep than were white men those promises made to red men, as surely some of these protestors were also red.

Three weeks later as a climax to many smaller meetings, a mass meeting of the starving and unemployed workers in New York City had been assembled on January 13, 1874—unlucky day for them, but no doubt any day would have been unlucky in these tempestuous, torrid, disturbing and disturbed times—at Tompkins Square on the Lower East Side, New York, not far from St. Marks in the Bowery and not far from Cooper Union, which had been founded by Peter Cooper as a forum for free speech.

The people meeting at Tompkins Square that freezing day had not seemed individuals isolated from each other and so wholly helpless or unaware of their rights that—as the people before the American Revolution had seemed when Thomas Paine, who would be a beloved icon to Debs, first came to these shores as a corset fitter in flight from the corset makers—they could be led by a thread or governed by a reed.

The soapbox speakers who had addressed the masses of people packed inside the gates of Tompkins Square had included John Swinton of the eminently respectable *New York Sun,* the Reverend Myron Reed, a friend of social justice, a future master spirit in the life of Eugene Victor Debs, who at this time, still a locomotive fireman with the hailstones dashing against his face and the burning cinders dashing against his back, had spent his times of rest in the railroad sleeper reading the newspapers in order to try to find illumination upon those who, greater in violence than such train robbers and murderers as the Reno boys and James brothers and Molly Maguires, were the czars of coal and iron and steel and rails.

The violences at the Tompkins Square convocation of those for whom America had not fulfilled the promise of democracy had been not those of revolutionary deeds but those of the most incendiary words imaginable, as an eccentric radical named Tom-ri-John, then turning out a steaming little East Side journal which was so radical in its messages that it burned like burning ashes in a man's hand and deserved its name *Volcano,* had passed with his wife through the crowd selling the sheets which should have caused puffs of smoke and yet had not done so.

The sheets were bright yellow, and the print was done in that bright-red ink the use of which, among antireds, was in itself a crime of sedition against the ruling powers, just as was the display or waving of any kind of red flag other than that which on railroad tracks warned of wrecks ahead.

Mrs. Tom-ri-John, a very intense creature, was dressed like a man, seeming a derelict bloomer girl at best and a tramp grave robber at worst, one who would open graves and let out the dead souls of America and shove the monopolists in and put the sod over their heads as she walked about distributing the *Volcano* to buyers and who, although she did not have a gun upon her hip, did carry a large staff with which to beat the head of any man who might have the foolhardiness to attack her, be he a police-man or a rapist who could see beyond her mask.

The most disastrously eruptive thing about the communist or socialist couple who put out the *Volcano* and were interested in all kinds of reform was that they had three daughters whose names were Eruptor, Vesuvius, and Emancipator, none spouting fire and brimstone—indeed, the girls seemed rather deprived because of their being fed by their parents on scraps such as might be found in gutters—perhaps old bread as hard as stone.

All kinds of poor ragbag people were here. A publication asking for help from the government in the establishment of public-works projects for the benefit of the starving poor men and women, their eyes burning like fires in those deep eye sockets which seemed like holes which had no eyes in the thin, drawn faces which were the skulls of the living dead, had been that edited by two visionary men—Lucien Saniel, whose life as a member of the Socialist Labor party and editor of *The People* until his eyes were clouded over by the approaching blindness caused by a chronic state of semistarvation would be devoted to lifting from the neck of the American people the yoke of capitalism—and P. J. McGuire, who was no relation to the Molly Maguires and whose worthy, God-fearing father had been so offended by his godless socialism, as it had been described to him, that he had openly denounced the depraved thing and had renounced his son on the steps of the Catholic church as one who had gone over to the prince of darkness and had turned his back upon heaven's light and was the sheep who had strayed from the fold to join the wolf fold, it had seemed.

P. J. McGuire would one day found, with the help of Debs, the Brother-hood of Carpenters and Joiners, as he would also be the founder of the first Labor Day, May 1, 1886, when the eight-hour day which had been post-poned year after year by the profit-seeking mutilationists of workingmen as if it were a dead letter in the post office although in the national law for nearly two decades, it was as unrealizable as the always postponed socialist millennium which no capitalist in his right mind could smile upon. An eight-hour day would have brought all progress to a halt.

President Chester A. Arthur, the former Prince of Spoilsmen, when approached by eight-hour brotherhood petitioners in 1882, would turn to them a face as cold as an unmelting iceberg with the declaration that he did not think that the eight-hour law was constitutional and that no power on earth could make him enforce an unconstitutional law—the fact that he denied the law having been what gave momentum to strikers.

[147]

AMONG THE STRIKERS at Tompkins Square had been Samuel Gompers, a future founder of the American Federation of Labor who at this time was a cigar roller peacefully rolling in the only unionized cigar factory in the city and had been taught by the ex-revolutionary Scandinavian cigar maker who was his boss that it was all right to attend the meetings of socialist radicals, to listen to what they said and try to understand, but that it would be wise to avoid any philosophy which was tainted by utopian communistic or socialistic philosophy so theoretical and fantastical that any union leader who turned into such visionary bypaths away from the realm of common sense might risk the loss of many improvements which, step by step, might be brought to men who kept within the ranks of labor unions and did not seek to transform the entire nature of the world of man.

The radicals at Tompkins Square that day had been of every stripe or spot or check or color there was, some so motley that they might have been communists, socialists, and anarchists all at once and were running in all ways and with no sense of direction. The crowds were still descending on Tompkins Square and singing the "Marseillaise" and waving the red flag for perhaps the first time in a public place of such magnitude in America, when suddenly, in outrage because the meeting was taking place even though permission for it had been withdrawn, but too late to keep the crowds away, the police had charged inside the fences of the park, knocking down those who were stampeding like cattle toward the narrow gates, while policemen on horseback had stormed through the streets, riding pell-mell upon crowds whom they also clubbed, and Samuel Gompers with his cigar burning between his lips had narrowly escaped having his head bashed in, cigar burning to a mere ash.

The police brutality had made Gompers cautiously stick to his cigar makers' craft union and would make of him a labor conservationist as it would make of John Swinton an uncompromisingly humanitarian believer in the solidarity of the skilled with the unskilled. It would be recalled by the cigar-smoking man many years later when he was looking backward that he had seen how all the professions of radicalism and sensationalism had brought into concentration all the forces of organized society against a labor movement and had nullified in advance that which should have been normal, necessary activity. "I saw the danger of entangling alliances with intellectuals who did not understand that to experiment with the labor movement was to experiment with human life."

It seemed to him that for the radicals the spreading of propaganda was the chief end of life, that their desire had been and would be to play a great part, that they were unwilling to do the quiet and unostentatious things that made for real progress. Samuel Gompers, throughout his long labor career, had chosen to be guided by his reason in times of labor wars, which must always have been going on somewhere.

It had been necessary to help his people in a way that would not jeopardize or wreck the legitimate unions of craftsmen such as would be absorbed into the American Federation of Labor, which had not yet been founded at the time of the exposure and prosecution of the mining union agitators in the Pennsylvania anthracite barrens when no rational resolutions could help save them from an irrational fate, which, greatly to the contempt of the fused corporation heads, would cause the bog Irishmen of America to fill the bogs with their tears and would increase the numbers of bogs of despair in men's night dreams.

Samuel Gompers was simply dedicated to his own craft unionism which had no room for tramps. His establishmentarian conservatism or, as some would call it, his craftiness would be such that he would always consult his labor chart as he ventured under chartless stars and would not steer his labor craft directly into the heart of any labor storm by which it might be wrecked, would stand aside, would stand at the edge.

In *Seventy Years of Life and Labor,* Samuel Gompers would remember, in explanation of the Tompkins Square riots, a plot which might have been concocted by Allan Pinkerton with his idée fixe that the nonstriking Knights of Labor were half Mollies, half communists, six of one and half a dozen of the other. Not to Allan Pinkerton, however, but to the methods of espionage borrowed from continental Europe would Samuel Gompers attribute the charge of the police upon the crowds which included the sick and the halt.

George Blair had been a box maker by trade and was a member of the Knights of Labor when that body was a still secret body and underground. The international communists had accused George Blair and others from the workingmen's union of having warned the police that they were dynamiters trying to organize a commune, this accusation having hung around for years before it was thrashed out in the central labor union caucus, which found no evidence of Blair's having ever been a stool pigeon, of which there were more then than passenger pigeons.

Samuel Gompers always believed him to be honest and loyal to the best interests of labor: "He may have asked for police protection to have the workers properly protected—but I am perfectly confident he betrayed no trust."

THE CONFLICT between Wealth and Want, it would be labeled by Henry George, who had begun in San Francisco the manuscript of *Progress and Poverty* in 1877, the year of the long strike, which had raged from coast to coast as the first great strike of national magnitude, although it had not seemed to indicate its power or its longevity on the day that it began.

Staying at the Brevoort House in lower New York, then a fashionable watering hole for gilded Republicans whose horses were better fed than gelded workers even when employed, John W. Garrett, president of the Baltimore & Ohio Railroad who with other presidents of railroads had the government in their back pockets and were also armed, had been perfectly confident that he could go home to sit at the bedside of his dying mother and leave to the vice president of the railroad, who was John W. King, his son-in-law, the stopping of the strike of the firemen and brakemen who had done a more terrible sin than if they had violated all the generally recognized Ten Commandments at once.

"Thou shalt not abandon thy trains upon the rails" was the commandment that should have been observed by workingmen who showed that they would drop a tablet of stone and a mountaintop upon the railroads if they were not given that increase in pay which the railroad company in these depressed times could not give—not even the cent for an extra chicken's wing.

The heads of the Baltimore & Ohio, in anticipation of the strike of firemen, brakemen, engineers, conductors—whatever employees were abandoning trains at Camden Junction just a few miles outside of Baltimore and in the city's railroad yards—had already arranged to have at their beck and call the company supervisors and forty policemen to escort the scab firemen to the fire hogs, scab engineers to the engines which many might never have piloted before, scab conductors and whatever other scabs were needed to show that business was in power and the members of the Trainmen's Union or other violent malcontents should be fired.

But to the probable surprise if not astonishment of Garrett, the railroad president, the strike had been stopped at Baltimore as effectively as if shot down by a marksman's gun, and yet before the day was done the strike against the B & O had reappeared at Martinsburg, West Virginia, a junction on the line from where—endowed with more miraculous power than Mark Twain's Remarkable Leaping Frog of Calaveras County—the supposedly somnolent strike had leapfrogged to Pittsburgh, a major city upon the Pennsylvania Railroad lines on which president Tom Scott was unable to keep the peace unless by assistance of the United States government's force of arms against the strike, which was characterized by him as an insurrection.

Had the government ever betrayed a trust—a capitalistic trust—and would it do so now in the great conflict between Want and Wealth, the Want of the many, the Wealth of the few, or would it attempt to understand the chronic extremities of longstanding social and economic injustices which were the cause of this wildly increasing foment in which it seemed that the entire nation might be taken over by the lowest elements rising to the surface?

The historian James Ford Rhodes, son of an Ohio coal operator who had suffered financial losses during the long strike, would remember how it had come like a thunderbolt out of a clear sky, seemingly threatening the chief strongholds of society and at the same time shaking the delusion that such uprisings belonged to Europe and that there was no reason for their occurrence in a free country where there was space enough for all to have a chance to rise.

What evidence could Pinkerton have found for the attribution of the long strike to European Marxist disturbers of the American peace and not to agitators of native origins and the simple cry of the children for bread in a society of extreme, even flamboyant, wealth where there were thousands of homeless tramps upon the roads of rural America and where in the congested districts of the homeless poor in great cities there were thousands upon thousands of revolvers, called revolvers not because they carried these weapons on their hips as did Pinkerton's operatives but because, although in the hot summers they slept under no shelter but the sky, in freezing winters they were given turns in great flocks revolving, sleeping for a night upon the floors of police stations or churches before forced to move on so that others might take their place?

RED FLAGS, of course, had been flown that day of the riots at Tompkins Square, as some of the newspapers had almost facetiously complained upon the subject of Samuel Gompers's opéra bouffe.

Perhaps some were the torn shirts of poor men who had suffered from this necessary police action when the charging, marvelously concerted police had descended suddenly upon them, but never catching the Marxist communist speakers who had fled from their posts as if they had been tipped off that the men in blue were on their way to the bull pen where the masses waited for the slaughter.

Of course, there had been proof of terrorism against the police when a little old German radical carpenter, his dwarfed body stronger than his brain, had come to the battle equipped for war and had struck out madly with his clawhammer at a tall young police sergeant and had felled him and then, when he was lying on the ground with his skull split open and blood spilling from his wound, had struck with his clawhammer again before he was disarmed and taken to jail. The dying dwarf had explained that he had been told that he must either fight upon the battlefield or starve, and he had foolishly decided, because of his intellect which was of no great magnitude, that he would rather die upon the battlefield than die of starvation.

THE PENNSYLVANIA postmortem legislative committee, viewing the dead long strike as if it were the body of a dead striker or woodchuck, would acknowledge that the causes had been the general depression of business which had caused vast unemployment and the reduction of wages paid to the employed.

The long strike, which had broken loose at Martinsburg, West Virginia, and had been more like the American Revolution against the British Empire than like any other revolution, had been covered by the press from the beginning as not so much a strike as the railroad war or a civil war, with issuance of frequent bulletins from the battle fronts in the appropriate military language which the besieged capitalistic powers had wished to inspire against the Trainmen's Union and other malcontents who had not accepted the eternity of suppression which had previously been inflicted upon those who asked for that bread which was the staff of life.

Garrett of B & O had not only not had the time of day to spend with visiting firemen who had sought to ask him for the wages—even if he was thought to be by some men (who believed that God had imposed hard labor upon man from the day that He had closed the gates of Eden) no doubt something like a capitalist who was kicking out a picker or a would-be picker of an apple from the railroad tree—he had also fired the firemen.

When the firemen at Martinsburg, informed of new slashes by the B & O, had begun to abandon their fire hogs at Martinsburg and had succeeded in taking brakemen and engineers and conductors and others with them, they had had the sympathy of many in their town who had known of their economic deprivations and had perhaps shared them and were very tired of hearing of the problems of the starving heads of the starving corporations and their starving stockholders and their starving lapdogs and their starving racehorses and the way they were all about to lose their golden coronets or would if the firemen and the brakemen should take over.

After all, although the magnificence of the rich was probably beyond the imagination of most rural folk, where even the affluent might wear old blue jeans and slop around in the mud feeding the hogs, it was so well known to the starving poor in great cities like New York that Colonel Vanderbilt, for example, dared not take a stroll in Central Park for fear of being clawed at by hordes of the starving unemployed.

Since, in spite of obstacles in communication set up by the B & O to forbid telegraphers to spread the news, the news had run like wildfires along the rails where no trains or freight cars moved and strikers in other West Virginia towns had joined, the *New York Times* had reported on these wild creatures—"They are more pugnacious than ever in their talk and declare themselves willing to fight any power for the sake of maintaining what they call their rights."

They uncoupled cars, slipped rods out of eyes, poured salt water into already rusted engines, removed keys from locks, drove cars into roundhouses which thereafter should be locked as if they were the houses of the dead which would not open again until the millennium, mutilated some already mutilated equipment, removed lamps, cut pump hoses between tenders and locomotives, and surrounded railroad yards with picket fences of which the pickets were human beings.

When Governor Henry M. Matthew, at his wit's end, had called in state troopers to protect railroad property, he had found that it was highly unwise to place any trust in them on behalf of the trust that the trusts had placed in him, for either the troopers were as drunk as loons, were whirling like whirligigs, were brothers and cousins and cousins' cousins and cousins' cousins' cousins of many of these strikers, and in any event had no sympathy with the B & O, which everybody knew was crueller than cruel. This was rebel country.

Governor Matthew, finding that his state troopers could not be relied upon to stamp down the rebellion in a state that had been a part of the Confederacy and still contained the worshipers of Robert E. Lee and Stonewall Jackson and remembered the occupation by federal troops, had appealed to the Republican president in the White House in the federal capital to send troops, and this was what he had immediately done.

Hayes had been put into office by the Grand Old Party, of which certain leaders at the last moment had conspired to steal the election from the booze-drinking, ever gullible Democrats—but now, when he had removed the old occupation troops which for so long had waved the bloody shirt, he had sent in new occupation troops equipped with great Gatling guns and bayonets with which to put down the insurrectionists who had taken over the B & O property at Martinsburg.

Scab engineers had driven the locomotives bearing the troops through enemy territory to Martinsburg, where after three days the strike had been put down, and from there the troop trains going on to other strike points had traveled on rails lined with men, women, and children throwing pebbles. At Cumberland, of the sixteen troop trains which had tried to penetrate masses of the unemployed, only one had succeeded.

Thousands of trains were soon brought to a standstill as upon the appeal of the B & O thousands of National Guardsmen were sent in with Gatling guns and bayonets with which to subdue the seething, storming multitudes blocking their way from the Armory to Camden Station, from where they were supposed to embark for other battlefields.

The crowds blocking the railroad station were not railroad strikers but simply those men who were unable to understand the wealth of the rich and the poverty of the poor and were beating against the doors when all suddenly and without warning and to the lasting astonishment of some of them they had been fired upon by hailstones of the great Gatling guns many had not known contained live ammunition until they fell.

Among the permanently astonished had been a certainly nonstriking middle-aged vote registrar who could scarcely have failed to know that the presidential election had been disputed. Another was an itinerant Irish tinner with a bullet hole through his stomach which was beyond repair by any doctor coming like a tinsmith to cover him up with a piece of tin and set him on his way again like some poor old tramp all patched over with pieces of tin, tin over the hole where there had been an eye, tin over the ear, tin over the place where the heart had been. A young girl and a boy who had made the mistake of strolling through these daisy fields had been knocked down into a gutter with the blood streaming from their sides.

And then there had been a raggedy newsboy who had made the mistake of not being a Horatio Alger, Jr., newsboy who had stood on the right street at the right time and had sold a newspaper to the right rich man and for his alacrity and courtesy and kindness had received a large tip, perhaps as to where there was a hidden gold mine, and by a series of miraculous transformations had lifted himself up to become the president of the United States.

A bystander who was killed was identified simply as an Arab, probably a native of Araby and not one of that native variety of Arabs who were then the homeless wanderers in the desert wastelands of this nation's life. Every great city was filled with such street Arabs as these, and some were only three years old.

Someone—perhaps a crazy old Locofoco—had struck a match and lighted fire to the depot, but the fire had been put out as the city waited the night through.

The temperance-loving President Hayes, the next day, had sent troops of soldiers and Marines from such far-distant places as New York and Washington for the protection of the B & O rail yards and properties against the incendiary and bloodthirsty mobs who had gathered in the streets.

Toward nightfall the battle between the troops from the North and the unpatriotic, unarmed rebels of the South had broken loose again, with the burning of a string of cars loaded with oil, the burning of a lumberyard, and an attack upon the foundry where the molten metals poured into vats were those into which sometimes poor workers fell.

The loss of material property, the expenditure of money by the capitalists and of money by the government for their protection against starving strikers was of far greater magnitude than if the far from immoderate demands of the workers had been met. As to the loss of that cheaper merchandise that had cost nothing and was easy to replace from an endless supply, there had been, besides many who were wounded some with visible wounds to the body and some with invisible wounds to the ego or soul, the loss of altogether thirteen lives body and soul before the law of the railroad, conjoining with the law of the government, had restored the semblance of order—only the semblance.

The lid had blown off the cauldron of hell in Pittsburgh, where the superintendent of the Pennsylvania Railway at this point had followed instructions from the top by issuing, not long after the fires had been started by the demons at Martinsburg, the imperial command that double-headers should be run over the Alleghenies in the eastern haul, two iron horses to pull twice as many freight cars as they had done before, the engineers and firemen to remain in their cabs—for of necessity, some human intelligence had been required—but half the brakemen and half the conductors were to be left by the side of the rails without any more concern for them than for those who perished every year in railroad and other industrial accidents without so much as a funeral wreath from Tom Scott, who was so professorial as he explained the necessity for financial austerity such as must be imposed by the company in these hard times which were like a season of drought and surely not eternal drought that he had seemed permanently to overwhelm and mesmerize labor union delegates who had come to his headquarters to beg for no further reductions of their pay.

The Brotherhood of Locomotive Engineers, which had been organized in 1863, had accepted in 1867—as a result of the fact that their union, when on strike against the Chicago & Galena and the Michigan Southern, had had its head cut off, its back broken, its legs severed at the hips, its hands thrown overboard—the ideal of the improvement of their efficiency in the intricate science of piloting, which would bring voluntary increases of pay from the managers, whose efficiency, however, was a mythology which had exploded so many times that it was a wonder it could be believed by even the most innocent believer in an unbridled progress.

So what the Brotherhood of Railroad Engineers had become was a benevolent order providing benefits which necessarily no company of railroad kings could afford, not even those harps of flowers or pillows of lilies and other funeral expenses which would be paid for by the Brotherhood of Locomotive Firemen when, as its membership increased in this world, its memberships increased also in the world of the dead, as Debs could see.

The Brotherhood of Railroad Brakemen had not yet been born but was that to which Debs would be midwife as to other labor unions for which his help would be given in the drawing up of constitutions which had relationship to the constitutional rights of man in a democracy and not a monarchy run by despotic czars of American railroads and steel and iron and oil and coal which neglected baptisms of the newborn unless in seas of fire and neglected funeral rites for those who died young or those who died in middle age or those who died old—those who died at every minute around the clock.

[1 4 8]

THE ENGINEERS and firemen who were to run the doubleheaders through the northern Alleghenies had been expected to do so with that calm which might seem less the calm of rugged men than that of men who recognized how almighty were Tom Scott and the railroad and coal and steel and iron magnates and how small was the individual in relation to monopolistic powers immovable as mountains of stone or any great monolith of industry and finance and government.

Had they not learned to keep their peace from the moral example of what had happened to the low-down, murderous Molly Maguires? And did they not know that Pinkerton's police were fighting with the help of the railroad lords and the government to put down strikes against the B & O, the Philadelphia & Reading, and any infernal rail there was?

Since the South, even where there had been no great plantations with black slaves, had suffered decimation during the Civil War and had suffered from the carpetbaggers who were the agents of the railroad powers, regional differences might have accounted for the Stonewall resistance of the South to the new invasion of federal troops sent by the president to protect not the poor workingmen who were in every way victimized, kept in a state of semistarvation, plucked by the pluck-me stores, overcharged for dwelling places with roofs full of holes and not even old surrey hoods or old umbrella tops to spread over their beds at night as if they were forever travelers on rutted roads and not even so much as a pot in which to catch the rain but were sent to protect the poor, starving, abused, beaten, battered imperial corporations whose heads were crowned with silver and gold and whose teeth were gold and silver planks, not a wooden plank among them, and who lived in a luxury unimaginable to those starving in the southern Alleghenies, poor folks who could not know how the rich magnates lived unless, of course, they should dream that they were rich.

The troops coming in from New York had been warned that in the South they might evoke memories of the Civil War. Regional differences had been transcended, however, by the almost irrational bond of union, of solidarity which had seemed to unite the strikers in the South with the strikers in the North.

The resistance to the federal government had been even more intense than in the cities of the South, partly because some could remember that they or their fathers had worn Lincoln's dog tags while the railroad corporation heads had profited during that Civil War as they were profiting during this extension of the Civil War.

One flagman who had refused to mount the doubleheader had been like that small thing, the rolling of one pebble which may cause a mountain to move, century-old snow to fall in great, roaring avalanches, as now when others of his crew joined with him and that act of rebellion which might have resulted in the breaking of an anarchic workingman was suddenly become a vast upheaval, dislodgement, roaring as other crewmen joined and the mass movement of the great strike was on in the city built of many levels, the rich at the top and the poor at the bottom, the city of Allegheny coal and steel and locomotives and freight and passenger trains and volcanic chimneys and roaring furnace fires where the Monongahela and Allegheny rivers join together to form the beautiful Ohio River, from which, it was already hard to believe, vast populations of water travelers—Indians and fur traders and explorers and missionaries and seekers after the earthly paradise and founders of utopias and real estate agents and soap salesmen and lace salesmen and founders of empires and the parents of Debs, who would found no empire on earth—had journeyed into the western world, then so largely unknown, now so largely known and owned by the great combines of capitalists that there was scarcely a pebble where a bird could set its starfish foot left to the thousands of dispossessed broken workingmen.

What could not possibly have come as a shock to the well-upholstered gentleman in the well-upholstered railroad office in New York who had kept his skeleton crew of engineers, firemen, conductors, brakemen, men of the footboard at peace or that which passed for peace when they had scarcely a foothold, scarcely a place for one foot and would lose even that place if they should show signs of rebellion against the united railroad powers to whom God had given the task of running this nation as if it were a train was the way the shortsighted businessmen of the middle class in Pittsburgh, instead of showing sympathy for the Pennsylvania president in this which justifiably was likened to the hour of his Gethsemane as the victim of lynch or lynch artists had been perfectly willing to nail him to the rails in this strike, which, wildly spreading, threatened to be a universal boycott upon Old King Coal and the kings of Cork—not Irish—and all the kings of rails and steel there were.

After the American Revolution, seven out of nine representatives from Pittsburgh had voted against the adoption of the federal Constitution because it had not seemed an unwinding parchment which would provide, like an umbrella spread over all citizens alike, protection for the plain people and simple artisans like shoemakers, blacksmiths, tinsmiths, but rather had seemed to favor business interests and property owners and those of privilege, the few and not the many who were or would be made shelterless in a land where the ruling of the state presumably and of the federal government and the poor were exposed to the storms blowing from all sides.

And now in this new revolution which was in many ways an extension of the old, small businessmen who were of that generally contented American middle class which had seemed to make these shores an unlikely place for the sowing of the seeds of Communism and to make this land seem, to many foreign communists, a land offering few revolutionary possibilities and hardly the place in which to try to establish a demonstration of the Marxist world which had appeared as yet in no part of the world, the businessmen of Pittsburgh had showed themselves to be in virile sympathy with the strikers against the Pennsylvania Railroad and not because they were necessarily altruistic.

The businessmen of the middle class had seen that their position between the very high and the very low was impossible to maintain, that they were not rising but were sinking because unlike the government or a corporation they had no sinking fund and were likely to fall back into the mud from which they had once pulled themselves up by their own bootstraps.

Great crowds, among them numerous businessmen, had gathered along the rails cheering the strikers who had refused to take the double-headers over the mountains and had engaged in this rampant insurrection against the rule of a foreign empire which was not an isolated place hidden somewhere in the United States but extended to its outermost boundaries and threatened to turn this entire nation of rails and machineries into a stone age where the rails and trestle bridges rusted and the machineries stood as still as the bones of dinosaurs.

The police force, having been cut to half by the economies necessitated by the depression, even at this same time when Pinkerton security men were helping to put down mobs of strikers wherever they appeared, had seemed content to stand by, allowing fate to take its course as if what was now happening were as inevitable as the working out of a law of nature not recognized by the Pennsylvania Railroad, for whom poor men were moles, skunks, rats, and ought to be killed.

There were men in City Hall who seemed to think that the votes of poor men were many, there being more poor men than rich men, and thus had been unwilling to move against the men on strike.

The governor had been absent on a vacation in California, so had not been available to commit himself to a move that might be popular with a few rich men, a minority he was bound to protect, but would not be very popular with the many who were instigated and led on by old army men, some of whom had worn Mr. Lincoln's dog tags, some of whom knew how to carry on this railroad war by those strategies which would bring the capitalistic exploiters of white wage slavery to their knees.

When the governor's office had sent in a division of state militiamen to protect the business interests of President Thomas A. Scott, former assistant secretary of war under Abe Lincoln, their number including many who had worn his dog tags or had been the sons of men who had worn his dog tags, they had been slow to assemble, slow to come—had wished to fraternize with the strikers and the sympathetic crowds from the mills— had seemed unwilling to ride down upon these men who were unwilling to wear President Scott's dog tags and who in the view of those who stood for the most corrupt capitalism as if it were lily white, were wild beasts, scoundrels, dirty dogs.

A workman addressing a united crowd of strikers and mill men at Phoenix Hall had stated, to the cheering multitude, that what was happening could well be the beginning of a great civil war in this country between capital and labor. The former assistant secretary of war would have agreed, although this present eruption—which called only for the restoration of the last diminishment of wages and no more doubleheaders with a reduced staff and the taking back into the fold of the strikers who had struck for bread—was supposed to have been an attempt to reproduce the situation of the Paris Commune in Pittsburgh and in all other cities and in all villages and probably every lonely junction where no trains came, every Pebble Scratch from here to kingdom come. The American apple was threatened to the core.

America was about to see that end of the world which it had always been prophesied living Americans would live to see—hail and fire and brimstone dropping from the clouds, volcanic eruptions, seas of fire.

Until at the request of President Scott the first division of militia made up of thousands of the state's National Guardsmen along with workers and the unemployed were called in from the City of Brotherly Love to put down the strike of the Pittsburgh proletaire, there had been no war between poor men and poor men but only this tensely waiting state.

The Philadelphia troop trains had been molested by crowds throwing rocks, coal, bricks, pebbles in Harrisburg, the industrial center of coal and iron into which many immigrants of European origin had streamed since the Civil War and which was still many decades from the building of a capitol in which the statuary at the entrance would depict the burden of Life and Labor and Brotherhood—and they had been stoned at Johnstown, where, narrowly encircled by mountains, there had been chronic floods from the earliest time pouring upon a city where capitalists had built no ark and where there were burning fires caused by the melting of iron ore and the mining of that black gold which was coal—and they had been stoned at Altoona, an industrial diamond set in the midst of mountains where the Pennsylvania Railroad was the chief employer and where had been located its base for the pioneer work of building the first railroad and sending the first train over the unfriendly Allegheny Mountains, which had spawned the Molly Maguires—and they had come along the rails into Pittsburgh with seventeen sheriffs marching as their advance couriers into the coming storm and bearing with them warrants not for the arrest of the government and railroad powers with their railroad and coal and steel rings but for the arrest of eleven of the most vocal and active ringleaders in this strike of the many against the few.

A few boys had tossed chunks of coal at the Philadelphia troops, and the chief of the Pennsylvania Railroad had been given a black eye when he had tried to turn a switch to set the train upon its way in the sacred name of all the bureaucracies of whom the bureaucrat was the representative, but the mettlesome Philadelphia troops who had not considered that they were going to a picnic had advanced with their bayonets drawn and had begun shooting when there had been no order given by their major general to shoot into the ranks of mad dogs who were trying to bar the passage between the army and the trains.

Twenty civilians had been killed within five minutes and many more had been wounded, including fifteen militiamen whose sympathies were with the strikers, one woman who had made the mistake of not staying at home, three children who now would never become the president of the Pennsylvania Railroad or the less important president of the United States or a labor agitator, and more than seven scores of bystanders had been dragged away and hidden by their people as the shrapnel fell like brimstone, against which the government had provided no constitutional umbrella of protection but a parchment strangely shriveling in the heat of the sun for men whose crime was that they had refused to work under death-dealing conditions or allow the trains to pass until they were given not the philanderings of reason but the deep recognition of man's instinctive need to live.

The promise had been made by the Pittsburgh labor strikers that they would fight on even if it meant sending back to Philadelphia every soldier in a box—but naturally that last journey could occur only when the striking railway workers and hordes in sympathy with them had triumphed over the many-taloned Pennsylvania Railroad as they would permit no string of trains to run under the oblique guidance of scab engineers, scab firemen, scab brakemen, scab sleeping-car porters who should attend the freights when they were sleeping cars for cattle, no doubleheaders cut to a skeleton crew, and no trains if all trains in these yards and elsewhere throughout this nation should be burned and all rails should be torn up and all roundhouses and firehouses should be burned and owls should perch upon the chimneys of rusted locomotives and the sun of progress should stand still. The only alternative to this prospect of desolation would be the triumph of the labor strikers who had asked only for the hours and wages permitting survival at a level which was still far below the threshold required by the middle class.

President Rutherford B. Hayes, the dry-as-dust temperance man and hymn singer in the White House, had been in close communication with the former assistant secretary of war who had asked for additions of troops as the strike roared with a Babel of tongues including old Irish brogue of old Hibernian antilandlords, Italian, Polish, German, Russian, Magyar, and such tongues as those with which God had confounded the bricklayers, carpenters, and builders who had attempted to build a tower to heaven which was probably the precinct of a railroad.

And yet these men of various tongues had seemed to understand each other by various signs older than those of any language and very well might soon be climbing over the picket fence which the railroad powers had built around the universe and might take it over if not stopped dead in their tracks. Not only were the strikers setting fire to such highly inflammable material as freight cars loaded with gasoline—there were some wild tramps who were making themselves into living torches by drinking entire casks of the blood-red wine they had stolen from freight cars.

President Hayes had very seriously weighed and considered asking his cabinet to declare that there existed in Pennsylvania a state of insurrection against the government, and he naturally did not refer to the empire of the former assistant secretary of war but to the rebels upon whom the militia had turned more great Gatling guns which were still not enough, more having been required with every passing hour.

When the strike had been broken because of the greater fires with which to create greater combustion, when the lid which had been off hell had been put back on again so that the Pennsylvania Railroad could resume its functions, the president of the United States had acknowledged that the strike had been put down by force and force alone. When the federal troops had arrived on July 23, six more days had been required before the first trains could be moved again, and one of these had been wrecked in the mountains before it could reach its official terminus.

A POINT OF VIEW on the Pittsburgh strike differing radically from that of the military was that which would be described in the autobiography of the Irish firebrand Mother Mary Jones, when she looked back upon her career which had been devoted to the Christ-like struggles of labor unions to be born and to live and not to be crucified by capitalists.

She had been in Pittsburgh at the time of the B & O strike, had known the labor strikers intimately, had seen with her bright eyes which would never be dimmed as to labor struggles the burning of one hundred railroad locomotives of the Pennsylvania Railroad and of the roundhouse when the burning boxcars had lighted the sky and had turned to flames the steel bayonets of the soldiers. It had been common knowledge that the fires had been started by hoodlums backed by the businessmen of Pittsburgh because of the discrimination against their city in the rates for freight. She had known that the labor strikers were to be charged with arson although their members who might run amok and commit an act of violence were subjected to discipline. "Then and there I learned . . . that labor must bear the cross for others' sins, must be the vicarious sufferer for the wrongs that others do," she would tell Debs in the later years when they were travelers together through the coal country trying to save other strikers from burnings as from sorrows which were immeasurable. Would the sorrows never end?

[1 4 9]

IN THE EARLY SEVENTIES, John Hay had married the daughter of Amasa Stone, whose wedding gift to the newly bridled couple had been a substantial stone house on Cleveland's prestigious Euclid Avenue, where the American despots who lived in an atmosphere of Medici magnificence, the coal and iron and steel and oil barons or kings or emperors of emperors were undergoing or had already undergone the aurification which permitted them to wield unholy powers over the lives and deaths of poor men, but which did not arouse the outraged moral disapproval of Old Dirty Socks Abe Lincoln's former secretary, who now, while watching over his father-in-law's business interests from his office at One Cushing Block as he had promised to do, had spent most of his time working on his biography of Lincoln, the Great Commoner—his only relaxation having been his sending whatever comforting news there was on the strikes, which, raging in Pittsburgh, had not bypassed the city of the magnate, who suffered from dryness of bones and, vacationing, was taking the waters in foreign spas.

Hay sent his father-in-law news of the strikes that were going on back home in America and even in Ohio—just as if the old oaken bucket that came up from the well were loaded with sticks of dynamite and matches set aflame by labor strikers, as if all the rich folks were going to be piled into a hell-bent battered old surrey and dispatched over the hills to the poor farm. "Since last week," according to John Hay's comforting report to the anxiety-ridden Amasa Stone,

> the country has been at the mercy of the mob, and on the whole the mob has behaved rather better than the country. The shameful truth is now clear that the government is utterly helpless and powerless in the face of an unarmed rebellion of foreign working men, mostly Irish. There is nowhere any firm nucleus of authority—nothing to fall back on as a last resort. The Army has been destroyed by the dirty politicians, and the State militia is utterly inefficient. Any hour the mob chooses it can destroy any city in the country. . . . Fortunately, it has not cared to destroy any but railway property.

The day before this letter was written, a regular panic had prevailed in the city as freight men had refused to let merchants have their goods, which were spoiling at the Cleveland depot. But the resumption of work by the rolling mills had helped matters somewhat—and so Hay had decided to risk staying on here with Amasa Stone's darling daughter and grandchildren, who were the apples of his eyes.

> The town is full of thieves and tramps waiting and hoping for a riot but not daring to begin it themselves. If there were any attempt to enforce the law, I believe the town would be in ashes in six hours. The mob is as yet good-natured. A few shots fired by our militia company would ensure their own destruction and that of the city. A miserable state of things which I hope will be ancient history before you read this letter.

The next day things had become more quiet—and passenger and mail trains would begin running as soon as possible. It had looked as if the railroad companies were about to surrender to the demands of the strikers, and this fact could only rouse John Hay's ire as he apparently had elected to have no understanding of the rebellion of wage slaves, whether white or black—certainly no understanding of the labor agitators who, according to one of his fateful witticisms, were called leaders only because they could always get a mob to follow them.

The future chief of imperialists had now reported to Amasa Stone—"There is a mob in every city ready to join with the strikers and get their pay in robbery, and there is no means of enforcing the law in case of a sudden attack on private property."

When the country had passed through a week of great anxiety, the son-in-law could report to the father-in-law that it was nearly at the end of the greatest danger. But his feeling was that the profound misfortune and disgrace which had fallen on the country could not be wholly remedied. One astonishing feature of the whole affair had been that there had been very little fall in stocks. In the agony of the riots Rock Island had gone down a little but had recovered while a mob was still rampant in Chicago.

Until the troops arrived, there was no safety in buying, for the rioters might destroy millions [in] property in an hour. . . . The Democrats have tried to curry favor with the rioters in their platform without, however, daring to approve their outrages—and the Republicans will also have a milk-and-water resolution in favor of law and order without daring to condemn the strike.

Distrustful of both parties, he did not advocate the abolishment of both parties or say with what form of government the presently inept two parties should be replaced—did not suggest a monarchy such as he did not approve of anywhere on the American continent or anywhere on any other continent or island over which it should have dominion, be it even a turtle's back—for he would stand for the expansion of the golden American democracy everywhere, and with haughty oblivion to the irresponsible views of anti-imperialists in every walk of life and walk of death for whom the fiscal interests of coal and steel and iron emperors were not the dominant interests presiding over every aspect of man's fugitive existence as it might seem to be or become under that rule of that form of government which was described as democracy at home and was despotism abroad.

Lincoln's private secretary, John Hay, had seemingly not understood such conciliatory attitudes so hopeless of enactment—nor had he understood the draft riots in the North—the fact that poor boys had been forced into a war for a democracy they had not enjoyed, unlike the rich, whose fathers had been able to buy their way out so that many hardly knew there was a war as they passed their time playing croquet or polo, the sport of kings, which might be likened to croquet on horseback.

His experience with the upholding of the class structure with the few rich at the top and the many poor at the bottom during the Civil War, which had greatly increased the distance between them although this could not have been the martyred president's intention, had probably been a greater cause for his favoring the capitalists and disparaging the rebel labor strikers who wanted their share of the cherry pie than was the fact that he was married to the daughter of a tycoon and was not himself entangled in any business by which to rake in money. The ability to make dollars had been quite lacking in the character of a poet who was proud of his lacrimosity, his ability to shed tears over the deaths of Shelley and Keats. His true love was the Lincoln history which was his major concern during this year of the railroad riots. He once merrily observed, when allowing Robert Todd Lincoln, future Prince of Nails, as he would be called during the Pullman strike, or Debs's strike, as it was called, to check on the manuscript for any changes of spirit or flaws of fact he wanted to be removed, that he would be a Republican until he died but that when he got to heaven, he would try a monarchy perhaps.

Looking up from his manuscript on the Civil War to report to Amasa Stone on this new civil war which had been brought to a peace in Cleveland, he had been disgusted not only with the Democratic gubernatorial candidate—and quite correctly, for it was he who by appeal to the labor votes would win when the votes were counted—he had also been disgusted with the Republican gubernatorial candidate in spite of his having modified some of his idiotic talk at Cleveland. "All his sympathies are with the laboring man and none with the man whose enterprise and capital give him a living. He condemns the use of force against strikes and opposes the increase of the Army."

Still later, knowing that Amasa Stone must be sickened by the folly and cowardice of public men on both sides, he could see only gloomy prospects for both capital and labor. "The very devil seems to have entered into the lower classes of working men, and there are plenty of scoundrels to encourage them at all lengths."

The author of *Pike County Ballads,* John Hay was much embarrassed by the popularity of "Little Breeches" with both political parties and its constant reprint all the way from the East to the West Coast. "Little Breeches" had followed him everywhere, was like a rattling tin can tied to a dog's tail, was the most awful doggerel for which he felt that he ought not to be held responsible in a life increasingly sophisticated and concerned with matters on a world scale. He had placed only his initials on the original publication and was surprised that they had not worn off. He could still take pride in his fatherhood of "Jim Bludso" with its tale of the riverboat engineer who weren't no saint but had deserved praise for the heroic act which, appearing in the last two lines, he had written with the moral sentiment which Whitelaw Reid would some day claim had been added at his suggestion— "Christ ain't going to be too hard / On a man who died for man."

To his father-in-law when he was at home and John Hay was resting abroad, from eternal dyspepsia and headaches no waters could cure—for he was worn down by wearing the iron crown of an American mogul who would bend all little people to his will—he had written on March 11, 1883, of the horror of body and soul which had been visited upon him because of the anarchic uproarings to which he had been a witness in Paris.

"A demonstration took place day before yesterday on the Esplanade des Invalides which might easily have become very serious. A few bakers' shops were pillaged, and a crazy creature named Louise Michel tried to get the mob to march to the Tuileries, but the quirassiers came on the ground and dispersed them. . . . The laborers have had the mischief put into their heads by trade unions, etc. . . . Paris is a poor place to live in." As usual, he had been painfully impressed by the fact that these troubles were caused by insubstantial politicians so eager for their advancement that no government could last more than a few weeks.

In response to the railway strikes and riots of 1877, Lincoln's former secretary had written, under the spell of his sardonic muse, *The Bread-Winners,* a work of fiction which he had published anonymously and which he would not clasp to his nonpatriarchal bosom even when, probably to his surprise, it became a literary sensation of the day.

A lady living in New York City on East Twenty-seventh Street, thus not far from the neglected author of *Moby Dick,* had written to the aggrieved father that she would be happy to take in the motherless and fatherless orphan and take care of it only if he would cede to her the legal title and the royalties which would surely, of course, pay for its board and keep many thousands of times over.

Part of the charm of *The Bread-Winners,* no pioneering trailblazer of any kind, was that the public which interested itself in these matters did not know who the author was. He had been as remote, as withdrawn as if he had not only not written the book but had not turned its pages. He had refused also to hide himself away under a woman's name and petticoats and no doubt not because he was as revolutionary as some last-ditch literary Molly Maguire. He was conservative and bold, and was that mentality a crime?

The book, one of the first economic novels of native origins but thinly veiled by its love story, was no great work of art and very antirevolutionary in its very rational, unambiguous propositions as to what was or should be the nature of the world which was the property owners' world and breadbasket. The themes, which were the defense of the rich in a world which was essentially moral of nature and should be conducted according to law and order by those who knew best what was good for the majority of mankind, were the opposites of those in *Les Misérables* or *The Mysteries of Paris* or *Uncle Tom's Cabin*—the latter a revelation of the black man as one of *les misérables*.

Although there might be individual capitalists who were of darkest colors, villains of the deepest dye, yet honest laborers had nothing of which to complain—and socialistic and anarchistic panaceas were not, in this view, the nepenthean cure-alls which some charlatans seemed to promote, sincerely or insincerely, for magical use in relation to human ills—old coughs, old croups, old scars, old scabs unhealed, old joints out of joint—but rather were those which would poison the body of society from the head to the toes—and thus the radicals were these true criminals who engineered a war between the masses and the men who were responsible for this country's progress from the darkness to the light.

The arguments of the incendiary novel, if one believed in such inhibitions of freedom of speech and writing as capitalists attempted to place the lid of the Lazarus tomb over mad-dog anarchists who were opposed to the lords of high finance and military power they seemed to be trying to overthrow when actually what they had asked for in 1877 and earlier and would ask for through a long, long afterward were a loaf of bread and an eight-hour day—the latter request about as outrageous as if the entire dial system of the universe should run on an eight-hour day on their account— had reflected the attitude of other respectable people and had helped to pave the way to the Haymarket martyrdom as surely as if *The Bread-Winners* had carried no basket of mother's old-fashioned home-baked bread but a basket of that loaf of dynamite which was a bomb thrown by a person never to be identified and believed by anarchists to have been a secret agent of the capitalistic powers for whom all who spoke out against their rule should be muffled and gagged and silenced—should keep a silence as silent as the silence of the grave. In nineteenth-century literature, a very noisy place as almost everybody knew, the greasy apostle of labor, asking what the workers were, defined them as slaves, as "Roosian scurfs." "We work as many hours as our owners like; we take what pay they choose to give us; we ask their permission to live and breathe."

John Hay was also one of the anti-inflationary men opposed to populism and Greenbackism—the argument that, according to some American humorists, Greenbacks were the most democratic dollars there were as they flew so rapidly from hands to hands that they settled never in one place, were not in one man's hands long enough to put into his pants pocket, were not the kind of wealth which like gold and silver could be piled up in safety vaults as something which would be of value until that time when gold and silver came to dust even as would great kings.

[1 5 0]

GENERAL PHILIP SHERIDAN, far from believing that the buffalo hunters should be outlawed as had been urged by humanitarian legislators who because of their attempts to protect the buffalo herds had been called Indian lovers, thought that a coin in their honor should be struck off with a dead buffalo on one side and a poor Indian on the other. How could the buffalo herds be welcomed when they had been known to stand against trains like strikers trying to stop their passage through lands where the grass burned?

The buffalo herds were so rapidly disappearing that they were or would soon be as rare as the rapidly disappearing red men who soon would be so rare in the old Middle West that most people had never seen any Indian but the wooden cigar store Indian in Chicago against whose cheek Debs's friend Bill Nye struck a match and was surprised that the cheek twitched.

According to General Sheridan, for whom the only good Indian was a dead Indian, buffalo hunters had done more to settle the vexed Indian question in two or three years than the entire regular army had done in thirty years. "They are destroying the Indians' commissary. . . . Send them powder and lead . . . but for the sake of lasting peace"—and what a strange ideal lasting peace was as it usually meant lasting death and might mean, in the ultimate sense, universal death—"let them kill . . . until the buffaloes are exterminated."

In Louisville a tall black man who should have identified himself with the buffalo rather than with the buffalo hunter but who called himself Buffalo Bill had led a flock of stampeding blacks upon a wild trek in which he and his people had demanded a dollar and a half a day for an eight-hour day as repairers and cleaners of the drainage system in the districts of the rich. Crazily dressed in rags and patches, armed with no weapons but sticks and stones and burning torches made of bulrushes, the blacks had rampaged through the streets smashing streetlamps and the windows of rich men's houses and setting fires, thus giving substance to Allan Pinkerton's judgment upon the mercurial nature of this childish and ignorant race who, reacting to the veriest trifle, showed their unfitness for immediate acceptance into this civilization which was purportedly based on law and order. Pinkerton had closed his eyes to the rebellion by former wageless slaves against wage slavery which had given to them an insufficiency of bread and meat and no shelter. They lived in mud holes along the river banks. Kentucky nights in the long winters were freezing cold.

In West Virginia the fraternizing of poor rednecks with poor blacks as they had protested against the railroad powers had shown that the class struggle and not the race struggle was what was at stake and could only cause alarm among those who by using the blacks as scabs had given substance to the idea that the races were divided in their interest, that those poor rednecks who had never owned plantations or had black men to weep for them when Old Marse was planted in the ground should be opposed forever to the blackbirds who were the lowest birds on the totem pole. The blacks had been longer in nature's ovens than the reds—so why should all not burn?

As the strikes had leapt from city to city, yard to yard, line to line, and as Pinkerton's men and other private detectives were engaged in seining for the ravenous fish who, keeping to darkest waters, were the labor union leaders, as Washington's public buildings were guarded by Marines, the lake city of Chicago had come into the complete possession of the communists who, of course, lived there and thus were natives either of the city or of America, as was not noted by the *New York Times,* for whom these natives were as alien as to other capitalistic presses in a day when labor organs were so small and weak that they did well if they had the lead blocks for all the letters of the alphabet, particularly after a police raid.

The portrait drawn by the war reporters of the *New York Times* of the railroad strikers was altogether unflattering. These strikers for bread in their baskets were certainly not living skeletons with nothing left but their great lantern eyes, as some sentimentalists would like to believe—they were certainly not the good elements such as respectable citizens were—

they were the disaffected elements roaring wild in Chicago—roughs, hoodlums, and adventitious robbers—suspicious-looking individuals, blacklegs and looters and communists, rabble and labor-reform agitators and drunken section-hand men, incendiaries and enemies of society and felons and idiots—worthy apparently of any name that was fit to print—but what was really appalling was that there were so many of them not only in Chicago but elsewhere.

When President Hayes had contemplated announcing that this entire country was in a state of insurrection, the holocaust blowing from shore to shore in a way to give pleasure to Allan Pinkerton as if his wildest dreams were about to be realized, if Gowen had had at a deeper level than the conscious any stain of guilt, it had been covered over by the government-sponsored mass slaughter when the troops had shot into the crowds at Reading, his own bailiwick, and where there would have been more murder and mayhem if the members of the Sixteenth Regiment had not threatened to decimate the members of the Fourth Regiment if they molested the workingmen any further with their quail shot and where the occupation forces might have required an entire population of the anarchists that Americans essentially were and have left the railroad powers as a small minority under siege behind their castle walls such as the Larches, or all might have had to take refuge in holes in the ground.

As the strike raged with particular intensity in Chicago, the city of the roaring winds where everything that occurred in other cities occurred with exaggeration, magnification, greater wildness to which winds and waves contributed, the Chicago Board of Trade which was made up of the respectable railroad kings and merchant princes and not of the disaffected elements, boodle artists and looters and labor agitators and skulking characters who would have killed their mothers for a piece of silver or gold or twenty cents, had begged the governor of Illinois and the president of the United States for troops in a city where not a train moved and not a streetcar moved and the sailors on the freighters in the harbor had refused to move as the crowds were beyond control and the city which had been destroyed by fire once before might be destroyed by fire once again and the lake turn to fire.

The secretary of war, determined to evade a premature Apocalypse, had dispatched couriers to General Sheridan, then busily killing off the Sioux with his marksmen. Helping to restore law and order had been Lieutenant Colonel Frederick Dent Grant, son of Ulysses, while as troops were rushed to other trouble points they were not emptied from the nation's capital itself and further troops were brought from Norfolk by ships as two ironclads were ordered to stand by lest thousands upon thousands of bums should decide that God helps those who help themselves and should descend upon the dome and carry it away or sleep in Abraham Lincoln's bed or hang their rotted clothes on the wash line in the Blue Room as Dolley Madison had done or storm into the United States Treasury and carry away the capitalistic ears of the gold corn, ears of the silver corn, or start printing their own paper money like the scrip that was issued by some businessmen to the workers in company towns where the pluck-me stores were those which plucked the feathers from the chicken workers by charging twice as much as other stores charged.

Not only had President Scott refused absolutely to negotiate with the strikers at Pittsburgh, he, the most corrupt of railroad powers, had called for the militia to give a rifle diet to the strikers on his lines for a few days and see how they liked that kind of bread—and when the strike on the four great lines was over and at a cost which would have provided bread for workingmen, had asked in the September issue of the *North American Review* that from now on, in view of the great conflagrations which were raging as he wrote, federal troops should be called out without a governor's request and that there should also be a redistribution of forces throughout the nation so that they might not be at long distances from the places where the insurrections broke out.

The governor of Pennsylvania upon return from his California vacation had had to send troops by wagonloads into the forbidding mountains where the Molly Maguires seemed never to have died.

The Reverend Henry Ward Beecher had rhapsodically, euphemistically, expressed to the congregation at the Plymouth Church where there were not only stockholders clipping their railroad coupons but stockholders clipping their stock in God, and surely it was gilt-edged no doubt like the Bible, his sense that the importation of communistic and like European notions were abominations with their notions and theories that the government should be paternal and take care of the welfare of its subjects and provide them with labor.

The American doctrine is that it is the duty of the Government merely to protect the people while they are taking care of themselves—nothing more than that. "Hands off," we say to the Government; "see to it that we are protected in our rights and in our individuality. No more than that." . . . Good has intended the great to be great and the little to be little. No equalization process can ever take place until men are made equal as productive forces. It is a wild vision, not a practicable theory.

As others, of course, would agree.

No DOUBT from the point of view of the Darwinian social evolutionists in opposition to the Marxist social revolutionists, it would be necessary, before equality could be established, for all cloud-topped mountain pinnacles to disappear through ages of erosion and all great Rocky Mountains to wear themselves down to the level of molehills and even farther down until there should be that endless plain on which all workingmen should be made equal as productive forces and, if there should still be those incapable of survival by self-support, should be paid in relation to their need. The ideal would evolve ultimately into the idea of the pan-labor unionist Debs.

While the riots raged, the respectable Chicagoans had scarcely dared to close their eyes in sleep lest they should never open their eyes again in a red dawn streaked by the volcanic fires of labor riots which might make a buried Pompeii of America, a continent covered from sea to sea by forever burning ashes and lakes of fire burning like the eyes of birds, and would do so if the capitalists of the great combinations and conspiratorial apparatuses backed by the powers of state should have their nonblessed way of keeping everything fixed, static, absolute, unchanging according to their belief that there should be no combination of lowly laborers but only those of the omnivorous trusts for whom gilt-edged securities were their security against such chaos as the labor strikes raging under the leadership of men whose maps and charts for a New Moral World were foreign to the spirit of true enterprise.

The year 1877 was that in which Thomas Edison heard for the first time on the phonograph the sound of human speech which was the pastoral nursery rhyme so dear to the hearts of little children who slept not under the beds of trains or at the bottom of coal mines: "Mary had a little lamb, / Its fleece was white and snow, / And everywhere that Mary went / That lamb was sure to go."

But surely the American dream of a machine-powered society had no room for a labor leader whom the laborers should follow, and the labor leader was less like a man with human dimensions than a mad old ram leading the hobbledehoy masses over the edge of the viewless abyss, that which opened at men's feet as truly as if the earth had swallowed them.

Had the ideals of a revolutionary democracy been a material importation from Europe, they never would have been permitted to pass the inspectors at the customs house. The harm of the labor riots in great industrial cities would be attributed generally to the agitations of the foreign-born who had not lived through the evolutions of democracy before coming to America. Much of the darkness of the times was caused by the large numbers of poor Civil War veterans who, although they had had the honor of fighting for the preservation of the Union, seemed ungrateful for this privilege as they cried out for their share of the nation's wealth which should take the form of higher and higher pensions which were now so low that they could hardly sustain human life and for which they sought increases, a nation of parasites within the nation of workingmen who were expected to give to them their eternal support.

But if not all had been unwilling conscripts, if some had been willing to risk life and limbs for the Union cause or had understood what it was, yet had they made their great sacrifice for the benefit of the war profiteers who now turned great guns on them as in Chicago when the great army officers came in with some of their old companions to shoot at them?

The use of the judicial ukase, which in Russia under the czarist regimes was an edict or order having the force of law as was any decree issued by an authority or official and which might even have the power to stop the course of the sun, as some of the czar's little pigeon workers thought, and which in America was known as the writ of injunction, requiring a person or persons to refrain from doing certain acts—should he refrain from breathing, and should he put a stoppage to the beating of his heart?—was one of the mighty engines employed by the great corporation combines on a large scale from 1877 onward and with no decreasing power as a means of settling industrial disputes as was the use of state and federal troops and volunteer citizens as special deputies and watchmen, some who came in from tennis courts to contribute their services in the ping of war of the capitalists which should be followed by no pong of the starving workingmen.

This vast strike history of which Debs was the magnetized witness, the watcher on many fronts, was a very important factor in the education of his heart but was only one of many injustices playing before this on his imagination, stretching his taut nerves like harp strings—and many would come afterward. There was this music where the man was. There was not the silence.

[1 5 1]

THE BEDLAM OF the Chicago strike when workers of many tongues were making themselves understood by signs had begun when by discord the workers had sought to reach concord with their united employers—to shake the great golden apple of concord from the trees which had yielded to them only the apples of discord—to shake, indeed, the unshakable conviction of the capitalists in these dark ages of the American democracy that the only utopian dreams which might be realizable upon earth were their own according to their profound conviction that the profits of corporations were not in any way within the province of the lowly children of the common clay to judge and bore no relationship to the wages paid to them and that the wages were correctly founded upon no law but the immemorial law of supply and demand for that labor which was on sale on the marketplace just like any other merchandise and was as necessary as the law of progress by which nature itself operated its machine.

In the pastoral America before the Civil War, Thoreau had heard the creaking of the axle rod of the wheel upon which this old world turned and had thought it perhaps needed greasing, but such sentiments even if still nostalgically entertained by the good and respectable people had little place in a world which had departed from what was natural and was now itself the machine, the roaring locomotive which should not be brought to wreckage by men on strike, the dead souls of America whom the labor organizers were trying to lead from the darkness into the light, as if through ages of darkness the children who had been born in darkness and had lived in darkness and should die in darkness should still find their way from the darkness to the light. The strike had begun because some cogs in the great machine were loose and the engine was busted and the train would not move.

The strike at Chicago, in response to strikes against the great trunk lines in other cities whose heads were meeting in New York with the head of the Pennsylvania Railroad for the purpose of establishing their own version of a union or brotherhood against the Brotherhood of Locomotive Engineers and the Trainmen's Union and all other unions real or potential had begun in the last week of July at the Michigan Central freight yards and had passed from there, wave by wave, to other yards with such intensity of conflagration that it might seem that the city was in danger of being destroyed again by fire and ashes.

All the streetcars were stopped on the South Side in this new crisis threatening the city with incendiaries swarming about like lightning bugs feeding on the body of a dead horse. All business which depended on transport by locomotive wheels had come to a halt. The streets had been hot enough to fry men's brains like eggs. Policemen on horseback had attacked the strikers with clubs and guns at the Michigan Central freight yards— had shot into the crowds at the Chicago, Burlington & Quincy roundhouse, where three people had been killed and seven wounded—had shot at a crowd of ten thousand people at the Halstead Street viaduct, with the toll of many more lives taken by the capitalistic toll keepers, many wounds paid to workers instead of the coins which were owed. Altogether between thirty and fifty people had been killed and about one hundred wounded before the strikers who had had no weapons but sticks and stones with which to defend themselves had been put down by the peacekeeping squads whose diversity of membership had been composed of all kinds of troops determined that the structures of capitalism should not perish in a universal carnage against the men who were themselves the perpetrators of mass carnage in mills and mines and railroad yards—this triumph over the desire of dead souls for resurrection certainly seeming to be living proof that the capitalistic brigand Jay Gould had been correct in his boast that he could hire half the workers in America to kill off the other half at any time.

The forces which had triumphed over the strikers in the city by the dunes had been six companies of the Twenty-second Regular Infantry, the North Regular complete down to its last man, a battery of artillery out to shoot whatever crazy seagull workers there were and bring them down into the sand and the mud, several companies of soldiers on horseback charging upon a mob, five thousand special deputies who—previously lawbreakers themselves who had been in flight from the law—were now given power to arrest the men who sought by work stoppage to challenge the enactments of economic royalists for whom the workers were replaceable in an endless supply, five hundred veteran soldiers who were now at war with fellow veteran soldiers with whom they had once been shipped off in boxcars to the battlefields of the South, and members of such patriotic organizations as the Ellsworth Zouaves, and also the federal troops which had come in from service against the Indians who were supposed to be the scalpers, whereas the true scalpers were the corporations scalping the heads of poor men and quite ready, it would be seen, to wear their scalps draped over their military bonnets.

It was too early for the irreverent Mr. Dooley, the sage of Archey Road, to explain to readers of the *Chicago Evening Post* in the capital city of muckrakers what high finance was. "High finance ain't burglary, an' it ain't obtaining money by false pretenses, an' it ain't manslaughter. It's what ye might call a judicious selection fr'm th' best features ov them ar-rts."

In the mass hysteria caused by the refusal of the corporation Apache barbers to give up their scalpings of the wages of poor workingmen, Mr. Dooley, the fictional old Irish saloon keeper of the many-faceted intellect with his brogue which allied him with anarchic creatures of the bog and elicited the love of Debs (the creation of the fictional journalist Finley Peter Dunne, a second-generation Irishman), might have had his old Archey Road bar closed and hung permanently with his funeral wreath and his neck wrung for such an incendiary, riot-inspiring, antisentimental sentimental statement as this upon the nature of high finance or his definition of rights as those a man ought to take and for the simple reason that a right which was handed to him for nothing had something the matter with it.

Mr. Dooley was surprised, in the eighties following the Haymarket strike in the city of wild garlic and wild hogs running wild which the muckrakers would make into a capital city, when the ever-ignorant Hennessy wanted to know the meaning of the open shop which was then the subject of much discussion in the newspapers. "Sure, 'tis where they kape the doors open to accommodate th' constant stream of min comin' in t' take jobs cheaper than th' min that had th's jobs."

To Hennessy's pointing out that the open-shop men were for the unions if the latter were properly conducted, the wise old owl Mr. Dooley's answer was to agree with them but then to ask, in a way to keep the conversational ball rolling—"An' how would they have thim conducted? No strikes, no rules, no contracts, no scales, hardly any wages, and damn few members."

It was not too early, however, for President Scott and others of the industrial lords to whom the government had prostituted itself to believe that dynamite eggs should be used against workers when they went on strike and to look upon the present suppression as a preparation for the outbreak of union agitation and agitators and anarchists in whatever future civil war battles might occur.

It was not too early for the suppression in Chicago of Alfred Parsons, who was among other literate radicals rounded up and warned by Mayor Monroe Heath that he should stop addressing the strikers and go back to where he had come from—and that was not a foreign country but was the state of Texas, where many citizens had gone originally in flight from the long noose of the law in this country and where many still preferred to think that theirs was still a foreign country—for if he persisted in Chicago, the gentlemen of the Chicago Board of Trade would as soon hang him from the next lamppost as not.

And yet the leaders of the Workingmen's party in Chicago, of whom he was the most vocal spokesman, urged strikers, in the name of their fledgling labor organization which was strong on its feet although only one year old, to remain strong in their refusal to work on presently murderous terms but to engage in no incendiary acts.

One of the lines which was most often quoted by Parsons until the warning of Mayor Heath that the Board of Trade would hang him was that of Thomas Jefferson at the time of Shays' Rebellion:

God forbid we should ever be twenty years without such a rebellion. . . . What country can preserve its liberties if its rulers are not warned from time to time that this people preserve the spirit of resistance? Let them take arms. What signify a few lives lost in a century or two? The tree of liberty must be refreshed from time to time by the blood of patriots and tyrants. It is its natural manure!

Such Jeffersonian agrarian and historical imagination was not that enjoyed by the members of the Chicago Board of Trade during the railway strikes of 1877 turning the great hub into a wheel with spokes and its outmost rim, that reaching over the nation, into a rim of fire and its spokes into rims of fire when the anarchists of European philosophy were so few that the labor strikes would have raged without them as they had not demanded the total reform of society, nor would it have been welcomed unless as an excuse for the hanging of the Haymarket martyrs from the great capitalistic tree of death, surely not that of life, as a moral example to all who might wish to show the workers at least the first two or three steps away from the moral bog by hanging the long, lank frame of the man who had headed what would be labeled the Debs Rebellion and who was believed by some people to be no better than Jesse James for his leading the strike against the emperor Pullman of the sleeping-car palaces whose idea of utopia did not conform with that in which all American agitators should be mesmerized into sleep and dreams, pleasant dreams from which there should be no awakening.

After the great Chicago fire more than one million dollars had been contributed to the relief of the homeless poor who had camped along the water's edge.

Two thirds of this vast allotment of money had stuck like honey to the

fingers of members of the Chicago Board of Trade for investment in their
own companies at bargain interest rates, it was believed, the magnate mul-
timillionaires who had refused to hand out relief to the maggoty Chicago
homeless poor, including such self-elected excellencies as George Mortimer
Pullman, Marshall Field, Rufus King, and other civil and financial bigwigs
whose sympathies were not even passively given to the raiders on the railroad's roundhouses and trains, the furious strikers of the worker bees
against the burning hives of the capitalistic beekeepers. How could Debs
not come into conflict with them although he was weak and they were
strong?

[1 5 2]

In St. Louis, where the long strike would be, in the immediate sense,
short-lived, it had raged with widespread revolutionary fervor: pilots on
steamboats were stopped on their voyage down the Mississippi, the unpredictable river which, like history, sometimes changed all shorelines by
departing from some settlements and inundating others, burying them
under seas of mud; and steamboat whistles had been stopped, and trains
and train whistles had been stopped, so that there was transport neither by
water nor land; and the executive committee of the well-organized United
Workingmen's party had announced that there could be no middle
ground, evidently no place like a ridge of dry land between raging torrents
where the river split and divided into two rivers, not even a dry spot large
enough for the foot of a crane, for there must be absolute victory or absolute
defeat no matter how long the war between the rich and poor should continue, and as was recognized by those who understood the long history of
the spirit of reform and the opposition by fire and flood to its resurgence,
the true threat to this democracy came from the rich corrupter and not
from the masses of the poor—the rotten-potato poor.

The executive committee of the United Workingmen's party had called
a mass meeting in which all the blood shed in the strikes was blamed upon
President Hayes, the God-fearing man in the White House who had sent
troops to put down men fighting for rights at a minimal level. When the
governor, closing all places of business, had threatened to declare martial
law in the city, it was already overrun by an army of one thousand citizen
volunteers equipped with munitions by merchants and businessmen who

were losing dollars because of this strike of dollarless men and who, if they yielded an inch, might be confronted by endless rising of demands, as there were also eight thousand musketmen from the Rock Island Arsenal which was on the site of the old Fort Armstrong, the long-ago guardian of the Mississippi, which during the Civil War had manufactured weapons for use against the Confederate and had had also on its grounds one of the largest prisons for Confederate prisoners of war.

The executive committee's letter to the governor when the city was threatened by carnage had expressed labor's demands for the righting of wrongs which were certainly not too far different from the descriptions of the economic injustices of the turbulent seventies by Herman Melville, author of the neglected, never best-selling poem "Clarel," whose lines—if ever they were read—could not have endeared him to the American worshipers of gold, such as Jay Gould, who was not by any means, as Debs would point out, the chief of sinners:

> *Ay, Democracy lopes, lopes, and where's her planted bed?*
> *The future, what is that to her who vaunts she's no inheritor?*
> *'Tis in her mouth, not in her heart. . . .*
> *But in the New World things make haste:*
> *Not only things, the state lives fast—*
> *Fast breed the pregnant eggs and shells, the slumberous combustibles*
> *Sure to explode. 'Twill come, 'twill come!*
> *One demagogue can trouble much! How of a hundred thousand such? . . .*

The St. Louis executive committee members had asked for the speedy cooperation of the governor of the state of Missouri and all citizens for the passage of the eight-hour day and its enforcement and for an end to the employment of children under fourteen years of age in factories and shops and in other uses calculated to injure them. Living wages paid to the railroad men would bring a peace and prosperity such as had not been seen for the last fifteen years. Nothing short of compliance to this just demand which had been made purely in the interest of the national welfare would arrest this tidal wave of revolution, the executive committee had warned, that neither threats nor organized labor would turn the toilers of this nation from their earnest purpose but would rather serve to enflame the passions of the multitude and tend to acts of vandalism.

The executive committee had also demanded food for the starving workers and had offered to pay for it.

As the B & O had been conquered and the tidal waves of revolution had been put down elsewhere, the United Workingmen of St. Louis, where the revolution had lasted only five days, one day less than the time God had taken to create out of nothingness a new world, had found that greater time and greater effort would be required to create out of the capitalistic framework of this old, rotten state a new world premised upon even the simplest economic justice, for they were surrounded on all sides and invaded from all sides by the combined military forces mustered by the mayor, the governor of Missouri, the governor of Illinois, and the president of the United States when he was put into the White House as the chief executive representing the chief executives of mills and mines and railroads who did not starve, as their children also did not starve for lack of bread as did the humped children of the poor whether the times were good or bad as the grain of the harvest was not for them.

In 1876, in the race against the Republican presidential candidate Hayes, Slippery Sam or Soapy Sam Tilden, a tricky railroad lawyer, had been helped to his defeat by a lawsuit brought by the Terre Haute, Alton & St. Louis Railroad. A sworn affidavit filed in the case in 1862 had given his fee from the railroad as ten thousand dollars, although in his tax return for that year he had told Uncle Sam that he had made altogether only seven thousand one hundred and eighteen dollars. When found out, he had explained that he had given large sums of money to his brothers.

To the *Toledo Sunday Democrat* this excuse was not considered valid. He might as well have given to his brother Lo, the poor Indian, a hat full of rain. The Republicans had answered that his income was his income, no matter to whom he had passed it along.

The *Toledo Sunday Democrat,* representative of the whiskey-drenched Irish, had quickly dug up the fact that the supposedly pious Hayes had failed to mention, in his local tax reports of 1874 and 1876, the fact that he had had a fund of fifty thousand dollars for three years and was the holder of several mortgages which were unwept, unhonored, and unsung, and—what was really scandalous—he had kept secret from the government the fact that he had had a magnificent piano of which the ivory and ebony keys rippled with the music of such hymns as "A Mighty Fortress Is Our God."

As the strikes were snuffed out in St. Louis, there had begun in Chicago in a nation in which both major parties recognized no labor party's rights to strike, concerted raids on the union headquarters at Schuler's Hall, and the arrest of the members of the executive committee of the United Working-men's party on charges that they had engaged in that conspiracy against the state, which fortunately at this time would result in no sentence of hanging for which, it had seemed, the times were not ripe. The intention had been merely to break the legs of all poor workers who by this moral example would learn to give up their foolish dreams of human solidarity, it was perhaps not even hoped in spite of this temporal triumph, for the threshers who objected to being torn to shreds by the great threshing machines would surely go on flailing against them and all other reapers of men, and preparations must be made against other conflagrations starting up or even an undying ember like the eye of a tramp who, achieving a greater miracle than that of Jesus Christ Who had walked on water, could walk under water.

On July 23, a mass meeting of workers in San Francisco who had gathered to express sympathy for the workers in Pittsburgh had turned into a prolonged riot against the heathen Chinee who had helped to build the railroads but now in hard times deserved to be beaten into grains of sand, according to the sand lotters, whose name was taken from their meeting place.

Denis Kearney, an ex-sailor and ex-drayman who had not understood that the Irishmen who had been killed on the rails were of the same order as the heathen Chinee of Bret Harte's poem, had established his leadership over a large number of Hogans and Brogans and others of the auld sod for whom there was little or no employment by proposing certainly no kind of utopian balm by which to cure society's ills in a way which would recognize the needs of all regardless of the color of the skin, no quest for a socialist El Dorado in this land where the capitalists had found gold, but rather a little hanging here and now as the best course to pursue with the capitalists and the stock sharps who were robbing the white men by hiring the yellow men at lower wages than any white man would work for.

At a meeting on Nob Hill where the rich lived like mandarins with coolies to wait on them and bring them their mandarin ducks for dinner on plates of gold, he had announced that the corrupt railroad owners wallowing in their wealth had only three months in which to get rid of all Chinese laborers unless they wished to dance at the ends of ropes.

"Remember lynch law," he had cried out with his bullhorn to the railroad owners whom he was going to make into new Reno boys and James brothers and Molly Maguires and at least partly in memory of them. He was going to dig the graves of a great many people who were now in high places.

[1 5 3]

WILLIAM HENRY VANDERBILT had been named by the old Commodore who had given names of presidents to all his sons but one, who had turned out in his judgment to be an absolute lunatic and unworthy of the name of the man who was surely the greatest commodore who had ever sailed up the Hudson since Henrik Hudson had reached the present site of the state capital at Albany.

When President William Henry Vanderbilt was told that the employees on the New York Central Railroad were determined to stop the trains unless they received an increase of pay over the going rate which they claimed gave to them not enough for bread, he had expressed his confidence that they understood very well the identity of interests prevailing between themselves and the company. If they should stand firm in the present crisis which came from the hard times faced by business, it would be a triumph of good sense over blind fury and fanaticism.

Despite such rational considerations as seemed to be his in the thought that all should be the sharers of misfortune if not of fortune, Vanderbilt had still persisted in the view that the trains had been stalemated not by the authentic workingmen, who were no malcontents, but by rioters charging over the rails and into the yards and shops.

"The desperate men who have done this"—he had told a reporter at Saratoga Springs, where he was taking the medicinal waters from blessed Indian springs where the Great Spirit flowed while the iron horses thirsted for one drop—"are not the Central men but probably men out of employment who would like the situation of those at work." It was an accusation covered with the hoarfrost of age and had some truth in it in a nation of starving men.

"Our men feel that, although I may enjoy the majority of stock in the Central"—President Vanderbilt had explained—"my interests are as much affected in degree as theirs—and although I may have my millions and they the rewards of their daily toil, still we are about equal in the end. If they suffer, I suffer—and if I suffer, they cannot escape."

That was why he could not give them their living wage which for the very skilled was one dollar and a half and for the unskilled from eighty cents to a dollar per diem, scarcely enough to keep a man with a family alive and not enough with which to buy a wedding veil of mosquito netting for his starving, flea-bitten daughter when she was married to her starving bridegroom and not enough for a tin tiara for his old, mangy, flea-bitten tramp dog if he had one following him around the way a tramp would follow a tycoon. And although he had closed his eyes to the strike as if he were closing his eyes to the sun, he had farsightedly asked for the governor to dispatch his troops to the sore spot as had been swiftly done, with the result that the freight cars had been moved.

A young brakeman named John Van Hoesen, who had cried out at a rally of workers in a public park that if they who were asking for bread should be given a diet of bullets, they would answer with bullets, had been arrested, along with other strike leaders, and thus the strike had been broken as effectively as if some old, patient turtle which had suffered much from its tormenters had been turned upon its back and left to right itself in the mud.

A notice which was not unlike a coffin notice had been nailed onto the walls of depots and shops that those who did not report for duty at eight o'clock on Monday morning, July 30, 1877, would be considered as having left the services of the company unless they could give a good excuse for their failure to appear.

The mayor of Albany and prominent citizens had promised the broken workingmen to present a petition to President Vanderbilt for the restoration of the pay scales to which they had objected, but the train of time had rattled along its track without their keeping their promise.

President Vanderbilt had continued at the death-dealing pay scale but had promised an increase at the moment when the business of the country could give justification to it and had ordered that a purse of one hundred thousand dollars should be split among the workers as their reward for loyalty to the railroad, each to receive a share proportionate to his position. And thus the engineer on the right side should receive greater reward than the fireman on the left side and the fireman greater reward than the brakeman and the brakeman greater reward than the wheel wiper, who so easily might be wiped away himself by the wheels passing over him—as would be pointed out time and time again by Debs of *The Locomotive Firemen's Magazine*.

When President Vanderbilt's heart went on strike, striking for the last time, when all the railroad lamps went out for him because the lamp lighters were on strike, when the engine died, when the wheels turned no more, he would come to the end of this life's journey in the midst of a heated discussion with John W. Garrett over the rights of the Baltimore & Ohio Railroad to enter New York.

[1 5 4]

THE GOVERNOR of Indiana in 1877, James D. "Blue Jeans" Williams, when he was running for office in the campaign of 1876, seemed to be God's answer to the Democratic party's prayers in its opposition to the Republican candidate, Godlove Orth, to whom the malodorous scandals of the Grant administration stuck like the odor of a skunk.

In Washington, the discovery of Blue Jeans Williams had seemed as phenomenal as if a gold creek had been discovered in the Hoosier hills. Politically unknown, an ugly, well-to-do, six-foot-four-inch farmer from Wheatland, Blue Jeans Williams, or Uncle Jimmy, as he was sometimes called, was described by the *Evening News*'s Washington correspondent, Regulus, as a man who knew nothing of diplomacy and the disreputable wild shifts of small politicians and was of the people and had always identified with them and their most intimate interest.

Judge Walter Q. Gresham of Indianapolis, urging upon Republicans the necessity of their moral uplift, had stated—"I don't believe that Orth is an honest man. . . . Certainly we will be overwhelmed with corruption at no distant day if the people continue to ignore the duties of citizenship in the blind adherence to party leaders."

Blue Jeans Williams, a political stump orator who wore sun-streaked, rain-faded overalls and an old straw hat and seemed as old-fashioned as if he had just stepped out of the antebellum world of little old farms before there were railroads, was boastful of the fact that he had never gone too much to the little red schoolhouse because he had been too busy plowing, sowing, feeding the chickens and the hogs. As to his Lincolnesque height which made him seem even taller when he was on the stump, he could only explain—"I just grew up between two corn rows." Although he was often seen with manure on his boots and the streak of clay on his shirt and mud on his blue jeans, it was not because he had been feeding himself at the trough of corruption like Godlove Orth.

This horny-handed son of toil, who would wear his blue jeans and raise his lank form in every Hoosier county so that a unified democracy could rally around Uncle Jimmy with the seeds of grain hanging in his beard, was the choice of the independent *Evening News* for winner of the gubernatorial contest over Godlove Orth, who was belled like the cat by the Grant administration, especially for his participation in the Venezuelan swindlers' ring, and was chased around by the *Evening News* for dodging an investigation. "He had prostituted his office to that of procurer for thieves and swindlers. . . . He had not scorned to cover his real purpose by the use of a man of straw."

Abandoned by party bigwigs and especially by the Republican power broker and ex-governor Oliver Morton, the waver of the bloody shirt, Godless Orth had withdrawn on August 2, 1876, as if he were the only one who was corrupt and had not God's love, and telegrams of appeal to come to the rescue of the Grand Old Party had been sent to the conductor of every southbound train to hand to General Benjamin Harrison, who was on his way home from fishing for blue bass in the waters of northern Lake Michigan and was astonished when finally after two days of fishing for him the Republican central committee landed their hook on him to inform him that he was the big fish whom they wished to lift out of clear waters and put into muddy waters as their candidate for governor.

The *Indianapolis Journal* had already described this favorite Republican son as not only one of the ablest but also one of the purest and best men in the state—and had not seemed to know that they were giving him the kiss of death by praising him as a man of splendid intellect. Their nostalgia for the way things used to be and had never been had carried them back to older times when intellect had not been a hazard to a political candidate.

"Kid Gloves" Harrison, as he was sometimes called because of his sartorial elegance, which was in keeping with his elegance of intellect, had not heard of his unanimous choice for candidate for governor by the central committee in the Hoosier capital city's United States courtroom until his train had pulled in at Fort Wayne, from where he was traveling on the beeline to Indianapolis to receive showers of congratulatory messages for a candidacy he had not accepted although a party of Republicans as awesome as any lynch party had jumped on board his train at Muncie to persuade him that he ought to take Godlove Orth's place. The local band struck up a tune that would recall Lincoln: "We Are Coming, Father Abraham."

All along the way, at every whistle-stop where ordinarily the proud iron horse would not have stopped even to pay a courtesy call, the train had been stopped and there had been huge bonfires lighting the way, until finally, many hours late, the general had arrived at Union Depot, where he had been greeted by a volley of cannonballs left over from the Civil War and huge crowds and various volunteer bands playing old Civil War marching songs which were enough to break the heart of any crippled Civil War veteran, should he be above the ground or under the ground within hearing distance.

The general had explained that he needed time to think, yet the impression he had given to his hearers was that he would not be able to withstand the unanimous will of his people. He himself had said that he saw no way to get out of his running. But all through the night and all through the family's prayers the next morning and all through services at the Reverend Myron Reed's First Presbyterian Church, he had mulled the matter over in his mind, had turned and turned somewhat like a fish unable to get off the hook.

His old Ohio father (one day to be the victim of grave robbers) had written to him his serious regret that the responsibility of choice had been thrown on him by his party—although, as was said by the Negroes, they had gone and done it, and he would be compelled to decide between party obligations and his private and personal interests. "I am curious to know what horn of the dilemma you will choose."

The horns of the dilemma were that Harrison could make more money as a practitioner of the law than as a governor, who, the servant of his people, would be administering, upholding the law, for the benefit of all, of course, and not of various party horses.

A lawyer had written from Richmond, Indiana, the Quaker stronghold—"I hope before I die to be permitted to vote for you for President of this Nation and have expected it for some time, but it is my conviction that you made a mistake and missed reaching one of the stepping stones when you declined the race for Governor during this campaign."

An Indianapolis bank president had cried out from the Republican amen corner: "*Vox populi, vox dei!*" And still another had promised a campaign for Big Ben which in this hour of peril would bring back the glorious campaign of 1840 when his grandfather had triumphed over all inclemencies. By sunset, the general had made up his mind to run.

"Give Harrison a kid-glove client and a two thousand dollar fee"—had sneered the Democratic *Daily Sentinel,* which was naturally backing Blue Jeans Williams as its champion boxer in the gubernatorial sawdust ring— "and no matter how guilty the culprit may be, his intellectual grasp will really separate crime from such respectability."

The former vice president Schuyler Colfax, once called Smiler but not smiling since the disgraces of the Grant administration had caused the tears of self-pity to erode his once smiling face, had warned—"You will exchange congenial professional labors for public life which—in its best estate—is full of toil, exactions, and misrepresentations."

A former trooper of Harrison's brigade had joined with others in the amen corner by writing to the general that what they heard today was the same old cry as had greeted them at Resaca, Kenesaw, and Peach Tree Creek, and that they well knew the meaning of the old command that they must tighten their belts, boys, and give them the cold steel.

Morton, although joining with Godlove Orth in congratulating General Ben for his candidacy, had helped his old rival almost not at all, confining his two-hour congratulatory speech at Danville, the little capital of Hendricks County, to an attack upon the Democrats and no proposition of any kind as to how to solve the country's financial woes which were so many in those days that drovers of a generally Democratic hue would cry out to their horses not "Whoa, whoa, whoa" but "Woe, woe, woe." And everybody knew that the old oaken bucket which came up from the well had been filled with golden coins for the Wall Street pumpers and nothing for poor workingmen with their patched blue jeans and their hats full of holes.

The rain had been pouring all night long at Danville before the general's arrival with his party in five cars provided by the Indianapolis & St. Louis Railroad for their conveyance from the capital city's Union Depot to the land of the Hendricks corn. The rain had been good for the corn.

The rain had stopped, but no sooner had the general mounted an open-air platform than the rain had fiercely poured down upon the man who was not seeking the office—"The Office Seeks the Man," according to a motto outlined in evergreens on a trellis above him, which gave no protection from the storm—and the crowd and the reluctant candidate had been forced to run for shelter to the county courthouse.

"We will have some fraud in office until the good time comes of which the Bible tells us when the evil doers shall go to their own place," the general had promised, with that sense of reserve which was always his. "As the Scriptures say, offenses come, but the motto of the Republican party is 'Woe unto the man by whom the offense cometh!'"

The *Indianapolis Journal* had already predicted the general's victory from the shores of Lake Michigan to the Ohio and from the Wabash to the eastern boundary, and although at the rally at Danville that day when the heavens had conspired with the Democrats to be rent apart by thunderclouds, to pour the buckets of rain upon the general as if he with his patriotic fire could be squashed like a lightning bug by a dark flood, had not lost faith in him by any means when it reported—"In the light of the rallies at Danville and Anderson, it was not too much to say that the fires of 1840 were being kindled from the Lake to the Gulf."

In Morgan County, which had been rebel country, the general had chosen to be under guard by a battalion of old, gray-haired Civil War veterans of the kind who had not already heard taps, had not come out of their graves to hear him say, with ringing pride, that he accepted the banner of the bloody shirt. "I am willing to take as our ensign the tattered, worn-out, old gray shirt, worn by some gallant Union hero, stained with his blood as he gave up his life for his country."

In September, the Civil War veterans of the nation had flocked to the Hoosier capital city as if it had suffered no division of pro-war Republicans and antiwar Democrats during the Civil War, when Dr. Gatling had been the Southern watcher of the Northern boxcars coming back with their wounds bleeding through the loosely planked floors onto the railroad beds and ties and rails. Coming in now to the old Union Depot, every veteran had brought, as instructed, a torch, two blankets, and a tin cup, the latter not for begging but for the coffee which was provided by the wholesale grocers of the city for brewing in barrels at the wash house of the Asylum for the Blind.

Only two weeks before the election, the presence of Civil War veterans in the streets and at rallies in public parks had made it seem an act of patriotism to vote for the Republican candidate and not for the Democratic Blue Jeans Williams.

Campaigning throughout the state after the veterans who had heard reveille, had heard taps, had gone home or crept back into their graves, the general had shouted that all in the nation would go down together in one vast abysmal depth of beggary and ruin if Confederate representatives were aided by enough Democrats to obtain hold of the administration and the Treasury, so anyone might conclude that it was they and not God's Own Party which had been responsible for the purloined carbuncles of the thieving Grant administration, which had taken place because he was as innocent as a baby as to what was going on.

A monster celebration of the grand old pioneer days had been held in September at the Tippecanoe Battleground in Lafayette for the purpose of bringing back to life Old Tip, who had sold whiskey bottled in a miniature log cabin and had never been a sharer of a pioneer's life.

Although the true log-cabin party of that day had been that of Blue Jeans Williams with the holes in the soles of his shoes, there had been a grand show of log cabins on wheels—just such which, as a matter of fact, had been used by those original perambulatory pioneers who had always been moving on from one place to another toward the western glow, and there had also been canoes on wheels, as many old voters for Old Tip had managed to wheel themselves out in wheelchairs in an effort to bring back the old log cabin which was associated with Old Tip and not because he had been pouring its chimney fires down his throat. Anson Woolcott, the Independent Greenback candidate, a former Republican, had taken at the last hour his hat out of the ring lest by his continued candidacy he should inadvertently deprive the people of Indiana of a candidate who had been a Union soldier and who was a man of tried patriotism, pure character, and splendid intellect and learning in all the lore of statesmanship, a man whom the office would not exalt but who would dignify the office.

This switching of the Greenback candidate had aroused from the Democrats the cry that the Republicans and the Greenbackers had entered into the sale of the gubernatorial office by unholy collusion against Blue Jeans Williams, the farmer's friend, the honest farmer.

The Democrats who had been in the Greenbackers' fold, which was in favor of folding money, had put forth a next-to-the-last-hour candidate to try to bring the Hoosier state into the Greenbackers' fold of all those poor men who did not care what the currency was, whether it folded or folded not, just so they could pay for bread.

Judge Walter Q. Gresham, even before the charge that the national election was stolen from the Democrats by the backers of the honest Rutherford B. Hayes, had been of the conviction that Woolcott had been purchased. But the honest Benjamin Harrison had gone right on around the clock with his Republican speeches striking in every town like a railroad clock. And what had been the result when the sheaves were counted at the harvest?

For a while, the results had hung in doubt. But finally, all the sheaves having been counted, it was dapper Ben who seemed the gruesome scarecrow even the crows would avoid in a barren field—for he had lost while Blue Jeans who was the lowliest fellow that grew up tall between two rows of corn had won and was crowned king.

Party members, according to the self-congratulatory *Sentinel,* were soon singing a merry song to celebrate Blue Jeans Williams's walk over the political grave of Old Tip's grandson, Kid Gloves Harrison. But the *Journal,* which was the Republican trumpet, had cried out, perhaps because someone had been reading Robert Browning on the failure of success, the success of failure, that there was such a thing as a defeat which was greater than victory.

The defeat of the general had occurred less than five years before his election to the United States Senate and only two elections before his election to the White House which was as cold as an iceberg in wintertime and should have been called an icehouse and where he would have to accompany him in his walks through rooms where the chandeliers were icicles a

Siberian bloodhound which was so huge that someone remarked to him—"It looks like a very over-fed monopoly"—and he agreed.

The triumph of Williams over Harrison which had occurred in spite of all the Republican money flowing in from the East to overthrow the man of common clay had been, according to the Democrats, the triumph of Blue Jeans over blue blood. Many of the common clay had thought that the general's blood must be blue and not red because he was so very cold, formal, remote.

The "deer publick," as Josh Billings had called it, had not known that while convalescing from the lost gubernatorial campaign Harrison had worn for a few weeks, while piled up under blankets in his four-poster bed in his North Delaware Street mansion, some very fancy nightshirts, which had been sent to him by a family friend in St. Louis, Cousin Meg, to whom he had written in his thank-you note in early January, 1877—"Mrs. Harrison thought I would not wear ruffled and pleated 'robes de nuit' and was surprised to see how kindly I took to the finery." Strange as it might seem to Cousin Meg, he had never had a more unruffled sleep.

His was not to be an unruffled sleep for long. He had helped himself along in his recuperation of strength by making a tour of key coastal cities in the East, where—when not shading himself and his wife and daughter and son under the very large beach umbrella of his protection from the blazing light of the sun as they looked out over the waves of the sea—he could observe at close hand the unjust conditions under which the laborers worked in factories and railroad mills and railroad yards, the long hours for which they were given short pay, and so it had happened that he had been on a tour combining pleasure with duty when the four eastern trunk lines had announced the ten percent wage shave for which they had conspired together as if their four heads were one with but a single thought, and that was profit.

When the strikes of the railroad men had broken loose, sweeping the country with oceanic storms, the Harrisons had managed to ride ahead of the conflagration into that safe haven which should have been the Union Depot in Indianapolis where, of course, the hackman had been waiting to take them in his hack to their North Delaware Street mansion as the city was not burning yet and about the only insurrections which there were might be caused by a swarm of bees disturbing the peaceful traffic flow by landing on the nose of a hackman's horse or on a hackman's red nose which they had mistaken for a flower.

The Sunday peace on the morning of July 22, 1877, when the city was boiling not only with its usual heat but with fears of conflagrations breaking out here in God's own city, had been definitely ruffled by the distribution to churchgoers of the kind of literature far more fearful to them than if they had been told that Jehovah was about to break loose with His thunderbolts and shower down His meteors and bring this old earth to its end so that there might be a new heaven and a new earth, as had been promised so often before that the promise could be ignored by rational men as something not to be feared or, if they were not rational men, could be heartily welcomed.

> Attention, railroad men! Rise up and assert your manhood. There will be a meeting held in the State House Yard on Monday evening, July 23, 1877, at eight o'clock sharp, for the purpose of sympathizing and taking action with our starving brothers in the East who are now being trampled under the feet of railroad bond holders. Everybody invited that believes in equality and justice to all mankind. Let us have a hand in the breaking of the railroad monopoly.

The trouble was that in sympathy with the railroad owners elsewhere, there were only thirteen soldiers guarding the United States arsenal in the Hoosier radiating railroad city, and thus there was no real protection against raiders who might attempt to steal away munitions with which to carry on this new civil war which only the discerning might recognize as an extension of the old Civil War. This city had not been a battlefront during the Civil War, although it had been a city of divided sympathies. There were only a few bullet marks on little gingerbread houses on Guisendorf Street, which was not far from the old red mill overlooking the canal and not far from the Military Park, where were piled up pyramids of cannonballs where tramps slept hiding away from the night watchman during the long nights and which had not yet been removed because of the tramps who after a long night of sleep, purple sleep, washed their feet at dawn in the central fountain near a children's merry-go-round.

General Harrison, upon his return from the Civil War with the sounds of battle still ringing in his ears, although sometimes the enemies had been only shadows moving in the fog as also his regiment had seemed to them, had realized the unrest of poor soldiers who, sometimes with arms and legs missing, had returned home to find that their little homesteads with pea patches and beanpoles and gourds hollowed out for mailboxes had been run over, appropriated by the race of hard rich men who had been able to hire the poor boys to fight for them while they gathered in the golden sheaves of the war profits—and yet he had asked whether even one of those who had fought for the Union would exchange the proud consciousness of having imperiled his life in defense of his country for all the gain which had been piled up by those who had stayed at home, it having been his passionate conviction that this proud consciousness was better than bank stocks, houses, or bonds.

Harrison had relied even then upon his politically useful habit of warning against wartime traitors who—the worst were those rebels of the North who sympathized with the southern rebels—would sneak in upon the Union patriots while they slept and steal away the fruits of the bloody contest. And now although he had always thought that the Republicans, Lincoln's party, should be the workingmen's party, Harrison's sympathies were on the side of the property-holding class, the railroad bondholders, the railroad monopoly to the extent that he would wish to protect the sacrosanct trains and roundhouses and railroad yards which were held for the public weal from needless damage by those who worked for the public woe. But where were the troops?

Must the rich answer to the call of arms by coming out of their rose gardens to do battle with the poor wage slaves who were striking for what they considered their minimal economic rights in a democracy where everything was measured by the cost, the cost to the rich and not to the poor? Was the Hoosier capital to be subjected to the torch like Atlanta?

It had been boasted that wherever Sherman had passed in the South, agriculture could not be revived for a generation, the policy having been that of the scorched earth as in the Indian lands which were being stripped of their mantle of grass and flowers and their buffalo herds.

Blue Jeans Williams, the Paul Bunyan farmer with the clay on his blue jeans, could not have cared less than he did for the federal government and thus had refused to protect the trains which were running under its protection, even though manned by scabs, and had not given an owl's hoot what happened to the mail trains in the baggage cars, which did have a tendency, as some were rehabilitated cattle cars or troop cars, to spill the mailbags along the way to some of the nowhere towns where no town ever was and for which he would assume no responsibility if they were mired by this strike with the result that there would be many letters lost, decades sometimes passing between the posting and the delivery and many a poor old mother long in her grave before she heard from her dead soldier son that he lived and would be coming home soon—and so would she not cease her mourning, keening for him?

Considering the magnitude of the theft of the presidency from Tilden which had occurred at about the time of the attempted theft of the body of

Abraham Lincoln, considering also the fury of the Democrats who had promised to march on Washington should Hayes, who was favored by Harrison, be placed in the White House, Blue Jeans Williams, having threatened to join with them with pleas for bread and meat, the down-to-earth governor could only feel that as a representative of the majority whose will had been sacrificed upon the altar to the will of the minority railroad owners, it was not only morally but politically perceptive to favor the poor because there were so many of them, as many as the grasses of the fields.

The mayor of the city and the chief of police took the same view of the railroad strike and would protect only private property if it should be under threat. The Greenbackers, instead of voting for their candidate, had secretly voted for more Democrats than Republicans because of no reason but that they knew who the poor man's friend was.

The Farmers' Declaration of Independence in 1873, a resurgence of the original Declaration, had stated—"The history of the present railway monopoly is a history of repeated injuries and oppressions, all having in direct object the establishment of an absolute tyranny over the people of these States unequaled in any monarchy in the Old World and having its only parallel in the history of the Medieval ages when the strong hand was the only law."

The general had called in a group of leading citizens to discuss the best ways of handling the strike, what might be done to move the trains, the gentlemen of the council including Judge Walter Q. Gresham, Colonel A. W. Hendricks, and other representatives of law and thus, but not necessarily, representatives of order.

The gentlemen on the Harrison council, putting their heads together, had all said yea with no dissenting nay that, as the army was out of town, camping on some other battlefield than that which this city might become, a volunteer citizens' army should be called up for the maintenance of civilized order if Blue Jeans Williams and John Caven, the latter of an old Hibernian name, should continue in their present policy of failing to act, playing the fiddle while Rome burned or, as Debs's friend Bill Nye would have said, playing Rome while the fiddle burned.

The general had ensured that a telegram was tapped out to Washington by a telegraph operator who was not asleep or on the side of strikers to authorize his call to arms of two hundred volunteer citizen soldiers for the protection of government property. Perhaps he had had in mind transporting them on the mail trains, for he could not possibly have thought that the government owned the railroads—even if he had not been reading any red literature, he must have recognized that the railroads owned the government.

And was not the government under great debt to the railroads for bringing together the East Coast and the West Coast, although, as the anti-train Riley used to say to the pro-train Debs, if God had intended for them to have enjoyed such proximity with each other, He would have drawn the Atlantic Ocean and the Pacific Ocean together and left but a thin strand, probably just enough for a long-limbed bird to stand on.

[1 5 5]

GENERAL HARRISON's belief was that there should be negotiations between capital and labor and not confrontation as of two opposing armies meeting in the darkness of night—no doubt that night caused by Stygian stupidity—the spirit which he favored being that of the laying down of arms by rebels against the railroads and the sacrifice of absolutes through arbitration in a spirit of compromise until the harmony of labor with capital should be reached, everyone to make some concession for the sake of equilibrium, and the workers to understand that if they strangled the goose of capital it would be unable to lay the golden egg in any tramp's old hat as the strikers seemed to think.

Harrison was unable to make a sentimental appeal to poor men such as was made by the dogmatic Democrat Blue Jeans Williams when, as in the campaign in which he had created hell on the Wabash for Republicans, he had gotten himself, as he described his oratorical methods, chuck full of his subject, knocked out the bung, and let nature caper as if there had never been a Washington, D.C., or a larger country than the Hoosier land.

Although Judge Gresham had issued the invitation to the respectable citizens who were interested in self-protection to meet with him and others of the council at the federal courthouse, not all who came out of their rose gardens with fear that if the anarchic elements should win, then even the lawn sprinklers would go on strike and not a drop of water would be left with which to put out a lightning bug's fire, let alone the fire of a labor strike, could agree that the organization of a volunteer army would have the desired effect.

Some responsible citizens had genuinely considered the possibility that if it was known that a volunteer army was forming, that fact alone might bring war instead of peace. What, indeed, would be thought if men of the white-gloves society, as the Democratic *Sentinel* had labeled the respectable class, should be engaged in battle with men with bleeding hands, brakemen who had perhaps already lost a hand or two before the strike began, firemen who had lost their eyes or engineers who had lost an eye or two—possibly three?

Such considerations might have given any politician pause, just as to go to war now would be to advance the career of the low-down thieving governor with the clay on his blue jeans and his nose as yellow as the buttercups he had been smelling when out cavorting in the bog lands with the rag-patch Irish crew who would set the trains on fire and in all ways disrupt the usual course of events.

Kid Gloves Harrison was not an old-time Hoosier sentimentalist who mistook homespun sentiments for truth or exaggerated them for political purposes, it did seem, was not one to pull out the bung and let the foam flow as the bucolic Blue Jeans Williams was wont to do. The general's argument, precise and to the point, had been that in the present crisis all attempts to interfere with operations of the railroad in violation of the law must be suppressed at any cost. And thus although he would wish to be known as the great conciliator, his was not what was sometimes mistakenly called tactfulness or the kid-glove approach to the problems of labor which he seemed to think it was.

His two kids, as Democratic papers had quipped during the last campaign, had lost him the election—to the man who, of course, had been the man of the people and never afraid to soil his hands, which were no better than those of the common clay which were workingmen's hands if they had hands—or, if they were valued only for their hands and, as we know, seldom referred to as men.

Very militant, the general had not seemed to be counting noses of future voters who might come in for him as Blue Jeans Williams with his old plow handle had certainly done, although the general in this new civil war knew that fewer Hoosiers had ridden on trains than had not ridden on trains and that for many insulated poor folks Cincinnati or St. Louis might as well have been on another planet and probably was.

General Harrison's belief that Lincoln's party was or should be the workers' party was that which had prompted him to see that there were two sides of the strike question, as could not be admitted by capitalistic absolutists for whom there was no side except their own, of course, and even though few things come in packages as pure as the snow which melts before it touches earth.

Kid Gloves Harrison's proposal that a mediation committee should be formed for the hearing of the strikers' grievances was not one which exposed the city to danger, for the soldiers who were defending capitalism were already in the streets. The two companies of volunteers, for the seventy-two hours in which the strikers met with him in his office from which the streets could be seen, had been bivouacked in the Federal Building and other public buildings which certainly had not been meant for private armies, be they even those of great caesars by the ton, although fortunately as they were capital city residents, mainly from the fashionable northern half of the mile square, they had not come by horseback and had not brought their horses into the courthouse to sleep where there were the scales of justice or injustice.

At the back of the post office where the sacred mail was piling up because of the profane strikers who had stopped the movement of the trains which were the sacred cows of the government so that no poor old bog mother might write to her lost son at a nowhere post office somewhere out in the far West to ask him where he was and no fine lady could order a bolt of silk which would not be just another lightning bolt caused by mad strikers disturbing the heavens and the earth, there were tarpaulin-covered wagons loaded with great Gatling guns and Beecher's Bibles in this city where had been Beecher's pulpit long before the Civil War, and its new pulpiteer when he had gone east to his upper-class Brooklyn church was the pro-labor, pro-utopian Reverend Myron Reed, former fisherman of Newfoundland's Grand Banks who would be a friend of Debs's and Riley's and who had been hooked and brought here by General Harrison.

Another of the military men in charge of the citizens' army had been General Lew Wallace, who was to write *Ben-Hur* in answer to the atheism of Robert Ingersoll, it may be remembered, his maledictions against Democrats so great that, according to the grammar-fracturing Petroleum V. Nasby, he should be forgiven for his attacks upon God or Christ for his having shown that the only way a Democrat could achieve immortal fame was by being hung next to Christ upon the cross as one of the two thieves who died with Him.

At the first meeting with the strikers who had expressed to General Harrison their litany of grievances, he with the help of General Albert Porter had counseled exact obedience to the law but had agreed that the wages paid to the men were too low. At the second meeting, to which upon his instructions they had brought written statements covering wages paid to all men on the rails from the top engineers clear to the bottom where the lowly wheel wiper was if he had not been wiped away when the wheels moved, the general had been under as much pressure as a locomotive steam boiler building up steam without a safety valve from which it could escape, for there were actually members of the Safety Committee who believed that to attempt to come to reasonable terms with these belligerent labor strikers was not only futile but a thing beneath contempt—and thus at any moment the general's army might leap to the battle before he gave the word that the peace was lost and that the war was now to be carried to the front which happened to be this city.

The general had stated to the Committee of Safety, which had wanted the citizens' volunteer army to jump from the frying pan into the fire, that he absolutely did not propose to go out and shoot down his neighbors when there was no necessity for doing so. To the representatives of the strikers with their written demands, he had pointed out that by stopping transportation, they were also destroying the property which belonged to the businessmen whom they had brought to the brink of bankruptcy by the stopping of their drafts.

The strikers had not been persuaded to sympathize with the businessmen and had started to walk out but had returned when called back by their strike leader, Warren Sayre, to hear the general's arguments to their conclusions but without faith in his promises of redress which were supported by guns.

They should go back to work for the reduced wages which had caused the strike, he had sincerely, seriously, advised, and, if they did so, then he and others of the Citizens' Mediation Committee would seek to influence the railroad to raise the pay to a living standard and give to them other benefits at a time when they had neither life or death benefits. But could his promises be believed by poor men who knew the history of greed and surely also that Croesus was not Jesus?

The general had warned that citizens would not long tolerate mob rule and that it had been tried again and again and had failed. The sooner they went back to work, the sooner they would regain the sympathy and confidence of the public and would attain to their just ends.

[1 5 6]

UNFORTUNATELY, the Committee of Public Safety had been riding a Hamiltonian horse while the Committee of Mediation had been riding a Jeffersonian horse in an America which, while supposedly for the little men and the little farms and pea patches, was for the big men and the big farms like those of the railroad and coal and coke and steel and other monopolies and Wall Street, a narrow man-made canyon which in its relation to its financial powers should have been wider and deeper than the Grand Canyon in a time when the viewless abyss was widening between the rich and the poor and the way ahead was darkness and whirlwind, as it would continue to be, with particular blows dealt out to labor movements and racial minorities, the latter sometimes discriminated against by the unenlightened poor white men like those who in the long strike of 1877 in San Francisco had devised the anti-queue laws according to which no poor "Chinaman" was allowed to neglect shaving his head bald unless he wanted his long queue to be cut off, to be used as a musical instrument to gong and bong him. And it was against the law for a "Chinaman" to walk through the streets of San Francisco carrying over his shoulder a long pole with a bucket of water at either end, although the constellation Aquarius which was the water carrier with a bucket of stars continued to cross the heavens and let spill sometimes those stars which dropped like rain to water the crops.

Looking back upon the depression which began when this country was cast into a period of financial bankruptcy, industrial stagnation, and economic gloom, the onetime editor of the elegiac *Locomotive Firemen's Magazine,* Eugene Victor Debs, would remember—"The sheriff's hammer was heard everywhere beating the dolorous funeral marches of departed prosperity. . . . It was during this panic that the tramp became a recognized factor in our social life."

That for which the poor worker had asked in the long strike of 1877, which was in actuality so short, was that the government which had devoted itself to the protection of life and liberty and property should be more concerned with life and liberty and less with property and property rights.

The capitalists apparently could not agree with each other as to the best way of cutting the strikers down—whether by force of reason or by force of arms. General Harrison's Committee of Public Safety had been unable to agree with General Harrison's Committee of Mediation, his white kid gloves somewhat at odds with his military sword, over which, however, should surely be draped, as he marched into war, no lilies of the valley in memory of some young brakeman, the son of an old neighbor of his, who would be mowed down if all reason failed and an action had to be taken against destroyers of government property down at the newly white-washed Union Depot which might soon be red with blood.

Kid Gloves Harrison of the Committee of Mediation had called upon the Committee of Public Safety to march in a dress parade headed by General Harrison as a way of warning the stubborn strikers what would be their fate if they persisted in their strike.

The attorney Albert Porter, a spokesman for mediation at a new meeting with the labor strike leaders who like labor agitators in other strike centers were being depicted by the newspapers as red, red in tooth and claw, had calmly informed the workers that their calling of public attention to their grievances was all that their rebellion could possibly achieve—and so he had convinced them that as further effort would be futile, they should accept the conciliatory terms offered to them by their fellow citizens who entertained toward them, naturally, no revengeful spirit for this ruffling of the civic peace in which good citizens must have feared that every crackle of a twig was caused by the stealthy approach of an assassin and had not dared to close their eyes lest they should awaken to the fate of a Pittsburgh Sodom. The naïve who had followed a flamboyant leadership would be forgiven if they would just lay down their arms.

And after all, as must have been plain to anyone who had seen the dress parade near the arsenal, men who were equipped with sticks and stones and pebbles and croquet mallets stolen from the lawns of their masters would have about as much chance against these well-to-do, affluent, and sometimes staggeringly rich guardians of civic and moral and economic virtue with their wagonloads of munitions as the quail had had long ago to escape riddling by great Gatling guns in the abandoned Noble Street graveyard.

The strike leaders had given up just as Blue Jeans Williams, seeing that the peace had been declared, decided to call out the militia which would not now be necessary but might save him from accusations that he was and had always been a bloody traitor to the United States government and not, of course, to the railroads for which poor soldiers were asked to die. Little doubt and more important, he because of this delay had been spared being put into the agonizing position of mowing down the numbers of voters who would bring in the sheaves for him at the next election harvesttime.

Although General Harrison's staunch resistance to the multitudes of the poor men striking against the railroad powers which had wished to seem beatific and well intentioned to those who submitted to their will as if it were the will of God had had the effect of making him the most important spokesman for the big wheels of the Republican party, which favored the big wheels of the railroad trains running over wheel wipers as if they were rags, their loss to society counting very little or not at all to the profits of big business, his indifference to a political future was believed by his enemies to have been prompted by the very remarkable thought that he could not afford a career in politics either local or national, that there was less money to be found in the upholding of government than in the practice of law.

His loss of the race for the United States Senate in 1878 to the Tall Sycamore Daniel Wolsey Voorhees, whom Blue Jeans Williams had previously appointed to take the senatorial chair vacated by Morton and who would be an icon in the tree-shadowed life of Debs, had left him with his peace undisturbed even although the return of Blue Jeans to the governorship and the victory of Tall Sycamore of Terre Haute had been undeniably a landslide about which there would be no doubt.

"If our people prefer Blue Jeans and Dan V———, let it be so," Harrison in his ruffled white nightgown had written with unruffled calm to Cousin Meg in St. Louis. "My law practice is a more important field for me."

President Hayes and his wife had been entertained in the garden of Harrison's mansion in Indianapolis after the long strike, where no Irishman of the Rebel party had been hired to pull out the bung from the whiskey barrel or dance to the tune of the devil's fiddle some old Irish bog song or song in memory of the Molly Maguires.

General Harrison's firm had been hired by Chicago and New York railroads, which necessitated his long-distance or short-distance travels, which he made wherever possible by Pullman parlor cars, a means of transport which was a luxury unimaginable to most poor people who, like those living at Lonesomeville, as in one of old Pop Riley's antirailroad poems, watched the trains go by, as he would tell the pro-train Debs, and how sad and strange a thing the sound of the whistle was, it sometimes seeming that there might be a whistle where there was no train—none coming or going.

[1 5 7]

I N 1888 General Harrison would run for the presidency as the Republican party's hope against democracy, the flesh, and the devil, his premise that the law is that which throws the aegis of its protection over all was to be his uncritical message two years after the Haymarket bombing and martyrdoms, which would radicalize generations of Americans. Of the law he had stated with unctuous certainty—"It stands sentinel above your country and homes to protect you from violence—it comes into our more thickly populated community and speaks its mandate for individual security and order.... To the law we bow with reverence. It is the one king that commands our allegiance. We will change our king, when his rule is oppressive, by those methods appointed and crown his more liberal successor."

He would say in his "gates of Castle Garden" speech that the tide of emigration from all European countries had always been and was toward our shores. "The gates of Castle Garden swing inward. They do not swing outward to any American laborer seeking a better country than this."

But how degrading it was, how altogether malicious, from his point of view, when along the Erie tracks in Steuben County there had appeared thousands of tracts screaming accusations, all of Democratic origin, all as lowly as if they were made by the everlasting Molly Maguires or other children of hanged men, that in the Indianapolis railroad strike of 1877 he had told the strikers that a dollar a day was good enough for any workingman and that he had barked out to them then like a dog—"I would force you to work by the bayonet, or I would shoot you down like dogs"—charges which, when made in the Hoosier state where he was well known, he had refused to dignify by a public denial, but which were not difficult to believe in the East and other places where he was unknown.

Spread by a presumably mad labor agitator whose name was unhappily Edwin F. Gould were such stories as that when General Harrison had marched with the private citizens' army to the Union Depot with the latest model of Springfield rifles to break the strike by force, Governor Blue Jeans Williams, trying to stop the expedition, had been told by the general—"We'll shoot the dogs anyway—hanging is too good for them."

What Harrison himself, stumping again, would say of the dollar-a-day story and all its satirical appendages was that it was not a perversion of anything he had ever said—it was a false creation.

When the accusation was made during the presidential campaign of 1876 by an old Irishman in the audience at Bloomington, Illinois, that Harrison had given his praise to all nationalities except for the Irish, of whom he had said that if it were not for them we would not need half our penitentiaries, for the jails were almost full of them, and they had no intelligence, and they were only good to shovel dirt and grade railroads and that they received for this work more than they were worth to the American people, he had coldly denied these allegations as the guards had leapt upon the old man and carried him from the hall and wheelbarrowed him away, throwing him out into a cinder yard where the likes of him belonged. Perhaps they had broken his already broken bones.

[1 5 8]

WHEN HARRISON, as thick as he was short and still wearing the style of beard that Ulysses S. Grant had popularized, was running for the White House, having won the nomination over all other contenders, including Judge Gresham—whom he had privately accused of having promised to those who would favor his nomination everything from the office of secretary of state to White House coachman, complete with horses and plumes, depending on his preference—he had done so as one who would be faithful to the religion of big business, which favored a high and not a low tariff.

On the other hand, he had been accused by his rival, James G. Blaine, of having asked, when he was a senator, for thirteen more diplomatic posts than there were upon the whole department list—it being a wonder that thirteen countries had not been added to the list, so that some old Hoosier retired senator or gentleman of military bearing with walrus mustache might be sent, or that diplomats were not sent to some parts of this country which were treated as foreign empires under the rule of despotic gold and silver and copper and lead and coal companies whose ambassadors were not only in Washington but in the Congress and the Senate, no matter what administration was in power.

If Kid Gloves Harrison had been a dyed-in-the-wool friend of the legitimate laborer in 1877 as he claimed, if he had been unjustly maligned by legends confusing him with Reverend Beecher and was not the follower of the Reverend Reed, lover of the lost utopian prospects, yet the history of

President Harrison in the White House would show him still to be that incorrigible law-and-order man who, in the season when he was doggedly running for his second term, would send to Coeur d'Alène, Idaho, upon request of the governor whose state militia had been unable to put down the strike, federal troops to triumph over the victorious strikers who had won out against blacklegs and seized the mines as once the labor union agitators had seized the old Union Depot where there were now clocks telling the various times in the various time levels throughout the United States but where none should ever strike the correct hour for labor strikes against great and ever-coordinated corporation powers, their clocks always the same, their agreement with each other best exemplified when they were in conflict with any attempt of the workingmen to unite themselves and not to divide under the pressure of tragic events not necessarily foreseen by them although they were the kinds of men who risked their lives every day in their dangerous employment and so might consider that there was no greater risk taken by striking against blacklegs than by death by accident or by the erosion of all their vital parts—their organs, pipes, lungs, heartstrings, skins, sense of manhood. The trouble with these wild jackasses was always that they dreamed of being or becoming men.

Open shop would be forced upon the western strikers by the federal army sent by President Harrison to do battle against these wild human jackasses during the time when he would be running for reelection to the White House which he called the Ice House but probably without too much desire to sit upon the ice throne for another four years if his indifference to political considerations was as real as he claimed, so very real that he would sacrifice himself and his possible popularity to his unchanging ideals which would favor a minority block of powerful businessmen to a majority which was made of a nondescript rag-and-patchwork rabble seemingly incapable of entertaining profundity of thought, all living for the immediate gratification of their desires.

Undoubtedly, he would rather have gone duck-shooting for a string of wild ducks than have sent an army out for the killing of labor strikers, but the voice of duty was sterner than the voice of conscience or even of consciousness.

Herds of the labor strikers at Coeur d'Alène, many hundreds, would be driven out of the mines into barbed-wire bullpens where they would be left to starve, rot, pine away like the mournful pines for many months, pine with a sound which would be heard by Debs and every lover of poor men in America who understood anew now or had always understood that the law which was king was that representing the corporation kings, their power steadily increasing behind the mask of a government representing itself as rational but no more rational, when the crisis came, than the law of the talon.

Eighty-five miners would be indicted for contempt of court and twelve who had been in the jail would be convicted as open shop triumphed and blacklegs triumphed and under the supervision of the military machine the members of unions were turned away, henceforth to be hounded like those cranes whose legs had not been broken and should never be allowed a place to land on earth in any mill or mine or on any railroad or train or even the top of a boxcar.

The interesting timing of this intervention was that the strike at Coeur d'Alène had begun on the very day when, in answer to the plea from a capitalist which no state governor could resist, the governor of Pennsylvania had sent thousands of troops to enforce the open shop at Homestead, where, as Allan Pinkerton had unfortunately not lived to see this almost conceivably worst fulfillment of his dreams of the attempted takeover of America by legions of reds, Pinkerton's army had charged against the strikers who, including members of the Amalgamated Association of Iron and Steel Workers, the very kinds of aliens who had crowded through Castle Gates to get into this country and not out of this country, were now locked behind the fences at the Carnegie works for having struck for an improvement in pay, a new contract which had been refused to iron workers up until then engaged in building structural iron for fireproof buildings, some to be embossed with wreaths or frames of flowers or bunches of roses and some to show also shadows of men burned when through their ineptitude they fell into pits of fire, and also were the manufacturers of plate armor for massive ships of war although the wars going on then were domestic wars to which, as there was quite often no water passage across wheat- and cornfields, no ships of war could be sent.

[1 5 9]

DEBS—THE RECIPIENT for years of letters to *The Locomotive Firemen's Magazine* from Tired Tool, Loose Bolt, Arctic Blast, Loose Screw, Broken Wheel, Screech Owl—always believed that Brainy Ben or Big Ben or Little Ben or Kid Gloves Harrison had been—whether in the Senate or in the White House—the ever-malleable, ever-adjustable, ever-judicious mediator in behalf of the steel kings for whom the workingmen made the steel armor, the railway kings whose iron horses they shod, the coal and coke and blast furnace kings in whose furnaces they burned—and was not the friend of workingmen—when, and only after years of unmitigated sufferings they had attempted in a great surge like fires which fed upon themselves to take over the property of hardworking, industrious, dedicated men who in building this nation from the ground up and the ground down were responsible servants of God and obeyed the capitalistic property laws which were sacred unto Him down to the last blade of grass or pebble scratch or sand grain—and had not the exile of our mythic first parents from Eden been a great freeze-out against just such apple thieves as these?

As Debs had known by a thousand, ten thousand, multitudinous details as time went on how altogether fallacious had been Allan Pinkerton's account of the Pittsburgh riots of 1877 in his curious volume of now-forgotten lore entitled *Strikes, Communists, Tramps and Detectives* with its frontispiece embellished by the portrait of P. T. Arthur, grand chief of the Brotherhood of Locomotive Engineers, who at that time had been regarded as a firebrand among labor agitators but had shown himself to have been a traitor to a truly humanitarian socialistic concept of the brotherhood of men with man. It had been clear to Debs at the time that the late President Benjamin Harrison, ten years before his elevation to the White House, had been in charge of duplicitous events when he was acting for capital and labor but especially for capital.

This struggle had been the first in which the powers of the federal courts had been evoked to break a railroad strike, according to Debs's recollections of the former president who as a general had organized the company of soldiers and had made speeches against the strikers, his words so incendiary that if words could have burned, they would have burned, and then as a lawyer had prosecuted the strikers in the federal courts of the Hoosier capital and had secured prison sentences for them. And afterward the labor agitators had been blacklisted, of course—their punishment never to cease.

"The loss of the strike was a staggering blow to organized labor, and many unions passed out of existence. Upon the railroads the mere suspicion of belonging to a union was sufficient grounds for instant discharge," Debs recalled.

The blotting out of the long strike of workers who had aroused the rabid reactions of the corporation powers—and were accused of supposing that they could strangle the goose of capitalism and still receive golden eggs which would be dropped into empty hats of tramps who had always been famous for stealing eggs—had been ironical because it had been done under the aegis of a Republican candidate whose party had stolen the office from the Democratic candidate, Samuel Jones Tilden.

In Terre Haute, as of June 1877, the members of the Brotherhood of Locomotive Firemen's Vigo Lodge, where Debs was the youthful organizer not by any means solely devoted to benefits for the widows and children of dead firemen had they lived long enough to attain to fatherhood, for out of the world of the dead would come the world of the living as expressed by labor unions which should be dedicated to the preservation and development of human life, and this was and would have been his most vital intention even when there was only one spark of life, had suffered wage cuts of twenty-three percent between 1873 and 1876 and ten percent between August 1876 and May 1877. These deductions would soon be taking away from a man more than had ever been given.

The men of Vigo Lodge, those whose grievances Debs had heard night after night when he went down to the railroad yards to ensure that his interests were not merely parochial, that he sought to understand the world beyond the horizon, had feared that Riley McKeen—whose mother, née Paddock and who owned fine paddocks of blooded breed horses and was the president of the Vandalia line with its iron horses of not so fine a breed as his mares and his stallions but were finer than his workers who, being human, were in the eyes of most but not all opportunistic corporation heads the lowest, the most dispensable breed there was, a cheap merchandise upon the labor market—would automatically follow General Scott's playing of stacked cards against the living wage of train men by dealing out a run of euchres of his own in relation to the depressed times in which the affluent gave up no crumb of the cake in the union of capital with government to the poor workingmen waiting for a piece of the cake.

The firemen, hats in hands, had presented to Riley McKeen a request only for that fifteen percent raise; they gave him only the rest of his day and the night, in which it was hoped that he could peacefully yield to their certainly reasonable demand and peacefully sleep, but if he failed to yield to them with their own desire for sleep and dreams, then the very next morning, when the firemen who had never yet gone on strike against stoking up coals of the burning sun that there might be, as God had perhaps intended, another dawn, these very earthbound firemen of this very mortal brotherhood would not mount the Vandalia fire hogs and would not allow freights to pass out of the Terre Haute yards, would bring railroad time to a standstill.

They had promised that all would be orderly—for inasmuch as they were under a generally observed oath of temperance while employed, so also they would not imbibe of the demon wine with which to quench the thirst of their rusted throat pipes when they were on strike and soon would be not only thirsting—would be starving if the strike went on.

McKeen had failed to respond, good intentioned though he was, for he really had not known what to do. Six hundred men of the Vandalia repair shops had laid their tools down. He had stopped all trains except the mail trains and thus had seemed to be in some harmony with the strikers, who had expressed their faith in him and had promised to guard the railroad property from men who were unemployed and to whom it had probably not yet occurred that they should also have their union or their rights of protection by this government for whom they were as dispensable at this time as if they were herds of buffaloes striking against Gould's trains.

Who needed such madmen as these, often drunk, their eyes red with rage and drunkenness—and were they not anarchists as much as were the union men, all doomed to defeat by the only true anarchists there were in America, the big capitalists who did as they pleased, made the laws, enforced the laws, and were as efficient in breaking and destroying little capitalists as they were in putting strikers down wherever they appeared?

The union men recognized that the Vandalia line was not their enemy. "We are not making war upon women and children," they had announced in refutation of General Brainy Ben's thesis that the true victims of such labor agitations were women and children who, unlike the members of the citizens' army who when it was bivouacked at the arsenal in the Large Hub had received fried chicken and hot red Indian corn and red ripe tomatoes and apples and grapes and home-baked bread brought to them by their mothers' servants, had often not so much as a heel of bread and were left to starve like birds molting their feathers and skins forever and not in preparation for new feathers and new skins.

We are warring to break down the gigantic Eastern monopolies, the Pennsylvania Railroad—in two words, we can put it—Tom Scott. It is not particularly upon Riley McKeen or Mr. Pebble that we are warring. They, like us, are under the thumb of this road, and when they take up their thumb, they say "Jump!"

The attempt had been made to recognize the solidarity of human beings in Terre Haute, the identity of interests binding the capitalist employer and the labor striker, to refuse on each side to paint the other side as either the devil or the devil's messengers bringing fires to Terre Haute, and specifically to refuse to take out on Riley McKeen or Solomon Pebble revenge for the infernal works of Tom Scott and others of his power who had the backing of Hayes—a man with butter in his mouth.

That man in the White House had already shown, during a strike of coal miners when he was governor of Ohio, his iron resistance to the idealistic expectations of labor strikers when he had sent the state militia to break, as if they were large chunks of coal which should be broken into small chunks of slag or dirt, the labor strikers at Masillon, from where General Coxey's army would one day start out to walk the long way to Washington in order to ask the president for the assistance of the government through the employment of the unemployed and the unemployable and whose numbers would include enough freakish characters to give consolation to anyone who placed his faith not in the government but in that great god who helps those who help themselves and look not to anyone for a handout as did, of course, many a capitalistic bigwig, including Tom Scott.

[1 6 0]

WHEN THE FEDERAL TROOPS were sent to Indianapolis and Terre Haute—the former partly under the command of General Daniel Macaulay, who was a friend of Longfellow's and would one day write a letter of introduction to him for James Whitcomb Riley, author of "To an Old Sweetheart of Mine" and whose neighbor he was in Lockerbie Street, and who was a bosom friend of Debs's—the then secretary of the navy Richard W. Thompson, distinguished citizen to be praised along with McKeen and Debs, had been far from peaceful in his mood.

The trouble with Terre Haute on the Wabash was that the interlocking canal and river system having been long ago displaced by the railroad, it was not a seaport with direct waterway to France as it should have been. Secretary of the Navy Thompson, who had been at one time chief counsel for the Terre Haute & Indianapolis Railroad, had been sorry that he could not send to Riley McKeen for protection of the Vandalia a company of Marines.

Absolutely outraged by what was happening in God's own country or rather what was not happening in Terre Haute, where no cannonballs had roared although there were those federal troops which Riley McKeen had not wanted to be withdrawn, for there might come an outbreak of chaos to the city on the high mound worse than anything that had been seen since Big Ben's grandfather, William Henry Harrison, future president of the United States, had built his fortress against the red men high on the bluffs above the Wabash and had driven them out of their holes where the shedding of their blood had caused the red flowers to come up out of the ground in the spring.

The uprisings of the workers in Terre Haute and elsewhere had been nothing more nor less than French Communism and had been so entirely at war with the spirit of our institutions that it must be overcome—no matter at how high a cost, including the sacrifices of many innocent lives.

Although Riley McKeen had promised not to fire the strikers against the Vandalia, the property which he would sell out to the Pennsylvania line in 1893, he had not felt bound to his promise and at their trial in the Indianapolis courthouse under the murals depicting Justice had testified for the prosecution of the labor agitators for a strike that had been brought about by the oblivion of the government to the rights of workingmen.

The Locomotive Firemen's Magazine, then under the editorship of Brother W. M. Sayre of Indianapolis, when Debs was still confined in the warehouse and trying to understand as best he could the trials and turmoils of labor, had reported in its issue of August 1877 that the cuts which from time to time had been dealt to the railroad workers had reached that state in which they could no longer support themselves and their families. Besides this, payments were in arrears, although they should have had priority over payments to stockholders.

President Hayes had sent troops to put down the strikers, mainly firemen and brakemen, at a time when Debs from his experience and every responsible citizen knew that a brakeman creeping over the roofs of cars from brake to brake received from a dollar and a quarter to a dollar and a half a day for a trip so far away from home that the men had to provide food and lodging out of the small pay.

Also, as would be pointed out one day by Debs, some were so afraid to spend money that they slept on railroad benches and would eat almost nothing in order that their wives and children would not starve. And that was why there were living skeletons manning the trains and rails owned by the major capitalists.

In September 1877, when Debs had become an assistant editor, reference was made in *The Locomotive Firemen's Magazine* to the fact that there would be a united strike on June 17 and that if it failed, there would be another attempt. The free press had said—"Oh, Sayre is a Communist and won't tell nothing—but we are afraid he knows the day, the hour!" An article in the *Chicago Tribune,* written by a lady in Bureau County, Illinois, had denounced members of labor unions as wholly unfit to serve with Christians.

Brother Timothy Fagan, having visited Brother Sayre in Indianapolis, had contributed to *The Locomotive Firemen's Magazine* a bird's-eye view of what went on in the interior of the Indianapolis courthouse which Brother Debs knew so well as one who was already what he would always be, a critical student of human justice or injustice. "For instance, in the criminal court is represented the man branded with murder; his hands and feet are shackled; he has a downcast and degraded appearance. He appears entering the court room accompanied by a guard—in front of him sits the Judge—Justice is there, in her left hand the scales, in her right hand the sword. His wife and mother, pleading for him, are personified by Mercy."

Mayor J. T. Caven had told Brother Fagan of the confidence he had placed in the men during the great strike. They had promised him to preserve, as much as in their power, the lives and properties of the citizens of Indianapolis, the railroad companies' shops, the engine houses, et cetera, and had faithfully kept their word—not a railroad spike had been destroyed.

Although the Brotherhood of Locomotive Firemen was for the protection of the Protestant, the Catholic, the Greek, and the Mohammedan and thus had believed itself in perfect accord with American institutions as well as an observer of the Golden Rule—"Do unto others as we would have others do unto us"—yet there had been not only exclusions of bad men on the premise that to take bad men into the brotherhood would be like putting leaven into an unleavened loaf—there had not been the hands of friendship reaching out to accept minorities—and this fact as much as any other would contribute to the chafing of Debs's spirit as if he wore heavy chains.

From North Platte, Nebraska, in June 1877, when the great strikes were on and some of the fighters against Indians had been brought out of the West to fight against Chicago reds, *The Locomotive Firemen's Magazine* had carried a correspondent's report on what had happened to a poor red devil who had gone out to the Indian territory. This account of the tragedy that befell Lo, the poor Indian, was surely not the kind of bedtime story mothers would want to tell to children as they combed the tangles from their hair and put them into bed for God's keeping throughout the journey of the night:

> One little Indian got on track, tried to chase train—Indian got on horseback following him. We crossed bridge and as a natural consequence boy fell in, his stomach resting on a tie—horse followed suit and fell on top of boy—old Indian remains on horse. Dead boy.... If the government would only make all of them good Indians, it would help this part of the country. I have only seen six good Indians—they all were dead.

[1 6 1]

A S TO SUCH munitions makers as Krupp in Germany, the *Boston Sunday Herald* had published early in 1889 an article on Krupp which had seemed worthy of note to the essentially pacific editor of *The Locomotive Firemen's Magazine,* who would cling to the illusions of progress through reason as long as he could, no doubt longer than he could.

The name of Krupp was that which struck fear in the hearts of men and with good reason. "The misfortunes of others, as a rule, prove blessings to him. To the minds of the peace-loving community, there is something very terrible in even his name, for it has the savor of what the gifted author of 'Childe Harold' would stigmatize as 'blood and thunder, thunder, wounds and blood.' "

As would be pointed out at a later date in history by the anti-imperialist William James, there were utopias and utopias—and a state of perpetual war would be a state of perpetual utopia for munitions makers and military men. Indeed, as Debs already recognized, if there were no war, none like that against the feathered reds in the West after the Civil War and no red labor agitators to fight, then the munitions makers and military men would certainly go to seed.

Redress of grievances in courts of law might take a long, long time, as it was told in one of the numerous antilaw jokes that Debs collected along with reports on mortal accidents suffered by railroad men. For example, a man who had a case in court had cheerfully said that if he lost in the court for common pleas, he would appeal to the Supreme Court—and if he lost there, he would appeal to the United States court—and if he lost there, he would appeal to heaven. "And then," a friend of his had said to him, "the case will be dismissed, for you will not be present to answer for yourself, and no attorney is ever admitted there."

As between heaven and hell if they were the ultimate or immediate goals of man when the journey of his life was over and the journey of the next life had begun, Debs would always rather not have been in heaven with the munitions makers and the capitalists who would tear up its streets of gold if there was any financial profit to be made, would blow the moon out of its orbit, would derail this earth from its star belt or track, with the antilabor legislators and antilabor agitators and labor spies and great detectives of supposedly all-seeing eyes who would spy upon the poor man's desire to lift himself up from deepest mines, with the great Hobbes economists for whom the state was the all-powerful Leviathan, with the great Malthusians who believed in the necessary or desirable reduction of the world's population by volcanoes and glaciers, volcanoes spewing fire and glaciers spewing ice, by mass starvation and individual starvation as the mass is composed of individuals and is not simply one great glutinous and undifferentiated crowd, by child labor in mills and mines and other forms of industrial infamy with their continual mechanical innovations, including war—would rather be in hell with Shelley and the anti-Malthusian lovers of mankind who knew that the fruits of earth were provided in abundance for all, would rather be with the lowest elements there were and had always said so.

In 1878 Debs had been elected associate editor of *The Locomotive Firemen's Magazine* at the brotherhood's convention in Buffalo and had begun, with renewed dedication, his organization of the brotherhoods of railroad workers, that crusade which was for the retrieval of railroad workers' rights including the rights of life before all could be lost beyond retrieval.

"It has been a mercy that man was not made too imaginative, or otherwise the knowledge and the realization of the woes and troubles of others would make life intolerable"—according to an unsigned editorial in May 1880, when he was writing the unsigned editorials or was responsible for their content—"but the feeling of self-protection and of brotherhood has been likewise implanted in us for a divine purpose."

The tragic railroad accident to which Debs then referred as that statistician of the deaths of railroad men which were caused mainly through the negligence of the czars of the cars and out of which would grow the American socialist movement was that of the daring engineer and fireman going down into the dark waters when the timbers of a bridge over the river gave way.

Worthy of record in *The Locomotive Firemen's Magazine* was the tale of a cat in Brooklyn who had lived in a basket with a dozen newborn chicks and had not molested one of them.

[1 6 2]

M RS. WHISTLER would enjoy more fame or infamy for the portrait which, called by her son James McNeill Whistler *Arrangement in Gray and Black No. 1: The Artist's Mother,* but generally called by others *Whistler's Mother,* was revered in God-fearing homes as a saintly character but was vastly caricatured in saloons where sometimes the face of Susan B. was substituted for hers and sometimes she sprouted a patriarchal beard such as a Russian bishop would have worn in old St. Petersburg and sometimes in her lap was shown a great Gatling gun or a bottle of whiskey distinctly not contributing to the reverential mood of a stiffly corseted lady who had been in Russia a Bible thumper of an evangelical reformist spirit such as would characterize the American presence in unenlightened, backward, primitive, or pagan foreign lands.

Interested in casting the Russian soul into a new mold, she had not been one to be inhibited by the iron czar for whom her husband laid the rails for the flying samovar or she-devil hissing steam. She had strongly disapproved of all heathen ways, including the Russian Orthodox view of God or the devil and had been appalled by the museum where were the stuffed bodies of dead Arabian racehorses caparisoned with jewels, all so real that they might seem ready to start up at the sound of a starter's horn beneath the gilded, frescoed ceilings—for excesses of imagery in art had also displeased the lady who would be a serene, somewhat cold-blooded *Arrangement in Gray and Black*—a mother whom few wine bibbers could love although some might pretend to do so when they saw her portrait hanging above the bar.

She had handed out Bible tracts to railroad workers and soldiers right under the nose of the czar, and he had seemed always not to notice and to look the other way, just as she with her fervid hope that the Word of the Lord which she spread about would bear fruit, and what she had happily not found out was that the way it had borne fruit was that poor, freezing serfs and soldiers had saved their souls by walking on it, stuffing it between the soles of their shoes and the soles of their feet to give some slight protection from the snow where those who were the soleless had left the marks of their bleeding feet.

Mrs. Whistler, upon hearing of the Chartists' uproar in London, had firmly believed that her husband's mission, which was the building of the railroad for the czar in Russia had been God's mask for the far more important mission that was hers—that of converting the Russians over to Simple Simon Bible truth, American style, the text in Russian so simple that not only a Russian serf but a Russian muley cow might understand, and she did not believe in the necessity of any music to accompany the simple Word of God unless it should be the music of the harp.

Mrs. Whistler was less sympathetic with the white serfs than her husband was and was also less realistic in her optimistic and yet melancholy survey of the prospects for reform, the way she laid her ruler straight upon her map and marked out with her compass no circles, no arcs for age-old mythologies which arose out of the necessity to endure in patience what had taken long to come into the world and might take longer to go out of it than she could foresee. She was impatient. She feared the white serfs whose state of ignorance seemed to her not Christian but all too pagan and artificial to be real, even as she feared scrofulous beggars in the streets, some without noses, street musicians and clowns, sinister-looking wayfarers who seemed to keep no business hours. She had forbidden her sons to attend the Royal Theatre until she had found out that the actors on the stage were wooden puppets pulled by invisible puppeteers. Although outraged by the institution of white slavery which prevailed in Russia, she had not stopped to think of the white wage slaves in Lowell, Massachusetts, and other mill towns or those who worked in mines and mills or worked along the rails in the land in which one man's opportunity was the loss of opportunity for ten thousand other men.

Mrs. Whistler had been able, as a good North Carolinian, to justify the ownership of wageless black slaves in the American South by the sanctimonious thought that it had been arranged for the holy purpose which God had had in mind and had recalled to her and others of her missionary zeal, that of educating some future generation of black men to go to the African jungles and throw out Bible tracts for the instant conversion of bush natives—and no doubt also elephants and giraffes and cranes—over to the Christian faith for the sake of their immortal souls just as she was doing with her Bible tracts in the city of Peter and in the bogs along the rails right under the eyes of the military czar who always seemed, only seemed to be looking the other way, not noticing what he noticed—but fortunately for him or for her, she had not known all the intrigues of which he was capable.

Had she accepted the czar's heartfelt invitation to bury her husband in St. Petersburg and allow his two living sons to be brought up as members of his court to whom would be given the education and privileges and responsibilities attending rank—had she been willing to sacrifice her life as an impoverished railroad engineer's widow in the land of that democracy where all men were equal, of course, and some more equal than others— had she continued in Russia with her constant remarks upon the superiority of all things American to all things Russian, Russia seeming to her to be in the cruelest orbit there ever was, then her son might never have become the painter he became when transferred to a land which did not arouse his visual sympathies and had apparently no need of painting of dead lilies by dried-up streams.

[1 6 3]

WHEN JAMES McNEILL WHISTLER, lover of the Winter Palace and all the beauties of art and theater he had seen in Russia, had wanted to be an artist with paint and brush, his mother had discouraged this ambition as unfit for an American of good family, scientific gifts, and military history, and had wanted him to be captain in the army of God. The pay would be big.

She had promoted his entrance at West Point, where his father had done so well but where the son had given considerable trouble to the academy's commander, Colonel Robert E. Lee, and where he had failed his chemistry examination as he had mistakenly identified silicon with gas, thus disappointing his mother's hopes although encouraging his own.

If silicon had only been a gas instead of a metal, as James Whistler would many times laughingly remark, he would have become commander in chief of the army. Perhaps in that case the future human butterfly would have been blown away by cannonballs—and possibly by those from the Union side. He had favored the Southern Confederacy.

His friend Jefferson Davis, then secretary of war, had been wise enough to do nothing to change the exodus of the butterfly from West Point, and so he had escaped the iron mesh.

For a time serving as a reluctant, dreaming draftsman for the Winant Locomotive Works at Baltimore, Maryland, he had raised all chaos and brought himself into social disgrace by ruining designs of many machines with his blottings out of drawings with which he had whiled away his time, the smudges he had left over safety valves and engine parts and chimneys and wheels—and then for a while had continued his infernal mischief as draftsman for the Coast Survey in Washington, adding to the abstract maps of coastal topographies such images as an old woman's head in Boston harbor, portraits of himself whose spirit and signature would be the butterfly, signifying ego or soul or mannikin—the empty space on a map seeming to him a space which must be filled.

When he left the Coast Survey, he had refused to be taken back repentant to the Winant Locomotive Works—would rather have died, little doubt, as a daisy or a butterfly or a peacock along the margin than have died with his face upon the rails of monotony, endless monotony.

As an artist in exile in Paris and London who would not yearn for return to America where he had had no fixed roots and no home but that of a drifter in a world he never made, the aesthetic creed which he evolved was that the artist was a monument of isolation, always somewhat lonely and taking no part in the progress of his fellowman—for art was limited from the beginning so that there could be no progress from the beginning.

"We have then but to wait—until, with the mark of the gods upon him—there comes among us once again the chosen—who shall continue what has gone before. Satisfied that, even were he never to appear, the story of the beautiful is already complete—hewn in the marbles of the Parthenon—and broidered with the birds upon the fan of Hokusai—at the foot of Susiyana."

He was not given over to the altruistic socialism which his ego-centered aestheticism did not necessarily preclude, all depending upon a painter's vision and the arrangement of light and shadow.

As he was always proud of his brief career at West Point where if he had survived he might have enjoyed an honorable military career and have become a director of a railroad with its locomotive chopping up the yellow daisies or smearing over yellow butterflies as its oiled wheels turned upon the faintly gleaming yellow rails through the yellow fog—he was also always proud of his having been an art student in St. Petersburg, where art was an extension of the world one lived in, the Venice of the North where were jewels shining like eyes in stones and where when the ice broke with wildly musical sounds upon the previously slumbering Neva, an attendant would bring to the czar of czars a cup of water which he would drink or pour out and return filled with wine or golden coins.

Whistler's poverty as a young man had been so great that he sometimes described himself as a starving character in a ditch. Once as an art student in Paris when he found a hole in his hat, he had refused to have it darned or patched and had punched it into a larger hole in order to make the impression not of suffering from chronic, premeditated poverty such as might be suggested by repair but rather that of suffering from an altogether unpremeditated accident.

Wealth was necessarily not unimportant to him who found his wealth in painting and proclaimed that he was indifferent to the fate of the lumpen proletariat. The fate of the artist was what concerned him.

Starvation, however, was not conducive to the creation of the finest flowers and fruits of paintings, according to a man who was as capable of being a butterfly without a sting as a wasp with a sting.

When *The Yellow Buskin, La Princesse du Pays de la Porcelaine,* and *The Fur Jacket* were chosen for hanging in the British Exhibition at the Chicago World's Fair in 1893, masterpieces of Whistler's paint and brush which travelers from Europe and other travelers would see, among them Eugene V. Debs of *The Locomotive Firemen's Magazine,* former fireman for the old B & O, as they would see the façade of Pullman's utopia which was the earthly paradise founded by an enlightened businessman without reliance upon any divinity unless his own, the butterfly Whistler who had been the discontented draftsman for the B & O would describe a little street boy to whom his friend William Makepeace Thackeray had suddenly given a penny and whose surprise had been more ready than his gratitude.

Capitalists in America, providers of an endless gold rush into the cups of painters when the silence of winter sleep was broken because they had at last achieved some kind of recognition for their paintings, the flowers under ice and snow, were important to Whistler only for the gold they at last gave for his gold dripping from his paintbrush onto the fog of his shimmering canvases which moved and stirred as if animated by a secret life of their own and reflected irises of eyes staring at them through this moral fog which he illuminated as he illuminated their recognition of fugitive beauty made forever both fixed and fugitive. Starving workers on a canvas in his *Nocturne* had not been starving workers to him but only arrangements in blobs of dark blue and gold.

He would remember that the serfs in Russia had tried to work their way out of the bog by their beautiful paintings at St. Petersburg under the patronage of the czar, and some had succeeded in coming to the surface just as Whistler had done. But what bogged him with resentment was that the American czars, men of great wealth and infinite resources in trains and oils and gold who had bought his paintings for a trifling sum when he was poor and then had sold them for ten times the sum did not put an urn or a coffin of gold upon a cushion and bring it to him in recognition of the money they had made upon him when he was poor and to fame and fortune unknown.

When he was rich enough to employ a broker to watch over his capital on the American Stock Exchange and see to it that the gold poured into his buckets in the bucket shops, it would be said of Whistler that when he had attained fame as a portrait painter he had sacrificed the floating gold of his canvases to gold in a metallic form by painting Vanderbilts and other tycoons of railroads and gold and silver and copper and tin or their wives or their coronet-hunting daughters when he should have remained true to the arrangements and harmonies of that floating world which in the beginning some critics had thought ridiculous and trivial.

The main influences upon him were the dreamlike Oriental art and the satiric Hogarth—these influences along with many others had combined into the production of that which was his own and could only arouse the envy of others whose paint drops did not seem to achieve the same magic.

Voyaging to America, passing the customs house duty free as he was an American, the paintings but not the painter had journeyed by train through the wild, rough, crude, rude landscape which the transcendent butterfly painter had avoided although he had been paid his weight in gold, for they were used by great czars of the age of industrial progress to decorate not only the drawing rooms of their palatial houses but the drawing rooms of private Pullman palace cars furnished with pianos, harps, and organs, their appointments as luxurious as palaces in the land of the Romanovs which Whistler remembered so well.

One of the ways in which the *prince des papillons* amused his friends was to shuffle about with his bright walking stick in his left hand and twiddle on it with the finger and thumb of his right hand as if he were playing the banjo as he sang old darky songs, camp meeting songs, digging songs, spading songs.

One, entitled "De History ob de World," was very popular in American minstrel shows in which the singers, although the black men were the greatest singers of their sweet songs and should not have been deprived of this employment of native gifts arising out of deep suffering, were white men painted black. The song was one which Debs knew and heard sung by the white minstrels painted black before coming to the understanding of this injustice:

De world was made in six days
And finished on the seventh.
According to de contract
Should have been de eleventh.
But de masons dey fell sick
And dey joiners wouldn't work
And so dey thought de cheapest way
Was to fill it up with dirt.
Walk in, walk in, walk in, say
Walk in de back parlor and hear de banjo play. . . .

[1 6 4]

M RS. WHISTLER's chief concern had been and always would be for man's preparation for the next world, to which good Christians should attain by the simple act of bowing to God's will—just as the czar had also believed—for had he not advised his people to be meek and let their eyes not wander away from their work? Strikes had been forbidden in his secular but sacred realm where the serfs had laid the rails under the direction of Major Whistler, the nontheological and nonpolitical American engineer and, once they had dug the holes, had not filled them up with dirt again unless instructed to do so by the representative of God on earth—for God was only a greater engineer, and His instructions were not easily to be set aside and must be followed every step of the way. He had shown His plans to the eye of the czar, had whispered into his ear.

Mobs of the starving poor were roaming at this time over the Russian steppes in search of food where there was none or, as would have been said in America where the red men were being killed, not so much as a prickly porcupine from which to make one's soup.

As revolutions raged in European cities and might break like a flood through a dam, the governor of Moscow submitted a proposal to build no new factories or mills or mines whatever in Russia and thus to eliminate masses of men for whom there was no place on earth, to extinguish these wild hordes of homeless wanderers for whom there was not a grain of wheat for bread. Should those who rebelled against the laws of the czar be thrown into the bottomless pit as in the past they had been—and not only in Russia but probably in every country where the rich reigned supreme and provided whatever should be the destiny of the poor as that which reflected, in one way or another, the will of God—even though there might be no God?

"The government should not permit the concentration of homeless and immoral people, easily attracted to any movement aiming at the destruction of the public and private tranquillity"—the governor of Moscow had advised from the city of golden onion domes.

PIERRE-JOSEPH PROUDHON, the French philosopher and political economist whose work was to be a great influence upon Debs, and who in 1840 had drawn down all the hounds of heaven upon himself for having answered, on the title page of his most important work, the question "What is property" with a treatise providing the flaming answer "It is theft"—along with works by Voltaire and Victor Hugo and various other skeptical philosophers, most particularly Saint-Simon, Charles Fourier, and Robert Owen, the main inspirers of American utopias of a secular and not religious nature—had been held responsible by the ever-vigilant czar for the virus of the revolutionary spirit which he feared more than seven plagues sweeping over Russia like the bubonic plague which felled the serfs along the rails and would be responsible for the death of Major Whistler, his body going home by rail and ship as his spirit remained cutting through frozen silences like the whistle of the train, just as the czar had said.

The train in the view of Western-oriented believers in progress was a winged horse, a Pegasus which might suddenly take to the sky with wings, as would long be remembered—but for incorruptible Slavophiles it was the carrier of disease just as some old-timers were sure that comets and meteors were carriers of infectious diseases showering on men in the same way as Beelzebub had originally fallen with burning eyes from clouds— and the train was the she-devil, never the he-devil, and was the devil's ram—as the rails were laid out through that spirit of pride which was in competition with God Who had laid out the original old plank roads in darkest Russia without the help of man and perhaps also without the help of God. Man's Promethean spark should be squashed out before it set the world on fire—as surely a child of three should be able to understand.

The czar—requiring the train for military causes and not intending by its use to let the Russians out of his fortress but rather only to keep foreign invaders from coming in—could only feel himself very vulnerable when he saw a world in which there was no safety, no trust which he dared place in anyone.

At the customs house on the borders, watch must be kept to admit no dissonant music or foreign thought to shake and stir and crack the brains of men. As the czar knew, for his spies could smell a foreign thought a mile away as if it were not the perfume of a rose but that of a skunk, these mad shakers and movers who fondly imagined that they could blow him off his throne and change the face of the world and possibly the universe had been meeting for some time in a secret cell in St. Petersburg for the study of the falsely utopian, altogether untenable thoughts of the ridiculous revolutionary Charles Fourier, all very disturbing to the peace of mind of those who believed in the ancient Russian Christ complete with purple robes or His chief vicar on earth who was as good a stand-in for Christ as could be found—and in fact, there was no other but Himself with His colors glowing in His shadow as in the icons bearing His image in gold mosaics and stained-glass windows almost anywhere one looked.

Upon the Nevsky Prospect in Major Whistler's Russia had been a lonely, forlorn, fugitive figure who, although he thought of himself as a burning volcano of a man, a fiery genius who had not yet erupted, was both burning and shivering in the cold of the city of St. Petersburg, the Venice of the North upon the marshlands with their waterways. He would go down sometimes to watch the progress of the railroad station, sometimes with a fellow Fourierist of the secret study cell which he had joined because of his yearning for intellectual fellowship and his fear that in his isolation he might die of boredom and the need for recognition of a genius which had not yet found itself or explored, at so early an age, its unknowable dimensions but which he might find in a tentative way through conversations with this presumably anarchic group at its weekly meeting under cover of a mystery like everything else in the czar's Russia where a freezing, coughing carriage horse could not cough without inspiring a written report as to what the coughing meant, whether or not it was a threat against the present state by the drover or the passenger or the horse, was a well-known mystery.

The man who went down to watch the railroad station as it was going up and who would do most to immortalize the mortals of the Nevsky Prospect by exploration of the divinity and the criminality of man and with less interest in the sufferings of martyrs than in the complexities of executioners not only in Russia but beyond its borderline had been Fyodor Dostoyevsky, a universal genius through the very burning intensity of that fact.

He had, with the dream of paradise on a grand scale, the almost detached certainty that unless the suffering multitudes who were the serfs were given their freedom, they would rise up and take it by bloody revolution even as those who had murdered his father for his gold, surely that which may have been a few spoons or knives or forks or cups but nothing by comparison with the czar's gold.

In his novel *The Possessed,* which was written in response to the violent murder, on November 25, 1869, of a young student of the Moscow Agricultural Academy whom fellow conspirators had thrown into a fish pond, Dostoyevsky would bring into the text memories of the illicit Fourierist cell of dreamers to which he had once belonged and whose ideals he would mix in with subsequent revolutionary plots and movements in a way the early group did not deserve as all their crimes had been, if crimes they were, those of words and not of deeds, those of having engaged in the attempt to enjoy, even if shrouded with silence, freedom of thought and speech. *The Possessed* recalled also the words of an old folksong which Dostoyevsky must have heard in those early days in St. Petersburg when liberals, often at odds with each other, were dreaming of revolutionary reform, albeit that which the intellectuals and not the serfs should devise, and no doubt it had been written by a landowner with a prophetic social conscience and not by some poor child of nature to whom had been given no voice—"The peasant with his ax is coming. Something terrible will happen."

Dostoyevsky's companion on the walks to the railway station through various phases of its scaffoldings had been the intensely visionary socialistic or anarchic dreamer and critic Vissarion Belinsky, known among some of his fellow writers as Vissarion the Furious and so called also by the far more hesitant, seemingly almost slow-witted Dostoyevsky, for whom the abyss was always opening at his feet so that he must walk with care lest he should fall with whirling into a fit caused by all that was divine and all that was criminal in life and the irrationality of reason itself in the face of the great enigmas which man's reason alone could not solve, he thus differing from the man who was so rapid in his thoughts and was so rapid in his espousal of every theory which might bring improvement to man upon the road to humanistic progress such as he without hesitation had thought would be brought by the rails which would be laid over the sleeping, yet slightly stirring Russian land as the dead moved.

As the railroad station was being laid from the ground up, no roof before there could be the necessary support of pillars which would not float away in a city built on marshes, dissolve like a dream of a Prospero in mists and clouds, the old critic in the squirrelly overcoat which no Gogol's thief, if in his right mind, would have snatched—for it looked as if it had already been torn to pieces by howling, screaming packs of wolves who had leapt upon this strange animal in a treeless world of everlasting polar snow— would escape being exiled to the czar's Siberian icehouse with other deranged Fourieristic plotters of reform only because of his dying of the ravages caused by the white plague before he could be deported as he would have been if there had been only one spark of life left in his mortal frame.

Coughing as Dostoyevsky also shivered in his tattered overcoat and felt himself at times to be nothing more than a skeleton or at least had felt his nakedness of flesh before Belinsky's discovering of him, he had said, with his usual rapidity and impatience, that he found it difficult or almost impossible to wait calmly for the last stone to be set—for that which he utterly believed, as the train would bring an end to travel by carriage over lost or impassable roads, was that the rays of the headlights, even as was believed in America by those optimists for whom the old lost roads through lost worlds were best—would light the dark plain with radiance as the locomotive would bring Russia into the age of progress. He had been sure that the railroad which the czar had intended to be a part of military linkage to protect Russia from invasions by revolutionary Europeans or other aliens of movements either real or imaginary would be the linkage which would bring the Russian bear from the frozen sleep of ages into the heavenly folds of Western civilization and allow not only economic and social improvement but the flowering of humanistic culture.

Dostoyevsky had predicted that there would come a time when there would be trains bringing firewood from the remotest regions of Russia to provide heat for the unheated houses of St. Petersburg and Moscow when it became an important railway center.

The revolutionary firebird Belinsky could not believe that the new form of transportation would not be used for the transformation of the lives of the poor children of the clay of which all men were made and whom he idealized for their power to stand up and be men in the new world which was yet to come and would be that ruled by science and reason—whereas to Dostoyevsky when he looked back as one who had suffered both transportation to the freezing Arctic wasteland and that spiritual illumination which had come to him in the czar's icehouse, the long-faced old Christ of Russia would endure and it would be that land which was most productive of the seeds not of rationalism but of the irrational, mystical, ever-dreaming god who expressed the soul of His people. And all that Belinsky had proposed to take the place of the suffering Christ weeping tears of pearls had been an upright man in a rational state guided only by reason and the power of the idea of man's essential good.

Belinsky, the white plague in the White City tearing like wolves' teeth at his lungs, had once been an aesthetician, a worshiper of beauty for its own sake, but upon finding that he was totally suffocated by the rarefied atmosphere in which he had indulged himself with the splendid thought that there was no existence possible save inner existence—even as was believed in America by many who could not endure to look upon the brutal wildernesses of external realities and so had turned their eyes inward and explored harmonious and almost supernaturally divine wildernesses of self-centered realities which took no necessary cognizance of poor beggars freezing to death in the winter winds and snow—he had gone out of himself into a new work of suffering, as he had explained his progress from egoism to altruism in a letter to a friend. He had come to the not flickering, not fickle conviction that literature, in order to justify the time and effort given to its creation, must convince members of the privileged aristocracy, those few who were at the top and lived in gilded palaces as did the rich in other countries, that they should recognize their brotherhood with the poor serfs such as those whose frozen bodies, when railway tracks were being laid, were piled up like cordwood waiting for mass burial, as surely every intellectual knew unless like the czar with his all-seeing eye and his all-hearing ear he was blind, deaf, dumb, even more indifferent to human sufferings than stones might be.

Belinsky had been an undeviating worshiper of Nicholai Gogol's *Dead Souls,* the tragicomic epic of the adventures of a corrupt salesman whose purchase of the names of dead serfs from serf-owning landlords in strange, wild villas, set in the midst of perpetual fogs scarcely penetrated by sunlight, shows every type of corruption and cupidity there is, all the sins of Russia as the dead souls under discussion become the most vivid and beautiful actors seeming, as they have never been embalmed, literally to rise up from their graves—this novel of social consciousness to be someday, along with *Les Misérables* and *The Man Who Laughed* and *The Wandering Jew* and the novels of Balzac and Dickens as well as philosophic works like those of Voltaire and Rousseau and Proudhon, among those which the father of Eugene Victor Debs would contribute to the magnification of consciousness in the mind of the former locomotive fireman who would become the youthful editor of *The Brotherhood of Locomotive Firemen's Magazine* when he was writing or collecting elegies for locomotive firemen out of which would steadily grow his vision of socialism, that which had taken root in a grave and yet would grow.

[1 6 5]

DEATH, IT SEEMED, had preceded life. For Belinsky had believed, as he was a materialist and an agnostic—hence, in Dostoyevsky's view, a snob—that the portrait of the living dead in *Dead Souls,* which was also a national portrait, would stir up utopian or reform movements in a Russia which would go over from the orbit of death to the orbit of life in a temporal and not otherworldly sense.

This kind of belief must necessarily have removed the man with the wolf-torn overcoat and white wolves tearing at his lungs in the white light of the White City from its fulfillment which he expected in an almost millennial sense without recognition of the mysticism inherent in a wholly unsupernatural faith in the imminence of the age of progress as that which would give happiness to mankind—although so far as Dostoyevky would live to see, upon not one square mile had a utopia founded wholly upon reason and science given witness to its ability to survive the winter blast and not be cut down like the phantom and the dream it was.

Dostoyevsky would claim that, although he had never been a socialist, he had enjoyed consideration of every form of utopian thought which might present itself to the human mind—whereas for Belinsky the illusion must be made into the real, the word, to take on flesh, and abstraction was not enough for the satisfaction of his obsessive desire for improvement of life in the here and the now when the revolution should be realized and the errors of the past be put away, in the words of Robert Owen, like a mistaken dream.

Belinsky's praise for *Dead Souls,* in spite of all the contradictory weathervanes there were in the wildness of Russia where was no real sense of order but that of blind chaos ruling over blind chaos, had been for some time the unchanging North Star of his life. For he had believed that *Dead Souls* revealed a road from death to life as it explored the diseases to which the land was subjected by cruel landlords in their mad villas falling, crumbling into miasmic mists and fogs like the House of Usher, some people would say, as also America under the iron rule of the iron czars would be compared with the falling House of Usher or with the rule of the iron czar Nicholas I.

Nothing that did not advance the cause of empirical socialism as transplanted to Russia from the Western world was justifiable in the bloodshot eyes of the ailing Belinsky—there was no place in all of Russia for any tinsel-crowned Christ like that one which, carried through the streets, had made Dostoyevsky, then half in love with atheism and half in love with religion, nearly fall into that great abyss which was the fate of the epileptic to whom was given no aura of forewarning, no crown of light by which to know that the experience in pseudo-death was at hand.

He had felt himself to be a somnambulist walking through this life of phantoms and shades, although some sense of his own value had been reported to him by Belinsky's recognition of his genius as the writer of *Poor Folk*.

To Gogol Belinsky had given a praise not given to any but the sharers of his socialist-oriented views. *Dead Souls* was to become the bible of the modern revolutionaries as truly as if the author had been a firebird of egalitarian consciousness who intended to ignite the dead firewood into living sparks.

Upon the publication of Gogol's turncoat *Correspondence* and greatly to the ironic amusement of Dostoyevsky in retrospect as to the turning away of the once-revered author into a world of increasing supernaturalism, Belinsky reminded Gogol of the love which he had given to him but which was now withdrawn by the fastest man in Russia. "Yes, I loved you as only man bound to his country by red blood"—was not Vissarion the Furious always coughing, spitting up blood?—"can love the hope of that country, its honor and its glory, and one of the great leaders of its conscience, its developments, and its progress. . . . You do not realize that Russia's salvation lies not in mysticism or pietism but in the progress of civilization, in the maturation of that human dignity which for centuries has been dragged in mud and dung. . . . Look at your feet, they stand at the edge of the abyss."

Gogol's portrait of the nation in *Dead Souls* could only have seemed all too darkly pessimistic for a man of optimistic spirit to have entertained, although on one side of the coin of his genius was the muse of tragedy and on the other side was the muse of comedy, and they were aspects of the same world.

Gogol was to go over the abyss as a suicide in 1852, which Belinsky did not live to see and as he probably would have interpreted as the result of

Gogol's departure from the humanistic belief in egalitarian rationalism which should be the new world. The plummet line of simple truth dropping with the anchor heart was that in which the believers in a rational world must surely believe or ought at least to seem to believe, even although they might best know the all-devouring abyss.

Belinsky's admiration for Dostoyevsky's *Poor Folk* had been founded on his need to believe that the humane was the only sacred thing. *Poor Folk* had seemed to reflect his own very biased views that the bedrock upon which the new world should be built was socialistic and that all other philosophies were as trivial as tinsel or smoke in the wind or phantoms which would dissolve in the light of truth.

As to what Belinsky had seen in *Poor Folk* to elicit his recognition that it was a socialistic novel as he had believed *Dead Souls* was, even if not quite a masterpiece of the same stature, what was needed for the author was naturally the time in which to develop from this seed or cocoon, as it may be called; it was quite simple. "Some worthy fools believe that love of mankind is the pleasure and duty of every man. They do not understand what has happened when the wheel of existence with all the well-established privileges crushes and pulverizes their flesh and bones. That is the tragedy! What characters!"

Dostoyevsky had been lifted up from the mud of oblivion by Belinsky's praise of *Poor Folk* and had found himself, the shabby aristocrat, invited to gilded drawing rooms. But he was deeply depressed when rival writers accused him of stealing *The Double* from Gogol's *The Nose* and *The Overcoat*. Because of these false accusations, he had felt like a living skeleton, not for the first time nor for the last time, and had wanted to die, simply to dissolve into mists and fogs. He had thought of the desirability of simulating insanity as a way of escape from a world which was, little doubt, all too irrational for him to endure. He had written his brother Mikhail that he lived as in a fog. "I do not see life, I have no time to recover my senses. My art is being ruined for lack of time—I should like to stop."

[1 6 6]

IN THE AGE-OLD pattern of insertion of an informer or various informers in the insurrectionist camps, as would happen when the American czars of railroads and mills and mines would employ Pinkerton detectives to spy like the all-seeing eye upon the embryonic organizations of unions which should be strangled in the womb of time before they could emerge, as would be observed by Debs, for the womb was supposed to be their grave over which the clods of earth had been permanently placed to be forever barren of even one disturbing seed of hope breaking into flower, an official of the ministry of the interior had been ordered to find and insert into the Fourierist circle which met in a little Russian fairy-tale house where there was only one candle burning to its stub with flame fluttering in the high gale of revolutionary talk a spy who was not to be, of course, some poor serf like a clod hopping away from the czar's harrow which harrowed him but a man of intellectual luminosity and thus above suspicion, certainly not of that low order which might be the candle already burned down with his red-rimmed eye sockets already burned out as would be some of the revolutionaries in America, when not the intellectual but the poorest blasted broken fireman or brakeman or miner or puddler with his face seared by fire and blackened by mud and dust would rise as the potent force to lead man from the darkness to the light.

An Italian was found to come to the clandestine meetings with his paintbrush and paint the intellectuals as red as the red dawn which was so prematurely feared, and no one had seemed more subversive than he or more dedicated to revolutionary projects such as, if they succeeded, might be like some great hurricane shattering all the chandeliers in the Winter Palace, causing them to fall with the weight of galaxies, causing thousands of porcelain rosebuds and feet of cherubim and ears of cherubim to fall on the czar's head.

As for Dostoyevsky, he had often felt as if a weight of stone as heavy as a mountain was hanging over his egg head and was about to fall although he had felt helpless and unable to move and perhaps had felt fascinated also by the sense of impending doom.

The year in which Dostoyevsky had read aloud Belinsky's letter to the author of *Dead Souls* was 1849, the year of the accelerated gold rush to California. "The church presents itself as a hierarchy, that is to say, as a personification of inequality, a courtesan of established power, an enemy and a wrecker of brotherhood among men." And yet although he had heard his voice like a stranger's voice emanating from him and had read loud enough for others to hear as a flame flickered but did not quite go out, he could not possibly have wanted, God have mercy on him, the golden Christ to be harassed or hammered down into gold dust.

Later, the well-intentioned Petravesky, the chatterer and mountebank and prince of fools who had prided himself that the czar's police were looking for him as the guilty party under whose sheltering wings the utopian chicks were hatched, had announced, at a dinner in celebration of the birthday of the antirevolutionary Fourier, from whose philosophy they were receiving infusions of revolutionary spirit, that the old society with all its errors and woes had been condemned to death and that the only problem now was to carry out the death sentence, which, of course, was different from a life sentence. The czar's spy, who had been welcomed by the addlepated fool as the real thing and not fool's gold, had been fascinated to hear.

That which had been courteously demanded by the revolutionists, who had no army and no guns and who hoped that the czar would grant their wish of his own volition so that he and all that he represented would not be killed by a random arrow or a thousand arrows, had boiled down to the demand for the abolition of private property, which should be shared by all men in equal brotherhood—the abolition of the present presumably sacred marital state, which was prevalent less in reality than in practice—an end to the servitude of women who were beaten like workhorses by cruel drovers—and the abolition of the present government, the army, and all the traditional things there were, all of which were for the preservation of the upper pyramid.

Dostoyevsky had not been present at this fatal banquet which had given to the czar's all-seeing eye and all-hearing ear the evidence which would provide to a wise emperor of an empire so vast that it reached beyond his firsthand knowledge an opportunity to close in upon potential troublemakers whose programs of instantaneous reform would bring on, if they were not untrammeled in their way, the storming of the Winter Palace or the carrying out of the death sentence upon the czar who, like every other czar, no doubt including the czar rooster in the barnyard, knew not who his true enemies were and so had to guard himself from those within the gates and outside the gates.

As for the arrest that had been recommended by the secretary of interior, whose loyalty to the czar was necessarily demonstrated by the numbers of plotters he found within the amorphous boundary lines of this old Russia sleeping under the shell of the mother-of-pearl sky—"Go to it, in the name of God"—the czar's pen had written on the margin of the detective's report—"and let thy will be done." Of course, to let God's will be done did not signify trust in God or fate but rather the enactment of the will of the purple czar.

The czar who had pointed out with his ruler to Major Whistler the way the railroad should be laid as straight and shining as a thread through a needle's eye and not with such difficulties as those which a rich man finds in passing through the pearly gates of paradise which are as small as the needle's eye to him could only have considered the large-headed but small-brained Dostoyevsky in his evaluation of himself and his genius as a withered, shrunken seed in its shell—something unable to bloom.

The clouded indistinctions drifting through Dostoyevsky's cracked mind had caused him to be, when a student at the Engineers' Castle, more interested in its builder, the Emperor Pavel Petrovich, who had been murdered with the foreknowledge of the crown prince and whose death had been attributed by him to heart failure, a very common cause, than a man of his passions and depths and heights could possibly have been in presumably materialistic sciences such as military engineering, algebraic equations, and geometric arcs and angles and triangles and endless circumferences valuable for their relation to no spiritual premises but fortification against the enemies within and the enemies without and foundation stones and stone walls and castles not sinking into bottomless lakes at a wild crane's cry, a loose pebble rolling upon a known shore which was the unknown, topographies which were abstractions when marked on a surveyor's map.

Dostoyevsky had been a conscientious student but had not shown the brilliance of the great and many-faceted crystalline dome which would be his in the inexact science of human nature.

He had found his life in the engineer's castle as a student of conventional mathematics at odds with his potential but unrealized and perhaps unrealizable talents and had complained to his brother Mikhail—"Only that which is freed from earthly materialism and happiness is beautiful."

In the esteem of the young scholar—who was called Photus after the founder of the Russian Orthodox church whom he revered as he would always have a special place in both valves of his heart for religious seers and madmen and none for shaky engineers of merely temporal constructions sealed from their beginning by doom because founded on injustice—as he had added to his brother Mikhail, "I think that the world has taken a negative direction and that high and beautiful spirituality has become a satire."

His correspondence was that of a man who was in the inferno and yearned to get out, at the same time that he who was burning was also freezing. "I am surrounded by an icy, polar atmosphere without a ray of the sun." When he had failed to pass an examination in algebra, mainly because of absent-mindedness, as the subject bored him, he had blamed the persecutory spirit of his professor of mathematics for what seemed a conspiracy against him and had cried out—"I would like to crush the universe." As a second lieutenant assigned to the engineering blueprint division, he had felt surrounded by a stone wall and had determined to become a stone in that wall.

His sense of isolation, already so great that he had felt as if he were living on the back side of the moon, had been greatly heightened by the rumor that he was to be transported with a corps of engineers on an expedition many moons away from the White City, St. Petersburg, and the Nevsky Prospect, or great white way, where the streetlamps could scarcely cast their rays through the fogs, where he moved like a phantom shadowed by a phantom and where his cries were answered by cries—and who was he? Was he himself or the other one—or was he both?

[1 6 7]

DETERMINED TO ARREST this moon-faced fool and other inane plotters for whom nothing in Russia was good enough, their dissatisfaction with the world never to be satisfied, the czar had had thirty-four persons rounded up by eager-beaver policemen who raided their dwelling places in the early dawn of April 22, 1849, impounding their books and papers and letters and other not reliable evidences of revolutionary intent—gathering up the conspirators whom they had found indoors, some in bed, some about to go to bed—and also those who were outdoors and might be found upon various street corners under streetlamps gleaming like fallen moons in the districts of the rich but already extinguished by the lamplighter in the districts of the poor, those fellow conspirators who for one reason or another had not been at home sheltered from fogs and mists and from the coldly falling rain of a spring which had come so late it almost had not come.

The tears of heaven were falling for these errant fools with their quixotic ideals which had manifested themselves in the realm of words, words, which were not deeds but were likely to be dreams, and some of these plotters who were the quick and not the dead must have dreamed, like the slow-witted Dostoyevsky with his love of beauty and art, that someday they in recognition of their services would be entertained by harps and horns and harpsichords and fiddlers stepping on clouds and more orchestral instruments than most men had ever dreamed of or had ever heard, including the music of silent horns in the czar's palace by the great czar himself, there probably having been few or none who would have committed that regicide which was the ultimate patricide and in America would be the murder of a president.

The prison which was the Peter and Paul Fortress and had been built by Peter the Great, and in its cold dungeons had housed the conspirators organized by his son who had been tortured to death for his failure to agree with his father's will, could not have surprised Dostoyevsky very much by its silence and his separation from others, as he had already felt, through years of loneliness, what it must have been like to be Lord Byron's "Prisoner of Chillon." He had found himself suspended in a state in which it was difficult to find the dividing line between life and death, waking and sleeping—just as, like Edgar Allan Poe, the author of "The Raven," he had always feared that when he seemed to be the corpse as dead as stone, yet he might not be dead but only sleeping and might be buried alive—might awaken too far under earth to claw himself out—might die with the cold clods of earth upon his face. He was after all a military doctor's son to whom the opening eyelids of the dead and the suddenly burning sparks in their eyes were as familiar as fireflies gleaming in twilight over meadows and fields when the harvest was done. He had felt a strange sense of peace.

The trial of the presumably anarchic plotters was like the many blades of iron harrows slashing the accused for crimes which—like the pronouncement of a death sentence upon this mistaken historical past, like the glad tidings of Robert Owen upon the banks of the Wabash that the old immoral world was dead and that the new moral world had been born (some might have heard it already crying in its crib), that the Rubicon between capitalism and communism had been crossed—had not yet occurred and were ones they had shown no tendency to carry out except in realms of sentences which were made of words.

Should men be mutilated or destroyed not because of what they did but what they said? Should they be suppressed and stamped out by the unlawful forces that were called law and order and must be observed by the czar, as if freedom of thought and speech were the equivalent of universal murder and might draw meteors down from the sky? In darkest Russia, such rigged injustices could occur, even as in an enlightened democracy such as America where lynch law prevailed in relation to black men whose little frog and mice and owl songs had been songs in code, and neither was there pity for yellow or red.

The investigating committee had found, after five months of investigating the men who were accused of socialism, no organized cell for the propagation of revolution, no more individualistic and ego-centered anarchy nor any kind of program nor calendar for the enactment of the death sentence upon the old world when the millennium of the new world should begin.

A military court including both military and civilian members had enacted in September the role of the many-armed czar by sentencing seven prisoners to deportation, fifteen to execution, and six to release into the freedom of the silence which they must maintain unless they wished to be picked up again.

The emperor who was the czar of all the czars, still not satisfied, very much annoyed by this failure in cooperation against those would-be communist cooperators, had transferred the case to the auditorial general, whose staff had extended their clemency by commuting sentences of exile to sentences of death, with the closet recommendation to the emperor that he in all his glory, poor puppet that he was in view of greater forces, just as an American president might also be forced to dance on strings pulled by the promoters of industrial imperialism, should extend the largesse of his all-embracing clemency by commuting sentences of death to sentences of exile, as the condemned in the bowels of the Peter and Paul Fortress had not known.

Silence prevailing, the cell of Dostoyevsky had been filled only with the memory of the music he loved, the choral voices of priests, the music of the piano as played by Liszt, the music of the violin as played by the sentimental folk musician Ole Bull, with a tossing mane as he would be elegized some day by James Whitcomb Riley for having played the strings of his violin and the strings of his long white beard which were caught among the strings in a shipwreck on the Ohio River, where, lifting his arm with his fiddle above the waves, he had swum to shore, the legend would be told, and had aroused the admiration of Debs, most particularly as he was a believer in a mystical order of cooperative communism in the Far West, and the memory of Dickens and Poe and Balzac and the perfect saint who was Victor Hugo. Dostoyevsky had naïvely supposed with a naïveté which was almost incurable that he and others would be released from the cells of a prison which, like many prisons, was a hive where no honey was.

The doors of the cell had been opened at last, and the prisoners in their overcoats and hats—dressed as for a long journey but surely not one from earth to heaven, which would require no overcoat for a naked animal such as every man and even great czars must be, in the eyes of God—had been taken to a scaffold in a military field, of all the places in the world, had not been told that they were free to go home.

There was an unreality about it all. It was all so bizarre, so out of this world that it was hard to believe the evidence of one's remaining senses.

Dostoyevsky had seen the fool Petravesky waiting for a verdict. A black-robed priest with a silver cross was in attendance waiting as if to hear confessions and give last rites. The military officer was wrapped around by shawls of fog. The words read by him in a muffled voice, those which might make dead pigeons fall with muffled thuds from the sky the mottled color of pigeon's breast in this month of December seemingly as fit for Decembrists as for the birth of Christ, were those of a sentence to death and were read three times—no doubt once for Father, once for Mother, once for Son of Holy Ghost.

Dostoyevsky was among those chosen for instant dispatch to another world by the czar. This death sentence was probably not a comment upon his literary work, most of it in the future which would never be his past. What he had written the czar had not admired.

Of his experience before he, kneeling in the snow, was hooded for the execution by the firing squad, Dostoyevsky's recollection would be that he had felt no sensation at all of the freezing cold and had trembled not at all. Simply, he had felt peace—and after all as he had always felt near to death, this time had been not the confrontation with extinction it might have been for some—it had not seemed to bring him any nearer to an absolute as might have been the case if he had been the atheist he once had said he was—when he was in debt to one who did not believe in God.

Perhaps the freezing cold had caused a languor to creep like a cloud over all the luminous cells of his body at once and he had been at the ever-moving boundary line between sleeping and dreaming which was marked only upon the map dividing, although with eternities of variables, consciousness and unconsciousness, even as every true topographer of the human being must come to know and socialists of humanitarian instinct like *The Locomotive Firemen's Magazine*'s elegiast Debs would come to know when he was recording the deaths caused by the negligence of czars or cars like those falling through the thin crust of earth into the deep pits.

Standing beside poor Petravesky at the edge of the abyss into which all men must precipitate themselves at the end, some sooner than others when their lives were cut short by the evils which, perpetrated by not truly thoughtful men, far outnumber those in the essential nature of things mortal and transitory and subject to improvement, Dostoyevsky had kissed the silver cross in the hands of the peripatetic black-robed priest when he had lifted it to his mute lips. He was soon to pass from the mobile to the immobile state, if, indeed, there is such a thing as an immobile state possible in the invasive cosmos. He would recall of this crucial experience—"I thought I might perhaps have five minutes more to live, and awful those moments were. I kept staring at a church with a gilt dome which reflected the sunbeams, and I suddenly felt as if these beams came from the region where I was to be myself in a few minutes."

As Dostoyevsky and the others had knelt in the white snow while the executioner was placing black hoods over their eyes, three had been tied to the posts to wait for the hail of artillery which should come with the commander's thunderous bark—but there had been only the ominous silence broken by no sound, no sound at all. Petravesky, whose intellectual curiosity had brought him to this theater of doom in the first place, a fool who would risk that retribution which was to be executed twice, once when he was dead, had peeked out from under a corner of his black hood and had seen the firing squad, at a sign from the commander, withdrawing from their line to go in all ways.

The death sentence which had been followed by the priest's prayer for the repentance of these doomed socialists so that God might show to them some mercy in the world to which they were about to go, whether upward with the repentant or downward with the unrepentant, had most strangely, most mysteriously omitted the hearing of the confession of one of the men and the last sacraments for which he had asked—for would not the carrying out of the czar's theatrical pseudo-masterpiece to such a realistic or surrealistic extent have been an act of sacrilege?—had been followed by the commander's reading aloud to the men who had already suffered the psychic and physical agonies of confrontation with an unbelievable extinction which was believable the commutation of the impending death sentence to a life sentence in Siberia through the infinite clemency of the czar.

By this macabre joke upon writers and other miscreant practitioners of plots against the czar, by the introduction of the Italian painter as the informer who had noted the speeches of miscreants and painted them as red as blood with his paintbrush, by the rigged jury which had brought these madmen to the scaffold for pockmarking by riflemen—but then with a sudden shift of design, which had been presided over by the czar as to every measurement of every man for his coffin and every turn of every screw, they had been sentenced to that exile in the Siberian wasteland from which they would not return alive or dead, in all likelihood—the czar had shown that an active man not given over to such profundities of thought as theirs might concoct plots outdoing those of harebrained writers like Dostoyevsky, the purloiner of *The Nose* and *The Overcoat* and *The Double,* and that all screw-brained utopists or riotous anarchists or nihilists or revolutionaries were utterly inept in the productions of fictional utopias by comparison with nonfictional utopias such as that he had just robbed them of.

Dostoyevsky and the others who had undergone the agonies of pseudo-execution as if they were actors had been given hoods for the journey into the polar night where the nights were six months long and had been put aboard open sledges with horses pointing to the land where would be the material for *The House of the Dead*. They had worn ankle chains, each weighing ten pounds, which might as well have weighed twenty pounds, each leaving permanent scars upon the frail body of the man who would express not only the genius of the race in Russia but of the human race.

Later, they who had been guilty of no crime but freedom of thought and speech had been put into covered sledges for the long journey through lands as frozen as might have been the surface of a star beyond the reach of man.

The place of Dostoyevsky's exile was Omsk, between two rivers in the Central Asiatic wilds of the Russian province of Armolensk, a land of steppes seeming to reach on and on without exit, a land seeming itself that infinity and that eternity united here as nowhere in any temperate zone. The only exit might be burial under a frozen lake when one's spirit, as the ice groaned, should be translated upward like a vapor or breath. Unfortunately for Dostoyevsky, who was to suffer pseudo-death many times, he had not the ability of the hibernating frog or owl. His deaths were to be many and one more than would be followed by his awakening—so far as may be known.

The work which the gaunt, thin-boned Dostoyevsky performed in the freezing cold had included clearing away with an ice pick of ice and snow which the rainbow-bedazzled Fourier would have melted away by the manufacture or magical evocation of a second aurora borealis so that there might be flowers with bird bills and birds who were made of flying flowers like those dreamed of by exotic poets and the rising up of alabaster blocks of cathedral size from lakes of ice.

Once Dostoyevsky had glimpsed, on the other side of the Irtysh River in the distance from which came the songs of nomadic shepherds, a skin tent from which arose curlings of smoke mixed with vapors, and there was a woman tending her sheep. Of communism in its pure form, he would one day observe that it had been the age-old society of Asiatic nomads.

Doubtless there was nothing new under the sun. So also communism had been the age-old society of Indians who in America had spared shooting with their arrows the caravans of Brigham Young and his fellow Mormons when they, in flight from the burned-out Nauvoo, had been trying to find their way out of America toward some new land where they, pietists of mystical vision and in some ways Fourieristic romanticists and in other ways Owenite empiricists, could live according to their communitarian religious and economic beliefs and without harassment by surrounding capitalistic murderers like those who had killed the God-inflated Joseph Smith and his brother and others at Nauvoo—a city which would be one of the lost utopias where Debs would study fallen pillars and broken angel wings and cherub ears.

The sleep of the men in the czar's freezing bullpen or icehouse for the human cattle herded there had been rudely disturbed night after night by Eight Eyes, the drunken overseer who with his cracking bullwhip had taken great pleasure in awakening men who had turned from sleeping on their right sides to their left sides or flailing from side to side had whispered like little children to their mother or cried out for her in dreaming states beyond the control of consciousness. The unconscious knew no rules.

Bedbugs had crawled over the men who had no blankets to protect them from the icy, flailing frost and cold coming in through chinks. Dostoyevsky's feet had frozen in an atmosphere where quicksilver froze, and yet his thoughts under his own cracked crystal dome had run about in all ways like quicksilver when he had no intellectual outlet or employment but to think.

One of his achievements had been to teach a convict from the Caucasus to read the New Testament in Russian from a tattered Bible which had been given to him on his way to the arid icehouse by the black-garbed widow of a Decembrist exile, one of the many heroic women who had lived in vain waiting for either the living or the dead to emerge from the land of snow and ice for which some would continue to wait even when their men were dead and in all probability would not return.

The words of the Russian testament and especially the beatitudes were those which were embroidered in threads of finest gold and silver on finest linen pillows fringed with silver and gold for the divans in great palaces where horses were better housed than were the poor, even as would be true in the America of the great tycoons who would come up after the capitalistic opportunity which would be theirs because of the Civil War which would enlarge the realm of railroads and their baronies and their dukedoms at the expense of black and white, yellow and red men who would be characterized by Debs as Uncle Sam's orphans.

While in the prison which would be characterized as "the house of the dead," where a man's hands might fall off or his eyeballs freeze and where, with the top of his head shaved completely bald by the prison barber, half his mustache shaved away and all his beard shaved away so that the loss of the individual life would seem more nearly complete than it already was and he, if trying to break his chains, would be recognized as the anonymous convict guilty of any awful crime which might cross the mind of any noncomprehensive man who saw him and felt himself to be different from this wild beast, Dostoyevsky had not been under any further compulsion to be the atheist who owed a debt to society for his sacrilegious spirit and, in a sense far more profound than that of the mechanical czar, had remained true to the Byzantine icons of the beloved Russian Christ, and perhaps because such icons had been in chicken yards in the days of his childhood this Christ had not been for him an aristocratic Son of God but the lowly and simple Christ of the workingman or farmer whose wife gathered up the eggs which were the hen's eggs and not the rooster's eggs as they might be in certain out-of-this-world utopias.

This humble Christ had come to him with radiant visions transmuting Arctic grayness into bands of rainbow light. As a hod carrier increasing every day, for the exercise of his muscles, the loads of bricks he had carried from the kiln to a military building under construction, the punishment had seemed to him to be greater than the crime which he had not committed and to be less in its constant repetition day after timeless day not always divided from the night, had seemed less burdensome to him than the condition of forced labor which was performed not as one's choice by a man with freedom of will but with threat of punishment by the mutilation of one's already mutilated body, even by hackings of one's ears or one's nose away.

He had not resented the failure of the military overlords to recognize and respect a social difference between the political prisoners and the lower elements, the thieves and murderers who were in the same pit with him and other literary or artistic or intellectual men and who in turn, instead of embracing these brothers who were sharers of sorrows in a great mutuality where social differences should have seemed irrelevant and should have disappeared, had placed them lower than themselves and at the bottom of the heap.

It had been almost impossible for men of the lower class in the prison population, many or most of whom were illiterate and came from the most impoverished and most underprivileged strata of society, to believe that the political prisoners, gentlemen of noble class, were genuine socialists or communists wishing to extend brotherhood to them and were guilty of no greater crime than to dream of a New Jerusalem on earth where all men would be brothers and embrace each other in an act of what might seem or be eternal love.

One may well imagine that a serf who had cut an aristocrat's windpipe must have been startled and disbelieving when brought into association with rich men who, if they could follow the dictates of their hearts, would steal all private property away from the landlords who were petty czars themselves or representatives of the czar of czars doing his will and hand over every acre to them, every horse pond, every thistle and every flower, every cocoon and every butterfly.

Dostoyevsky had found that his fellow convicts with their heads shaven bald like his and their faces sometimes branded by hot irons, their noses sometimes mutilated or their ears cut off, had been that which should have been valued by human society and not dismissed as dirt. The convicts with whom he had wished to share his feelings of the commonality of brotherhood were not to be dismissed as unworthy of compassion and understanding. Isolation in prison might protect the world from their depredations but had in no way contributed to their moral improvement.

"What a wealth of young manhood lies here buried to no purpose! What a wealth of vigor lies annulled within these walls! Yet truly it may be said that these same convicts were splendid men—perhaps the best, the most virile, the most gifted of all we possess—whereas their powers and faculties lie ruined abnormally, irrevocably, and illegally!"

He had seen that the imprisonment under inhumane conditions did nothing at all for the redemption of men who were society's outcasts. "We were squeezed in like herring in a barrel," according to his recollections to his brother in St. Petersburg. "The convicts were like pigs. 'Since we are living beings,' they said, 'how can we help being piggish?'"

In the Arctic prison he had felt as if he were cut off like a slice of frozen bread from all those beauties and works of art which had been his in the past. Yet he would always believe that the prison had killed many things in him but had made others come into bloom.

As for the four years which he had spent there, he would come to regard them as a period when he was buried alive and locked into a coffin from which he had emerged. He would also hold to the conviction that there was not one four-by-six territory on earth which under the influence of materialistic science and without recourse to spiritual beings had ever succeeded in the demonstration of utopian social perfection.

Resurrection and redemption and everlasting life, the awakening of the dead would be found by those whose boats were so strongly anchored in the love of Christ that they would not be swept away by storms. The world itself and all the nations of the world would be redeemed at the end by the Russian Christ Who had come to him in visions and dreams when he was in the Arctic pit.

[1 6 8]

THE IRON CZAR could not have failed to be pricked by iron pins and thorns when he saw the eternally hopeful revolutionary description of him which showed him to be no great beauty with angels embroidered on his robes and no golden pillars upholding holy icons as should befit one who was the representative of a god in whom he did not necessarily believe as God should have a care for the lowliest creatures on earth, but rather as a European reaction to the French Revolution and all other outbreaks against his scepter and his crown—a stumbling block in the path of the revolution ready to face all comers.

The situation had been explosive indeed, that of social ferment caused by the yeast of revolution which, as was also true in the America of the railroad czars, was threatening to blow up the entire pan of the dough which was the rich man's dough. The familiar image of the pan would be employed by Debs when he, a spokesman for the workers of the Gilded Age, which was more appropriately called the Gelded Age, because he became a revolutionary spokesman from the time of the Pullman strike onward if not before when his mindless jackass brain was seething with discontentment in a land ruled over by the American czars of mills and mines and rails. The image was timeworn, and it was international.

A cartoon of that nonhalcyon time, in which the ever-dying Major Whistler, a long and lonely whistle ringing in his ears because of the freezing winter winds in which the freezing, snow-freezing, snow-furred serfs were crawling like white lice over the inert, immobile, frozen body of Mother Russia who from horizon to horizon and as far as the befogged eye could see was laid out like a corpse in the snow, had shown three symbolic bottles labeled France, Prussia, Russia which could be read aloud to those who could not read.

France was a bottle of champagne, the cork blown out as upon the shooting spurts of the effervescent liquor which was the drink of bubble-headed kings who were a covey of kings and princes and cabinet ministers, all perishing when the wind blew. Prussia was a bottle of beer, and also uncorked, letting out a dull cascade upon which were streaming the king, his margraves, archduke, and his dukes. But Russia was a bottle of vodka, and the bottle was not uncorked, and nothing was escaping as the cork was tied down by a rope like a noose and sealed with the double-headed eagle which was the sign of the imperial czars—even as in America when the strikes were raging against the great capitalists, it would be suggested by anti-imperialists that the American eagle should also be doubled-headed like that of the great czar of all the Russias who had had the power of life and death over his people.

The old saying among the unemployed poor who starved in Russian cities as did the serfs employed on the railroads, which had been described as "an experiment in training people not to eat," was that Jesus Christ would have been a thief like the thieves who died on either side of him if His hands and His feet had not been nailed to the cross. He would have gotten off and walked away with the cross to make firewood of it, little doubt, and why not? For firewood was what it was going to be when he was burned. Or he would have given the cross to some poor old Russian mother for her firewood with which to cook a tough old hen in the pot if she had one or even its head.

It was a matter of awesome and yet not extraordinary fact that railroad ties, when joined together by iron nails, made excellent crosses for the hanging and nailing of any railroad Christ whose egregious mistake had been that of expressing fraternal sympathy for the devil himself or the abused, starving, almost bloodless poor—the kind who, when they were ill and shaking from head to foot and so emaciated as to be almost bloodless, had received only the attention of a doctor with his buckets of leeches coming to draw out the blood to the last drop upon the snow and the grass. The true leeches upon the poor, however, were the landlords and other capitalists whom even the iron czar had feared he might displease.

Was this enforced labor of starving, fainting, falling men who would be shot if they showed the slightest sign of rebellion characteristic only of the land under the imperialistic rule of the czar of darkest Russia, a land which the headlight of the B & O locomotive could not light up? Or was such tyranny only more flagrant in Russia than in democratic lands claiming enlightenment?

Czar Nicholas I was not fond of the conservative and watchful landlords who were the upholders of his iron rule over his realm—for were they in his employment, or was he in theirs who might swarm over his dead body like flies if he in any way disappointed them?—and were they not the quellers of the czar's little pigeon serfs if or when they should show any sign of rebellion against an age-old system by which they lined their pockets with gold coins while the workers were reduced to skin and bones and dared not ask the great father for a loaf of bread or even a few crumbs which would not be stone?

Because of such puzzles, the landlords could not be the recipients of his affection of which he gave little or nothing and gave less of nothing to the sprouts upon their old family trees, their rebellious sons whose revenge against their fathers might be likened to that of his elder brother against Paul or that of the erratic son of Cromwell who became an upholder of Charles Stuart and wore his hair in long gold curls.

For the rebellion of these Russian scalawags against their property-owning fathers did not necessarily stop with their drinking and gambling and whoring and clowning around all night with total disregard of curfew laws—their debaucheries either including or seeming to include the dream of patricide upon a vast and perhaps universal scale which might result in their refusal to inherit their fathers' estates and their serfs when their fathers gave up the ghost—always with a long and rasping note which caused the stars to sigh as they fell from heaven to earth—or they might attempt, by hidden and subterranean ways, to instigate a revolt against the greatest father of them all, the czar who was the vice-regent of Christ on earth and czar of all the czars and landlord of all the landlords.

There was the possibility that these rebel sons might try to force from him a written contribution by which to make muley cows into prize cattle or prize cattle into muley cows, sows' ears into silk purses, onions into lily bulbs, as in some of their crazy dreams of overnight utopias—perhaps turn the earth from west to east upon its axis—so that the uncertain czar with his divine sense about him was filled with the dreadful presentiment that not from the lower world but from the higher world the revolution might come—perhaps was already on its way.

Although to the iron czar who was God's first if not His last word and who was a servant of the deity and thus could take no direction leading him away from the lodestar of the tradition-haloed past which had survived so many disasters, serfdom was an evil, palpable and obvious to all—as was certainly recognized by him—yet to touch it would be to bring on a world of chaos such as could be seen in countries where the popular rage for revolution and change of age-old institutions prevailed.

Contributing to Major Whistler's illness in Russia had been the inequality of a society in which white people owned white people. The major had grieved greatly over the Mexican War for which he could only hope that if the invasion succeeded, America would be forgiven for its imperialism by its European critics for exercising its power over its small neighbors and ousting despotism.

He had known that black slaves were owned by railroads at Vicksburg and that the red men of the west were in the process of being murdered or driven farther into the sunset glow in accordance with a policy which was inevitably, unless there should be some miracle, linked with the extinction of the feathered bird men who were dispensable in the expanding coloniza- tion policy as were the wild birds of America whose cries could still be heard—the wild ducks, the goldeneyes, the long-limbed cranes, the whistler swans, and droves of albatrosses who could be seen far inland.

He had known also at first hand of the sufferings of Irish workers on rails of whom Thoreau, the inspector of snowstorms, the track inspector of the universal rail, had pondered much, and had asked himself and others the question, the profoundly moving question—"Did you ever think what those sleepers are that underlie the railroad?"—and then had answered— "Each one is a man, an Irishman or a Yankee man. The rails are laid on them, and they are covered with sand, and the cars run smoothly over them. They are sound sleepers, I assure you. And every few years a new lot is laid down and run over—so that, if some have the pleasure of riding a rail, others have the misfortune to be ridden upon."

It did seem that there were two classes—the few who were the living riders such as the iron-heeled czar and the many who were the dead souls and were ridden upon as their faces were stamped down into blood- streaked ashes and dust.

The mythology of the workers sleeping in the beds between the rails— turning and tossing until they could turn and toss no more—was based on fact and would not only prevail among Russian liberals but would endure for many decades in the folklore of American train travel, where it had begun.

A sudden bump to a train so that it would seem ready to jump off the rails was that which was caused by an Irishman turning on his bed between the wheels—as would be said by Riley and Debs and many a locomotive brakeman, fireman, or engineer who had good reason for cultivating and cherishing the elegiac sense.

As for Debs with his faith in a better future, how long would the elegiac sense continue in him? It would continue for as long as he lived and per- haps long afterward. As will be seen.

Afterword

AMONG THE BOOKS most fascinating to the visionary Debs from the time when he was a locomotive fireman were not only those describing fictional utopias such as the volumes by Plato, Sir Thomas More, or Victor Hugo but also *The House of the Dead,* which he would see at large and magnified in America from the 1870s onward, long before he knew that he would be a prison bird.

Debs would remember of the early history of the trade union movement which was the fruit and flower of the nineteenth century the pioneers of progress who had paved the way for the twentieth-century workman. Many whose names were forgotten had laid the foundation of the labor movement when they had had but the vaguest conception of what their real mission was—but were those to whom Debs paid such continual tribute that his entire life, although keenly innovative in the work for the founding of a better world, would be spent in memory of early and late martyrs and the names which he wished to be rescued from the darkness of oblivion.

"The writer"—Debs would recall in his "Essay on Unionism and Socialism"—"has met and known some of these untitled agitators of the earlier day, whose hearts were set on organizing their class or at least their branch of it."

The organizer of that era's unions had still to face innumerable difficulties, and yet as a rule the ground had at least been broken for his approaching footstep.

Far different was it with the pioneer who left home without "scrip in his purse," whose chief stock consisted in his ability to "screw courage to the sticking point" and whose privation and hardship only consecrated more completely to his self-appointed martyrdom. . . . Our pioneer, leaving home, in many an instance never saw wife and child again. . . . Repulsed by the very men he was hungering to serve, penniless, deserted, neglected, and alone, he became "the poor wanderer of a stormy day" and ended his career a nameless outcast.

Indeed, he filled an unknown grave.

In the thirty years of trade unionism that had begun after the Civil War with its swift and vast concentrations of capital and unprecedented industrial activity—that is to say, from the seventies to the close of the nineteenth century—Debs had seen the tide of unionism sweeping over the land and rising steadily higher, notwithstanding the efforts put forth from a hundred sources controlled by the ruling class to stamp it out of existence:

> No strike has ever been lost, and there can be no defeat for the labor movement . . . and only the scars remain to bear testimony that the movement is invincible and that no mortal wound can be inflicted on it. . . . The union has been a moral stimulus as well as a material aid to the worker; it has appealed to him to develop his faculties and to think for himself. . . . Although these things have as yet been only vaguely and imperfectly accomplished, yet they started in and have grown with the union.

Trade unionism had always been guilty of a certain elitism or exclusiveness in the eyes of the labor union organizer Debs, an essentially millennial socialist long before his emergence as one of the most powerful spokesmen for universal economic and political and social justice this old world would have, a man of that passionate vision which would not permit him to neglect—even if socialism should become almost universal—one coal pit or pea patch to which it did not pertain.

There were reasons that the trade union movement had not been sufficiently progressive of spirit to keep up with the forward march of events. Rebellion against the employing class, wherever it had appeared, had been suppressed.

> This was kept up for years—but in spite of all that could be done to extinguish the fires of revolt, the smouldering embers had broken forth again and again, each time with increased intensity and vigor. . . . The working class alone does the world's work, has created its capital, produced its wealth, constructed its mills and factories, dug its canals, made its road beds, laid its rails and operates its trains, spanned the rivers with bridges and tunnelled the mountains, delved for the precious stones that glitter upon the bosom of vulgar idleness and reared the majestic palaces that shelter insolent parasites.

Debs would write in the essay "Socialism" of the capitalists who spent their time gambling at Monte Carlo, drinking champagne, choosing judges, buying editors, hiring preachers, corrupting politics, building universities, endowing libraries, patronizing churches, getting the gout, preaching morals, and bequeathing the earth to their descendants—"The other side do the work, early and late, in heat and cold; they sweat and groan and bleed and die. . . . They build the mills and all the machinery; they man the plant, and the thing of stone and steel begins to throb. They live far away in the outskirts in cottages just this side of the hovels where gaunt famine walks with despair and 'Les Misérables' leer and mock at civilization."

He had seen that when the mills shut down and the workers were out of work or out of home, or when old age began to steal away their vigor and their step was no longer agile and they were no longer fit for the labor market to make profit for their masters, they were pushed aside into the human drift emptying into the gulf of despair and death. The system as he saw it was an unmitigated curse. "It stands in the way of progress and checks the advance of civilization. If by its fruits we know the tree, so by the same token do we know our social system. Its corrupt fruit betrays its foul and unclean nature and condemns it to death."

Debs had known more of the dark side of the lives of workers than almost any man might know unless he was a worker himself, and perhaps not even then would he know the entire surrounding social circumstance by which he was isolated to his lonely life and death in the darkness of that oblivion to which he had been consigned from the day of his birth.

Looking backward on the nineteenth century, as in his essay "The American Movement," he could believe that it had evolved the liberating and humanizing movement in which he had become an active participant from the time of his joining the Brotherhood of Locomotive Firemen onward—how long ago it must have seemed in objective time as kept by the train upon the rail from station to station as from hour to hour, year to year upon the clock. Out of the misery of the past would surely rise the civilization of the future.

In the progression of the first nineteen centuries, there had not been one century of true progress. "From the very first tyranny has flourished, freedom has failed, the few have ruled, the many have served, the parasite has worn the purple of power."

Had Debs been a total pessimist as to the possibility of man's reaching the goal of socialist millennial reform within the purlieus of mortality, he could scarcely have dedicated himself to the search. The pessimist was present in his character but not allowed to throw the steel net of delay around the optimist he sometimes seemed, although he knew as a matter of his direct and indirect observation the tragic ground on which the future must flower.

Victor Hugo's words while in exile in 1864 would come to Debs many times when perhaps his spirit would have failed without them, the assertion of faith in humanity's unquenchable resources in realms of resurrection, redemption, transformation from the old world of capitalism to the new world of socialism. They inspired him to write:

> The transformation of the crowd into the people—profound task! It is to this labor that the men called Socialists have devoted themselves during the last forty years. The author of this book, however insignificant he may be, is one of the oldest in this labor. If he claims his place among these philosophers, it is because it is a place of persecution. A certain hatred of Socialism, very blind but very general, has raged for fifteen or sixteen years and is still raging most bitterly among the influential classes. Let it not be forgotten that true Socialism has for its end the elevation of the masses to the civic dignity and that, therefore, the principal case is for moral and intellectual elevation. . . . If, as we are quite ready to believe, the twentieth century realizes the prophecy of the French poet and "bursts full-blossomed on the thorny side of time," it will be the denouement of the Socialist agitation that began in the preceding century—the fruition of the international Socialist movement.

Debs's search for utopia, which he did not expect to be granted in a millennial sense with instant transformation of the old world into the new, had begun at that time when the fringe-topped surrey which like a troika could lose its way in an enchanted wood or take the long way and not the direct way home as the driver grew old was being displaced by railroad traveling as speedy as the arrow in flight, so rapid that some people thought that the molecular agitations and displacements caused by long-distance traveling could permanently addle a man's brain, the flowering geranium which could think, or his entire nervous system.

Oh, don't you remember Norman Thomas's elegiac portrait of Debs— the long-armed, long-legged man in the gray business suit with his properly tied necktie and folded silk handkerchief patrolling this planet— keeping watch—walking the star belt—his shoes splashing through galaxies of firefly stars—stars brushing his sleeves, his coat, his vest, his trousers as he goes on and on, this world always half in darkness?

Editorial Note

EUGENE VICTOR DEBS's first prison term: In 1895 he was sentenced to six months in prison for contempt of the federal injunction stopping the strike against the Pullman Palace Car Company in Chicago, also known as the Pullman strike, the Debs strike, or the Debs Rebellion. The court injunction destroyed the American Railroad Workers Union, which Debs had founded to consolidate all the diverse craft unions to work toward the same goals. It was while serving his prison term that Debs first read Marx and reread old favorites, notably Victor Hugo's *Les Misérables*. His experience of prison conditions heightened his awareness that labor issues were inseparable from social issues. Later, when he read Dostoyevsky's *The House of the Dead,* he felt a shock of recognition. As with Thoreau, whose night in jail changed his view of society, Debs began his critique of capitalism in prison and this in turn started his consideration of socialism, which eventually became a lifelong commitment.

Index

Index

Index

Index

A NOTE ON THE TYPE

THIS BOOK was set in Granjon, a type named in compliment to Robert Granjon, a type cutter and printer active in Antwerp, Lyons, Rome, and Paris from 1523 to 1590. Granjon, the boldest and most original designer of his time, was one of the first to practice the trade of typefounder apart from that of printer.

Linotype Granjon was designed by George W. Jones, who based his drawings on a face used by Claude Garamond (ca. 1480–1561) in his beautiful French books. Granjon more closely resembles Garamond's own type than do any of the various modern faces that bear his name.

Composed by North Market Street Graphics,
Lancaster, Pennsylvania
Printed and bound by R. R. Donnelley & Sons,
Harrisonburg, Virginia
Designed by Virginia Tan